etic Screening Smart Garments Biowarfare Climate Change Non-Le
pons Telemedicine Cloning Artificial Intelligence Gene Therapy
ns Fashion Cryonics Automatic Face Recognition New Drug
orgs Future Evolution Wireless Shopping Smart Houses
chemical Computing Artificial Life Information Visualiz
oscopic Computers Smart Materials Smart Applia
estic Robots Smart Cars & Roads e-Relationsh
iversity Life Extension Space Exploration M
nes News Cancer Research Infertility Mil
bs Personal Transporters Wind Power
age Advertising Movies Privacy Mon
rmation Visualization Augmented Real
Cells Smart Cars & Roads Garbag
ons Floating Cities Deep Sea Expl
sroom Collaborative Tools Solar
art Cards Museums Cyberwarfa
thermal Energy e-Government
nate Change Non-Lethal Weapo
cines Automatic Face Recognit
onics Wireless Gene Therapy
art Appliances Quantum & Bio
oscopic Computers Cellular
rgy Lie Detection Augmente
nputers Smart Cars e-Relat
ce Exploration Biowarfare
ironments Video Games Ca
tary Robots Artificial Organs
vs Digital Paper & Ink Art
ies Privacy Money Architec
Exploration Smart Cars & Roa
me Investigation Prisons Lie D
Travel Floating Cities The Class
l Energy Smart Cards Deep Sea
erwarfare/Cyberterrorism Literacy
etic Screening Smart Garments B
apons Telemedicine Cloning Artific
ns Fashion Cryonics Automatic Face
orgs Future Evolution Wireless Shopp
chemical Computing Artificial Life Inform
oscopic Computers Smart Materials Smar
estic Robots Smart Cars & Roads e-Relation
diversity Life Extension Space Exploration Muse
mes News Cancer Research Infertility Military Ro
bs Personal Transporters Wind Power Music Art E
rage Advertising Movies Privacy Money Architecture B
rmation Visualization Augmented Reality Biotech Food Crime
l Cells Smart Cars & Roads Garbage & Pollution High Speed Rail
ons Floating Cities Deep Sea Exploration Nuclear Energy Air Travel
SKYCAR
ASIMO
HONDA

TechTV's Catalog of Tomorrow

Edited by ANDREW ZOLLI

650 Townsend Street
San Francisco, California 94103

201 West 103rd Street
Indianapolis, Indiana 46290

TECHTV'S CATALOG OF TOMORROW

International Standard Book Number: 0-7897-2810-9
Library of Congress Catalog Card Number: 2002107982
Printed in the United States of America
First Printing: September, 2002
06 05 04 03 02 7 6 5 4 3 2 1

Interpretation of the printing code: The rightmost double-digit number is the year of the book's printing; the rightmost single-digit number is the number of the book's printing. For example, the printing code 02-1 shows that the first printing of the book occurred in 2002.

QUE

Publisher
David Culverwell

Editor-in-Chief
Charles O. Stewart III

Editors
Andrew Zolli
Karen Whitehouse

Image Editor
Alice Martina Smith

Product Marketing Manager
Judi Wade

Managing Editor
Thomas F. Hayes

Project Editor
Tonya Simpson

Production Editor
Megan Wade

Indexer
Ken Johnson

Cover Designer
Sandra Schroeder

Interior Designer
Allison Cecil

Graphics Conversion
Tammy Graham

Page Layout
Heather Stephenson

Team Coordinator
Sharry Lee Gregory

TechTV

VP Strategic Development
Glenn Farrell

Managing Editor
Andrew Guest

Marketing Coordinator
Anne Leuthold

Table of Contents

OUR SOCIETY

ABOUT THE CONTRIBUTORS

ANDREW ZOLLI, editor of the *Catalog*, is a futurist working at the intersection of design, technology, culture, and futures research. He specializes in helping institutions see and understand complex change and develop and implement compelling visions of the future. Previously, he helped start the new media practice at Siegelgale, a leading strategy, brand, and new media consultancy and has developed forward-looking products, services, and businesses for Netscape, Kodak, American Express, Silicon Graphics, and many other organizations and institutions. Andrew writes, speaks, and teaches widely on the subjects of technology, design, communications, and long-term forecasting. He can be reached at editor@catalogoftomorrow.com.

LESSLEY ANDERSON is a freelance business and technology journalist living in San Francisco. She was a staff writer for *The Industry Standard* for 3 years, covering the digital entertainment industry and pop culture. Prior to *The Industry Standard*, Anderson worked at *Wired* magazine.

JOHN ARQUILLA, Ph.D., is professor of defense analysis at the United States Naval Postgraduate School in Monterey, California, and a consultant to RAND. He and David Ronfeldt were among the first to explore the issue of information technology in warfare and coined the terms "cyberwar" and "netwar."

CLEMENT BEZOLD, Ph.D. is president of the Institute for Alternative Futures (IAF) and president of IAF's for-profit subsidiary, Alternative Futures Associates (AFA). A leading health futurist, he has developed concepts that have accurately described aspects of how the health care system and therapeutics will evolve. Dr. Bezold is presently overseeing a major process for the Department of Defense on the future of military medicine. He is also consulting with both WHO/Geneva and the Pan American Health Organization (PAHO) on enhancing their ability to use health futures in their operations to support WHO's vision of health for all.

CHRIS BORLAND is co-founder, president, and CTO of Information in Place, Inc., a leading developer of augmented reality technology. He has been involved in vision research at Indiana University for more than 12 years and has 20 publications. He joined the WorldBoard Forum in 1998 as its technology director. He has a strong background in research and interests in contextual intelligence and augmented reality.

CURTIS J. BONK, Ph.D., is an associate professor of educational psychology as well as instructional systems technology at Indiana University. He is also a core member of the Center for Research on Learning and Technology at IU where he co-directs a rural teacher technology integration program. He is also a senior consortium research fellow with the Army Research Institute. Dr. Bonk received the Burton Gorman teaching award in 1999, the Wilbert Hites Mentoring Award in 2000, and the "Cyberstar" award from the Indiana Information Technology Association in 2002. He is president of CourseShare.com.

GARETH BRANWYN has written about near-future technologies for *The Futurist*, *Wired*, *Yahoo!*, *The Industry Standard*, *Details*, *Esquire*, and the *Baltimore Sun*. He wrote the first book about the Web, *The Mosaic Quick Tour*, and created the early 1990s e-book *Beyond Cyberpunk!*, a critically acclaimed compendium of near-future sci-fi and early Net culture. He also runs the popular geek watering hole Street Tech (www.streettech.com).

MICHAEL BRAUNGART, Ph.D., is coauthor with William McDonough of *Cradle to Cradle: Remaking the Way We Make Things* (North Point Press, 2002). Dr. Braungart is a chemist and the founder of the Environmental Protection Encouragement Agency (EPEA) in Hamburg, Germany. Prior to starting EPEA, he was the director of the chemistry section for Greenpeace. Since 1984 he has been lecturing at universities, businesses, and institutions around the world on critical new concepts for ecological chemistry and materials flow management. Dr. Braungart is the recipient of numerous honors, awards, and fellowships from the Heinz Endowment, the W. Alton Jones Foundation, and other organizations.

TIFFANY LEE BROWN is a former editor of *Future Sex*, *Anodyne*, and the *Fringe Ware Review*. She is a regular contributor to *Wired*, *Bookforum*, *Bust*, *Venus*, and the *Mercury*. Brown's work has also appeared in *The Guide to the New Girl Order* (Penguin, 1999) and a multitude of pop culture 'zines.

JUNE COHEN, former VP of content development at Wired Digital and founder of Webmonkey, is now a freelance writer and consultant living in

New York City. Prior to joining Wired, Cohen was a journalist, receiving her B.A. from Stanford, where she served as editor-in-chief of the award-winning *Stanford Daily*.

CORY DOCTOROW is an award-winning science-fiction short story writer, frequent contributor to *Wired* magazine, blogger, and outreach coordinator for the Electronic Frontier Foundation. Winner of the John W. Campbell Award for Best New Science Fiction Writer, Doctorow is coauthor of *The Complete Idiot's Guide to Publishing Science Fiction* (Alpha Books, 2000).

FRANK DRAKE, Ph.D., is chairman of the Board of Trustees of the SETI Institute and a professor of astronomy and astrophysics at the University of California at Santa Cruz. In 1960, as a staff member of the National Radio Astronomy Observatory, he conducted the first radio search for extraterrestrial intelligence.

MARK FRAUENFELDER, a writer and illustrator living in Los Angeles, co-founded *bOING bOING* magazine and was the founding editor-in-chief of *Wired Online*. He writes a monthly column for *Playboy* called "Living Online" and was the co-editor of *The Happy Mutant Handbook* (Putnam-Berkley, 1995).

RICHARD "LORD BRITISH" GARRIOTT is one of the pioneers of the computer gaming industry, best known for his mega-successful Ultima role-playing game series, developed at Texas's Origin Systems. To date, there have been over a dozen sequels, plus countless other products, including children's cartoons, comic books, novels, and songs.

ANDREW GUEST is managing editor at TechTV where he has worked since its inception in 1997. In addition to his work on the *Catalog*, Andrew is a contributor to Que Publishing's *TechTV Leo Laporte's 2003 Technology Almanac*.

POLLY HARROLD holds down the fort as information director for her state's art agency. A poet by nature, with graduate studies in art and critical theory, she has written about the arts, science, and technology for over 10 years. Her first big interview in 1992 with video-art pioneer Nam Jun Paik abruptly ended when his cell phone died.

RICHARD KADREY, author of *Metrophage* (Ace, 1988) and *Kamikaze L'Amour* (St. Martin's Press, 1995), is a veteran science-fiction writer, former editor of *Signal: Communication Tools for the Information Age* (A Whole Earth Catalog Book), and contributor to *Wired* magazine. Kadrey is also the author of *Covert Culture Sourcebook* and *Covert Culture 2.0*.

BILL KASZUBSKI is a writer, editor, and researcher. A graduate of the technical communication program at Rensselaer Polytechnic Institute, he was first published in *The New York Times* in 1989 and then took a long respite to work as a graphic designer, business process analyst, and software architect. Now living in West Hollywood, he has returned to thinking and writing about science, politics, technology, and their interactions.

SONNY KIRKLEY, ABD, is the director of the WorldBoard Forum at Indiana University's Center for Research on Learning and Technology. WorldBoard envisions a global infrastructure for delivering augmented reality experiences. He is also co-founder and CEO of Information in Place, Inc., a leading developer of augmented reality technology. Kirkley's research interests include innovative learning environments, human-computer interface design, and human factors research.

PAUL KRETKOWSKI is a San Francisco-based writer and researcher who has written for *The New York Times Magazine*, *Wired News*, and *Mother Jones Online*. His current focuses are Middle Eastern affairs, information warfare, and rowing.

ANDREW LAWLER has covered space, medicine, biotechnology, archeology, as well as government and university politics for *Science Magazine* since 1994; since 2001 he has been the Boston correspondent for the weekly publication. Before joining *Science*, he was a reporter with *Space News*, *The Futurist*, and other magazines based in Washington. His freelance stories have appeared in *Air & Space*, *Astronomy*, and *Discover* magazines.

PAT MACKE is a writer and creative marketer, with experience on the client and agency side of the creative continuum. For the past 5 years, he has served as creative director of Fuse Interactive, writing and shaping creative ideas for the award-winning agency.

ALEX MARSHALL, a recent Loeb Fellow at the Harvard University Graduate School of Design, is a freelance journalist in New York City, who has written about urban design for *The Washington Post*, *George*, *Metropolis*, *Planning*, and other national publications. He is perhaps best known for *How Cities Work: Suburbs, Sprawl, and the Roads Not Taken* (Univ. of Texas, 2001).

VIVIEN MARX is an award-winning freelance science and technology writer based in Boston, Massachusetts, and Frankfurt, Germany. She has written for *Science Magazine*, *The Economist*, *The Wall Street Journal Europe*, *Red Herring Magazine*, and national newspapers and magazines in Germany and Switzerland. She has worked as a senior TV producer for a multilingual joint venture between German and French public television called ARTE and has written books about optical Microelectromechanical Systems (MEMS) and reproductive medicine.

STEFANO MARZANO is CEO of Philips Design. He holds a doctorate in architecture from the Politecnico di Milano. Marzano is a professor of strategic design in the Faculty of Architecture of the Politecnico di Milano and chairman of the Supervisory Board of Faculty Industrial Design at the Technische Universiteit in Eindhoven. He regularly participates as a juror on international design competitions and as a speaker at design and business conferences worldwide.

WILLIAM MCDONOUGH is coauthor with Michael Braungart of *Cradle to Cradle: Remaking the Way We Make Things* (North Point Press, 2002). The founder of William McDonough + Partners, a design and architectural firm dedicated to environmentally intelligent and economically responsible projects, McDonough received the Presidential Award for Sustainable Development in 1996. *Time* magazine named him "A Hero for Our Planet" in 1999.

PETER MERHOLZ is one of the founding partners of Adaptive Path, a user experience consulting company in San Francisco. He also works as a Web problem solver for Phoenix Pop Productions, where he focuses on usability and interaction design. Merholz has also worked at Voyager, Studio Archetype, and Epinions.

MICHAEL MILLER is a writer, a consultant, a musician, and the president/founder of the Molehill Group. As the best-selling author of more than four dozen nonfiction books and numerous magazine articles, Mr. Miller writes about a variety of topics, ranging from computers to consumer electronics to music. From his first book *Ventura Publisher Techniques and Applications* (Que, 1988) to his latest title *Management Secrets of the Good, the Bad and the Ugly* (Winding Stair Press, 2003), he has established a reputation for practical advice, technical accuracy, and an unerring empathy for the needs of his readers.

MICHELLE PENN is a novelist, poet, journalist, travel writer, and translator. She lived in Paris for 7 1/2 years, where she was a writer and creative director for three French companies. She also earned master's degrees in French and comparative literature from the Sorbonne. Her writing has recently appeared in *Pharos*, *Directions Immobilières*, and *Adam*. Currently a San Francisco resident, she is working on her second novel and a poetry collection.

CHRISTINE PETERSON is co-founder and president of Foresight Institute, a nonprofit organization that educates the public, technical community, and policymakers on nanotechnology and its long-term effects. With Eric Drexler and Gayle Pergamit, she wrote *Unbounding the Future: the Nanotechnology Revolution* (1991), and with Pergamit she coauthored *Leaping the Abyss: Putting Group Genius to Work* (1997).

JEF RASKIN teaches at the University of California at San Diego. Raskin is also VP, Interaction Design, at Telocity, Inc. His current and recent contributing editor positions include *Wired*, *Mac Home Journal*, and *Pacifica Tribune*. Raskin is also a regular columnist for *Forbes ASAP*. Best known as the creator of the Macintosh computer project at Apple, he is the author of the critically acclaimed *The Humane Interface: New Dimensions for Designing Interactive Systems* (Addison-Wesley, 2000).

HOWARD RHEINGOLD is a professional virtual community builder and perhaps the preeminent expert on cyberculture. Some of his most popular books include *Tools for Thought* (1984, 2000), *Virtual Reality* (1991), and *The Virtual Community* (1993, 2000). Rheingold edited *The Millennium Whole Earth Catalog*, was the first executive editor of *HotWired*, and launched Electric Minds in 1996. His new book, *Smart Mobs*, is due out in November 2002 from Perseus Publishing.

MARGARET RIEL, Ph.D., teaches at Pepperdine University and is a noted expert on educational technology. Riel has studied interactive learning environments with a focus on collaborative learning, facilitated, but not controlled, by technology. She is the coauthor of *The Beliefs, Practices, and Computer Use of Teacher Leaders*.

DOUGLAS RUSHKOFF analyzes the way people, cultures, and institutions create, share, and influence each other's values. Rushkoff is the author of eight best-selling books on new media and popular culture, including *Cyberia*, *Media Virus*, *Playing the Future*, *Coercion: Why We Listen to What "They" Say*, and the novels *Ecstasy Club* and *Exit Strategy*. He has served as an adjunct professor of virtual culture at New York University's Interactive Telecommunications Program for the past 4 years, as an advisor to the United Nations Commission on World Culture, on the Board of Directors of the Media Ecology Association, and as a founding member of Technorealism.

ZAHRA SAFAVIAN is a doctoral student at the University of Baltimore whose research focuses on the creation of gender-neutral electronic games. Safavian also works as an interactive multimedia designer and developer. She has done design work for a variety of companies, including *The Wall Street Journal*, The League of Conservation Voters, and The Make-A-Wish Foundation of the Mid-Atlantic.

PAUL SAFFO is a technology forecaster studying long-term information technology trends and their impact on business and society. He is the director of the Institute for the Future, a 30-year-old foundation that provides strategic planning and forecasting services to major corporations and government agencies. Saffo serves on a variety of boards and advisory panels, including the AT&T Technology Advisory Board; the World Economic Forum Global Issues Group; and the Stanford Law School Advisory Council on Science, Technology and Society.

WENDY SCHULTZ, Ph.D., teaches at the University of Houston-Clear Lake as a visiting assistant professor in futures studies. Her research experience has included designing group scenario-building for Hawaii's planners, creating a visioning process for U.S. state courts, developing Hawaii's Ocean Resource Management Plan, planning for sea level rise in the Republic of the Marshall Islands, and forecasting world natural gas trade.

MARK F. SEIFERT, Ph.D., is a professor of anatomy and cell biology at Indiana University School of Medicine. He is a highly regarded teacher and director of human anatomy instruction to first-year medical and doctor of physical therapy students. He serves on the editorial board of *Clinical Anatomy*, the official journal of the American Association of Clinical Anatomists. His research includes the biology of osteoporosis and the nutritional effects of dietary lipids on bone cell function and skeletal metabolism.

NATHAN SHEDROFF, a well-known information and interface designer, is the author of *Experience Design 1* (New Riders, 2001). He focuses on developing online experiences, building online brand strategies and business models, and developing online communities. Shedroff founded Vivid Studios, a decade-old pioneering company in interactive media.

MARTIN SIEGEL, Ph.D., is a professor at the School of Education at Indiana University. He is also the director of the Human Computer Interaction Program at the Indiana University School of Informatics. Siegel is among a group of pioneers in computer-based training and education, beginning with his work in the 1970s on the PLATO system. His current research focuses on the design of digital learning environments, and he leads a doctoral research group on e-learning. He is also the founder, chairman, and CLO of WisdomTools, Inc.

JOANNE SILBERNER is a health policy correspondent for National Public Radio. She covers medicine, health reform, and changes in the health care marketplace. Prior to NPR, she spent 5 years covering consumer health and medical research at *U.S. News & World Report*. In addition, she has worked at *Science News* magazine and *Science Digest* and has freelanced for various publications.

JOHN SMART, author of *SingularityWatch.com*, is a scholar of accelerating and increasingly autonomous computational change. He has a long generalist history of studying science and technological culture with the aim of better understanding the future, his professed passion since the age of five. He has a B.S. in business from UC Berkeley, a grounding in the liberal arts, and 7 years of full-time university coursework in biological, medical, cognitive, computer, and physical sciences at UCLA, UC Berkeley, and UC San Diego. He's now completing an M.S. in future studies and will start a Ph.D. in science and technology studies in fall 2003. He is also finishing *Destiny of Species*, his first book on the technological singularity and organizing a Conference on Accelerating Change at University of Houston for March 2003 (details available at the SingularityWatch site).

RORY STEAR is the chairman and CEO of the Freeplay Energy Group, based in London. Stear founded Freeplay in 1994 along with Christopher Staines. Both men were named Top Entrepreneurs of the Year in 2000 by *Business Week*.

MAURICE STRONG is a senior advisor to U.N. Secretary General Kofi Annan and has been described by *The New York Times* as the "Custodian of the Planet."

GONG SZETO is an award-winning design practitioner and strategist based in New York. He has studied architecture and computer science at the University of Texas at Austin and MIT, and has owned and worked for both small and large design firms in his 12-year design career. He is currently the editor of GAIN, the AIGA's new online publication on business and design, and serves on the board of trustees of the American Institute of Graphic Arts and the Van Alen Institute for Public Architecture. He is also a partner of Szeto Partners Ventures, founded with his brother Nam, also a successful designer and entrepreneur. He was featured in *ID Magazine's* ID Forty List in 1996. Szeto was recently awarded his first U.S. patent in interactive television, work he did with Sony Corporation.

J. CRAIG VENTER, Ph.D., is the former president of Celera Genomics and currently president and chairman of the TIGR Center for the Advancement of Genomics (TCAG), the Institute for Biological Energy Alternatives (IBEA), and the J. Craig Venter Science Foundation. Venter is also the founder and chairman of the Board of The Institute for Genomic Research (TIGR), a not-for-profit genomics research institution located in Rockville, Maryland.

ACKNOWLEDGMENTS

No book of this scope could be created without the input and support of dozens of people. Developing the *Catalog of Tomorrow* has truly been a team effort.

In addition to the gifted writers and thinkers who contributed pieces to this volume, the editor would like to gratefully acknowledge and personally thank Frank Carsey, John Priscu, Dan Gillmor, Joel Hagen, Laurence Dewhurst, Doug Vakoch, Haley Ashland, Sandy Burchsted, Amy D'Angelo, Jay Forrest, Jeff Waldo, Glenn Hough, Alexandra Montgomery, Ramon Ascoroberta, Martin Humphreys, Marianne Kestenbaum, Pero Micic, Zane Ney, Beth Price, Wendy Schultz, Chris Jones, John Smart, Ruud Van Der Helm, Tim Macfarlane, Kim Heismann, Ben Fry, David Swofford, Geoffrey Harvey, Justin Belobaba, Scott White, Eileen Claussen, John Trotti, Cindy Eikenberg, Ariya Akthakul, Jennifer Carlson, Gerardo Ceballos, Alexis Rockman, Carole Wagemans, Gary Liss, Karen and Graham Hawkes, Franz Himpsel, Chaz Miller, Pat Franklin, Max Carcas, Miguel Encarnacao, Nicola Hoare, Jan Zastrow, Marylin Nemzer, Elise Boulding, David Small, Chris Reiter, Heather Kowalski, Marian Brown, and Keisha Hutchins. Their behind-the-scenes efforts, large and small, were invaluable. Special thanks to Chuck Stewart, Karen Whitehouse, Allison Cecil, Bill Kaszubski, and Alice Martina Smith for their extraordinary ideas, efforts, and long hours throughout, especially down the final stretch.

The publisher would like to thank the following individuals, friends, family members, and colleagues, whose ideas, enthusiasm, suggestions, and interest contributed to the making of this extraordinary work: Joe Gillespie, for the brainstorming lunch at COMDEX that planted the seeds of this endeavor. Jim Louderback, whose whiteboard diagram of space tourism showed how a complex subject could be explained with a simple illustration. Laura Culverwell and Eric Culverwell, for suggestions about subjects that would appeal to their respective generations. Wendy Boswell, for her exhaustive promotional efforts, her input along with Tom Boswell's on the original outline and content, and their work along with Chelsea Culverwell's in contacting many of the companies whose products we discuss. John Scardino, for his excitement about the idea and his promotional genius. Steven Hammersly and Peter Hammersly, for their unflagging support and diplomatic skills. Glenn Farrell, for his article-by-article review and insightful commentary. Karen Whitehouse, for her publishing and organizational acumen and whose editorial contacts led to a host of brilliant thinkers and contributors. Chuck Stewart, friend, co-conspirator, and "idea guy" who relished the challenge when I said, "The Catalog doesn't have to be perfect, but it must be great!" Chuck's passion for doing things right went a long way toward ensuring this book's excellence. And, lastly, researcher Alice Smith, whose daily exuberance and unrestrained outbursts as she made new discoveries gave this project a passion few books ever see. To each of you, my highest gratitude.

What's in Your Future?

"Prediction is difficult, especially when it is about the future." Yogi Berra's immortal quip amounts to nothing less than a one-sentence user's guide to this *Catalog of Tomorrow*. Prediction is indeed hard, and the history of future-speculators is littered with realities missed and visions that never came to pass. Anticipators in the 1950s foretold a world of personal helicopters and atomic planes, while experts like IBM chief Tom Watson cautioned that the future market for computers was miniscule. Two decades ago, pundits anticipated a world of ubiquitous "interactive TV," but utterly missed the imminent arrival of the World Wide Web. And in the late 1990s, we were told to expect the Dow to soar to 20,000 in a new age of "friction-free" capitalism and happy globalization. No one mentioned Osama, and Afghanistan was 78th on the State Department's list of countries to worry about.

One could not assemble a more impressive collection of experts than is contained in this book, but only one forecast is certain: They will do no better than their predecessors. A decade or two from now, this book will seem as dated as a dead dot-com and the visions that evoke wonder today will likely trigger giggles and wistful recollections of more innocent times.

The authors' forecasts will fall short because prediction is not simply difficult; it is impossible. This is good news, for prediction is possible only in a world in which the future is preordained and unchangeable. Such a world would be grim indeed, inhabited by bystanders, who even if granted a peek into tomorrow, could do little more than watch their inevitable fates unfold.

The miserable record of would-be forecasters is welcome proof our future is anything but preordained. At any given present moment there is a myriad of possible outcomes, and it is our actions that determine which become future reality. We are not bystanders, but full participants shaping the future we will occupy. The authors of this catalog are not prognosticators, but guides, and ultimately advocates. The value of their visions lies less in their ultimate accuracy, but in the options they reveal and the thoughts and actions they provoke.

All this does not mean that we can't gain more than an inkling of what awaits us in the decade ahead. A decade is not a long time, and many of the issues we will face are easy to identify because they have already appeared on the horizon. In the tools space, these include the evolution of old friends such as computing, the arrival of long-awaited revolutions like the biosciences, and the emergence of entirely new disciplines like nanotechnology. Each area is framed in a Horizons Essay by a leading expert and explicated in supporting articles.

Think of the *Catalog* as a map, an abstraction built on expert, but incomplete, information with some areas completed in great detail and others left as the sketchiest of white spaces. Don't just read, but question the contents and attempt to fill in the gaps. This is especially important when it comes to forecasting the impact of new tools on our lives and society at large, for even in the case of the simplest of innovations, implications tend to proliferate endlessly and the timing of outcomes is uncertain at best. As Arthur Clarke once observed, "Predicting the automobile was easy; anticipating the traffic jam was another matter."

But one fact about human nature offers a navigational star amidst all the uncertainty. As uncertain as the outcomes may be, even in periods of seemingly great change, the volume of things that don't change is vastly greater than the things that do. This is due in no small part to the fact that underlying ever-changing social novelties is a constant set of human needs and desires, such as security, certainty, and the desire to provide for one's offspring. More often than not, seeming innovations merely reflect the novel expression of old, unchanging needs and desires. A century ago, the sudden popularity of "living rooms" reflected the desire to maintain family cohesion in the midst of the swirl of modern society. More recently, email and instant messaging have caught on with techno-peasant adults as a means of staying in touch with college-age kids and globe-trotting children.

In fact, we reject vastly more novelties than we accept. Innovators propose, and populations dispose. If in doubt, conclude that a novelty will fail — it is usually the safe bet. But just because something has failed in the past, don't write it off entirely, for many ideas take a couple of runs at society before they catch on. Simply put, most ideas take 20 years to become an overnight success. Television took over three decades from invention to catch on, and the Internet was almost exactly 20 years old when the public began to embrace it in the late 1980s.

More than a few of the topics in the *Catalog* look ripe for overnight success. Home robots have been anticipated since the 1920s, becoming a humorous stereotype in the 1970s film *Sleeper*, even as we are still awaiting the home robotic reality. Smart appliances were the backdrop in the 1950s GE Kitchen of the Future exhibit, site of the spontaneous 1959 "kitchen debate" between Nixon and Khrushchev. Will this be the decade our appliances get brains and robots invade our homes, and if so, what further surprises will they lead to in how we live and what we eat?

Like all good maps, the contents of this *Catalog* amount to an abstraction in which its usefulness is determined as much by what is omitted, as what is included. As you read on, ask yourself what has received too much emphasis or too little, and above all, what is missing? Also, read with a pen in hand, adding your notes in the margin. Don't just confine your remarks to what may happen; also consider how you will act if the forecast should come to pass.

It is easy to lampoon the wrong-headed forecasts of yesterday, but what the jokes miss is that the authors of many a wrong forecast, like Tom Watson of IBM fame, went on to make fortunes and change the world, exploiting the very things they were initially so wrong about. Their experience reflects an important lesson: If you must forecast, then forecast often. Don't just read this book once and put it on a shelf. Come back in a year and read it again. Look at your notes and revise them. Consider what still feels right and what has passed off the horizon of possibility. And last, but not least, reflect on how you will respond. After all, you are not a bystander, but a participant, in all that is to come.

—Paul Saffo

Progress Toward What?

THE HUMAN TALENT FOR CREATING and using tools has changed our brains and altered our social relations. You are decoding the symbols that make up this sentence instead of stalking game or fleeing predators at this moment because our scrawny primate predecessors learned how to amplify their brains. Sharpening rocks and bringing down mastodons kept our forebears fed; the skills required for spear-making and hunting in groups changed their thought processes and their society in the process. New social structures and mental constructions emerged as soon as axes, agriculture, and alphabets made them possible. We've used our problem-solving tools and talents to master the energies that light the stars and invoke the forces that drive evolution. Immortality and extinction loom as mutually exclusive but real possibilities for this generation or the next. If we are to avoid intentional or unintentional extinction in the near future, we're going to have to turn our problem-solving power on ourselves: Can humans crack the secret of cooperation?

Perhaps the sources of the destructive behaviors of homo sapiens can be understood, just as science has rendered visible other secrets of nature, once unknown. Continuing survival of our species is a compelling goal but not the end of the challenges posed by our technological prowess. If we can somehow learn enough about the architecture and processes of cooperation to stabilize the human population, preserve the global ecosystem from further damage, and provide basic health and nutrition resources to everybody, the human race of the 21st century faces the most formidable questions our evolutionary lineage has faced since some great-great-great-grand-amphibian flopped onto dry land: Given the power to control our future evolution, can and should we try to restrain that power? If not, exactly what should human nature become? What kind of coevolution will occur with the ubiquity of computers and the networking of minds, tools, and cultures?

Buckminster Fuller knew early in the 20th century that we were within range of having the technical means to enable every human to live like a king: "Now in the 1970s we can state an indisputable proposition of abundance of which the world power structures do not yet have dawning awareness," Fuller proclaimed in *Synergetics: Explorations in the Geometry of Thinking*. He wrote: "We can state that as a consequence of the myriad of more-with-less, invisible, technological advances of the 20th century, and employing only well-proven technologies and already mined and ever more copiously recirculating materials, it is now technically feasible to retool and redirect world industry in such a manner that within 10 years we can have all of humanity enjoying a sustainably higher standard of living—with vastly increased degrees of freedom than has ever been enjoyed by anyone in all history."

Fuller wasn't just a dreamer. He was an engineer, most famous for his invention of the geodesic dome and dymaxion house and car. He believed that what we needed was not a new technology, but a new way of conceiving, building, and applying technologies, a "comprehensive design science." J. Baldwin, a former student of Fuller, had a habit of stopping conversations with a loud exclamation whenever the word "progress" was used to justify some new development. "PROGRESS TOWARD WHAT?" he would roar. Then he would raise his eyebrows at all the faces that were turned his way and smile quizzically. It's still a fundamental question. How about making the answer simple, if enormously challenging? "Progress toward a decent way of life for everybody" seems like a worthy goal to me.

Fuller's hopes haven't materialized, even three times 10 years later. Human behavior, not technical capability, is the limiting factor. One key element Fuller had not adequately accounted for was the difficulty getting people to do the right thing, once we've figured out how to do it. One of the obstacles Fuller did understand was the maze of invisible walls that kept knowledge compartmentalized into disciplines.

A few years after Fuller wrote the words quoted previously, in 1979, a political scientist named Robert Axelrod started using game theory to explore the nature of cooperation. Quietly, starting in the early 1980s, evolutionary biologists, economists, mathematicians, and computer scientists have been unraveling some of the secrets of cooperation. Parallel research in sociology, inspired by the work of Elinor Ostrom and others into the way humans govern the use of shared resources, has uncovered some of the reasons some groups cooperate to maintain public goods and others fail to do so.

What is the strategic importance of cooperation? In 2000, I noticed high school students in Tokyo forming "thumb tribes," knit together by their appropriation of mobile text messaging. I started looking more deeply into the future of mobile media when I noticed students the same age in Helsinki flocking to social gathering places, using the same medium, a few months later. My investigation led me to the laboratories in Tokyo, Stockholm, Seattle, and Silicon Valley, where tomorrow's media gestate. As soon as I saw how mobile communications and pervasive computing were converging, I started to notice how other phenomena fit into an emerging pattern. The peer-to-peer file sharing of Napster and Seti@home, eBay's online reputation system, wireless networks, location-aware devices, radio-networked microchips, the blogosphere, and wearable computing are all a part of an emerging phenomenon I came to call "smart mobs." I saw that the personal computer of the 1980s and the Internet and mobile telephones of the 1990s had built upon and modified each other to create a platform for the third and most dramatic change in the way people work, socialize, learn, communicate, and entertain — the coming era when the Internet leaves the desktop and pervades every aspect of our lives and every part of the material world.

We know far more about how to create powerful new tools than we know how to design, deploy, use, and regulate them. Just a few centuries ago, nobody knew how to think about the material world, so people believed diseases were the result of sin and that flying through the air could only be accomplished through witchcraft. The "new method" of thinking espoused by Descartes and Bacon and exercised by Newton and Galileo led to modern medicine and aviation. Perhaps a new method of thinking about the way we and our tools coevolve could enable us to cure or at least salve some of the ailments of technological society, and to fly into the future instead of stumbling into it.

—Howard Rheingold

"How's That Jet Pack Workin' Out For Ya, Futureman?"

When I mentioned in casual conversation that I was working on a book about the future, a man in his 60s who had grown up with Buck Rogers and *his* image of the future uttered those words. Imprinted on his psyche at age 9, the future had utterly failed to materialize. As far as he was concerned, the furthest "The Future" had progressed was the swooping, rocket-like tailfins of his father's '57 Ford Fairlane. And then the world moved on, never quite delivering on its promises, at least not in the jet-pack department.

The implication of his reproach was clear. Why would one want to engage in effort as risky as writing about the future? After all, for every Leonardo daVinci, who sketched the submarine and the helicopter in the 16th century, or H.G. Wells, who envisioned World War II 50 years before it happened, aren't there are a thousand modern-day cranks, false prophets, and infomercial charlatans? Predictions are cheap, and you get what you pay for.

Our collective view of the future does play a vital role in our lives and our society, for better or for worse, propelling us *somewhere*. As the late sociologist Fred Polak noted, we inherit what we prophesy. If a society jointly holds a pessimistic view of its prospects, then that view will likely become its destiny. And the gloomy predictions don't have to be accurate to be destructive: The behaviors they encourage can be sufficient by themselves to bring about decline. The opposite is also true: If a culture holds positive views of its future, the resulting spirit of optimism and progress can lead to a better way of life. Consider, as peace researcher Elise Boulding has noted, that most government services we enjoy today, like Social Security or free medical care for the poor, can trace their origins to the then-utterly-ludicrous notions of 18th-century Utopian novels. Imagination has its rewards.

Ideas about the future permeate the American story and are embedded in our language, culture, history, and geography. An unflappable faith in "A Better Tomorrow" first brought many of us here and then led us over the next hill toward the western horizon. The first mention of California, in the Spanish novel *The Adventures of Esplandian* published in 1510, described it as an island flush with gold. In that light, the gold rush of 1848 wasn't just a compulsion; it was a confirmation: For dreamers of every stripe and motivation, the glittering future lay due west. Is it any wonder Silicon Valley and Hollywood, those twin engines of futures — real and imagined — are located where they are today?

Many of the ideas in this book have been around since the 1950s, when the space race and the Cold War fueled a massive boost in science and technology research, and post-war optimism was at its height. A few are even older than that, and collectively they've cycled through our culture to become kitsch icons — like the robot, they are idealized symbols of our 20th-century yearnings. The difference between then and now is that, in many cases, half a century's worth of research and development has started to make these earlier visions a reality. Today, we can watch gladiator robots built by schoolchildren battle for our pleasure on television — a purpose probably unimagined by the engineers, if not the science-fiction writers, of yesteryear. Likewise, tomorrow's surprises will not come just from technological advances in areas like bioscience or nanotechnology (although there will be plenty of those), but in the unforeseen cultural impacts of those technologies as they become commonplace. In a sense, then, this book is a report card on our previous century's image of the future — how far we've come in realizing it and the unforeseen paths it is starting to lead us down. It's also about the beginnings of a new image of the future, still in its infancy, which will be our generation's contribution to tomorrow.

...

This book favors raising questions about the future over making hard-and-fast predictions about it. Yet in assembling the work of more than 40 contributors and the input of dozens of interview subjects and advisors, certain themes emerged again and again that seem likely to define significant dimensions of change in the coming decades and lead to provocative questions.

The first theme is **new domains of design.** From the genome to the individual atom, human beings are extending our will into entirely new dimensions of the physical world. We are making things in new places and in the process recasting the very nature of both *thing* and *space*. We will not just split atoms, but build with them; we will not just patch DNA, but invent with it. Are we fit for a world of our own making? How much of nature's happenstance is good for us, or necessary?

The second theme is **hybrid areas of knowledge and invention.** As these new domains of design come to the fore, they will recast traditional disciplines from agriculture to zoology. We'll see fields like psychopharmacological geneticists (people who make mood-altering drugs based on your genes) and genetic cryptologists (people who use DNA to encode and decode secret messages). More and more, advances in one field will transform another, cascading like an explosion in a fireworks factory. How should we teach and learn in this new environment?

The third theme is **the rising power of the small.** From warfare to journalism, individuals and small groups will increasingly compete against and collaborate with larger institutions, taking advantage of their strengths and weaknesses. For both good and bad, the small, the fringe, and the amateur will become increasingly networked and powerful and will permanently alter commerce, democracy, and society. Will we achieve some kind of new synthesis? What will it look like?

The fourth theme is **the rise of new agendas.** For a century, most of our important innovations have originated with the marketplace and military needs of the developed world, even if they didn't always stay in their service. But the need for food, clean water, shelter, education, and meaningful work in the rapidly growing developing world, and the unsustainability of many current "first-world" practices, are likely to lead to a shift in priorities. Will the environment take pride of place in our innovations? Will the developing world demand its due? Will our children need to be taught Chinese in grade school?

The final theme is **the centrality of values.** The future will amplify some parts of the human experience, even as it diminishes others. It will present us with questions that traditional systems of ethics were never designed to address. And it will make our choices more important than ever before. What efforts are the most critical? How do we keep the future human and humane? And ultimately, who should decide?

...

More than 600 years ago at the dawn of the Age of Exploration, the first maps of the larger world were beginning to be assembled by cartographers in Europe. These first efforts tended to correctly identify the shape of a landmass or correctly measure its distance, but rarely both. And those early maps of the globe were invariably filled with sea monsters — manifestations of travelers' half-glimpsed fears of the unknown — as well as lands paved with gold and alluring fountains of youth, the incarnations of the traveler's hopes and dreams.

Similarly, maps of the future tend to get the timing of major changes right or their impact, but rarely both. And just like their geographic cousins, maps of the future inevitably contain imaginary Kraken (a mythological Norse sea monster) that, under scrutiny, dissolves into driftwood, as well as promises of bounty that fail to materialize in quite the way we expected, if at all. This book will be no exception. But, as Jim Dator says, useful statements about the future should seem ridiculous. When encountering an idea that seems absurd, avoid thinking "that can't be true" and consider what the world might be like if it were true.

As more people traveled the globe, the better the geographical maps eventually became. Likewise, the more people think about the possible, the probable, and the preferable futures that we individually and collectively face, the better our map of the future becomes.

In that sense, every reader is a contributor to the larger conversation of where we're going, whether or not we should be going there, and how to best get there or change course. To accelerate this conversation, we've put together a Web site, www.catalogoftomorrow.com. It contains exclusive content, interviews, information, updates, links, and polls. We want your help in crafting the next edition of this book, which will begin development as this volume goes to press. You can always email us directly at editor@catalogoftomorrow.com.

Ultimately, ideas about the future are like trampolines. We bounce off them to more interesting places. If we get a little practice, we can control our bounces and achieve art in the motion.

On behalf of all the contributors, happy bouncing.

—**Andrew Zolli**
New York City
August, 2002

Our Tools

Bioscience

- Horizons Essay
- Genetic Screening
- Gene Therapy
- Cloning
- Biotech Food
- New Drugs
- New Vaccines
- The Future of Evolution

Computing

- Horizons Essay
- The Internet
- Broadband
- Wireless
- The Future of Software
- Artificial Intelligence
- Quantum and Biochemical Computing
- Artificial Life
- Information Visualization
- Haptics
- Ubiquitous Computing

Nanotechnology

- Horizons Essay
- Nanocomputing
- Cellular Robots
- Smart Materials

Genomics and Our Future

THIS HAS TO BE ONE OF THE MOST exciting times in human history. We live in a world where there are limitless tools and opportunities at every turn. Computers and the Internet alone have dramatically changed the way we live our lives. Everyone from young children to octogenarians now takes for granted the ability to log on and communicate by email, download any fact, or purchase something with the click of a mouse.

Advanced computers, along with new mathematical algorithms, were the key technological advances that allowed my team to sequence the human genome faster than anyone ever thought possible. Now the three billion letters of the human genetic code and the genetic code of more than 100 other species are available as a resource for scientific discovery and research via your desktop. This breakthrough has brought us to the beginning of the genomics era.

Contained in the four seemingly simple letters of the DNA code is our evolutionary history and some of the keys to our future. Genomics has the potential to change life as we know it. Through full knowledge of the human genetic code we will usher in the era of preventative medicine by empowering individuals with knowledge about their own genetic makeup. Not only will we help eliminate racism, but for the first time we will fully understand the evolutionary events that led to our existence and where we as humans fit into the biological continuum. Imagine planning your diet and life activities on predictions from your genetic code in order to prevent future disease. And imagine the impact if we viewed each other as nearly identical members of the same race — the human race — because we now know that race is a social concept and is not based entirely on the genetic code. This code is the common bond for all six billion of us on this planet.

The knowledge we have gained from the revolution in microbial genomics has given us the tools to develop new vaccines and therapeutics against the world's most devastating infectious diseases. Microbes can be used to enhance CO_2 sequestration and provide new mechanisms for developing clean and efficient fuel sources. Imagine the positive economic and political, let alone the environmental, impact of switching to a hydrogen-based economy. This could all be possible in what scientists have deemed the genomics era. But we have only scratched the surface of the powerful potential that this information holds for humanity.

In February 2000, my team at Celera published our first analysis of the human genome. We learned some surprising facts from sequencing the human genome. We found there are approximately 30,000 human genes — about the same as a mouse and twice as many as a fruit fly — far fewer than the 100,000 or more that many predicted. We have basically the same genes in the same order as all other mammals. We are only 1.27% different at the genome sequence level from chimpanzees, and the human X chromosome is only 0.9% different from the chimpanzee X chromosome. A key study recently published showed that protein expression in chimpanzees and humans was essentially the same in all tissues except for the brain. So why were so many people perplexed and dismayed at the notion that we have fewer genes? The conventional wisdom was that because we are clearly complex organisms there must be one gene for every human trait, characteristic, and disease. As a society we seem to view life in a genetically deterministic fashion. People want their genes to absolve them of all flaws and foibles. With only 30,000 genes, we cannot possibly be just the sum total of our genes.

In my view, one of the most important outcomes from our sequencing of the human genetic code is clear support for the notion that race is a social concept, not a scientific one. We sequenced the genomes of five individuals, three females and two males, of self-identified ethnicity as Chinese, Hispanic, African-American, or Caucasian. Looking at the genetic code, we can tell who is male and who is female, but we cannot determine who is Chinese, Hispanic, African-American, or Caucasian. There will be those who want to continue to use the genetic code as a means of discrimination, but with education we will all learn that our life outcomes are not genetically predetermined.

Modern science has and will continue to present us with many ethical and social issues. Rather than something to be feared, this should be viewed as a wonderful opportunity for all of us to learn from and to engage in an open, public dialogue. For this dialogue to be meaningful, we clearly need better public understanding. We all should be excited and energized by the vast array of new research information and tools at our disposal today — more than at any other time in human history. But I continue to be concerned that we will not be able to reap the potential societal and health benefits of this vast new expanse of knowledge because of public fear of the unknown. We need to assure the public that genetic information will not be used as a weapon of discrimination. Carefully crafted legislation can provide this reassurance so that society can benefit fully from these scientific breakthroughs.

Genomics is only one area that has opened up new possibilities for new treatments and cures for disease. The use of stem cells and therapeutic or non-reproductive cloning techniques have the potential to treat some of our most devastating illnesses like Parkinson's disease, Alzheimer's disease, diabetes, and cancer. This research is still in its nascent stage; however, I am extremely concerned that the current climate in our government will prevent us from moving forward in the pursuit of this essential knowledge. The scientific community must mobilize to educate our legislators and work to ensure that basic research is not criminalized.

We are still faced with these sobering statistics: One in eight American women will get breast cancer in her lifetime; global warming is occurring at a faster rate than expected due in large part to our continued increase in fossil fuel consumption; more children die in the world from infectious disease and malnutrition than ever before; despite some improvements in lessening world hunger, there are still 800 million people in the developing world who do not have sufficient food; and in this country we still have more than 40 million citizens without healthcare coverage.

The world has advanced greatly, and we are fortunate to live in one of the most technologically, medically, and scientifically advanced societies, but clearly we still have much to work to do if we are all to live up to our full potential. I believe that genomics has the power to dramatically change some of these negative outcomes and be a force for positive change in the world. I look forward to helping to lead this charge into the genomics era of science and medicine.

—J. Craig Venter, Ph.D.

GENETIC SCREENING...

If you compare the human genetic code to a book – it may be an overused metaphor, but it works – scientists have known what the letters are for decades. Today, with the human genome essentially figured out, they know the order of the letters. They are in the process of reading the book – spelled out by the genome. A single cell – an egg cell, or a cell from an embryo, or a fetus, or a child, or an adult – can at least theoretically reveal an entity's medical fate.

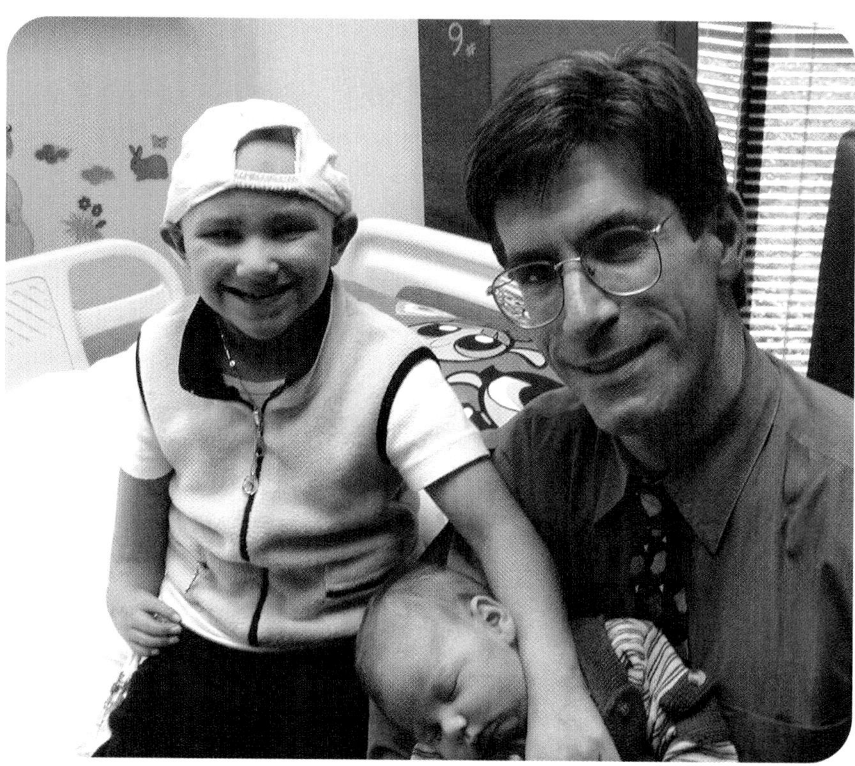

FAMILY TIES. *The Nash children with Dr. John Wagner, the doctor who performed the stem cell transplant from Adam's umbilical cord.*

Photo by Mark Engebretson for the University of Minnesota/Newsmakers

What does the ability to read the entire book mean? Being able to read parts of it has already eliminated a fair amount of human suffering. For years, along with a slap on the rear, babies have routinely gotten their heels stuck with a lancet. The few drops of blood collected on a filter paper enable technicians to search for misspelled words – genetic defects – and determine whether the baby has one of a variety of metabolic disorders. Discovery routinely allows early and effective treatment of conditions like phenylketonuria, which could otherwise cause retardation, and galactosemia, which can cause liver or brain damage.

Discovery of problematic genes is possible even before birth. That's the whole idea behind amniocentesis and chorionic villus sampling, done with samples from the placenta or amniotic fluid of a weeks-old fetus; but what about a days-old embryo – one that's outside the body, one that has fewer than dozens of cells? The procedure is called preimplantation genetic diagnosis. It's already been used to detect at least 50 genetic conditions, perhaps most famously in the case of the Nash family from Colorado.

Daughter Molly had Fanconi anemia, a rare and serious blood disorder. She was in dire need of healthy blood-making cells, but her parents could find no immunologically compatible donor for bone marrow transplantation. So they decided to make one. They donated sperm and eggs for in-vitro fertilization. Yury Verlinsky, director of the Reproductive Genetics Institute in Chicago, examined individual cells from the resulting embryos. He selected genetically healthy, immunologically compatible embryos, and he implanted several into Molly's mother.

After baby Adam was born in the summer of 2000, cells taken from his umbilical cord cured his sister.

Verlinsky has already gone a step beyond. He's used unfertilized eggs

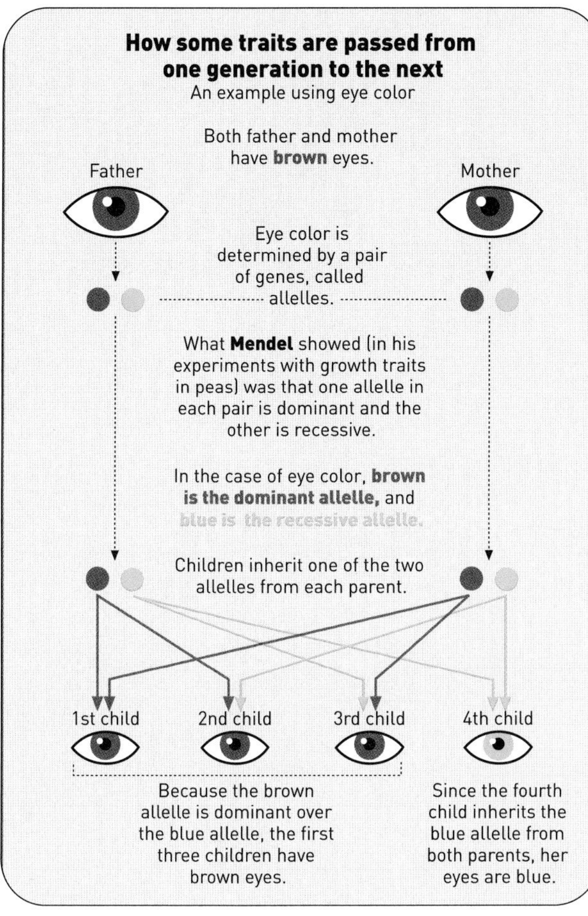

How some traits are passed from one generation to the next
An example using eye color
Both father and mother have brown eyes.
Father
Mother
Eye color is determined by a pair of genes, called allelles.
What Mendel showed (in his experiments with growth traits in peas) was that one allelle in each pair is dominant and the other is recessive.
In the case of eye color, brown is the dominant allelle, and blue is the recessive allelle.
Children inherit one of the two allelles from each parent.
1st child
2nd child
3rd child
4th child
Because the brown allelle is dominant over the blue allelle, the first three children have brown eyes.
Since the fourth child inherits the blue allelle from both parents, her eyes are blue.

Graphic by Nigel Holmes

collected from a woman whose father and brother were struck by Alzheimer's disease while they were in their late 30s. Had she had a child naturally, the baby would have had a 50% chance of the same fate.

Verlinsky performed molecular tests to select eggs that didn't carry the problem gene. He fertilized some of those eggs with the woman's husband's sperm and implanted four of the embryos. In the year 2002, at the age of 30, the woman bore a healthy baby girl – a girl whose mother may not be alive in 10 years.

Genetic screening has led to a whole new field called pharmacogenetics, the study of how genes interact with pharmaceuticals. The goal – figuring out how to identify the genes that cause 2 million Americans a year to be hospitalized with untoward reactions to properly prescribed drugs. When the particular genetic aberrations are known, doctors can prescribe drugs only to people who will be helped.

Already, a trial headed by Mary-Claire King at the University of Washington has shown that a breast cancer drug works in women with one genetic makeup, but not another. The researchers studied cancer-free women with one of two mutations, BRCA1 or BRCA2. Tamoxifen didn't protect the women with BRCA1, but it reduced the incidence of breast cancer 62% in women with BRCA2.

With thousands of detectable genetic diseases known, and more being learned every day, genetic screeners could be quite busy in the future, helping parents select embryos that will grow into disease-free adults. Some ethicists are a bit uncomfortable with all this. There's the question of creating or gathering embryos and eggs that will be discarded. And there's the chance that parents will demand these sophisticated new techniques not for health reasons, but to engineer an especially intelligent or athletic child. At the moment there's little federal oversight of the experimental procedures – decisions about what should and shouldn't be done are in private hands.

Legislatures, though, have taken an interest in genetic screening in the workplace and that by health insurers. Twenty-two states have some sort of law covering genetic testing. Businesses, people, and insurers…they now are going to have to decide whether they want to use the ability to read an individual's genetic book, and skip to the ending.

PROVOCATIONS…

Could genetic modification affect the Olympics in the future?

Will genetic screening lead to new forms of depression for those who learn they are at risk for a disease?

Will singles demand to know the genetic risks of a potential life partner?

– Joanne Silberner

WANT MORE?

DNA FILES FROM NATIONAL PUBLIC RADIO
www.dnafiles.org

BIOEXCHANGE – FOR-PROFIT PORTAL SITE
www.bioexchange.com

PRESIDENT'S COUNCIL ON BIOETHICS
www.bioethics.gov

NATIONAL CENTER FOR BIOTECHNOLOGY INFORMATION
www.ncbi.nlm.nih.gov

EUROPEAN MOLECULAR BIOLOGY LABORATORY
www.embl-heidelberg.de

NATIONAL INSTITUTE OF GENETICS
www.nig.ac.jp/home.html

GENE THERAPY... TINKERING WITH CELLS

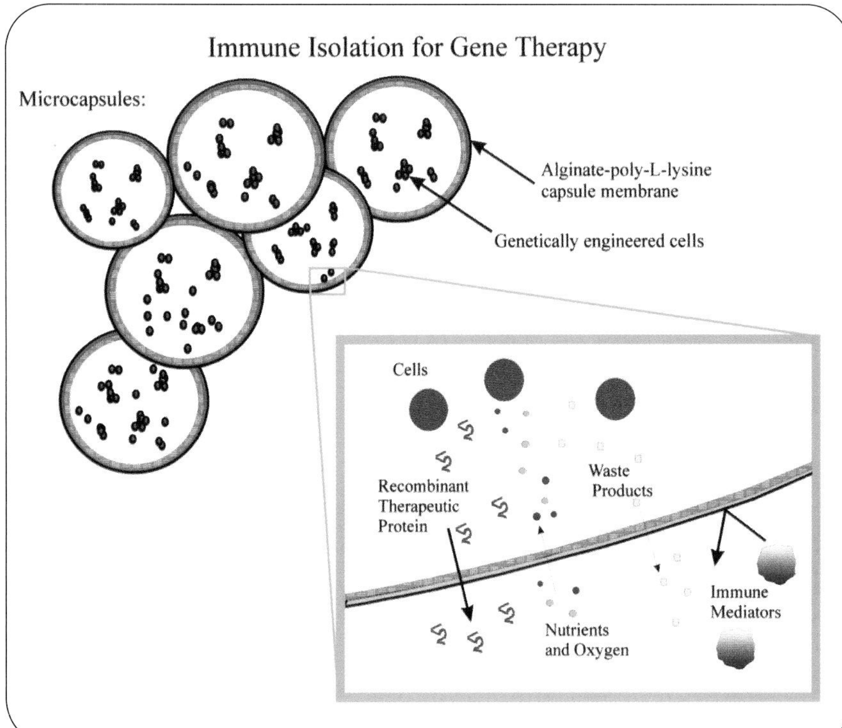

GENE STRATEGY. *Researchers at McMaster University are working on a nonviral approach to introducing genetically altered cells into the body. They encapsulate the cells in a semipermeable membrane that prevents the body from rejecting the new cells while allowing the beneficial proteins created by the cells to enter the body.*

Image courtesy of Patricia L. Chang, McMaster University

"PSST. COME HERE. I DON'T WANT TO TALK TOO LOUDLY. *I've got a sure cure for your cystic fibrosis; it's just not approved by the government yet. I've built a virus that can help you. I made it out of Ebola virus and HIV. C'mon, let me infect you with it. What do you have to lose?"*

Such a composite virus, already built and animal tested, may be the answer to one of the biggest hurdles for gene therapy: figuring a way to shepherd helpful genes into target cells. Gene therapy has long been touted as the cure for hundreds of genetic diseases, and it's long been stalled by the lack of a way to get good genes into cells.

It's not that scientists haven't been trying. Within a year of the discovery of the cystic fibrosis gene in 1989, scientists loaded up defective lung cells with a healthy version of the gene and implanted the doctored cells into the lungs of CF patients. But the new cells didn't last long enough to make much of a difference. Other gene targeting approaches have failed, too, because they didn't get enough genetic material into target cells, or once there, the genes didn't produce.

So scientists have been tinkering, and coming up with ideas like using two of the world's deadliest viruses, HIV and Ebola, as sherpas to carry genetic material into target cells. The Ebola virus excels at locking onto lung cells. The human immunodeficiency virus is hardy. So researchers at the University of Pennsylvania took the genetic material of these viruses apart like tinker toys, throwing out the killer parts and hanging onto the genes with the desired characteristics. Then they added a gene that can take over for the damaged CF gene. Robert Gallo, credited as co-discover of the virus that causes AIDS, said at the time of the announcement, "I wouldn't want this thing put into me."

But other scientists contend that once HIV and Ebola are taken apart, their genetic subunits can be safely used. Parts of HIV have already been used to carry an anti-sickle-cell gene into mice ... and it worked. But there are lots of hurdles for the hybrid-virus approach. The virus might insert the genetic material right into the middle of another gene, or the genetic components of HIV could be

DNA, THE TINKER TOYS OF GENES.
Inside the nucleus of nearly every cell in the body, a complex set of genetic instructions, known as the human genome, is contained in 23 pairs of chromosomes.

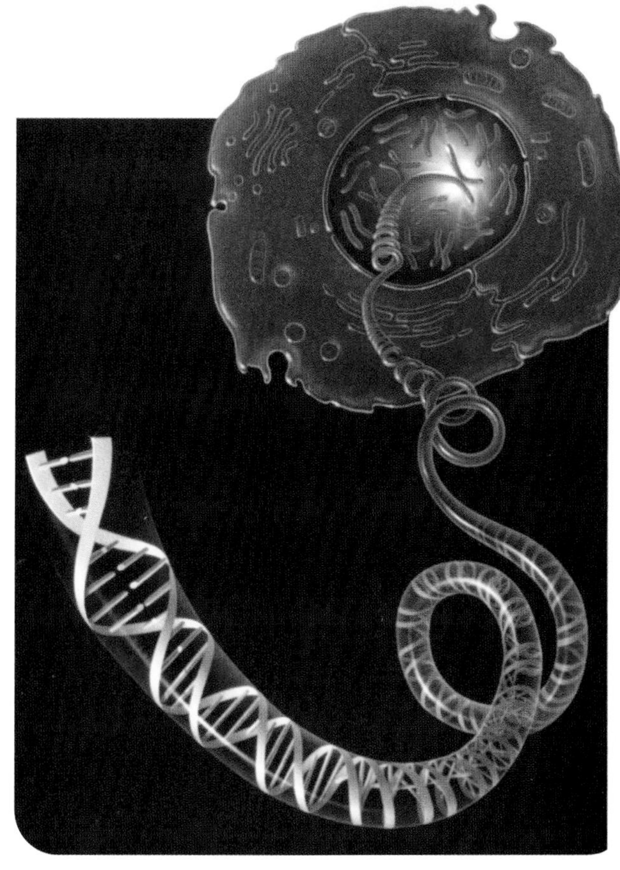

picked up by other viruses, making them as hardy as HIV.

Still, the approach has worked in mice. But it will go no further, at least at the University of Pennsylvania's Institute for Human Gene Therapy. The government won't let the scientists there try any human gene therapy technique, and the reason is related to gene delivery problems. The Institute was the home of the first death directly linked to gene therapy: Jesse Gelsinger, who had a metabolic disorder, died after receiving a corrective gene loaded onto a usually harmless virus that somehow caused multiple organ failure. The Food and Drug Administration ordered the Institute not to work with people any more.

Some researchers are working on gene delivery techniques that don't expose people to potentially harmful viruses. The idea is to take problem cells out of the body, fix them in the laboratory, and then send them back into the body. Lots of groups are trying this approach with immune cells, "infecting" them with a virus that's been saddled with a helpful gene, and then the altered cells go back into the body. It's worked in a few children with severe combined immunodeficiency disease – in fact it's the only full-out cure credited to gene therapy.

Options on the drawing board include building a new, 47th chromosome that would act on its own. Gene guns – which are guns that bombard cells with DNA – are another hot item in the laboratory. Researchers at Case Western Reserve University have figured out how to pack DNA into tiny fat globules that can diffuse into the cell's nucleus, and they're testing it on a dozen people with cystic fibrosis.

Image courtesy of National Human Genome Research Institute

Of course, there are some ethical issues any time you work with genes. Most research efforts so far have been aimed at cells that aren't involved in reproduction ... cells that will, eventually, die with the recipient. Repairing genes in sperm and eggs would be permanent, not just for the recipient but for the recipient's offspring as well. So far scientists have been staying away from that area. The ability to make germ-line changes brings on a whole new level of questions.

"Fixing" traits permanently is still a long ways away. Scientists are focusing first on diseases. They can boast of lots of success in treating cells in culture and laboratory mice. They've cured rare types of immune disorders. They're working hard on cystic fibrosis, and there's been limited success for some types of heart disease. And if the HIV/Ebola virus combination works or the gene gun succeeds, there are likely to be a lot more.

PROVOCATIONS...

Will there be no more short people?

Could genetic manipulation affect the Olympics in the future?

Will we ever screen for softer traits, like musicality or the innate susceptibility to ideas?

—Joanne Silberner

WANT MORE?

UPDATE FROM THE HUMAN GENOME PROJECT
www.ornl.gov/hgmis/medicine/genetherapy.html

AMERICAN SCIENTIST MAGAZINE
www.americanscientist.org/articles/99articles/kmiecgene.html

INST. FOR HUMAN GENE THERAPY
www.uphs.upenn.edu/ihgt/index.html

AMERICAN SOCIETY FOR GENE THERAPY
www.asgt.org

CLINICAL GENE THERAPY TRIALS
www.clinicaltrials.gov

CENTRE FOR GENE THERAPEUTICS, MCMASTER UNIVERSITY
www.fhs.mcmaster.ca/cgt/home.html

Cloning... We, Myself, and I

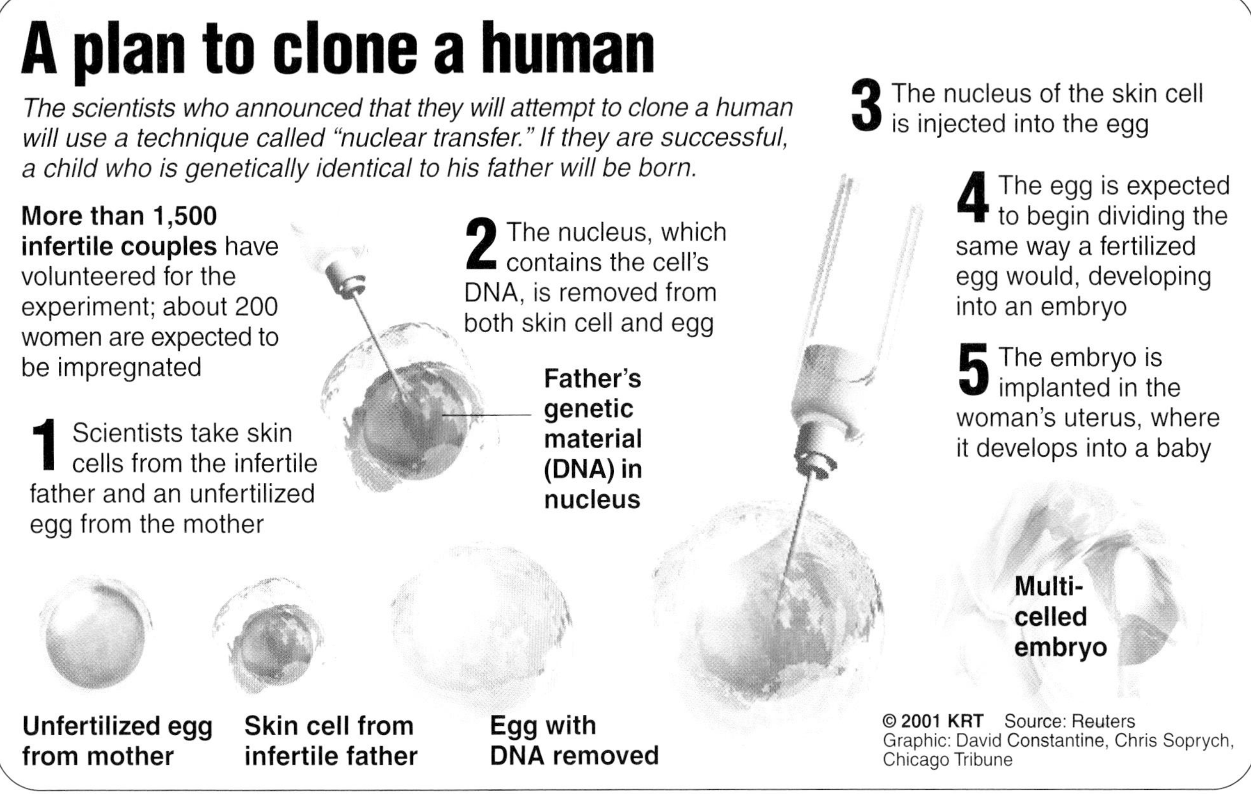

A plan to clone a human
The scientists who announced that they will attempt to clone a human will use a technique called "nuclear transfer." If they are successful, a child who is genetically identical to his father will be born.
More than 1,500 infertile couples have volunteered for the experiment; about 200 women are expected to be impregnated
1 Scientists take skin cells from the infertile father and an unfertilized egg from the mother
2 The nucleus, which contains the cell's DNA, is removed from both skin cell and egg
Father's genetic material (DNA) in nucleus
3 The nucleus of the skin cell is injected into the egg
4 The egg is expected to begin dividing the same way a fertilized egg would, developing into an embryo
5 The embryo is implanted in the woman's uterus, where it develops into a baby
Multi-celled embryo
Unfertilized egg from mother
Skin cell from infertile father
Egg with DNA removed
© 2001 KRT Source: Reuters
Graphic: David Constantine, Chris Soprych, Chicago Tribune

CLONING EVOKES BOTH FEAR AND FASCINATION IN MANY PEOPLE TODAY. PERHAPS WE CAN *trace part of that trepidation all the way back to a fear of twins in the world's ancient cultures. The Igbo tribe of what is now Nigeria used to abandon twins to the wilderness. Rome was said to have been founded by Romulus and Remus, twins who were cast off by their civilization only to be suckled and raised by a cooperative she-wolf. Although the modern world regards twins as part of a natural process, one in which an embryo simply splits after fertilization, cloning exposes our fears about scientific methods whose complexity leaves us uneasy.*

Make no mistake about it—cloning by scientific means is a tremendously complicated process. Dolly the cloned sheep made worldwide headlines in 1997. Since then, a veritable menagerie of animals has been duplicated — cows, pigs, and even a kitten. Lost in the successes of Dolly and her subsequent heirs is the incredible failure rate in such animal cloning experiments. It took 277 tries for Dr. Ian Wilmut to produce that first cloned lamb at the Roslin Institute in Scotland. But that's not to say that 1 in 277 attempts is the ratio for successful cloning. Perhaps Dr. Wilmut's team was lucky. There just isn't enough data to show how successful such cloning will be. But what evidence does exist points to about a 2% to 3% success rate.

The advent of cloning as an accepted medical technique is perhaps inevitable. Drugs and surgery do not always provide the solution to medical problems. Donor organs and transplants frequently cause problems of host rejection. And there are those for whom procreation is an unattainable goal, even in an era of in-vitro fertilization. Although some argue that any type of cloning is unethical, many scientists seek to separate the purposes of cloning research, distinguishing between therapeutic and reproductive cloning.

Therapeutic cloning seeks to produce stem cells that can then be manipulated to grow organs, tissue, or other replacement parts. Reproductive cloning, of course, seeks to create a living human being. Given the failure rates of animal cloning experiments and the increased complexity of human physiology, reproductive cloning has encountered the most resistance on both moral and practical grounds.

The next breakthrough in cloning technology will likely come in the therapeutic realm, when human tissue is cloned and then manipulated in the service of disease prevention or genetic therapy. Although there is resistance to therapeutic cloning as well, the latter has more champions than does reproductive cloning.

People may have a justifiable fear of science gone awry, but when the benefits of a measured advance in cloning for disease prevention become more apparent, the term "clone" may evoke less ambivalence. Just as identical twins have become almost commonplace in the human community, so the facts of cloning as a well-researched procedure will become just another step in our scientific understanding of life.

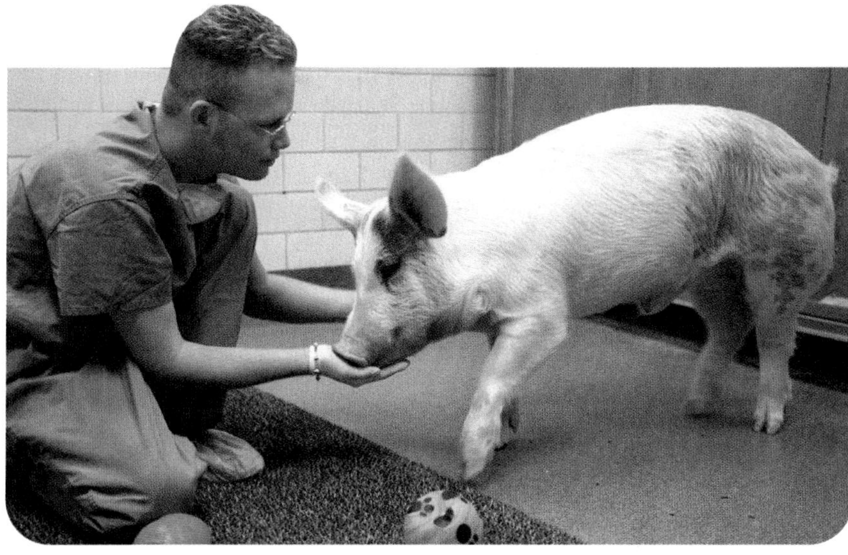

SPARE PARTS. *One of the world's first cloned transgenic piglets carrying a human gene, bred at a Wisconsin research facility. It is hoped that these piglets will provide whole organs and spare parts for human transplantation.*

PROVOCATIONS...

If we could bring back an extinct species through cloning, should we?

Will there be a boom in pet cloning?

Will you ever be able to really "know yourself"?

— Andrew Guest

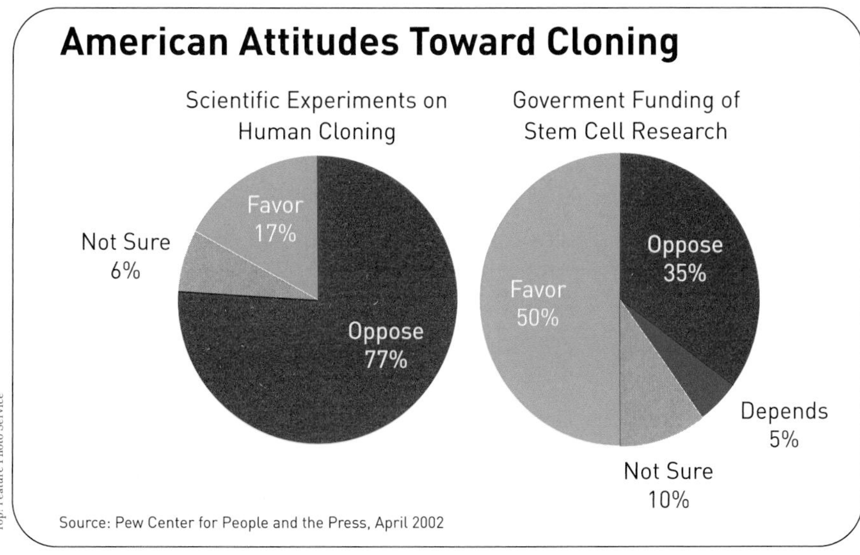

WANT MORE?

HOW STUFF WORKS CLONING PAGE
www.howstuffworks.com/human-cloning.htm

HELLO DOLLY (FROM WHY FILES OF UNIVERSITY OF WISCONSIN)
http://whyfiles.org/034clone

JAPAN'S CENTER FOR DEVELOPMENTAL BIOLOGY
www.cdb.riken.go.jp/english

ANDROLOGY INSTITUTE OF AMERICA
www.aia-zavos.com

ADVANCED CELL TECHNOLOGY
http://advancedcell.com

ROSLIN INSTITUTE
www.roslin.ac.uk

Top: Feature Photo Service

Biotech Food... Future Food Fights

FEW THINGS GET PEOPLE SO WOUND UP AS WHAT *they put in their stomachs. Think of Jewish and Muslim repugnance toward pork, the fabulous rice-planting festivities on Bali, or the intense devotion given to those little wafers doled out at Catholic Mass. Or, perhaps just as famously, the recent worldwide outcry against genetically modified (GM) organisms. That outcry is radically reshaping the future of food.*

Photo courtesy of Monsanto Corporation

Look for a tossed salad of technologies: GM soybeans and corn already are part of some 70% of the food on American supermarket shelves—and they are likely to stay there for some time. But GM inroads into fruits and vegetables and even animals, say researchers, is likely to be overtaken by methods that use old-fashioned cross-breeding and modern genetics but avoid the gene splicing which gives GM foods the deadly moniker of "Frankenfoods." Meanwhile, there is an increasing tempo in efforts to alter plants to improve nutrition, introduce more anti-cancer substances into the foodstream, and produce vaccines. At the same time, the organic market is growing by leaps and bounds and seems likely to coexist with its more industrial cousin.

"What you won't see are a lot of strange and unusual fruits and vegetables," says Susan Harlander, a biologist and consultant to food companies. By bypassing the tedious tradition of breeding one plant with another, researchers envisioned future fields of everything from wheat to melons to tomatoes to unknown varieties in between, impervious to bacteria, pests, viruses, drought, or severe cold, and which could remain fresh long after conventional foods rotted. And corporations envisioned huge profits.

PUBLIC FEARS

What neither imagined was the fearful public response, which took off in Europe in the 1990s and spread quickly around the world. That reality, which has led to an increasingly stringent set of regulations, is prompting companies to back off from their wilder dreams. "The real check on progress is not the science, but the regulation and consumer demands," says Roger Beachy, a biologist at Washington University's plant science center in St. Louis.

It is also true that the big gains in GM foods have come from inserting single genes into grain commodities that can kill pests, a technique used successfully by Monsanto and other agribusiness giants. But altering fruits and vegetables to make them crisper, fresher, and tastier is another matter. Such traits typically involve many genes. To complicate the picture, fruits and vegetables typically come in a large number of varieties tailored for specific climates. That makes GM techniques expensive and risky. The GM FlavrSavr tomato, for example, crashed and burned once it reached the market; consumers simply didn't find it significantly more appealing than non-GM varieties.

THE THIRD WAY

Those scientific and political barriers are opening the door to what researchers are calling an enticing "third way." In the past 5 years, advances in decoding the DNA of organisms are offering a whole new way of improving the food supply. Traditionally, farmers have crossbred different varieties of plants to produce hardier or tastier grains and fruits and vegetables — a slow and difficult process. But by pinpointing those areas — called DNA markers — which distinguish specific varieties, researchers can conduct cross breeding in a far more efficient way — without directly inserting alien genes as is done in genetic modification. "This could make both camps" — GM opponents and proponents — "happy," says journalist Ken Roseboro. Those plants with favorable traits can be bred, producing non-GM varieties.

But the battle over GM is far from over. Though a GM potato and other products have been put on hold, transgenic animals — animals with genes inserted from other species — are provoking new outcries, and a transgenic salmon is undergoing FDA testing now. Hogs and poultry, now typically raised in a more industrial form than a few decades ago, also are targeted for genetic modifications. Consumer reaction may be overwhelmingly negative. "There's no People for the Ethical Treatment of Soybeans," notes Rebecca Goldburg of New York's Environmental Defense Fund. And how consumers react will determine whether companies will stake funds of new research.

IMPROVING NUTRITION

But research is unlikely to slack off when it comes to improving nutrition — which the new Golden Rice claims it can do — for poor people around the planet. Some are working to increase the antioxidant content of foods to stave off cancer and degeneration from old age. And scientists like Charles Arntzen at Arizona State University in Tempe are busy examining how they can use common plants to manufacture vaccines in the field, providing protection from viruses by a simple pill rather than injections. The fields of developing countries could grow plants producing vaccines, which then would be harvested and ingested as pills — requiring no needles, sophisticated health care professionals, or expensive manufacturing facilities. Arntzen hopes he can find a philanthropic organization to foot the $50 million to $60 million bill for growing hepatitis B vaccine, which he hopes to have available by the end of this decade.

None of this means that small farms or sustainable agriculture are history. Organic farmers have established a small but growing presence in mainstream supermarkets, a trend that shows no sign of withering.

Looking beyond the next few years, some researchers foresee a day when your DNA code can be matched to the bar code of a particular fruit or vegetable — some GMs, some not — in the supermarket that would be best suited for your particular body. "This will tell me what's good for me to eat," says biologist Beachy. "And this could be very effective in preventative health care." Where food is concerned, however, it is a question of what technologies consumers are willing to swallow.

Do you favor or oppose genetically modified food?

	Protestant	Catholic	Jewish	Muslim
Favor	37%	42%	55%	32%
Oppose	57%	52%	35%	46%
Not Sure	8%	6%	10%	22%

Source: The Pew Initiative on Food and Biotechnology

PROVOCATIONS...

Will the world divide into GM and non-GM eaters?

Will farming require a license, a lab, and a Ph.D.?

—Andrew Lawler

WANT MORE?

MONSANTO
www.monsanto.com

PEW FOUNDATION
http://pewagbiotech.org

UNION OF CONCERNED SCIENTISTS
www.ucsusa.org/food/0biotechnology.html

ENVIRONMENTAL DEFENSE FUND
www.environmentaldefense.org/home.cfm

COUNCIL FOR BIOTECH INFO
www.whybiotech.com

GREENPEACE
www.greenpeace.org/campaigns/intro?campaign_id=3992

NEW DRUGS...

New Elixirs for Old Scourges

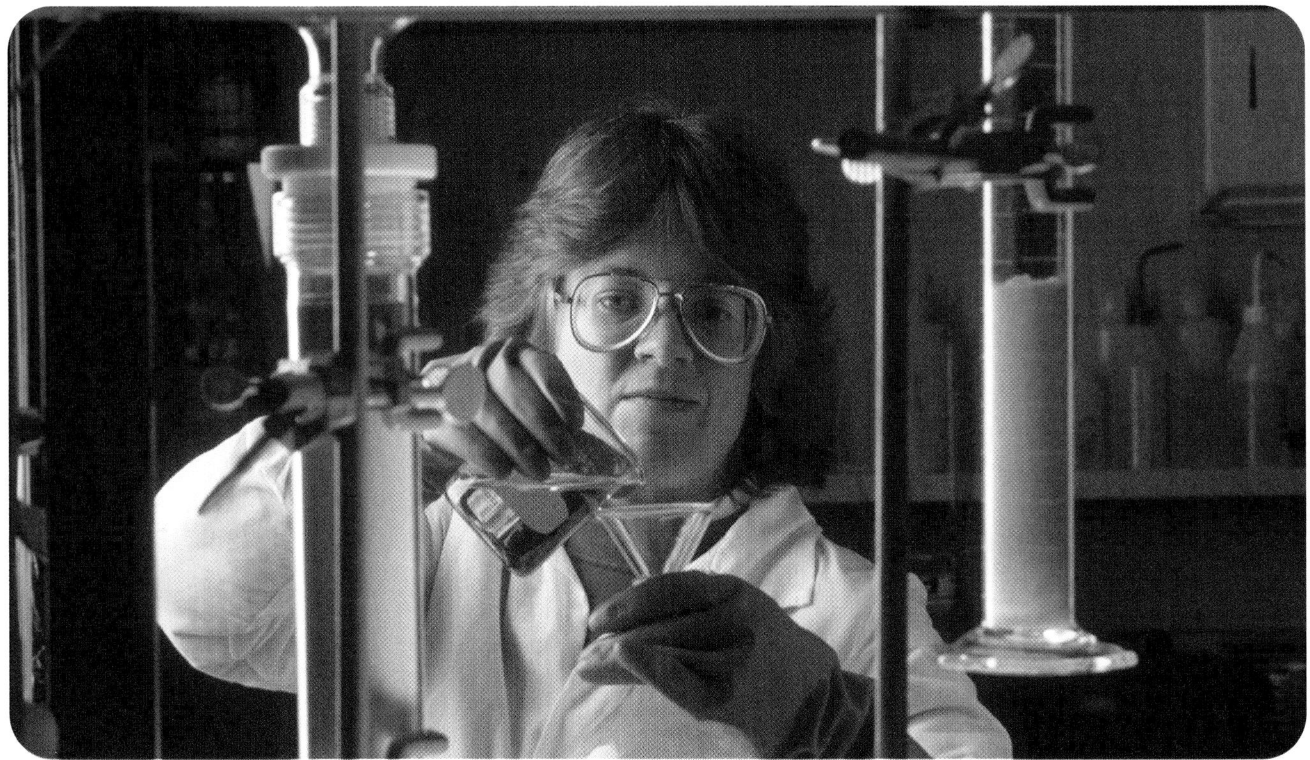

Photo courtesy of Monsanto Corporation

PHARMACEUTICAL COMPANIES AND PATIENTS HAVE IN COMMON THE FACT THAT THEY WANT *drugs that cure disease, alleviate symptoms, and cause few, if any, side effects. Patients with diseases that are currently difficult to treat, with age-related disorders, or with cancer can hope to see new and better treatment options.*

Often, new treatments work well in animals but not in humans. Cancer, for example, seems easier to cure in mice than in humans. New compounds called antiangiogenesis drugs, now in clinical trials, work in mice by starving tumors and preventing new blood vessels from sprouting as the tumor's supply lines. Yet these drugs have not delivered results worthy of the hype.

Another new approach to cancer-drug treatment is antibody compounds that harness the body's immune system to fight cancerous cells. Reviving an older technique, a number of companies are developing a drug class called monoclonal antibodies which are engineered versions of proteins in the body's defense system lineup. Because they are so specific, at least theoretically, they could handle many human diseases. Currently, one in five biotech drugs in development is a monoclonal antibody.

Another novel approach is glyco drugs. New research shows that sugars are pivotal in the complex communication among cells. Many companies and research groups involved in glycomics are working on promising sugar-related drugs for the treatment of various diseases, including Gaucher's disease, cancer, and various bacterial and viral infections.

Specificity, the ability to zero in on the cause of a disease, is one major characteristic of new drugs being developed for cancer and heart disease, the most frequent causes of death.

MOLECULAR MEDICINE

One new drug development is based on genetic knowledge that reveals how a disease starts. As this new field of molecular medicine evolves, the drug industry is reinventing itself. Consequently, there is a lull in the drug pipeline as companies switch to new methods of drug development. As this change occurs, the patents on some classic, best-selling drugs are expiring, which means cheaper generic drugs will replace them. That is good news for the patient's wallet. While generic drugs are not new cures, next-generation drugs just might be.

These new drugs will make it out of research and to market faster. Pharmaceutical giants and the teeny and the not-so-tiny biotech firms are revving up to use novel methods to shorten drug development cycles. The goal is to cut the current 10- to 15-year lab-to-bedside path in half. This acceleration is a boon for patients, as well as a good business practice since a patent will travel further if a drug hits the market sooner. Estimates of drug development costs vary greatly, but according to the Tufts University Center for the Study of Drug Development, it runs about $800 million.

The human DNA sequence gives an inkling of the genetic foundation of a disease and provides drug developers a target, a kind of bookmark. Genes are not straightforward blueprints; they turn on and off and get involved in cellular events in many ways. Finding a lead-in drug discovery involves comparing genes and their activity in healthy and diseased tissue and cells. Next-generation drugs will result from looking at what genes do and the proteins they produce. This is a blossoming field of research called proteomics.

Hunting genes and proteins in this fashion requires new tools, and the result is that biology, chemistry, and informatics are merging. Primarily, drug developers will use bioinformatics to determine whether they have selected the correct gene, its product, and function; have tested it well; have tweaked the compound chemically to enhance its activity; and have experimented to see if it has the desired effect, both in the test-tube and in patients. Now and in the future that work is all about navigating through traffic jams of data.

LIFESTYLE DRUGS

They are called patient-initiated prescription drugs, rejuvenation pharmaceuticals, or lifestyle drugs, and they are for people keen on remedies for a non-life-threatening condition. Drugs to treat depression, obesity, and skin aging were the first lifestyle drugs; then the blockbuster Viagra was introduced as a novel treatment for erectile problems in men. Because of the success of these treatments, investment is growing and new marketing concepts are being explored such as direct advertising to consumers for prescription lifestyle drugs.

In addition to weight-loss drugs for the seriously obese, drugs in the development pipeline will address baldness, wrinkles, hair loss, smoking cessation, premature ejaculation, and the early stages of addiction. Progress in reproductive medicine is leading to new drugs for contraception as well as for infertility treatment. Drug development is expected to rise in all areas associated with anti-aging products. After all, over the next 30 years the number of elderly is expected to increase by 300%. They will enjoy increased life expectancy and will seek to control the non-disease-related effects of aging.

PROVOCATIONS...

Will there be as many new drugs developed for women as for men?

Will doctors use genomic information to design drugs for a single patient?

How will liability be assessed if something goes wrong?

—Vivien Marx

WANT MORE?

NATIONAL INSTITUTES OF HEALTH
www.nih.gov

FOOD AND DRUG ADMINISTRATION
www.fda.gov

FDA CENTER FOR DRUG EVALUATION AND RESEARCH
www.fda.gov/cder

PRESCRIPTION DATABASE
www.nlm.nih.gov/medlineplus/druginformation.html

CENTER WATCH DRUG TRIAL LISTINGS
www.centerwatch.com/patient/trials.html

NEW VACCINES...

Eradicating the Plagues of Mankind

THEY DRANK VENOM, so the story goes, as an attempt to become immune to its effect. The results of this experiment by Indian Buddhists in the 7th century remain murky, but their experiment shows how far back the idea of using immunization reaches. More recently that concept has taken on a new urgency. The release of anthrax spores through the U.S. mail in the fall of 2001 was the first attack of its kind. It led to the deaths of five people from inhaling anthrax. In each case, the bacteria managed to distribute its toxin in these people's bodies, unhindered by the administered antibiotics. The anthrax attack has been a forceful political and public health argument for better therapies and better vaccines. The good news is that new insights into how viruses work and how the immune system operates are jump-starting vaccine research.

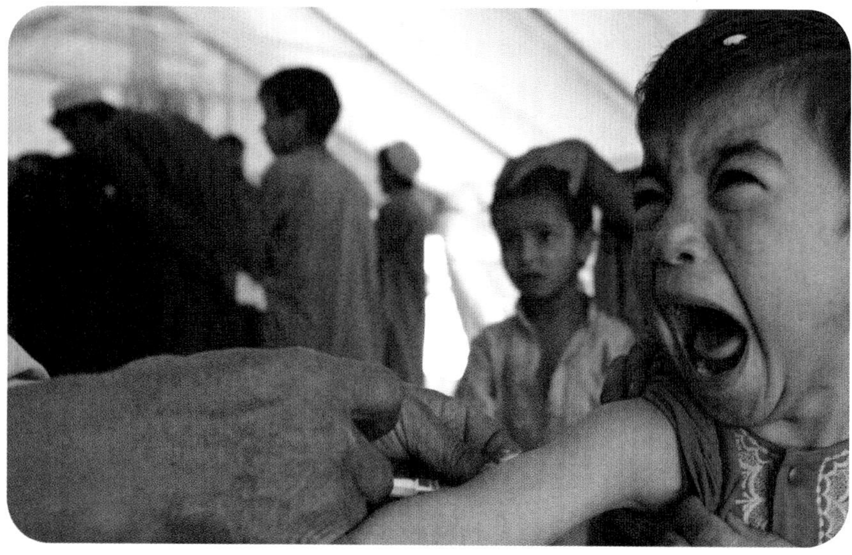

SHRIEKING IN PROTEST. *An Afghan refugee receives her measles vaccination at a refugee center outside Kabul. Among all vaccine-preventable disease, measles is the largest killer of children in Afghanistan.*

All vaccines — the ones for diphtheria, tetanus, influenza, measles, mumps, rubella, varicella, and smallpox, in addition to anthrax — are not in plentiful supply in the U.S. or around the world, a situation slated for change shortly. Currently, there are few vaccine developers and, of those, some are plagued by manufacturing problems. This shortage has in turn rekindled discussion about establishing a National Vaccine Authority that would oversee production and distribution as well as research on vaccines.

THE POLITICS OF VACCINATION...

The prestigious Institute of Medicine, which is part of the National Academy of Sciences, has come out in favor of establishing a National Vaccine Authority, which would be a government authority that could step in when vaccine needs are not met by the private sector. The pharmaceutical industry opposes the proposal and foresees more industrial activity in vaccine research, now that national complacency about infectious diseases has waned. It is likely that a cooperation between the public and private sectors will be set up to develop vaccines in the future, building on new insights in this field. Right now, in addition to a handful of pharmaceuticals in vaccine production, smaller biotechs are revving up to fill in the gaps.

Photo by Natalie Behring Chsiholm/Getty Images

HOW VACCINES WORK

Some researchers call the body's immune response choreography, a concerto. First reactions to an invader involve a general disposal team of cells. The following reactions are more specific with a line of defense that can target particular invaders. It involves producing antibodies, tailored proteins that match the proteins on the invader, such as a bacterium or virus. The antibodies lock into the invader, which marks it for destruction by other specialized cells in the body's immune system. Vaccination helps the body train for a potential attack, priming the immune system to what an invader looks like, allowing a quicker and more effective response.

A novel and potentially powerful vaccine type, DNA vaccines are made from a snippet of genetic coding for a protein that will activate the body's immune system. These vaccines are easier to manufacture than traditional vaccines. Research is underway on both the injecting of naked DNA, as well as DNA that uses a vehicle to enter a cell, such as a specifically engineered virus.

NEW VACCINES, OLD DISEASES

An AIDS vaccine is long overdue, given the large number of deaths and HIV carriers. But even decades into HIV research there is still no vaccine against the tricky virus that undermines the body's immune system. Of late, federal funding for HIV vaccine research has increased, and the pipeline now holds about 12 potential vaccines entering clinical trials. One important new vaccine research approach being applied to HIV and other diseases is called prime-boost. It aims to combine different types of vaccines to induce complementary double-punch immune responses.

Vaccines that protect against parasites are a fast growing market, especially in the animal health pharmaceutical market where they're mainly used to treat livestock. But as more people seek chemical-free food and as concern for animal well-being rises, vaccines are increasingly being explored as ways to ensure animal health, both for livestock as well as pets.

Then there are the trickier parasites, which make the quest for a malaria vaccine difficult. One challenge is the parasites' complicated life cycle. Each life cycle presents different hurdles to the immune system. Researchers are scanning the recently sequenced genomes of the parasites to identify what could be used as vaccine targets to either prevent or lessen the severity of malaria.

There is an anthrax vaccine available. The only FDA-approved vaccine, AVA, for Anthrax Vaccine Adsorbed, does the trick by stimulating the body to produce antibodies that wipe out the bacterium's toxins. But the vaccine is expensive to produce, is in short supply, causes side effects, and must be given 6 times over 18 months and annually after that. So other vaccines are in development to protect the body from the toxin-producing bacterium. Efforts are ongoing to chemically tweak and weaken the toxin so it can be used in a vaccine.

To help the body fight off existing cancer or to stop a cancer from recurring, cancer vaccines are being tested. Just as in the case of other vaccines, what it does is stimulate the body's immune system to build a targeted force of molecules that seek out and destroy tumor cells. Tumors carry signposts, tumor-specific proteins or antigens. For example, PSA, prostate specific antigen, is one protein specific to prostate tumors. A number of labs and companies are trying to use these signposts to prime the immune system to attack the tumor.

VACCINES NOT NEEDED?

Are there diseases for which vaccines are no longer needed? The smallpox campaign has shown that global eradication of a disease is possible. Three infectious disease candidates for global eradication are polio, measles, and rubella. In the year 2000, for example, there were less than 3,000 cases worldwide of polio. Now that researchers have reassembled the polio virus from scratch, eradication appears doubtful. Immunization is a cheap way to deal with public health challenges, the old ones and the new ones.

PROVOCATIONS...

If new vaccines cure addiction, should the government compel addicts to take them? Will Colombian drug lords develop anti-vaccines to stay in business?

—Vivien Marx

WANT MORE?

THE IMMUNIZATION GATEWAY
www.immunofacts.com

THE VACCINE PAGE
www.vaccines.org

CDC
www.cdc.gov/od/nvpo

ALLIANCE FOR VACCINE
www.vaccinealliance.org

CHILDREN'S VACCINE PROGRAM
www.childrensvaccine.org

VAERS (VACCINE ADVERSE EVENT REPORTING SYSTEM)
www.fda.gov/cber/vaers/vaers.htm

DNA VACCINES INFORMATION
www.dnavaccine.com

The Future of Evolution... Revolution in Evolution

"As for a future life, every man must judge for himself between conflicting vague probabilities."

– Charles Darwin, *Life and Letters*

FUTURE FARM. *This painting by Alexis Rockman shows what could result when we apply biotechnology to our allied species, ensuring their survival and making them even more useful to us.*

ALTHOUGH DARWIN was talking about the afterlife when he wrote this, his assessment could be applied just as easily to the future of life on Earth, especially in light of the evolutionary theory he founded. Unlike most of the other topics in this book, evolution's progress is invisible in a human lifetime – the timeframe in which it operates is simply too large. However, we can look at the current state of life on Earth, think about the forces influencing its progress, and construct "conflicting vague probabilities" about evolution's future.

One thing that's certain about future evolution is that it will be driven by the ecosystems in which it takes place – the nature in natural selection. If we want to think about the paths evolution is likely to take, we'll first need to think about the world in which it will take place. Of course, it's a bit simplistic to think of the world's ecosystems as just a theater for evolution; instead, it's a reflexive process, as changes in life on Earth trigger and reinforce further changes in life on Earth. What's different these days is the wildly disproportionate effect that one animal – homo sapiens – is having on all the other lifeforms on Earth. Mankind has reshaped the Earth through construction and mining, changed the composition of the atmosphere and water, reduced the diversity of plant and animal species in most ecosystems, and asserted its dominance with consumption and population.

It's a good thing nature is so tough. Life on Earth has survived ice ages thousands of years long, meteor impacts that resulted in year-long rains of fiery impact fragments, and decades of dust-driven darkness, even other dominant species that stood atop the food chain for millions of years. Given beneficial genetic mutations, natural selection, and a few billion years, life keeps improving itself, finding the best ways to survive in the world it inhabits.

So the plants and animals most likely to be the next winners of the evolutionary lottery are those best adapted to the Earth that humans are creating. The most obvious of these is, of course, mankind itself. Barring a nuclear, climatic, or biological Armageddon of our own making, humans will remain Earth's dominant species. We're simply too good at too many things to encounter a situation we can't make the best of. An asteroid slamming into our planet might dramatically reduce our numbers, but those who survive would figure out how to live on the Earth that's left.

Other winners will likely be our allied species: rice, wheat, and corn; cows, pigs, and salmon; dogs, cats, and grass, to name a few. We've stacked the odds in favor of these species – leveled forests to plant our crops, tamed wolves to keep us company, and depleted aquifers to create steaks and golf courses. Now that we have the tools of biotechnology at our disposal, we're likely to increase diversity within these species, even as we reduce diversity among species in general. We'll have 50 varieties of pig, each created to serve a specific need – from bacon pig to pancreas pig to pet pig – but we'll no longer have the wild boar, which lives on land that could be farmed and really serves no purpose, after all.

Or perhaps the boar will find a way to adapt to us. As we've created a more hospitable world for ourselves, and the species on which we depend, we've also created opportunities for other, less desirable species. Our cities, with their abundance of sewers, garbage dumpsters, and other dark places, have proven to be ideal environments for the Norway rat and the cockroach. Our vast fields of homogenous plant life have attracted a host of "pests," like the boll weevil and the corn borer, who are just taking advantage of what are for them ideal places to live. And our global transportation systems have shrunk the size of the Earth, making it possible for alien life forms – the zebra mussel, the snakehead fish, the West Nile virus – to find new habitats where, without their natural predators, they can thrive. They will continue to thrive, along with any other species who can find ways to adapt to the crowded, toxic, agricultural, and overexploited world that mankind is creating.

The same situation will likely hold true in the world of flora – the survivors will be those plants we humans deem necessary to our survival and those plants that can figure out how to hitch a ride with us. In both worlds, the losers will likely be those lifeforms that get in our way. From the Moa to the Heath Hen to the Bigleaf Scurfpea, evolution has little tolerance for those species that cannot adapt to a changed survival situation. Human-created deforestation, species exploitation, and ecosystem disruption have become the most powerful forces of evolution, to both good and ill effect.

We've even begun to take the reins of our own evolution. Changes in lifestyle have resulted in a doubling of our lifespans over the last 1,000 years, finding this potential within ourselves far faster than truly "natural" selection would have. Now we're beginning to directly manipulate our genomes. The first modified human could appear in the next 100 years, certainly within the next 1,000 – an eye blink in evolutionary time. We will take over for nature, replacing risky reproduction and mutation with the risk of making changes to a system we only superficially understand, in the hope of becoming better adapted to the world we're creating.

Of course, all of this could be wrong. Completely wrong, dead wrong. In 100,000 years, humans could be the servants of elephants who, under the intense survival pressures we applied to them, evolved higher brain functions and tool-using abilities. Or polydactyl housecats could develop opposable thumbs and wreak unimaginable havoc. Or some transgenetic crop could hybridize with a nanomachine spore, drowning the world in a flood of bionic daisies. Or we humans could eventually realize just what kind of an effect we're having on ourselves, our world, and its other inhabitants, and decide to act differently. What seems certain, though, is that in some form, and in the ways it has for the past 3.8 billion years, life will prevail.

PROVOCATIONS...

Will pets evolve to do housework?

Are "flaws" likely to disappear in human nature, or are they the very things that make us human?

—Bill Kaszubski

WANT MORE?

EVOLUTION TV SHOW
www.pbs.org/wgbh/evolution

PALEONTOLOGY MUSEUM
www.ucmp.berkeley.edu/history/evolution.html

EVOLUTIONARY DYNAMICS
www.santafe.edu/sfi/research/focus/evolutionaryDynamics/index.html

INTERNATIONAL JOURNAL OF ORGANIC EVOLUTION
http://evol.allenpress.com/evolonline/

Matching Machines and Minds:
SAVING THE FUTURE OF COMPUTERS

THE COMPUTER AND OTHER TECHNOLOGY interfaces we use, like the spoken and written languages we use, mold how we think, and how we think — consciously or unconsciously — determines how we view and interact with our technology. It also colors how we see the world: I remember overhearing two teenage boys looking out over the Pacific at a beautiful sunset, "Takes a lot of pixels to do that," said one. "Yeah, the sunlight scattering and the surface modeling is perfect," replied the other, in awe of the beauty and only half-joking.

They see fog as a way to save having to render distant objects (a strategy employed in *Myst*, written when computers were less capable than they now are). But even we more mundane users are affected by our use of computers. An elementary school teacher with a class that uses word processors feels free to require rewrites to correct details and even change things around. Without word processors, students might be asked for one revision, or just have to read the teacher's comments.

How we behave depends on the tools in front of us. How we use computers doesn't depend much on the processor inside. We have transcended the physical; the real interest should be in the software — not in the hardware.

Oddly, most of the attention of the digerati focuses on the latest hardware, its case color, or movie versions with futuristic readouts and handwaving inputs. Direct mind-to-machine communication is hot, if unaccomplished, but wearables and stealth eyeglasses that invisibly (to others) deliver a full-screen view to you bring us closer to that dream. Microprocessors infect every device in which electrons move, giving them undreamed of abilities to confuse and upset us. Whoops. Let's play that last bit back slowly.

...undreamed of abilities to make things easier and faster. There, that sounds more like a *Catalog of Tomorrow* sentence. Unfortunately, it is not uniformly true. Do you find it hard to remember which of those four symmetrically placed buttons on your digital watch does what? Do you get a new piece of software and then realize that you dread having to learn it?

Just when you get comfortable with version 5.3 of something, are you forced to upgrade to 6.0 because some other program or service you use every day demands it? And then do you have to get a computer with more memory and a faster processor to run it all, even though your "old" computer was the latest thing three years ago and would otherwise be perfectly satisfactory?

The last time computers got easier to use was when the Macintosh was introduced in 1984. That was the year my first child was born, and he's now a sophomore in college. Ever since then, digital devices have gotten harder to use. And it's not only because we're doing more with them. Even the tasks we did way back then, such as word processing, are now harder to learn and have become impossible to master.

We need a new revolution. And it won't originate on the hardware or software side — it will come from the study of how the human mind works. For example, when I spent time at Xerox PARC in the early 1970s, I watched people confused at using the mouse. To select some text, you had to press one button here and another button there. When I designed the Mac, I wanted to treat text (which is just a picture with lots of little squiggly things, if you think about it) the way I treated images, so I invented "click-and-drag" where you just sweep from one end of the selection to another, and whereby you can just latch onto an object and move it around. This changed our mindset from text as a sequence of characters to text as an object with geometric properties, something only graphic artists had considered up to that time.

When machines were mostly mechanical, the engineering discipline of ergonomics was born. Ergonomics studies how big and small people are, how strong they are, how fast they can move, and other physical properties. Cognetics is the mental analog of ergonomics. It is a new discipline because only in the last few decades have machines that interact with our intellects become widely available.

Cognetics studies questions such as how long can you remember a message, what causes a computer user to make mistakes, what makes us comfortable or uncomfortable with a widget or interface feature, how long will it take us to do a task with this method versus that method, how efficiently can a job be done, and how close to the maximum efficiency is the method we are using?

Cognitive psychologists, computer scientists, and practical interface designers have made some suprising discoveries over the last decade. They've learned that we are not aware of many of our own mental limitations. Because of this, most of the common user interface techniques, usually called "GUIs" for "graphic user interfaces," actually impede our use of computers. For example, adding sounds, such as those accompanying opening and closing windows and other system actions, slows down the user. Even harder to believe, but borne out by many experiments, is that we can pay attention to only one thing at a time. This accounts for many of the errors humans make using computers. The designers put up an indicator (like the light on the caps lock key), but we often don't notice the indicator because we are concentrating on getting some task done.

People often blame themselves for the problems they have using computers, PDAs, fancy cell phones, and the like. Time and time again, I hear users say, "How stupid of me, I knew better than to do that." In almost every case it was not stupid of the user, but stupid of the designer. An architect who does not know the strengths and weaknesses of materials is a danger to anybody who inhabits a building he or she designs. A software architect who does not know the strengths and weaknesses of the human mind is a danger to anybody who has to use their software.

Many things keep the industry from changing. The biggest problems are complacency (we're making billions, that's good enough) and fear (if we make any big changes, our customers will stop buying our product). The tools that come with computer languages and development systems embody the mistakes of the present generation of interfaces. They force you to build bad products because they have built-in widgets that replicate the mistakes of the past couple of decades. To do something different is technically difficult. Programmers trained in using the present toolsets have to learn new techniques in order to do better.

When I am hired to improve the usability and learnability of software, I am told, "Make it distinctive, very easy to learn and use, give it a feel that will set our company apart, go beyond the state of the art." Then I am asked, "Are you familiar with the Windows guidelines?" because they expect me to keep to industry standards.

At this point, I go into a *Sesame Street* routine where I explain that for something to be better than a competitor's, it has to be different from their product. If you want something a lot better, then it is going to be very different.

In the next 5–10 years new ways of using digital devices will appear alongside of today's boring and tedious menus. They will coexist for a while, and there will be compromise and composite systems that will satisfy nobody. Eventually, the new methods will be nearly universal, and only a few old diehards will continue to use software that looks like Windows. We will not think in terms of applications, the desktop, or operating systems (my definition of an operating system: the program you have to hassle with before you get to hassle with the application). Our work will be in terms of the creative content and the particular transformation we wish to bring upon it.

—Jef Raskin

THE INTERNET... The Planet Grows a Mind

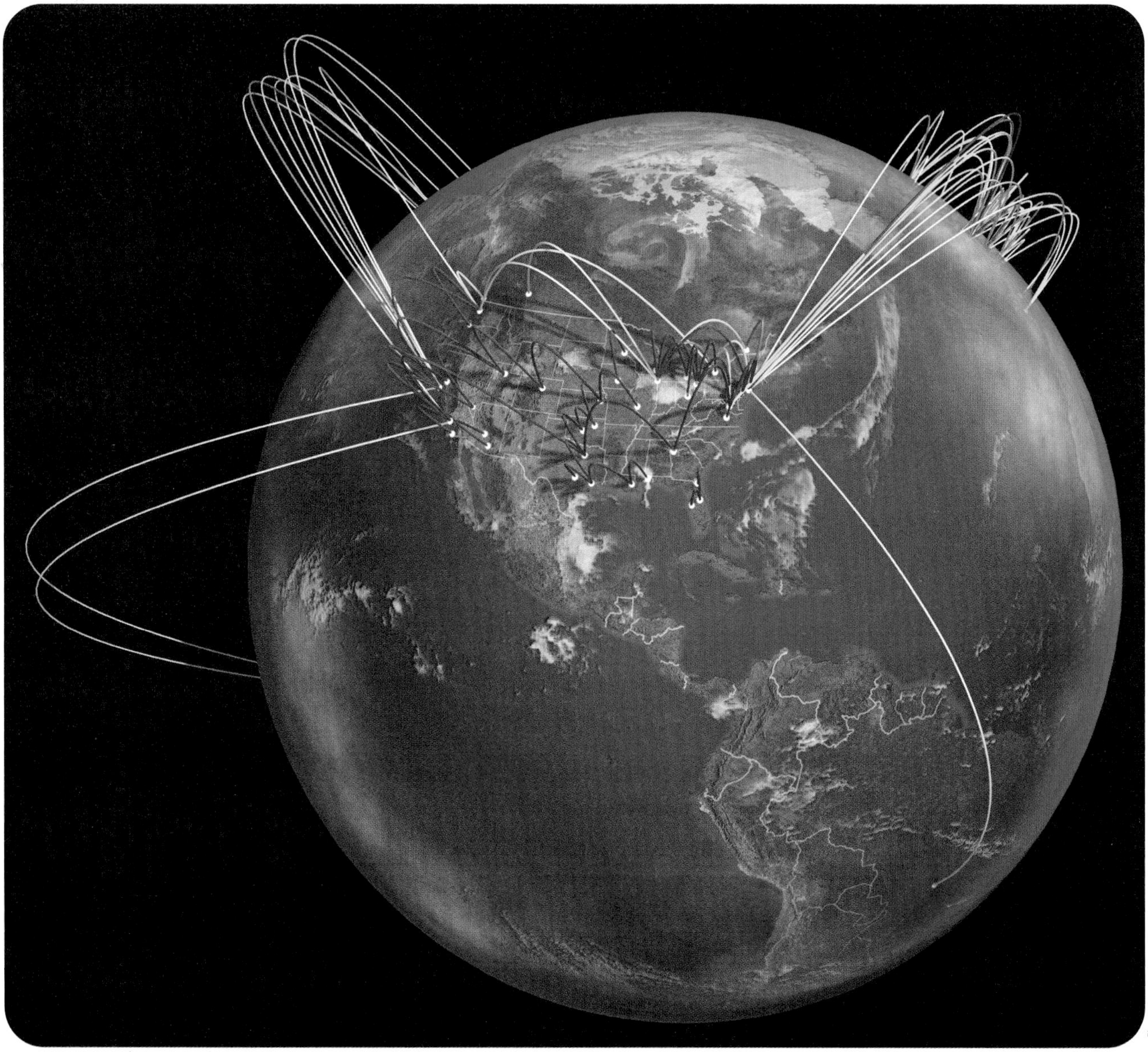

Image courtesy of Peacock Maps, Incorporated. Artist: Irena Slage.

If there's one certainty about the future of the Internet, it's that it will continue to grow — and become more important in our day-to-day lives. The history of the Internet is one of unprecedented growth. According to NUA, the number of Internet users worldwide increased five-fold in the five-year period from 1997 to 2001, from 101 million to 527 million. This extraordinary growth is expected to continue, with the Computer Industry Almanac projecting 945 million Internet users by 2004, and 1.4 billion users by 2007.

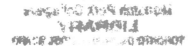

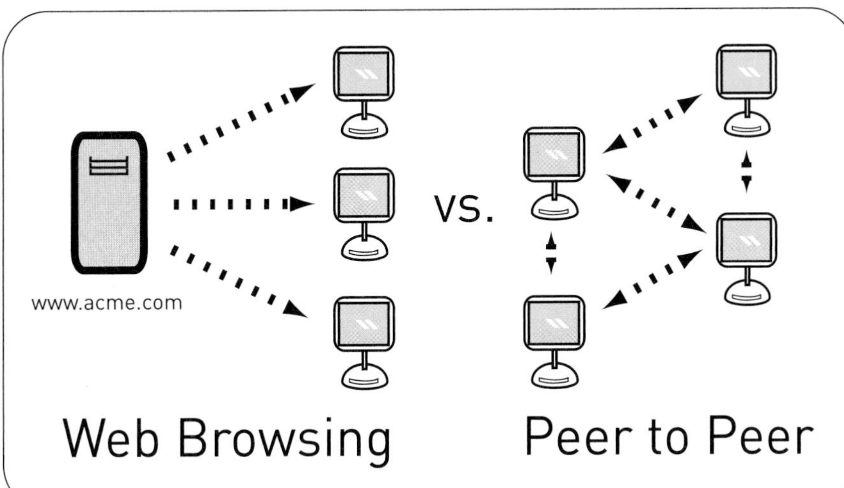

NO CENTRAL SERVER. *Peer-to-peer computing eliminates central file servers and lets individual PCs share data directly.*

Equally important, the future will bring more Internet connections. The days of one individual having one connection to the Internet are already gone; today, we connect to the Internet at work, and we connect at home. (That's two connections per person.) Tomorrow, we'll also connect when we're between work and home — via Internet-enabled PDAs, mobile phones, and maybe even *Star Trek*-like personal communicators.

This type of constant connection will be enabled by the increased availability of fast wireless Internet access. According to the *Computer Industry Almanac*, 46% of U.S. users (and 67% of European users) will have wireless Internet access by 2007. Wireless access via cell phone is already a big deal in Japan, where subscribers use third-generation (3G) phones to fetch their email and graphically surf the Web.

When the Internet is always available, there will be less need to carry data with you, or to store it locally. A constant Internet connection provides instant access to any information stored online, no matter where you are or what you're doing.

PEER-TO-PEER COMPUTING

This doesn't necessarily mean that there will be a single giant database of information for you to access. Just the opposite; data will be dispersed among thousands or even millions of individual computers. This concept of eliminating central file servers and letting individual PCs serve the data is called *peer-to-peer (P2P)* computing. Most of us got our first taste of P2P with Napster, which created a massive file-sharing system using millions of subscribers' PCs. Even though Napster was eventually shut down (for sharing too many copyrighted files), P2P continues in services like Music City Morpheus and Madster.

Of course, P2P isn't limited to sharing digital music files. P2P technology can also be used to store and disseminate information without being tapped, traced, or monitored in any way, shape, or form. This concept is being pioneered by Freenet, a P2P network that constantly moves data from one computer to another, in total anonymity. A file might reside on one computer today and a totally different computer tomorrow — which makes the data stored on Freenet both anonymous and censorship proof.

INTERNET2

The Internet, as you know it, will soon be obsolete.

A consortium of major universities, government agencies, and high-tech corporations (including Cisco and Nortel) are building a new Internet, dubbed Internet2. This new Internet is designed to connect select academic and government users outside the increasingly cluttered and unreliable current Internet.

This new Internet will be faster and more reliable than the current version. To that end, Internet2 will run over two backbones provided by Qwest and the National Science Foundation and connect to participating universities and agencies at gigapops — network points of presence capable of transferring data at an eye-popping rate of 1 gigabyte per second.

While the average home or business user will not have access to Internet2, we will all benefit from new applications developed for the new Internet — and from the bandwidth freed up by organizations shifting to Internet2 connections.

PRIVACY AND SECURITY

The desire to keep information out of the hands of any central authority will be increasingly important as Internet users grapple with the growing conflict between security and privacy. Government entities want increased powers to monitor Internet-based communications, under the pretext of stopping future terrorist attacks and criminal activity. Freedom-of-speech advocates view these changes as unwarranted

BUSY CYBERCAFE. *In a typical week, approximately 35,000 users will anonymously access the Internet from this New York City cybercafe.*

GROWING THE INFRASTRUCTURE

Just as the growth of phones, pagers, and faxes created a shortage of phone numbers and the creation of new area codes, so too has the explosion of Internet-connected devices created a shortage of Internet Protocol (IP) addresses. The current Internet Protocol, version 4, has room for about 4 billion addresses — which seems like a lot, even though it isn't nearly enough to assign an address to every computer or device currently connected to the Internet.

The solution is a new protocol, IPv6. This new protocol has room for about 35 trillion addresses — enough to provide an individual address to every grain of sand on Earth.

And the more Internet connections there are, the more bandwidth will be necessary to service all these users and devices. According to Insight Research, the amount of total Internet traffic per day is expected to increase from 20,000 terabits in 2001 to 1.5 million terabits in 2006. To handle this increased traffic, the major Internet bandwidth providers — Sprint, GTE, Qwest, et al. — are busy laying thousands of miles of extremely high-bandwidth fiber-optic cable and installing tens of thousands of new routers, switches, and other connecting devices.

invasions of privacy, and reject any attempts to increase online surveillance. Any entity trying to control the Internet will find massive resistance from the increasing base of Internet users.

One of the most visible threats to the daily working of the Internet comes from computer viruses and worms. According to ISCA Labs, the rate of virus infection in North America in 2001 was 113 infections per 1,000 computers; most users can expect to find at least one infected email a month in their inboxes.

Another significant threat comes from hackers and crackers executing attacks on computer systems and networks. According to the Computer Security Institute, 90% of U.S. businesses and government agencies suffered hacker attacks within the past year, resulting in $455 million in damages. The average cost of each attack topped $200,000; major attacks can shut down individual Web sites and whole ISPs.

A more innocuous threat comes from what experts call *unrequested commercial emails* (*UCEs*), or what lay users call *spam*. Spam is the online equivalent of junk mail, and too many spam messages can clog your inbox and make your email unmanageable. As if you couldn't tell, the spam problem is major; according to Jupiter Media Metrix, the average Internet user receives 700 pieces of spam a year — for a total of 206 billion individual messages. This number is expected to double by 2006, if not before.

While you can use antivirus and

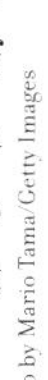

personal firewall software to minimize your personal risk, experts somehow have to stop these threats at the source — or risk a catastrophic collapse of the entire Internet.

VIRTUAL COMMUNITY

The Internet encourages the development of virtual communities, with users from all around the world joining together to engage in like activities. No matter what your field of interest, the Internet enables you to associate with other hobbyists in different cities, states, and countries, in real-time, without the expense of a long-distance phone call or plane ticket; distance is no longer a limiting factor. In fact, users in these virtual communities often develop closer ties than they have to neighbors or colleagues in their physical communities — and the extension of the Internet further around the globe will only increase the importance of online community.

As our online relationships become more important, what becomes of traditional face-to-face interactions? When we're constantly wired, will we spend less time talking to real-world friends and family?

It's impossible to know the long-term impact of the Internet on our day-to-day activities and relationships. All we know is that in a short 10 years the Internet has become an important part of our daily lives; in the future, it's likely to become more integral to what we do — and to how we do it.

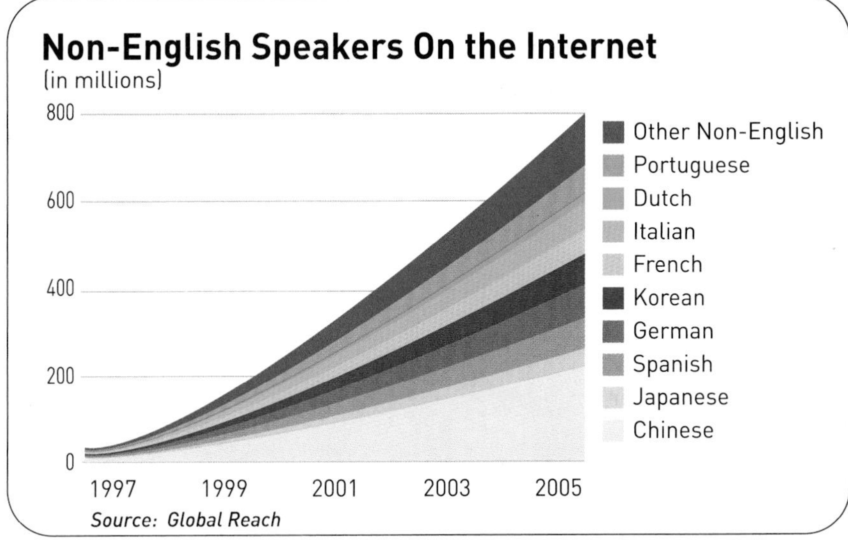

PROVOCATIONS...

As our online relationships become more important, what becomes of traditional face-to-face interactions?

When we're constantly wired, will we spend less time talking to real-world friends and family?

How will we manage to maintain the balance between an increasingly commercial Internet and the the "shared commons" nature of the Internet as it was originally conceived?

—Michael Miller

WHERE WIZARDS STAY UP LATE

Where Wizards Stay Up Late: The Origins of the Internet, by Katie Hafner and Matthew Lyon (Touchstone Books, 1998).

This remarkable history of the invention of the Internet is a must-read for anyone who wants to understand how the most complicated invention humankind has ever built came into being. *Where Wizards Stay Up Late* traces the history, circumstances, and personalities that conjured the Internet into existence, drawing heavily on the first-person accounts of the wizards themselves. Hafner weaves these personal stories into a gripping narrative of the moment of grace that enveloped a group of lucky geniuses who assembled the building blocks of the Internet from scratch.

WANT MORE?

ELECTRONIC FRONTIER FOUNDATION
www.eff.org

SATN WEBLOG BY INTERNET PIONEERS DAVID REED, BOB FRANKSTON, AND DAN BRICKLIN
www.satn.org

MADSTER P2P SERVICE
www.madster.com

THE FREE NETWORK PROJECT
www.freenetproject.org

INTERNET2
www.internet2.edu

OPENP2P
www.openp2p.com

TREND MICRO VIRUS INFORMATION CENTER
www.antivirus.com/vinfo

EMAILABUSE.ORG
www.emailabuse.org

BROADBAND... Faster Is Better

It's all about speed. When the Internet moved out of the university environment, users had to find some way to connect their home and business computers to the growing Internet. The easiest way to connect was to let someone else do it — via Internet service providers (ISPs) that had their own connections, either direct or indirect, to the Internet backbone. Consumers used modems to dial into their ISPs, via normal phone lines, and were then plugged into the Internet itself, via the ISPs' connections to the backbone.

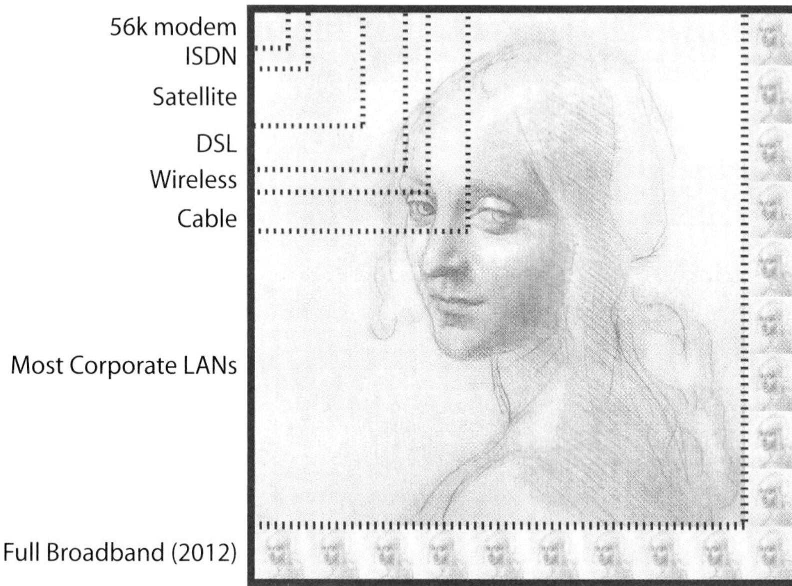

Source: *Special Edition Using the Internet and Web* (Que, 2002)

HOW FAST IS FAST? *If the image above is 1 megabyte (about the size of an average digital photograph), here's how much of it will download in 1 second using various kinds of Internet connections.*

IS BROADBAND GROWING — OR DYING?

Experts predicted a rapid shift from dial-up to broadband access; the experts were wrong. Not only has the move to broadband been slower than projected, some experts now believe that the number of broadband subscribers may have already peaked.

The cost of broadband (roughly twice the cost of dial-up access) is one factor; another is the slow and unsteady roll-out from the major Internet service providers. The past few years have seen numerous DSL and cable service providers go out of business or file for bankruptcy protection, leaving millions of broadband users in the lurch. For a cable company or telco offering broadband service, the economics are daunting; it currently costs far more to connect a new broadband customer than any company can hope to recoup. And, to make matters worse, the telcos and cable companies behind broadband are woefully underequipped to handle the complexity of providing the service. (In some areas, it can take months to get a new broadband connection up and running.)

As you might expect, this combination of high prices and poor service is universally unappealing, and many users simply don't see the benefits of a broadband connection. As of the end of 2001, 85% of U.S. Internet subscribers were still accessing the Internet via a dial-up connection — because many dial-up users either don't see the need for speed or don't want to pay higher monthly fees. (Jupiter Media Metrix reports that fully 76% of current dial-up users were uninterested or neutral about broadband.)

While broadband will undoubtedly be part of the future of the Internet, these pricing and performance issues must be solved before the mainstream audience switches from their more affordable and, in most cases, more reliable dial-up connections.

The big problem with dial-up access, of course, is that it's slow. It's also not always available; you have to manually dial up whenever you want to access the Net. Fortunately, dial-up access isn't the only way to connect to the Internet. When you're tired of slow-loading Web pages and impossible-to-play real-time audio and video, you can switch from a dial-up connection to a faster broadband connection.

Broadband isn't a single technology; there are several different ways to increase the speed of an Internet connection. The two most popular types of broadband today are digital cable and DSL (Digital Subscriber Line), which offers fast connections over standard telephone lines. Broadband is also available via two-way satellite (using the small dishes popularized by DIRECTV and the Dish Network) and wireless transmission.

Depending on the type of broadband connection you have, your connection speed will be anywhere from 6X to 40X faster than a typical 56Kbps dial-up connection. In most cases the speed will be faster downstream than upstream; this type of asynchronous communication provides a bigger pipe for the data you download to your computer, based on the assumption that most "mouse-potato" users download more data than they upload.

This speed comes at a price. Most broadband plans run about $50 a month, compared to the $20-$25 per month rate of a typical dial-up plan. For that price, you get both a faster connection and one that's always on, no manual dialing necessary.

When you have a broadband connection, your Internet usage patterns change. It's a simple fact — when the Web is faster and always accessible, you spend more time online. According to J.D. Power and Associates, users who switched from dial-up to broadband registered 23% more time spent online, 25% more individual Internet sessions, and 130% more page views.

With the Web server software that ships with every new PC, you can run your Web site from your own house. Attach it to a $30 Webcam and you can keep an eye on your cats from your desk at work. That monstrous router of the past has shrunk to a $50 "broadband gateway." Plug it into your DSL or cable modem, connect all the computers in your house to it, switch it on, and presto! The entire house is wired. Want to listen to an Internet radio station in the kitchen or broadcast one from your living room? You now have the tools.

As more users move to broadband, we'll see new applications developed to take advantage of the increased bandwidth. It's not just about faster-loading Web pages; the future of broadband will include multimedia presentations, two-way videoconferencing, real-time audio and video streaming, and pay-per-view movies on demand.

PROVOCATIONS...

Will certain people only move to communities with high-speed connections? When will we see DSL modems at Goodwill?

—Michael Miller

THE DOWNSIDE OF BROADBAND

When you're always connected to the Internet, as you are with a broadband connection, you put your personal computer at higher risk of attack. Hackers can force their way into your system, viruses and worms can infect your hard drive, and unscrupulous sorts can monitor every keystroke and mouse movement you make.

It's not that PCs with dial-up access can't be attacked; it's just that the longer you're online, the more visible you are to potential attackers. An always-on broadband connection makes your computer particularly visible, and thus particularly vulnerable.

The best way to protect your computer against outside attackers is to install a firewall between your PC and the Internet. A firewall is a piece of software that acts as a barrier between your computer and the Internet; attacks are stopped at the firewall, before they can reach your PC.

Personal firewall software is both affordable and easy to use. There are many low-priced commercial programs available, such as BlackICE PC Protection and ZoneAlarm, and there's even a bare bones firewall built into the Windows XP operating system.

WANT MORE?

BROADBAND GUIDE
www.broadband-guide.com

BROADBAND REPORTS
www.broadbandreports.com

HOME NETWORKING
www.homenethelp.com

HOME PC FIREWALL GUIDE
www.firewallguide.com

ICSA FIREWALL COMMUNITY
www.icsalabs.com/html/communities/firewalls/index.shtml

WIRELESS... The Anywhere, Anytime Connection

Since Marconi's first transatlantic radio broadcast in 1901, technologists have evolved millions of applications for radio, communicating with and controlling devices at great distance without wires. But no application is more compelling than wireless Internet access — the anywhere, anytime connection.

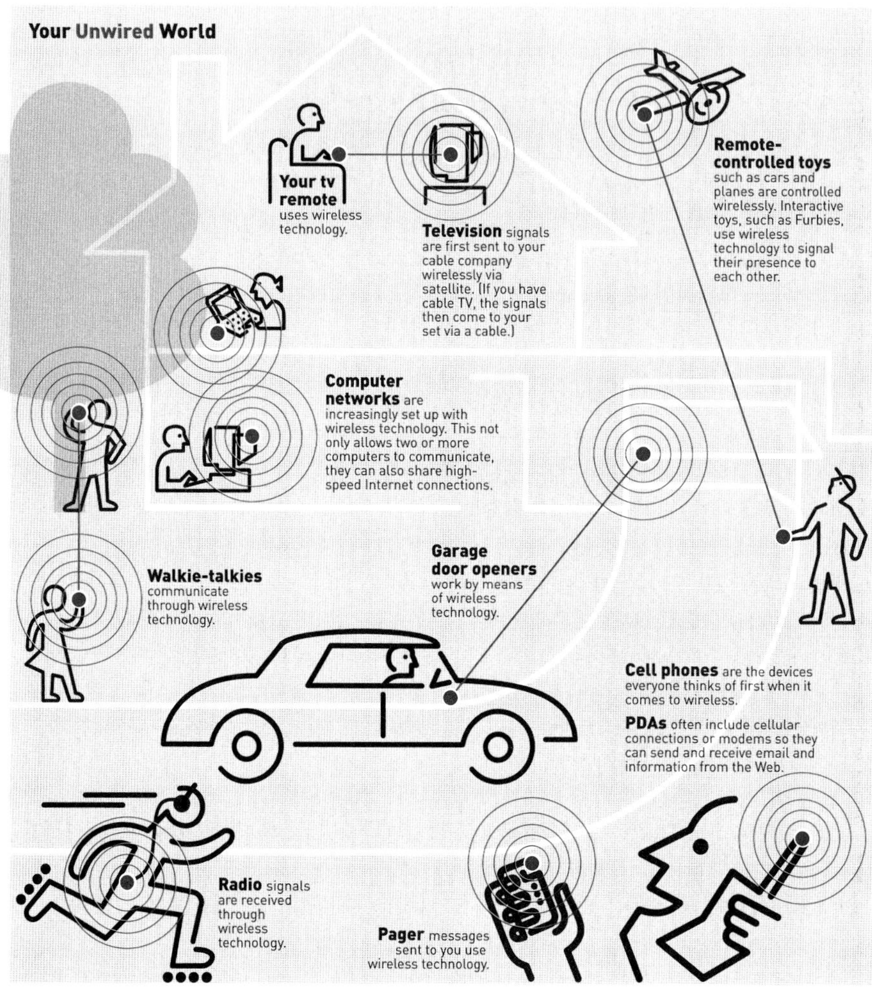

AN UNWIRED WORLD. *We live in a world increasingly characterized by wireless communication devices, from garage door openers to sophisticated PDAs.*

Graphic by Nigel Holmes

Although the wireless Internet hasn't caught on in the U.S. as it has in places like Japan, where more than 2 million people use their wireless handsets to send email across the Internet, wireless applications are certainly growing in the U.S. At the TechXNY expo in New York City in June 2002, vendors and developers discussed the build out of wireless "hot spots" in large venues such as airports and stadiums. Cisco Systems has worked with the Ochsner Medical Institute in New Orleans to create a "wireless hospital." Denver, Colorado, will be the first city in the U.S. with complete wireless Internet coverage. Ricochet Networks is supplying the city with 1,000 wireless modems and unlimited service for its law enforcement agencies. At Disney World in Florida, wireless technology is used for everything from point-of-sale transactions, such as food carts, to headset units for foreign guests that provide simultaneous translation into multiple languages. And Federal Express uses wireless technology to provide up-to-the-minute information about every shipment they process.

According to *Wireless Week*, there are something like 300 million handsets in use around the globe. By 2005, this number is expected to hit 1 billion. Gartner's Dataquest Inc., predicts that there will be more wireless handsets than televisions and PCs combined by 2005. That's a wireless explosion, perhaps even a revolution. The newest generation of wireless devices — including RIM's Blackberry — integrates telephone, email, Web browsing, calendar, and personal information management into a hand-sized device.

BUILDING THE WIRELESS NET

The FCC is at the center of the wireless revolution. It sells off slices of the radio-frequency (RF) spectrum to licensed carriers — mostly cellular companies — who've been promising for years to use

WIRELESS SUPPORT. *The NYC Wireless collective created an instant ad-hoc network in the wake of the 9-11 disaster.*

KRT Photograph by Susan Watta/New York Daily Times

their apportioned airwaves to deliver high-speed Internet access in the form of third-generation (3G) networks. These networks are envisioned as a kind of cell phone for computers, providing wireless Internet connections to computers and handheld devices. 3G has yet to bear any fruit, however, and there are those who remain skeptical about its future.

Instead of the phone companies, we may need to look to ordinary citizens to build the wireless Internet. The FCC has opened up some small pieces of the RF spectrum for unlicensed use. Traditionally, these unlicensed bands have been known as the "junk bands," because so many different devices—from microwave ovens to cordless phones — share them, but their presence has spurred a worldwide revolution in low-power wireless networking.

802.11B - "WI-FI"

These radio free-fire zones have been fertile breeding grounds for "community wireless" projects, where groups of public-spirited geeks are slowly blanketing major cities around the world with wireless data networks. These networks have been made possible by a free wireless standard called 802.11b, or Wi-Fi, for wireless fidelity. While these networks have severely limited ranges, they are so cheap and popular that they have overcome their short range. Many companies have sprung up to provide commercial wireless access through "hotspots" in airports and cafes. These WISPS (wireless ISPs) compete with the free community networks that are mushrooming to provide Internet access everywhere, not just where the business elite congregate.

802.11A – A FASTER STANDARD

802.11a offers wireless connections at five times the speed of Wi-Fi. The low cost of 802.11a, combined with its high speed, makes it an ideal candidate for replacing the long-haul, high-speed backbones currently used to connect most ISPs' customers to the Internet. Disaster-relief agencies, municipalities, and commercial providers are eyeing 802.11a as the ideal way to extend Internet access to corners of the world that have been neglected due to the economics of laying high-speed wires in the ground.

COMMUNITY WIRELESS

The NYC Wireless collective swarmed downtown Manhattan after the 9-11 disaster, connecting open 802.11b access points to working Internet connections in homes and businesses, creating an instant ad-hoc network that was employed by emergency services, displaced victims, and businesses that had lost phone and Internet service. The BAWUG wireless group in the Bay Area is launching a high-speed, high-reliability 802.11a network for emergency services and scientific research. Nearly every industrialized city has a loose-knit band of wireless hackers who are building and deploying low-cost wireless Internet access points. The community wireless network phenomenon may be the wave of the future.

PROVOCATIONS...

What are the risks and rewards for a corporation of having employees scattered around the globe using wireless devices? Will our email and other personal data be secure from hacking, prying, and eavesdropping when everything is transmitted wirelessly?

—Cory Doctorow and Charles O. Stewart III

WANT MORE?

RESEARCH IN MOTION
www.rim.net

CISCO SYSTEMS
www.cisco.com

RICOCHET
www.ricochet.com

WIRELESS DEVCENTER
www.oreillynet.com/wireless

802.11B NETWORKING NEWS
http://80211b.weblogger.com

BOINGO WIRELESS
www.boingo.com

SPUTNIK WIRELESS
www.sputnik.com

SKYPILOT
www.skypilot.com

NYC WIRELESS
www.nycwireless.net

PERSONAL TELCO
www.personaltelco.net

ULTRA-WIDEBAND WORKING GROUP
www.uwb.org

THE FUTURE OF SOFTWARE... FROM PRECISION ENGINEERING TO GARDENING

SOFTWARE DRIVES THE *modern world; it is the symbolic instruction that brings computers to life, combining with electricity to transform a computer from an inert hunk of silicon chips into the most flexible tool the world has ever seen.*

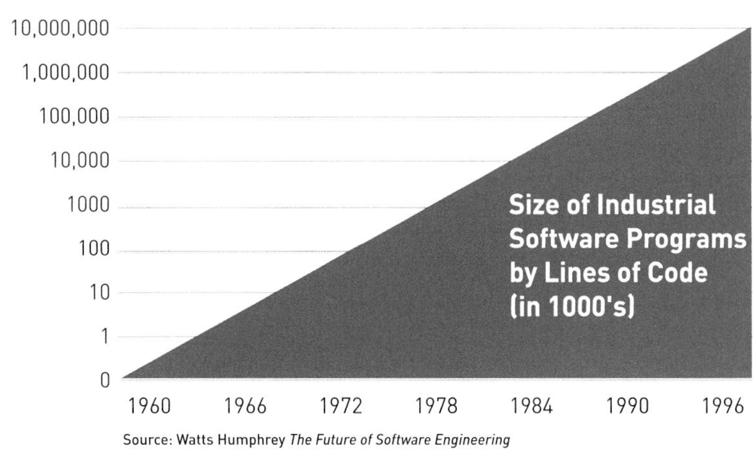

Watts Humphrey, of Carnegie Mellon University, estimates that the size of the software used to accomplish any computer function grows 10 times every 5 years. A byproduct of this growth is that bugs in software, assuming they are unavoidable, will grow more prevalent over time.

For two generations, the paradigm of computer programming has been rooted in deterministic notions of precision engineering. Code is exact: Built by hand, bit by bit, it faithfully fulfills every word of its instructions — blindly following the letter of its creators' commands. And as the developers' facility with software has increased, so has our appetite and expectations for their products. We yearn, and are fulfilled — or frustrated — in code.

As raw computing power has increased, the domains of human effort in which software plays a role have become more abstract — computer programs have exponentially increased in both complexity and sloppiness. The complexity is unavoidable, an artifact of the very complex tasks we expect the computer to perform. The sloppiness is a byproduct of market forces, the need to deliver a (mostly) working product before the competition does. Our world is shaped by the result: commercial software both magnificent and maddeningly buggy.

But don't blame the software developer; not even a vast team of geniuses working in a top-down manner could anticipate every bug. Even NASA uses "double fault tolerant" software systems, conceding that failure in code of sufficient complexity is impossible to predict.

In the coming decades, software will be created, used, and understood in ways that are very different from today. The first crack in the "precision engineering" orthodoxy has come with the rise of open-source software, where quasi-leaderless groups of programmers self organize to develop public domain software products that rival (and often route) the best efforts of commercial firms. This "bottom-up" approach allows for greater innovation by taking advantage of swarms of motivated talent that swaps fixed control for community involvement, thereby eliminating the time-to-market forces that degrade so many commercial efforts. The open-source software movement has inculcated the software engineering community with the power and value of cooperation, and provided a vehicle for doing so.

The next step in this progression toward decentralized software engineering may come from an entirely new paradigm called *genetic programming*. This is the use of software to write software — the human programmer provides the desired results, and the computer, borrowing a theme from Darwin, iterates and mutates its way to the desired solution. With genetic programming, as it's called, the software engineer doesn't "program" in the usual sense, she "gardens": pruning the growing program, selecting desirable results, and making way for new growth. This approach, still in its infancy, has already produced a myriad of results, from protein analyzing programs that are better than those created by professional molecular biologists to data-searching algorithms that are faster than any devised by theoretical computer scientists. In this world, the winning approach the computer takes to a programming problem may be unknown, perhaps even unknowable, even to the programmer himself, who posed the original question. And the approach isn't limited to the dry world of algorithms, everything from art to music to software interfaces could be evolved and optimized using the same technique.

And over this horizon is the evolution of "evolvability" itself – the ability to not only perform, but to do so in a wide array of computational and networked environments and in conjunction with many other programs as part of a larger whole. As the bandwidth of the Internet improves, many software applications in the future will likely not be delivered intact, but assembled on-the-fly from highly evolved parts. You may simply "scoop" word processing, or drawing and painting, from the software-enriched environment — wherever you happen to be, at a PC, in your car, or walking down the street.

And ultimately, as software manifests itself in the real world with increasing frequency, it may change our notions of physical space altogether – we may come to see code as part of the world, an aspect of the environment like color, shape, and texture.

PROGRAMMERS: THE NEXT GENERATION. *The demand for professional software programmers is at an all-time high – the most conservative estimates put the need at more than 300,000, a 50% increase over current levels. One answer to the gap might lay in programs like ToonTalk, a completely new kind of software – both a state-of-the-art programming language and a video game designed to teach the basics of programming, including constructing, debugging, and running programs.*

PROVOCATIONS...

If commercial software largely writes itself, will programming revert to being a hobbyist's pastime?

Will there ever be a Nobel prize for programming?

—Andrew Zolli

SOFTWARE THAT MAKES SOFTWARE

As computing power has relentlessly doubled and redoubled, radical software theorists have latched onto a new way of "writing" code. Instead of methodically plotting out the optimal way to accomplish some task, these theorists write a program that generates thousands of new programs at random. Each one is given a test set of data. For a sorting program, this data may consist of hundreds of random numbers. After each program has executed its randomly generated instructions on this test data, 10% of the results that are closest to a correct solution are used as the basis of a new generation of random programs. After a few hundred generations — which can be run in seconds in parallel by a powerful computer — clear winners emerge, randomly "evolved" programs that sort data as well as, or better than, any human-authored one.

WANT MORE?

GENETIC PROGRAMMING, INC.
www.geneticprogramming.com

TOONTALK
www.toontalk.com

XML
www.w3.org/XML

ARTIFICIAL INTELLIGENCE ... "If I Only Had a Brain"

THE PROBLEM WITH ARTI-*ficial intelligence isn't the technology, but the movies. Because of Stanley Kubrick's HAL (Heuristically programmed ALgorithmic computer) in* 2001, *Spielberg's* AI, *and* Star Trek*'s talkative computers, we tend to associate artificial intelligence — human-like cognitive abilities or the appearance of them — with machines that look and sound like us. Machines that can chat with us over lunch, like HAL or* Star Trek*'s tan-challenged humanoid robot, Data. The truth is that AI is all around us; it just doesn't look like the AI in the movies. Real AI is much more subtle. In fact, it's mostly invisible.*

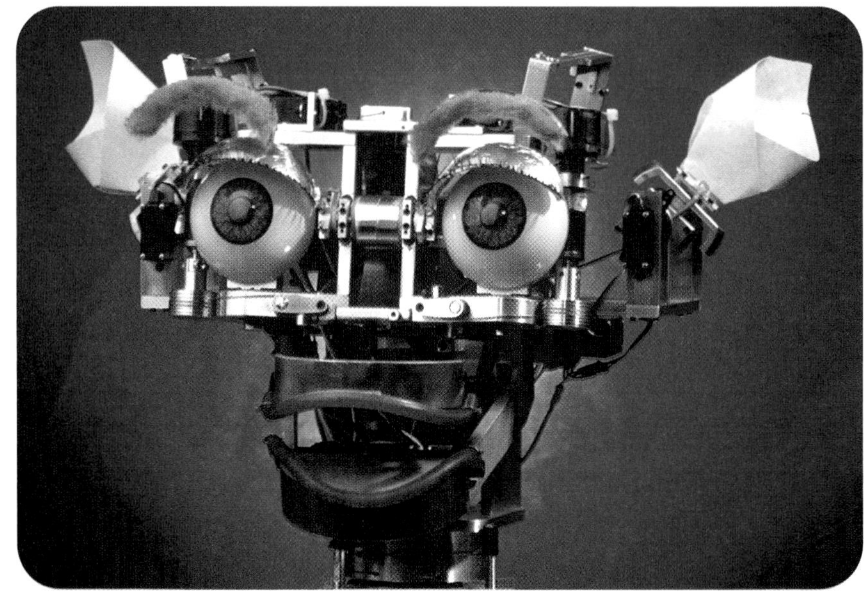

SOCIABLE MACHINES. *Kismet, one of the anthropomorphic robots at the MIT Sociable Machines Project, engages people in natural and expressive face-to-face interaction.*

The voice-recognition software that routes your calls through phone systems or takes airline reservations learned to understand speech using AI algorithms. In offices, AI-based probability model software can prioritize workers' email, phone messages, and appointment books based on their past choices. Web-based chatbots use "natural-language processing" to converse with users and point them to Help files or other Web content.

To find something close to a HAL-like AI supercomputer, however, you have to look first at IBM's Deep Blue, the machine that defeated Russian world chess master Gary Kasparov in 1997. Deep Blue isn't as smart as a human. It isn't even necessarily a great chess player. Deep Blue beat Kasparov not because it was clever, but because IBM kept upgrading the size and speed of its processors to the point that it could evaluate 200 million chess positions every second. This is the "brute force" version of intelligence.

THE FUTURE OF AI

The future of AI probably doesn't lie in brute force, but in a more subtle approach that has been quietly under development for 18 years in Austin, Texas. The project is called Cyc (pronounced "psych"). The brainchild of computer scientist Douglas B. Lenat, Cyc is a system that has "learned" 1.37 million discrete ideas — including names, descriptions, root words, and abstract concepts. Cyc can find complex information for a user by way of a normal conversation. To help it converse, Cyc comes equipped with a kind of built-in common-sense engine that lets it communicate clearly and distinguish between different meanings of a single word ("in love" versus "in the car"). Funded by a consortium of private corporations, individual investors, and the Pentagon's Defense Advanced Research Projects Agency, or DARPA, Cyc is a knowledge base program. This is an attempt to create AI not by the traditional method of modeling the human brain, but by creating a common pool of knowledge that any intelligent entity would need to function and communicate.

Not only is Cyc the most robust AI system ever built — able to answer questions conversationally, asking its own questions when it's unclear on something — it's the first large-scale AI to generate marketable products. Cycorp, the company that developed Cyc, is selling CycSecure, a system that combines a huge

FUZZY LOGIC

"Fuzzy logic," which is a form of AI, enables many common devices, from washing machines to cameras, to "think" for themselves. Video cameras use fuzzy logic to adjust the focus and cancel image jitter. Fuzzy systems have been used in automobiles for air conditioning systems, anti-braking devices, transmissions, and fuel injectors, for example. Subway cars in Japan are piloted during peak hours by fuzzy systems that outperform human operators.

database on common computer network vulnerabilities with known hacker strategies to detect security holes in a customer's network before outside thieves can find them.

Of course, not every researcher has signed on to the knowledge base-model of AI. Rodney Brooks, director of MIT's Artificial Intelligence Lab and founder and chairman of iRobot, his own robotics company, believes that as our machines become smarter and more human-like, humans will happily become a bit more machine-like. In a February 2002 interview in *Salon*, Brooks said, "As these technologies become more and more available, we're going to start implanting them in our bodies. So we as humans are going to drift in the robotic direction, as the robots get more intelligent. Where that ultimately leads is a little harder to predict."

INTELLIGENT AGENTS

When you talk to your computer, does it talk back? It can, if you want it to. In fact, in the not-too-distant future, you'll probably wonder how you ever got along without being able to chat with your desktop machine.

Intelligent agents come in all sizes and flavors, though few programmers or researchers can agree on a definition. What we can say about intelligent agents is that they have to be able to take input (a question or a command such as, "Book me on a flight to New York this Friday.") and respond with an answer or results, such as a plane ticket. Agents take requests and ask question when they don't understand something, using "natural language" processing. It's a conversation — or a pretty good simulation of one.

These are collaborative agents, and they're all about autonomy. They glide across networks and out into the Web to work on your behalf with other agents.

Carnegie Mellon University's Pleiades System divides collaborative agents into task agents (that do things) and information agents (that find things). If you need some corporate financial data, an information agent can scan hundreds of databases, having learned over time what you want. A task agent can take the data and turn it into a new database.

Real machine/human conversations go back to 1966 and a program called Eliza. Dr. Joseph Weizenbaum at MIT used only 240 lines of code to create a program designed to simulate a conversation with a therapist. Eliza would zero in on keywords, fit them into one of several standard responses, and give her reply instantly. A "therapy session" could look like this:

> Bob: I thought about my mother today.
>
> Eliza: What did you think about your mother?

WANT MORE?

CYCORP
www.cyc.com

RODNEY BROOKS' HOME PAGE
www.ai.mit.edu/people/brooks/index.shtml

MIT AI LAB
www.ai.mit.edu/index.shtml

MIT HUMANOID ROBOTICS GROUP
www.ai.mit.edu/projects/humanoid-robotics-group

MIT LIVING MACHINES GROUP
www.ai.mit.edu/projects/living-machines/index.shtml

MARVIN MINSKY
http://web.media.mit.edu/~minsky

HANS MORAVEC ON MACHINE INTELLIGENCE
www.transhumanist.com/volume1/moravec.htm

SRI'S AI CENTER
www.ai.sri.com

THE INTELLIGENT SOFTWARE AGENTS LAB
http://www-2.cs.cmu.edu/~softagents

ISR INTELLIGENT AGENTS
http://more.btexact.com/projects/agents.htm

ALICE AI FOUNDATION
http://alice.sunlitsurf.com

AGENTLAND.COM
www.agentland.com

BOTSPOT
www.botspot.com

ASK ALEX
http://jurist.law.pitt.edu/alex.htm

NETBOT
www.bot-in.net

A.L.I.C.E. *The creation of Dr. Richard Wallace, A.L.I.C.E. (which stands for Artificial Linguistic Internet Computer Entity) won the 2000 Loebner Prize for being the most lifelike machine of the year. The prize uses the Turing Test, named after British mathematician Alan Turing, to determine if responses from a computer can convince a human into thinking it is a real person.*

Bob: I hate my mother.

Eliza: Why do you hate your mother?

Eliza didn't have a lot of imagination, but she was the first generation of what are now called *chatbots*, a kind of agent designed primarily to talk with people. The top chatbots can hold very human conversations. One of the best of the best is a bot named Alice, the award-winning digital offspring of Dr. Richard Wallace.

Today, users from all over the world chat with Alice over the Web, asking her about her life, proposing sexual liaisons, and confessing their deepest, darkest secrets to this seemingly intelligent program. Was Dr. Wallace surprised at how easily people fell into conversation with his creation? "Consciousness is an illusion," Wallace says. "Most people, most of the time, are not really as self-aware and original as we would like to think. We are all robots."

Aside from the fun of chatting with a machine, intelligent agents, and chatbots in particular, are developing an important technology. We're close to a time when there is simply too much information for any one person to deal with. Having a personal agent that can handle some of your more mundane tasks will be essential in the next few years. "When you think about Alice as the talking computer of the future, with no keyboard, no display, no WIMPy interface, then it becomes clear that all applications can be done through natural language. Surfing the Web, sending an email, playing a game, balancing your checkbook, managing your schedule, filing your taxes, almost everything you do with a computer today, will be done through a voice-style interface tomorrow," says Wallace.

But balancing your checkbook won't be the end of the line for Alice and her kind. "The shared vision of many people in the Alice and AIML (AI Markup Language) community is the Hal/*Star Trek* talking computer of the future," Wallace says. "The problem is, we don't know if it will take 5 years, 10 years, or more."

CYBER VIXEN. *The friendly Cybelle, who resides at agentland.com, uses body language in addition to text to converse with visitors to the site (left).*
BOT FILM STAR. *Ruby, one of Dr. Richard Wallace's favorite online intelligent agents, has her own portal and stars in the film* Teknolust *along with Tilda Swinton* (Conceiving Ada, The Beach, Orlando, Female Perversions).

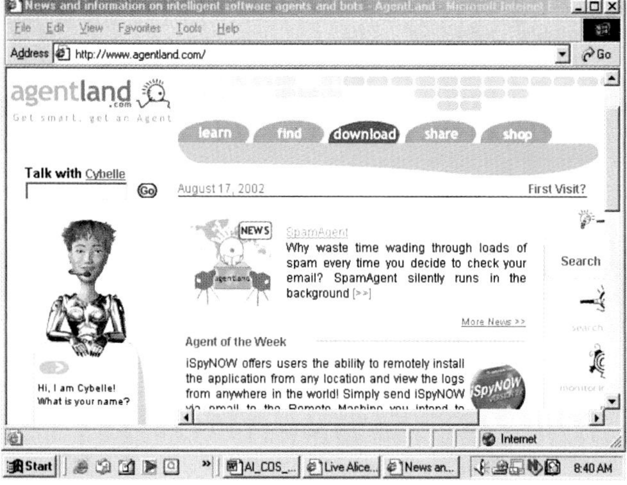

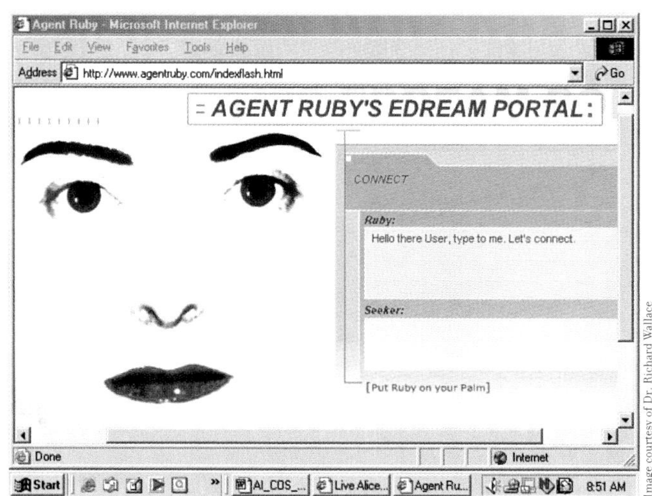

Image courtesy of Dr. Richard Wallace

Chatbots aren't the only agents around today. AgentLand.com, for instance, hosts dozens of specialized bots that will play games with you, work as your personal assistant, perform specialized Web searches, monitor sites for you, and search for products you might want to buy. You can even build your own agent. And don't forget Cybelle, AgentLand.com's cyber vixen chatbot. Technically, she's an avatar because she has a body and uses gestures while talking. These small head, eye, and body movements make Cybelle seem disturbingly alive.

CREATE YOUR OWN AVATAR

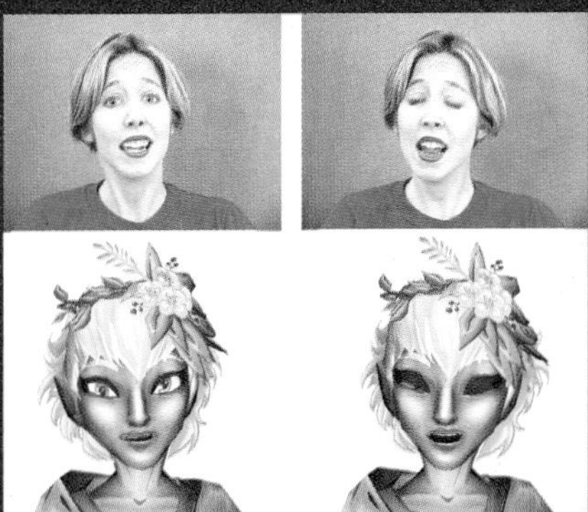

Eyematic is using computer vision tech to create avatars with realistic facial movements, at a fraction of the cost and skill set required for traditional techniques. With Eyematic FaceStation, animators capture actual human facial expressions using a standard camcorder or Webcam and use this data to animate avatars in games, television shows, and feature films. For the masses, Eyematic is developing avatar-based multimedia messaging and digital assistant applications. These applications allow users to interact and communicate with animated 3D avatars on color-screen cellular phones, mobile handhelds, and personal computers.

AVATARS

Avatars are what comes from the collision of AI and computer animation. In the next few years, avatars will become our embodied assistants and representatives online. They'll perform all the same jobs as task and information agents, but you'll be able to interact with them face-to-face. Eventually, you'll become an avatar yourself.

Avatar Me, for example, has developed AvatarBooths for places such as malls and libraries. Using two cameras, the booths photograph people in four poses. The captured data is used to create 3D photorealistic avatars that will place you in computer games and home walk-thrus and allow you to try on clothes in online stores using a service such as FashionMe.

Agents are also invading the business world. Avatar Me and Televirtual are developing videoconferencing software called AvPuppet. People located thousands of miles apart can use their avatars to hold online business meetings, using their own voices.

Eyematic Interfaces is using facial recognition tech to create avatars with realistic facial movements, at a fraction of the cost and computing power required for traditional techniques. With their FaceStation software, animators can record facial expressions with a standard camcorder and import the data into any 3D rendering package. While it's popular with the gaming industry, Eyematic is also developing Shout Messenger, a messaging service to be used with the next generation of full-color wireless devices. Shout Messenger lets users send 3D animated avatars, complete with changeable facial expressions.

PROVOCATIONS...

If a chatbot tricks you into thinking it's human, should you be able to sue its owner for false advertising?

Will students use bots to sit in for them in distance learning classes? Will teachers?

Will a computer beat a human at the game of Go during our lifetime?

Will you buy a dress because an intelligent agent says you would look sexy in it?

—Richard Kadrey

WANT MORE?

THE INTERNET FIRSTBORN BOT
www.the1stborn.net

FASHIONME
www.fashion-me.com

AVATAR ME
www.avatar-me.com

BT AVATAR DOWNLOAD
www.talkzone.co.uk/NEW_AVATAR_Index.html

EYEMATIC
www.eyematic.com

BOOKS

UNDERSTANDING ARTIFICIAL INTELLIGENCE (2002, WARNER BOOKS)

THE AGE OF SPIRITUAL MACHINES BY RAY KURZWEIL (2000, PENGUIN)

FLESH AND MACHINES: HOW ROBOTS WILL CHANGE US BY RODNEY BROOKS (2002, PANTHEON)

Image courtesy of Eyematic

Quantum and Biochemical Computing...Beyond Silicon

EARLY ELECTRONIC COMputers, *which used vacuum tubes to enable calculations, were so large that they filled entire rooms. In the mid-1950s, transistors contributed to the miniaturization of machines, and later the "integrated circuit," a collection of transistors on a single chip, collapsed computers into yet a smaller space. In the early 70s, the microprocessor, essentially an entire computer on a single chip, gave birth to the first desktop machines.*

Since then, there's been a race to miniaturize components. Twenty years from now, many researchers believe that we will reach the limits of how small we can make the components for traditional chips. The good news is that computer researchers are already moving beyond traditional materials for computer components into the sub-miniature world of nanocomputers, which are devices that use incredibly small, incredibly fast components to perform calculations.

Three big ideas have emerged from this tiny world: biocomputing, quantum computing, and carbon nanocomputing. While none of them work in any practical or commercial way—yet — they hold extraordinary promise for the future. When these technologies become commonplace, the tiniest appliance — from your cell phone to your MP3 player to your PDA — could be smarter than the smartest computer now in existence.

7 QUBITS! *Dr. Isaac Chuang at the IBM-Almaden Research Center, in San Jose, California, has developed a 7-qubit quantum computer, meaning he can manipulate 7 qubits at once. While this is a small number, Chuang's device is the most powerful quantum computer yet constructed.*

Photo courtesy of International Business Machines Corporaion. Unauthorized use not permitted.

DNA: WET COMPUTING

The idea of using bits of DNA instead of silicon chips to run computer tasks is hard to imagine. To understand DNA computing, forget your standard image of a computer: the gray box, keyboard, mouse, and monitor. DNA computing is wet computing — that is, everything takes place in a test tube and at a microscopic level.

A DNA computer uses the genetic information "programmed" into DNA, which is found within structures called nucleotides. Within each nucleotide are combinations of four acids: A (adenine), C (cytosine), G (guanine), and T (thymine). Combinations of these acids program DNA to create every structure in our living bodies. By chemically manipulating how nucleotides combine with one another, researchers can now trick them into performing complex computations.

What makes a DNA computer unique is that while a silicon computer spends its

TAKE A FANTASTIC VOYAGE...

Some researchers have big plans and expectations for nanocomputers. Ray Kurzweil, Artificial Intelligence researcher, inventor, and businessman, sees the day when we'll all have microscopic computers in our bodies and brains. These tiny machines will augment our sensory and cognitive abilities, expanding the finite number of neural connections in our brains. Nanocomputers could hide out near the sensory processing centers in our brains and replace the input and output, connecting us via a wireless network to the whole world with no other equipment than what's in our bodies.

time calculating what it thinks is the right answer, DNA computers compute every possible single answer for a given problem. So to arrive at a final answer, researchers chemically bathe the DNA strands to wash away the incorrect combinations, leaving only the correct answer.

DNA molecules function like little microchips. They're so small you can have a tremendous number of them in a small space—in fact, there are around 10 trillion in the space the size of a marble. And, unlike most electronic computers, DNA computers perform all their calculations in parallel. Most silicon computers operate linearly, sorting through a single problem one at a time, before moving on to the next one. Because it's a massively powerful parallel processor, DNA computers can quickly solve problems that would take a conventional computer hundreds of years to solve—if at all.

Usable DNA computers are a good 10 years away, according to most experts, and when they arrive, because of their unique ability to analyze combinations, they will probably be used by the government for cryptography and the airline industry to route planes.

THE BIRTH OF SPINTRONICS

Quantum computers take computing to a truly small scale by using subatomic particles instead of silicon chips and lines of programming. Of course, when you get down to the subatomic level, quantum laws take over. So little is certain, and what is certain, isn't certain for very long. This new *Alice in Wonderland*-style science is called "spintronics," or "spin-based electronics."

Conventional computers perform calculations using binary bits, 1s and 0s. Quantum computers, powered by the spin of subatomic particles, use quantum bits; or qubits (also known in the biz as quantum dots). For instance, if a particle's spin is up, it can be read as 1, and when the spin is down, it can be read as 0. Qubits are special, in that — because of the laws of Quantum Uncertainty — they can be simultaneously up and down, so they can be 1 or 0 or somewhere in between. This state is called "superposition," and because a quantum computer can exist in this multiple state, it can perform many calculations at once, far surpassing the power of any conventional computer.

CARBON NANOCOMPUTERS

Think your PalmPilot is small? Imagine a computer so tiny, you can see it only with a microscope. This is what happens when the worlds of computing and nanotechnology meet. Theoretically, there are two types of carbon nanocomputers.

ELECTRIC. These are the closest to current computers. Using nanolithography, lasers inscribe nanoscale circuits onto chips, creating tremendous computing power in a tiny space. MECHANICAL. These computers use tiny moving nanogears to encode data, like the old analog adding machines. Mechanical nanocomputers would be extraordinarily complex, with millions of moving parts. Because of this level of mechanical complexity, many researchers believe that they are unworkable.

Computers running on these new molecule-scale components could be thousands of times faster than today's machines, hold more data, and consume a fraction of the power. A single battery could last for days or weeks at a time.

PROVOCATIONS...

What would you do with a pocket supercomputer?

—Richard Kadrey

WANT MORE?

BIO-COMPUTING...

LAB FOR MOLECULAR SCIENCE
www.usc.edu/dept/molecular-science

BIOLOGICAL NANOCOMPUTERS
www.weizmann.ac.il/mathusers/lbn

DNA COMPUTING FAQ
www.usc.edu/dept/molecular-science/fm-dna-computing-faq.htm

DNA2Z.COM
http://dna2z.com

QUANTUM COMPUTING...

SPINTRONICS AND QUANTUM COMPUTERS
www.qi.ucsb.edu/qcc/index.htm

IBM QUANTUM COMPUTING
www.almaden.ibm.com/st/projects/quantum/nmr

THE QUANTUM COMPUTER BY JACOB WEST
www.cs.caltech.edu/~westside/quantum-intro.html

INSTITUTE FOR MICROSTRUCTURAL SCIENCES
www.sao.nrc.ca/ims/programs/explore-e.html

QUANTUM COMPUTING FAQ
www.qubit.org/oldsite/QuantumComputationFAQ.html

CARBON NANOCOMPUTERS...

NANOTECH PLANET
www.nanotechplanet.com

NANOELECTRONIC CHIPS
www.lucent.com/press/1101/011108.bla.html

PROF. CHARLES M. LIEBER'S GROUP AT HARVARD
http://cmliris.harvard.edu

Artificial Life...

TECHNOLOGIES LEARN FROM BIOLOGY

ARTIFICIAL CREATIVITY. *A-life is being used to create movies, games, and art like this painting by Kevin Mack.*

ARTIFICIAL ORANGUTAN

Steve Grand, creator of the hit a-life computer game Creatures is making an orang-utan robot using a-life technology. The robot, called Lucy, has a brain, muscles, a voice, eyes, ears, and senses of balance and body temperature. Grand hopes Lucy will learn to talk and function in the same way that a real baby learns.

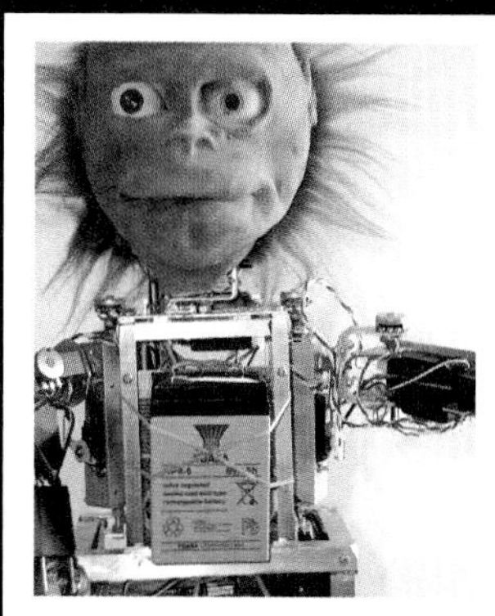

WHEN PEOPLE STOPPED USING HORSES AND STARTED *using cars, they gained a lot. Cars are faster than horses; they require less maintenance; they carry more passengers and cargo; and they're ultimately less expensive. But consider what people lost when they made the switch from using an intelligent animal to a dumb machine. Horses were like co-pilots. They knew the way home all by themselves. They knew how to avoid potholes in the road. They knew how to prevent collisions with other horse-drawn carriages. Imagine a car that could think like a horse. Imagine a home security system as smart as a bulldog.*

Artificial life (a-life for short) is the science of designing things and systems that breed, adapt, grow, develop, and learn like living creatures. The principles behind a-life are already being used to route telephone calls, synthesize new proteins, optimize software, and make realistic animated characters for movies. In the coming years, a-life will provide the brains for sophisticated robots and manage the huge repository of information on the Internet.

Artificial life is not the same thing as artificial intelligence (AI), which is primarily concerned with making databases of facts and rules that can be used as "artificial experts." As opposed to this top-down approach to creating intelligence, a-life takes a bottom-up approach to creating life-like behavior. In other words, a-life starts with the small and the simple and then lets the system evolve itself into something big and complex.

In the same way that humans evolved from one-celled creatures, a-life scientists hope to evolve intelligent and useful programs from simple starting conditions. One of the fundamental kinds of a-life is called the genetic algorithm. An algorithm can be thought of as a recipe or step-by-step formula for accomplishing a certain task. For example, a sorting algorithm could be used to arrange a list of words in alphabetical order. Typically, a computer programmer would be hired to write a program to sort the words. But a programmer doesn't write a genetic algorithm. It is evolved inside a computer, using a "survival of the fittest" method. Here's how it works. First, the computer generates dozens or hundreds of sets of random numbers. Since computer programs are really nothing more than a series of 1s and 0s, each random number set can be considered a kind of computer program. Next, the computer applies each random number set to the task of sorting the list of words. Of course, none of the random number sets will do a good job of sorting the list, but a couple of them might be able to put one or two words in the proper order. The other sets are discarded, and the survivors are used to breed a new crop of slightly mutated number sets. Once again, they're applied against the list of words, and the fittest ones are allowed to live and mutate. This goes on for hundreds, thousands, even millions of iterations. (On a fast computer, this entire process can happen in a flash.) Eventually, you'll end up with a very efficient sorting program, one that no human wrote.

Artificial brains made using a-life technology will one day be housed in robotic bodies and put to work doing things humans are unable or unwilling to do – clearing toxic waste dumps, exploring deep space, searching buildings for bombs planted by terrorists. Further out, a-life will be used to extend our capabilities beyond our biological limits. One day, people may be able to download their consciousness into an adaptable robot body designed to colonize planets on distant stars. We'll connect memory enhancers and language translators to our brains. As Marvin Minsky, the head of MIT's Artificial Intelligence Lab says, "We will find ways to replace every part of the body and brain. Needless to say, in doing so, we'll be making ourselves into machines."

PROVOCATIONS...

Should we include a-life in our biodiversity programs?

Does killing an a-life create bad e-karma?

—Mark Frauenfelder

ANTS!!!

MCI is using "ants" (tiny, intelligent agent programs) to route telephone calls around bottlenecks or other congestion in the phone network. Recently, MCI has reprogrammed the ants, enabling them to breed with each other, so that new generations of ants – each as unique as an individual child – can adapt to the changing nature of the phone network.

ARTIFICIAL ACTORS

Kevin Mack is an Academy-award winning visual effects supervisor. Besides using a-life techniques to create the effects for movies such as *Fight Club*, *The Grinch*, and *A Beautiful Mind*. Mack is working with a neuroscientist to develop artificial worlds with intelligent virtual creatures. He hopes to make animated cartoons populated by evolved characters that write their own stories.

WANT MORE?

ANT COLONY SIMULATOR
www.drizzle.net/~goldbay/boid.html

DISTRIBUTED COMPUTING
www.demo.cs.brandeis.edu/pr/golem/download.html

BIOMIMICRY
www.biomimicry.org

ZOOLAND: A-LIFE DIRECTORY
alife.ccp14.ac.uk/zooland/zooland

LUCY
www.cyberlife-research.com

KEVIN MACK'S ART
www.mackarts.com/kevin_mack.htm

Information Visualization...
When the Visual Makes Us Smarter

THE WORLD PRODUCES more information than we can possibly handle. The need to make sense of this flood has led to the emergence of the information visualization field, whose members attempt to create meaningful imagery and interaction from abstract data.

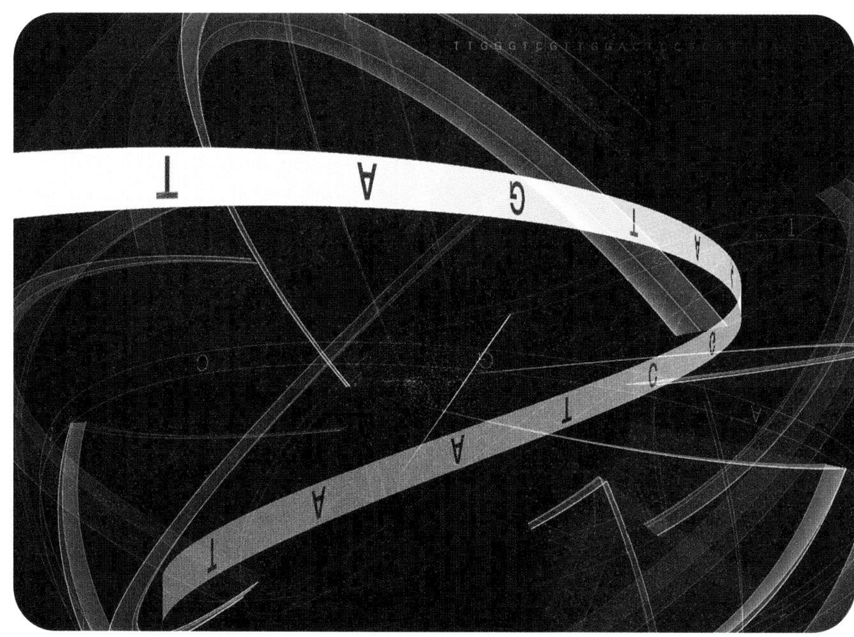

"VALENCE." *Software sketch visualizing biological data, by researcher Benjamin Fry of MIT, part of a series that explores the structures and relationships inside very large sets of information.*

"Valence" by Benjamin Fry MIT Media Laboratory, Aesthetics + Computation Group 1999–2002

Information visualization sets out to exploit humans' perceptive strengths, particularly visual pattern recognition and spatial memory. The point is "using vision to think," to apply the cognitive capabilities developed through adaptation to the new information jungle.

Turning the patterns of data into pictures is nothing new, as information design pioneer Edward Tufte illustrates in his classic book on statistical graphics, charts, and tables, *The Visual Display of Quantitative Data*. In fact, William Playfair developed scatterplots, bar charts, and pie charts in the late 1700s. What successful information visualizations offer are two primary advantages: immense amounts of detail in a single image and interactive capabilities that allow users to get at the desired specifics without being overwhelmed. This follows human-computer interaction researcher Ben Shneiderman's now-canonical mantra: "Overview first, zoom and filter, details on demand."

This developing field has had 20 years of navel-gazing because information visualizations tended to be ugly, too complicated, rendered in 3D, and not well-suited to any real task or problem. These issues were all addressed by the first widely successful visualization, SmartMoney.com's Map of the Market. A single screen offers a wealth of data on over 500 stocks, exploiting size, color, and placement to quickly present market capitalization, percentage change in value, and industry. The basic simplicity of this patchwork model, called a "tree map," is proving fruitful in variety of contexts, including photo libraries, conversational analysis, and coffee sales.

The Web has proven an irresistible lure for "info viz" designers who consider the Web's lack of structure a problem to be solved. The renowned *Atlas of Cyberspaces* is filled by the efforts of researchers and designers the world over, who have developed visualizations to overlay a spatial framework in order to highlight relationships and strengthen recall. Tools include Inxight's Star Tree, which presents massive hierarchical systems, and Antarctica's Visual Net software, which creates map-like images showcasing major themes. Yet such systems have not caught on, for the simple reason that instead of providing clarity, they add another layer of abstraction, requiring users to learn yet another arbitrary scheme for organizing and presenting information. While no one would argue that finding information on the Web is a worthwhile problem to address, different tools need to be created.

Perhaps the most rapidly evolving visualization is found in the burgeoning field of social network analysis (SNA). In order to see how complex human systems really work, SNA depends on maps that depict connections between people in a given environment. These have proven extremely valuable within corporations, where organizational researchers can identify which employees are the most connected, where there are gaps in the flow of communication, which people serve as bridges among different departments, and so on. It follows that Web visualizations begin to make sense when documents are no longer treated semantically with attempts at assaying their meaning, but socially, by following how they are connected through links. Visualization tools like TouchGraph, which borrow from network analysis diagramming to depict Web site connections, benefit from the proven effectiveness of social network visualizations.

Moving forward, information visualizations will follow a path perhaps unique in software — they'll get simpler. Straightforward visualizations that address specific problems will become more widespread, many aping the success of the Map of the Market. 3D visualizations will disappear from all but scientific visualizations. Instead, 2D applications will come alive through animation, as people go beyond the information snapshot, studying systems over time.

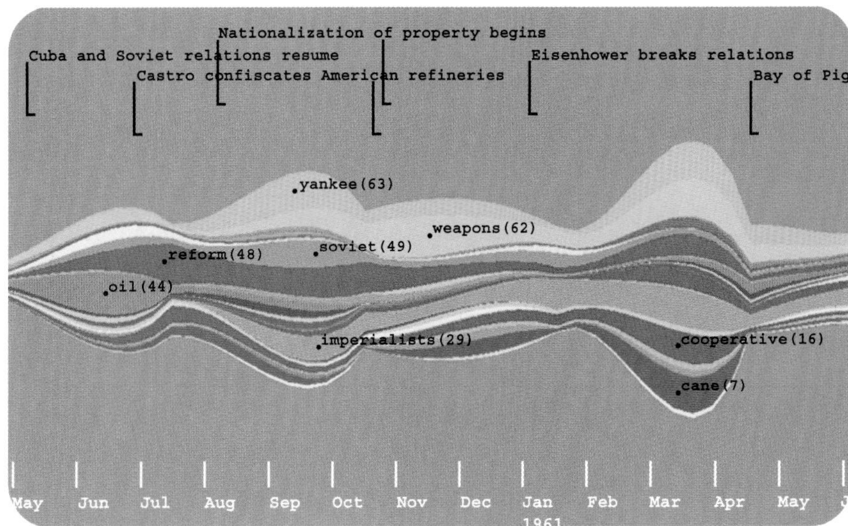

INFORMATION AS A RIVER. *The ThemeRiver™ visualization, from Pacific Northwest National Laboratory, helps users identify time-related patterns, trends, and relationships across a large collection of documents. The themes in the collection are represented by a "river" that flows left to right through time.*

PROVOCATIONS...

Will better visualization change the way people and companies play the stock market?

Will it improve their performance?

— Peter Merholz

WANT MORE?

ATLAS OF CYBERSPACES

www.geog.ucl.ac.uk/casa/martin/atlas/atlas.html

INFORMATION VIS RESOURCES

www.cs.man.ac.uk/~ngg/InfoViz

INFOVIS.NET

www.infovis.net/MainPage.htm

SPOTFIRE

www.spotfire.com

EDWARD TUFTE

www.edwardtufte.com

INXIGHT

www.inxight.com

THEY RULE

http://theyrule.net

INFILTRATION VISUALIZATIONS

The tragedy of 9-11, and the subsequent awareness of what the intelligence community faces in making sense of the data they gather, has prompted an exploration of how information visualizations can assist counter-terrorism activities. Starting from the commonly held assumption that the 19 hijackers were part of a network of terrorist cells, social network analyst Valdis Krebs drew upon publicly available information to create a diagram showing their connections. Though drawn by Krebs in hindsight, he points out that much of this information was available to the intelligence community before well before 9-11. Perhaps had analysts employed such depictions, action could have been taken to prevent the attack (for Krebs's full essay, see http://www.orgnet.com/prevent.html). Informative visualizations alone are not enough. As information science researcher Marti Hearst points out, "You have to understand the context in which the visualizations are used."

Haptics... Reach Out and Touch Some Data

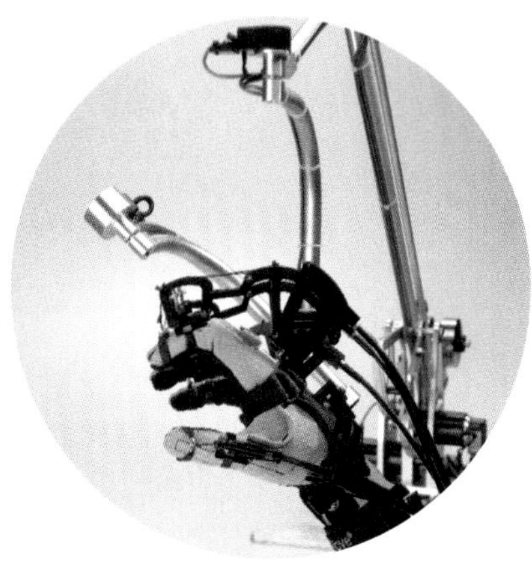

IMMERSION MEDICAL'S CATHSIM

Immersion Medical's CathSim uses tactile feedback and a computer representation of a human arm to instruct nurses and doctoral students on how to insert a catheter through the skin of a patient and guide it through an artery. Students can feel the "pop" of the needle as it penetrates the skin and enters a vein.

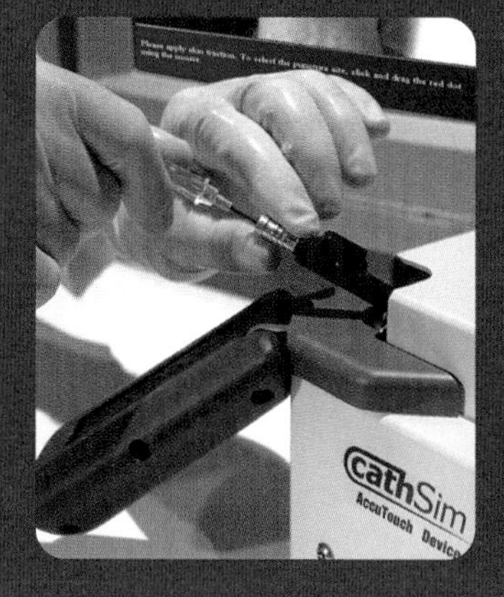

Clockwise from top left: Ryan McVay/Getty Images · Image courtesy of Immersion Corporation · Image courtesy of Immersion Corporation

UNTIL RECENTLY, COMPUTERS COULD ONLY SEND *information to your eyes or ears. A new technology, called haptics (from the Greek word haptikos, "to touch"), is giving computers the capability to send information to your hands, too. Haptics equipment uses vibrators, electromagnets, motors, and brakes to add a variety of tactile sensations to human-computer interfaces, so you can actually feel information.*

Today, video gamers are using haptics-equipped mice, joysticks, and steering wheels that deliver jolts and rattles synchronized to the games' events. When players drive over a bumpy road, or get hit by a plasma torpedo, they'll feel it. Animators are using special gloves equipped with force-feedback mechanisms that enable them to sense the resistance of virtual blobs of onscreen clay that they can mold into cartoon characters. Car manufacturers are including dashboard controls that vibrate, stick, and click so that information is imparted to drivers' fingers, instead of forcing drivers to take their eyes off the road.

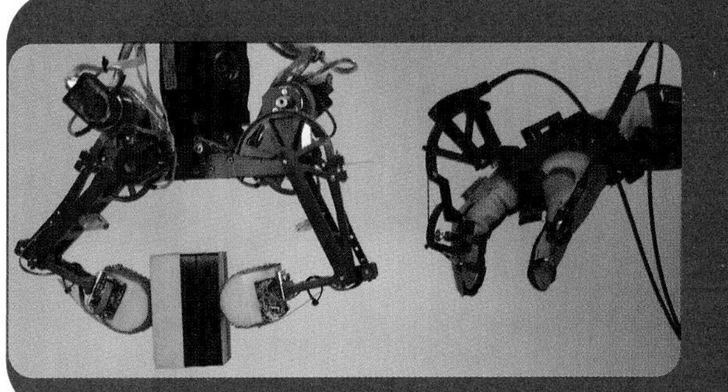

CYBERGLOVE

Designed by Dr. Mark Cutkosky at Stanford University's Dexterous Manipulation Lab, the Cyberglove remotely controls a robot arm. The robot arm does whatever the user's hand does. A force-feedback system in the Cyberglove allows the user to "feel" objects at a distance.

In the near future, haptics will have its greatest impact in the field of medicine. Doctors are learning how to perform complicated and risky surgical procedures by practicing on machines designed to mimic the sensations of prodding, cutting, and guiding surgical instruments in the human body. Immersion Medical, a Gaithersberg, Maryland, company that manufactures haptics-based medical training equipment, has sold hundreds of devices to teach doctors how to use vascular catheters and endoscopes. Immersion's CathSim uses tactile feedback and a computer representation of a human arm to instruct nurses and medical students how to insert a catheter through the skin of a patient and guide it through an artery. Students can feel the "pop" of the needle as it penetrates the skin and enters a vein. The software can simulate a variety of different kinds of patients, from a child with small veins to an IV drug user with toughened veins. In years to come, haptics devices will be used to help doctors perform real surgery on patients hundreds of miles away.

Looking beyond, haptics could be used to help online shoppers get a feel for the quality of materials used in merchandise offered for sale on a Web site. Early prototypes of "texture simulators" use dozens of tiny metal pegs arranged in arrays of columns and rows. Depending on the data the device receives, certain pegs will protrude and other will recede, providing the illusion of corduroy, sandpaper, polished wood, beard stubble, or any other textured surface. Because the heat transfer characteristics of materials are an important part of accurately simulating a surface, the pegs can be heated or cooled to the appropriate temperature. So far, textural haptics aren't ready for prime time. Major design challenges lie ahead before shoppers will be able to feel the difference between a silk purse and a sow's ear.

LOGITECH'S iFEEL MOUSE

Logitech's iFeel mouse uses a motor to send distinct vibrations to users' hands when they guide the cursor over elements on a computer display. For example, the mouse will create the sensation of a "speed bump" when crossing the border of a window. Other elements on the desktop can be customized to feel "metallic," "rubbery," or "spongy."

MODELING SYSTEMS. *Sensable's Freeform modeling system allows industrial designers, sculptors and 3D artists to mold computer models as they would from a block of clay. Designers at Adidas, Disney, Hasbro, LEGO, and Honda use the company's haptics modeling systems.*

PROVOCATIONS...

Will people add haptic content to their home pages?

Will lovers be able to hold hands remotely with haptics?

– Mark Frauenfelder

WANT MORE?

MIT TOUCHLAB
http://touchlab.mit.edu

IMMERSION
www.immersion.com

SENSABLE TECHNOLOGIES
www.sensable.com

Clockwise from top left: Image courtesy of Stanford University Dexterous Manipulation Laboratory · Image courtesy of Immersion Corporation · Image courtesy of Logitech, Inc.

Ubiquitous Computing...
INVISIBLE COMPUTERS EVERYWHERE

TINY SPECKS OF MICRO-chips are embedded in a bedroom window. They're so small you can't even see them. A few of the chips are photosensitive. So when the sun hits the glass in the morning, these chips send a wireless radio signal instructing the blinds to open automatically. Another chip senses that the window is heating up rather quickly, so it tells the air-conditioning unit to kick in before the room gets too warm. After the owner of the house leaves for work, a burglar breaks the window. The window's sensors trigger an alarm, lock all the deadbolts in the house, and call the police. Our bewildered burglar has only enough time to crawl through the window, grab a stack of Blu-ray discs and a laptop, and hop out the window with his swag. Unfortunately for him, no one will want to buy the discs because they all have tiny smart tags embedded in them that prevent them from being played on a machine that doesn't have the key to unlock the tags. It doesn't matter anyway, because by the time the thief gets a few blocks away, the cops have pulled him over. How'd they know? The laptop had a homing device that was activated by sensors in the window frame when the burglar carried it out of the house.

NEVER "TOO" HOT. *HotClock is a watch and a program that warns you with a "beep" sound, when the liquid in the MediaCup is too hot to drink. The HotClock either communicates directly with the MediaCup or can use the network infrastructure to access information about the cup's status. In either case, the communication is accomplished wirelessly, via infrared.*

Image courtesy of Teco, University of Karlsruhe. www.teco.edu

This scenario depicts the near-future world of ubiquitous computing (ubicomp for short), in which every object of value is embedded with microprocessors, low-cost miniature sensors, and radio transceivers. The idea of ubicomp is to endow everyday objects — books, furniture, shampoo bottles, banana labels — with the capability to sense changes to themselves and in the environment and then communicate

SMART DUST – NOTHING TO SNEEZE AT

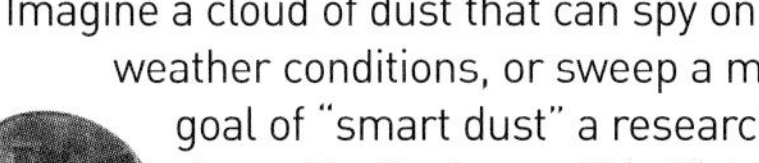

Imagine a cloud of dust that can spy on people, report on weather conditions, or sweep a minefield. That's the goal of "smart dust" a research project being conducted by Professor Kris Pister at the University of California, Berkeley, School of Engineering. The "motes" that Pister and his graduate students have built so far are not as small as specks of dust – they're more matchbox-sized – but they're getting smaller by the month (the mini-mote is shown here). So far, the motes are able to sense and report on changes in temperature, humidity, barometric pressure, light intensity, tilt, vibration level, and magnetic field. Pister envisions sending smart dust into the air with tiny rockets. Once deployed, the clouds of smart dust will act as a floating surveillance network.

Photo courtesy of Seth Hollar and Christina Adela, University of California at Berkeley

those changes to other objects.

UBICOMP CHALLENGES

For ubicomp to really become ubiquitous, a couple of technological barriers must be broken. The first is size. Today's devices are much too large to be embedded into small items, like socks and paper money. But since ubicomp sensors are made primarily of silicon, it's likely they'll get smaller with each passing year, just as memory and microprocessors have.

Another barrier is power. In order for a device to send a signal, it needs a power supply. Traditional batteries are no good, as they are too bulky. An Israeli company, Power Paper, is working with International Paper to create batteries that can actually be printed like ink onto labels, boxes, and other objects. Fuel cells, which use methanol or butane, could provide even longer lasting power to tiny transceivers. And for objects that require permanent power, there are piezoelectric generators that produce energy from ambient vibrations in building structures.

UBICOMP TODAY AND TOMORROW

Even though full-blown ubicomp is years away, there are working examples that exist today. Bluetooth is a low-power wireless network standard that allows computers, peripherals, and consumer electronics devices to talk to each other at distances of up to 30 feet. For example, if you have a Bluetooth mobile phone and a Bluetooth laptop, the laptop can use the phone to dial into your Internet service provider even though the phone is stashed in your briefcase.

In the future, FedEx shipping labels might come with cheap, disposable GPS units so that you can watch your order from Amazon move in real-time across a map of the United States. Large office buildings might have hundreds of tiny sensors mounted all over the wall and ceilings, reporting on the temperature and ventilation conditions. A fruit bowl might have a MEMS odor sensor that can sniff the produce it holds and alert the people in the house that they have 24 hours to eat the avocado before it spoils.

PROVOCATIONS...

What are the privacy issues surrounding ubicomp?

How much are you willing to pay to never have to lose your car keys again?

What kinds of military applications can you imagine for ubicomp?

—Mark Frauenfelder

VIBRATION PARASITES

The typical building never stops shaking. Air conditioners, computer fans, and heaters create tiny vibrations in walls, floors, and ceilings. This ambient hum is usually too slight for us to notice, but for the tiny "vibrational energy scavenger" under development at the Berkeley Wireless Research Group at UC Berkeley, it's enough to produce 70–80 microwatts of electrical power. The scavengers will be used to power tiny "PicoRadio" transceivers that can be attached to surfaces throughout a building for monitoring environmental conditions such as airflow and temperature. The radios form ad-hoc wireless networks and transmit their monitoring data to a central computer that can adjust the environmental conditions based on the data it receives. Better than batteries because they don't run down, and more practical than wired power, the scavenger uses a piezoelectric crystal and a weight attached to a springy cantilever to convert mechanical stress into electricity.

WANT MORE?

THINGS THAT THINK
http://ttt.media.mit.edu

BLUETOOTH
www.bluetooth.com

UBICOMP ROUNDTABLE
www.computer.org/internet/v2n2/round.htm

UBIQUITOUS COMPUTING GAMES
www.playresearch.com/ubigame

UBICOMP AT XEROX PARC
http://sandbox.parc.xerox.com/parctab/csl9501/node2.html

Nanotechnology and Molecular Manufacturing

Ever since humans first existed, we've worked to rearrange atoms, from our earliest efforts at chipping flint to today's high-tech etching of silicon wafers into computer chips. The end of this improvement process still lies many years ahead, but can now be envisioned — the coming ability to build devices and products with every atom in a designed location. Because every physical thing is made of atoms, the ability to control them can literally change everything. This ultimate control of atoms and molecules will reshape our world to its foundations.

Nanotechnology isn't just about smallness, about building unimaginably tiny structures. It's about using that ability to make a difference for things we care for at the human scale: our bodies, our environment, every physical object we can see and feel.

NANOTECH: EXCITEMENT AND CONFUSION

Today there's tremendous excitement surrounding this new field. The race is on: the U.S., European Union, and Japan compete to determine which will have the biggest annual budget for its nanotech program. As this is written, each is nearing $1 billion, with a comparable amount said to be spent by private industry.

In parallel with the excitement, there's confusion about what nanotechnology is and when we can expect to see results. Partly this is because we humans aren't good at understanding things that happen at a size we can't see, but more of the problem is due to how we use the word nanotechnology itself.

Researchers use the term for an ambitious goal — as the U.S. National Science Foundation puts it: "The essence of nanotechnology is the ability to work at the molecular level, atom by atom, to create large structures with fundamentally new molecular organization." They envision building from the bottom up, with every atom in a specified location, as close to perfection as physical law allows. When achieved, we'll be able to build large objects with a precision of under 1 nanometer — one billionth of a meter. While extraordinarily challenging, the goal is clear and understandable.

Unfortunately, the business community now slaps a nanotech label on anything where smallness matters — any product where the arrangement of atoms makes a key difference. Because the qualities of all physical objects depend on the arrangement of their atoms, this includes practically everything: certainly all of chemistry, materials science, and even biotech. Used this way, the word is just a marketing term for products that can be made today, atomically precise or — more often — not.

But we needn't let this confusion bother us. Sexy new terms often stray from their original meanings — we can view these incompatible definitions as different stages of nanotech development.

NEAR-TERM NANOTECHNOLOGIES

What near-term products are being developed under the umbrella term "nanotechnology"? Within 5 years, money is expected to be made — according to *Trends in Nanotechnology Weekly* — in drug delivery, solar energy (photovoltaic or direct hydrogen production), batteries, displays and e-paper, nanotube and nanoparticle composites, catalysts, coatings, alloys, medical implants, insulation (thermal and electrical), sensors (bio and chemical), filters, glues, abrasives, lubricants, paints, fuels and explosives, textiles, hard drives, computer memory, and optical components.

But don't let this avalache of products lure you into thinking there's a "nanotechnology industry" — there isn't. The incremental technical advances in the products above often have no connection to each other, apply to unrelated processes, and don't add up to a coherent "industry."

MOLECULAR MANUFACTURING: ADVANCED NANOTECHNOLOGY

While near-term results attract attention, the real power of nanotechnology will be seen only later. Predicting the future of any technology is notoriously difficult, but there are a few tools that can help if used carefully.

Physics, chemistry, and biology are understood well enough to give us assurance that the long-range goal of building with atom-by-atom precision is a reasonable one. The laws of economics, and of human nature itself, tell us that the momentum on this pathway will continue. The result, over time, is technological advancement to the limits allowed by nature.

Today, we can build very small objects with atomic precision or larger ones without it — we can't do both at the same time. Long-term nanotech will give us this direct control down to the molecular level, enabling us to precisely change the structure of all physical things, including the human body.

We'll do this by copying the strategy that nature uses to manipulate matter — molecular machines. Animals and plants are full of these machines, which carry out the complex processes inside them. Today, researchers are learning to redirect these natural machines to do other tasks. But what happens when we learn to design and build our own new systems of molecular machines, not modelled directly on nature's and not floating around in water as they do but instead cooperating closely, like a tiny factory?

These molecular nanosystems will be used to rearrange atoms and molecules as we wish, to make objects that are themselves made of molecular machines. Instead of the things around us being made of fairly simple materials, as they are today, it's more accurate to think of future products as collections of active devices. These "smart," reconfigurable objects will sense, move, and compute at the molecular scale.

THIS CHANGES EVERYTHING...

The results should be abilities similar to those seen with nature's manufacturing methods: an extreme decrease in direct manufacturing cost — to the level of crabgrass — an extreme decrease in pollution, and an extreme increase in product complexity. But we should be able to improve on nature, building stronger structures and doing a better job of repairing molecular machinery when it breaks. This latter ability is important in medicine, where it will enable us to reconfigure diseased cells into healthy ones, and even reverse the aging process itself — if we can write the needed software to direct the repair process, no easy feat.

Once deployed, the effects of these powerful, inexpensive manufacturing and repair abilities should be felt throughout the economy, from transportation and energy to environmental remediation and the human settlement of outer space. Enabling humanity to spread into space will help relieve the burden on Earth's environment, while ensuring that life spreads beyond one precious, vulnerable planet. Meanwhile, nanotech-based computation should have enough raw computing power to do a "brute force" model of the brain, bringing the prospect of artificial intelligence — if it hasn't been achieved earlier by more clever means.

Yes, this all sounds like science fiction. But that's what we should expect when we look at the future of technology. If it didn't sound like science fiction, we'd know our long-term projections were definitely wrong.

A technology this powerful could be abused, raising ethical issues. The two main challenges are preventing accidents and preventing deliberate abuse in war and terrorism. The former has already been studied, and draft safety rules have been issued by the Foresight Institute for community review. The latter — deliberate abuse — looks far tougher.

Some say that such a powerful and potentially dangerous technology should not be developed. At first this seems a viable option, but given the number of countries and companies on the pathway, the positive payoffs at every step along it, and the hard-to-detect nature of the research, the chances of a complete halt are roughly zero. Instead, the safest course is to move quickly, before the R&D costs of developing these abilities drop to a level that rogue governments or even small, secret groups can afford.

The remaining question is about timing — when should we expect to see these revolutionary advances change our world so dramatically? Any date is just a guess. Current guesses are circling around 2020. Try to hang around until then if you can — things should get very interesting indeed.

—Christine Peterson

Nanocomputing...

The Massively Minuscule World Beyond Silicon

IN THE NEXT 10 OR 20 years, the rapid miniaturization of computer processors will screech to a halt. Components — already shrunk and densely packed — are nearing the limits of how fast electrical impulses, and therefore data, can travel between them. More compact circuits make for faster chips but also for mounting temperatures, and eventually, the wires simply melt. In an attempt to sidestep this problem, scientists at UCLA, Hewlett-Packard, and IBM are pioneering new computers based on "molecular circuits." They hope to create transistors only a few nanometers in size to replace silicon-based electronics.

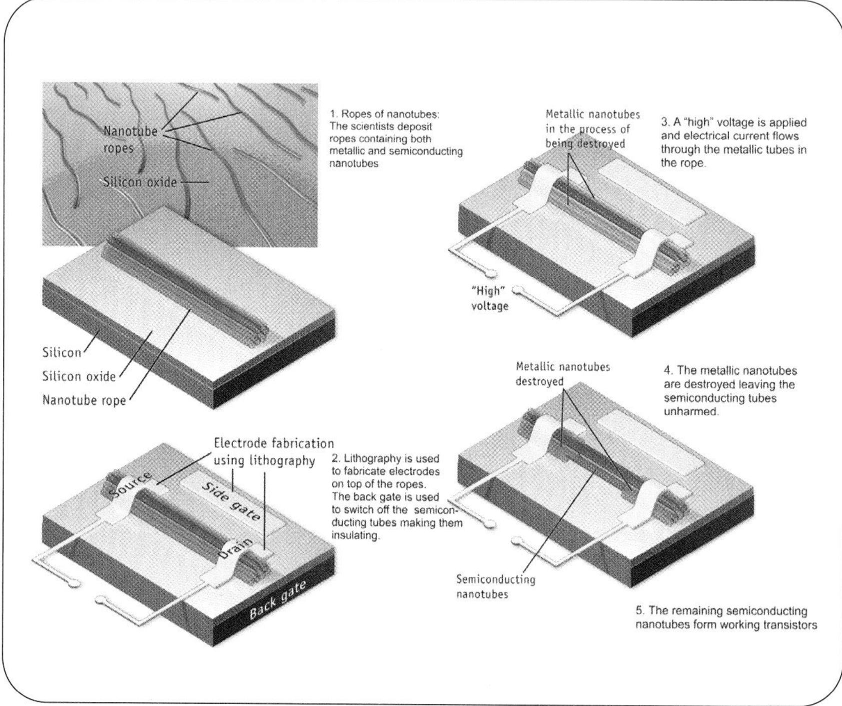

NANOTUBE TRANSISTORS. *IBM used "constructive destruction" to produce carbon nanotubes with the electrical properties needed to build ultrasmall, superfast, and low-power transistors.*

The heart of these components is the nanometer-wide "carbon tubule." Nanotubes have high levels of electrical conductivity and heat-resistance. Stretched into nanowires, the foundation for molecular switches, the tubules set down a grid, marked by individual molecules at each intersection. Each nanotube amplifies electrical surges and the switch reacts to that input, flipping to either an open or closed state. Using combinations of single-molecule switches to configure logic gates, such as AND and OR, nanoprocessors will perform complex operations, just like today's silicon CPUs.

A SMALLER CHIP

A silicon chip can fit on a fingernail, but a nanochip will measure a scant 100 nanometers across, smaller than a bacterium. It will have enormous processing capacity, conducting trillions of operations in seconds. In Engines of Creation, Eric Drexler envisions networks of nanocomputers carrying out 10 quad-rillion (or 10 million-billion) operations per second. (Today's supercomputers can boast 30 trillion, while workstations generate 64 billion, and desktops 13 billion.) Molecular computers will also be ultra power-efficient. Aside from superior conductivity, nanotubes offer less resistance than silicon, reducing electricity loss. Imagine a laptop that will function on a single battery charge for days or even months.

Business Wire Commercial Photo

This vision of nanocomputers represents a fundamental shift in thinking. Existing technology follows "top-down" reasoning: Engineers design a small number of ever-smaller components from bulk materials, like sheets of metal, while trying to make those materials stronger and lighter. In contrast, "bottom-up" logic parallels biology and chemistry, exploring molecular structures atom by atom with the goal of controlling the way they form larger entities. Nanocomputers are based on a "bottom-up" approach, yet take into account a future of powering complex machines that have previously been built by "top-down" methods. In building nanocomputers, scientists exploit the habitual bonds between molecules to coax them into transistors and circuits, "growing" the machine, molecule by molecule.

THE FIRST STEPS

Early-stage nanocomputing is moving toward reality. In May 2002, IBM created a transistor out of carbon nanotubes. Hewlett-Packard plans to integrate its own molecular electronics into conventional silicon devices over the next 2–3 years. Samsung is already replacing the cathode-ray tubes and liquid-crystal panels in its computer monitors with nanotubules. And Bell Labs is constructing circuits from organic compounds for use in flexible computer screens and airport baggage-tracking tags.

But functioning nanocomputers won't be a fixture of daily life for several more years. Companies like Carbon Nanotechnologies are producing tubules, yet face exhorbitant costs: A single gram of carbon atoms costs about $1,500. Even when prices drop and quality and purity become consistent, scientists will have to tackle the challenges of programming even a single nanocomputer, let alone coordinating several million to communicate in a network.

PROVOCATIONS...

How will scientists construct hack-proof and virus-proof nanocomputers? If knowledge is power, how will society prevent the minds behind molecular computers from becoming too influential?

—Michelle Penn

NANOCOMPUTERS AND NANOMACHINES

Nanocomputers won't simply store and process information, they will be the brains commanding microscopic machines, complete with molecular motors, arms, and conveyor belts. Powered by sunlight or organic catalysts, teams of these assemblers will forge any product for free, from a bagel to a building.

How? The computer will be programmed with an object's "blueprint" and instruct different assemblers to carry out specific tasks. For a bicycle, one assembler might construct carbon tubule-based fibers for the frame, while another might amass molecules to fashion the gears. This process of positional assembly will take only hours, making it possible to cut production times significantly.

Nanomanufacturing will take recycling to new heights. Assemblers will find the molecules they need by deconstructing and then rearranging atoms from sewage or landfills, putting an end to dumping and depletion of the Earth's resources. Special replicators will assemble copies of themselves, allowing a nanofactory of one billion atoms to duplicate in hours. Theorists hope that one day, nanomachines will create enough food to nourish the planet's population, making poverty — and its related social problems — part of the past.

WANT MORE?

FORESIGHT INSTITUTE
www.foresight.org
http://nanodot.org

TECHNOLOGY REVIEW MAGAZINE
www.technologyreview.com/nanotech.asp

INSTITUTE FOR MOLECULAR MANUFACTURING
www.imm.org

SMALL TIMES
www.smalltimes.com

NANOTECHNOLOGY MAGAZINE
www.nanozine.com

NATIONAL NANOTECHNOLOGY INITIATIVE
www.nano.gov

MOLECULAR ELECTRONICS CORPORATION
www.molecularelectronics.com

ZYVEX CORPORATION
www.zyvex.com

IBM
www.research.ibm.com

HEWLETT-PACKARD LABORATORIES
www.hpl.hp.com

CARBON NANOTECHNOLOGIES
http://66.28.45.185/cni/index.cfm

BELL LABS
www.bell-labs.com

SAMSUNG ADVANCED INSTITUTE OF TECHNOLOGY
www.sait.samsung.co.kr

Cellular Robots… Your Body, Your Robots

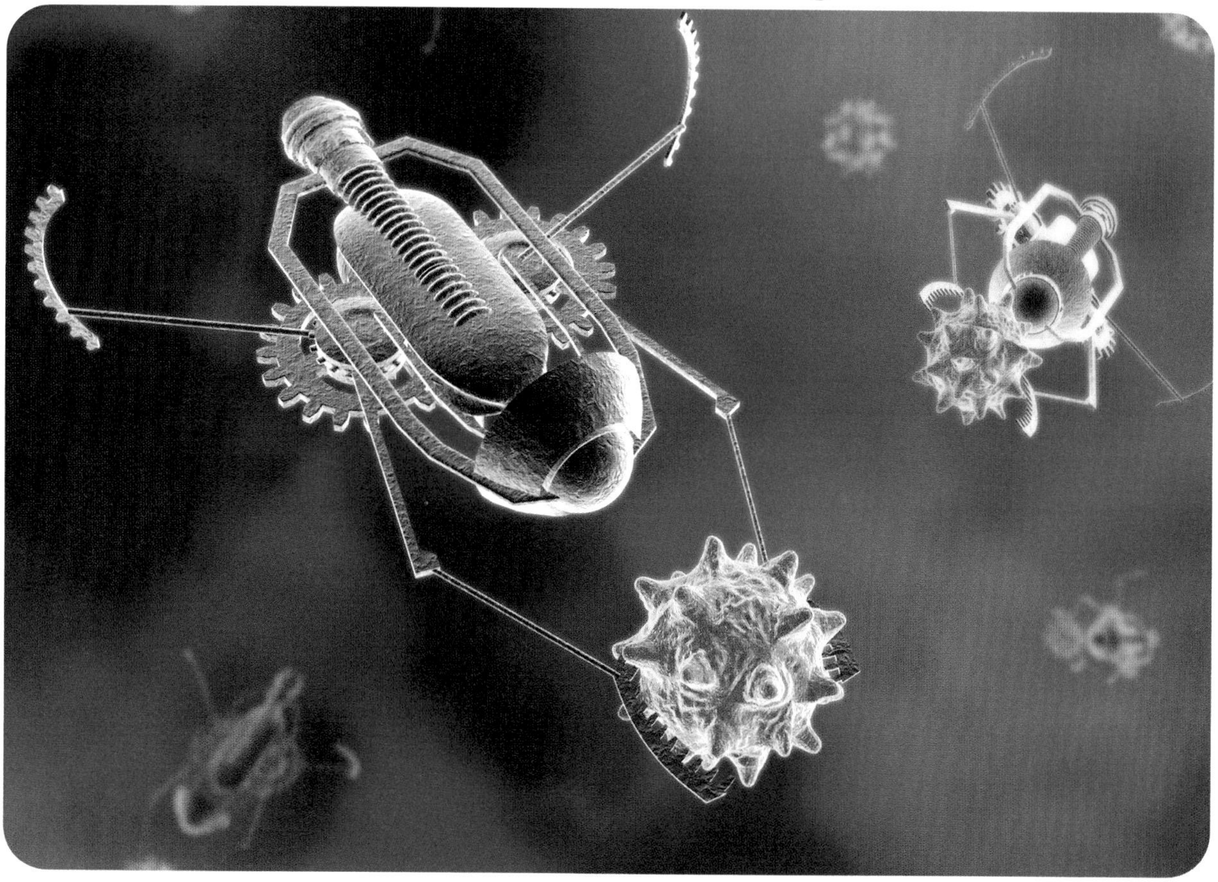

NANOBOTS. *Mechanical-looking medical nanorobots navigating the bloodstream pursuing viruses.*

IN THE PSYCHEDELIC 1966 FILM *FANTASTIC VOYAGE* A *surgical team and their military submarine have themselves shrunk and injected into the body of a scientist who has fallen into a coma. Their adventures send them zooming through the heart, lungs, and ear before they reach and repair the blood-clotted brain.*

It's 2016 now, 50 years after the film's release. You're in the doctor's office, where you have just been diagnosed with cancer, but you aren't worried. Your physician will simply inject a few minuscule devices into your bloodstream, which will target the diseased cells and destroy them while leaving healthy cells intact.

This scenario might seem to be just another fantastic voyage, but nanomedicine will soon be reality. Combining biology with molecular electronics, scientists are exploring ways to build robots 1/100th the size of a cell. These nanobots will propel themselves through the body, following instructions from onboard computers. External nanowires will act as sensors, changing electrical states when they come into contact with specific disease-marking molecules (or signatures). They'll be able to obtain accurate readings from only a drop

Clockwise from top left: Graphic by Jeff Johnson; Graphic by Jeff Johnson

of blood or body fluid and then communicate that information to physicians for diagnosis — all in seconds and without technicians or expensive equipment.

Such diagnostic precision will help doctors tailor medication to each patient. Robots will deliver smart drugs — designed to act only under specific circumstances — to the affected cells. This method will revolutionize cancer treatment because, unlike during chemotherapy, healthy cells won't be poisoned, which translates into fewer side effects.

In addition to ridding the body of disease, nanobots programmed with the host's DNA will act as repair crews, mending anything from a skinned knee to a malfunctioning kidney. Placed inside arteries, their miniature lasers will shave away dangerous plaque deposits. They'll even offset the aging process. Beyond rebuilding sun-damaged skin and tightening sags painlessly, they'll reverse osteoporosis, muscle atrophy, and other age-related conditions. People will look and feel 30 while in their 70s, 80s, and beyond.

Preventative medicine will undergo radical change. Robots will regulate diabetics' glucose levels, signaling problems before the first symptoms appear. They'll burrow into cell nuclei to rectify genetic irregularities, putting an end to inherited conditions including cystic fibrosis and Down syndrome. They'll even carry out what Robert A. Freitas, Jr. has called chromosome-replacement therapy, in which robots will substitute chromosomes from diseased cells with new ones to direct reconstruction.

Nanobots inside our systems will also protect us during life-threatening situations, such as fires and chemical leaks, by monitoring blood oxygen and compensating for toxic vapors. Freitas has designed a prototype of an artificial red blood cell called a *respirocyte* that will regulate oxygen and carbon dioxide levels and either take in or pump out the necessary molecules. This type of robot could keep body tissues oxygenated for hours following a heart attack.

In addition, teams of robots will circulate through the bloodstream, reinforcing the body's natural immune system. Comparing what they sense against the patient's DNA, they'll identify and annihilate any toxin, virus, parasite, or bacteria within minutes.

Of course, having a robot (or a few million) circulating inside your cells may sound terrifying. But the body already has its own natural nanobots: white blood cells.

Still, nanomedicine will hardly be a risk-free venture. The immune system could reject a robot in much the same way it might reject a transplanted organ, a reaction that could be harmful or even fatal. A nanobot inside an artery or brain capillary could crash, disrupting normal functions, perhaps irreversibly. And robots that begin to self-replicate uncontrollably could lead to what expert Raymond Kurzweil terms "non-biological cancer."

Cellular robots may come into existence around 2020 — to lead humanity on its own fantastic voyage. Nanorobots could challenge our very definition of ourselves.

PROVOCATIONS...

Is harboring an internal robot akin to having a pacemaker, a device that steps in when individual functions falter?

Is it any different from a transplanted human organ?

—Michelle Penn

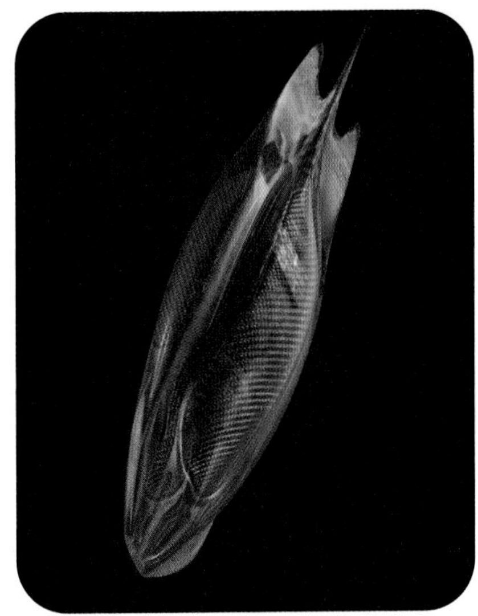

CELL ROVER. *Just microns in length, this bioengineered cell rover swims through the human body delivering drugs or removing wastes or toxins.*

Artists Forrest Bishop and Scott Maxwell, Cell Rover was conceived and designed by Forrest Bishop

WANT MORE?

NANOSYS, MANUFACTURER OF BIOSENSORS
www.nanosysinc.com

MOLECULAR NANOSYSTEMS, NANOSENSORS FOR MEDICAL AND OTHER USES
www.molecularnanosystems.com

USC LAB FOR MOLECULAR ROBOTICS
http://lipari.usc.edu

NANOTECHNOLOGY MAGAZINE
www.nanozine.com

GENERAL NANOTECHNOLOGY
www.nanotechweb.org

FORESIGHT INSTITUTE
www.foresight.org

NANOTECHNOLOGY EXPERTS
www.kurzweiltech.com

ZYVEX CORPORATION
www.zyvex.com

Smart Materials... Creating Smarter Stuff

IMAGINE YOU'RE HOSTING *a party and a guest is describing a camping trip. To enhance the story, you tell your walls to become deep forest green. Nanocomputers embedded in the paint's molecules instruct them to rearrange and reflect light differently. Then a friend lights up a cigarette. Your paint senses the change in air quality and filters out the toxic particles. Suddenly, someone knocks over a metal sculpture, leaving a gash in your now-green wall. But the paint simply mends itself.*

FLEXING YOUR MUSCLE. *Bendbots, Electroactive Polymers (EAP), are under development today.*
FOGLET. *These nanorobots can simulate hard and soft materials (below).*

Your paint is an example of a smart material. These emerging ceramics, plastics, composites, and gels can respond to variations in their environment, such as changes in temperature or light. That response is an alteration in shape, viscosity, or electrical conductivity. Yet the material reverts to its original state once the stimulus is removed.

Smart materials are engineered in much the same way that nature creates. An abalone absorbs the calcium carbonate that forms chalk and mixes it with protein to construct a shell 3,000 times more resistant than calcium alone. Similarly, scientists manipulate molecules, atom by atom, taking advantage of natural bonds and reactions. Combining these molecules with existing materials, they can alter thermal or structural properties.

There are two basic types of smart materials: actuators and sensors. *Actuators* bend or change dimensions when they react to external stimuli, such as temperature or magnetic fields. They're a key component of the helicopter rotor blades being developed jointly by Boeing, Pennsylvania State University, MIT, and DARPA (Defense Advanced Research Projects Agency). Smart materials allow each blade to twist, thereby reducing vibrations and contributing to a more supple, aerodynamic aircraft. In the future, actuators will suppress shivers in everything from bridges to optical instruments, leading to unprecedented levels of comfort and precision.

Clockwise from top left: Image courtesy of NASA/JPL/Caltech - Image courtesy of J. Storrs Hall

Sensors respond to their surroundings through variations in viscosity, conductivity, or other properties. Molecules that transmit current, such as carbon nanotubules, "sense" by reacting electrically to the presence of other molecules. Incorporated into intelligent food packaging, they'll monitor bacteria and signal stores to remove affected products from the shelf. Similarly, tires will alert drivers when they need replacement.

Special sensors outfitted with microscopic computers, will also act as effectors, able to interact with their environments and manipulate the matter around them. If your blender spurts margarita mix onto the wall, the paint molecules will quiver, ridding themselves of the foreign particles. Apply a similar mechanism to concrete and it will survey and repair its own cracks.

Some effectors, such as utility fog, will create objects on demand. Billions of snowflake-shaped nanorobots, or foglets, will simulate hard and soft materials, as well as liquid, gas, and empty air. If you're short a chair for your party, you'll select its model from the fog's library. The foglets will not only mimic each material, but they will adjust to support the weight of the seated person. After the party is over, you'll command the fog to return to its "invisible air" program. In "Utility Fog: The Stuff That Dreams Are Made Of," creator J. Storrs Hall writes, "Virtually, anything you can imagine can be given tangible reality in a utility fog environment."

Smart materials will transform manufacturing. Carbon nanotubules, which are as resilient as diamonds yet virtually weightless, will be incorporated into composites of astonishing strength, leading to everything from unbreakable glass to lightweight, fuel-efficient cars.

Smart materials will also participate in ubiquitous computing, in which chips will be embedded in every conceivable object. Intelligent appliances and intelligent materials will communicate with each other and share information. For example, sensors inside a smart juice carton will react to low supply by signaling the refrigerator, which will automatically order more through the Internet.

Graphic by Thomas Nissen. www.designinsite.dk

SMART POLYMERS. *Gels consist of a cross-linked polymer network inflated with a solvent, such as water. They can swell or shrink up to 1000 times their volume.*

Adaptive materials will impact the internal world, as well. Impulse-conductive smart gel will form artificial muscles. Gel implants will deliver insulin to diabetics. Someday, carbon mesh may be woven through bone marrow to reinforce skeletons. You might fall from a balcony without suffering even a hairline fracture.

Your clothing won't suffer from your tumble, either. Intelligent fabrics will be able to clean themselves and mend their own tears. As with smart paint, computers will instruct the molecules to swish dirt away. They'll also dispatch nanorobots to mend damaged fibers. While this kind of adaptive textile won't be available until about 2020, scientists at Nano-Tex are currently marketing fabrics that repel stains, water, and perspiration.

Other smart materials are already changing consumer products. K2 and Active Control Experts have introduced vibration-softening skis, while Nanophase Technologies produces zinc oxide nanoparticles for transparent sunscreen. Voridian employs clay nanoparticles into shatterproof plastic, and other companies are developing materials for everything from tires to tennis balls.

Some branches of nanotechnology may take 20 years to come to fruition, but today, ordinary materials are becoming much, much smarter.

PROVOCATIONS...

Will houses organically adjust to changing seasons?

Will smart garments wash themselves, or us?

Will smart materials change interior design?

— Michelle Penn

WANT MORE?

K2
www.k2skis.com/skis/technology.asp

K2'S ACTUATOR/SENSOR DEV.
www.cymer.com

GLOBAL NANOTECH PORTAL
www.nanotechweb.org

SMART MATERIALS SITE
www.intellimat.com

NANOSIZED-CLAY MINERALS
www.nanocor.com

NANOCRYSTALLINE MATERIALS
www.nanomat.com

NANOMIX (FORMERLY CALLED COVALENT MATERIALS)
www.covalentmaterials.com or www.nano.com

QINETIQ NANOMATERIALS
www.nano.qinetiq.com

INMAT
www.inmat.com

NANO-TEX (FABRICS)
www.nanotex.com

NANOPHASE CORPORATION
www.nanophase.com

XEROX PARC
www.parc.com

Our Lives

The Digital Lifestyle

UNDERSTANDING TODAY IN TERMS OF the past is, perhaps, the best way to gauge how the future might be different for us. Consider for a moment what is important to people today — or to you, personally. Once you strip the present of its artifacts, and focus on the goals, understandings and desires of people, you quickly see that things have not changed at the deepest level of ideals, motivations, or emotions. Finding love, understanding the world, leaving a mark, having a family, creating works or acts of importance, peace — these are all universal conditions of our lives that have changed very little throughout our history, and we predict they won't change much in the future. Of course, how we express these goals and desires and what tools and artifacts we use to accomplish them will change radically; in many cases, our motivations, hopes, and fears — the very things that drive our decisions, attitudes, and expectations — probably won't.

With more computing power and speed, large devices will become smaller and small devices will become invisible. Already there are probably more computers and chips around you than you realize. Soon even complex devices will be so portable that they will merge into single devices (such as the illusory MP3 player/PDA/cellular phone/digital camera/Web browser). Some of these devices could turn into jewelry or clothing (such as the *Star Trek* communicators that are worn on the front of a shirt). Having this amount of powerful technology so integrated into our lives (since it will be with us all of the time and anywhere we go), will change conversations ("I don't agree with that, let me look it up right now"), contracts ("I've got that conversation recorded, you said exactly that"), and travel ("The closest restaurant where you can earn United Mileage Plus miles while you eat is up three blocks and to the left. It's next to an historic turn-of-the-century building that you'll want to see because currently there's a gallery show of your favorite artist.")

We'll be able to control our homes — even letting the dog out and the FedEx guy in — from our phones and wireless PDAs while vacationing on another continent. And our houses will increasingly control themselves. How our houses and buildings operate behind the scenes will be dramatic. More and more, they will act like living entities — with the intelligence equal to our favorite pets and, hopefully, without the idiosyncrasies. Your house will control its energy signature by regulating light and air in and out with piezoelectric blowers and LCD windows (that instantly turn opaque) and bargain for lower energy prices automatically, scheduling the laundry for off-peak times. It may power itself from both solar cells and solar water heating, using passive solar design in its construction (a trend started decades ago). Don't look for housing styles to change (we'll always be interested in the traditional as well as the new).

Homes and buildings will learn our habits and even identify individual use when we're in them, when we leave, and when we approach. They will customize environments for us much like car seats do today, heating the hot tub or cooling the bubbly. Offices (whether cubicles or actual rooms) will reconfigure themselves based on their occupants, making it more comfortable for temporary or travelling workers. Mobile devices will allow us to work anywhere more easily (satellite phones and collaboration software are just the beginning). We will travel with preference files that will be used by remote and shared computers to automatically reconfigure themselves to look and work exactly like what we're accustomed to using, and then clean up securely when we leave. Very soon, we won't be lugging even the lightest of today's portable computers.

Entertainment and health will be some of the major forces as they currently and often have an adversarial relationship. We will continue to seek elaborate and immersive experiences whether in theme parks, online, or in retail stores. The ideal entertainment experience is a multi-sensory, immersive reality much like *Star Trek*'s Holodeck. While the technology for such an experience does not exist — and likely won't for centuries, if ever — we can create something similar using live actors, interesting storytelling, and creative sets. Still, there's something too controlled, rare, and costly about these experiences that keep them from being satisfying for a long period of time. However, it remains a model that has infected our expectations for all kinds of experiences.

Meanwhile, decades of entertainment media have amused and amazed us while it takes more and more time away from our physical health. World health figures support both of these trends. In the future, the two will need to be reconciled. Health and fitness activities will need to be more entertaining, relying on virtual simulations not only in the gym, but out on the trail as well.

Our knowledge of healthy eating and nutrition will have to be more widespread. Perhaps, new technologies will allow us to be better fed despite what we put into our mouths (super vitamins, customized nutritional supplements, starch, sugar, and fat blockers, and so on), but our attitudes and culture will need to change as well. More people will be buying and using nutritional supplements, including more aggressive vitamins that exceed the minimums set by the FDA, meal replacement bars and drinks, and supplements with enough potency to be labeled "self-medication." These are already in common use, but they'll be more widespread than ever. We will be able to eat better more often, but eating right will still take initiative. There will be a wider rift between those who eat well and those who don't, and this will most likely fall along monetary lines. Those with money will tend to eat fresher, more organic, and more healthy foods, and those with little money will tend to eat food that is more prepared, more advertised, less fresh, and less nutritious.

Slowly, customization will take hold in our culture as we learn to customize everything from our breakfast cereal to medicines, music, and clothes. We won't have time to customize everything, but we'll spend time personalizing those things that are dear to us and opt for the Gap-style choice for the rest. Of course, everyone will have their own priorities, but more sophisticated software and the return of insightful middlemen (like real estate and travel agents) will help us manage the things for which we have no time, desire, or expertise. Though we can book our own flights online from a variety of Web sites, we still can't find the information that really helps us make decisions about where and when to go. Only experts (even though they're also known as "middlemen") have this knowledge; this kind of in-depth knowledge about an area will always lie with experts, and many of the best selections will never be listed publicly.

We will develop a new relationship with our bodies, seeing it in increasingly plastic and malleable terms. Those who strive for classic beauty will have a new assortment of tools and procedures to tuck, snip, suck, and tone. Today, Botox parties bring cosmetic surgery to the Saturday evening cocktail set: Just duck into the bedroom when your turn comes, and 15 minutes later, your lips and eyes look younger. Tomorrow, high-end doctors will make "housecalls" for all sorts of elective procedures (for those with the money, of course). As the healthcare system worsens, the wealthy will support high-end health co-ops that cost more but treat them with more respect, take less time, and are much better managed. These will become models for the next generation of HMOs. Don't be surprised if financial organizations that manage money for wealthy people (such as Merrill Lynch) start offering healthcare coverage and insurance coverage with the same level of service and reporting that they offer for their financial services. Instead of earning miles with their Visa cards, some of these customers will be earning points toward discounts for prescriptions as well as elective procedures not traditionally covered (e.g., laser surgery, facelifts, liposuction, in-vitro fertilization, or genetic screening). These same tools in the hands of new mavericks will, instead, transform their bodies into imaginative and original creations (with horns, appendages, additions, and colorings). Tattoos and piercings were only the beginning.

Though the importance of relationships won't change significantly, how we manage these relationships will. We'll be able to stay in touch with those we need to (like colleagues or employers) as well as those close to us (family and friends) more easily and more fluidly. Our communications devices will work seamlessly worldwide, translating between multiple media, and we will be more adept at fielding, managing, and prioritizing calls without our involvement. We'll have more conversations at once, though shifted in time (like in email or discussion forums), and we'll be more connected to people of other cultures.

New technology won't make us understand each other better or give us more tolerance, but it will give us the tools for interacting with others more easily and experiencing more people or different cultures. There will never be a utopia, and we will always have conflicts, but technologies that make distance less important and that put us in contact with ever-increasingly more people will continue society's path toward tolerance, diversity, and peace.

—Nathan Shedroff

Smart Garments...
INTELLIGENCE WITH A FLAIR

A STAPLE OF CHEESY *STAR TREK* EPISODES *and fantastical cyberpunk tales, the clothes of the future have been envisioned for years as lavish costumes or generic uniforms that can change color and monitor a strange planet's atmosphere. We're still not jet-packing through the skies encased in psychedelic second skins, but some smart garments — a.k.a. i-Wear, smart clothing, and intelligent garments — are ready-to-wear.*

PERMANENT PRESS? *Corpo Nove has designed a shirt that will automatically shorten as the temperature rises, in effect rolling up its own sleeves.*

Take for example, Corpo Nove's "intelligent shirt," which responds to temperature changes and requires no ironing. Georgia Tech has created a shirt that can be adapted to monitor soldiers, hospital patients, and infants and even administer medicines to them. MIT investigates 21st-century info-armor with its MIThril program ("mithril" is the magical chain mail forged by the Elves in J.R.R.Tolkien's books). From molecular manufacturing to processes inspired by archaeological digs, researchers are finding new ways to custom-fit, create, clean, and dye clothing.

The possibilities seem unlimited: Designers and excited journalists exult that our clothes may soon shield us from pollution, find our keys, read our email aloud, and release pheromones to attract the opposite sex. What we'll probably see first are practical items like breathable cottons that turn

SHAPE MEMORY ALLOYS

Wouldn't it be nice if your shirt returned to a wrinkle-free shape just by blowing it with the hair dryer — while you're wearing it? To the joy of travelers everywhere, Shape Memory Alloys (SMAs) make this possible; Italian clothing company Corpo Nove has already released an expensive shirt woven with the shape memory material Nitinol. It may not sound terribly "smart" or glamorous, but it's a reality!

Image courtesy of Corpo Nove

WEARING THE NEW MACHINES

David Forrest, President of the nonprofit Institute for Molecular Manufacturing and a materials engineer at the Naval Surface Warfare Center, has studied nanotechnology and its myriad applications since 1985, when he heard influential nanotechnology evangelist Eric Drexler speak. Much has changed since then, including the 1991 discovery of carbon nanotubes and recent progress in manipulating their conductive properties. The tubes' great potential for creating super-strong, thermally- and electronically-conductive materials has enticed a number of companies into a development race. "Textiles is such a natural place for these to be applied," Forrest says. "They look like fibers!"

But other applications, such as electronic devices, will likely fuel the evolution of molecular manufacturing. Then, according to Forrest, "whatever technology is available will be applied to making fabrics considerably more sophisticated, to the point where you won't be able to really define whether someone is wearing a material or a machine."

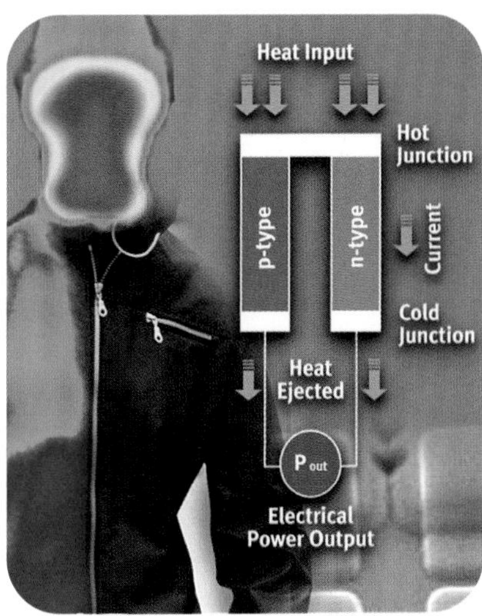

MAKING POWER. *Infineon's concept for self-powered clothing with body heat.*

water-repellent when it starts to rain; specialized gear for firefighters, police officers, medical uses, and outdoor sports; and super-fabrics for military and space programs, like the color-shifting and extra-strength textiles that researchers at Clemson University in South Carolina hope to produce.

Progress is well underway to make garments that look smart. Flexible electronic computer displays have already been unveiled by a new Lucent Technologies circuit-printing technique, which may someday result in outfits that change images, projections, and patterns. Temperature-sensitive fibers could be woven into "mood fabrics," and the military is financing research into the ultimate camouflage: "chameleon fabrics," with colors and patterns that would change in response to electrical commands.

How are these smart garments to be powered? Photovoltaic fibers, similar to the little cell on your solar calculator, could convert light for this purpose, as could heat from the environment. A firefighter's smart coat might simultaneously warn of a heat increase by changing color and then use that heat to power its various functions — like cooling down the inside of the jacket. Infineon Technologies' thermogenerator uses the difference in temperature between the human body's surface and that of the clothing itself to generate electricity — enough to power medical sensors.

Bacteria may also affect tomorrow's clothing. Some fabrics may be engineered to eat odor-causing chemicals and human sweat, others to secrete protective coatings. The past may also hold the key to the future: UK researchers looking for a more ecologically responsible way to dye clothing have found spores of the bacteria responsible for making indigo in Medieval times. Reviving the bacteria, they were able to replicate the centuries-old, indigo-making process.

Lasers have proven effective at welding clothes together, which works especially well for waterproofed seams. Eventually, however, we may see our pollution-resistant, self-cleaning, color-shifting unitards created by molecule-sized machines that can build fabrics and garments from the bottom up, molecule by molecule. It may not sound as sexy as a pheremone-producing tube top, but molecular manufacturing will likely determine the shape of clothes to come.

PROVOCATIONS...

Will your clothes grow as you do?

Will smart garments know the weather before you do?

Will smart garments help us locate them under a pile of dirty laundry?

—Tiffany Lee Brown

WANT MORE?

GEORGIA TECH'S WEARABLE MOTHERBOARD
www.gtwm.gatech.edu

MIT'S MITHRIL
www.media.mit.edu/wearables/mithril

CORPO NOVE
www.corponove.it

INSTITUTE FOR MOLECULAR MANUFACTURING
www.imm.org

Fashion... Much More Than a Matter of Style

IF YOU THINK OF FASHION ONLY AS STYLE, *there's no way to predict the future and, in fact, the future is mostly just a repetition and reflection of the past (hemlines up, hemlines down, hemlines erased, blurred, exaggerated, reduced, etc.). The 2001 New York Metropolitan exhibit on fashion throughout the past (and from many different cultures) described this kind of fashion very well.*

However, if you think of fashion as an industry of innovative manufacturing, materials, and methods, then the future becomes much more interesting and new. For example, Jhane Barnes, one of the leading high-end designers, applies high-tech software and the mathematics of fractals to create her stunning, one-of-a kind designs. Materials currently being developed by MIT's Media Lab are intended to not only reduce weight for soldiers, but

Left to right: Photograph © 2002 Fotographie Jean-Luc Valentin. Photograph © 2002 Fotographie Jean-Luc Valentin

HIGH TECH. *Jacket with integrated MP3 player, from Infineon Technologies.*

DESIGN BY THE NUMBERS

Former president Bill Clinton, musician Wynton Marsalis, comedian Jon Stewart, Los Angeles Laker coach Phil Jackson, and actor Don Johnson all swear by her one-of-a-kind menswear designs. The youngest person ever to win the COTY Menswear Award, leading fashion designer Jhane Barnes, uses technology and higher math to develop her distinctive patterns. Fractals suggest the underlying order or "geometry" of nature, and Jhane's designs have been inspired by such fractal patterns as the Koch curve, the Mandelbrot Set, and the Julia Set. Jane says, "Instead of thinking of patterns only in a visual sense, I now break them down to their simplest elements and think of them mathematically." When she creates designs with fractals, Jhane may start with a "fractal seed," a simple shape that gets turned into a fractal by applying a rule that replaces the seed with a more complex shape. Seeds beget seeds, and you end up with a complex shape that can look remarkably like the things we see every day in the world around us. Jhane manipulates the image until she has a unique design that could end up on a shirt, tie, sweater... or even on designs for seating, office systems, and walls for the office.

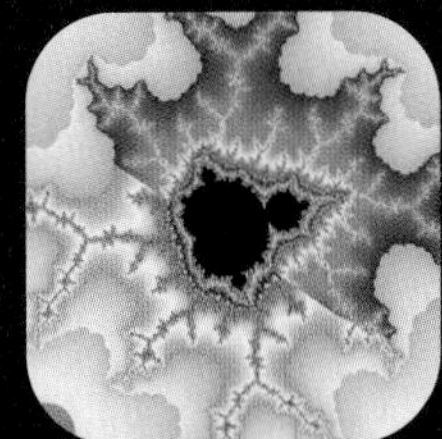
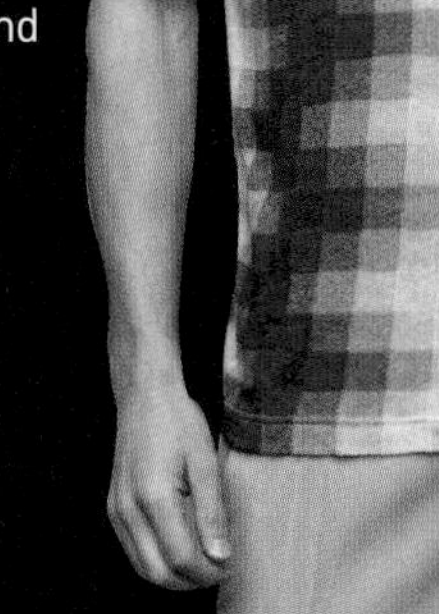

stiffen immediately upon conduction of an electric current to form an automatic cast for an arm or leg. Other materials are being developed to have conductive qualities for wearable computer components, changeable surfaces for dial-in camouflage, and even displays for showing advertisements (and you thought those subsidized cars driving around town were bad enough).

Perhaps the most interesting fashion arena is that of manufacturing. For years, manufacturers have been developing printing systems to color and print cloth as it rolls off the spool. This would allow patterns and colors to change at a moment's notice, driving the costs for custom designs down to that of mass-manufacturing and creating a boom in personalized clothing, accessories, and other wearable objects. Many clothes will be spun and cut from spools of pre-sewn or sealed fabric, like Issey Miyake's A-POC (A Piece of Cloth) system now being sold for high-end dresses, shirts, and sweaters. Each item comes perforated on a spool but can be customized in how it's cut from the roll, creating instantly personalized items, again at a mass-market price.

Clothing in the future will be designed with our digital lives in mind. Already, Dockers sells e-pants with extra pockets in the seams for storing PDAs, cell phones, and MP3 players. IDEO Japan has designed a show full of fashions that provide guides for headphones to weave through a jacket, jewelry that mimics the wearer's heartbeat (think mood rings but with an elegance and metaphor), and clothing with multiple functions (it's a jacket, a rain coat, and a sleeping bag all in one!). We'll also see a rise in disposable clothes that meet the specific needs of healthcare and relief workers, as well as security personnel, with much more sophistication.

PROVOCATIONS...

How will smart garments change our dress code?

Will garments be ad-supported, in the way that Web sites are?

—Nathan Shedroff

WANT MORE?

JHANE BARNES
www.jhanebarnes.com

ISSEY MIYAKE
www.isseymiyake.com

THE MIT MEDIA LAB
www.media.mit.edu

CHARMED TECHNOLOGIES
www.charmed.com

I-WEAR
www.starlab.org/bits/intell_clothing/index.html

AVANTEX
www1.avantex.de

Wearable Computers... "SLIP-ON" CYBERSPACE

BULKY LAPTOPS THAT WEIGH MERE OUNCES *may soon be a thing of the past. Ask nearly anyone on the street what they think of the latest generation of lightweight laptop computers, and chances are they will find them to be the future of computing. Ask the same question at one of the several wearable computing companies and labs cropping up across the world, and even the most microscopic laptop will suddenly seem as gargantuan and old-fashioned as the room-filling mainframes of the 1950s.*

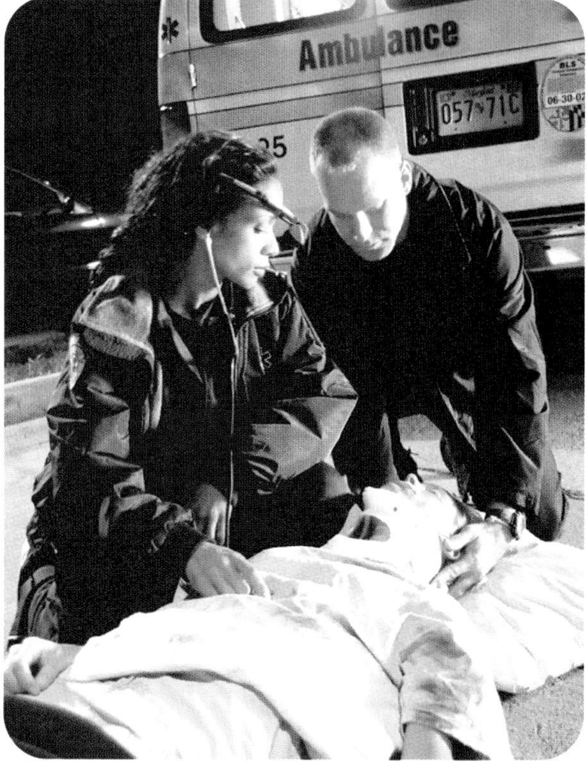

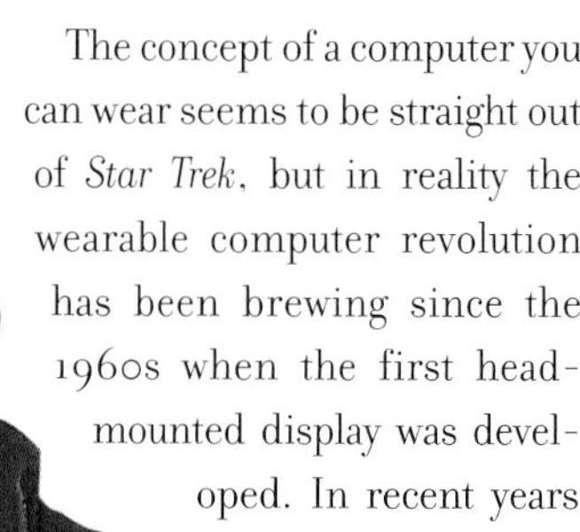

FASHION. *Charmed Technology sponsors a series of "Brave New Unwired World" fashion shows that showcase the future look of wearable computing.*

The concept of a computer you can wear seems to be straight out of *Star Trek*, but in reality the wearable computer revolution has been brewing since the 1960s when the first head-mounted display was developed. In recent years, several wearable computers have hit the market. Xybernaut®, one of the largest developers of wearables, recently released the Poma, dubbed a "personal multimedia appliance." As one of the first devices in the field to be marketed to the general consumer, the Poma gives users access to email, the Internet, music, videos, and games using a computer that can fit in a pocket, a hand-held optical mouse, and a head-mounted display that weighs only 3 ounces.

While devices like the Poma are breaking ground in the world of mobile computing, the truly revolutionary wearable computer of the future is still in development in research facilities across the world. Charmed Technology, for example, is developing wearable computers that are literally wearable. Their "Brave New Unwired World" fashion shows preview computing devices that are embedded in clothing or take the form of jewelry or other fashion accessories. Not

Clockwise from top left: Photo courtesy of Xybernaut Corporation. Image courtesy of MIT Media Lab. Model Sumit Basu; photo by Rich DeVaul

only are these wearables destined to be the fashion accessory of the future, but they will also be a necessity as work environments become increasingly mobile.

Perhaps some of the most forward-thinking research in the field is taking place at the MIT Media Lab, where the focus is on human-computer interaction. Size is definitely an issue in mobile computing. In order to be useful, a wearable computer must be lightweight and easy to transport. More importantly, however, wearables must break from the paradigms that have dominated computing since the very beginning.

To date, most computers have failed to move beyond functioning as glorified calculators and word processors, and nearly all of them are far from intuitive. MIT's Wearable Computing group believes that computers should not only be completely mobile, but they should also act as "intelligent assistants." This seems to be the path wearable computers are taking. Through the use of sensors and intelligent agents, these devices will be able to sense the user's environment and act accordingly, presenting users with an augmented reality— a view of the world that is enhanced with useful information.

Engineers, for example, could use wearables that project blueprints onto their field of vision while on the worksite. Speech recognition software would allow them to interact with intelligent agents that would answer questions as they arise, and wireless technologies would make communications from the field easier than ever. The possibilities don't stop there. Wearable computers have the potential to change the face of nearly every industry, from medicine to firefighting. And as sensor technologies improve, they will also help us take care of our bodies. As these technologies become more commonplace, the logical next step will be to use the embedded sensors to monitor our vital signs and warn us of any impending health problems.

For decades, the idea of wearable computing has conjured up images of cyborgs from a distant future. In reality, wearables will be almost invisible, integrating seamlessly with our everyday clothing and accessories, making our day-to-day tasks easier. While these devices may seem to be the stuff of science fiction, they are fast becoming fact, and resistance is undeniably futile.

Clockwise from top left: Photo courtesy of Xybernaut Corporation; Photo courtesy of Xybernaut Corporation

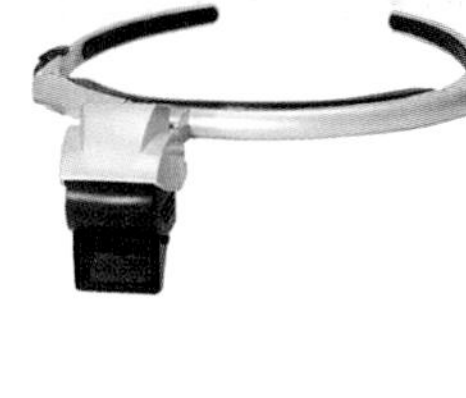

POMA. *The Poma is one of the latest releases from Xybernaut®, one of the largest wearable computing companies in the world. About the size of a paperback book, this computer comes with a handheld optical mouse and a head-mounted display and gives users on-the-go access to email, the Internet, gaming, and more (above).* **ON THE MOVE.** *This Xybernaut® wearable can be customized to give your mobile workers the tools they need to keep moving (bottom left).*

PROVOCATIONS...

Will users bump into each other more... or less?

Will people be forced to turn off their wearables when they drive?

— Zahra Safavian

WANT MORE?

INFORMATIONWEAR
www.ingineo.net

WEARABLE COMPUTING AT THE MIT MEDIA LAB
www.media.mit.edu/wearables

THE WEARABLE GROUP AT CARNEGIE MELLON
www.wearablegroup.org

XYBERNAUT
www.xybernaut.com

VIA WEARABLE COMPUTERS
www.via-pc.com

CHARMED TECHNOLOGY
www.charmed.com

EXTREME COMPUTING
www.extremecomputing.com

PEN COMPUTING MAGAZINE
www.pencomputing.com

E*Relationships... THIS IS YOUR VIRTUAL LIFE

DURING THE ASCENT OF the Internet in the mid-to-late 90s, it was common to hear "content is king!" Hundreds of business models were predicated on this new medium, sitting alongside books, movies, radio, and television as a vehicle for one-way transmission. As the millennium dawned, the fallacy of this approach became apparent: People were unwilling to pay for content, yet forked over money to ensure contact with others. Communication, not content, is king.

As people grew to realize the importance of communication, concern about the impact of these new technologies on interpersonal relationships commensurately rose. Initial discourse ranged from depressing (Internet use leads to social maladjustment), to fear mongering (your child might be "chatting" with unsavory characters), to salacious (teledildonics will allow you to enjoy many partners, guilt- and disease-free!).

Until recently, rampant speculation won over reasoned research. Happily, the balance is shifting, as more social scientists address this topic. What are they finding? That the reality is far less sensational and far more subtle than previously acknowledged. (They're also engaged in that time-honored practice of disagreeing with each other, so don't assume certainty about what follows.)

Carnegie-Mellon's HomeNet Project dropped a media bomb in 1998, when its research showed that greater Internet use led to declines in sociability and increases in depression—supporting the common perception of the computer user as maladjusted nerd. Making less of a splash was their subsequent 2002 report that revealed the Internet has generally positive effects on users' sociability. Although the report also indicated the Internet produces a "rich get richer" trend, where extraverts heightened their sociability and introverts lessened their sociability.

NYU Professor Katelyn McKenna's

PEOPLE WHO SAY BROADBAND HAS IMPROVED "CONNECTIONS"

To their friends	76%
To their family	71%
To meet new people	20%

Source: pewinternet.org

Stone/Getty Images

work has shown that not only is it common for relationships to form over the Internet, these connections are remarkably lasting, often surviving the move to the "real world." Seemingly paradoxically, this is due to the anonymity afforded by the medium — people more readily overcome initial social anxiety and more quickly present their "true selves" online. This leads to a more solid foundation as the relationship moves offline.

Increasingly, these technologies are being used to help people find mates. Bolstering the claim that "communication is king" is how magazines are morphing into community platforms. Unable to generate any real revenue with articles, many now host paid personals and are nearing profitability. Product designers are cleverly addressing this need, with gadgets such as the Japanese "Lovegety," a device that alerts you to other people in your proximity interested in making contact.

From a technological standpoint, perhaps the most interesting truth about interpersonal relationships is the extreme simplicity of the most popular tools used to support them.

Email and instant messaging are the digital equivalents of two cans and a string. Many attempts have been made to enhance these tools (videophones, videoconferencing, virtual reality meeting spaces, and so forth), but none has taken hold. This suggests that successful future technological developments likely will focus on improving the usefulness of these basic technologies.

A key trend in this regard is incorporation of social technologies into mobile devices. The massive success of SMS overcame the pronounced awkwardness of typing with a phone keypad, proving the power of combining simple contact with mobility. This evolution continues with the "buddy list," the heart of any instant messaging program. This personalized one-to-one chat space on the PC has definitely had a subtle, yet profound, impact on sociability. These lists are migrating to mobile phones, which not only show whose phone is turned on, but its location as well. Such technologies strengthen our sense of connectivity with others.

What's particularly clear is that "e-relationships" do not stand on their own. People desire to turn online connections into real-world ones and, subsequently, use online technologies to bolster them. It's a truism that humans are social beings, and people will always find ways to use technologies to enhance their relationships.

UNINTENDED USES

People have a tendency to transform, and even subvert, the intentions of designers in order to manifest social capabilities in their tools. Prof. McKenna noted, "People change the use of our various technologies to fit their own needs. The Internet was originally touted as 'the information super-highway' but people found it far more useful as a means for social interaction."

The ARPANET, the precursor to the Internet, was invented for the sole purpose of sharing extremely valuable computing resources across a network, but users exploited the physical connectivity to support social connectivity via email.

The Web was developed as a means for publishing physics documents, and well into its popularity, was often analogized as an enormous library. Yet the one standard-bearing successful "pure-play" site is eBay, a simple conduit connecting buyers with sellers.

Online games were originally conceived to support the efforts of individuals battling each other. In short order, "clans" began to form, perhaps reaching its apex in the Korean phenomenon "Lineage," where whole armies of people work together to beat other armies. And Lineage is most commonly played at PC bangs, cyber parlors where teams gather, blurring the distinction between online and offline contact.

In Japan, where the mobile buddy lists (see main article) are quite popular, a cottage industry has developed where businessmen will hire someone to stand in the place where they're supposed to be, fooling their employer, and freeing them up to go elsewhere.

PROVOCATIONS...

Will more e-relationships bring about a resurgence in the art of writing love letters and verbal romance?

Will e-group therapy be successful, and will e-psychology boom?

— Peter Merholz

WANT MORE?

HOMENET PROJECT
http://homenet.hcii.cs.cmu.edu/progress/index.html

PEW INTERNET AND AMERICAN LIFE REPORTS
www.pewinternet.org

JOURNAL OF SOCIAL ISSUES, VOLUME 58, ISSUE NO. 1 (WINTER 2002).

SMART CARDS...

IT'S AS EASY AS ONE, TWO, THREE, SWIPE

THE U.S. GOVERNMENT *has considered creating a national I.D. card based on the Social Security system as far back as 1971, and the issue has been raised in every presidential administration since then. As cliché as it now sounds, the 9-11 terrorist attacks have impacted everything. Once considered a gross invasion of privacy, national IDs have now gained an unprecedented amount of support among the American public, and smart cards have become one of the hottest technologies.*

Smart cards are plastic, credit-card-like cards with microprocessor chips embedded in them. Unlike the magnetic stripes commonly found on credit cards and identification cards, it is difficult to copy, erase, or overwrite the information stored on a smart card's chip. This is especially true when biometric technologies are involved. Hong Kong, for example, plans on distributing national ID cards to all of its citizens by 2007. In addition to biographical information and a photograph, these cards will have the cardholders' digital signatures and thumbprints embedded in a microprocessor. When a citizen makes the trip from Hong Kong to mainland China, they will simply insert their ID in a kiosk and press their thumb against a screen. If their thumbprint matches the information in their card, they can continue through. In addition to thumbprints and

'Smart card' replaces ID, cash and keys

Microchip cards, or smart cards, come in two

Contactless cards use a small antenna to transmit data, for example to pay a highway toll

Contact cards are inserted into a reader, such as one on a door lock

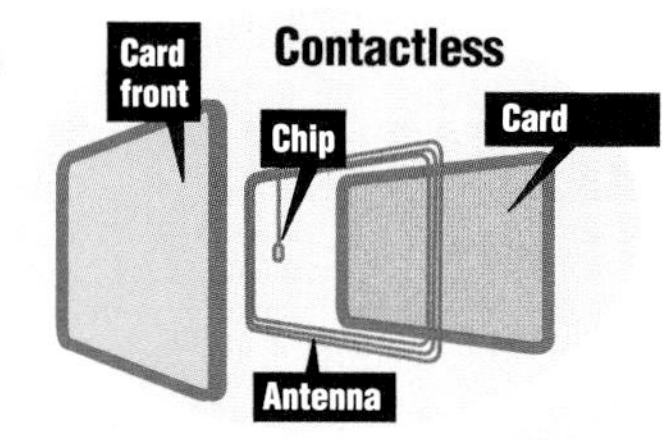

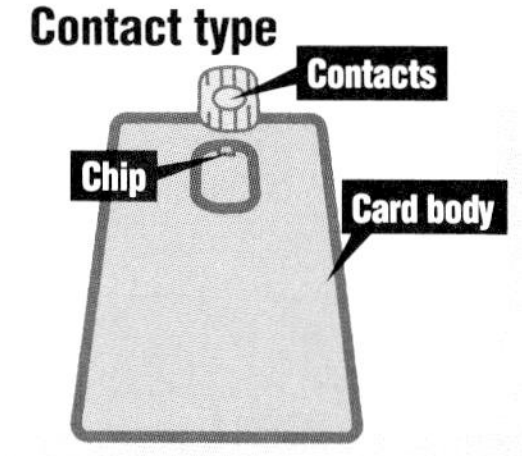

Memory cards differ from microchip cards because memory cards simply store information like a floppy disk, but in a secure manner; an example is a prepaid telephone card with a set

Smart cards in everyday life

Smart cards can store photos, digital thumbprints and other information. When presented, the information on the card is compared with a central database. Possibilities of smart card technology:

Holds passwords that let you log onto your computer

© 2001 KRT Source: The Dallas Morning News research
Graphic: Guillermo Munro, The Dallas Morning News

Graphic from the Dallas Morning News/Staff Illustrator Munro

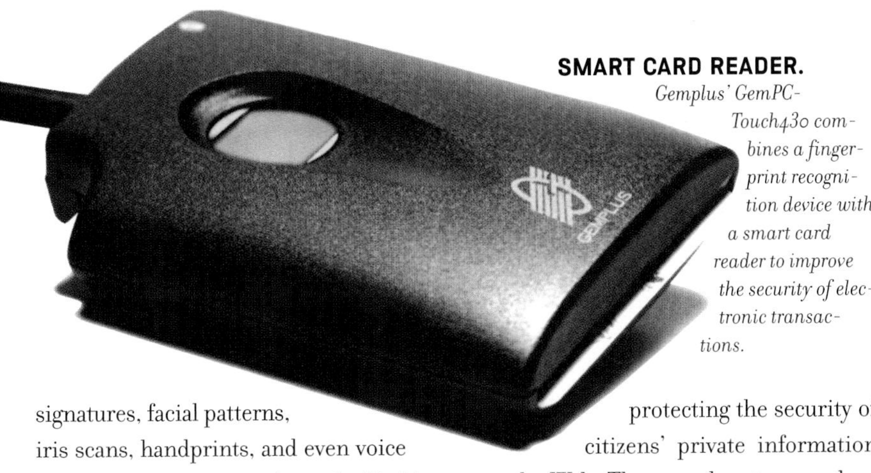

SMART CARD READER. *Gemplus' GemPC-Touch430 combines a fingerprint recognition device with a smart card reader to improve the security of electronic transactions.*

signatures, facial patterns, iris scans, handprints, and even voice recognition patterns can be embedded in a smart card's microprocessor.

Smart cards have other applications, as well. The U.S. military, for example, is instituting smart card identification programs for all of its employees. These cards will contain identifying information, including some biometrics, in addition to access keys. When military employees attempt to log on to a computer network or enter a secure building, they will use their cards to gain access.

The most widespread application of smart technologies will likely be in e-commerce. Finland, one of the most wired countries in the world, has made the FINEID card available to citizens since 1999 for the sole purpose of protecting the security of citizens' private information on the Web. These cards act as an electronic identity for users when making online financial transactions or when transferring sensitive information, credit reports, or health records. In the future, these cards may be expanded for other applications, such as allowing telecommuters to remotely log on to their companies' networks.

In the U.S., American Express recently released their Blue cards, a series of smart cards that are built with online purchases in mind. Used with smart card readers that can be connected to any PC or laptop and a PIN number, the Blue cards ensure that only the cardholder can use the information on the card. Several companies are working on similar cards for online usage.

In a world where more of our personal information is in open circulation than ever, smart cards have become the most popular solution to security problems. Many European and Asian countries have already adopted these technologies, in the form of national identification or "electronic purses" that allow the secure transaction of money, online or offline. The United States, on the other hand, is still embroiled in the debate. Civil liberties organizations worry that smart cards will not only fail to protect, but they will make our most personal information — our biometric data — vulnerable to theft.

For the most part, the American public has agreed with the ACLU and the Electronic Privacy Information Center (EPIC), two of the most outspoken voices against smart cards. In the past year, however, popular opinion has swayed to the other side. As the Department of Transportation prepares to set national standards for state-issued driver's licenses, pressing a thumb against a screen or getting an iris scan will more than likely become a common occurrence in the U.S., and 9-11 may also be the day the smart card industry was officially launched into the American public.

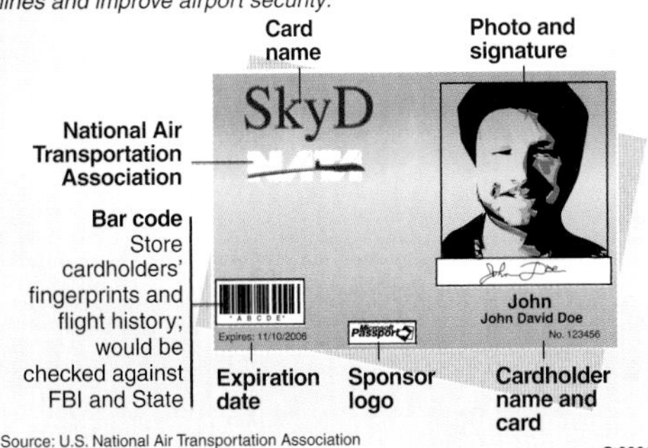

GOODBYE LINES. *The airlines have proposed the Flight ID card for the convenience of their passengers.*

Clockwise from top left: Image courtesy of Gemplus S.A. Image from Knight Ridder by Cassio Furado

PROVOCATIONS...

What will we do when our smart cards break?

What services will we decide we don't want linked to such cards?

—Zahra Safavian

WANT MORE?

SMART CARD ALLIANCE
www.smartcardalliance.org

GEMPLUS
www.gemplus.com

SMARTTRUST
www.smarttrust.com

ELECTRONIC PRIVACY INFORMATION CENTER
www.epic.org

EGOV
http://egov.gov

The Future of Shopping...
SHOP 'TIL YOU...FIND WHAT YOU WANT

As arguably the *most materialistic nation in the world, American identity is often expressed through its brands – Coke, Nike, Disney. Similarly, the changing values and desires of the American people can be viewed through the lens of how and where we're shopping. In the plentiful post-war years, Americans moved to the suburbs, embraced car culture, and liked to shop where they could park conveniently. The mall was born. At the end of the go-go 80s, baby boomers ditched their Izod shirts and designer jeans in favor of cheaper generic brands that fit the leaner times. The discount superstores, also known as Big Boxes were born – Wal-Mart, Home Depot, Costco, and others. When tech got sexy in the 90s, and Americans' wallets fattened,*

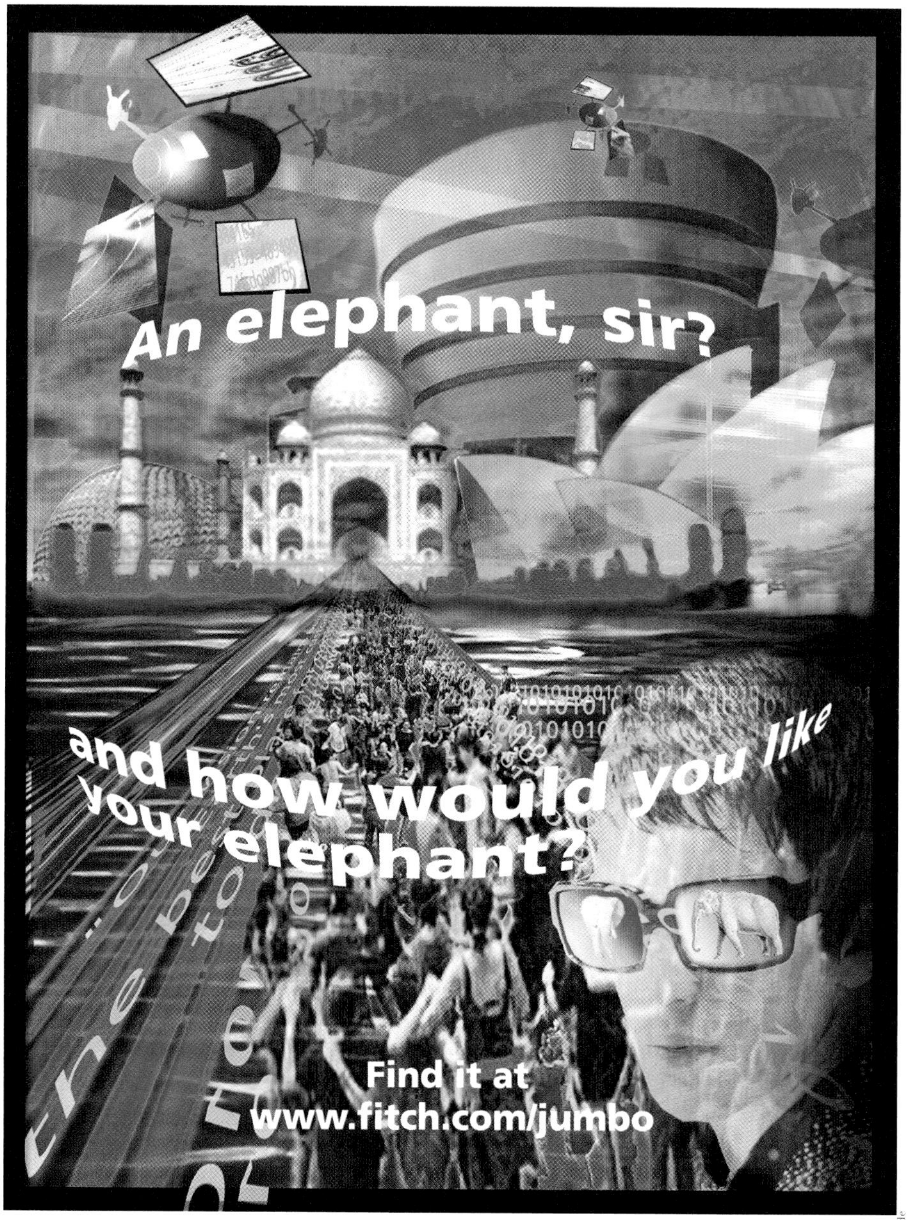

AMAZON'S FUTURE? *Designed by Fitch: Worldwide, this prototype concept for an online 3D store includes avatars who greet you personally and lead you through a bazaar-like shopping experience that blurs the distinction between "bricks and mortar" and online shopping.*

Image Courtesy of Fitch: Worldwide

MAIN STREET USA

Town Center Drive is a new kind of mall that's designed to look like an old-fashioned Main Street full of independent retailers, and even housing. You can drive down the street and park in front of stores, (though a big parking garage is also hidden in the back), watch hired street performers, or attend the sidewalk art festival. The intention is to give shoppers a fulfilling sense of "place" and "community" that will keep them there – and shopping

Web-based stores like Amazon.com opened their doors. Offline "flagship" stores for apparel makers like Levi and Nike displayed nothing but its product, in high-tech, museum-like surroundings.

WHITE GLOVES

Future retailers will take cues both from the hospitality industry's white-glove customer service, and the old-fashioned corner store where customers chatted and clerks greeted you by name. The phenomenally successful Central Market grocery stores in Texas offer a glimpse into the future of retail. At 75,000 thousand square feet, Central Markets are like mini World's Fairs of food. The store offers 600 types of cheeses and 80 varieties of fish. Shoppers can sample any product in the store, watch cooking demos, take cooking classes, send their kids to cooking camp, or get advice for their next dinner party from "foodies" who cruise the aisles in green aprons, like docents or tour guides.

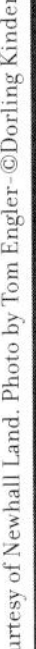
Photo courtesy of Newhall Land. Photo by Tom Engler-©Dorling Kindersley

In an increasingly fast-paced future, where fear of terrorism and war will cause us to seek the comfort of personal connections with one another, we will shop in two ways. When we want something quickly, increased use of the Web and innovations in bricks-and-mortar payment systems will get us products conveniently. And, when we want to browse, retailers will bend over backwards to make the experience pleasurable, engaging, and personal, with opportunities for us to connect with each other and feel like a community. Ann Satterthwaite, author of *Going Shopping: Consumer Choices and Community Consequences* (2001, Yale), identifes the following trends for the future of shopping: fast-and-easy and bargain shopping; remote shopping (automated and online); tourism and entertainment shopping; and sociable, service, and communal shopping.

Solely competing on price or merchandise won't cut it in the future. Today cultural anthropologists are being hired by future-thinking retailers to do things like analyze video of shoppers recorded by hidden cameras. They note shoppers' body language, as they pass by certain displays or encounter salespeople, to see whether they are relaxed or stressed out and suggest improvements. Minneapolis-based retail consultant firm Experience Engineering works with Fortune 100 companies to identify the subconscious responses shoppers have to retail environments that make them want to come back or run screaming. The firm puts test shoppers in "good, bad, and ugly" shopping situations and then hooks them up to a PET scan to watch their brain waves.

According to retail experts like Geoffrey Booth at the retail think tank The Urban Land Institute hermetically sealed malls are a thing of the past. The future is in "lifestyle centers" – outdoor malls designed to look like Main St., USA. A recent report by the International Council of Shopping Centers identified about 30 such projects open today, with many more in the pipeline.

Some new outdoor malls have gone a step further by offering residential living, too. The future success of these mixed-use developments depends on the dismantling of traditional zoning laws, which separate retail and residential in most communities, and even more

BODY DOUBLES

Retailers of the future will build Web sites that try to immerse their customers just the way offline stores do. The Lands' End Web site allows you to create a 2D virtual model of yourself by supplying your measurements. You can then try on Lands' End clothing on your model, approximating the experience of a real store.

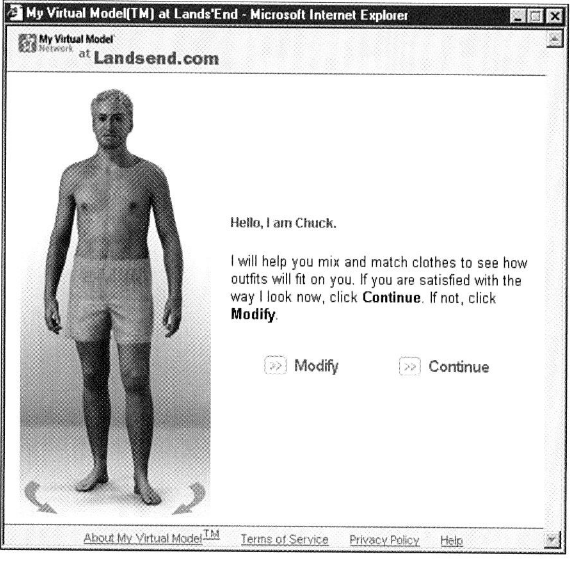

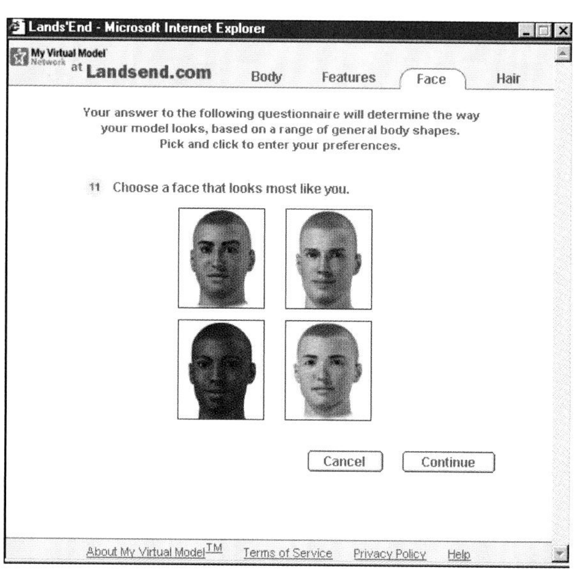

AMAZON'S 3D "NOTCOM" STORE

Imagine, for a moment, that it is tomorrow. You don't distinguish between shopping online or going to the mall: Early 21st-century distinctions between "bricks and mortar" and "e-commerce" seem quaint, anachronistic. Freed from the burden of purchasing commodities and necessities (most done virtually and automatically for you), your shopping experience has become luxurious, lateral, bazaar-like, random, and even visceral, like foreign travel, a favorite sport, or a mode of entertainment. The store has become the place where you learn what you want to buy, a reversal of the late millennial habit of researching purchases online but buying in-store.

Avatars who know your every preference and proclivity greet you at the store's entrance. Shopping with you, these hologram-like guides indicate a path to what you like based on a profile built from thousands of your clicks. Personality management software enables these helpers to propose store journeys customized to your whims or needs, always drawing from your digital character sketch to cross categories freely and cluster purchases based on past experience. These guides can provide you with curator-like commentary on your Limoges porcelain collection or on the eco-friendliness of solar-powered devices. Bank balance checks and shopping-to-earning ratios can also be voice-activated, and *Consumer Reports* charts materialize when necessary. Shopping for birthdays and holidays is particularly breezy because your avatar has profiles of relatives and friends and your entire gift-giving calendar. Shopping carts have given way to voice-activated avatar ordering, enabling you can shop unencumbered, free to try out or try on everything.

interestingly, on how well people and brands will coexist. What if school kids want to demonstrate in the "town square," which is not really public space but part of the privately owned retail development? They would not be allowed their First Amendment right of free speech in a traditionally sealed mall — but then, they would not be living there.

Online shopping will continue to grow — in 2001, holiday shopping rose 34.5% from the year before, despite the economic downturn, according to e-commerce research firm Bizrate.com. So far, consumer privacy concerns have

SHOPPING, IT'S THE EXPERIENCE, STUPID

Take art, entertainment, and high technology, and what do you have? You wouldn't expect to answer "a store," but that's what you have with Prada's newest store, set to open in September 2002. Taking a hint from Issey Miyake, who had Frank Gehry design his Tribeca store, Prada hired pretigious architect Rem Koolhaas to provide a provocative and futuristic shopping experience. The New York store, one of five new flagship stores, located in SoHo has all the technological gadgetry any geek could hope for — Prada is just hoping high-end retail shoppers will want them too. Wanting to provide the ultimate in customer service, Prada staff, at the flick of their handheld reader (a "style scanner" from Texas Instruments), lets the customer immediately know whether the color and style is available in her size. Sales staff also use the device to read tagged products (to maintain that real-time inventory), and to control video screens throughout the store, which will show collection photographs and designer sketches, while providing more information about fabrics and materials used to create the couture.

The store's futuristic interior includes transparent display cases hung from a network of motorized tracks on the ceiling — the push of a button can reorganize a store to make room for a runway show or party. The transparent glass doors on the dressing room, though, are the coup de gras. Once the patron enters the dressing room, the doors turn opaque — thankfully, for those of us who are body conscious. The dressing rooms are outfitted with video screens rather than mirrors. You can use the dressing-room computer to find matching items, check sizes, and check stock. The dressing rooms will also be equipped with cameras and high-resolution video screens so the shoppers will be able to see a full-view of themselves on a TV screen as they try on clothes and then view the selections later from home.

stymied retailers in their attempts to use new technologies like the Web to track and widely share information they gather about customers' shopping habits. To do so would allow them to market new products tailored towards our individual preferences. In the future, customers will be slowly but surely desensitized to sharing information with retailers because doing so will get them discounts or faster or more personal service. Foreshadowing of this can be seen in today's widespread use of "loyalty programs" like grocery store club cards — i.e., in exchange for a few pennies off, your purchases are tracked and used by grocers in making purchasing decisions and marketing products to you.

Wireless technologies, like Bluetooth, in the next 5 years will be tested by retailers as a way of communicating with shoppers' PDAs or cellphones. Five years from now, all customers who want to will be able to buy movie tickets on their cell phones. With the current FCC-mandated advent of location-based identification services, over the next year, carriers will be able to know your location. This means customers will soon receive special coupons or deals from their cell phone carriers based on where they are physically positioned in the city. If consumers become accustomed to using wireless services as part of their shopping experience, retailers may be able to ask for something in return. A consumer's PDA, for example, could communicate profile information about her likes, dislikes, and the date of her boyfriend's birthday to a sales rep when she walks in the door, in exchange for receiving deals and special treatment.

New payment systems that work like quick-pay, toll-pass systems on the freeway will make shopping ultra-convenient. Also, combinations of Web-based ordering and home delivery, and self-scanning checkout lines — already entering high-tech grocery stores — will make incursions into nearly all kinds of offline retail environments in the next 20 years. Likewise, when digital TV services and/or cable set-top boxes come down in price and cable companies begin widespread rollouts gradually over the next 20 years, consumers will be able to buy things by clicking on their televisions.

PROVOCATIONS...

Will we buy admission tickets to stores in the future?

—Lessley Anderson

WANT MORE?

LAND'S END
www.landsend.com

CENTRAL MARKET
www.centralmarket.com

VALENCIA
TOWN CENTER
www.valenciatowncenter.com

FITCH:WORLDWIDE
www.fitchworldwide.com

EXPERIENCE ENGINEERING, INC.
www.expeng.com

COUNCIL
OF SHOPPING CENTERS
www.icsc.org

When Our Environments Get Smarter

There used to be a time in which life, at least for most people, was quite linear. You were born in a family with a father and a mother, grew up in the place of your birth, went to school if you were lucky, and then to work. You married, raised a family of your own, worked at the same place for most of your professional life, retired, and then died. Such was the life that my grandparents lived, as did my parents.

But this is not the life that I am living, nor is it the one that my children will experience. Something has happened. Sometimes it feels as if this "something" has made the world shrink and has compressed time, allowing us to live many lives, in many different places, at the same time. Sociocultural researchers at Philips Design refer to this phenomenon as "mosaic" living, a life in which we are allowed to be different people at the same time, while still maintaining our core selves. Between birth and death we now have many choices and possibilities before us that were unavailable to previous generations.

This "something" that has turned the world around is technology. Telecommunications has allowed us to experience the world almost at our fingertips. Global air travel has enlarged our horizons, literally and figuratively. Miniaturization has allowed us to do more in less time, and with less cluttering hardware. When I sit back and think of the past, I feel that this development, which I certainly welcome and embrace, has not come without a price. We can now communicate through computers, but we may miss sharing ideas and friendly chats face to face with our neighbors. We can now travel far and fast, but we seem to spend more time in faceless airports rather than enjoying cultural exchanges with people. We can do more in half the time, but we miss having some time to do nothing, such as just sitting under a tree and thinking.

We have to choose our own future and not be forced into something we do not want. Our most noble purpose as a species has always been to improve the quality of our collective life. We owe it to our ancestors and descendants to continue to do the same.

I work for Philips Electronics, one of the largest technology companies in the world. As such, I have an informed sense of our technological future. Whether we like it or not, technology companies are all working toward the same goal: Some call it "ambient intelligence," others "ubiquitous computing," others a "connected world." What it all boils down to is the fact that we will soon live in a world in which many objects will become "smart," able to respond, react, and anticipate on our needs, wants, and desires. In such a world, technology will play an even greater role than it plays in our lives today.

At Philips we have developed an approach to design based on understanding people and developing solutions that ultimately aim to improve the quality of their lives. We want to develop a future in which technology empowers people in subtle ways, leaving them able to experience life on a human scale — one that they can grasp. Our goal is to create solutions that are relevant, meaningful, and understandable for people, from a personal and cultural point of view.

Homes in the future will look more like homes of the past than those of today. A typical contemporary home may be strewn with remote controls, switches, buttons, cables, and screens. Because of its own limits, technology is not able to provide us at present with solutions that meld gracefully into the domestic environment. This "cluttering" of technology is not just an aesthetic problem. Think of the way we interact with technology. Do you know how to program all your devices? Do you find it easy to remember all the functions of your numerous remote controls? When there is too much hardware in the home, it is difficult to remember how to operate this or that device.

At Phillips Design we want technology to be operated intuitively. We want hardware to disappear. You may think it is funny to hear this from one of the largest hardware manufacturers in the world, but this is our vision, the direction that we are taking. "Ambient Intelligence" for us is an environment in which people are free to use technology without perceiving its presence, without seeing it or needing to think about how to interact with it.

For instance, you may think of coming home and being recognized by a camera on your door. The door will open automatically and then lock itself behind you. While you relax, you can keep an eye on your children playing in the garden, thanks to a GPS system inserted in their clothes that transmits their positioning and well-being to you. You also will not need to go to the grocery store if you don't want. Whenever an item is missing from your kitchen, it will appear automatically on an online shopping list, which you will be able to send by voice command to the supermarket for home delivery. You will be able to communicate with people far away not only through voice, but also through images and possibly even smells. For example, a friend sitting in a restaurant could share ideas with you about the menu while you are enjoying a quiet night at home! Or a friend could transmit images to you from a retail store of the two dresses that she feels suit her best, and you could advise her on which one to choose — all while lying in your bath!

Similarly, in the office of the future we will be able to do more with less. Teleworking will become commonplace and will be a very smooth process. In the future, I will be able to sketch the design for a product directly on the surface of my desk, which will have replaced the conventional computer screens of today. I could then simply send that drawing electronically to my colleagues on the other side of the world, who would receive it instantly, with no long file download. By means of videophone and video conferencing, we would converse and finalize the design as if we were next to each other.

In the future, we will no longer need to carry around mobile phones or PDAs. Our clothes will have embroidered keypads and integrated microphones, and we will be able to communicate in total comfort and freedom. Data from your daily agenda could be displayed on your sleeve, thanks to the use of flexible display screens. Intelligent devices and networks will unobtrusively embrace our entire domestic and work experiences, allowing us to perform tasks better.

But technology (functions) and design (the capacity to integrate functions in objects that are culturally relevant) alone are not enough for people anymore. In Abraham Maslow's (1954) well-known hierarchy of needs, people satisfy basic physiological and safety needs before moving up to "higher" needs such as love, esteem, understanding, beauty, self-actualization, and, ultimately, a kind of transcendence in which one helps others find self-fulfillment. As we progress up this scale of needs, practical solutions are taken for granted and people begin to search for something more. The next challenge for designers is to focus on creating experiences and establishing new relationships. The "human touch" is missing in the scenarios described previously. The systems solutions that we develop must take into account the need for people to interact with each other. We do not want people to avoid physical contact and to communicate through devices only. We must conceive of technology solutions that foster new physical relationships and social groupings, allow people to create rather than to passively use, and enhance sensual experiences.

At Philips Design we have taken up this challenge. We are now working on open systems that understand and support the rituals of our living and adapt themselves to people through time and places. We have developed environments that respond to the totally unpredictable physical behaviors of the inhabitants — environments that adapt continually to support the activities and states of being of the inhabitants. For example, we have developed a bedroom concept in which two people sharing a bed change, through their movements, the settings of the room, such as the wallpaper and the lighting. We have designed interactive tools that allow children who are playing together to build a common story through visuals and sounds. We have also developed another system that allows members of a physical community to share information and meet each other as a consequence of using the tool.

The greatest challenge in this area is for interaction designers. In these active environments, interfaces will disappear. In the bedroom concept you see nothing but a bed. The interface is embroidered on the duvet. The whole environment will be an interface; the whole environment will be reactive. We will no longer interact with just our fellow humans, but also with technologies that will be able to learn, grow, and change in time — just like children. Interaction design will play a key role in designing and enabling these new types of relationships and interactions.

—Stefano Marzano

Smart Houses...
THE AUTOMATED HOME

IMAGINE coming home from work to a house that has turned on the heat to your preferred temperature, switched on the lights, and cooked the casserole you left in the oven. The smart house is by no means a new concept. Since as early as the 1950s, creative minds have envisioned homes that take care of the daily necessities of our lives, from The Jetsons' Skypad Apartments to Ray Bradbury's Happylife Home. With the advent of broadband Internet access, these future visions are quickly becoming a reality.

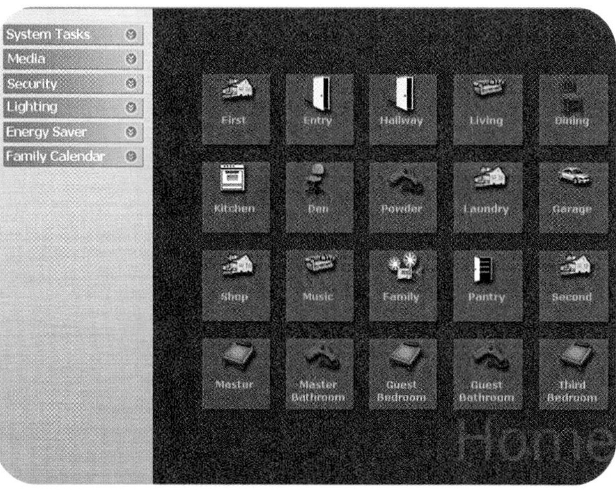

THE JETSONS' HOME IS HERE. *The home of the future has technology at its core to support, drive, and maintain its sophistication. New electronic systems tie a home's audio, video, alarms, phones, and lights into a single control. Premise Systems' SYS automation software (shown here) combines different types of systems into a single unit regardless of who made them.*

The Internet Home Alliance, a diverse group of technology-related companies working together to bring an awareness of the digital lifestyle to existing and future homeowners, is currently testing the OnStar at Home system in 100 houses in Detroit, Michigan. With this system, homeowners have always-on, broadband Internet access that allows them to integrate automation, home security equipment, and monitoring products from various companies into their homes. And OnStar provides several ways for you to access (control) your system: through its in-vehicle voice system, the Web, a cellphone, or a wireless-enabled PDA. Projects like OnStar at Home are taking place across the world, from Silicon Valley to Singapore, and experts in the field believe intelligent houses will become the norm as more homeowners take advantage of the convenience and the time and cost-savings of connected technology. Bob Vila thinks so. He's showcasing on his

WHAT'S THE HOLDUP?

An Internet Home Alliance survey identified two major factors that have dampened consumer excitement over the connected home: technical complication and security. The technical difficulty of setting up a wireless home network, however, is quickly getting easier, thanks for the emergence of 802.11b, or "Wi-Fi," as the wireless standard of choice among major high-tech equipment manufacturers. Wireless networking hubs called "gateways" should further simplify network management by controlling all devices from a central, Web-enabled box.

Security is a stickier issue. Home automation is powered via the Internet, and with any Web-based venture comes questions of privacy. What's more, the same viruses that plague PCs could be programmed to infest entire home networks. If a network gateway gets infected, could the system go beserk? For now at least, such concerns don't seem to discourage the tech dreamers who see smart homes as the wise way of the future.

Photo courtesy of KRT

AGING IN PLACE…AT HOME

If smart homes take off, they will also make it possible for the elderly and the disabled to live at home rather than at care facilities. This is the goal of the Georgia Institute of Technology's "Aware Home of the Future," and the University of Rochester's Center for Future Health, which includes features such as cameras in bathrooms that can detect melanomas and sensors that collect information to let people know if their elderly parents are well or if they need help.

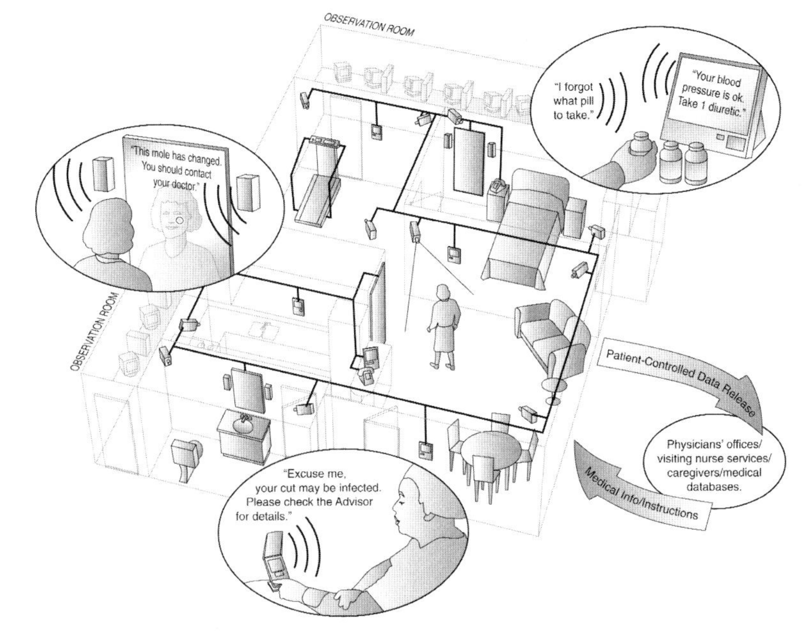

Image courtesy of Future Health University of Rochester, Rochester, NY

Web site the dotCOM dreamHOME, a 10,000- sq. foot luxury home just completed in Las Vegas, which uses innovative building technologies and advanced communications. This 21st-century home has technology at its core to support, drive, and meet the needs of today's (and tomorrow's) busy household. Its presence may be subtle, but technology is everywhere. Vendors have teamed to integrate lighting, audio/video, home security, communications, and the Internet seamlessly into the home's décor with control panels, communication centers, touchscreens, Web pads, and handheld devices. Everything functions invisibly via a complex electronic network within the walls.

While smart house developments in high-tech areas of France and Korea are proving to be successful, the widespread acceptance of intelligent houses will require easy-to-use interfaces and a significant price drop. The average user should not only be able to control all appliances and features in a house with one interface, but should also be able to add new appliances and features easily and cheaply. Hand-in-hand with ease of use is the issue of control. Unless users feel like they are in control of their houses, smart homes will be an unlikely reality.

Clearly, much work is required before smart homes become a part of mainstream culture. However, tremendous growth in broadband and networking technologies are an indicator of society's eagerness to not only be digitally connected to the wealth of information the Internet has to offer, but also to control this information. As networking and interface technologies are developed and prices drop, people will gain more control over the devices and information stored in their own homes, in ways more exciting and advanced than Ray Bradbury ever envisioned.

PROVOCATIONS…

Will the new real-estate mantra be "Smartness, Smartness, Location"?

Will a smart house keep you from watching "dumb" TV?

Would you rather live alone?

—Zahra Safavian

WANT MORE?

PREMISE SYSTEMS
www.premisesystems.com

DREAMLG
www.dreamlg.com/en/index.jsp

INTERNET HOME ALLIANCE
www.internethomealliance.com

THE CISCO INTERNET HOME
www.cisco.com/warp/public/779/consumer/internet_home.html

HOME AUTOMATED LIVING
www.automatedliving.com

HOMESEER TECHNOLOGIES
www.homeseer.com

ECHELON
www.echelon.com

BOB VILA'S DOTCOM DREAMHOME
www.dotcomdreamhome.com

Domestic Robots...

YOUR VERY OWN DROID

TO VIEW ONE OF THE MUCH-PUBLICIZED DEMONstrations of Honda's ASIMO humanoid robot or Sony's SDR-4X is to stare into the face of the future. It is both an exhilarating and a highly unsettling experience. Looking at one of these amazing machines, you'd almost swear that you were looking at a small child traipsing around inside a plastic space suit. The balance, the dexterity, the limb articulation is unprecedented ... and quite uncanny. These are the prototypes for the first generation of true domesticated robots — or at least that's what their manufacturers, and others like Fujitsu and NEC, are hoping.

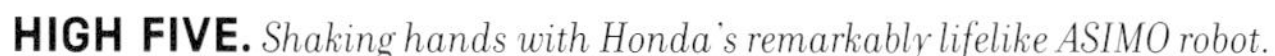

HIGH FIVE. *Shaking hands with Honda's remarkably lifelike ASIMO robot.*

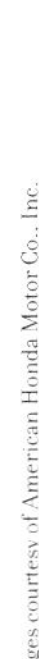

Images courtesy of American Honda Motor Co., Inc.

The race to create the first generation of real-world C3POs is not what you'd call a tight one — it's not even what you'd call a race. It is an extremely diverse arena of developmental activity, moving in fits and starts, with staggeringly different ideas of what even constitutes a robot, what users want out of a mechanical domestic, what the best path to widespread marketability should be...the list goes on and on. Some, like the Japanese companies previously mentioned, are taking a high-end (and high-priced) humanoid approach, while others, many of them scrappy U.S. firms, are taking a more bottom-up, utilitarian tack (think: R2-D2). The first real-life Rosie the Robot will probably fall somewhere in between. And while you likely won't be removing her from her shipping crate and handing her the feather duster anytime soon, recent developments from many quarters of the robot world point to that future happy day.

SURF'S UP! *Sony's latest diminutive (23" tall) singing and dancing (and apparently surfing) robot.*

MAY I TAKE YOUR HAT AND COAT?

To date, Sony and Honda's prototypical humanoids amount to little more than the concept cars of the robot world, but they are innovating technologies that will likely be found in future home robots. The SDR-4X has 38 articulated joints that can respond, in real time, to changing environmental conditions such as carpeting and rough surfaces. It has two color-camera eyes that can identify and respond to faces and guide the 'bot around objects (also in real time). Multiple microphones in its head allow it to follow sounds and voices as a human would. Sony hopes to put a version of the SDR on the market in the near future, but sales will be limited to those who can afford an "entertainment robot" that'll sell for the price of a small luxury car. Honda has recently begun renting ASIMO out to corporations as a receptionist and hospitality robot.

THE KILLER APPLICATION

One of the questions that needs to be answered before the home robot revolution can begin in earnest is: What will the "icebreaker market" be, the product area

THIS ROBOT'S A NO-BRAINER

In the last few decades, many robot designers have turned their attention to nature for cues to successful robot design. No "school" of robotics has taken this to a greater extreme than BEAM. Created by Los Alamos National Laboratories robotics engineer Mark Tilden, BEAM (which stands for "Biology, Electronics, Aesthetics, Mechanics") not only focuses on biologically inspired designs but also on bottom-up 'bots that have little-to-no brains (i.e. no onboard computers). BEAM designers cleverly orchestrate sophisticated insect-like behaviors by creating "nervous nets" out of basic analog electronics (capacitors, resistors, etc.) and solar power cells. Tilden sees a possible future in which swarms of tiny BEAMbots wrangle the dust bunnies on your floors, munch the dirt on your windows, and perform other thankless household chores.

CUDDLY AS A PUPPY? *Sony's best-selling AIBO ERS312, now in its third generation.*

that will help bootstrap a full-blown industry? Sony has focused, with significant success, on the robot entertainment business. Its best-selling AIBO robo-pet is on its third generation, with each new version sporting more sophisticated features, more user access to programming tools, and greater robot autonomy. Recently, nursing homes and others who care for the elderly have begun using AIBOs as companions and as a tool to help stimulate aging imaginations. Fujitsu has run with this idea, creating a robotic teddy bear for elders that can play with them, remind them to take their meds, and even alert the staff if their human master stops talking mid-sentence (possibly a sign of trouble). Developers are working on more sophisticated nursing care helpers that can, for instance, escort elders around a nursing home (one of the most time-consuming nursing home activities). High-end robot toys and tireless mechanical companions (despite the obvious inherent controversies) are likely to continue to be potential breakout markets. Sony is using the success of (and much of the technology from) AIBO to develop its SDR series, and, one can imagine, will use any market gains of the SDR to develop more sophisticated, more useful future home robots.

ZIPPY RUG SUCKERS AND GRASS MUNCHERS

Perhaps with the freakish exception of Martha Stewart, most of us loathe housecleaning. Many futurists expect that cleaning capabilities will be the domestic robot killer app, but so far, workable solutions have been elusive. British vacuum trendsetter Dyson and Eureka (Robo Vac™) in the U.S. have been showing off zippy rug suckers for years now, but they remain more-or-less stuck in the prototype stage. Probotics has delivered the goods with Cye, an affordable ($2,995) multipurpose entry-level robot domestic that does light vacuuming (with hit-and-miss success) and dirty-dish hauling, but it's still a hobbyist's platform. Robot lawn mowers have fared a little better, with examples such as the Toro iMow and the Husqvarna Auto Mower, but these manufacturers see it as a novelty market rather than a near-term direction for their industry. Price, ease-of-use, and reliability are all issues that will need to be addressed before robotic cleaning help becomes commonplace.

ROBOTIC CONTROL SOFTWARE

Bill Gross of Evolution Robotics believes that what the robot world needs is a standard platform — sophisticated, easy-to-use robot control software that companies can use to develop many different types of robots. His company has developed such a program, called the Evolution Robotics Software Platform, that he hopes will become the industry standard for accessible home robotic control, like how "the Netscape browser

LEAN, MEAN, CLEANING MACHINE. *Dyson's DC06 "dual cyclonic" robotic vacuum prototype.*

Clockwise from top left. Image courtesy of Sony Electronics, Inc. Entertainment Robot America. Image courtesy of Dyson Ltd.

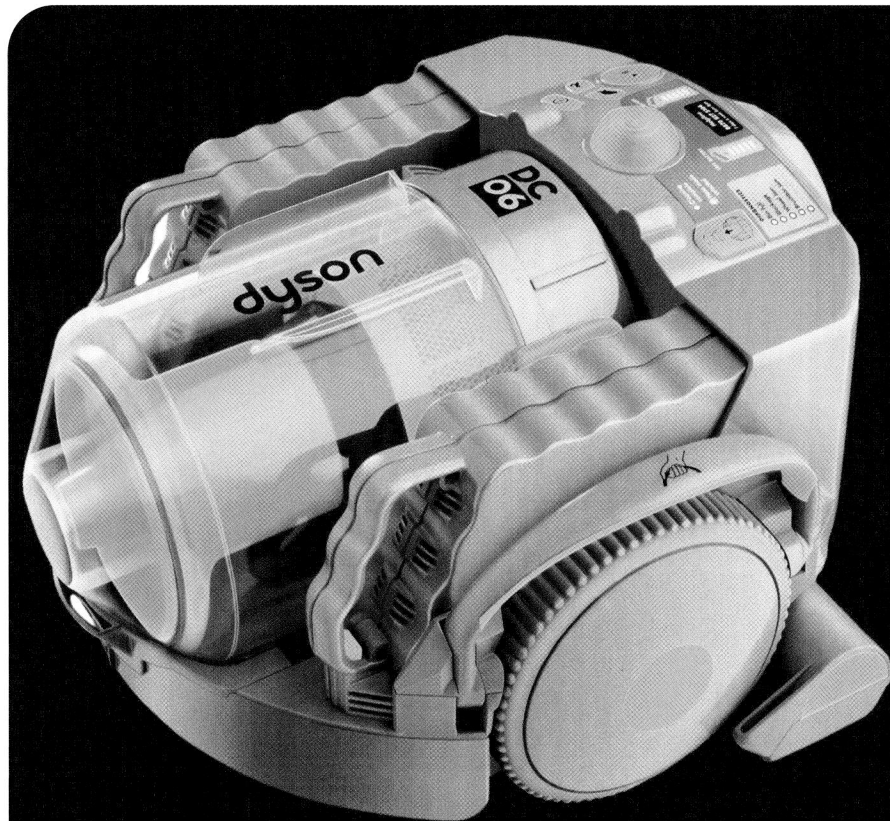

BUILD YOUR VERY OWN 'BOT

The Evolution Robotics ER1 is an affordable personal robot system that you train to do useful and fun things around the house. All that's needed is a laptop running Windows. With the ER1's Evolution Robotics Software Platform, you can train your 'bot to do many things, such as recognize objects and places, send email, take pictures and video, respond to voice commands, monitor the house, teach a foreign language to children, and more. The kit includes stepper motors, a USB camera, a CD with the ER1 Software Control Center, and the XBeams™ aluminum building system. The kit is reconfigurable to different shapes and accessories.

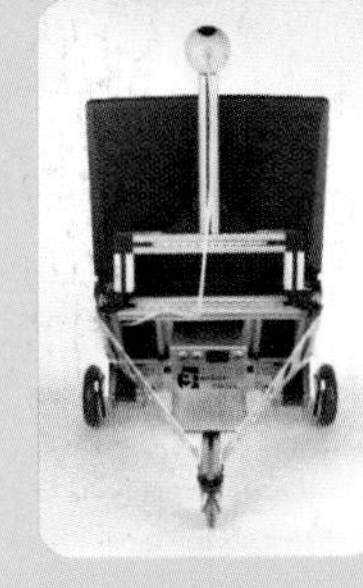

LAPTOP NOT INCLUDED. *Evolution Robotica's ER1 Personal Robot System.*

made the Internet accessible to the masses." Unfortunately, the EvoVision source code is proprietary, but the company does provide tools and a commercial license so that third-party developers can easily create additional applications for it.

LEFT FIELD AND "BATTLEBOTS"

Then there's left field. Could the domestic robot killer app be a killer robot? The phenomenal success of "robotic combat" TV shows like *BattleBots*, *Robot Wars*, and *Robotica* has sent thousands of would-be gearheads to their garages to pore over robot manuals and cannibalize the family mower in hopes of 15 minutes of fame in the robot arena. Like NASCAR champs, winning *BattleBots* designers now enjoy big corporate sponsors, the proceeds from which they're using to build better 'bots. Some combatants who work in high-tech industries claim that they've already incorporated innovations from their combat robots into their work in fields like animatronics and prosthesis engineering.

Could the widespread popularity and acceptance of robotic sports be a doggy door into the home robotics market? Only time will tell. Or will your robotic future be brought to you by LEGO®? The popular building-block company's MINDSTORMS™ Robotic Invention System (think LEGO products with motors and brains) has created a quiet revolution among robot hobbyists (and university engineering departments) who share breathtakingly clever hardware hacks and robot programming tools online. The literal building-block approach to robotic design and engineering has been hailed as a godsend by budget-strapped universities that use the system for teaching and rapid prototyping.

PROVOCATIONS...

How would robot domestics affect the labor market?

If you could have a robot domestic do all your household chores, would you still do any?

—Gareth Branwyn

WANT MORE?

ASIMO
http://world.honda.com/robot

AIBO
www.aibo.com

EVOLUTION ROBOTICS
www.evolution.com

BATTLEBOTS
www.battlebots.com

SOLARBOTICS
www.solarbotics.com

ROBOT.NET
www.robots.net

LEGO MINDSTORMS
http://mindstorms.lego.com

HUSQVARNA
www.husqvarna.com

TORO
www.toro.com

DYSON
www.dyson.com

EUREKA
www.eureka.com

CYE PERSONAL ROBOT
www.probotics.com

Images courtesy of Evolution Robotics

2000 2005 2010 2015 2020

risks  rewards 

Smart Appliances...

HI, MY NAME IS BOB, I'LL BE YOUR TOASTER

WHAT IF YOU COULD *surf the Internet from the comfort of your own kitchen? Sharp's RE-M210 microwave oven allows users to do just that and more. Every year more and more appliances are being developed to take advantage of the wealth of information available to us through the Internet. The RE-M210, for example, allows users to download recipes, including a list of necessary ingredients and preparation and heating instructions, to a "Cooking Data Box." The microwave can then use the data to automatically select the appropriate cooking temperature, time, and sequences to prepare the food. While currently available only in Japan, Sharp and several other companies are working on bringing such robust appliances to homes worldwide.*

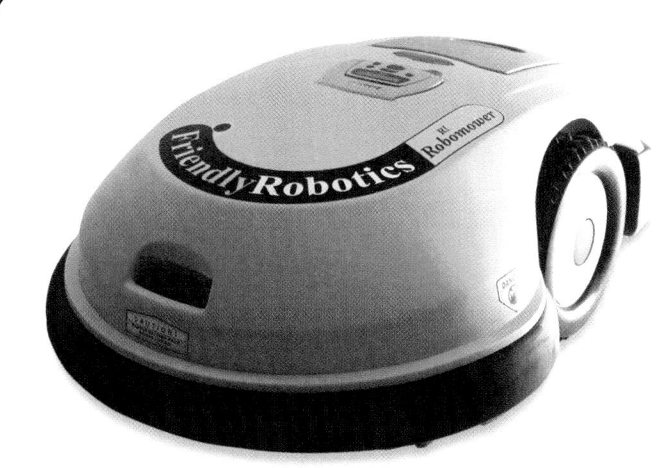

ROBOMOWER... WHERE'S MY LAWNCHAIR?

Once you set up the robomower, there is little else to do. Just lay the wire around the outer edges of your lawn. Then connect it to a small perimeter switch. Because the wire will soon be covered by grass, you'll never know it's there. But the Robomower will, and that's all that matters. Now turn on the perimeter switch and find yourself a comfortable chair or hammock. Since it operates on rechargeable batteries, there's no need for oil or gas — making it environmentally friendly. And because it mulches as it mows, there's no need for backbreaking grass bagging either. Finally, it's so quiet, you'll hardly know it's there — that is, until you see the results of its handiwork.

Clockwise from top left: Photo © Bettmann/Corbis · Image courtesy of Friendly Robotics

Smart appliances are not a new concept. The 1960s cartoon *The Jetsons* envisioned a fully automated home complete with a robot maid and appliances that took care of the mundane activities of everyday life. Until recently, such devices were an unrealistic dream. Today's high-speed Internet access and wireless technologies have made appliances that work together and lessen our workload a distinct possibility. Over the past few years, several home appliance companies have developed prototypes for products ranging from alarm clocks that can tell your coffee pot to start brewing to dishwashers that let repair people know that they need repair.

For the most part, these appliances will enhance our lives by collecting information about the way we live and then storing it for future use. For example, an oven might use information from your last blood test to let you know that your dinner will raise your cholesterol. With the amount of information the average person juggles on a daily basis, appliances that do some of our thinking for us clearly would be helpful. However, critics believe that consumers will find such products to have few added benefits that are worth their significantly higher prices. They also worry that using the Internet to store our personal information for use by these appliances will result in widespread invasion of privacy. As a result, appliance companies have begun to develop cheaper, customized computer chips and processors that have security features to ensure protection of a user's personal information.

In light of recent developments in the field, many industry experts believe that smart appliances will infiltrate a majority of homes within the next 10 years. Until then, manufacturers are developing appliances that are smarter than their predecessors, even if they aren't networked or Internet-ready. Whirlpool and GE, for example, have both developed appliances that save time and are more energy-efficient. If this growth in the industry continues, we will soon be able to enjoy our homes more, and work in them less.

SMART APPLIANCES TODAY

Several companies are developing smarter appliances today. They may not talk to you or let you check your email, but they do save energy and make life a little easier. The following are a few appliances available on the market today.

WHIRLPOOL'S POLARA REFRIGERATOR RANGE

This stove is both a refrigerator and an oven. Using easily programmable timers, it allows you to put a meal in the oven (up to 24 hours prior to eating), and it keeps it cool until the designated cooking time. Once cooking is complete, it will revert to warming mode.

GE'S PROFILE ARTICA REFRIGERATOR

The latest GE refrigerator has a special bin that will cool beverages and foods in a matter of minutes. This bin also has an "ExpressThaw" setting that will thaw meats in a few hours. Even with its high-tech features, the Profile Artica is more energy-efficient than more low-tech models.

WHIRLPOOL'S DUET WASHER AND DRYER

This washer and dryer combination uses 68% less water and 67% less electricity than standard washers. It can fit a 17% larger load than most washers, and the dryer will dry the clothes in the same amount of time as the washing cycle. The washer also has a sanitizing cycle that claims to eliminate 99.9% of common bacteria.

PROVOCATIONS....

Will your appliances compete for attention and upgrades?

What would you want a smart appliance to learn (or forget) about you?

—Zahra Safavian

WANT MORE?

ROBOMOWER
www.robomower.com

ELECTROLUX HOME APPLIANCES
www.electrolux.com

WHIRLPOOL
www.whirlpool.com

GE
www.ge.com

MAYTAG
www.maytag.com

SHARP ELECTRONICS
www.sharpusa.com

Tomorrow's Office...

ADAPTABLE WORKSPACES FOR EMPLOYEES OF THE FUTURE

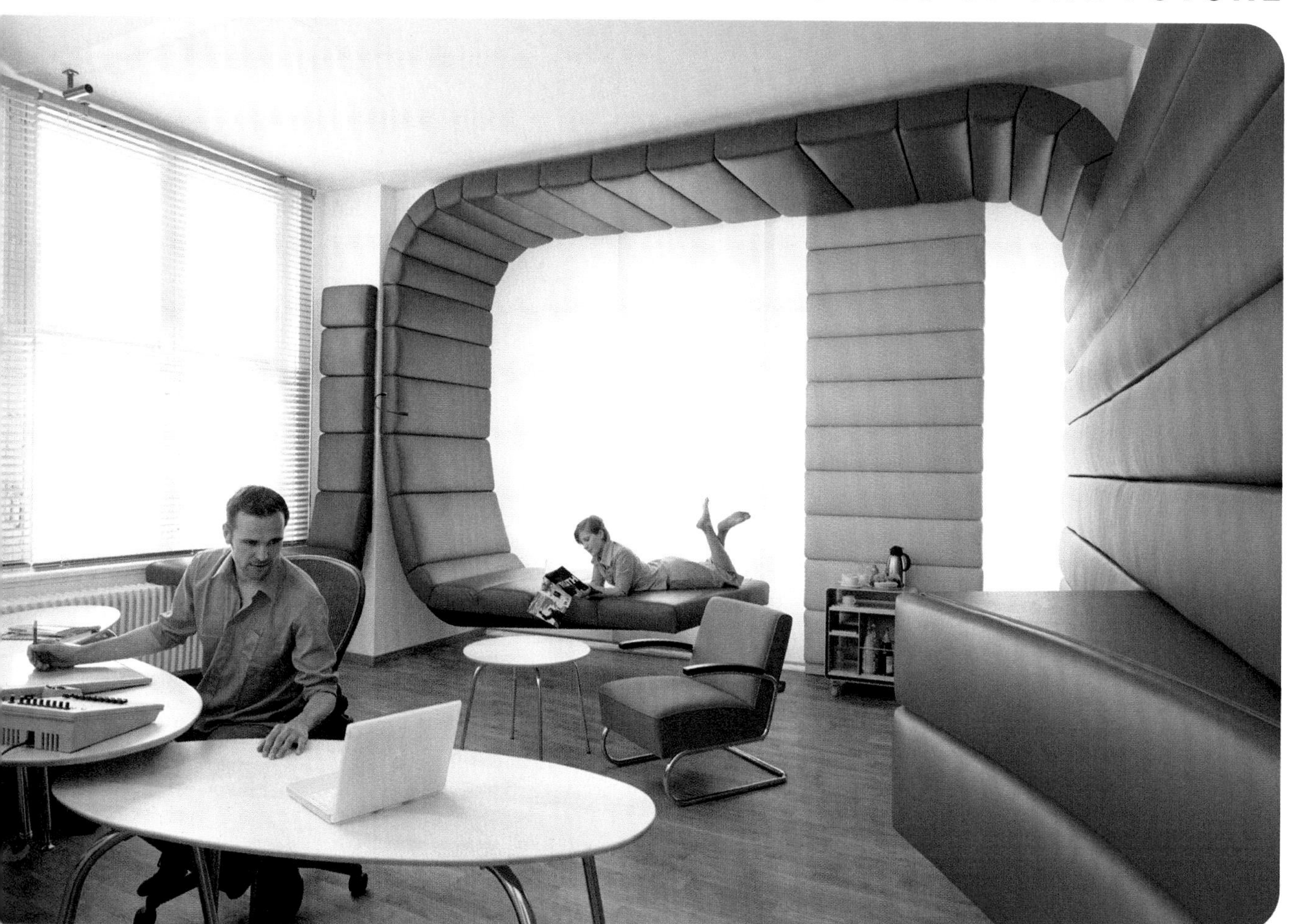

Projekt: "Das Werk Berlin" by MARTINI, MEYER. Foto: Arwed Messmer

PEOPLE WILL RIDE "GYRO-COPTERS" TO WORK AND ZAP "MICRO-MAIL" TO PEERS, WHILE *machines throughout the city talk to each other. Automatic doors and self-correcting typewriters will save time, and some employees will use TV-phones to talk to people across the country or even the world. People will work only 24 hours a week and will earn up to $12,000 a year. This was the scene that greeted visitors to the 1962 World's Fair at the "World of Tomorrow" exhibit — an exhibit that touted the home and office in the year 2000. The year 2000 has come and gone, and most office workers have a much longer work week, a much larger salary, and a car ride through rush-hour traffic to get to the office. Still, the futurists of 1962 were not that far off.*

WORKPLACE COMFORT. *Designed by Martini, Meyer of Berlin, with the goal of providing an environment that would satisfy the needs of employees, many of whom work in excess of 30 hours straight, the suite is set up so clients can work on a laptop or view work on monitors integrated into the wall (left).*

The introduction of the computer and the Internet have clearly changed the way businesses work. The Internet has allowed people worldwide to successfully collaborate on projects, such as the Human Genome Project, making it apparent that working in teams produces more creative solutions faster. Improvements in communications technologies are allowing more people to work on the road or from home. These changes, as well as the rising cost of corporate real estate, are leading to a dramatically different architecture in the workplace — both physically and philosophically.

Future@Work, the Office Innovation Center, and other interactive exhibits on the workplace are now illustrating the landscape of tomorrow's office. The Office Innovation Center, for example, contains no fixed furnishings or furniture. Employees have portable containers for their personal documents and possessions, and they receive portable phones when they check in every morning. Computer projection technologies are utilized to turn any surface into a monitor. Workers in an office setting such as this would be able to move with ease throughout the office, from individual work situations to group sessions.

Group Goetz Architects, for example, have created hotel-like spaces for many of the offices they have designed. Employees can reserve an individual office that meets their specific needs when they require a private workspace. Companies that adopt such systems use technologies

MOBILE TABLES. *Many of these products, such as InteracTable®, will use wireless networks and independent power supplies so that they are completely mobile (above & below).*

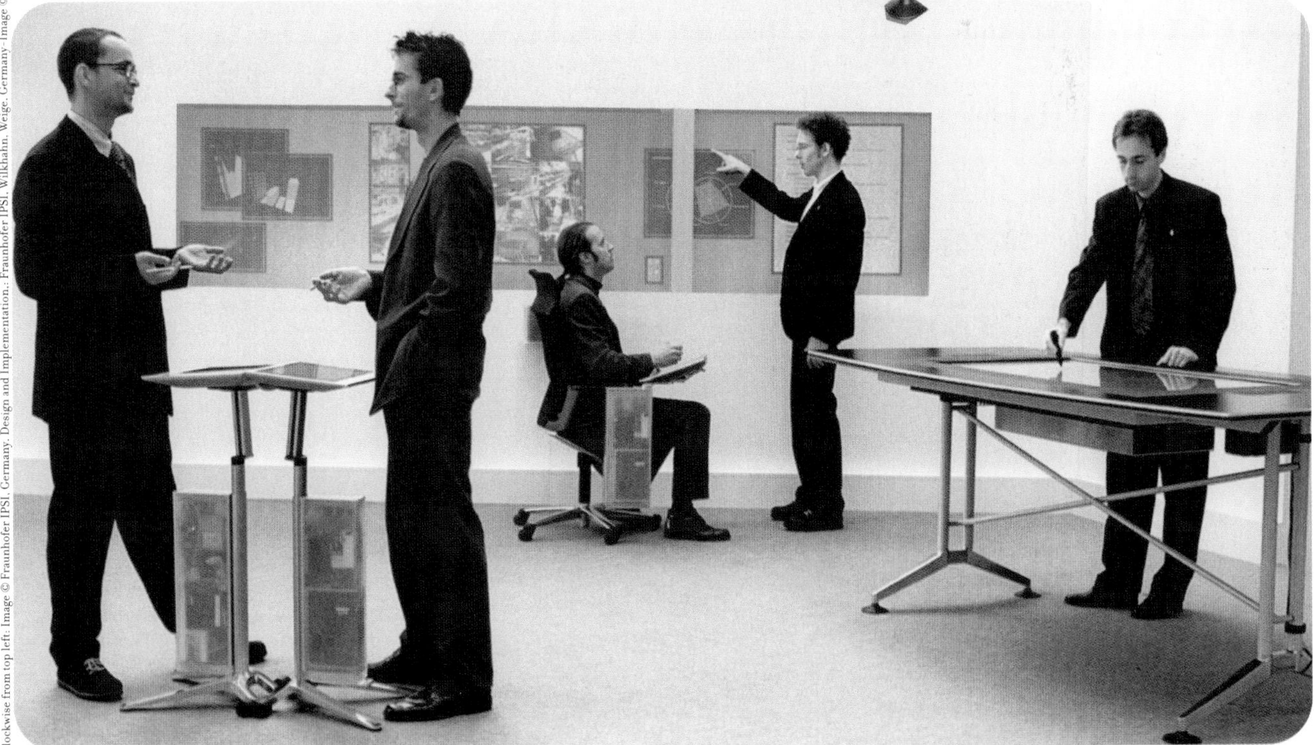

such as Johnson Control's Personal Environment Unit to allow employees to personalize the spaces they temporarily inhabit by adjusting their temperature, lighting, and other qualities to suit their needs. Additionally, since the majority of an employee's time is spent in meeting spaces, they are designed to be larger and more comfortable and to serve multiple purposes.

Designing more productive and utilitarian spaces is not enough in the Information Age, however. People in offices have come to rely extensively on the Internet and communication technologies. As employees spend less time at their desks, corporations must find ways to ensure they have access to the information and people they need to perform their jobs. For some, this means installing more cabling in offices to ensure that every space, even a lunchroom, can be used as a workstation. For an increasing number of businesses, however, this means the adoption of innovative wireless technologies, which allow employees to connect to the Internet or communicate with their co-workers with one device and without cables.

Accommodating collaboration has become another area of focus in the development of technologies for the future office. As more and more work is done in teams, it becomes increasingly important for computer technologies to allow multiple users. Academic institutions and technology companies alike have adopted the idea of ubiquitous computing (a system that accommodates multiple users and multiple inputs) as they develop new computing technologies. These technologies are also concerned with becoming more a part of the physical architecture in which we work. Researchers at the Ambiente research group in Darmstadt, Germany, for example, are developing Roomware®, a number of computer-augmented room elements that enable multiple people to work together on computers that blend seamlessly into the architecture of the room. As these types of technologies become a part of offices everywhere, not only will they make collaboration an

DILBERT CREATOR TAKES ON THE CUBE FARM, RAT MAZE, OR SLAVE CAGE

Sixteen percent of America's workforce calls the office cubicle their home for hours upon hours, day in and day out. *Dilbert* creator, Scott Adams, accidentally became the world's leading expert on what's wrong with cubicles with thousands of fans writing every year, complaining about their 8-by-8 foot boxes. The standard cubicle is cold, mechanical, and very drab looking. Adams and Ideo, a leading design firm, have teamed up to build a prototype of *Dilbert's* Ultimate Cubicle. The customizable cubes are basically thick building blocks you can use to build your own cube. You can build nooks and spaces to keep a coat, an aquarium, a TV monitor, or a punching bag of the boss — there's really no limit to what you can do. Adams and Ideo also bring outdoor elements indoors. For example, special lighting mimics the sun travelling from east to west across your cube throughout the day.

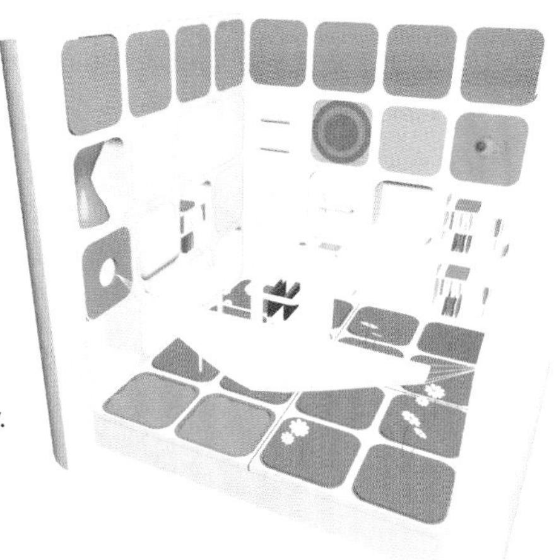

Clockwise from top left: Image courtesy of Steven Moeder. Image courtesy of IDEO

NETSURFER. *Designed by the award-winning Swedish design firm SNOWCRASH (www.snowcrash.se), the Netsurfer abandons the conventional combination of chair and desk and rethinks our relationship to the computer and our surfing requirements. The semi-reclining position with the screen at eye level is designed to be comfortable for long periods. Pillows support the neck and lower back; arms and legs are supported on adjustable arms and footrests. Designer Illka Terho comments, "We came up with this idea based on a motorcycle and the way you have the engine between your legs. It was a bit tongue in cheek; all those phrases, like the information highway, were in the air at the time."*

easier task, but they will also make the office look less like an office and more like a comfortable living space.

The 1962 World's Fair demonstrated that predicting the future of the office is not an easy task. Today's architects and office-solutions companies have stopped trying to predict the future and have started designing workspaces that work in the present but evolve with future changes in the way people work. With flexible designs that blend innovative architecture and technology to create spaces with a range of possible uses, these companies are making the office of tomorrow a more productive and enjoyable place to work—especially since the 24-hour work week is clearly a dream of the past.

PROVOCATIONS...

How will we goof off in the office of the future?

Will open workspaces mean more or less office romance?

—Zahra Safavian

THE EMPLOYEE STILL WILL BE NUMBER 1

An April 2002 survey conducted by the Opinion Research Corporation on behalf of Steelcase, a leading world office furnishing company, revealed that working adults spend the majority of their day away from their desks in meetings and other collaborative work situations. The result is workplaces with offices and meeting rooms that are unused for much of the day. As real estate prices rise to astronomical levels, businesses are looking for ways to conserve space. While they are generally not taking such drastic measures as illustrated in the Office Innovation Center, they are reducing the size of individual spaces and increasing the size and flexibility of common areas, such as meeting rooms. The money saved on real estate is spent on the most valuable asset of today's company – its workers.

WANT MORE?

FUTURE@WORK
www.future-at-work.org

OFFICE INNOVATION CENTER
English site:
www.oic.fhg.de/english/index.html
German site:
www.oic.fhg.de

STANFORD INTERACTIVE WORKSPACES PROJECT
http://iwork.stanford.edu

WORKPLACES 2010 (EXHIBIT ENDED DECEMBER 2001)
www.workplace2010.com

BARCLAY DEAN
www.barclaydean.com

CALLISON ARCHITECTURE
www.callison.com

GROUP GOETZ ARCHITECTS
www.gga.com

NBBJ (ARCHITECTS)
www.nbbj.com

JOHNSON CONTROLS
www.johnsoncontrols.com

SPARLING
www.sparling.com

STEELCASE
www.steelcase.com

HERMAN MILLER
www.hermanmiller.com

BOOKS

Duffy, Francis. *The New Office.* London: Conran Octopus Ltd., 1997.

Peters, Tom. *Liberation Management - Necessary Disorganization for the Nanosecond Nineties.* New York: Alfred A. Knopf, 1992.

Entertainment + Media/Technology = ?

Dynamic. Iterative. Global. Fascinating. When I think of adjectives to describe the entertainment industry, these words come to my mind. Early forms of entertainment — from storytelling and poetry to books, operas, and plays — provided people with a way to forget the drudgery of normal life, to relax and be amused. Modern entertainment — from radio and TV to video games to music — seems to have gone one step further. The industry is not just a conduit to relaxation and fun; it has infiltrated regular life. It drives what people talk about, how your hair should look, what clothes you should buy. Gadgets like portable DVD players and wireless services that send news headlines or games to a cell phone, pager, or PDA are being created daily so that we don't have to miss our entertainment or media fix. No longer a mere diversion, modern entertainment has become another way to experience life.

The technological developments of the last 20 years have been key to this change. Prior to radio, people had to carry information, ideas, and forms of entertainment from place to place, making the proliferation of ideas slow and the availability of options limited. The information age has expanded entertainment possibilities faster than even those of us focused exclusively on this segment could imagine. We can hardly keep up with innovations in our own offices, much less predict and keep up with what others are doing. It's an exciting time to be a part of it.

My career in the computer games industry started in 1974, more than half my life ago, and at about the beginning of the computer games business. I began writing games before CDs existed, before hard drives were generally available, before floppy disks were common — even before personal computers themselves were popular. When an industry has come so far in its mere 20-year lifespan, imagining what the next 20 years will bring can be a challenge. But looking back can give us some ideas on how to track the future.

My first games, in the 1970s, were written on a teletype that punched holes in a strip of paper tape. There were no graphics. Only hard-core gamer types or real computer enthusiasts (frequently the same pool of people) were exposed to computer games. In the early 1980s, electronic games rose rapidly on the back of the personal computer revolution. Technology improved and a whole new world in digital graphics and music was born. This affected book and magazine publication, TV, movies, music, and electronic games, among many other industries. Processor speed, graphics technology, sound technology, and storage all continue to get bigger, better, and faster.

ENTERTAINMENT BEGETS ENTERTAINMENT

Technological developments have allowed those in the entertainment and media industry to roll out enhanced products with more realistic settings in games, movies, TV, and digital music. These developments have also made easier the replication and sharing of content and ideas. So, while we do see some original thoughts and ideas in the industry, each segment has been able to re-create ideas from other segments. Books, comics, and cartoons get turned into movies and games; games get turned into movies, comics, books, and music CDs; movies get turned into books, games, music CDs, and so on. The entertainment industry, the mother of pop culture, feeds on itself. Its dynamically iterative nature is only enhanced by technology that can make games and movies look and sound and feel more like real life. Like never before, audiences can submit to being visually brought into another reality.

But the most powerful technological success of late has been the advent of the Internet.

THE INTERTAINMENT INDUSTRY

Since the latter part of the 1990s, the Internet has become a vastly important tool to all first-world countries. We began to see the convergence of different types of content — information in general, and entertainment specifically — onto one platform. We can search and gather information, read news and media reports, order items to be sent to our home, check our email, chat with friends and family, give feedback to our congressmen, play games alone, play games with others, watch or download movies, and listen to or download music in one, vast forum.

With respect to the computer games industry, I see this as a natural societal progression. People are social animals. People have played games together since the earliest times. Computer games prior to the Internet robbed people of an important aspect of high-quality gaming: socialization. The development of the Internet as a tool to reach broad — even global — audiences with varied types of content made sense. And so my industry added another genre: the multiplayer online game.

But many forms of entertainment permeate the online world: news magazines, entertainment industry 'zines, books, music, movies from big studios, documentaries, and shorts from hopeful independents. Even individuals with the right equipment can make a film and publish it on the Web. The Internet has become an amazing forum that enables us to get our fill of whatever we want, when we want it. This trend will continue in the future.

NO BOUNDARIES

Although many tend to concentrate on how computers and the Internet discourage us from socializing with each other, I think of it as another venue to do so. Where else can you talk to people half way around the world without bankrupting yourself in phone charges? Not only does the Internet provide another way to be social, but it facilitates our exposure to other cultures and could potentially help bridge the gap in subcultures.

The gaming industry is a subculture. Within it are many other subcultures or genres: fantasy, sci-fi, heroes, and the like. Each area of entertainment (movies, TV, music, books) has its own subculture. That entertainment gives birth to other forms of entertainment, as technology (digital, in particular) continues to advance, coupled with the way we use the Internet, it not only reduces the gaps between many cultures and subcultures, but has the potential to close them! Twenty years ago, if you referred to someone as a "gamer," most people conjured a vision of some guy in high school or college who didn't know how to act around other people, wearing black concert t-shirts and keeping to himself as much as possible. Today, there are many women, jocks, computer geeks, intellectuals, and hipsters who play games online. Not only does this medium allow the industry to reach global audiences, but it allows individuals the opportunity to have new experiences they wouldn't otherwise have, to make friends they wouldn't otherwise make, and to learn about other cultures to which they wouldn't otherwise be exposed.

SOCIAL IMPLICATIONS

As TV, movies, and computer games have become better crafted, they have also become more compelling. Like gambling or drugs, they can easily become a habit that takes people away from important aspects of real life, such as interacting with others, work, and school. The Internet holds the key to electronic entertainment moving from an interesting distraction to compelling and socially positive forms of entertainment.

Many consider entertainment in the form of movies, television, and computer games a waste of time, or a bad influence. In fact, these venues can be used as valuable teaching tools. We can teach problem-solving techniques and appropriate social interaction through role-play.

Through the Internet we are now creating games where, instead of playing alone at home, you play with millions of other players around the globe. And instead of just shooting and killing everything in sight, you are cooperating with other real people to accomplish goals. Good social skills are being reinforced because the player communities will not tolerate antisocial behavior online any more than they will in real life.

Deep, lifelong relationships are being made between people in these environments. Never before has such a large number of people been exposed to each other in a meaningful way. In some cases, they even fall in love for life. Clearly, there is something very socially powerful going on.

Yet we have only scratched the surface.

WHERE DO WE GO FROM HERE?

Another important issue in contemporary entertainment is violence. I am a strong believer in responsible content creation. This is not to say that there isn't a place for games and movies where destruction is a focal point, but it is important that the audience be considered in this process. Playing games and watching movies can be a great teaching tool, but they can also be an unwitting teacher of inappropriate behavior. I have witnessed young children playing kung-fu fighting games, only to put down the controls and try kicking each other. Despite the fact that online games currently don't make many social demands or help develop interpersonal skills, my hope is that this will improve in the coming decade.

Entertainment and the media will continue to grow as an industry and affect all of our daily lives. This industry will continue to use technology to create superior products and market them to the widest possible audience. There will be an explosion of gadgetry and devices that will carry entertainment-related content to us anytime, anywhere. My dream for the future of the entertainment industry is the responsible development of other realistic, fascinating, and beautiful worlds where people can meet, play, work together, relate, and enjoy life.

—Richard Garriott, a.k.a. "Lord British"

Advertising... "Way Beyond the Banner"

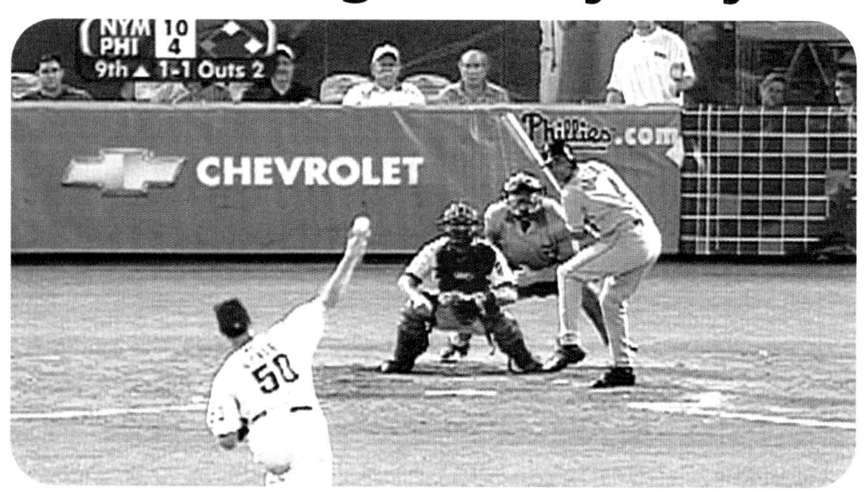

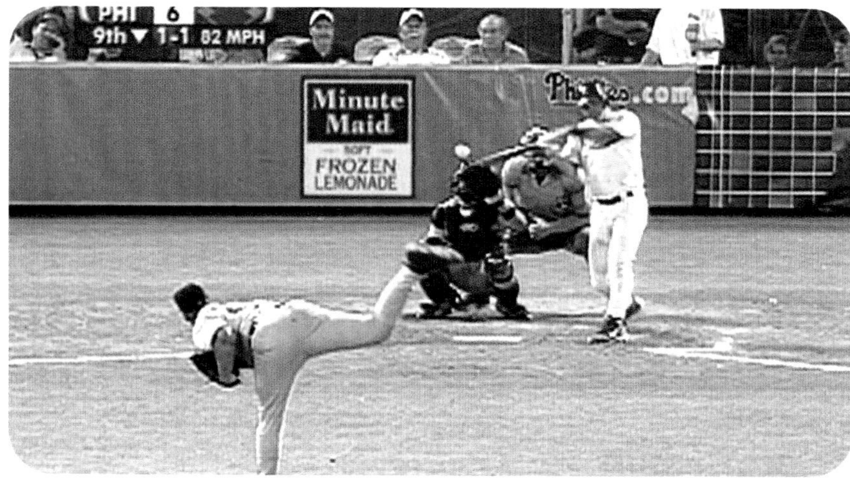

IT IS THE YEAR 2004. Network 23, the largest TV network in the world, creates commercials that last only a few seconds and not only prevent viewers from changing the channel, but also embed themselves in their minds. There is a small glitch, however — sometimes these "Blipverts" cause viewers to spontaneously combust. Thus begins the first episode of the cyberpunk cult classic Max Headroom. *¶ We're a long way from such a dystopian mediascape (or so the optimists among us would argue), but the metaphor remains potent. Most people have a strong ambivalence about advertisements; we love a cherished few and (at best) tolerate the rest. Despite the fact that the average person is exposed more than 3,000 ads every day, the vast majority simply fade into the background of our lives;*

NOW YOU SEE IT, NOW YOU DON'T. *Virtual product placement from Princeton Video Image inserts products into your favorite TV shows — whether they were there to begin with or not.*

Images courtesy of Princeton Video Image

a swirling vortex of shiny and alluring promises to which we simply don't have the time or interest to pay attention. As a consequence, advertisers always seek entrée into the quieter and more private moments of our lives (where they have less competition for our attention) just as they seek to create experiences we will have a hard time ignoring.

Great advertising will always provoke and engage, amuse and flatter, entice and excite us. And in the coming decades, advertisers will use new technologies to do just that and to create products more fantastic, compelling and, some would argue, more insidious than ever before.

THE MALLEABLE MEDIA STREAM

One place we're sure to see major changes is in the use of "virtual advertising." Princeton Video Image, Inc., has mastered the ability to digitally insert advertisements (and products) into our favorite television shows. Image a baseball game where one "real" set of ads plastered around the infield is seen by the people at the park, and another "virtual" set is seen digitally inserted by the people watching on TV. The owner of the team, and the network, get to sell the same advertising space twice — quite a windfall. Imagine what this does to reruns: That can of Coke on your favorite sitcom character's table sure looks real. But it may be a computerized image inserted after the program was shot. Even more amazing: That can of Coke may – poof! – be a can of Mountain Dew the next time the episode is aired.

The ability to digitally modify programs by inserting new and different "advertorial" content every time a program is aired raises questions about the relationship between programming and advertising, and the use of profiles to determine what those insertions are. If a family sees an image of a station wagon inserted into a program, while a single person sees an image of a sports car, does this make a difference? Will people deem this an invasion of privacy? Or will they come to see this as a valuable service — making the ads they see more relevant?

MARKETING AN EXPERIENCE

If you can't bring the product to the customers, bring the customers to the product. And since the days of P.T. Barnum, advertisers have known that the best way to do that is with rich, theatrical experiences. Since the 1800s, world's fairs contained rides sponsored by Industrial Age corporations. In the 1950s, Walt Disney created the first theme park, an entire environment in which visitors could experience the fantasy world of the Disney movies and television shows.

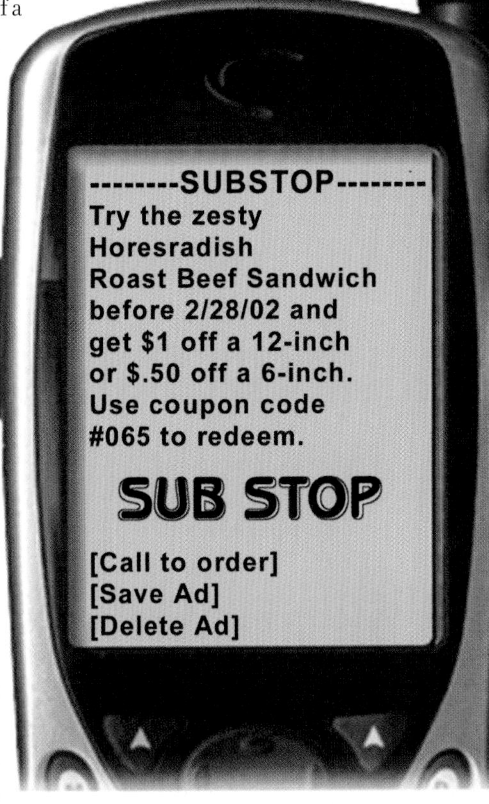

HUNGRY? *Your cell phone may be the advertising vehicle of the future.*

Image courtesy of SkyGo, Inc.

SPONSOR MY NOVEL, PLEASE

Fay Weldon has written what is widely considered to be the world's first sponsored novel. *The Bulgari Connection* was commissioned by the Italian jewellers of the same name and features the firm and its products on many of its 200 pages.

Weldon, the award-winning author of more than 20 books, says the novel is "a good piece of advertising prose." In the book she has broken down one of the last barriers dividing art from advertising, accepting money to publicize a company in her work. Hollywood films, radio, and television shows have taken product placement fees from companies for decades. But until now the world of literature had remained immune.

Weldon was required to mention Bulgari at least 12 times, but she far exceeded that requirement with a string of direct plugs. In a passage that reads rather like a catalogue of the jeweller's products, Weldon describes in detail the £18,000 necklace that a businessman buys for his wife. The protaganist picks a "sleek modern piece, a necklace, stripes of white and yellow gold, but encasing three ancient coins, the mount flowing the irregular contours of thin, worn bronze."

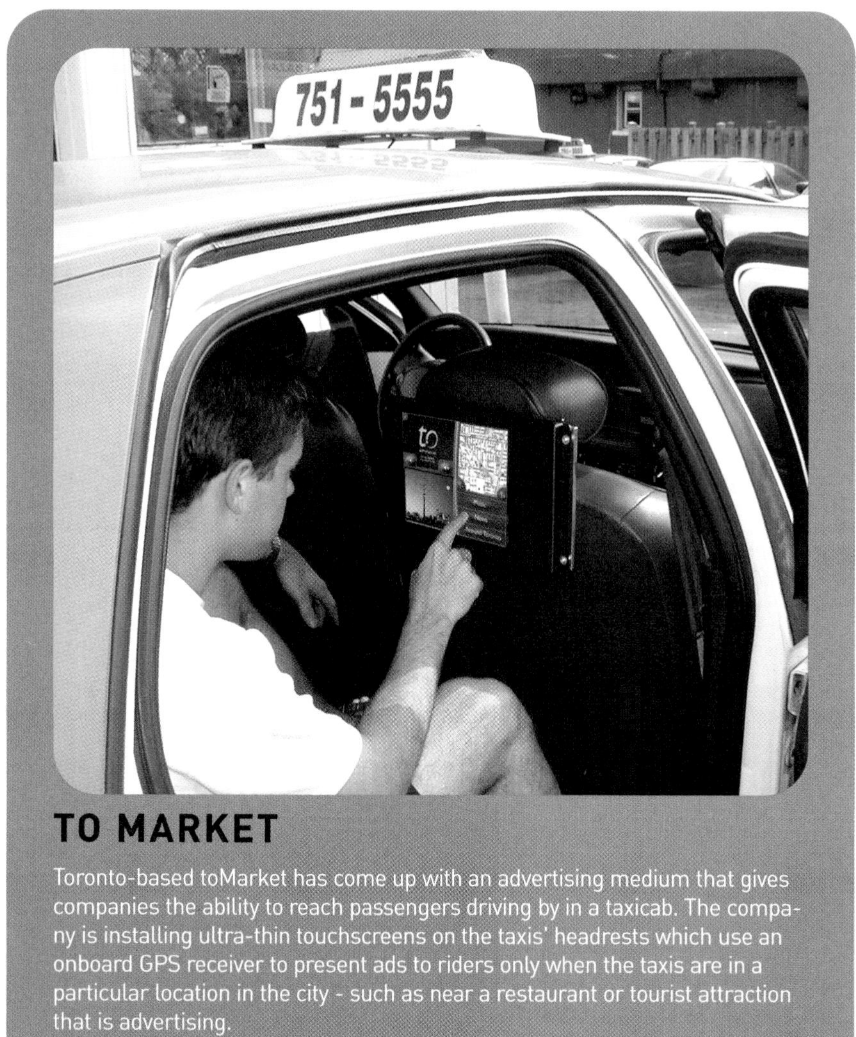

TO MARKET

Toronto-based toMarket has come up with an advertising medium that gives companies the ability to reach passengers driving by in a taxicab. The company is installing ultra-thin touchscreens on the taxis' headrests which use an onboard GPS receiver to present ads to riders only when the taxis are in a particular location in the city - such as near a restaurant or tourist attraction that is advertising.

Photo courtesy of toMarket

That's the tack that Nike, Disney, and other consumer brands have taken with the development of their megastores. These "monuments to the brand" are experiential advertisements — physical manifestations of the ineffable values that companies stand for, achieved with a blend of cutting-edge media, technology, and architecture wrapped up into a compelling and ever-changing experience.

Other companies, such as Philips and Delta Airlines, are attaching their names to experiences rather than creating their own. At the Philips Arena in Atlanta, Delta Airlines invites a few frequent fliers to lounge directly over center court, where they can sit in leather seats exactly like the ones in first class. This kind of experience is the perfect advertising vehicle — rich, sensory, and absolutely unique.

CONTEXT, CONTEXT, CONTEXT

The nature of "mass media" advertising has remained the same for a century: Market the same message to the same person regardless of who they are, where they are, and what they're doing. The otherworldly phantasms of Times Square beam the same radiant messages whether you're a family on its way to see *Beauty and the Beast*, a cop on the beat, or lovers on a stroll. But new wireless technologies promise to add an important layer of context to these real-world advertisements.

As GPSs (global positioning systems) become a standard component of PDAs and cell phones, it will soon be possible to track users' locations, sending them advertisements based on where they are and what they're doing. Happen to have a free hour in your schedule? Why not stop in at that Starbucks across the street — and if you do, Maggie Smith, you can take 10% off any coffee drink in the shop. Flipping through a book at your local Barnes and Noble? You might get a text message offering you a combined discount if you buy that one and another, recommended by

THE TRANSPARENT "FUN" FACTORY

In the same vein as Philips and other companies attaching their names to arenas and sporting events, Volkswagen recently created Die Gläserne Manufaktur – The Transparent Factory. Part factory, part theme park, The Transparent Factory not only allows visitors to see firsthand Volkswagen's production methods, but it also includes a variety of high-tech experiences, including a virtual driving tour, a multimedia installation on the future of information, and a "car configurator" which uses the largest touchscreen in the world.

the staff, sitting on the shelf just to your right. This kind of "contextual" advertising will be big business: Technology forecaster Forrester Research predicts that such e-coupons and other mobile commerce will be worth between $20 billion and $30 billion by as early as 2004.

Of course, for any of these technologies to work, ordinary people will have to consent — and that means advertisers will have to work hard to convince us, by creating powerful and valuable media experiences. And they will need to curtail abuse, technologically or legislatively. For as most of us already know, as the cost of *sending* advertisements drops precipitously, it invites unscrupulous advertisers to push useless "spam" at us at a blistering pace — the "Hey, you never know!" theory of advertising writ large.

There is hope. For the very technologies that make it easier for advertisers to market to us to us makes it easier, eventually, for us to find out if those advertisers *keep* their promises, and if not, to opt out. And we're likely to hit the "off" switch long before the world of *Max Headroom* ever arrives.

PROVOCATIONS...

Will people pay extra not to be advertised to? How much?

Will personalization make enforcing fair advertising practices impossible?

— Zahra Safavian and Andrew Zolli

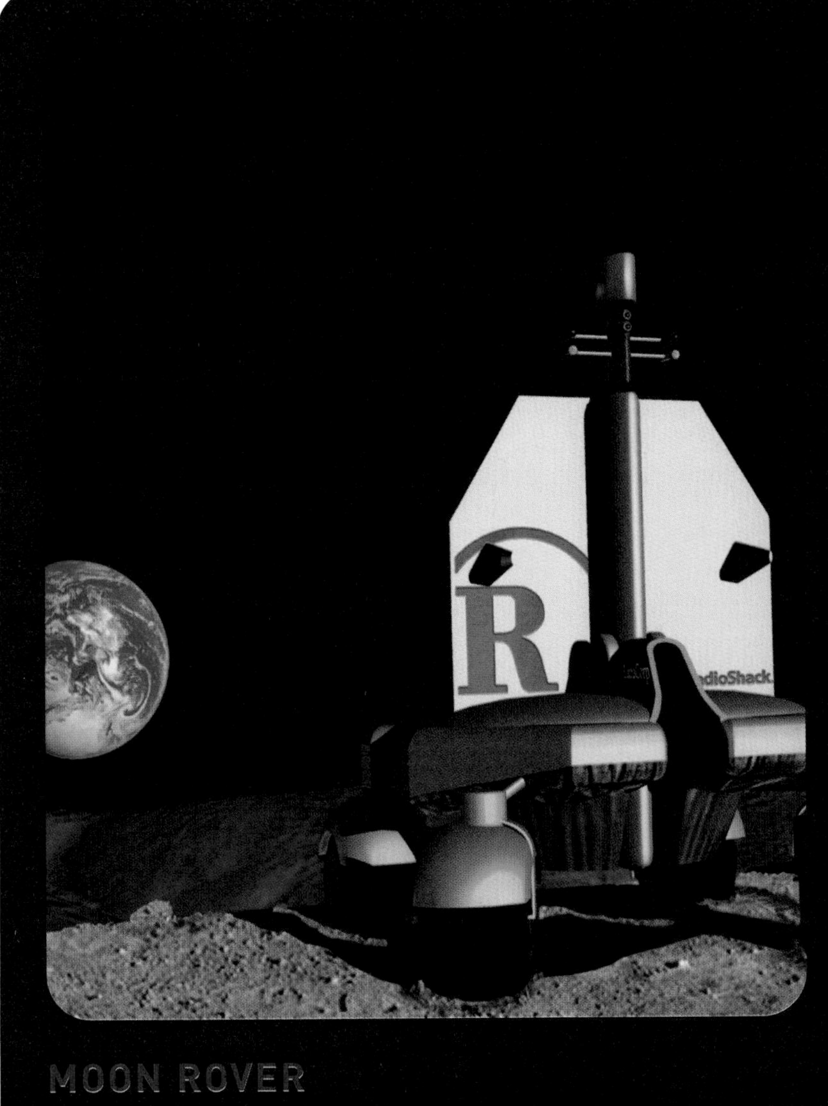

MOON ROVER

RadioShack is set to become the first U.S. business to back a commercial, sponsored mission to the surface of the moon. The rolling advertisement, planned for a launch by Virginia-based LunaCorp in 2004–2005, will search the lunar poles for ice — evidence of which would prove valuable to scientists and space-entrepreneurs alike.

Image courtesy of Luna Corp

WANT MORE?

PRINCETON VIDEO IMAGE, INC.
www.pvi-inc.com

JUNKBUSTERS
www.junkbusters.com

SKYGO
www.skygo.com

MOBILE MARKETING ASSOCIATION
www.waaglobal.org

DIE GLÄSERNEN MANUFAKTUR (THE TRANSPARENT FACTORY)
www.glaeserne-manufaktur.de

TO MARKET
www.tomarket.ca

LUNACORP
www.lunacorp.com

Cinema... Take Me Out to the Movies

"OPEN YOUR EYES, listen, smell, and feel — sense the world in all its magnificent colors, depth, sounds, odors, and textures – this is the cinema of the future!" In 1955, Morton Heilig, a Hollywood cinematographer, wrote of "experience theater" – movies that would stimulate all the senses to transport the audience into the story. Needless to say, Hollywood did not accept Heilig's ideas, he moved to Mexico, and little has changed in cinema in over 50 years – until now, that is. The growth of the Internet and digital technologies in the 1990s has spawned the beginnings of an evolution in cinema, from the studio to the movie theater.

DIGITAL BRUCE. *At Cinesite, Kodak's digital studio, digital technology drives every part of the moviemaking process, from effects to mastering.*

Certainly the art of making movies has steadily advanced. Colors are brighter and more true-to-life. Sounds are crisper and louder. Advanced computer systems create more spectacular special effects from companies like Industrial Light & Magic, a division of Lucas Digital. Yet it wasn't until the latest installment in the *Star Wars* saga *Episode II – Attack of the Clones* from George Lucas that the future of movie production and distribution truly began. Filmed entirely with a prototype high-definition camcorder created by Sony, the blockbuster became the first feature film to be completely produced with digital media from sound to special effects. In fact, in theaters equipped with digital projectors, the movie remained in a digital format for viewing

Nearly everyone in the movie industry agrees that digital cinema is the greatest innovation in movies since sound. Digital videotapes are a fraction of the cost of film, and they run for 50 minutes – five times longer than analog film reels. Actors can stay in character longer, and directors can view the performances on a monitor in real-time. With the next generation of digital camcorders, like the Sony prototype used by Lucasfilms, image quality will surpass that of 35mm film. In digital format, digitally created characters can be integrated more seamlessly into each frame, and colors can be corrected down to the pixel level.

Digital projectors have already surpassed the traditional film projector. Texas Instruments' prototype high-definition display, for example, uses thousands of nearly microscopic mirrors to reflect each pixel of a moving image onto a screen with absolute precision. Currently, very few movie theaters are equipped with digital projectors, but that will change in the next decade. Already

Making Digital Cinema Happen

From a "cinema hub" in Los Angeles ...via satellite ... to a movie theater in Des Moines ...to audiences.

1. The movie is digitized, then compressed and encrypted.
2. The film file is broadcast via geosynchronous satellite to movie theaters.
3. It is stored and decrypted for playback; data is sent back to the network.
4. The film is presented via digital film projector and sound sytem.

developing digital delivery systems, Kodak is expected to be one of the major players in the digital film industry. Kodak's system includes a server on which the movies are stored, an operating system to control when and where the movies are shown, and digital projectors.

Even theaters will change. The Sony Metreon in San Francisco is a multimedia complex with a sophisticated arcade and interactive exhibits to engage visitors before and after a movie. During the movie, viewers sit in plush, stadium-style seats that are tiered to allow everyone an unobstructed view. IMAX theaters have always created a more immersive moviegoing experience, and now they offer 3D movies on their 80-foot screens and Dome Theaters, which project movies onto a domed wall that surrounds the audience. Soon IMAX theaters will move beyond the museums and science centers in which they have always resided. With the recent culmination of nearly 5 years of research, IMAX can now convert feature films shot on much lower-resolution 35mm film into a higher-resolution digital format that can fully occupy an IMAX screen. *Apollo 13* will be coming soon to IMAX theaters across the country, and several more feature films will be re-released every year thereafter.

The digital revolution doesn't stop at the theater. Industry experts believe video-on-demand is right around the corner. Imagine being able to watch any movie, anywhere, anytime. With advances in interactive television, it will soon be possible to visit a movie studio's Web site, select a movie, and have the movie sent directly to your television, where it will be stored in a set-top box for a given amount of time. If you are on the road, you could have the movie sent to your laptop or PocketPC through wireless technologies.

Not since the birth of film has the movie industry been on the cusp of so much innovation. Digital technologies are invading every area of the movies, from filming to delivery. Movie quality will be improved, theaters will be more immersive, and watching a movie at home (or anywhere else) will be more convenient. Hollywood may not be where Morton Heilig believed it would be in the 21st century, but the digital revolution will soon take the movies somewhere Heilig never imagined.

PROVOCATIONS...

Will digital distribution mean movies will regularly be released all over the world on the same day?

Will the same system make it easier for immigrants to see movies from their homeland?

— Zahra Safavian

WANT MORE?

LUCAS DIGITAL
www.lucasdigital.com

KODAK
www.kodak.com/US/en/motion

ONLINE MOVIE RENTALS
www.reel.com
www.netflix.com

DIGITAL FILMMAKING
www.dfilm.com

MOVIES FOR HANDHELDS
www.mazingo.net

IMAX THEATERS
www.imax.com

News... For the People, By the People

"This... Is WeNN" Dateline 2007.

THE VIDEO FEED IS GRAINY, bursting with occasional static and jerking with the vibrato of its holder's adrenaline-pumped muscles – but its contents are unmistakable. ¶ A major earthquake has just hit Seoul, South Korea, and the story is broken, as it unfolds, via the most technically sophisticated newsgathering platform ever invented. ¶ A video-enabled, high-bandwidth cellphone – or, more specifically, thousands of such phones. ¶ In nearly real time, the feeds ping-pong through a network of global relays, spreading first-hand images of the quake across the globe. One such feed alights on a distant server, where it is piped to the community 'blog' (or Web log) of a distant friend, several relationships (and continents) removed from its original author.

SMART CELL PHONE.
Motorola's 3G Concept Model Video Phone.

Once posted, the feed inspires a frenzy of collective activity. One site member overlays the feed's GPS data onto a map of Seoul, pinpointing the quake's epicenter. Another runs the audio through an online auto-translator, while a third starts collecting other emerging accounts from a variety of professional and amateur sources. Their work ripples through the community – and is improved by it. Other members correct mistakes and improve on successes, as the group guides its own efforts. Without explicitly being told to do so, the group has amplified, clarified, and begun to contextualize the quake. News is born.

Welcome to the not-too-distant world of journalism 3.0, the term Silicon Valley journalist Dan Gillmor coined for a world where the technology in your pocket can turn anyone into a news reporter. Where the collective efforts of a loosely joined group of amateurs can complement, and occasionally trump, the most powerful news media organizations.

From its earliest days, the Web was seen as a new way to get the news out; it was initially lauded as a kind of hyper-efficient printing press. As the multimedia capabilities of the Web matured, news organizations began to see that the new medium expanded the possibilities of storytelling. Now, in the Web's adolescence, new dynamics are beginning to emerge. Individuals are empowered with ever more powerful multimedia devices. And new kinds of Web software are allowing regular folks to easily publish their own news stories and their interpretations of others' stories, and even to organize into their own novel forms of news organizations. This is participatory journalism on a grand scale, and it's eroding the traditional definitions and boundaries between journalists, events, and, in Gillmor's terminology, "the former audience."

Is journalism 3.0 an upgrade worth making? It depends on whom you ask.

New technologies have had a complex, and often paradoxical, impact on the business and experience of the news, and the promise is to continually reshape it in the future. The spread of both digital recording devices and tools for online community participation have bolstered the notion of the Internet as a "People's Press" that provides a new role for the passionate amateur, while offering people a huge variety of opinions and perspectives. However, like any highly democratized media, the digital "idea commons" is a noisy and sometimes misleading place. Quality is extremely varied, and insights are often couched in political rants and questionable rhetoric.

This variety guarantees that professional, standards-based news organizations will always be with us. But it's been more than half a century since people participated in media in this way, and those news organizations will invariably have to adjust to the presence, and expectations, of a wired populace.

In response, news organizations are working on new ways to personalize the news and tell stories in ways that are both novel and compelling.

There will be more subtle consequences of this revolution, though. No single news organization can compete with huge wired communities — they simply can't be in every place, every time. Thus, the rise of digital communities will shorten news cycles even further and may change the role of cable networks, much as their appearance transformed the role of newspapers. Perhaps the networks will cooperate, or further specialize. Perhaps they'll even put "bloggers" in their employ.

DIGITAL INK DISPLAY. *A prototype of a display from E-Ink and Philips, who hope to create electronic newspapers in the future.*

PROVOCATIONS...

Will ever-more personalized news erode our sense of a common truth?

In an era of lifelike digital recreation, will we trust what we see on TV?

Will news organizations put "bloggers" in their employ?

—Andrew Zolli

YOUR NEWS... ALL THE TIME, ANY TIME

The experiments are already beginning. ImmersiNews, a project of the USC Annenberg School for Communication, will deliver news stories that are customized in structure, narrative, and content according to user preferences and interests. The news will not only be tailored to the reader's background, it will also include multimedia experiences that are immersive and interactive. For example, users might be able to move through a 360-degree panoramic image of a sporting event and click on various parts of the image to get more information. USC Annenberg hopes to have a fully functioning prototype by 2006, and through partnerships with large media companies, news systems such as ImmersiNews could very well be the norm within 10-15 years.

WANT MORE?

MIT MEDIA LABORATORY'S INFORMATION
http://nif.www.media.mit.edu

USC ANNENBERG ONLINE JOURNALISM REVIEW "FUTURE OF NEWS"
www.ojr.org/ojr/future

IMMERSINEWS WEBSITE
http://imsc.usc.edu/test/research/immersinews.html

DAN GILLMOR
www.dangillmor.com

2000 2005 2010 2015 2020

risks  rewards 

Digital Paper and Pens

A NEW, MIGHTIER SWORD

WITH THE DAWN OF THE INFORMATION AGE, declarations that "print is dead" have been issued throughout the world, yet technologies such as e-books have failed to gain popularity in a world where paper still reigns. Readers still prefer flipping the pages of a tangible, printed book, and letters and notes are still scribbled on paper with ink pens. Researchers are finally taking note of these entrenched human preferences and are developing products that make pen and paper. ¶ Consider the typical business meeting. There are conversations and debates, and often, important decisions are made that affect other people. Generally, someone is on hand to record these decisions so that they can be transcribed into a more formal report at a later date. With the advent of PDAs, the additional tedious step of transcription seemed like a thing of the past, but the reality is that writing and transcribing is still easier than mastering most PDAs' shorthand alphabet or pressing the tiny buttons on their keyboards. Enter the digital pen.

HOW THE TECHNOLOGY WORKS

Dr. Michael McCreary, VP of research at E Ink, explains how electronic ink works: "Imagine a football field covered with beach balls that are filled with a dyed black liquid, and inside each beach ball are pingpong balls. If you looked at this from the air with the pingpong balls at the surface, it will appear white, and if you could push those pingpong balls to the bottom of the beach balls the surface would appear black."

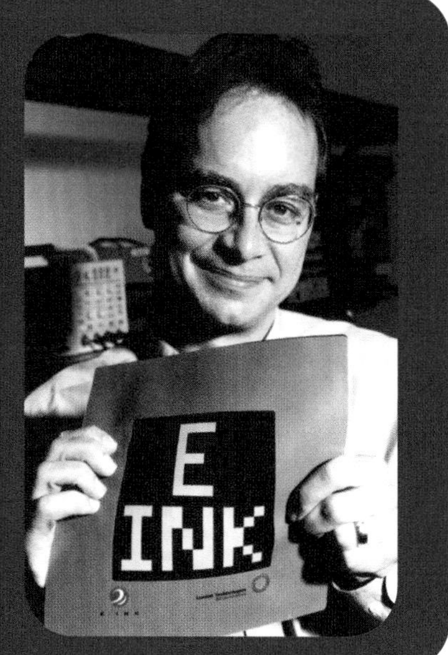

In the past couple years, a handful of companies has developed pens that record what you write as you write it. Some, like Digital Ink's n-scribe™, require users to clip a device, which receives signals from the pen, to the writing surface. As the user writes, the handwriting is converted into ASCII text, which can be uploaded to a computer, PDA, or cell phone to store, email, or print out. Other digital pens require the use of special paper that taps into wireless connections, such as Bluetooth, to transmit information to other devices.

OTM Technologies, developer of the V Pen, plans to add features, such as signature authentication, bar-code scanning, and text scanning, to its digital pen in upcoming years. Currently priced around $100, digital pens are already becoming an affordable way to interface with computers. As prices drop and functionality increases, writing may once again become a more prevalent way of recording information.

Digital paper is a much older idea than digital pens and perhaps a more innovative one. Basically, electronic paper uses circuits to apply electrical currents to charged ink particles so that they create patterns in the form of words or images. Originally conceived by Nick Sheridon at Xerox PARC in 1975, electronic paper did not become a reality until 1999 when E Ink developed cardboard-like display signs that could change messages. Because E Ink's product required rather thick, rigid circuit boards, these displays lacked one of the most important characteristics of paper – flexibility. However, the discovery of electrically conducting plastic in 2000 has made more paper-like products a possibility. Digital papers have a much higher contrast between text and background, like traditional paper, and are flexible and portable.

The applications of electronic papers are endless – from digital, interactive newspapers that look like traditional newspapers to wallpaper that can change its look with the push of a button. The ultimate goal of the few companies developing these technologies, however, is to create an electronic book within the next 10–15 years that looks and feels like a book but can display any work of literature.

e-Books, digital pens, and electronic paper are only the beginnings of the most exciting innovations in publishing since the invention of the printing press. From boardrooms to classrooms, these technologies promise to improve the ways everyone conducts business, and it is not hard to envision a future when the world's entire lexicon is available to anyone at the press of a button.

PROVOCATIONS...

Will Barnes & Noble still exist?

Will we see new paper-based art forms?

—Zahra Safavian

The ultimate in recycling:
Reusable electronic 'paper'

Synthetic "gyricon" paper being developed by Xerox Corp. and 3M Co. could be reused millions of times. Researchers say this and other "electronic ink" technologies may reach consumers within a few years.

How it works

1: Information arrives: News, photos or other information and images are downloaded from a computer into an electronic wand.

2: Paper scanned: The user runs the wand over the gyricon sheet, depositing an electrical charge that causes tiny balls inside the sheet to rotate, creating text and images on the page.

3: Image appears: The page holds the charge – and the image – until it is rewritten.

Roll of flexible "gyricon" sheet

Scanner wand

tech.life@inquirer

Designing the e-newspaper

Scanning sheet with wand deposits electric charge

Sheet with no image

The image can be letters, photos or other graphics and it can be changed with a swipe of the electronic wand.

Tiny half-black, half-white balls in sheet create image

Millions of polyethylene balls are embedded in each silicon sheet. Experiments are under way to add other colors.

In laboratory prototypes, the "gyricon" material is sandwiched between clear plastic sheets. The text is read through the plastic.

Wand

Electric charge

Plastic sheet

About as thick as a sheet of paper

Polyethylene spheres

Balls rotate in response

Silicon sheet

Making the sheet

The paper is formed by mixing tiny polyethylene balls in a syrupy liquid elastomer. The resulting mixture is formed into a thin sheet and heated. The sheet is dunked in oil. That makes the rubbery silicon elastomer swell and creates oil-filled cavities around the polyethylene balls. The balls rotate in the oil cavity in response to electrical charges.

Possible uses

Electronic paper could replace office paper in some applications. It could also be embedded with electrodes or transistors to create images without a wand.

The balls are currently 100 microns in diameter, about the width of a hair. Xerox is working on producing 30-micron balls.

100-micron ball

White side

Black side

30-micron ball

Image from Knight Ridder/Cothran

WANT MORE?

FUTURE OF PAPER & INK

http://todmaffin.com futurefile/paper.shtml

E INK

www.eink.com

GYRICON MEDIA

www.gyriconmedia.com

Music... More Than a Catchy Tune

FROM THE STONE AGE to the Digital Age, music has been a way to communicate stories, ideas, and emotions. With the growth of the Internet and digital technologies, this age-old art is undergoing major transformation, not just in composition and performance, but also in the distribution of music.

SYMPHONY OF THE IMAGINATION. *Developed by Teresa Marrin Nakra of Immersion Music, the Virtual Conducting Lab at Arizona State University allows music students to conduct a virtual symphony. The system reacts to body gestures and movements just as a real orchestra would, allowing budding conductors to hone their craft.*

Photo courtesy of Immersion Music/Webb Chappell

After years of mergers and buyouts, the music industry has been whittled down to a handful of big names from production to distribution. Four major record labels control the production end of the industry, and radio station conglomerates such as Clear Channel Communications, which owns over 1,100 radio stations in the U.S. alone, control the airwaves. Between major music stores like Tower Records and discount retailers like Wal-Mart and Target, independent music sellers are facing enough competition to put them out of business.

The result? The music industry has gone the way of Hollywood, with a few highly produced albums sung by manufactured personalities dominating musical culture. Everyone has heard their names — Britney, Pink, N'Sync, the list goes on — and more are on their way because these stars appeal to the market that makes record companies the most money, adolescents. Unfortunately, roughly 75% of the United States is over the age of 18, and they aren't, for the most part, into Britney Spears.

> Independent movies have taken Hollywood by storm, and independent music is about to experience the same success.

MUSIC AND THE INTERNET

Enter the Internet. In the 1980s, while CDs were infiltrating homes and cars across the U.S., researchers at the Fraunhofer Institute in Germany began working on an audio compression format, which they dubbed MP3. They also developed the first MP3 player in the early 1990s, but it wasn't until Windows offered the Winamp player in 1998 that the Internet music craze really took off. Within a year, Napster opened up shop and not paying for music was suddenly an option for the listening public. In 2002, Napster fell, but MP3 is growing into the predominant music format, and portable MP3 players are one of the hottest accessories. With the fall of Napster has come

PREPARING FUTURE COMPOSERS...

It has never been easier for a music lover to cross the line from listener to composer. Digital instruments and composing software allow almost anyone to create music. Venharis, for example, is a music and composition and generation software application that is designed like a computer game. By exploring the game environment and interacting with the alien characters, players create a fractal music composition. In order to create fractal music, the "composer" simply enters numbers, each representing a specific note, into mathematical equations. The numerical results of these equations, when strung together, form a musical composition. In addition to Venharis, several applications are available on the Web for the composition of fractal music.

The Opera of the Future (or Hyperinstruments) research group at the MIT Media Lab is developing innovative musical instruments and software with the goal of allowing anyone, even children, to create music. Its Music Shapers, for example, are soft, embroidered toys that play different notes depending on how they are squeezed, stretched, twisted, or pulled. With Hyperscore, a software application, users manipulate lines and shapes of various colors in order to create a visual composition, which is then translated into a musical score.

Photo courtesy of MIT Media Lab

the rise of peer-to-peer networks (P2P), such as Limewire and KaZaA, which allow music junkies to share files with other users. The expectation of free music is fast becoming the norm, and talk of change in the music industry is in the air and in the courtroom.

The beauty of the Web is that any musician without a recording contract can post MP3s on a Web site, and many of them are doing just that. In spite of what the music industry's lobbying groups say, the Internet is helping a lot of musicians make money. Consumers don't want to spend between $12 and $20 on a CD they haven't heard. They want to buy CDs they know they like. And, the Web is one of the only places consumers can hear non-mainstream music before they buy it.

Consider the story behind *Yankee Hotel Foxtrot*, the latest release of alternative-country band Wilco. After being dropped by their record label, the band bought the rights to their songs, which the label refused to produce, and made the entire album available for free on their Web site. Months later, the band signed with a small label and their album was released on CD. While thousands of people had already downloaded all the music, the album still debuted in the Billboard top 20 in sales.

Wilco's success is no fluke. It is part of a growing trend. Consumers will buy good music even if it is available for free. As musician Janis Ian has said, "Water is free, but a lot of us drink bottled water because it tastes better." The problem is the average American doesn't think the industry is making good music. The result is a backlash against mainstream music that parallels changes in the movies.

TAKING A CUE FROM HOLLYWOOD

Independent movies have taken Hollywood by storm, and independent music is about to experience the same success. Small labels, such as Matador, are selling more records, and no-label, local bands are gaining followings outside of their home towns. Bands like Pizzicato Five from Japan and Cat Power from Australia are reaching an American audience.

Whether record companies start catering to the public or not, these are exciting times for music lovers. Thanks to the Internet, music lovers have a greater variety of music available to them. And, while you still may not hear your favorite local band on the radio, the music industry of tomorrow will be more reflective of the cultural diversity of the American landscape.

PROVOCATIONS...

Will we ever have a number one song that is self-distributed on the Internet? Now that digital recording can be of any length, what does it mean to make an "album?"

—Zahra Safavian

WANT MORE?

MP3 DOWNLOAD SITE
www.peoplesound.com

MUSICIAN'S WEB PORTAL
www.hitsquad.com

SATELLITE RADIO PROVIDER
www.xmradio.com

FUTURE OF MUSIC COALITION
www.futureofmusic.org

Future of Art... Art Is Art. It Is What It Is.

IN MANY WAYS WE HAVE *more art than ever. Retail giant Target touts three-and-counting designers creating artful items with which you can brush your teeth, make toast, or scrub your toilet (although not at the same time).*

Art museums have become highbrow malls, punctuating their exhibitions with shops full of artist- and museum-branded wares. You have to make reservations to get into blockbuster shows, and ticket prices are into double digits. Friday nights at the museum look more like a singles bar — and sometimes they don't even bother to open the galleries.

Cities are "discovering" the economic impact of the arts (i.e., hotels and restaurant visits), and they are appropriating big dollars for marketing campaigns, even as they slash the budgets of the school arts programs developing tomorrow's arts audiences. What does it mean when an American consumer will drop $60 to see *Rent* once but considers $1 per capita annually too much public spending on the arts?

The rampant commercialization of art is hardly new — and neither is artists' resistance to it. Art trends start out novel, after all. The controversial artworks created in response are likewise to be expected. Consider that the Impressionist works that outraged both critics and public couldn't be given away in 1874. Today, these highly subversive works are available on tote bags and umbrellas for under $30.

AUGMENTED FISH REALITY. *This work of art is an in-process interactive installation that captures the natural behavior of Siamese fighting fish and translates it into fish bowls that move about.*

So, like they always have, popular notions of art continue to expand. It gets harder to be avant-garde in the 21st century. But we will still try. We'll bite the hand that feeds us. We'll use bizarre media, even mining our own bodies. We'll make art from refuse. We'll misuse technology in outrageous ways; subvert science into art, and vice versa. We'll rip art from its gallery context to render it unsaleable, or simply create works that have no value. And most shocking of all? Sometimes we'll just have a good time.

WATERBOY

San Fransisco-based assemblage artist Marcus Cornblatt had always mined the scrap heap for materials and inspiration. Silicon Valley detritus is pretty high-tech junk; excellent fodder for an artist

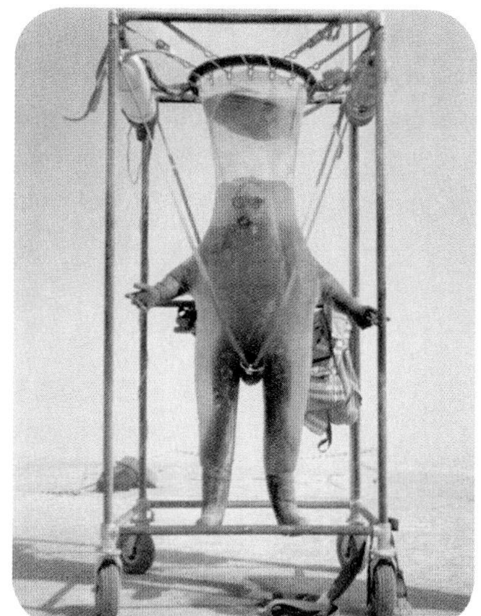

IRONIC, ICONIC, AND AVAILABLE FOR PARTIES. *Waterboy's bits and parts are mostly constructed from found objects and off-the-shelf hardware and technology. Cornblatt dons a scuba mask and tanks (and sometimes little else) and climbs inside.*

Top to bottom: Kenneth E. Rinaldo, Ohio State University © 1997 FalseGods Productions

MY ART IS FALLING APART...

A friend of mine was cleaning out a closet when she came across a disintegrating pile of fabric and rubber. It went out with the trash. It was a work by Robert Rauschenberg. Many other icons of 20th-century art, especially those made of experimental materials or new synthetics, face similar problems.

"Mixed media pieces are very vulnerable because they age differently," says Clark Bedford, Conservator of Paintings and Mixed Media Objects at the Hirschorn Museum. "Although 1950s and 60s works in plastic and polyester resin are also at risk." The stuff gets sticky, allowing dirt and dust to get into the piece. Other artists made their own acrylic paints of whatever they had on hand.

"Artists make temporary things that weren't meant to last - but then museums purchase and need to maintain them. We tend to think of the museum as a bank or storage vault. But the artists think of the moment," continues Bedford.

Contemporary pieces are even more esoteric. Consider preserving a bust of soap, or chocolate. A 3-foot wide wad of bubble gum; a tiny wad of poo. Isn't it part of the work to disintegrate or fall apart with time? "It is," admits Bedford. "But it better not happen."

exploring what it means to be human by transposing meat and machine.

"Being a component of a mechanical/biological entity is a unique experience," says Cornblatt. "It's not like being a performer in the traditional sense. It's more of an interaction – one in which you are both object and interpreter."

AUGMENTED FISH REALITY

Professor Ken Rinaldo's synthobiotic artworks explore "the confluence and co-evolution of organic and technological cultures." Science fiction made real, they're even about inter- and trans-species communication. Weird enough. Although "melding art and science is very old, " says Rinaldo, referring to a time when such distinctions were not made.

"Seventeenth- and 18th-century biologists were usually first considered artists. Art, nature, and biology have never really been separate. They're all about observing, conceptualizing, visualizing, and discovering," he says. "They're eternally connected."

Robotics, high-tech cameras, and specially written software allow hyper-aggressive fish to interact with each other and with the humans entering their space. It's also a selective breeding project. Less aggressive fish will be identified by their interactions with the world around them. Anticipated result: a kinder, gentler fish that no longer eats its bowlmates. And so, elegant and graceful, these robots and fish become sculpture. But the piece has an additional purpose that we usually don't expect from a work of art, however poetic — the creation of a different kind of fish.

ONLINE GALLERIES

Another place where contemporary art meets emerging technology is the Internet. But that's just the where – predicting the what is another matter, says Mark Tribe, founder and director of online New Media gallery Rhizome.org.

"What we can say is that whatever technologies do emerge, artists will be experimenting with them, pushing their limits, and generally using them in ways that were never intended – often to subvert the corporations that develop them," Tribe says.

As new media and fine art become amalgamated, there's no doubt we'll be seeing more cyber-based works. But there's a problem. No matter how good it is – by any artistic definition – it's hard to make money with it. It doesn't have the cabala of things that museums, collectors, and auction houses use to define worth: scarcity, individual ownership, authorship, uniqueness, and provenance. For a lot of people, this is also what makes it interesting.

No one can predict the future of art. And why would we want to? We'll know it when we see it, even as we shake our heads in disbelief.

PROVOCATIONS...

Do we like art, or do we just like to shop?

—Polly Harrold

WANT MORE?

ARTISTS AND SCIENTISTS
www.asci.org

NEW MEDIA ART COLLECTION
http://collections.walkerart.org

OPEN_SOURCE_ART_HACK
www.newmuseum.org

NEW TECHNOLOGIES ART
www.artfuture.com

TURBULENCE: NET ART
www.turbulence.org

EDUARDO KAC: THE EIGHTH DAY, A TRANSGENIC ARTWORK
www.ekac.org/8thday.html

AUGMENTED FISH REALITY
www.accad.ohio-state.edu/~rinaldo

WATERBOY
www.falsegods.com

MUSEUMS... More Hard Rock Café than Museum Mile

When Alexander the Great founded his Museum at Alexandria, he had big plans. Other museums of his day had modest goals: They were places of learning, where men found inspiration, studied philosophy, and created art.

But Alexander took it up a notch. His museum not only inspired great men to create great works (Euclid wrote his *Elements of Geometry* here), but also introduced the idea of collections (statues, maps, animal hides) and demanded of its scholars a comprehensive examination of, well, everything. Always ambitious, Alexander wanted his museum to take stock of all the world's knowledge, just as his army sought to conquer all its lands.

The Museum at Alexandria burned along with the legendary library in the 3rd century AD. But the fires didn't extinguish those human impulses to create, collect, and categorize.

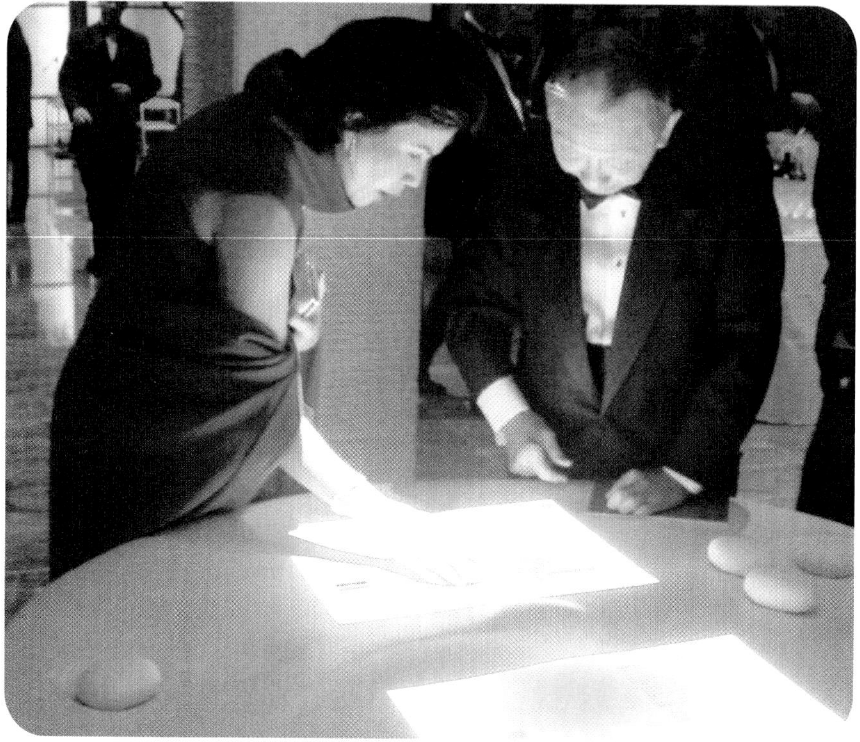

THE KNOWLEDGE TABLE. *Designed by Small Design and Andrew Davies for New York's Asia Society, this interactive exhibition presents visitors with tables on which digital maps of Asia are projected. By placing one of six differently labeled stones on the table, visitors can learn about various facets of Asian culture, from cuisine to history. Once placed on the table, the stones act as a mouse, allowing the visitor to zoom in on various countries for more detail.*

Photo courtesy of David Small/Small Design

"DEADLY DULL" MUSEUMS

When public museums emerged in Europe in the 1750s, they lacked the direction or inspiration of their classical counterparts. "Body-wearying and soul-stupefying" is how curator John Cotton Dana described the "deadly dull" museums of his day. Writing prophetically in 1917, he urged museums to break with tradition, focus on presentation, and take a few hints from retail on how to better serve their communities: "A great city department store is perhaps more like a good museum of art than are any of the museums we have yet established," Dana wrote.

IMMERSIVE EXPERIENCES

Decades after Dana's challenge, museums are finally taking the hint and watching how theme parks and superstores lure visitors. To compete with the Niketowns and Disneylands (to say nothing of PlayStation games and cable TV), many museums are modeling themselves after the immersive, multisensory experiences that Americans find so appealing. Focus is less on individual objects than the overall experience.

The influences of pop culture are sometimes obvious, as in the Smithsonian's excellent traveling show, "Star Wars: The Magic of Myth." More Hard Rock Café than Museum Mile, the exhibit explores the movie's roots in classical mythology, while surrounding the visitor with video clips, costumes, and music from the film.

But some of the most immersive museum experiences can be found in less likely places with more somber subject matter. The Museum of Jewish Heritage, for instance, weaves film projections, images, music, voiceovers, objects, and text to tell an unforgettable story of Jews before and after the Holocaust.

ILLUMINATING THE PAST. *Presented in a "virtual showcase" developed by the Fraunhofer Center for Research in Computer Graphics, the dinosaur skull is real — but the orange muscles overlaying it are digitally projected holograms. The virtual showcase can present objects not in the museum's physical collection, in effect creating "complete" objects from those that are broken or incomplete, or augmenting the information about a physical object being displayed.*

Image courtesy of Fraunhofer Center for Research in Computer Graphics

MUSEUM ACCESSORIES

Immersive environments may absorb and entertain, but they can only skim the surface of any given topic. A visitor's education is limited to what fits in the display case or on the audio tour.

But using new, digital displays, curators can provide deeper, on-demand information about every object or idea in an exhibit. These digital data wells are currently offered through computer stations or kiosks. But digital information will soon be integrated more seamlessly into exhibits, with the help of so-called "museum wearables."

Imagine looking at your favorite Picasso painting, while simultaneously viewing all the other paintings he completed during the same period. Want to learn what influenced him? Just make another selection (by simply shifting your gaze; the goggles' eye-tracking sensor will know where you're looking), and you can view the work of his contemporaries, the global art he owned, or the political and cultural events that shaped his world all without stepping away from the original painting.

While Sparacino's goggles tell the (extended) story behind an object, other simply allow you to see it more clearly. 3D-enabled glasses under development by Jorg Voskamp at Germany's Fraunhofer Institute for Computer Graphics allow visitors to view damaged objects — cracked pottery, faded clothes, statues with a limb lopped off — as they originally were. Or at least, as experts believe them to have been.

Using an object's image and 3D-modeling software, museum experts create a 3D, digital model of the artifact as it looked in its prime. The damaged object is then placed in a special display case, and the computer-rendered image of the missing elements is projected on it. This projection is invisible to the naked eye. But when visitors view the actual, noseless, armless statue through the glasses, they see it superimposed with a 3D shadow of its former self, allowing them to picture more clearly how it looked and what it meant.

THE ULTIMATE COLLECTION

If Alexander the Great were alive today, he would no doubt be scheming to reincarnate his Mouseion. With a large physical space, digital archives, museum wearables, and a lot of cash, he could finally build a MegaMuseum that catalogues all human knowledge.

This MegaMuseum would offer a vast collection of actual objects, narrated within an immersive, multimedia environment (imagine floor-to-ceiling video screens, interactive touch panels, digital sound) and augmented by digital archives accessible through a headset, which uses eye-tracking technology, voice recognition, and a smart searching system to understand and find whatever related information any individual visitor desires. Finally, all the information in the world would truly be at your fingertips, or your eyelashes, as the case may be.

PROVOCATIONS...

Will we stand in line longer to see a famous artifact or a famous technology that explains that artifact?

As technology allows us to create more and more convincing replicas, will original artifacts become less important, or more?

—June Cohen

WANT MORE?

MUSEUM PROFESSIONALS' SITE
www.utoronto.ca/mouseia/intro.html

MUSEUM CONFERENCE
www.archimuse.com/conferences/mw.html

SMITHSONIAN INSTITUTION
www.smithsonian.org

SMALL DESIGN FIRM
www.davidsmall.com

FRAUNHOFER INSTITUTE FOR COMPUTER GRAPHCIS
www.crcg.edu

CASSON MANN
www.cassonmann.co.uk

Video Games... Pushing the Envelope

LUSH AND SOPHISTICATED. *The graphics and artificial intelligence of 2001 bestseller Black & White are but a taste of the increasingly real game environments and characters of the future (above).* **WIRELESS PLATFORM.** *Games like Monkeystone's Hyperspace Delivery Boy are expected to accelerate developments in wireless technologies. While they still have primitive graphics reminiscent of the first console games, this emerging platform is expected to be a must-have in coming years (below right).*

FROM GRAPHICS CARDS TO WIRELESS TECHNOLOGIES, THE FUTURE *of the IT industry can be found in whatever direction electronic games are heading, and the gaming industry is gearing up for a wild ride.*

Electronic games have advanced light years beyond Pong and Pacman. One of 2001's hottest games, Black & White, features stunning 3D graphics and pioneering use of artificial intelligence (AI). In the beginning of the game, players can adopt one of three creatures and teach them survival basics. As the game is played, the adopted creature "learns" from the player in very much the same way children learn from their parents. If the creature notices that the player torments the villagers in the game, the creature will likely grow to be cruel.

While Black & White has broken ground, the lifelike creatures are just a taste of how AI will be used in games. Nonplayer characters (NPCs) will act and move more realistically. As voice recognition and language processing technologies improve, players will be able to interact with NPCs through speech rather than control pads or keyboards.

Not only will game characters be more true-to-life, but the actual game world will seem more real. Game characters will appear to have real skin and hair, and objects will seem to be made out of real metal or wood. Unlike animated movies, though, game graphics will

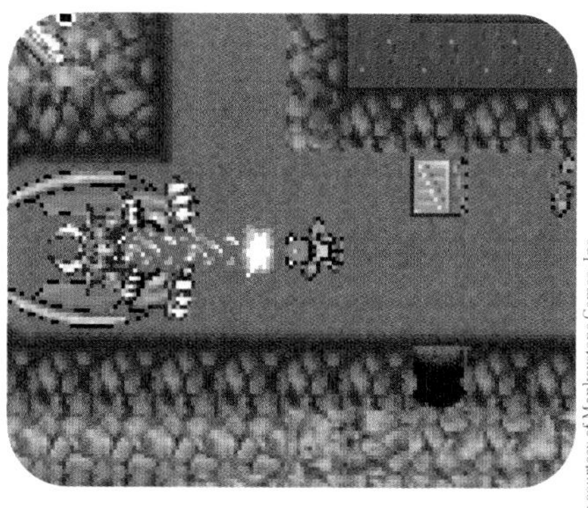

change in real-time based on the player's actions. Industry experts believe the next big innovation in game design will be highly advanced physics engines, the component of games that determines how inanimate objects react to the gamer's actions. Instead of interacting with only a set number of objects, players will be able to manipulate anything in the game world from a spaceship down to a bolt in a wall.

Some of the most exciting developments won't be in the games themselves, but in the platforms on which they are played. Online games have become big business in recent years. Driven by the widespread growth of broadband Internet access, the online gaming industry is expected to rake in up to $1.7 billion in the U.S. alone by 2004, and the console companies have taken notice.

Sony, Nintendo, and Microsoft all recently announced plans to venture into the online gaming environment with console networks. Xbox owners who also have broadband Internet access will soon be able to buy an adapter, complete with a headset communicator and access to Microsoft's Xbox Live service. With this service, users will be able to play games, such as the highly anticipated Star Wars Galaxies, against other gamers connected to the network using their consoles. The headset will allow players to talk to each other while playing. Playstation2 and the GameCube are now offering similar adapters, minus the network service. The next generation of console games, expected to hit the market around 2005, is expected to have networking capabilities built into them.

Even more exciting than the developments in consoles is the birth of the first new gaming platform since the development of consoles in the 1970s — wireless devices. In recent years, wireless games have been one of the fastest growing gaming segments in East Asia, where full-color mobile phones and PDAs are widely available.

Like the first console games, the first generation of wireless games uses primitive graphics and simple forms of interaction. However, the higher bandwidth of the emerging third-generation wireless networks will make it possible to develop games with more advanced graphics, higher levels of interaction, and multiplayer capabilities. Proponents of this new platform believe that these games will accelerate developments in wireless technologies much like electronic games did with the PC.

As with other fields of entertainment, the future of games is hard to predict. But, without a doubt gamers will continue to demand accelerated advancement in industries from computing to wireless communications, and the games of the future will be harder to pause, even for a second.

PROVOCATIONS...

When will a game designer be as popular as Steven Speilberg?

Will Spouses Against Everquest become the new Mothers Against Drunk Driving?

—Zahra Safavian

"REAL" MONEY FOR "VIRTUAL" ITEMS. *Ultima Online, a massive multiplayer game, is so addictive that people have literally started buying items that will give them an edge.*

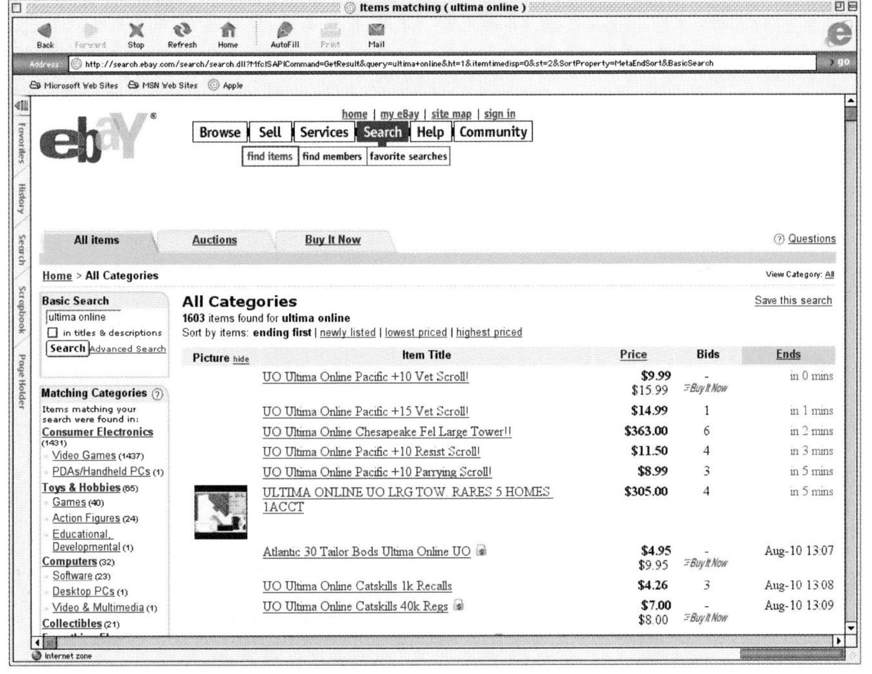

WANT MORE?

MOST VISITED GAMING SITE
www.ign.com

TECHTV EXTENDED PLAY
www.techtv.com/extendedplay

ELECTRONIC ARTS
www.ea.com

MONKEYSTONE
www.monkeystone.com

SORRENT
www.sorrent.com

GAME RESEARCH
www.game-research.com

GAME PORTAL, GAMENETWORK
www.gamanetwork.com

Envisioning the Future of Healthcare

THE NEXT TWO DECADES WILL SEE amazing technological advances affecting health, including control of cancer and heart disease, predictive medicine and virtual checkups, artificial organs and limbs, and other advances we can scarcely imagine. These advances can help us be healthier, both individually and as a society.

But these exciting new options from technology are just part of the story. For they will be used in the larger health systems we choose to create. The future of health lies in the choices we make about new technologies, the healthcare systems that deliver them, and in our personal and social behaviors. These choices will be shaped by our shared visions for health and will reflect ways in which we have "changed our minds" about what has come before.

The U.S. spends more per capita than any country on healthcare, yet is rated only 27th in the world in terms of the outcomes of its health system. It's clear that we have tremendous room to grow and improve — to make our shared investment generate greater returns for everyone. There are indicators that give hope that positive changes are ahead, but achieving such changes will mean overcoming the pessimism and fatigue of previous failed efforts at reform.

We missed an opportunity in the early 1990s. Amidst the politics and debate, the 1992 to 1994 national healthcare reform efforts failed, in part, because we never developed a shared vision of what we wanted our healthcare system to do. Such visions are critical to any large endeavor. They define our idea of success and are the point against which we measure progress. For example, do we want a healthcare system that both innovates, accelerating our ability to prevent and control disease, and ensures a basic level of effective health-enhancing care to all? Given emerging technology, how can we best deploy health professionals to ensure a basic level of care and allow those who can afford it to "buy up" to more upscale options, such as enhanced sexual performance, vision, hearing, or memory?

In this effort we will get the capacity for enhancement from genomics and other biotechnology, as well as from nanotechnology. Our economic system and our values will allow a great deal of variation, but precisely what kinds of research to publicly fund, how to set pharmaceutical and medical care prices, and how much of the advances to include in basic coverage are all issues for public and healthcare system decision-making. These opportunities will make it more important to have a shared vision to guide this decision-making in the future.

In the early 1990s, communities around the country were able to move further toward developing such shared visions and enhancing local health and healthcare, but only within the context of a relatively "visionless" national system. Some efforts, such as the Belmont Vision project, sought to raise the discussion beyond tactics and strategy (particularly financing) to the level of a shared vision. The Belmont Vision, signed by numerous leaders in the allied health fields, set out principles for a social contract and the outline for a design for healthcare based on a vision of what could be. As C. Everett Koop said in 1992 in his Foreword to the Belmont Vision document, "We can make our healthcare system far better, far more caring, and far more equitable for everyone." I believed those words when I helped develop the original vision in 1992, and I believe them still.

The options for better health and healthcare in this decade and the next are supported by the prestigious Institute of Medicine (IOM) of the National Academies of Science. The IOM report on "crossing the quality chasm" argues that healthcare must be looked at systemically and in light of what we want the health system to do. It proposes six aims for the healthcare system: safety, effectiveness, patient-centeredness, timeliness, efficiency, and equity. Would you want a healthcare system that meets these aims?

The call for healthcare systems that are equitable is reinforced by the World Health Organization's (WHO) Health For All Vision endorsed by every nation in the world. WHO argues that health will only be achieved when there is equity. (Equity in this context does not mean everything the same, but rather that there are not differences that are avoidable and unfair.) Likewise, the IOM aim reinforces the U.S. Healthy People 2010 Objectives for the Nation that sets forth two overarching goals for this decade, including the "elimination of health disparities." (The other overarching goal is "longer years of healthy life.") And there are significant health disparities in the U.S., based on factors such as race. As Harold Freeman, former chair of the

President's Cancer Panel put it, the cancer death rates in the U.S. could be interpreted as meaning that being black with cancer in America is an early death sentence.

Our approach to eliminating health disparities will ultimately require us to consider the larger issues of environment and the economy, particularly poverty. To be sufficiently committed to health to deal effectively with poverty will take a change of mind and heart. This change has happened before, and it could happen around equity. (Equity here means fairness, not sameness; it focuses on eliminating differences in health outcomes that are avoidable and unfair.)

In the last two centuries, humanity has generally improved the way that its societies work. For example, in the U.S. we "changed our minds" about slavery and women's rights. In the early 1800s slavery was accepted and common in most parts of the U.S. People in various states, and at different rates, "changed their minds" and opposed slavery. Likewise, reinforced by laws as well as community and marketplace practices, people "changed their minds" about women's rights. The right to vote for women came in the early part of the 20th century. Later in the 20th century, discrimination on the basis of race or sex was not only illegal, it was viewed as a negative social value in many settings. Discrimination did not disappear, but it has lessened.

Attitudes toward health in the 21st century are likely to reflect a similar movement. In addition to technology, we are learning more about the various factors affecting health. For example, over a life course, the four most important factors affecting differences in illness and their relative contribution are behavior (50%), environment (20%), genes (20%), and healthcare (10%). And we are coming to understand how our genes influence how we think and behave and how our thoughts and behavior in turn shapes our families, communities, and personal health. We are beginning to tease apart the mysterious relationships between biology, psychology, community, and society.

There is a mind shift underway and a set of choices each of us faces about how we deal with fairness in health and healthcare. In effect, we are not healthy as individuals and societies if there is a high degree of "unfairness" in health outcome. The future of health is about our choices. Trends suggest growing support for including equity in our definition of health and acting on it. But as Rene Dubos told us, trends are not destiny. Having health systems that work for all is a choice for each of us.

—Clement Bezold

Fertility... People, People Who Make People

THE NEWS THAT ONE HAS A FERTILITY PROBLEM OFTEN BRINGS HEARTACHE AND A DEEP *sense of loss to many individuals and couples. Several difficult decisions face such couples, including whether to pursue fertility services, adoption alternatives, or simply to remain childless. Age is definitely an enemy of fertility, especially in women. However, new procedures and advances are offering greater hope of conceiving than ever before. In addition, the development of new technologies is widening the path for people to conceive, who in the past could never have had the chance.*

WHAT "EXACTLY" IS INFERTILITY?
Infertility affects between 10% and 15% (approximately 6 million) of American couples. It is generally defined as the inability to conceive a child within 1 year of frequent and unprotected sexual intercourse. Physiologically, a woman is most fertile between 18 and 28 years of age, and then her fertility gradually declines until age 35. Thereafter, fertility dramatically decreases. Male fertility, on the other hand, declines only slightly over the years so men can father a child at nearly any age. Thus, fertility is more dependent on the age of the woman than the age of the man.

Photo by Jeff Widener

There are many factors that lead to problems with infertility. About 40% of infertility problems involve the female, 30% involve the male, and about 30% of infertility problems are unexplained.

It is very common for infertility to involve more than one factor. Once specific problems are identified, treatment can begin. Fortunately, the overwhelming majority (85%–90%) of infertility cases can be treated medically or surgically. Fertility drugs, such as clomiphene citrate (Clomid), are commonly prescribed for hormonal problems, which interfere with the production of eggs. Approximately 40% of women taking this drug become pregnant within 6 months. Only about 5% of infertility cases are treated by assisted reproductive technologies (ART).

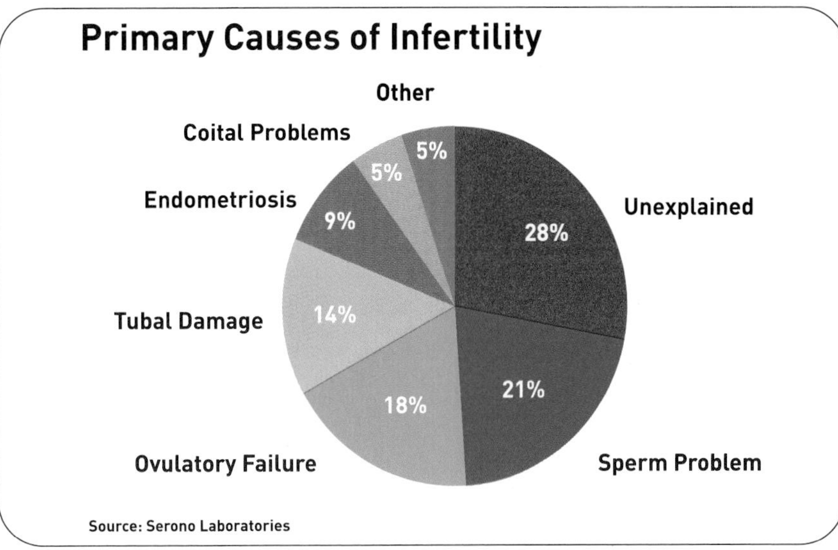

CONCEPTION TECHNOLOGIES

While most couples who try to conceive a child can plan and enjoy romantic lovemaking, infertile couples choosing assisted-reproductive technologies are forced to conceive in an impersonal world. There are approximately 400 fertility clinics across the U.S. specializing in assisted-reproductive technologies: in-vitro fertilization (IVF), gamete intrafallopian transfer (GIFT), zygote intrafallopian transfer (ZIFT), tubal embryo transfer (TET), and frozen embryo transfer (FET). Each ART cycle typically involves a 6-week period of multiple activities: multiple hormonal injections to stimulate and control egg production, multiple blood samples taken for assessing important hormone status levels, and multiple ultrasound exams to monitor follicle (egg) development.

There are basically three different procedures that fertility clinics currently use to help couples conceive.

IVF. The term "in-vitro fertilization" refers to fertilization performed outside of the body. The woman's eggs are induced to grow by hormone injections. Generally, eggs are retrieved from the ovaries by guided needle and are mixed in a laboratory culture dish with sperm. Fertilized eggs are identified through microscopic observation and then grown in culture medium for 3 – 5 days before two to four embryos are placed in a catheter and transferred to the woman. Additional embryos not transferred to the woman can be frozen and used for future transfers if desired (frozen embryo transfer, FET). IVF was the first of several cutting-edge, assisted-reproductive technologies and remains the most common. In addition, it is the only procedure available to women who have blocked fallopian tubes.

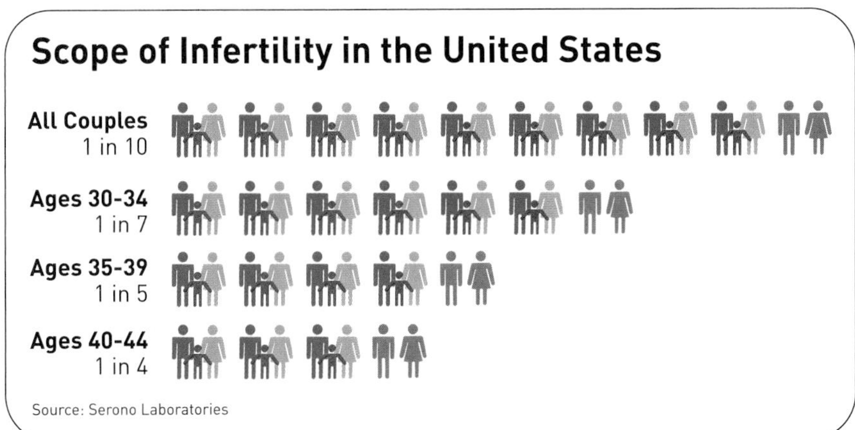

GIFT. Gametes refer to the sex cells, eggs and sperm. In this procedure, unfertilized eggs are collected from the ovaries and transferred immediately to the fallopian tubes where they are mixed with the donated sperm. Fertilization occurs in the fallopian tube (where it also occurs naturally), and the fertilized egg is conveyed to the uterus. This procedure requires laparoscopic surgery and general anesthesia.

SLOW DOWN THOSE SPERM!

Reseacher David Clapham and colleagues at Harvard University have discovered a protein, called CatSper, that gives sperm their pep. Mice without the protein are just as sexually active, but 100% infertile. Lack of the CatSper protein might make men as infertile as the mice. Taking a drug to temporarily block the protein could prevent conception, leading to a birth control pill for both men and women.

ZIFT. This procedure is initially performed like IVF. Within a day after fertilization the zygotes, the cells resulting from the union of the egg and sperm, are surgically transferred to a fallopian tube where they are subsequently conveyed to the uterus.

There is no higher incidence of genetic abnormalities in children conceived by these methods than by natural conception. Successful pregnancy rates using IVF range between 15% and 25% and are often higher in women patients under 30. Success rates for women over 40, however, are much lower, between 5% and 15%. Lower rates of success in older women are due to the decreased numbers of eggs produced and the decreased quality of the eggs. Donor eggs are the best options for older women and indeed, many women over 50 are able to become pregnant by this option. Between 30% and 60% of older patients undergoing IVF with young donor eggs produce successful pregnancies.

REPRODUCTIVE TECHNOLOGIES: TODAY AND TOMORROW

Recent revolutionary advances in micromanipulation and tissue-culture techniques are impacting both male and female factor infertility problems. In males, intracytoplasmic sperm injection (ICSI) is a new laboratory technique that involves a microscopically-guided insertion of a needle containing a single sperm into an egg to effect fertilization. Following a few days in culture, the resulting embryo is transferred to the prepared female partner's uterus. This procedure has yielded remarkable results and now enables men with very low sperm counts to father a child. Advances in microsurgical techniques now allow surgeons to retrieve spermatozoa via fine-needle aspiration. Sperm collected via these methods can be successfully microinjected into eggs. Experimental work being conducted in laboratory mice may eventually allow pre-pubertal boys who lose their testicles to cancer surgery or treatment to regain their ability to fertilize eggs as adults. Researchers have discovered that grafts of small pieces of testicular tissue or isolated immature sperm cells (germ stem cells) from different species into mice can produce normal sperm of the donor species. This creates the possibility that germ stem cells isolated from a male youth prior to cancer treatment can be frozen, stored, and then transplanted back into his testes as an adult once he has totally recovered from cancer therapy. Alternatively, grafting pieces of his testicular tissue into a mouse (serving as a "bio-incubator") would allow the production of normal human sperm that could then be collected and frozen for future use.

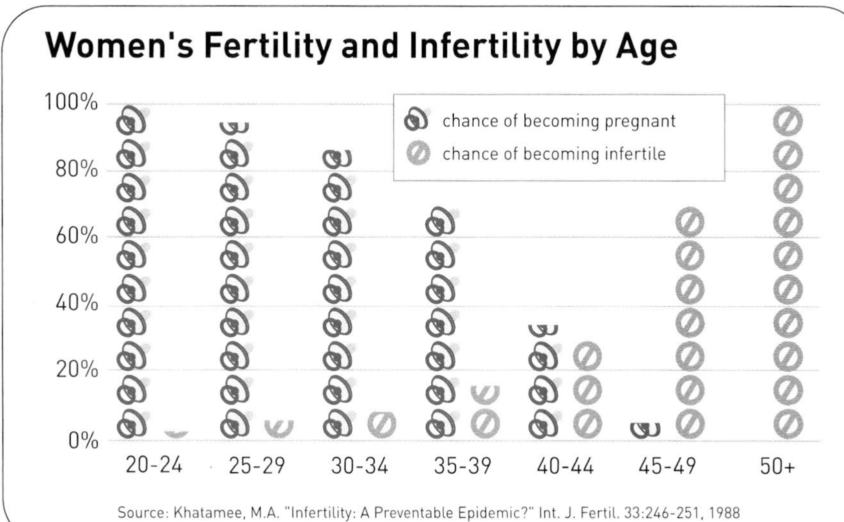

Similar techniques are being used to overcome female factor infertility. It is well established that egg production and egg quality progressively decrease with increasing age in women. A recent procedure known as cytoplasmic (or ooplasmic) transfer is attempting to recover the reproductive potential of an egg. In this procedure, a small volume of cytoplasm, that component of a cell exclusive of the nucleus, is removed from a younger donor egg and microinjected into an older recipient egg that is then fertilized by ICSI.

Recent developments in cryopreservation methods for eggs (such as

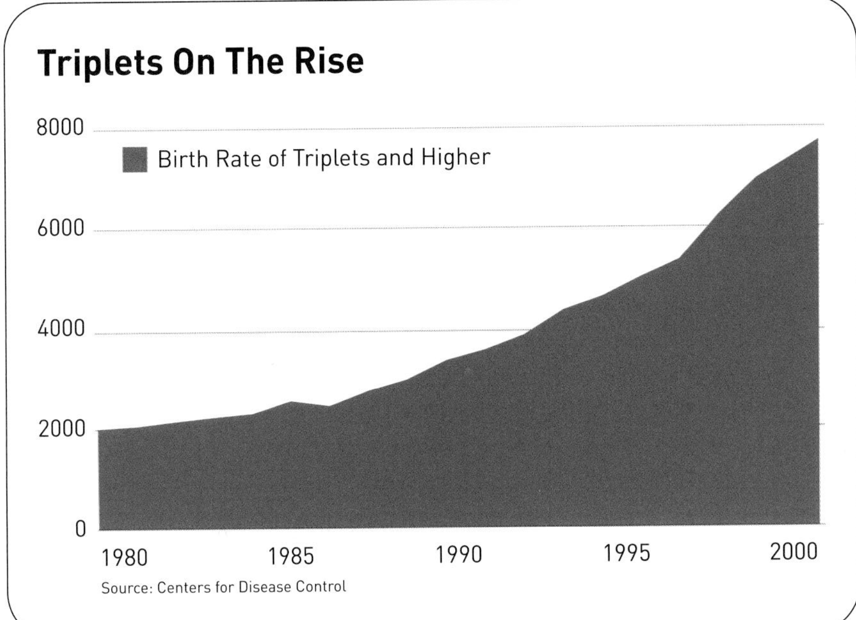

vitrification) and ovarian tissue may allow women, like their male counterparts, to "bank" their reproductive cells to preserve their future fertility either in the wake of aging or in response to fertility-damaging cancer surgery or treatment.

In addition to decreased reproductive potential of eggs with maternal age, there are also marked decreases in embryo implantation rates and increased rates of spontaneous abortion. This is principally due to age-related increases in chromosomal abnormalities. New sophisticated techniques such as fluorescence in situ hybridization (FISH) allow the detection of chromosomal errors in eggs prior to fertilization or in single cells removed from early-stage embryos prior to implantation — that is, pre-implantation genetic diagnosis (PGD). Such analyses could improve the odds of a couple having a successful pregnancy and a healthy child and decrease the costs of such services. These techniques could permit the transfer of fewer embryos (arguably, one) to the uterus, which would reduce the financial and psychological burden on parents who are trying for one child.

PROVOCATIONS...

Will marketers figure out a way to market a "pill for men" in a way that does not make them feel emasculated?

Could a massive upsurge in twins and triplets create havoc for facial recognition and fingerprint identification?

—Mark F. Seifert

TO WHAT LENGTHS?

Cytoplasmic transfer has been shown to increase egg vitality in experimental animals and has recently been performed in clinical trials in humans at St. Barnabas Medical Center in New Jersey that resulted in the births of nearly 30 infants worldwide. This procedure is fraught with risks, however, and has been criticized by many scientists and ethicists as a form of germ-line engineering. Present within the transferred cytoplasm are mitochondria that carry their own DNA (mitochondrial DNA). Thus, children born following such a procedure may contain DNA from three different people: the father, the mother, and mitochondrial DNA transferred from the donor egg. The short-term and long-term health risks to the offspring remain uncertain. There are over 40 known types of mitochondrial diseases, and genetic defects in mitochondria have been linked to a variety of human disorders, including cerebral palsy, hearing loss, Alzheimer's, and heart disease.

WANT MORE?

AMERICAN SOCIETY FOR REPRODUCTIVE MEDICINE (ASRM)
www.asrm.org

GUIDE TO ASSISTED REPRODUCTIVE TECHNOLOGIES
www.sart.org

WOMEN'S HEALTH INTERACTIVE
www.womens-health.com

INFERTILITY RESOURCES
www.ihr.com/infertility

CDC REPRODUCTIVE HEALTH INFORMATION
www.cdc.gov/nccdphp/drh

THE NATIONAL INFERTILITY ASSOCIATION
www.resolv.org

THE INTERNATIONAL COUNCIL ON INFERTILITY INFORMATION DISSEMINATION (INCIID)
www.inciid.org

AMERICAN INFERTILITY ASSOCIATION (AIA)
www.americaninfertility.org

Fitness and Exercise... TAKE A PILL AND RELAX

THE NEW WORLD OF working out integrates health and fitness into all areas of our lives, offering more from workouts than sweat and grim determination. ¶ Spirituality, stress release, and invigoration have become part of many Americans' workouts, along with social interaction — especially since 9-11, as Margo Faiman of the International Health, Racquet, & Sportclub Association notes. Americans are increasingly turning to yoga, spinning (on stationary bicycles), and time at the gym to reduce stress, build confidence, and treat pain, according to the American Council on Exercise.

While the Internet revolution suggested that computer networking would cause everyone to do everything at home, we're more likely to head away from home equipment and toward the education and community offered by gyms. Group classes use a myriad of methods and music; you can even take Punk Rock Aerobics. Hybrid

NIA... WORKING OUT FROM THE INSIDE

When people finish their first Nia class, they may talk in astonished tones about moving energy through their bodies, feeling a spiritual buzz, or having an emotional awakening — hardly the stuff of Jazzercise and treadmills. "The numbers are going to grow," says Carlos Rosas, co-creator of the Nia technique and co-author of Holistic Fitness in the American Fitness Aerobic Association (AFAA) training manual. "I see it everywhere I go, here in the U.S., Canada, and Western Europe." Nia blends movements and concepts from a diversity of cultures, borrowing elements of martial arts, t'ai chi, yoga, and dance to create "both fitness and wellness." Founded in 1983, Nia has kept a lower profile than other, more cardio-focused hybrids. But spiritual workouts are quietly amassing practitioners of meditation, yoga, and hybrid forms.

Eric Charbonneau / BEI, PRNewsFoto

A MAGIC PILL?

However healthy and holistic we become, the urge to cheat is hard to beat. We want pills that make us skinny and electronic gizmos that give us "six-pack abs." They usually turn out to be scams, but the discovery of the enzyme calmodulin-dependent protein kinase (CaMK) might mean that someday, our muscles can gain the effects of exercising — without the hassle. Researchers at Duke University School of Medicine and the University of Texas Southwestern Medical Center in Dallas have studied CaMK in mice, whose muscles behaved in many ways as if they'd been exercising after receiving CaMK. When a muscle contracts, calcium is released and elevated in cells, which activates CaMK. The enzyme then initiates a range of exercise responses. A CaMK drug would not just be an elixir for the lazy, notes *Science* magazine, but it would improve the lives of chronically ill patients and might help athletes gain endurance.

techniques like TaeBo, Nia, and Urban Rebounding continue to gain ground, mixing breathing and relaxation with martial arts and heart-thumping aerobic dance.

Gyms themselves are likely to fulfill more and more functions in our lives. Some clubs already provide services and comforts normally associated with pricey hotels; at Manhattan's Clay, members sit at gas-fired hearths, drinking espresso and answering email. Less exclusive clubs also set themselves apart with distinctive architecture, décor, and healthy touches. Seasonally depressed members of Resort to Fitness, a women-only club in rainy Portland, Oregon, can perk up in a eucalyptus-scented light therapy room. Expect the lines between day spa, meditation retreat, health education center, restaurant, home, cosmetic surgery clinic, and gym to blur even more in the next decade.

As for exercise equipment, machines will likely become simpler in response to customer demand, and technology for disabled and recovering patients may result in ergonomically sound, extra-safe workout machines for everyone. Pennsylvania-based HydroWorx has introduced a high-tech pool that contains an underwater treadmill, sophisticated hydraulic system, and computer controls for treadmill speed, water depth, temperature, and resistance. (Hydrotherapy lessens body weight, making it easier to exercise injured limbs.)

NASA scientists create next-generation exercise machinery in their efforts to keep astronauts healthy in space. You might strengthen your very bones with a vibration machine: NASA has discovered that barely perceptible vibrations stimulate the bones' stress response, causing them to grow. Treadmills inside "body chambers" are in the works to provide body weight in space. And researchers at the University of California at Irvine, in tandem with J.B. Witmer Co., have unveiled the Space Cycle. Described by Beyond 2000 as looking like "a scaled-down carnival ride," the chairs pivot as the riders pedal, and centrifugal force moves them outward; eventually, they end up horizontal to the floor, experiencing a force of 3G. Unfortunately, it makes some riders dizzy or nauseous, but it sure would look cool in the basement, sitting next to the old Thighmaster and the dusty Nordic Track!

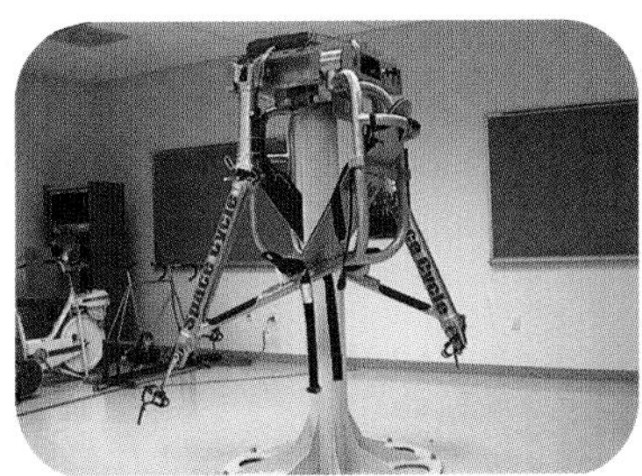

Photos courtesy of J.B.Witmer Company

A "SCALED-DOWN" CARNIVAL RIDE. *The Space Cycle holds two astronauts, sitting opposite each other in chairs mounted on a central pole.*

PROVOCATIONS...

If everyone gets a perfected body, will we have to reimagine our superhero characters?

—Tiffany Lee Brown

WANT MORE?

AMERICAN COUNCIL ON EXERCISE (ACE)
www.acefitness.org

PUNK ROCK AEROBICS
www.punkrockaerobics.com/index.html

TAEBO
www.taebo.com

THE NIA TECHNIQUE
www.nia-nia.com

URBAN REBOUNDING
www.urbanrebounding.com/about.html

HYDROWORX
www.hydroworx.com

NASA
www.nasa.gov

Cancer Research... Winning the Battles

Tiny cancer fighters

Nanotechnology is the science of building microscopically small chemicals and machines, sometimes one atom at a time, such as this experimental miniature "smart bomb" for treating cancer.

Antibodies

Radioactive atom

Cancer cell

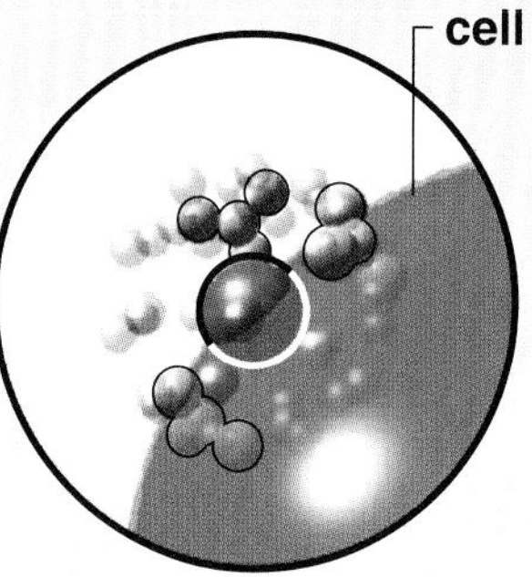

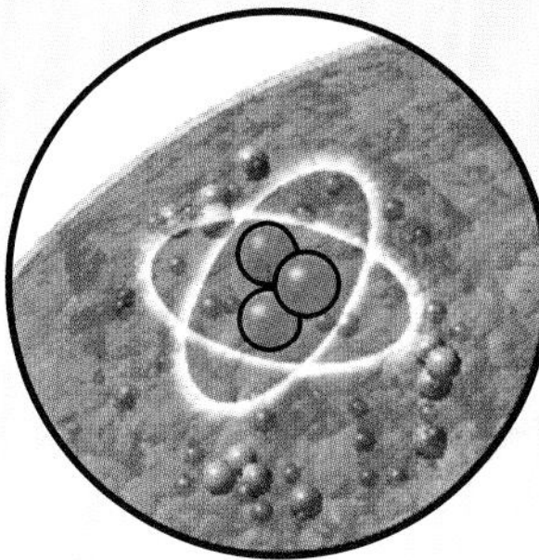

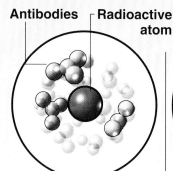

1 Scientists create a molecule to carry an atom of radioactive metal through the bloodstream

Antibody chemicals that react to cancer cells are attached

Molecule travels so rapidly that it doesn't adhere to anything or damage tissue

2 Millions of the molecules are injected into patient with syringe; molecules flow through blood vessels

When antibodies encounter cancer cells, they attach and penetrate cell membrane, pulling radioactive atom inside

3 Inside cancer cell, radiation from atom begins to kill cell

Radioactive decay gradually breaks atom down into smaller atoms, some of them radioactive

Radiation kills cancer cell and surrounding tumor

4 After cancer cell dies, radioactive metal, no longer dangerous, is naturally washed out of tissue along with rest of molecule

Source: Dow Chemical
Graphic: John W. Fleming and Heather Newman, Detroit Free Press

CANCER IS A WORD THAT STRIKES FEAR AND ANXIETY IN THE HEARTS AND MINDS OF MOST *people, and not without good reason. Cancer can develop in nearly every tissue in the body, and over 100 forms have been identified. Next to heart disease, it is the second leading cause of death among Americans and is responsible for one of every four deaths in this country. Since the "War on Cancer," announced over 30 years ago by President Nixon, progress against this foe has largely been modest, with some notable exceptions.*

According to the American Cancer Society, nearly half of all men and about one-third of all women in the U.S. will develop cancer over the course of their lifetime. Currently, lung cancer is the leading cancer killer in the general population. Breast cancer is the most commonly diagnosed cancer in women and the second leading cause of cancer-related death, while prostate cancer holds these dubious distinctions in men. Colorectal cancer counts as the third most common site of diagnosis and death in both men and women.

LOOKING BACK AND FORWARD

Over the past 25 years, investigators have made enormous progress in unlocking the intricate cellular and molecular details

Knight Ridder/Tribune

involved in the transformation of normal, healthy cells into abnormal, cancerous cells. This information has been used by drug developers to design therapeutics that more effectively target the specific dysfunctional gene or gene product. With the recent completion of the Human Genome Project in early 2001, medical researchers are rapidly cataloging abnormal genes expressed in cancer cells and at various stages of tumor development. To this end, in 1997, the National Cancer Institute created the Cancer Genome Anatomy Project that to date has catalogued several thousand genes expressed in most cancer sites in the body. Tumors have unique DNA fingerprints or genetic markers, and this information, for every kind of tumor, will profoundly change how cancer is viewed and clinically managed. Advances in the new fields of cancer proteomics and bioinformatics will enable researchers to identify the specific abnormal protein(s) or protein interactions in various cancers. Understanding the molecular profiles of specific cancers and their structural and functional defects will help doctors determine the best treatment plan for a particular cancer and will result in the production of better, "smarter" therapeutic warheads against these cancers.

Perhaps no less astounding have been the technological advances in radiographic imaging of the human body that have immeasurably enhanced patient diagnosis and treatment of cancer. The ability to visualize abnormalities of anatomic structure is vital to medical professionals when making precise diagnoses of disease, designing the best treatment strategies, and assessing effectiveness of therapy. Today, computer tomography (CT), magnetic resonance imaging (MRI), and ultrasound devices provide unprecedented clarity and resolution of structure. Newer, more powerful CT scanning devices are enabling clinicians to perform non-invasive, "virtual" colonoscopies and are presently being tested as screening tools for colon and rectal cancers. In addition, new technologies, such as positron emission tomography (PET) scanning, are enabling physicians to image functional activity of normal and pathologic tissues. PET scanning, therefore, has the potential of indicating if therapies are effective and detecting recurrence of disease earlier than anatomic imaging.

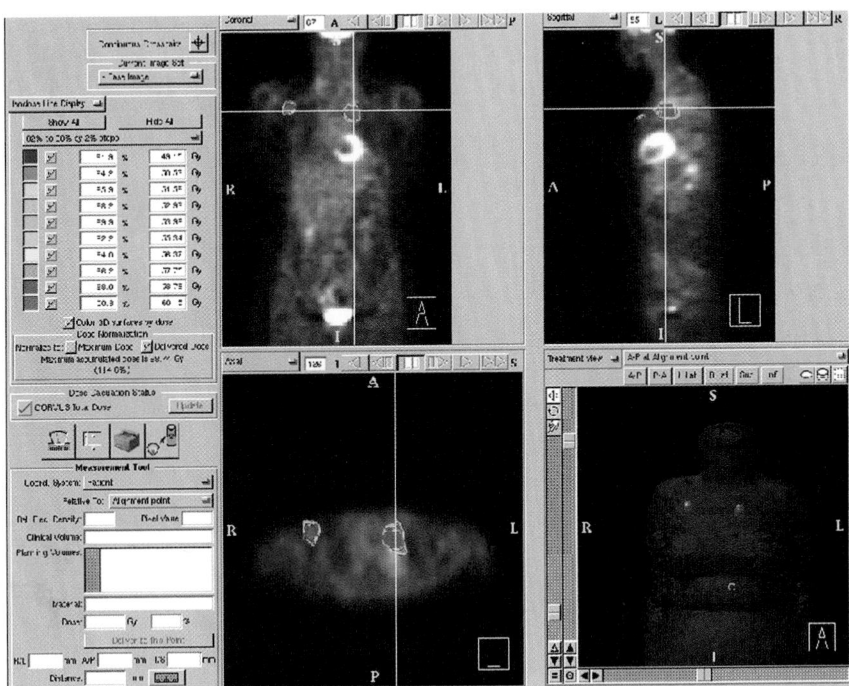

PRNewsFoto

3D PET SCAN. *With 3D imaging, a radiation beam can be directed to the tumor that conforms to the tumor's shape, thereby minimizing exposure of healthy tissue.*

Mammography is the standard imaging technology to detect breast cancer, but some tumors are still difficult to identify because of poor image quality, surrounding dense breast tissues, reader eye fatigue, or simple oversight. Currently, efforts are being made to design intelligent workstations based on appropriate algorithms in computer vision and artificial intelligence to assist radiologists in detecting the most challenging breast cancer tumors.

CURRENT TREATMENT OPTIONS

Major advances have been made in a variety of areas to support patient care and treatment. Most cancers currently are treated with surgery, chemotherapy, radiation therapy, hormone therapy, immunotherapy, or combinations of these protocols.

Advances in surgical techniques and instrumentation now allow surgeons access to the innermost recesses of the body in pursuit of tumors, while sparing as much normal tissue as possible and increasing patient recovery. It is becoming increasingly common to first shrink tumors with chemotherapy or radiation before surgery. New methods for removing or killing cancerous tissue continue

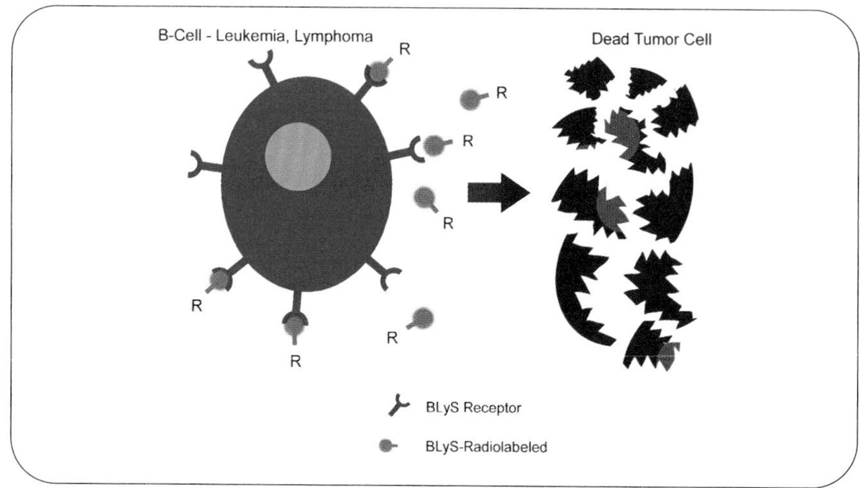

TARGET RADIATION. *BLyS protein attaches to a radioisotope, such as iodine 191, may bind to BLyS receptors on cancerous B cells, and kills the cells with low doses of radiation.*

to be explored including the use of high intensity focused ultrasound waves and microwaves to generate heat (hyperthermia treatment), but these are currently experimental and not widely used.

On the radiation front, one promising note includes external beam conformal radiotherapy. A procedure pioneered at the Radiotherapy Clinics of Georgia, it utilizes the advanced imaging technology of conformal radiotherapy, which first builds three-dimensional views of a tumor and then directs a beam of radiation that conforms to the shape of the tumor. This maximizes exposure of malignant tissue and minimizes exposure of normal, healthy tissue to the radiation.

The immune system is the body's natural defense system against a variety of diseases, including cancer. Immunotherapy is the latest member in the treatment arsenal and shows great promise in the development of the next generation of cancer therapeutics. Cancer vaccines are also being developed and evaluated in clinical trials against several types of cancer, including breast, prostate, colorectal, lung, ovarian, and melanoma, and many have produced dramatic results. This exciting and promising dimension in cancer treatment is still in its infancy.

UP AND COMING THERAPIES

The complexity of the life histories of cancers, from the mutation of genes to the mechanisms underlying tumor growth and metastasis, provide multiple opportunities to intercept disease progression. Here are some new, largely unproven strategies for treating cancer, many of which are being evaluated experimentally for their effectiveness.

ANGIOGENESIS INHIBITORS. Angiogenesis refers to the growth of new blood vessels. Tumors require blood vessels to deliver oxygen and the nutrients needed to support their continued growth. Drugs that could interfere with this process might be able to reduce tumor growth and size. The first angiogenesis inhibitor drug, TNP-470, was introduced in 1992, and several more currently are being tested in clinical trials. Angiostatin and endostatin are particularly promising anti-angiogenesis drugs. Although these inhibitors do not destroy tumors, by disrupting their blood supply they can shrink and limit their growth. Dr. Judah Folkman at Harvard Medical School has pioneered this exciting field.

GENE THERAPY. A novel experimental approach to treating diseases, including cancer, gene therapy involves the insertion of normal "therapeutic" genes into patients that have defective genes. This form of therapy has posed significant technical challenges. Research continues in the development of appropriate gene delivery vehicles (called *vectors*) that safely and effectively direct these genes to the desired target cells. Currently, there are over 300 early phase clinical trials listed in the NIH Human Gene Transfer Database pertaining to the treatment of different forms and stages of cancer.

ANTISENSE THERAPY. As confusing as the title of this therapy suggests, it aptly describes its intent — that is, to confuse a cell into thinking it has the goods to keep producing a particular protein when it does not. Before a new protein can be produced, a segment of a gene produces a single strand copy of the "manufacturing" instructions for that protein, called messenger RNA (mRNA). This mRNA is called the *sense* strand because when it is read it directs the assembly of the correct amino acids for the synthesis of a protein. The complementary strand of DNA is called the *antisense* strand. By knowing the nucleotide sequence of either of these strands, antisense molecules can be synthesized and used as therapeutic agents to block the synthesis of a particular defective protein. Genasense and MG98 are two antisense compounds currently investigated in

PRNewsFoto

clinical trials for patients with chronic lymphocytic leukemia, advanced melanoma, or a variety of solid tumors.

TELOMERASE BLOCKERS. Normal actively dividing cells pass through a limited number of population doublings before built-in mechanisms halt further cell division. With each division cycle, the DNA segments capping the ends of chromosomes, called telomeres, shorten a bit. At some threshold length, the shortened telomeres initiate a process that prevents the cell from dividing further. This process is circumvented in most cancer cells by activation of the enzyme, telomerase. This enzyme preserves the length of telomeres and allows the cancer cell to continue uncontrolled proliferation. Theoretically, if telomerase activity could be neutralized in cancer cells, telomeres would progressively shorten, causing the cells to stop dividing or to lead them to crisis and death. Researchers have recently produced vaccines against telomerase and found them to be effective in slowing the growth of skin, breast, and bladder tumors in mice.

MORE HOPE FOR TOMORROW

The stunning advances in molecular genetics and the anticipated contributions of proteomics research suggests that researchers are on the threshold of significantly impacting the diagnosis and management of cancer in this country. Technologies will continue to improve on several fronts increasing the ability to screen patients for disease, improving diagnosis, and providing patient-tailored programs of therapy according to their unique molecular fingerprints. Although much work remains to be done, the medical community is better poised than ever to make substantial advances on this adversary. Ultimately, it is the patients and their families that will benefit from this collective effort.

PROVOCATIONS...

Will a belief that a cure is in sight bring back bad habits like smoking?

Will 2050 usher in the first cancerless generation?

—Mark F. Seifert

Medicines in development for cancer*

type of cancer	
Bladder	9
Brain	26
Breast	59
Cervical	10
Colon	55
Head/Neck	27
Kidney	25
Leukemia	39
Liver	13
Lung	68
Lymphoma	32
Multipl e Myeloma	17
Neuroblastoma	3
Ovarian	34
Pancreatic	26
Prostate	52
Sarcoma	9
Skin	52
Solid tumor s	75
Stomach	14
Related conditions	38
Other types	14
Unspecified types	25

*Some medicines are listed in more than one category

Graphic by Nigel Holmes

WANT MORE?

AMERICAN CANCER SOCIETY
www.cancer.org

CANCER CARE, INC.
www.cancercare.org

CANCERLINKS.ORG
www.cancerlinks.org

CANCERNET
www.cancernet.nci.nih.gov

NATIONAL CANCER INSTITUTE
www.cancer.gov

CHILDREN'S CANCER GROUP
www.nccf.org

ONCOLINK OF UNIVERSITY OF PENNSYLVANIA
www.oncolink.com

ONCOLOGYCHANNEL
www.oncologychannel.com

ONCOLOGY.COM
www.oncology.com

THE CANCER INFORMATION NETWORK
www.thecancer.info

WOMEN'S CANCER NETWORK
www.wcn.org

CANCER SURVIVORS' NETWORK
www.cancer.org

Telemedicine...
Your Heart Surgeon's Ready to Operate Online

Doctors used to make house calls, and some still criticize them for abandoning the practice. If medical technology proceeds apace, doctors may soon not bother showing up at the hospital either. Will we see a future in which doctors telecommute to the office? Will ads for future long-distance medical technologies boast that surgeons will be able to operate in their undies (as ads for teleconferencing tools tease with today)? This may be exaggeration for effect, but "telemedicine" will obviously play a huge role in our medical future, offering patients in any location access to medical information, expertise, and cutting-edge procedures.

Image courtesy of NASA/JPL/Caltech

TELE WHAT?

Telemedicine is a catchall term for any form of clinical medicine (from doctor consults to heart surgery) performed remotely via telecommunictions technologies. Another term, *telehealth*, covers the nonclinical aspects of wired healthcare delivery, such as ordering drugs over a computer, accessing online patient information, participating in support groups, etc. The medical profession has, in fact, gone "tele-" crazy, with

WIRELESS MEDICAL DIAGNOSIS

Wireless technologies are revolutionizing communications, and the field of medicine is no exception. If tests being conducted at Brooke Army Medical Center at Fort Sam Houston, Texas, are any indication, in the future, the hospital may know all about your condition before you're even wheeled out of the ambulance. Doctors from the Center and engineers at the Southwest Research Institute in San Antonio recently transmitted a patient's echocardiogram (ECG) results, gathered with two handheld scanners, from an ambulance 20 miles from the hospital. Doctors at the hospital were even able to help direct the examination to make sure they got the data they needed. In the future, a whole series of tests could be performed by wireless smart devices and then sent to the hospital in advance of your arrival. Or you may not even have to finish the trip: "You can take Mr. Branwyn back home, it's just another of his infamous anxiety attacks."

nearly every field of medicine getting tele-prefixed (teleradiology, teledermatology, telepathology, and even the oxymoronic tele-homecare).

Not surprisingly, the two arenas from which telemedicine first emerged were the military and space travel. These disciplines continue to lead innovations in the field, but delivery of medical expertise to remote civilian locations has become the most common nongovernmental application. Just having an Internet-connected computer and a video camera in an otherwise remote corner of the world can be a lifesaver, bringing desperately needed medical attention across the wire. In India, for example, in the southern state of Tamil Nadu, a series of Internet kiosks has been set up. Villagers having eye troubles can come, explain their symptoms, have photos taken of their eyes, and then have the results emailed to doctors at India's prestigious Aravind Eye Hospital. The Madras Indian Institute of Technology has installed 30 such kiosks so far and plans on placing them throughout rural Indian within 10 years. The kiosks can also be used for nonmedical purposes, such as getting farming advice or applying for government loans.

VIRTUAL COLLABORATIVE CLINICS

Having one doctor on the line in a medical emergency is one thing, but how about a whole team of far-flung physicians? This is the idea behind virtual collaborative clinics. Being developed for NASA as a way of dealing with emergencies in space (e.g., on the International Space Station or a Mars mission), a virtual collaborative clinic will bring the best minds in medicine together, almost instantaneously, to discuss treatment options and view patient information and interactive 3D models of their body. A treatment course can then be collaboratively arrived at and beamed back to caregivers in space. By the time a Mars mission has touched down on the red planet, that caregiver will likely be a robot capable of doing everything from pinning fractures to performing complex surgery.

SMART DEVICES

Another development in space telemedicine that should eventually end up back on Earth is the medical smart device. Common medical testing, monitoring, and treatment devices such as IV pumps, ventilators, and vital sign monitors are being developed at Wyle Laboratories in Houston, Texas. These devices will wirelessly connect to onboard computers, which will not only record data, but will be able to offer a treatment plan via diagnostic software. There is already a semi-smart gadget on the consumer market, called the GlucoWatch®, which allows diabetics to track their blood sugar via a wrist-borne monitor and then download accumulated

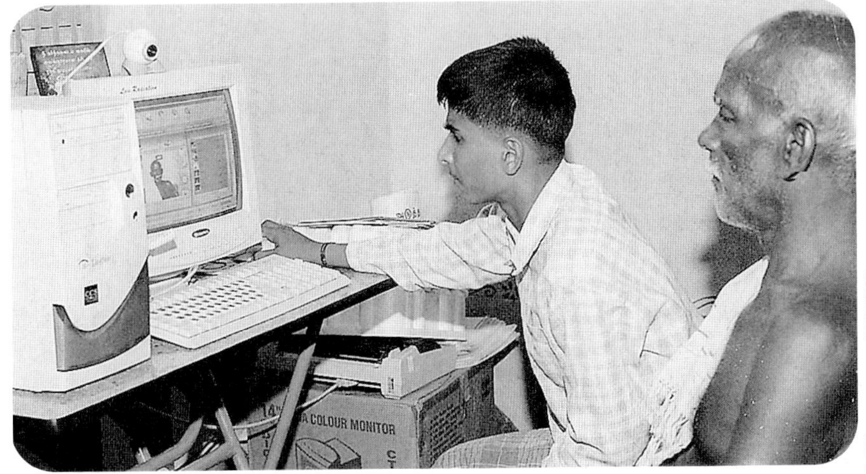

EYE "KIOSKS." *These allow doctors in India to interview and examine patients in remote villages.*

Photo by K. Ganesan, courtesy of THE HINDU

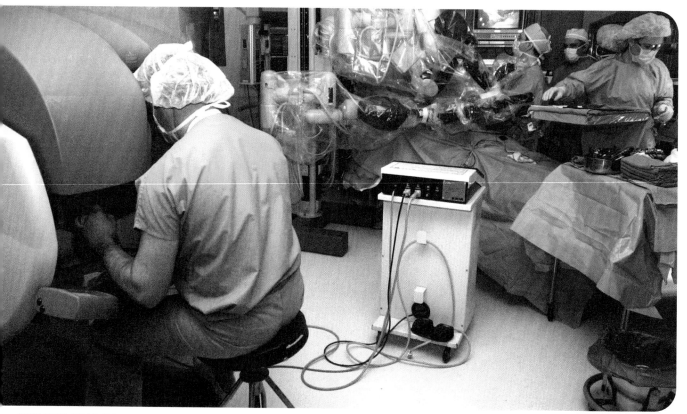

ROBOTIC GALL BLADDER SURGERY. *Dr. Andrew Boyarsky, seated left, uses a robotic surgery device called da Vinci Surgical System to manipulate robotic arms during a gall bladder operation about 10 feet away (in background) at Robert Wood Johnson University Hospital in New Brunswick, New Jersey. The machine allows the surgeon to do laproscopic surgery using robotic arms while looking at a three-dimensional image from cameras inserted into the patient's abdomen.*
TELESURGERY FROM 700 MILES. *Dr. Louis Kavoussi uses a remote-controlled robot camera to direct surgeons operating on a patient 700 miles away at the Johns Hopkins Bayview Medical Center in Baltimore.*

data to their PCs for analysis and emailing to their doctors.

TELESURGERY

The crowning achievement of telemedicine is, of course, surgery, the ability to cut into, repair, and then close up a human body regardless of whether the patient and surgeon are in the same room, the same state, the same country, or even on the same planet. In the last few years, remarkable developments have occurred in the field. In September 2001, a 68-year-old woman in Strasbourg, France had her gall bladder removed by surgeons operating 4,000 miles away, in New York. It was the first time that a complete remote operation of

Associated Press · Associated Press

THE STEADY HAND OF THE ROBOSURGEON

Telesurgery doesn't have to mean over great distances. Minimally invasive surgery is a type of in-the-same-room telemedicine that relies on cameras and remote-controlled instruments to operate inside the body. Researchers are now testing tiny robot surgeon hands that can even perform heart operations. The mechanical hands are steadier than human ones and require only a tiny incision, greatly reducing recovery times and the risk of infection. So far, the robo-hands have only been tested on dogs.

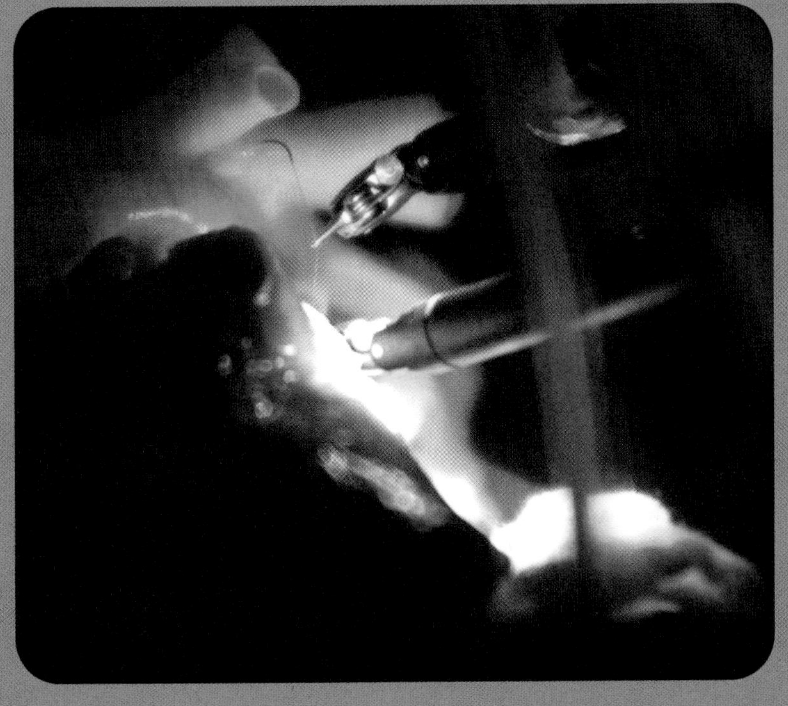

Associated Press

this magnitude (and distance) had occurred. One of the biggest impediments to telesurgery has been telecom time delay. In this case, the problem was overcome by a high-speed fiber-optic connection provide by France Telecom, which reduced lag time to an unnoticeable 150 milliseconds. Jacques Marescaux, who performed the operation, described it as the beginning of the third revolution in high-tech surgery, the first being camera-guided minimally invasive surgery (MIS), the second being computer-assisted surgery.

One looming roadblock on the telemedical superhighway is the insurance business. Insurers are not yet convinced that telemedicine will save them money. Since so much medical development money flows in the direction in which insurance companies point the funnel, telemedicine will have to prove its effectiveness before it'll get insurers' support (thus creating a chicken-and-egg problem). The issue of access also looms large. If, suddenly, high-quality, high-tech medicine can be delivered to any corner of the globe, which corners get served and which are left wanting care will be shown in even starker relief than they are today. These impediments aside, nearly everyone agrees that telemedicine will one day become so commonplace that "tele" will finally be unceremoniously excised from our vocabulary.

PROVOCATIONS...

How will telemedicine affect a doctor's "bedside manner"? Should they get media training?

Will telemedicine embrace Eastern medicine? Would you accept accupunture from a robotic arm?

Will the doctor's "waiting room" be in a chat room?

—Gareth Branwyn

WANT MORE?

TELEMEDICINE INFORMATION EXCHANGE
http://tie.telemed.org

INDIAN INST. OF TECHNOLOGY
www.iitm.ac.in/first.shtml

VIRTUAL COLLABORATIVE CLINIC
http://hsc.unm.edu/vcc

WYLE LABORATORIES
www.wylelabs.com

MIT TELESURGERY PROJECT
web.mit.edu/hmsl/www/Telesurgery

GLUCOWATCH
www.glucowatch.com

MEDICAL ROBOTICS GROUP – UC BERKELEY
www.robotics.eecs.berkeley.edu/medical

Body Modification
Piercings, Tattoos, and Horns, Oh My!

THE LIFESTYLE OF THE FUTURE *will encompass advances in personal care, along with cosmetic surgery and body modification. Trivial? Perhaps. However, they are the stuff of everyday life. We have machines for puffing up breasts, jackhammering cellulite, and suctioning penises. Strange formulations are created for hair, nails, soaks, spas, facials, and wraps; new razors and lasers appear and disappear like magic, but only a few items actually deliver the goods.*

SURVIVAL OF THE PRETTIEST?

Nancy Etcoff suggested in *Survival of the Prettiest: The Science of Beauty* (1999) that physical attractiveness has to do more with seeking signs of health and longevity in a mate, and media isn't to blame for what we seek. She popularized the notion of "ideal ratio," which is the ratio of hip and waist in a woman. The ratio, .7, is believed to signify a woman's childbearing ability. Too little a ratio suggests not enough fat — vital stored energy that is used during a pregnancy. Too much, and the woman is probably not as healthy as she could be.

On one reading, physical attractiveness is largely a sign of mate value, an assessment with ancient evolutionary roots. Researchers hypothesize that when humans were subject to varying periods of famine and plenty, the most reproductively successful females were the ones who were able to store surplus energy as fat. The extra fat, stored on the body, breasts, and buttocks, is said therefore to be attractive to males. The "waist-to-hip ratio," or WHR, is calculated by computing a ratio of the circumference of the waist to the circumference of the hips. The WHR for healthy, pre-menopausal women is generally between 0.67 and 0.80, but for men it is usually between 0.85 and 0.95. WHR has been shown to be a reliable morphological indicator of the levels of sex hormones, and also the risk of major diseases, reproductive potential, and premature mortality.

Research has also shown that body form, especially symmetry, conveys a subconscious message of fitness and initiates attraction. The theory goes that asymmetrical features give clues to underlying genetic problems, thus yielding less viable offspring. Such symmetry is used "as a means of ascertaining the stress susceptibility of developmental regulatory mechanisms"—in other words, organisms that maintain symmetrical features under environmental stresses also maintain healthy, unaffected genes. Symmetry is simply a way for an organism, including a human, to advertise that genetic fitness.

RADICAL SELF-EXPRESSION

Centuries before the first nose job, humans used the body as a "sacred canvas" for expressing tribal allegiance, religious devotion, or individual accomplishment. People currently sport surgically implanted horns, homemade subcutaneous insertions, and permanent fangs, in addition to the more common tattoos, piercings, brandings, stretchings, and scarifications.

Dr. Joe Rosen of Dartmouth Medical Center, a former scientific advisor to NASA, has infamously gone on record to say that within five years, people will be able to feel sensation in their surgically attached wings — though they won't be ready to take flight. Dr. Brian Kinney considers this possibility "speculative," but agrees with its spirit. "We need evolution," he says of cosmetic surgery's advances, but "we need revolution too." He notes that there may be topical lotions for staining the skin for several months, and not just in shades of tan: "We can have different colored hair, why not different colored skin?"

Sydney Biddle Barrows, author of the upcoming *Getting a Little Work Done*, extols the virtues of Botox, calling it a "gateway procedure" for new cosmetic surgery patients. By selectively paralyzing muscles, Botulinum Toxin smoothes lines. Off-label uses have blossomed, from patients and friends getting together for "Botox parties" to doctors treating excessive sweating with injections of this biological toxin.

But Dr. Brian Kinney, a Clinical Asst. Professor of Plastic Surgery at the University of Southern California who also holds degrees in engineering from MIT, worries what people's faces will look like after 10 years of regular paralysis: They could sag more or be less expressive. Botox is "not the final answer," and Kinney believes it could be outmoded by 2007. It may be replaced by more advanced injectibles: Chondroitin, hyaluronic acid (present in Restylane), elastin, collagen, and other materials present in normal cells will likely be recombined within the next decade, closely mimicking the spaces between natural cells, producing a more natural appearance.

In a scenario reminiscent of *Fight Club*, researchers have also come up with a controversial new use for the discarded fat from liposuction patients. The collagen-rich material contains each patient's own stem cells, which could be "banked" for the present and then used later to regenerate body parts or anti-aging materials. Stem-cell research continues to face ethical controversy, but having the cells donated to and by the self-same patient may overcome some concerns.

Australian researchers at the Bernard O'Brien Institute of Microsurgery in Melbourne have already grown breast and fat tissue in animals; they hope that women will be able to grow their own false breasts in the future, instead of using implants. Difficulties remain because fat frequently calcifies or disappears from the spot where it was originally placed to enhance the figure.

We're likely to see more tissue glues such as "fibrin sealant" and biological sugars, which minimize the number of sutures required to close a wound. Endoscopic surgery will likely increase in popularity; minimally invasive, it allows the surgeon to see inside the body via a small camera. And the French cosmetic company Sederma hopes to unveil a smart sunscreen using bacteria harvested from hydrothermal vents; Thermus thermophilus screens out UV damage even in high temperatures.

Nanotechnology even may have an application in the form of capsules that could burrow into a certain tissue area, either preprogrammed or on "remote control." These could release tissue factors under some radio-controlled feedback, perhaps from inside of a pod that could then migrate to another area of the body and release more chemicals to restore the skin's elasticity or change its look. For now, though, moderate advances in surgical and healing techniques are most likely to affect cosmetic procedures.

PROVOCATIONS...

Will we have to teach children how to make intelligent body modification choices?

Will schools have body modification codes as well as dress codes?

— Tiffany Lee Brown

WANT MORE?

AMERICAN SOCIETY OF PLASTIC SURGEONS (ASPS)
www.plasticsurgery.org

BOTOX™
www.botox.com

SURGEON AND SAFARI
www.surgeon-and-safari.co.za

SOUNDRELIEF STEM THERAPY
www.soundrelief.com

SEDERMA COSMETICS
www.sederma.fr

RESTYLANE
www.restylane.com

Artificial Organs...

Replaceable You, Part I: Engineering Mechanical Body Parts

IN THE EARLY 1980S, IT SEEMED LIKE EVERY paper, newsweekly, and pop science magazine was showing off a graphic depicting the coming cyborg body, with callouts to current and coming-soon bionic body parts. The diagrams looked impressive at the time, with metal hips and knees, cochlear hearing implants, artificial hearts, then-state-of-the-art prosthetic limbs, and a few bits of far-future tech like neural implants and bionic eyes. Today's body blueprint is far more impressive, with enough hardware and lab-grown parts to cover much of the body's real estate. A lot of the recent media attention has focused on the more cutting-edge realm of tissue engineering, but there is plenty of life-extending innovation occuring among those taking a more mechanical approach to body repair.

On April 16, 2002, Tom Christerson stepped from the front door of Jewish Hospital in Central City, Kentucky, to become the first human ever to reenter the real world equipped with an artificial heart. Christerson's much-publicized walk to his car marked the beginning of a new era in artificial organs. The miracle hardware he sports is an AbioCor™ Implantable Replacement Heart from AbioMed, Inc. The AbioCor is the culmination of all that scientists have learned about heart machinery since the Jarvik-7 trials in the early 1980s. The AbioMed heart features such 21st-century innovations as Angioflex, an astoundingly strong and flexible artificial heart material; internal motors and microprocessors (eliminating an external control console); and a portable external battery pack that transfers power through the skin, eliminating the risk of infection at the

REPLACEMENT HEART. *The Abi Cor mechanical heart from AbioMed, Inc.*

Clockwise from top left: Image courtesy Abiomed; Jim Leftwich

connection site. Mr. Christerson also has had his car wired so that it can power his heart as he drives. Five patients have been outfitted with the AbioCor to date (four are still with us), with a total of 15 implants slated for the first set of trials. If all goes well, and the FDA approves the AbioCor, thousands could be walking around with mechanical tickers within a decade.

Unlike the heart and the kidneys, a damaged liver can actually repair itself, if given the chance. Unfortunately, the body doesn't have the luxury of offering the liver downtime – enter high technology. Liver-assist devices like the Alin Foundation's Bio-Artificial Liver can give a patient's liver time to repair. The innovative external device uses animal liver cells but incorporates a synthetic membrane that keeps the patient's blood and the animal cells separate (eliminating the risk of rejection) while detoxifying the patient's blood. Recent experiments with fabricating capillary networks using computer chip-making machinery hold out the hope of constructing a fully implantable bio-artificial liver. The Alin Foundation also has developed a bio-artificial pancreas using a similar membrane-separated animal and human cell design – in this case, in an implantable substitute for the natural pancreas.

Lung transplantation, while extraordinarily difficult, has become a viable surgical option, with about 1,000 procedures performed each year. But like all organ transplants, donors are hard to come by and rejection is common. Eventually, artificial lungs may be the answer, but the impediments are great. One recent hopeful development is the University of Pittsburgh Medical Center Artificial Lung Laboratory's Intravenous Membrane Oxygenator (IMO). The device, which has been tested both in-vitro (externally) and in-vivo (internally), is an assistive device that can help patients with temporary respiratory failure or those awaiting lung transplantation. Eventually, scientists hope to use a "bio-hybrid" approach (combining tissue and machinery) to build a blood-air gas exchange system that exactly duplicates human lung function.

PROVOCATIONS...

Will we outsource our biological clock? Could replacement organs give us new senses (e.g., night vision, sonar)?

– Gareth Branwyn

DEXTRA

Up until now, artificial arms and hands could do little more than grasp and hold. William Craelius, Associate Professor of Biomedical Engineering at Rutgers University, hopes to change that. His "Dextra" hand is able to capture electrical signals generated by existing muscles and tendons and transmit them to a computer that operates the artificial hands and fingers. Craelius and his students believe Dextra even could allow its owner to perform such delicate tasks as typing or playing the piano.

LANGER LAB

Dr. Robert Langer is a true Renaissance man. He's a mathematician, a chemist, and an engineer. He and his star team at MIT's Langer Lab have had 380 patents issued (or pending) and have published some 700 scientific papers. You can't poke your head into too many areas of biomechanical and tissue engineering without bumping into the Langer Lab's far-reaching influence. Dr. Langer's almost casual brilliance and his endless enthusiasm have attracted some of the brightest young minds in biotechnology and related fields. One of the lab's most groundbreaking advances involves research into biodegradable polymer dissolve rates, which have been used to create polymer-based brain tumor drug delivery implants (which deliver the tumor drugs, at a controlled rate, right to the tumor site).

WANT MORE?

AMERICAN SOCIETY FOR ARTIFICIAL INTERNAL ORGANS
www.asaio.com

ABIOMED
www.abiomed.com

ARTIFICIAL HEART PROJECT
www.heartpioneers.com

ALIN FOUNDATION
www.alinfoundation.com

UNIV. OF PITT. MEDICAL CENTER ARTIFICIAL LUNG LABORATORY
www.pitt.edu/~wfedersp/alhtml.htm

LANGER LAB
http://web.mit.edu/cheme/langerlab

RUTGERS UNIVERSITY DEPT. OF BIOMEDICAL ENGINEERING
http://biomedical.rutgers.edu

2000 2005 2010 2015 2020

risks  rewards 

Artifical Organs...

Replaceable You, Part II: Growing Organic Tissue in the Lab

THERE ARE PROBABLY few medical advances that sound more like science fiction than the idea of vat-grown human organs. Certainly a liver, a heart, a kidney, or a lung are far too complicated, too precious to be cooked up in a pot like some Sunday stew? Increasingly, the answer is proving to be "No." In the last decade, in university biotechnology departments, hospital labs, and corporate R&D facilities throughout the world astonishing advances have been made in the science of "tissue engineering," the growing of human tissue, even entire organs. Some organs, such as skin, have become so commonplace (with FDA approval) that they have their own brand names, logos, and package designs and are sold by companies with names like Organogenesis, Advanced Tissue Sciences, and LifeCell. Skin manufacturing has become so mundane to Michael Ehrenreich of Techvest, an investment firm that tracks the biotech sector, that he has been quoted as saying "Skin. Big deal. It's proof of concept."

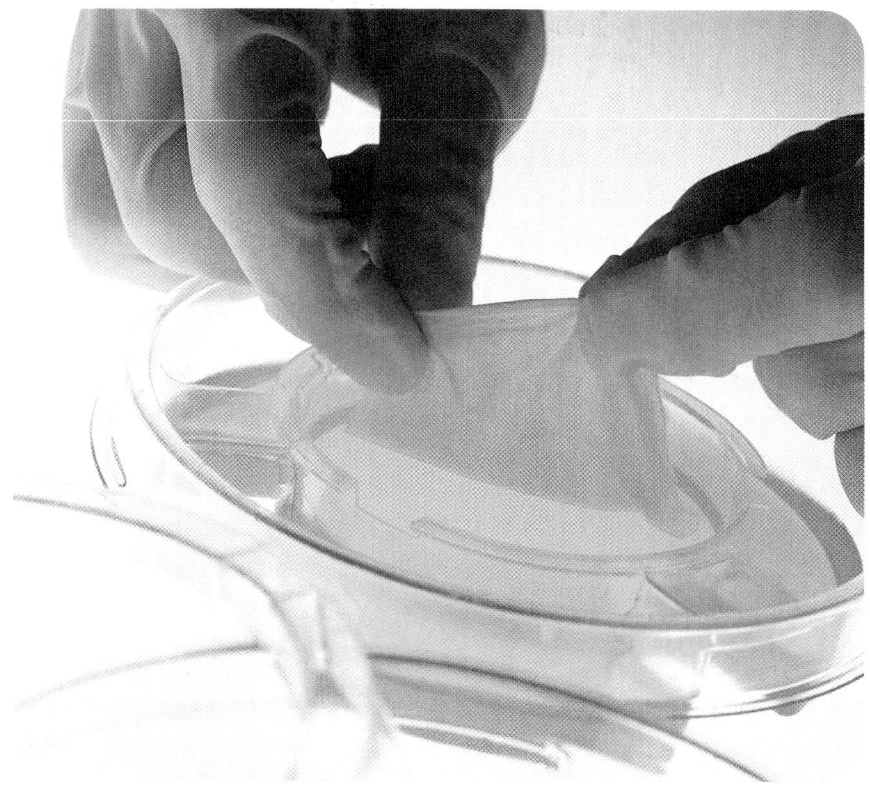

FAKE SKIN. *Attached Organogenesis' Apligraf® cellular, bi-layered skin substitute is the only mass-manufactured product containing living human cells to gain FDA approval. Here, Apligraf is shown being lifted from the dish in which it is shipped. The pink-orange material remaining in the dish is media (food).*

Photo courtesy of Organogenesis, Inc.

And proof of concept it is. The process for growing more complex organs starts with the same basic procedures. A biodegradable "scaffolding" is constructed in the shape of the organ, and appropriate tissue cultures are introduced (often taken from the organ's eventual recipient). The concoction is kept at the proper temperature and given the right nutrients in a device called a *bioreactor*. If all goes well, a shiny new human body part comes out of the reactor when the process is complete.

TOTAL BODY TRANSPLANTS

It sounds like something from a bad '50s horror film, but in the 1970s, Dr. Robert White of Case Western Reserve University transplanted a rhesus monkey head onto a different body. The monkey lived for hours afterwards and was able to see, hear, and eat, though there was no connection made to the body's spinal column. Dr. White believes that similar operations on humans could be possible within decades. The big stumbling block is spinal regeneration. An experiment conducted at the Massachusetts Medical Center several years ago may point to a solution. Researchers were able to remove part of a rat's spinal column and replace it with a tissue-engineered component that eventually restored the animal's motor function. Not surprisingly, all of this gives much of the public, and many health professionals, the willies. The Case Western Web site doesn't even mention Dr. White's controversial work.

WHEN PIGS FLY

While we wait for the organ factory to show up at our local strip mall, there's another organic alternative, and his name is Porky. Pigs are surprisingly similar to us genetically, and they are readily available. The problem with cross-species transplantation of organs (known as "xeno-transplantation") is a little something called "hyperacute or catastrophic rejection" — that is, your body says: "Hey, this ain't mine!" and attacks the organ. To combat this, biotech researchers are working on a number of schemes to fool the body into thinking that the pig parts are your own, which is being accomplished by immune repression or by tweaking the pig genes that trigger rejection in the first place. One scheme even calls for "introducing" the donor pig's and human recipient's cells to each other over a period of time leading up to the transplant so that each body's immune system treats the other as friend, not foe. If successful, this technique would save the recipient from a lifetime of troublesome (and expensive) anti-rejection drugs.

That's the theory anyway. Skin is relatively easy because it doesn't have so many differing cell types and there's no vascular system with which to contend. Even if it's not your own skin, tissue rejection is not a problem. With something like a liver or a heart, blood is everything. A lot of research is currently being done to find ways of engineering (or growing) blood vessels. Researchers are trying many innovative techniques. One group, headed by renowned tissue pioneer Joseph Vacanti at Mass General, is using computer chip fabrication techniques (which already deal in microns) to fabricate polymer scaffolding that will support the growth of capillary networks. It's conceivable that if such a method proved successful, a liver could be constructed by stacking thousands of layers of these capillary scaffolds, seeded with the appropriate blood and liver cells. Until there's a breakthrough like this, building large vascular organs will be impossible.

Your future replacement parts could start out life as a computer printout! A team at MIT has used a rapid prototyping machine (a.k.a. a "3D printer") to fabricate better tissue scaffolding. Usually used for etching out three-dimensional objects from computer-based designs, bio-engineer Linda Griffith and her colleagues have been using the machine to more precisely engineer the scaffolding using polymer powders. Besides giving tissue scientists more control over scaffolding construction, they also allow the integration of chemicals into the powders that "tell" the tissue cells where they're supposed to go.

It is these ingenious advances, and many more like them, that make researchers optimistic that we'll see many lab-grown parts (valves, ventricles, pancreatic islets, even bladders) within a decade, livers and hearts in two decades, and organs as complex as lungs by mid-century.

PROVOCATIONS...

Will alcohol have an extra "liver tax"?

Will we augment rather than replace our organs? Two livers? Two hearts?

Will we have Olympic organ contests?

Will this be the end of traditional breast implants?

—Gareth Branwyn

WANT MORE?

TISSUE ENGINEERING WEB WATCH
www-2.cs.cmu.edu/~webwatch

TISSUE ENGINEERING LAB AT MASS GENERAL
www.mgh.harvard.edu/depts/tissue/index.html

BIOTECHNOLOGY PROCESS ENGINEERING CENTER
http://web.mit.edu/bpec/index.html

ADVANCED TISSUE SCIENCES
www.advancedtissue.com

THE TISSUE CULTURE & ART PROJECT
www.tca.uwa.edu.au

2000 2005 2010 2015 2020

risks  rewards 

Cyborgs... Are We Assimilated Yet?

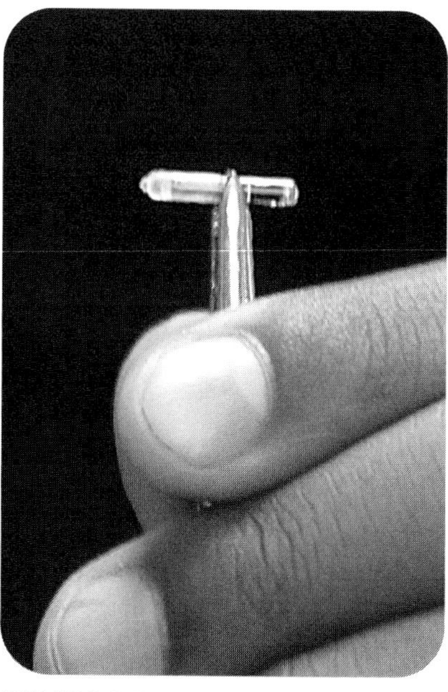

CYBORG 2.0 IMPLANT. *Professor Kevin Warwick shows off the external interface to his experimental implant (left).* **VERICHIP.** *About the size of a bloated grain of rice, the Verichip is the brainchild of Applied Digital Solutions.*

MICROELECTRODE ARRAY. *The tiny array implanted in Professor Kevin Warwick's forearm.*

Clockwise from top left: Image courtesy of Kevin Warwick–Wide World Photos–Image courtesy of Kevin Warwick

NIGHTLY, THE NEWS BRINGS STORIES OF ADVANCES IN *bionic eyes, plastic muscles, computer-brain interfaces, lab-grown human tissue, and other modern medical marvels. Artificial limbs and joints, cochlear implants (to restore hearing), artificial organs, and other forms of major body repair have become almost routine, with millions of successful procedures performed each year. Where this starts to get interesting (and troubling to some), is when we think about a swiftly approaching future, a cyborg (for "cybernetic organism") future, in which the sheer volume of technology starts to overwhelm our biology. Will a time come in which, rather than simply going in for replacement parts, we elect to* augment ourselves in true *Six Million Dollar Man* fashion, to make ourselves stronger, faster, better? For cyborg wannabes like the Jacobs family and Professor Kevin Warwick of Reading University that time has already come.

I'VE GOT YOU UNDER MY SKIN

Some might say that it starts with the soft stuff (as in: "the first implant's free") and then moves on to the hard. The Jacobs family of Florida made headlines in May 2002 when all three members, father Jeff, mother Leslie, and 14-year-old son Derek had computer ID chips implanted in their arms. The VeriChip from Applied Digital Solutions of Palm Beach, Florida, is about the size of a bloated grain of rice. Jeff is severely disabled and hopes that the chip could save valuable time, maybe even his life, in an emergency. Leslie and Derek got theirs as a show of support. Right now, the VeriChip is little more than a subcutaneous MedicAlert bracelet, containing a name, an emergency phone number, and a list of medical conditions, all of which are accessed by a special handheld scanner. ADS hopes to eventually get FDA approval on a next-generation chip that could contain a full medical history and insurance information (or at least the encrypted codes to access this data over a secure computer network). The VeriChip is also being used currently to help authorities identify Alzheimer's patients who become lost and disoriented.

And then there's Professor Kevin Warwick of Reading University in the U.K. He too started off with a simple subcutaneous chip, in this case, one that communicated his location to sensors throughout the hallways and offices of the Department of Cybernetics where he teaches. He has now "upgraded" to what he's dubbed Cyborg 2.0, a much more serious (and dangerous) experiment involving a chip array designed to send signals between his nervous system and a computer. No one has ever tried such an interface before or knows what the results might be. Warwick, a frequent face in the world media, plans on trying to "record" sensations (pleasure, pain, drunkenness) to the computer and then play them back to see what (if anything) he'll feel. If it works, Kevin's wife Irena plans to undergo a similar procedure. The couple hopes that the implants, moderated by a computer, will be able to transfer feelings from one of them to the other. Warwick is about to release a book about his past, present, and future experiments called *I, Cyborg*.

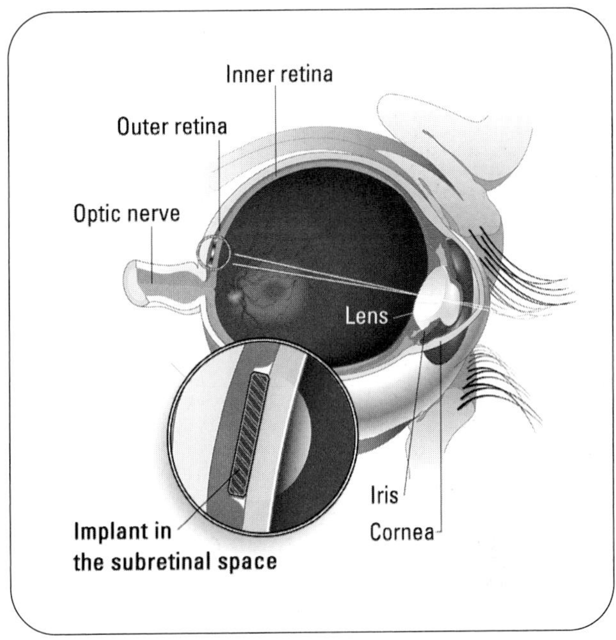

BIONIC EYE. *Developed by Dr. Alan Chow and Vince Chow of Optobionics Corporation, this groundbreaking retinal implant offers hope for those who are sight-impaired.*

Image courtesy of Optobionics Corporation

I SAW THE LIGHT...

Warwick's edgy "neuro-hacking" aside, most scientists take a more cautious approach to "neural prosthetics," or the science of getting information into and out of the nervous system (usually to repair damaged body parts). The tragedy of many cases of blindness, hearing loss, and spinal cord injury is that only a very small link in a chain of bodily systems is damaged. Using electronics to repair that link is what neural prosthetics is all about.

One promising example of such technology is the Artificial Silicon Retina (a.k.a. the "bionic retina"), developed by Dr. Alan Chow and Vince Chow of Optobionics Corporation. So far, the retinal chip has been implanted in six patients during clinical trials. The results are crude but encouraging. Implanted patients have only been able to make out

BORDER ARTIST

The Australian performance artist Stelarc has made a career out of exploring the increasingly permeable membrane between man and machine. In his unflinching desire to get people to question what makes us human and how far we want machines to encroach upon us, he has added a third robotic hand to his body operated by his own EMG signals), sent tiny sculptures into his stomach, let a computer manipulate his body (think inverse motion capture), and strapped himself into a six-legged walking machine. Some find the extremes to which Stelarc is willing to go distasteful, but you can't look at his work without having something to say about it, which is clearly the point.

basic lights and shapes, but when those lights and shapes are your spouse, the Christmas tree, and the house lights in your neighborhood, it's nothing short of miraculous. The bionic retina works by natural light stimulating microscopic-sized solar cells etched onto a microchip that's placed at the back of the retina (in the "subretinal space"). The excited artificial cells stimulate surrounding healthy retinal cells. Other developers are working on schemes that involve camera-equipped glasses that capture images and send them, via radio waves, to an array at the back of the retina, which then stimulates the nerves and generates the images.

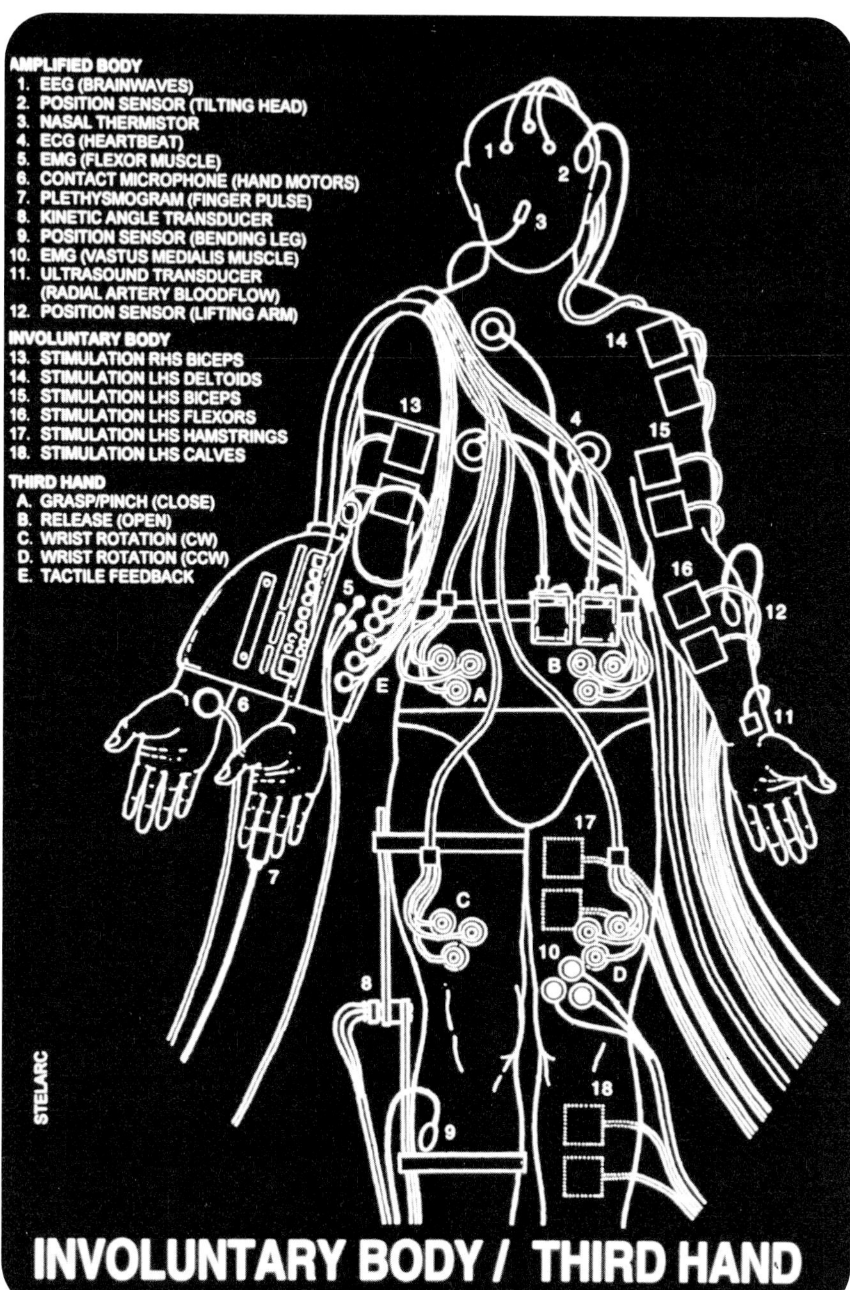

SING THE BODY ELECTRIC. *Amplified processes include brainwaves (EEG), muscles (EMG), pulse (plethysmogram), and bloodflow (doppler flow meter). Other transducers and sensors monitor limb motion and indicate body posture.*

Yokohama, Melbourne 1985 STELARC

Retinal repair is just one area of neural prosthetic research. Labs throughout the world are working on prosthetics to give voice to those who've lost their larynx to cancers, who've lost their sense of balance to inner ear problems, or who've lost the ability to move due to spinal cord injury. All of these researchers look to the success of cochlear implants for inspiration. Introduced in the mid-80s to restore hearing, cochlear implants were

THIRD ARM. *Artificial arm that functions as an addition rather than a prosthetic replacement (right).* **EXOSKELETON.** *A six-legged, pneumatically powered walking machine constructed for the body (below).*

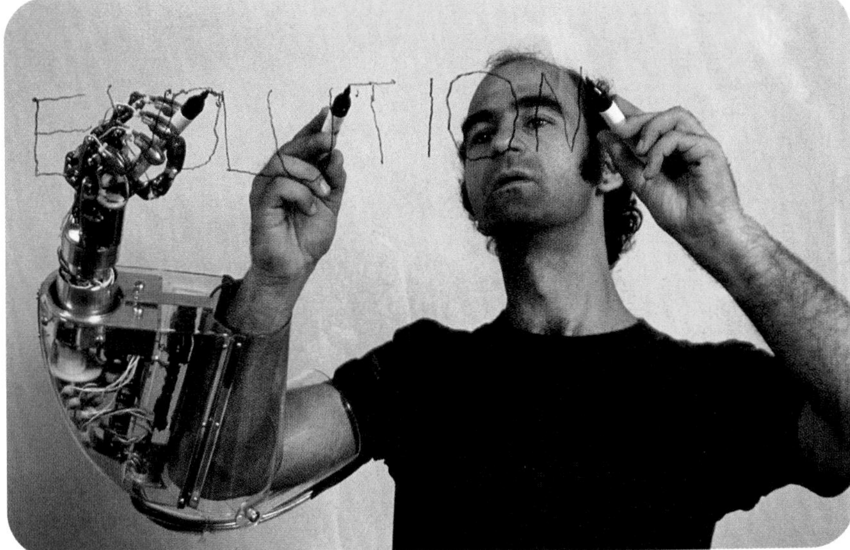

Clockwise from top left: Cyborg Frictions Dumpfzentrale, Bern 1999 Photograph: Dominik Landwehr STELARC-Maki Gallery, Toyko 1982 Photograph: Keisuke Oki STELARC

crude at best, and controversial, as they only improved hearing in 30%-40% of recipients. Today, these devices have become so commonplace and sophisticated that they're approaching the level of normal hearing. Reading accounts from the 1980s of early cochlear implantations, where patients talk about the immense joy they feel over hearing something as simple as a muffled doorbell, one can't help but imagine what wonders the next generation of bionic eye recipients will behold.

PROVOCATIONS...

Will we end paraplegia and quadraplegia in the next 20 years?

Will we invent new sports for augmented athletes?

—Gareth Branwyn

METAPHORICAL BLENDS OF HUMAN AND MACHINE

Although the word cyborg usually evokes futuristic images of sci-fi supermen or bleeding-edge medical technologies, some social scientists, such as the University of California, Santa Cruz's Donna Haraway, argue that we are already composite creatures of biology and technology. Every day it's getting harder to tell where we humans end and where our machines begin. The food we eat is as much a product of modern science, lab-tweaked supercrops, and agribusiness automation as it is of sunshine and Mother Nature. Our bodies are maintained by advanced pharmacology and world-class medicine, Nautilus machines help keep us in peak physical form, lasers correct our vision, scalpels rearrange our bodies, and even the shoes we wear are designed by engineers in a lab to maximize performance and comfort. And daily, without even thinking about it, we grab hold of a mouse to become nodes in a globe-spanning information and communications network where we exchange data between millions of computers and countless other humans who are simultaneously "jacked in" to an ever-expanding cyberspace. Haraway believes that the cyborg is the dominant "ironic political myth" of our time, and rather than being completely alienating, it can serve as a liberating organizing principle. If we think of ourselves as assembled rather than made, we can work harder to build the constructs that we desire rather than relying on what nature, society, and gender have preordained for us. Thinking this way raises all sorts of questions, both personal and political, about who our engineers are and who we want controlling our destiny.

WANT MORE?

PROJECT CYBORG
www.kevinwarwick.com/Info

KEVIN WARWICK WATCH
www.kevinwarwick.org.uk

APPLIED DIGITAL SOLUTIONS
www.adsx.com

OPTOBIONICS CORPORATION
www.optobionics.com

STELARC
www.stelarc.va.com.au

2000 2005 2010 2015 2020

risks  rewards 

Life Extension... LIVE FOREVER, OR DIE TRYING

HUMANS LIVE LONGER NOW THAN THEY EVER HAVE BEFORE. THE BIBLICAL LIFE EXPECTANCY *of threescore years and ten is routinely exceeded in the Western world, and there are now more than 50,000 centarians living in the United States. But of all human appetites, the appetite for life is the most voracious. Once reserved for the realm of literature, the quest for immortality is now the subject of serious scientific research. The research has taken three main paths: changing how we treat the body while it's alive to maintain a higher level of health for longer; making biochemical changes in the body to make it fundamentally less time-sensitive; and preserving the body when it does enter a fatal state, in hope that future generations will find a way to prevent or reverse the fatality.*

Most of the life extension humans have gained so far has come from our increased awareness how the body works and how to correct problems that do occur. Controlling infectious diseases, reducing death in childhood and childbirth, and increasing awareness of safety in our work and everyday lives — factors such as these have extended the average American's life by more than 25 years over the past century.

However, as our lifespan increased, we began to see the true toll that living takes on the body. Heart disease, cancer, and diabetes have emerged as significant health problems largely because more people are living to the age when these diseases begin to manifest themselves. Modern medicine has increasingly focused on lifestyle changes as the way to postpone this type of death. The Life Extension Foundation believes that "consumption of certain foods, food extracts, hormones, or drugs will help to prevent common diseases that are associated with normal aging" and has made a business out of providing its members with access to these substances and the research that identifies them. The CRON (Caloric Restriction with Optimum Nutrition) movement advocates a highly reduced calorie diet as the key to a longer life, a position substantiated by findings from the Biosphere 2 project. Research on these topics is serious, promising, and ongoing.

A more technical approach to life extension targets the body's constituent cells and attempts to extend their lifespans. The vast majority of the body's cells have the ability to divide only a limited number of times — a number known as the Hayflick limit. When enough of a body's cells reach this limit, the body itself will die. However, some cells have no Hayflick limit — stem cells, cancer cells, and human egg and sperm cells. These cells can divide an unlimited number of times, as long as their host is still alive. The difference between these two types of cells is thought to lie in their telomeres — proteins at the end of chromosomes that keep the chromosomes from sticking to themselves or other chromosomes. Each time a cell divides, its chromosomes' telomeres shrink slightly, until the cell is no longer capable of division. Researchers at the University of Texas Southwest Medical center have found that an enzyme — telomerase — is responsible for building new telomeres. By blocking this enzyme, they have been able to stop the growth of cancer cells; conversely, activating telomerase should make normal cells immortal. Practical tests are expected within the next 5 years.

Until our cells are immortal, our bodies will still eventually stop working. This may not be the end of our lives, however, if what proponents of human cryogenics believe is true. Cryogenic researchers and practitioners believe that if a body is deep-frozen shortly after it has stopped functioning, it can someday be revived and whatever caused it to stop functioning can be repaired. Of course, the process of bringing a body to –320°F will itself cause some damage — cracking of the tissues occurs at about –126°F. Cryogenic proponents believe that nanotechnology could be developed to repair this structural damage during the thawing process. Cryogenic companies establish trust funds to provide for the maintenance and revivication of their customers, and they do provide the option of freezing only one's head; however, they have not yet attempted to revive a frozen body. Many rumors to the contrary, Walt Disney's head is not believed to have been placed in cryostasis.

NANOBACTERIA AND AGING

Discovered by Nobel-nominated medical researchers Olavi Kajander and Neva Ciftcioglu in 1988, nanobacterium sanguineum are the world's smallest known self-replicating bacteria. These miniscule organisms — at 20–200 nanometers, only 1/1000 the size of regular bacteria — pass through any tissue with impunity, colonizing every part of our bodies.

Researchers suspect nanobacteria's calcified structures slowly build up in our bodies all our lives, causing "slow-down" degenerations and full-blown diseases now considered part of "normal aging" — from clogging arteries, heart attacks, and chunks of loose plaque causing stroke, to age spots, derm disorders, cataracts, glaucoma, arthritis, periodontal, kidney stones, PKD, multiple sclerosis, ALS, and Alzheimer's.

The identification of nanobacteria's role in age-related diseases holds the hope of revolutionary treatments and life extension. Dr. Gary Mezo at NanobacLabs is developing just such a treatment, NanobacTX. While still in clinical trials, this treatment appears to remove calcified nanobacterial plaque body-wide, causing a dramatic reversal of age-related diseases.

PROVOCATIONS...

Will longer lives mean older leaders? Would this be better or worse? How will having great-great grandparents around affect our notion of family?

—Bill Kaszubski

WANT MORE?

LIFE EXTENSION FOUNDATION
www.lef.org

CALORIC RESTRICTION
www.walford.com

HOME TO IMMORTALS
www.bjklein.com

FOUNDATION FOR INFINITE SURVIVAL
www.fis.org

TELOMERES INFORMATION
www.infoaging.org/b-tel-home.html

ALCOR
www.alcor.com

HOLLYWOOD FOREVER CEMETERY
www.forevernetwork.com

Cryonics... Timeship to the Future

SUSPENDED IN CAPSULES *under a layer of liquid nitrogen, 90 people are waiting for the future. Even though there is a good chance that they've done nothing more than turn themselves into human icicles, there are several hundred other people ready to join them. If they're right, however, they just might end up with immortality. Or, at least, a vastly expanded lifespan. This is cryonics, the art and edge science of freezing humans at the moment of death in hopes of reviving them sometime in the future. When in the future? That's anyone's guess.*

Clockwise from top left: Photo by Media Architects/Alcor. Photo by Media Architects/Alcor

HUMAN ICICLES. *Alcor's cryonic suspension chambers, or "dewars." Filled with liquid nitrogen, they cool an entire body — or just a person's head — to −320° Fahrenheit.*

The seeds of what would become cryonics were planted in 1940 by British biologist Basil Luyet, but they didn't bear fruit until the 1964 publication of *The Prospect of Immortality*, by physics professor Robert Ettinger. Ettinger's book proposed that humans could be frozen after legal death and bought back to life sometime in the far future when science had developed a cure for whatever had originally killed them. The idea seized the imagination of a lot of life extension activists and by 1967, the newly formed Cryonics Society of California had frozen its first "patient."

CRYONICS TODAY

Thirty-five years later, as cryonics develops and gains slowly in popularity, many of the problems that plagued its originators have been overcome. The biggest problem was the freezing process itself. With freezing, ice crystals form around cells, damaging the body and organs, including the brain. To eliminate this damage, cryonics has turned to "vitrification," a technology originally developed for preserving embryos and other small specimens. With vitrification, more than half of the water inside the body is replaced by an antifreeze-like fluid circulated through

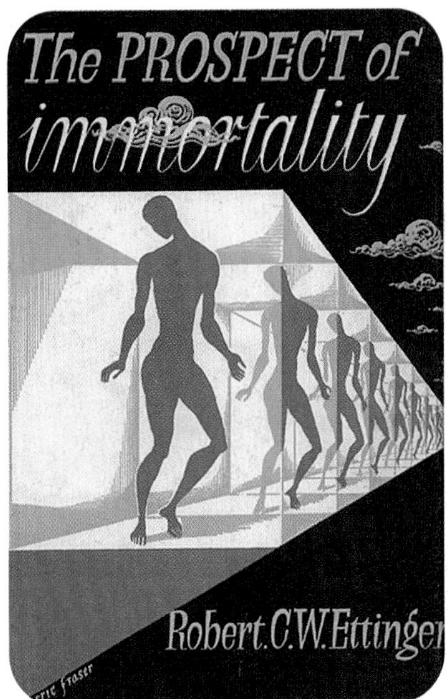

FROZEN MAN. *In this 1964 book,* The Prospect of Immortality, *physicist Robert Ettinger proposed that humans could be frozen and revived later, thus inspiring and popularizing the cryonics movement.*

HOW DO YOU FREEZE A BODY?

Techniques vary greatly among cryonics facilities currently operating in the U.S., ranging from simple and inexpensive freezing, to procedures involving surgeons and complex drugs designed to avoid ice formation completely. The following describes "best case" procedures of the Alcor Life Extension Foundation in Scottsdale, Arizona.

Ideally a team from Alcor will wait in a hospital until an independent physician pronounces legal death at the moment of cardiac arrest (stopping of the heart). The Alcor team then begins mechanical CPR and oxygen breathing. If performed within 4–6 minutes of legal death, this has the effect of restoring the brain to the same state as that of a living person. Drugs are administered to prevent the heart from restarting, maintain anesthesia, and reduce brain injury from any lack of oxygen. The patient is placed in an ice bath to begin external cooling, which further protects the brain.

Blood vessels in a leg are surgically accessed, and the patient is placed on heart-lung bypass. This means that a heart-lung machine replaces CPR compressions and lung ventilations for keeping oxygen-rich blood flowing through the patient. (The same technology is used during open-heart surgery in hospitals.) Relatively slow external cooling is now replaced by rapid cooling of blood in the heart-lung machine, which lowers the patient temperature down to 70° Fahrenheit in a few minutes.

As the temperature continues to drop, blood is replaced with an organ preservation solution that is specially designed for maintaining life at low temperatures. Upon completion of blood replacement and cooling to near 32° Fahrenheit, the patient is packed in ice for air shipment to Alcor. Published research shows that such procedures are reversible in animals for up to 3 hours.

Upon arrival at Alcor, the organ preservation solution is replaced over 4–5 hours by a gradually increasing concentration of antifreeze chemicals. The chemicals used are similar to solutions developed by scientists for preserving transplantable organs by "vitrification" (ice-free preservation), except that Alcor's solution is more concentrated and applied to the entire body. The body is then cooled as rapidly as possible to –200° Fahrenheit by cold nitrogen gas, causing the antifreeze-protected tissue to become a solid "glass". The body is then slowly cooled to –320° Fahrenheit for long-term storage in dewars or cryostats containing liquid nitrogen. The fine structure of the brain and other tissue can be maintained ice-free indefinitely at this temperature.

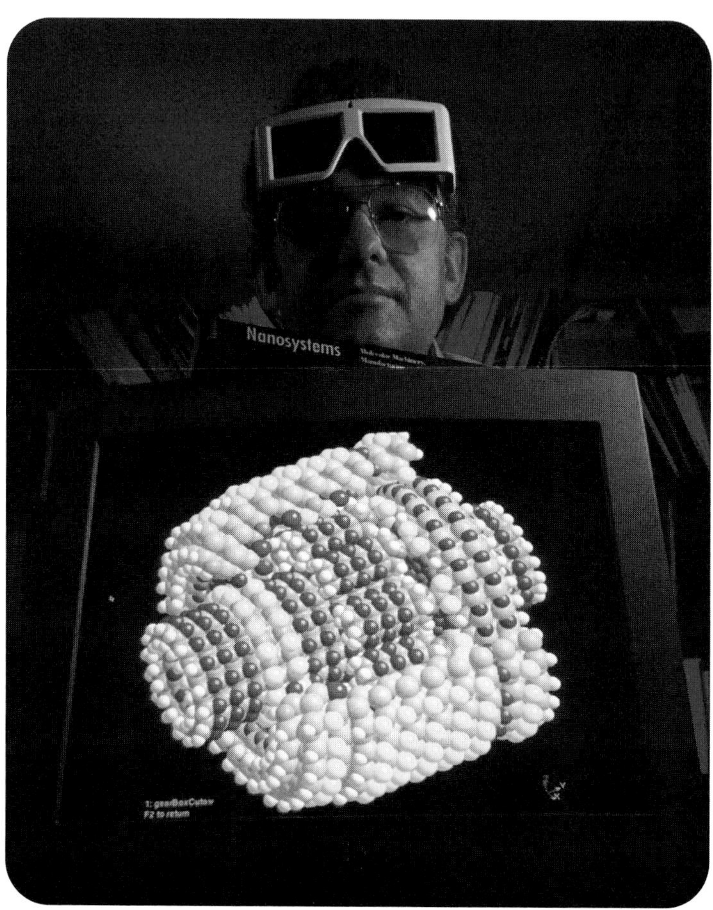

NANOTECHNOLOGY. *Researcher Ralph Merkle believes that nanotechnology is the key to making cryonics work. In theory, when a body is revived, nanomachines can enter the blood stream and repair damage done during the freezing process.*

the bloodstream. This process makes it difficult for water to freeze at all, so that a rapidly cooled body turns into a kind of glass instead. The process is currently irreversible because of the toxicity of the chemicals used, but it preserves cell structure and most chemistry far better than freezing.

The ultimate success or failure of cryonics relies on another edge science: nanotechnology. Dr. Ralph Merkle, nanotech researcher and a board member of Alcor, one of the oldest cryonics suspension facilities, believes that when someone is revived from suspension, nanodevices could be injected into the circulatory system to identify and repair cell damage. He's so sure this is possible that Alcor is encouraging its new members to forego full-body freezing for "neurosuspension," in which only the head is preserved. "In principle we need only repair the frozen brain, for the brain is the most critical and important structure in the body. Other parts of the body can simply be replaced...," Merkle said in a 1992 paper. In theory, some combination of nanotechnology and cloning will provide neurosuspended patients with bodies when they're revived.

THE TIMESHIP

At this time, there are only four groups offering cryonics services in the U.S., but a fifth group is ready to take cryonics to a new level. Timeship, a six-acre building now in the advanced design phase, will be the world's first comprehensive facility devoted entirely to life extension research and cryopreservation. Designed by visionary architect Stephen Valentine, Timeship will cryopreserve and store 10,000 individuals until they can be revived from suspended animation by advanced medical science and restored to full health and vigor. Timeship will also store sperm and ovum, fertilized embryos, and umbilical cords and other stem-cell tissues for DNA "family trees" for future medical cloning of organs. It will also house the DNA of thousands of near-extinct species.

Timeship will be one of the most advanced buildings built to date, using "green" design, ultra long-lived materials, highly efficient energy systems, onsite renewable energy generation for

CRYONICS GROUPS

When Timeship opens its doors, there will be five groups offering cryonics services in the U.S. Until then, four groups that have been around since the 1970s continue the work: Alcor Life Extension Foundation of Scottsdale, Arizona; American Cryonics Society, in northern California; Cryonics Institute of Clinton Township, Michigan; and Trans Time Corporation, also in northern California.

TIMESHIP. *Valentine describes Timeship as a "Fort Knox of friendly biological material." The Timeship will be one of the world's most advanced buildings, designed to withstand potential natural and human threats, keeping its cryopreserved treasures secure for hundreds of years.*

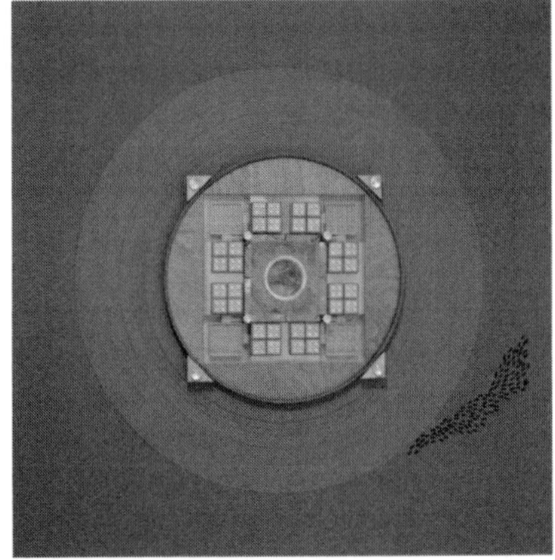

sustained self-sufficiency, and state-of-the-art security.

Because Timeship will be a bridge to the next stage of human existence, every effort was made by Valentine to have the building forms reflect a universal symbolic language through architectural metaphors that have recurred throughout history. Archetypal symbols from various cultures, including Mandalas, water, and sacred geometries, play major roles in the design.

Also on the Timeship site will be a conference center, a hospital, associated life-extension research facilities, and a hospice for people who want to enter cryonic suspension as quickly as possible after death. Site selection for Timeship is now under way based on highly rigorous criteria to ensure its security over the next several hundred years. Ground breaking is planned for the end of 2004.

PROVOCATIONS...

Will we no longer have wakes or funerals?

Would you rather be thawed as soon as possible, or on a certain specified date?

—Richard Kadrey

DESIGNING FOR IMMORTALITY. *Stephen Valentine, architect of the proposed six-acre Timeship facility. Timeship will not only study human life extension and cryopreserve thousands of humans, it will also preserve DNA specimens of near-extinct species (top left).*

SACRED GEOMETRIES. *Since the beginning, symbolic forms and patterns have mapped our understanding of life, eternity, and the cosmos. Valentine has used sacred geometries to design a timeless building that poetically incorporates symbols of rebirth that have recurred throughout human history. He does so in a manner that is both subtle and powerful, creating a "universal symbolic language." As shown here in a plan view, Timeship weaves mandalas, pyramids, cones, allusions to water (the source of all life), and the phoenix into the geometry of the building, layer upon layer (bottom left).*

Clockwise from top left: Photo by Andrew Sciaulino-Image courtesy of Stephen Valentine, Architect-Image courtesy of Stephen Valentine, Architect

WANT MORE?

CRYONICS FAQ
www-2.cs.cmu.edu/afs/cs.cmu.edu/user/tsf/Public-Mail/cryonics/html/overview.html

CRYONET
www11.pair.com/kqb/cryonet.html

FORESIGHT INSTITUTE
www.foresight.org

RALPH MERKLE'S NANOTECH SITE
www.zyvex.com/nano

ALCOR LIFE EXTENSION FOUNDATION
www.alcor.org/index.html

AMERICAN CRYONICS SOCIETY
http://AmericanCryonics.org

CRYONICS INSTITUTE
www.cryonics.org

TRANS TIME CORPORATION
www.transtime.com

TIMESHIP PROJECT
www.timeship.org

Our Society

Citizen of the Future
- Horizons Essay
- Digital Democracy
- Demographics
- Money
- Privacy

Places & Spaces
- Horizons Essay
- Architecture
- Building Materials
- Cities and Towns
- Augmented Reality

Transportation & Travel
- Horizons Essay
- Personal Transporters
- Bicycles of Tomorrow
- The Drive of Tomorrow
- High-Speed Rail
- Air Travel
- Floating Cities
- Space Tourism

Education
- Horizons Essay
- The Future of the Classroom
- Distance Education
- New Collaborative Tools

Security & Warfare
- Horizons Essay
- Army of the Future
- Non-Lethal Weapons
- Military Robots
- Cyberwar and Cyberterrorism
- Biowarfare
- Automatic Face Recognition
- Crime Investigation
- Lie Detection
- Today's Prisons

Citizen of the Future

DEMOCRACY IS A GREAT THING. I suppose a book about the future is as good a place as any to imagine whether one might ever, truly, come to be — and how.

Developing our collective autonomy — our shared responsibility for our unfolding reality — has been the great human challenge for ages and no doubt will continue to be one for ages to come. But thanks to a recent flurry of scientific, technological, and conceptual innovations, a unique opportunity for upgrading democratic participation may, in fact, be available to us today. We might even be ready to engage in something much closer to democracy than we may have previously imagined.

For the most part, democracies have been born out of revolutions. This is why, also for the most part, they haven't ended up functioning like democracies at all. Revolutions are just that — circles. They aren't usually fought by people with the ability to allow for anything particularly new to emerge; revolutionaries simply want to fight against whoever is oppressing them. Maybe that's why they usually end up simply replacing them. Perhaps there is nothing truly new, under the sun, anyway. The pronouncements of Next Big Things — as far as I can tell — are more useful for riling up crowds than providing us with a cogent plan for the future.

Renaissances, on the other hand, seem to recognize the fraudulence of the novel. Literally the "rebirth of old ideas in a new context," renaissances are simply moments when we recontextualize something very old from a new perspective. Renaissance innovations, from circumnavigation of the globe and calculus to perspective painting and the printing press, all involved increasing our concept of dimensionality, in one way or another. They increased our perspective on the stuff that we always had with us. This shift in perspective led to everything from the Protestant Reformation to the Enlightenment and republicanism.

The 20th century may have brought us through a renaissance, too. Photographing the earth from space changed our relationship to its dimensionality; so did gaining the ability to destroy it with nuclear weapons. Perspective painting finds its modern corollary in holographs. Calculus allowed us to describe one dimension in the language of another, while fractals gave us the ability to describe fractional dimensions. The Gutenberg press opened the world of reading to the masses, while the computer and Internet opened the world of writing.

Successive renaissances moved human beings from the roles of spectators to that of interpreters to that of creators. Each one increased the dimensionality of our orientation to the processes that steer civilization.

In short, the original renaissance gave individuals the ability to interpret and redefine their relationship to the institutions, ideas, and texts that guided their cultures. Our more recent renaissance gives individuals the ability to co-author them. Just as we moved from being able to encircle the globe to being able to blow it up, we are moving from the experience of our citizenship as a right to bear witness toward the sense of responsibility to participate actively.

Our many renaissance innovations, if we can call them that, provide new frames through which we can come to understand the nature of democratic participation and collective cultural engineering.

This is why so many people, on learning of the Internet, began to think of ways it could be used to enhance the participation of citizens in the affairs of their governments. The first and simplest visions were for something called "teledemocracy." To most people, this meant being able to vote in presidential and other elections through their home computers. Soon, even more elaborate visions emerged of citizens being able to vote on every issue coming before Congress — even replacing elected officials with daily, national votes.

These are noble but misguided visions. Just as executives must not micromanage their staffs, the voting citizens of a country must not micromanage their elected executives. This is why the system of representative democracy was invented. We elect representatives who can spend all day studying issues and then voting on them more intelligently than we can because we have full-time jobs doing other things. Representative democracy is not a surrender of authority but a concession to efficiency and specialization.

Most visions and implementations of teledemocracy, so far, suffer from the worst symptoms of consumer culture:

they focus on short-term ideals; they encourage impulsive, image-driven decision-making; and they aim to convince people that their mouse clicking is some kind of direct action. And anyone arguing against such schemes must be an enemy of the public will — an elitist. Teledemocracy is a populist revival, after all, isn't it?

Perhaps. But the system of representation on which most democracies were built was intended to buffer the negative effects of such populist revivals. Although they may not always live up to it, our representatives' role is to think beyond short-term interests of the majority. They are elected to protect the rights of minority interests — the sorts of people and groups who are still too often cast as "special interest groups."

The true promise of a network-enhanced democracy lies not in some form of Web-driven political marketing survey, but in restoring and encouraging broader participation in some of the networked world's more interactive forums. Activists of all stripes are gaining the freedom and facility to network and organize across vast geographical, national, racial, and even ideological differences. Indeed, democracy itself may soon outgrow the artificial boundaries of the nation-states that first spawned it.

For representative democracies in search of a sustainable future, the best course may well be a new emphasis on education, where elected leaders engage with constituents and justify the decisions they have made on our behalf, rather than simply soliciting our moment-to-moment opinions.

I can give you a few ways to tell if any particular innovation or opportunity for participation that our leaders bestow upon us is bringing us closer to participatory democracy.

First, you have to accept that the stories in our news media — from the heated debates on *Meet the Press* to gladhanding, "non-partisan" announcements in the Rose Garden — often have very little to do with what is actually going on. They are commonly exploited as opportunities to contextualize something that will happen in the future (hype) or to recontextualize something that happened in the past (spin). The only way to judge the integrity of what politicians say or do is to measure the extent to which they are willing to disclose their actual points of view. The more a politician claims he or she is "right," rather than simply explaining and defending an arbitrary but heartfelt strategy, the less democratic he or she is being.

Likewise, the more the political and legislative processes are mired by issues concerning flags, God, or national pride, the less likely they are to address the realities of governance. These are artificial ways of uniting large masses of people — not mechanisms for the development and expression of a multiplicity of points of view.

Real democracy is a negotiation. It is a way of orchestrating the collective will, while protecting the rights of minorities and individuals. Although nature provides us with many models for how such organic relationships can thrive — a coral reef, say, or colony of slime mould — these organic networks are generally cruel to the weak. Government, and civilization itself, exists to improve upon nature by replacing cruelty with cooperation.

The way to tell if a given innovation achieves this is to watch out for feedback and iteration. Does the new mechanism give people a chance to express their own points of view? If so, to whom? And how are they registered? Do they become part of some oversimplified, computerized schema, or are they actively digested and responded to? Real participation doesn't mean turning one's elected officials into marionettes, but rather engaging with them as human beings. The measure of our ability to participate democratically has as much to do with what the politicians say back to us as what we have the ability to say to them.

The other model we might use to gauge the development of a participatory democracy would be its networkability. I find that the most effective use of the Internet in the democratic process, so far, has been the rise of networked activism. Protestors, activists, and political educators have been able to engage both locally and globally through online bulletin board services and Web sites. They can discuss issues, inform one another, and even plan rallies and other activities. A scalable democracy is not a democracy with 6 billion individuals, but a myriad of overlapping interest groups and political affinities. Individuals find leverage through affinity and collective action; meanwhile, individuals express their individuality through their selection of networks with whom to affiliate.

So, rather than looking for a single headline, revolutionary concept, or breakthrough technology to herald a new era of democratic engagement, we might best look to the subtle ways in which our networks and affiliations more accurately reflect our own agendas. The more the world begins to look and feel the way we want it to, the better job we're doing.

— Douglas Rushkoff

Digital Democracy...

America's Second Revolution?

AMONG THE INTERNET'S MANY SIGNIFICANT *impacts on our society, it has forever increased our expectations. We now inhabit a world where we expect to be able to buy virtually any good or service in existence, from the comfort of our home computer, and to have it delivered literally overnight. If we send a company an email, we expect to be heard and responded to, and the inclined ladder of our expectations has continued to shorten the period in which companies "should" respond, from days to hours to moments. As we have all witnessed, adapting to these changes sent tremors through the world of business, changing the way we measure, value, and relate to companies and their products.*

GOODBYE, CHADS. *Successfully demonstrated in Texas during the November 2000 presidential election, Hart InterCivic's eSlate Electronic Voting System is a powerful next-generation voting system that promises to make voting extremely easy for all Americans, including the blind and disabled. A dial with an audible click lights up each candidate or ballot option.*

Image courtesy of Hart InterCivic, Inc.

As it has been with commerce, shall it be with government. From the way we receive social services, to the way we communicate with and vote for our leaders, "e-government" will transform the experience and expectations of American democracy in the coming decades.

There are important differences, however, between the world of Dot Com and the world of Dot Gov. Our need for security and privacy is much greater, as are the potential consequences of malfeasance or cyberattack. More importantly, there is a deliberative and representative nature to government, especially at the federal level, that intentionally resists the real-time expectations of the consumer marketplace. These two mindsets are on a collision course, and it's likely that both will be changed by the encounter.

On the surface, the Internet would seem tailor-made to improve democracy. The speed and ease of online communications could make our government more efficient, allowing us to deliver more social services to greater numbers of people (a traditionally Democratic concern) at a far lower cost (a traditionally Republican concern). The Internet can help make government more transparent, increase citizen satisfaction with government, reengage apathetic voters, and facilitate local initiatives. e-Government has other advantages as well. During a natural disaster or other emergency, for

THE CONGRESSIONAL CYBERCRUNCH

Want to get your voice heard in Washington? Paradoxically, you'd better pick up a pen, not a PC. The volume of email to congressional offices has risen dramatically over the past 2 years, and elected representatives are at a technical standstill. The House and Senate received 117 million inbound email messages in 2001 — if printed out on single sheets of paper, these emails would be more than 18 miles tall — and the rate continues to grow by an average of 1 million messages per month. Urged by activists of all stripes to "make their voices heard in Washington," advocacy organizations of every flavor often encourage the public to spam Congressional offices. The load is both crushing and confounding, and Congressional staff levels haven't risen significantly since the 1970s. Developing a policy to receive, weigh, and respond (or not respond) to that email will be a major battleground of e-government.

example, the phone systems are often overwhelmed with people seeking basic information. While such systems are taxed, Web sites can service many times the number of inquiries.

Citizens are clearly interested in e-government. A study by the University of Maryland in early 2002 found that 21% of Internet users polled have used the Web to conduct some form of transaction with the government, from paying taxes to applying for permits — a higher percentage than those who bank or buy online. The Council for Excellence in Government found in 2002 that 73% of citizens think that e-government should be a high priority, that 66% support the idea of a "technology czar," and that 65% favor using new technologies in the voting booth.

There is significant growth in e-government services, as local, state, and federal e-government portals take advantage of mature Internet technology. In one study of more than 1,600 such sites, Brown University found that 93% offered online access to government publications, 54% offered access to government databases, and 52% responded to email within one day. Even so, the e-government revolution will likely proceed slowly, given the politics of government employment, the post-9-11 need for cybersecurity, shrinking governmental budgets, and the as-yet unresolved questions of which new or existing agencies should be responsible for e-government and how they should be budgeted. In the near term, the true killer app of e-government may be paying parking tickets, a mundane task that is consistently ranked the favorite among citizens who use such services.

Ultimately we are not merely consumers of government, but also participants. The true promise of e-government will be realized when it is a vehicle not only for the delivery and receipt of governmental services, but when citizens use the medium to influence the very services they receive. As a "digital majority" begins to coalesce, we could experience a fundamental shift in the shape and mandate of governmental institutions. According to political scientist Max Blanck, that would represent "the most significant change in our democratic institutions since the New Deal."

PROVOCATIONS...

Will legislation be passed giving everyone an email address at birth?

Will a national leader be elected on a pro-e-government platform?

—Andrew Zolli

THE TOP TEN IN 2001

The Top Ten Most Wired State Governments:

Indiana
Michigan
Texas
Tennessee
Washington
California
New York
Pennsylvania
Florida
Ohio

The Top Ten National e-Governments:

United States
Taiwan
Australia
Canada
UK
Ireland
Israel
Singapore
Germany
Finland

Source: Taubman Center for Public Policy, Brown University

WANT MORE?

GSA'S E-GOVERNMENT PORTAL
www.egov.gov

THE SENATE E-GOVERNMENT PROJECT
www.senate.gov/~gov_affairs/egov

IBM'S INSTITUTE FOR ELECTRONIC GOVERNANCE
www.ieg.ibm.com

CONGRESS ONLINE PROJECT
www.congressonlineproject.org

Demographics...

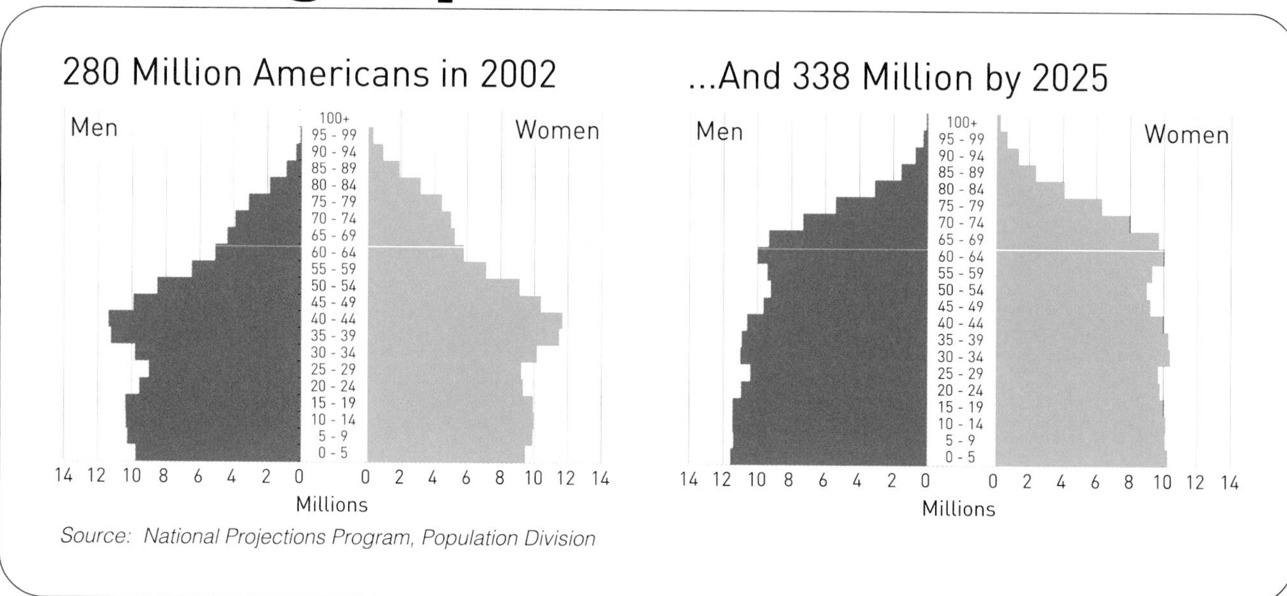

Source: National Projections Program, Population Division

THE NEXT 25 YEARS PROMISE DEMOGRAPHIC CHANGES THAT WILL RESHAPE THE FACE OF America *and transform the lives of all who live here. Like an explosion in a fireworks factory, these changes will amplify one another and deeply alter our national concerns, assumptions, and agendas.*

Much of this change is likely to be spurred by increased longevity. People are living longer today than ever before — more than 66% of all the people who have ever been over 65 are alive right now — and the numbers are going up. This boom in senior citizenship is coming just at the moment that the baby boomers, who at birth were the largest generation in American history, start to retire. By 2025, there will be 64 million baby boomers aged 61 to 79, a 90% increase in the size of this population from today. In 1980, the median age of the United States was 30. Today, it is 35. If present trends continue, "over 50s" will form a majority of adults in the United States sometime around 2050.

All those seniors are going to seriously stress current governmental and social infrastructure. Traditionally, societies have been structured like a pyramid, with a lot of young people at the bottom supporting far fewer seniors at the top. But by 2025, the American population pyramid will get far steeper, with relatively fewer young people to support their elders' increased needs, and expectations, for social services. The "gray lobby" will wield considerably more political, cultural, and marketplace power — a significant shift in a country that routinely caters only to the Britney Spears set.

This coming senior boom could affect our lives in unforeseen ways. We could see new intergenerational workplace politics, with "age diversity" becoming an important social issue, even while children and parents compete for the same management jobs. It will certainly affect domestic life: a 35-year-old woman in 2025 may end up caring for her mother longer than her mother cared for her when she was growing up. And it's

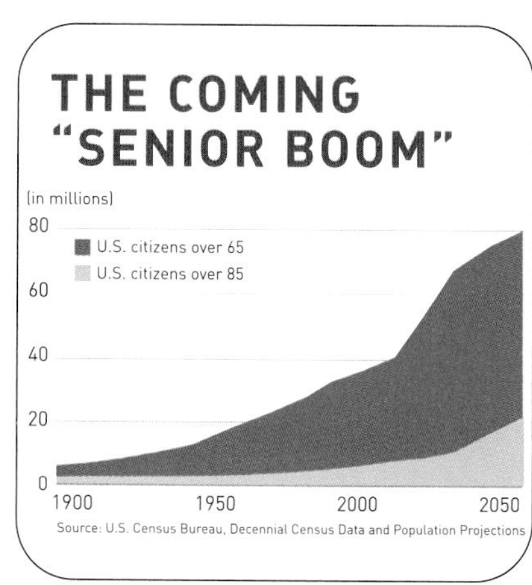

Source: U.S. Census Bureau, Decennial Census Data and Population Projections

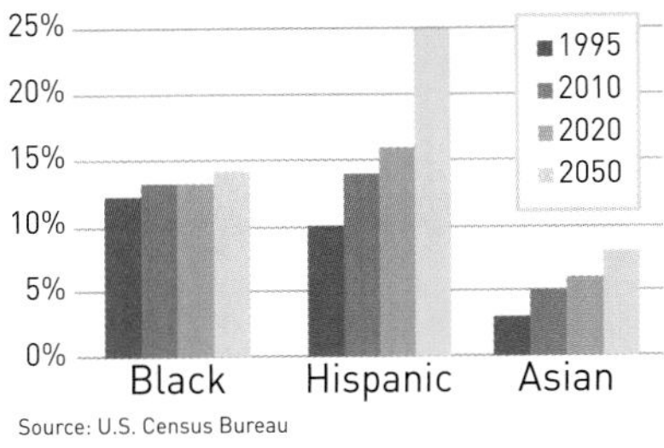

INCREASING DIVERSITY. *Minorities will become the majority by 2050.*

likely to lead to a major immigration boom, as the country imports labor to keep social services properly functioning.

The graying of America will be accompanied by a rainbowing. Latino, Asian, black, Native American, and other ethnic populations jumped from 23% to 30% between 1990 and 2000. By shortly after 2050, non-Hispanic whites may become a true minority. Hispanics are poised to overtake blacks as the largest minority group; Asians and Pacific Islanders could almost double their numbers by 2020. And interracial marriages will add children to the population who cannot be easily labeled using current categories. This is likely to lead to greater workforce and community diversity and a rethinking of our educational policies. In 2025, it simply may not be possible to function in America without knowing Spanish.

The family unit is likely to continue to change as well. The national average household size continues to get smaller — meaning fewer children and fewer parents. The household size of the average American family declined from 3.1 to 2.6 persons during the last 30 years and will reach 2.35 by 2020 — only one child for every three couples. Reasons for this include the decline in fertility, changes in the living patterns of youth, fewer overall marriages, a higher median age for marriage, and increases in the divorce rate.

Cohabitation is one of America's most recent and significant household trends. Between 1960 and 1998, America experienced a nearly 1,000% increase in unmarried couples living together. One-third of these couple households includes children. The percentage of never-married adults has consistently increased, from 22% in 1970 to 28% 30 years later. In the coming decade 4 million households will consist of unmarried couples living together.

These trends will intersect. The 21st century may find young minorities working to support an older and whiter population, spurring increased racial and ethnic tension across generational lines. As life spans increase, more and more people may give up the notion of lifetime marriage, choosing some form of serial monogamy instead. And there may be many more cuisine options alongside your local Chinese restaurant.

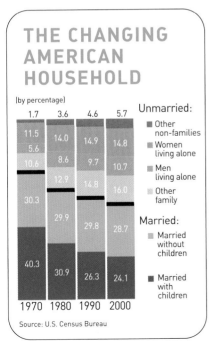

THE CHANGING AMERICAN HOUSEHOLD

(by percentage)

	1970	1980	1990	2000
Unmarried:				
Other non-families	1.7	3.6	4.6	5.7
Women living alone	11.5	14.0	14.9	14.8
Men living alone	5.6	8.6	9.7	10.7
Other family	10.6	12.9	14.8	16.0
Married:				
Married without children	30.3	29.9	29.8	28.7
Married with children	40.3	30.9	26.3	24.1

Source: U.S. Census Bureau

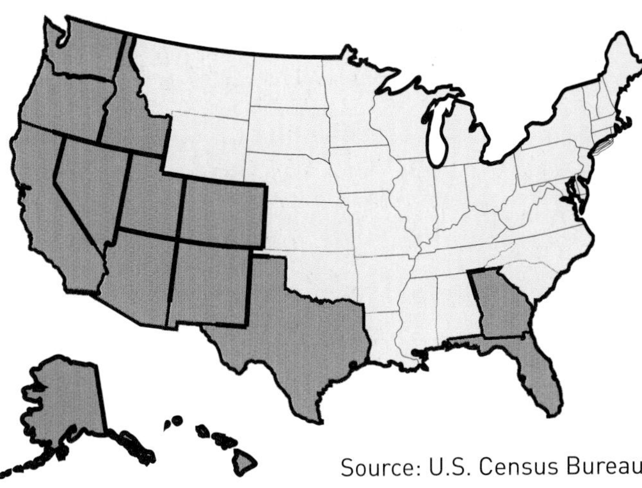

WESTWARD HO. *The fastest growing states 1995-2020.*

PROVOCATIONS...

Will the AARP Party replace the Democrats or the Republicans?

How will the Army cope with having proportionally fewer young people?

Will high school Hindi replace high school French?

—Andrew Zolli

WANT MORE?

MIT'S AGELAB
http://web.mit.edu/agelab/index.html

U.S. CENSUS BUREAU
www.census.gov

AMERICAN DEMOGRAPHICS
www.americandemographics.com

Money...Any Denomination You Want, As Long As It's Bits

OUR MONEY HAS MYTHICAL SIGNIFICANCE. LOOK AT A ONE *dollar bill. What stares back at you from the top of the pyramid? That's no less than the Eye of Providence, the benevolent force behind the founding of our Great Republic. Note the Latin "Annuit Coeptis," "He has favored our undertakings." Now consider "Novus Ordo Seclorum," or "A new order of the ages." These adages have been inspiring us for 10 generations. So what does providence foretell for money in the millennial generation?*

THE GREAT EYE IS UPON YOU. *In remarks to Congress about the symbolism of the Great Seal, it was said that the pyramid represented "Strength and Duration." Inside the capstone you have the all-seeing-eye, an ancient symbol for divinity.*

The more things change, the more they stay the same.

Today most transactions occur with paper currency, paper checks, and their electronic versions —intangible bits that fly around the globe in seconds between digital ledgers. Today's consumer is also increasingly comfortable using plastic (debit or credit, PIN or signature based) at the register, even as a substitute for spare change. Home banking and bill payment services, like Checkfree, are also allowing millions of us to move away from the monthly bill-paying grind.

But this transition is happening much later than was initially expected. Many predicted a "checkless society" (sound like the "paperless office"?) happening in the 1980s, yet U.S. check processing continued growing, albeit slowly, all the way up to 2001. The newest money on the block is stored value or "smart cards," with embedded microprocessors. Some of these, like MasterCard's Mondex, are gaining ground in Europe and Asia, in universities, and in the youth market. Carrying all their value on the card, they can be quickly swiped at the point of purchase for food, books, and other items without waiting that critical extra 20 seconds for online authorization (so where will you spend all those seconds you save?).

Does this mean the end for traditional currency? Don't hold your breath. We like our providential dollar bills, and there are still things we would rather pay for with our anonymous cash. At least one online alternative to credit cards, InternetCash, is even specifically designed to allow anonymous transactions. But how much longer will untraced finances survive in an increasingly security conscious society? At present there are no signs of significant changes on this front, at least with regard to person-to-person transactions.

> Money never made a man happy yet, nor will it. There is nothing in its nature to produce happiness. The more a man has, the more he wants...
>
> —Benjamin Franklin

Meanwhile, new quasi-currencies continue to emerge, from frequent flyer miles (a new form of corporate scrip), to "netmarket cash" (frequent-shopper credits for future purchases). For cash-poor businesses, excess inventories and underutilized services have reinvented barter on the Internet at such sites as BXI exchange. There are even a few paper currencies in local use, such as Ithaca, New York's Ithaca Hours, a community exchange scrip that contributes to Ithaca's "grassroots national product." Catherine England, a George Mason University economist, is among those who see a future where the Federal Reserve coexists with a number of "alternative currency" suppliers.

PRIVATE LABEL

More and more communities across the U.S. and across the world are developing their own "time currencies" to increase cooperation and community involvement. In upstate New York, Ithaca Hours can be earned by spending some period of time (often an hour) doing work for another resident, e.g., mowing the lawn, doing chores, and so on. The Ithaca Hours can be turned in for an equivalent amount of work from other holders of the currency.

That assessment, however, may be premature. Most attempts to create new money standards never get far off the ground (remember all those early e-currencies, like Flooz and Beenz?). If money is a community agreement to use something as a medium of exchange, such agreements are always quite slow to build, subject to counterfeiting and fraud, and in constant competition with other standards.

New Internet markets like eBay are allowing all our property to increasingly become tradable commodities, not only for expensive fine art — now even our kitschy art, broken equipment, and faded collectibles are almost as liquid as our bank accounts, once we snap a digital photo (noting any damage) and post it to the Web. Moreover, the digital currency of choice on eBay, PayPal, has skyrocketed in popularity and may itself become a new global standard.

As the battle for the most popular form of currency is fought in the coming years, issues such as speed, availability, fraud protection, and transparency will all be crucial. e-Commerce leaders like Siemens predict that our mobile phones will turn into ATMs, replacing today's PINs with encrypted digital signatures, emailing cash using voice commands, and the virtual end of number punching on keypads (uh, that last one may be a reach). We'll continue to do mostly online secured transactions, but we also may carry our offline, fastest-access cash in the digital wallet phones and smart cards that can activate only if our own thumb authenticates them, with balances that can be retrieved even if the hardware is lost or stolen. These cards, phones, and PDAs will have built-in firewalls, allowing our physicians access to one portion, our bankers to another, and with online data backups only a Web click away.

But like the checkless society, don't expect any of this overnight. Hunting in our pockets for change, building penny jars at home, and carrying our favorite crumpled, germ-carrying anonymous and story-laden dollar bills will also be with us for many years to come.

PROVOCATIONS...

Will digital cash reduce the incidence of muggings?

Will our wallets come with technical support contracts?

—John Smart

WANT MORE?

LESLIE BROCK CENTER FOR THE STUDY OF COLONIAL CURRENCY
www.virginia.edu/economics

JOURNAL OF THE RECIPROCAL TRADE INDUSTRY
www.barternews.com

BXI EXCHANGE (B2B BARTER)
http://bxinsider.com

COMMUNITY CURRENCY
www.ithacahours.org

ONLINE ANONYMOUS CREDIT CARD ALTERNATIVE
www.internetcash.com/index.html

MASTERCARD'S SMARTCARD E-CASH
www.mondex.com

PAYPAL
www.paypal.com

BOWIE BONDS

Perhaps the greatest success has come not in minting new money, but in new ways of "monetizing" our existing assets. In 1997, rock singer David Bowie made headlines by issuing $55 million worth of Bowie Bonds, securities drawn against his future earnings. Several other celebrities have since followed suit. The more connected we become, the more our economy moves from selling not just bread and butter, but also information, software, and services (55% of our economy in 1998), all of our so called "intangible assets." In other words, the more intangible wealth society creates, and the better our markets for intangible assets, the more money-like, or "liquid," all of our assets become.

Clockwise from top left: Bills courtesy of Ithaca Hours-PR News Photo

Privacy... In the Right Measure

If Big Brother finally arrives but is well mannered, will we welcome him? Stunning advances in computer technology allow recording and sharing of detailed information about every facet of our social and personal lives. We leave behind digital DNA in ATMs, supermarkets, credit card transactions, email, chat rooms — almost everywhere we go. Databases and lists build without our consent, or our "opting in." This data develop lives of their own, being continually incremented, correlated, merged, lent to, and bought by third parties.

Under surveillance

Most Americans support expanded U.S. law enforcement against terrorism, but six months after Sept. 11, their enthusiasm has waned.

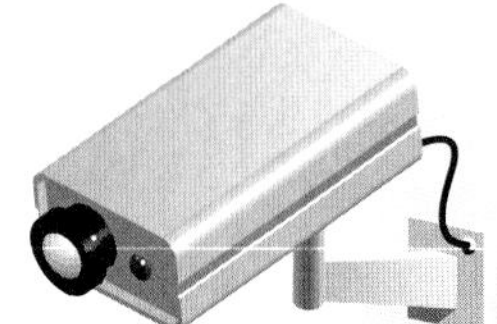

Type of surveillance	Sept. 2001	March 2002
More undercover work to penetrate suspicious groups	93%	88%
Face recognition technology to scan for suspected terrorists at public	86%	81%
Monitoring bank, credit card transactions to trace sources of	81%	72%
National ID system for all U.S. citizens	68%	59%
Camera surveillance on streets, in public places	63%	58%
Monitoring cell phones, e-mail to intercept communications	54%	44%
About law enforcers		
Very confident law enforcers will use expanded powers properly	34%	12%

Source: Harris Poll telephone survey of 1,017 U.S. adults, March 13 to 19; 3 percent error margin Graphic: Pat Carr, Pai

All this new data makes us increasingly interconnected. On the negative side, junk mail, spam, identity theft, and new forms of discrimination abound. We can now "google" most anyone to find oodles about their background. However, with this newfound power of information come responsibilities that we are just beginning to understand.

What's more, we aren't trying to jump out of this data fishbowl, at least not yet. Free encryption programs have existed for years, but few of us use them. Data security gets stronger as our computers become more powerful, except for the pesky human element. Even our personal computers are developing firewalls and immune systems to rival those of military installations. But curiously, we still seem to limit our use of privacy tools. For example, while transfer of electronic funds gets better protection, we don't see a simultaneous rise in "crypto-anarchy" or hacking. That's encouraging in a world of terrorist threats. It suggests we may be headed toward an implied social consensus of how much privacy we want and how much personal scrutiny we will tolerate in modern society.

Certainly secrecy and privacy remain important. Governments protect national security. Professions (e.g., law, medicine, education) maintain client confidentiality, corporations guard their strategic plans, individuals keep secrets (often on pain of discrimination if exposed: "Don't ask, don't tell"), since what we say in private has always been judged by a looser standard. With the Whistleblower, Freedom of Information,

Graphic illustration: Pai/KRT

and the USA Patriot Acts, and because of increasingly accessible credit and the availability of DMV, criminal, and other records, we are rapidly moving toward a "transparent society." That is, where our public lives are on display and even our private ones can be easily opened up to scrutiny, ideally only with just cause by appropriate parties.

> "Sacrificing anonymity may be the next generation's price for keeping precious liberty, as prior generations paid in blood."
>
> –Hal Norby

Here's the crux of the issue: How do we maintain personal privacy in an increasingly complex world where information is a commodity?

One problem is that our existing privacy laws are not up to the tasks presented by the new technologies. There is only a smattering of consumer data protection laws on the books. And, in the U.S., the privacy of medical records is left to a jumble of conflicting federal and state statutes. Today we allow insurers limited access to medical records and limited monitoring of our office email by employers, but abuses still abound.

A second problem is our need for better education on the proper ethical conduct with regard to sensitive data. Media are doing a lot of this work (e.g., watch *Law and Order* if you skipped civics classes in high school), but it takes time, and as our information society accelerates we are continually caught off guard by new technology. Consider that we don't even have a consensus on telemarketing etiquette (is that an oxymoron?), and now we're faced with cell phone telemarketers giving us personalized pitches via sophisticated information systems. As we move toward social and political debates on levels of public surveillance, information collection, database access and use, and adequate accountability and disclosure, there will be a market for simplifying and clarifying privacy issues.

Technology will continue to bring new privacy challenges. Today, some Internet sites (e.g., www.upoc.com) engage in live celebrity tracking in public via new Short Message Service text-messaging cell phones ("Madonna sighting on 7th and Broadway!"). Tomorrow we will live in a world where digital storage is so cheap and sensors so small that many of us may live "documented lives," wearing gnat-sized "lifecams" that create video and text streams of our entire life experiences, auto-archived for instant access at any time. With the advent of this year's "toothphone," the trend is toward increasingly unobtrusive ways to receive information. New laws and a new etiquette will be needed in that environment. New privacy issues will ensue.

As personal information becomes more ubiquitous and accessible, all the social players — government agencies, businesses, media, special interest organizations, and consumers — have an increasing responsibility to protect against the misuse of our ever-burgeoning information base. Perhaps the greatest danger is not the ubiquity of the information, but that we seem to care so little about it, nor are we thinking ahead about how to minimize abuses.

PROVOCATIONS...

Will there be a booming market for personal "privacy detectors" that alert you to when you're being snooped? Will local privacy protection laws influence where large numbers of people choose to live?

—John Smart

WANT MORE?

AMERICAN CIVIL LIBERTIES UNION
www.aclu.org

DEPARTMENT
OF HOMELAND SECURITY
www.whitehouse.gov/homeland

CENTER FOR DEMOCRACY AND
TECHNOLOGY
www.cdt.org

PLATFORM FOR PRIVACY
PREFERENCES (P3P)
www.w3.org/P3P

ELECTRONIC FREEDOM
FOUNDATION
www.eff.org

ELECTRONIC PRIVACY INFO.
CENTER ON MICROSOFT'S
PALLADIUM
www.epic.org/privacy/consumer/microsoft/palladium.html

PRIVACY RIGHTS
CLEARINGHOUSE
www.privacyrights.org

Buildings Like Trees, Cities Like Forests

When the architect and theorist Le Corbusier imagined the future of cities from the vantage of the early 20th century, he foresaw a new industrial aesthetic that would free design from the constraints of the natural world. For Le Corbusier, the city was "a human operation directed against nature" and the house was "a machine for living in." He imagined architecture worldwide shaped by a "mass production spirit." The ideal: "One single building for all nations and climates." Le Corbusier's friends dismissed his futuristic ideas. "All this is for the year 2000," they said.

It seems they were right. In many ways, our world is Le Corbusier's world: From Rangoon to Reykjavik, one-size-fits-all buildings employ the "engineer's aesthetic" to overcome the rules of the natural world. As uplifting as that might be for the spirit of Le Corbusier, it is becoming more apparent all the time that buildings conceived as mass-produced machines impoverish cultural diversity and leave their inhabitants cut off from the wonders and delights of nature.

But what if buildings were alive? What if our homes and workplaces were like trees, living organisms participating productively in their surroundings? Imagine a building, enmeshed in the landscape, that harvests the energy of the sun, sequesters carbon, and makes oxygen. Imagine onsite wetlands and botanical gardens recovering nutrients from circulating water. Fresh air, flowering plants, and daylight everywhere. Beauty and comfort for every inhabitant. A roof covered in soil and sedum to absorb the falling rain. Birds nesting and feeding in the building's verdant footprint. In short, a life-support system in harmony with energy flows, human souls, and other living things. Hardly a machine at all.

This is not science-fiction. Buildings like trees, though few in number, already exist. So when we survey the future — the prospects for buildings and cities, settled and unsettled lands — we see a new sensibility emerging, one in which inhabiting a place becomes a mindful, delightful participation in landscape. This perspective is both rigorous and poetic. It is built on design principles inspired by nature's laws. It is enacted by immersing oneself in the life of a place to discover the most fitting and beautiful materials and forms. It is a design aesthetic that draws equally on the poetics of science and the poetics of space. We hope it is the design strategy of the future.

THE HUMAN LEAF

If one unpacks the compressed verse of Einstein — E=mc2 — one finds poetry, beauty, the dynamic structure of the universe. Following Einstein's inimitable lead, we see in E=mc2 a kind of design koan. E is the energy of the sun — physics and planetary motion. M is the mass of the earth — chemistry. When the two interact at the speed of light, biology flourishes and we celebrate its increase — the growth of trees, plants, food, bio-diversity, and all the cycles of nature that run on the sun. Good growth. And when human systems support ecological health, that's good growth, too.

Applied to design, the laws of nature give architects, designers, and planners a set of principles that allow them to articulate in form a building's or a town's connection to a particular place. They allow us to create buildings that make the energy of the sun a part of our metabolism and apply it to positive human purpose — the building as "human leaf."

Waste=Food. The processes of each organism in a living system contribute to the health of the whole. A fruit tree's blossoms fall to the ground and decompose into food for other living things. Bacteria and fungi feed on the organic waste of both the tree and the animals that eat its fruit, depositing nutrients in the soil in a form ready for the tree to take up and convert into growth. One organism's waste becomes food for another. Applied to architecture, these cradle-to-cradle nutrient cycles can serve as models for the design of materials and building systems that eliminate the concept of waste. Materials designed for use in cradle-to-cradle cycles, for example, can be either safely returned to the soil or reutilized as high-quality materials for new products.

Use current solar income. Living things thrive on the energy of the sun. Simply put, a tree manufactures food from sunlight, an elegant, effective system that uses the Earth's only perpetual source of energy income. Buildings that tap into solar income — using direct solar energy collection; passive solar processes such as daylighting; and wind power, which is created by thermal flows fueled by sunlight — make productive and profitable use of local energy flows.

Celebrate diversity. "The tree" provides not just one design model but many. Around the world, photosynthesis and nutrient cycling, adapted to locale, yield an astonishing diversity of forms. Bald cypress, desert palm, and Douglas fir suggest a range of niches. The hundreds of tree species within a single acre of Southern Appalachian forest suggest the diversity of a single region. Architects and planners, applying a diversity of design solutions, can create buildings and cities that fit elegantly and effectively into their own niches.

KINSHIP WITH ALL LIFE

As architects and planners explore these principles — what amounts to a new conception of design — they will become more adept at creating fit and fitting spaces for human habitation. New benchmarks will emerge. Rather than overpowering nature or limiting human impact, good design will affirm the possibility of developing healthy and creatively interactive relationships between human settlements and the natural world.

With new benchmarks will come new practices, and a design process that is now rare will, we hope, become the norm. Design teams in many regions would begin with an assessment of the natural systems of a place — its landforms, hydrology, vegetation, and climate. They would tap into natural and cultural history; investigate local energy sources; explore the cycles of sunlight, shade, and water; study the vernacular architecture of the region and the lives of local fauna, flowers, and grasses.

Combining an understanding of building and energy systems with this emerging "essay of clues," designers would discover appropriate patterns for the development of the landscape. Building materials would be selected with the same care, chosen only after a careful assessment of a variety of characteristics, ranging from their chemistry to the impacts of their use, harvesting, and manufacture. We might also expect to see the industry-wide pooling of architectural products as builders begin to create closed-loop recycling systems to effectively manage the flow of materials.

With this emphasis on sustaining and enhancing the qualities of the landscape, architectural and community designs would begin to create beneficial ecological footprints — more habitat, wetlands, and clean water, not fewer negative emissions. We would see buildings like trees, alive to their surroundings and inhabitants, and cities like forests, in which nature and design create a living, breathing habitat. Vital threads of landscape would provide connectivity between communities, linking urban forests to downtown neighborhoods to riparian corridors to distant wilds. Cities and towns would be shaped and cultivated by an understanding of their singular evolutionary matrix, a new sense of natural and cultural identity that would grow health, diversity, and delight, setting the set the stage for long-term prosperity.

Changes such as these, many already afoot, signal a hopeful new era. Ultimately, they will lead to ever more places that honor not just human ingenuity but harmony with the exquisite intelligence of nature. And when that becomes the hallmark of good design, we will have left behind the century of the machine and begun to celebrate our kinship with all of life.

—William McDonough and Michael Braungart

ARCHITECTURE...

On Blobs, Shape-Shifting, Networks, and Theater

COMPLEX CURVES. *Only powerful computers can calculate the precise compound curves used to create the swooping forms of the Guggenheim Museum in Bilbao, Spain.*

Photo © Jose Fuste Raga/Corbis

BRICKS, MORTAR, GLASS, STEEL, STONE, AND SHEET *rock — these are the familiar materials that we find in buildings every day, and ones that have been used to build structures for thousands of years. The success with which a building withstands gravity and the elements usually determines how well, in part, architecture stands the test of time. But architects don't just think about ways to put materials together to make another house or office building. Architects also think about form, light, and human experience to drive their designs. In recent years, computer technology has been instrumental in allowing architects and engineers to create brand-new forms for buildings, forms that, up until today, could only be imagined in the mind's eye.*

GUGGENHEIM BILBAO. *Another view of this remarkable museum, which opened its doors to the general public in 1997. Less than a year later, the museum had been visited by more than 1,300,000 visitors.*

BLOBITECTURE

The future of architecture, with the aid of technological innovations in computer design, information technology, and materials engineering, will create brand-new forms of experience that will expand the ways we inhabit buildings and relate to the environment. Architects are now pushing the envelope in terms of new fluid, swooping, and dynamic forms, designing buildings that look more like "blobs" than boxes. Controversial for some time now, "blobitecture," as it is called, will continue to provoke discussion in architectural circles.

Frank O. Gehry's Guggenheim Museum in Bilbao, Spain, and Experience Music Project in Seattle, Washington, are both examples of dynamic and sculptural forms built at a massive scale with the latest in building techniques. To create and engineer these complex surfaces that can only be visualized on a powerful computer, Gehry's office uses the same software used by airplane designers. As impossible as these buildings may seem to build, they do in fact exist in the real world. "Blobitecture" currently defines the limits of our understanding about new forms of architecture and the tyranny of physical laws, but we will continue to see new forms as new discoveries are made.

Clockwise from top left: Photo © Yann Arthus-Bertrand/Corbis · Photo © Experience Music Project, photo by Stanley Smith · Photo © Experience Music Project, photo by Lara Swimmer

EXPERIENCE MUSIC PROJECT. *Seattle's dramatic example of dynamic and sculptural form built on a massive scale with the latest in building techniques (above and right).*

MALLEABLE ARCHITECTURE

Probably the most radical of recent innovations in architecture is where the building's envelope changes. This kind of "malleable architecture" is best exemplified in architecture firm Diller and Scofidio's Blur Building, part of the Swiss Expo 2002. Using computer-controlled mist generators that are integrated into the building scaffolding, this building behaves like a cloud shifting and changing with the wind. Sited at the base of Lake Neuchatel in Yverdon-les-Bains, Switzerland, and connected by two long pedestrian bridges, the Blur Building also incorporates state-of-the-art lighting to create a brand-new kind of experience for visitors of the pavilion. The Blur Building is a building that is ostensibly built from water in its many forms — through mist, dew, and fog. It is the ultimate in shape-shifting architecture that constantly changes and morphs. And because its envelope is primarily composed of mist, the Blur Building may very well be the lightest building on Earth.

NEW SOCIAL SPACES

Human experience stands at the forefront of most architects' thought when they design their buildings. Like artists, they have a palette of materials they employ

THIRST QUENCHING. *The ultimate in "shape-shifting" architecture made from mist, fog, and water (above, right, and below).*

and synthesize to create buildings that not only accommodate their functions, but reach new heights in allowing inhabitants to experience color, light, shadow, and movement. With the rise of Internet technologies, architects are thinking deeply about how to integrate these technologies into buildings that go beyond accessing email and surfing the Web. The "Remote Lounge," by architect Jordan Parnass, is a unique example of using new media technologies to create a new kind of bar that allows visitors to view other visitors at other tables. Remote cameras, networked peer-to-peer technology, and a series of consoles integrated into tables create a new kind of social space, one where you can see in detail what the inhabitants of other tables, and potentially other "Remote Lounges" around the world, are doing. Parnass has created a new kind of bar that isn't just about drinking and conversations — it's about expanding your experience of others that extends well beyond the limits of your own table top coaster.

ARCHITECTURE AS THEATER

Society has been fascinated with storytelling and drama for thousands of years. David Rockwell has mastered the art of "theatrical architecture" in which materials and light are used to create dramatic and memorable experiences for visitors and inhabitants of his buildings. In the Mohegan Sun, a vast casino in Montville, Connecticut, he transcends the typical garishness of casino environments and creates an atmosphere that pays homage to the Mohegan Tribe of North American Indians. The goal was more than to create an entertainment space, but to imbue the casino with symbolic elements of the history and mythology of this tribe. It is a spectacular and rich environment in which to play and immerse oneself in the culture of the Mohegan Indians. Rockwell's POD restaurant in Philadelphia, Pennsylvania, takes a very different approach in carrying the visitor off into another world. In POD, he designed a very retro-futurist environment that harkens back to science-fiction

All photos on this page are courtesy of Dillard & Scofidio

THAT'S ENTERTAINMENT. *Architecture can convey rich stories through materials and lighting. The Mohegan Sun casino combines elements of the history and mythology of the once nearly-defunct Mohegan tribe (right).* **RETRO-FUTURISM.** *Architecture that takes cues from science-fiction in TV and film (below right).*

and pop culture, from *The Jetsons* to Woody Allen's movie *Sleeper*. Through lighting and sleek forms, Rockwell creates a setting where restaurant-goers feel like they are experiencing the future of haute cuisine.

So what do blobs, shape-shifting, networks, and theater have in common? All are new ways of expanding the human experience beyond static walls and windows, beyond conventional notions of habitation. These new architectural directions point to rich new realms of experience that seek to expand, change, connect, flow, and inspire humans to relate to their natural and built environments and to each other.

PROVOCATIONS...

Will all buildings stop being square?

Will future buildings be about spectacle?

—Gong Szeto

I SEE YOU. YOU SEE ME. *Each table at this bar is a remote sensing station.*

Clockwise from top: Photo by Paul Warchol/The Rockwell Group- Photo by Paul Warchol/The Rockwell Group- Image courtesy of Jordon Parnass Digital Architecture (www.jpda.info)

WANT MORE?

GUGGENHEIM BILBAO
www.guggenheim-bilbao.es/ingles/home.htm

BLUR BUILDING
www.dillerscofidio.com

REMOTE LOUNGE
http://63.249.202.209/digital_architecture/indexpc.html

DAVID ROCKWELL
www.rockwellgroup.com

EXPERIENCE MUSIC PROJECT
www.emplive.com

2000 2005 2010 2015 2020

risks rewards

BUILDING MATERIALS...

Remaking Buildings, from the Earth Up

TO MANY, IT IS A DISCI-pline both mundane and foreign, the world of cement trucks, steel beams, and heavyset men in hard hats. But a major revolution is brewing in building construction that promises to remake the way we see, experience, and value the physical structures that surround us. ¶ Construction is among the largest ongoing endeavors in the world (the U.S. alone spends more than $1.1 trillion dollars on it every year), and it is responsible for a whopping 40% of the world's raw material and energy consumption. As such, construction has long been the subject of intense social, environmental, and political debate.

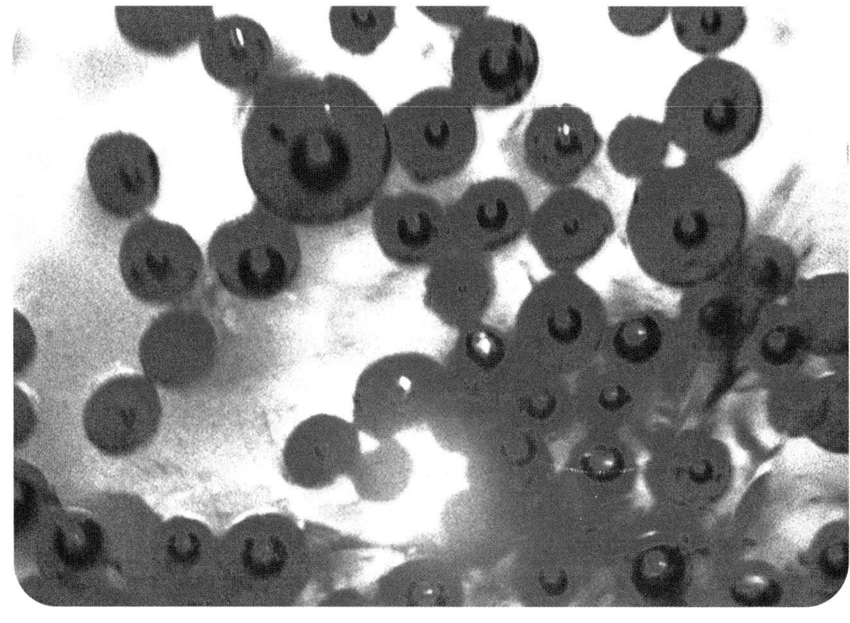

PLASTIC, HEAL THYSELF. *Researcher Scott White and colleague at the University of Illinois' Autonomic Healing Research Laboratory have created a revolutionary kind of material peppered with tiny capsules of "healing agent" that burst as a crack forms and automatically seal the rupture. This approach to self-healing takes it cue directly from nature.*

Images courtesy of Autonomic Materials Laboratory, Beckman Institute, University of Illinois

But when it comes to building materials, a generation-long battle between (so-called) "alarmist" environmentalists and (so-called) "backward" builders isn't being won or lost; it is being transcended. Engineering, technology, and industry have broadened the palette of materials with which we can make every kind of structure and have opened up new vistas for designers, builders, and the communities served by the buildings.

Materials innovations in building and construction are proceeding along two intertwining paths: the invention of radically new or improved versions of core building materials, and the rediscovery and reapplication of older, less environmentally damaging materials. New, environmentally sensitive construction management techniques are knitting the two together into a whole new approach to building.

For example, the National Institutes of Science and Technology (NIST) are using the Internet to create a virtual "concrete testing lab" that will dramatically accelerate the development of new forms of sturdier, more environmentally friendly concrete that creates less carbon dioxide and waste in its production. (Today, cement production is responsible for about 20% of all manmade CO_2 and about 5% of global warming.) Stronger concrete will mean less of it, both lowering its overall ecological impact and creating new architectural possibilities.

The Oak Ridge National Laboratory, in partnership with Habitat for Humanity, is testing another major innovation: building homes from "concrete" blocks made from 72% fly ash, a non-burnable residue that is expelled from coal-burning power plants. The blocks, produced by Babb International, weigh only 20% of regular concrete and are safe, strong insulators that can retain

RENAISSANCE MATERIALS

But not every innovation in building requires radically new materials. Some of our most important future building materials are among the most ancient. For example, glass, long considered so fragile and potentially dangerous that it could never be used for weight-bearing elements in buildings, is undergoing a renaissance, led by innovators such as Tim MacFarlane of Dewhurst MacFarlane and Partners. Counterintuitively, glass is actually 20-50 times stronger than steel if properly used and assisted by innovations in precision cutting and manufacturing, MacFarlane has been designing and building structures entirely out of glass. His breathtaking cantilevered subway entrance, built with Rafael Vinoly Architects in earthquake-prone Tokyo, seems to defy gravity and has already withstood several tremors without incident. MacFarlane believes we could be 10 years away from a new generation of super-strong glass; if so, we could see a resurgence of Crystal Palaces!

a home's heat long after the sun has gone down. Long used in industrial applications, their adoption in the consumer market could help absorb the millions of tons of combustion byproducts that coal plants produce every year.

Meanwhile, similar innovations are appearing in the domain of industrial textiles, used in everything from carpeting corporate offices to transportation and cruise ships. Climatex Lifecycle™ textiles, created by DesignTex, are manufactured in a "closed-loop" system, meaning that all the components that go into making the fabrics and all byproducts of the manufacturing process, as well as the products themselves, are completely biodegradable and compostable. The manufacturing system transcends "recycling" in the traditional sense; the water leaving the mill that produces the fabrics is as clean as the water going in, and the excess trimmings are used to insulate growing agricultural crops.

Even lowly polyester is going green. Interface Fabrics Group, a leading textile designer, is developing "synthetic" fibers but from organic, annually renewable resources rather than eco-unfriendly petroleum. So-called "bio-based" fibers have many characteristics of traditional synthetics but are derived from plants such as corn. These fibers require up to 50% fewer fossil fuels to produce than traditional synthetic fibers, emit less CO_2 during production, and can become compost in commercial facilities.

New models for directing building and construction projects tie these and a host of other sustainable building technologies together. Builders have been adopting a program called The Natural Step, a science and systems-based approach to organizational planning for sustainability developed by the Swedish cancer researcher Dr. Karl-Henrik. The system focuses builders on using locally available products, limiting overuse of synthetic materials, reducing the ecological impact of construction, and building in ways that are harmonious with the larger society.

As builders adopt such models, they are reversing the logic of the story of the three little pigs: In this version, it's the pigs that build from the most natural, readily available, and sustainable resources, strengthened by deep technological and scientific insights, that keep the big bad wolf at bay.

PROVOCATIONS...

Will houses grow their own insulation?

Will part of your house be edible?

Will houses self-repair or heal?

— Andrew Zolli

Photo © Kenji Kobayashi Photographer

WANT MORE?

ENVIRONMENTAL DESIGN AND CONSTRUCTION MAGAZINE
www.edcmag.com

THE NATURAL STEP
www.naturalstep.org

DESIGNTEX
www.dtex.com

DEWHURST MACFARLANE
www.dewmac.com

INTERFACE FABRICS GROUP
www.interfacefabricsgroup.com

Cities and Towns ... How They Will Change

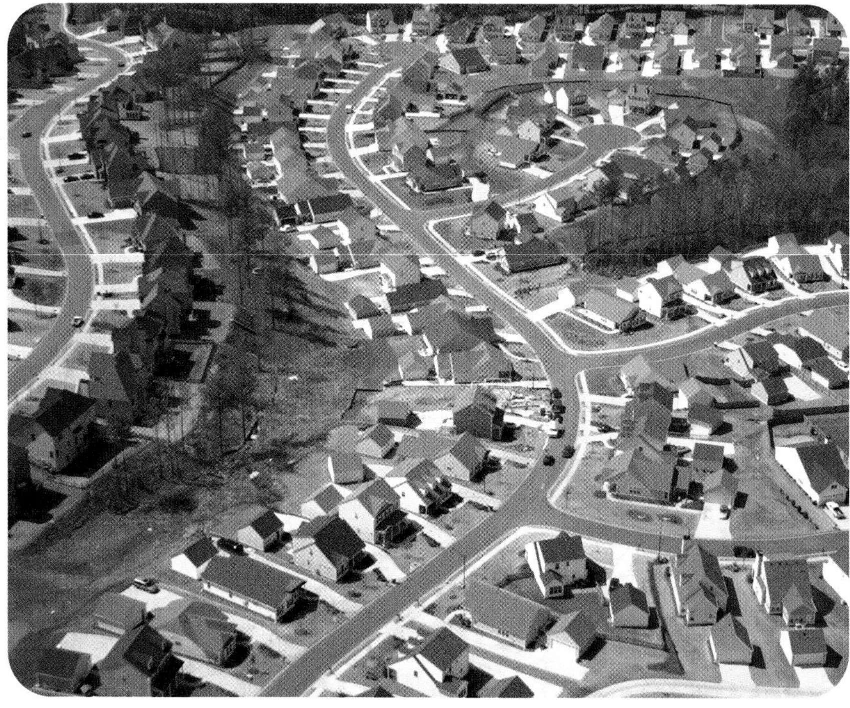

URBAN SPRAWL. *An aerial view shows houses built tightly together on former farmland turned subdivision in Kennesaw, Georgia, north of downtown Atlanta.*

Photo by Erik S. Lesser/Getty Images

A GENERATION FROM NOW, *where we live and how we live will change. Our cities and towns, the receptacles of our lives, will be different. In a generation, the cavernous 5,000-foot tract mansions on quarter-acre lots in the high-end suburbs will lay abandoned, or split into cheap apartments for immigrants. These now exclusive subdivisions will go through the same metamorphosis as the exclusive neighborhoods of urban townhouses built in 1890 in Brooklyn or Baltimore, built for the rich but eventually inhabited by the poor (and then sometimes, the rich again).*

Sprawl, that defining characteristic of American cites and increasingly the rest of the world's as well, will stop and pull back on itself, like an expanding universe that has reached its limit and begun to collapse.

The older inner-ring suburbs and the center cities will revive around a network of high-speed train lines that will connect major and medium-size cities. Small towns will come back as well under the influence of fleets of small jets that will easily carry people to and from them.

Cities and towns are a quaint duo of words, which really haven't been applicable for a century. A city, archetypically, is an urban center of offices, factories, and busy streets, while a "town" is a main street, a few homes, and some businesses. But these images have been outdated for a century. Cities and towns still exist legally and politically, but their form has changed beyond recognition. Our new "cities" stretch 50 or 100 miles, laced together by freeways and stretching from shopping mall to shopping mall. Our "towns" today are the agglomerations of subdivisions, office parks, and churches with 1,000-car parking lots grouped around the freeway exit ramps.

Silicon Valley in California, which stretches from the edge of San Francisco down to San Jose, is an example of a present-day city. It is the center of the top industry, computers, of our time. More fortunes have been created there than perhaps anytime and anywhere in history. Yet it is utterly unremarkable in appearance, a bland collection of subdivisions and shopping centers, without distinction.

But just as the form of Silicon Valley differed from New York of the 1920s or Paris in 1870, so will the city of 2025 differ from Silicon Valley. Why? What will prompt a change? Three things shape the form of our cities and towns: transportation, defense, and communication, with the first two being the most important. We no longer live in compact cities and towns because we changed how we get around. First came railroads and streetcars, and then came highways and cars. Because of this, the defining characteristic of change in cities and towns for the

LONDON 1800 Versus LOS ANGELES 2002

Some history provides perspective on the sprawl of the modern city. London in 1800 was the biggest city in the world and the capital of an empire. Yet with a million people within its borders, one could still walk from St. Paul's Cathedral to open countryside in 20 minutes or so. The entire city took up perhaps a few square miles.

Now, it would take several days if not a week to walk across a mid-sized American city. Los Angeles, the emblem of sprawl and with two dozen million people or so within its orbit, is called "the 100 mile city" by architecture critic Deyan Sudjic because it stretches at least that far from end to end.

WORST TRAFFIC. *The sun sets behind traffic in southbound lanes of Highway 101 during a lighter than usual commute east of Hollywood in Los Angeles. Recent studies support the long-standing Los Angeles record of having the nation's worst traffic and slowest commutes.*

last two centuries has been "more." If we were a family, it would be as if we had gone from living in a compact apartment, our possessions neatly arranged, to living in a sprawling house, with our possessions strewn around everywhere.

"The unit of the new city is not the street measured in blocks, but the 'growth corridor' stretching 50 to 100 miles," says urban historian Robert Fishman. "Where the leading metropolises of the early 20th century—New York, London, or Berlin—covered perhaps 100 square miles, the new city routinely takes up two to three thousand square miles."

Cities and towns have not only grown, they have grown exponentially. But the internal logic of this math suggests it cannot go on forever. Houston is readying to widen a principle freeway to 27 lanes but not unexpectedly is encountering opposition from the public, who question the wisdom of such a plan. Public support is drying up for new highways, which is what drives sprawl. Public support is building for new ways to travel, such as high-speed trains, which would redensify cities around these stations.

Other transportation revolutions are on the horizon. James Fallows, author of *Free Flight: From Airline Hell to a New Age of Travel* (Public Affairs, 2001), predicts that a new generation of small, fast, and cheap jets will become the equivalent of taxis, ferrying the masses hither and yon, using the 18,000 or so underutilized smaller airports that are now eclipsed by the overcrowded hubs. It will be a transportation revolution, he says, comparable to the introduction of the car. If so, then it will change our cities and towns in ways unimaginable. But one effect might be to revive now semi-abandoned small towns.

Our defense needs may change as well, and thus how we live. People used to live in walled cities because it was safer. If terrorists continue to bedevil us, we may retreat into walled subdivisions or concentrate more in center cities, under the watchful eye of hovering aircraft and radar.

Communication technology also shapes cities, but it's hard to predict how. In 1900, people thought an exciting new invention, the telephone, would save the family farm by connecting isolated families to the outside world. Instead, the telephone hastened the demise of the family farm by making larger factory farming more efficient.

The computer and the Internet are in the same position today. They are reshaping how we live, but predictions are tricky. Some predict that cities will die because the Internet allows people to live anywhere they want to. Others say cities will thrive because the Internet allows people to live anywhere they want to. You see the problem here.

What is probable is that we will change our cities and towns in the near future as much as we have in the past, which is a lot.

PROVOCATIONS...

Will walled subdivisions become cities in their own right?

Will you really live in Niketown?

—Alex Marshall

WANT MORE?

SMARTGROWTH ONLINE (EPA)
www.smartgrowth.org

SMART GROWTH AMERICA
www.smartgrowthamerica.org

SIERRA CLUB
www.sierraclub.org/sprawl

SPRAWL WATCH
www.sprawlwatch.org

SPRAWL BUSTERS
www.sprawl-busters.com

Photo by David McNew/Getty Images

Augmented Reality...

The Power of Extraordinary Perception in Our Daily Lives

A FAMILY IS IN THEIR *backyard, looking up at the stars for constellations and wearing special glasses that provide them with enhanced vision. With a simple voice command, they see the constellations outlined, just as they would in a planetarium, with names and distances labeling all the stars. They can find out more about a star by simply asking. Later that evening they decide to create new constellations by virtually drawing lines and connecting stars. The technology is called augmented reality, and in 10 years most of us will be using it every day.*

This may sound like a farfetched prediction, but millions of sports television viewers are already experiencing early versions of the technology today. American football fans see a virtual first-down line drawn across the field. Ice hockey fans can see the trail of the puck as it flies across the ice. Almost all sports fans see advertisements in the background that look like they are part of a

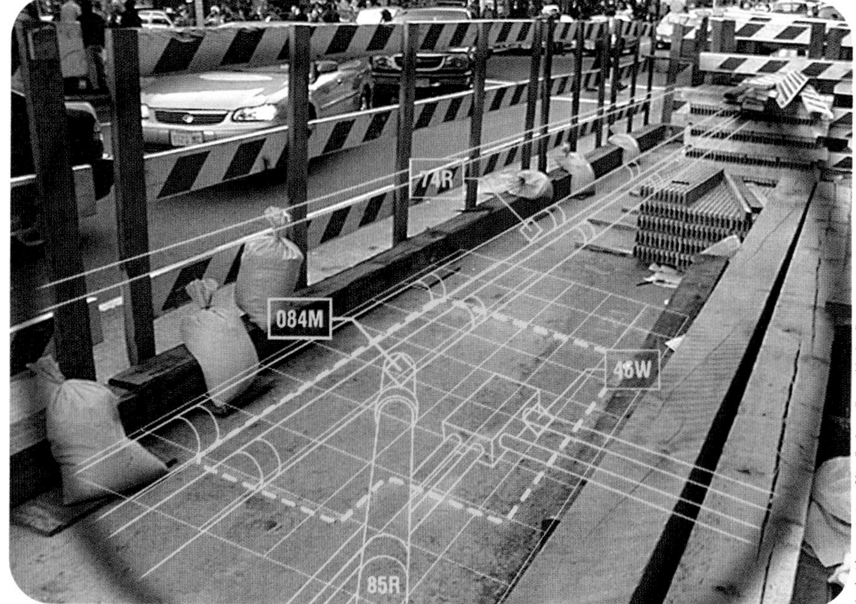

MOBILE GAMES. *Instead of playing games in front of the television, people will play in their backyard or local park. In this image two friends battle against a virtual dinosaur.* **CONSTRUCTION AND MAINTENANCE.** *Superimposing diagrams, models, and instructions enables hidden structures to be revealed. In this example, a construction crew can look at the ground and see the pipes below the surface.*

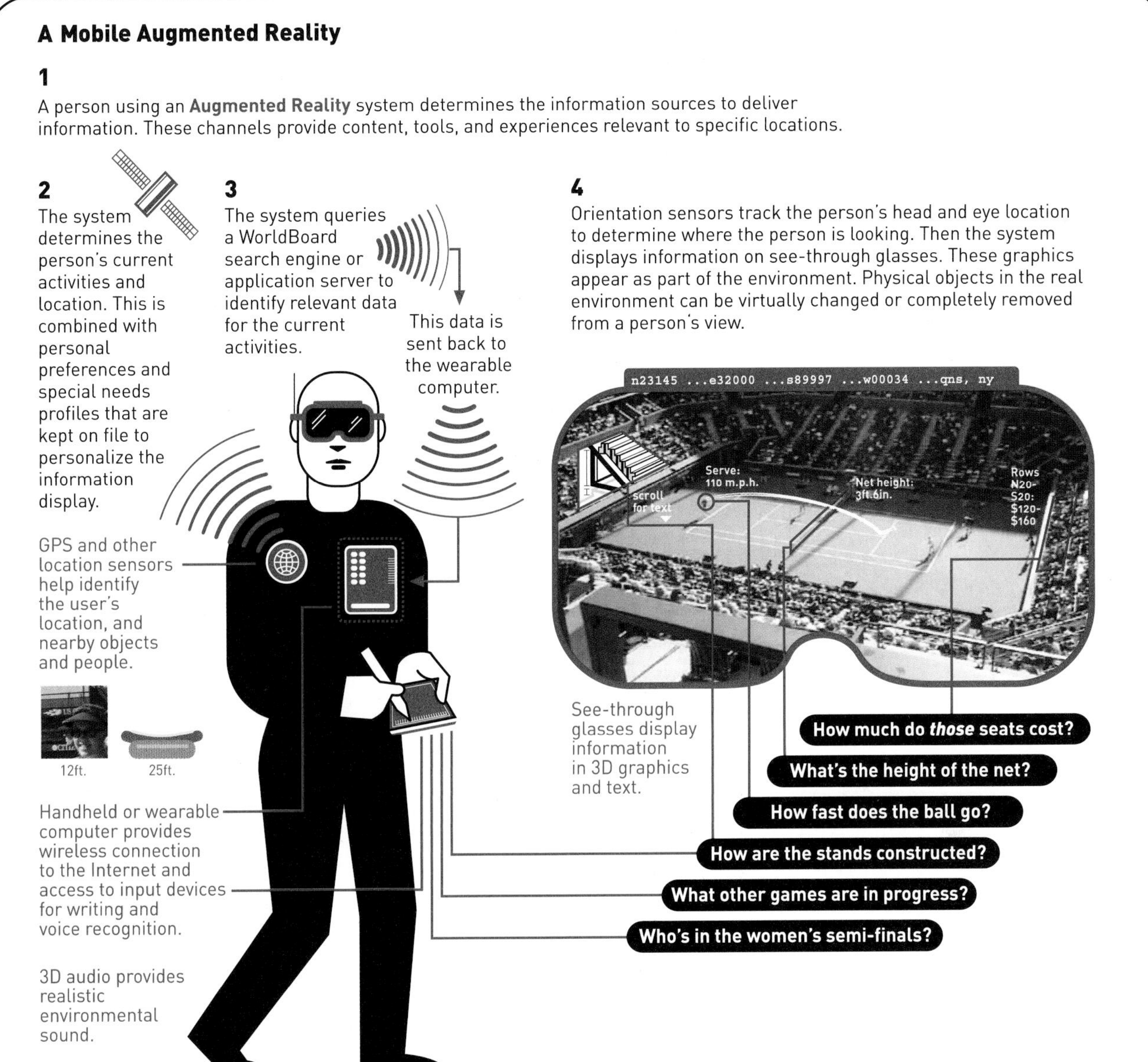

A Mobile Augmented Reality
1
A person using an Augmented Reality system determines the information sources to deliver information. These channels provide content, tools, and experiences relevant to specific locations.
2
The system determines the person's current activities and location. This is combined with personal preferences and special needs profiles that are kept on file to personalize the information display.
3
The system queries a WorldBoard search engine or application server to identify relevant data for the current activities.
This data is sent back to the wearable computer.
4
Orientation sensors track the person's head and eye location to determine where the person is looking. Then the system displays information on see-through glasses. These graphics appear as part of the environment. Physical objects in the real environment can be virtually changed or completely removed from a person's view.
n23145 ...e32000 ...s89997 ...w00034 ...qns, ny
Serve: 110 m.p.h.
Net height: 3ft.6in.
Rows N20- S20: $120- $160
scroll for text
GPS and other location sensors help identify the user's location, and nearby objects and people.
12ft.
25ft.
Handheld or wearable computer provides wireless connection to the Internet and access to input devices for writing and voice recognition.
3D audio provides realistic environmental sound.
See-through glasses display information in 3D graphics and text.
How much do those seats cost?
What's the height of the net?
How fast does the ball go?
How are the stands constructed?
What other games are in progress?
Who's in the women's semi-finals?

Graphic by Nigel Holmes

wall but are actually added to the scene before being broadcast.

Augmented reality (AR) blends the real world and digital information. A person sees digital text and objects and hears digital sounds as though they were part of the physical world around them, the reality they perceive through the five senses. For practical purposes, the near-term work is focused on vision, hearing, and touch (haptics). AR differs from virtual reality (VR) because in VR a person is immersed in a computer-generated world. In AR the real world is enhanced by adding digital objects. While with visual AR it is easy to illustrate and imagine, most uses of AR will involve the use of several modes simultaneously, especially 3D sound and graphics. AR will be experienced via head-worn displays and handheld devices, offering see-through capabilities like normal glasses and adding information to live video images.

Researchers have been working on augmenting human experience with computers since Ivan Sullivan's work in the 1960s. This was continued with work in military and university labs in the 1970s and 1980s, and the term *augmented reality* was coined at Boeing in the early

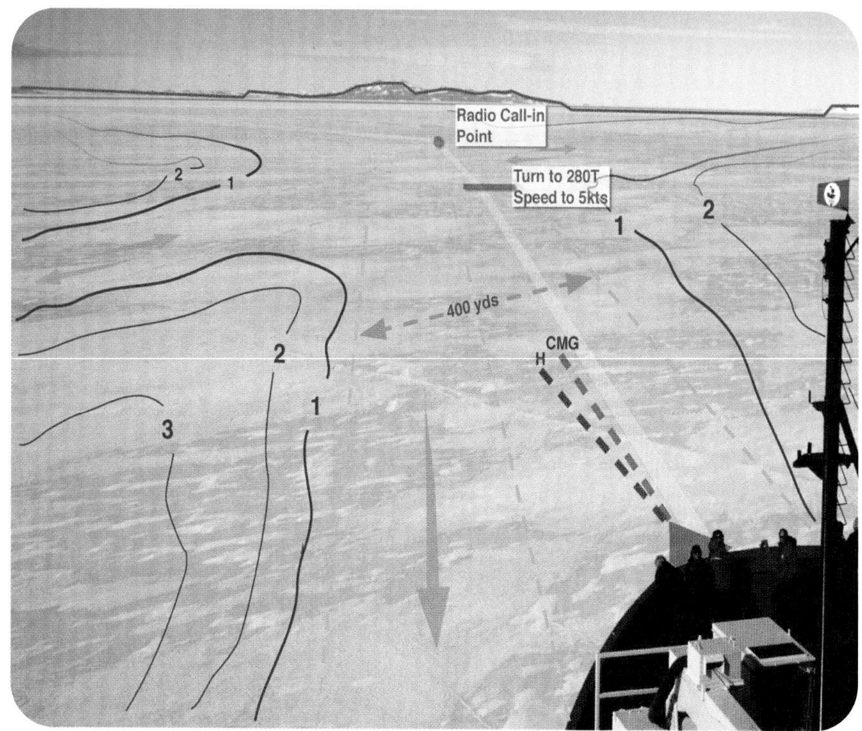

VIRTUAL HIGHWAYS. *Prototype system for overlaying information on the water for a navigator being developed by Information in Place, Inc., for the U.S. Coast Guard (left).* **VIRTUAL TOUR GUIDE.** *Animated characters and historical figures guide tourists on personalized tours. This image represents a visit to a Native American village complete with virtual reenactors and a re-creation of structures no longer in existence (below left).*

1990s to describe work they were doing on maintenance and assembly. Current work in AR can be divided into two focus areas: intelligent rooms and mobile AR. Intelligent rooms provide highly specialized systems for specific AR applications. These systems usually require extensive instrumentation where the system will be used, and the special tools, bulky size, and weight may force the person using the equipment to remain mostly stationary. A good example of these systems medical applications of AR, like those the University of North Carolina at Chapel Hill has been experimenting with since the 1970s. They have developed prototype applications that, like Superman's x-ray vision, let doctors see into the body of the patient by superimposing live medical data such as an ultrasound or MRI directly onto the patient's body.

Mobile AR systems focus on environments in which people move around frequently. These are less controlled environments and require different types of AR technologies that enable people to move around easily. The computer graphics group at Columbia University has developed prototype systems for tourists that provide information about the building they are viewing, historical events that took place at a location, and the ability to see a building that no longer exists but previously stood at the current site.

MERGING THE REAL AND VIRTUAL

For AR to work, a person must perceive digital information as part of the world. Scientists call this *co-registration*. For head-worn visual systems, this is achieved by tracking the person's head movement and exact orientation as well as location in the environment. This can be done with devices on the person and/or in the environment around them. Co-registration technologies enable the information to be overlaid precisely where it needs to be placed. Often this is partly behind or in front of real objects. In these cases the system has to occlude or block the view of the objects so that the digital information appears to be part of the environment. For instance, an interior decorator places a virtual chair behind a real table. The chair should only be partially showing because the person's view of the digital chair is partially blocked by the table just as it would if it were a real chair.

INFORMATION IN PLACES

While augmented reality provides the basic capabilities for a person to use and interact with digital objects, researchers at Indiana University have focused on how to enable a global infrastructure for delivery of AR experiences. Their work is inspired by a concept called WorldBoard, developed in 1996 by Dr. Jim Spohrer, then a researcher at Apple Computer. With WorldBoard, anyone is able to place any information at any location on the planet and have others access that information via AR. WorldBoard-like technologies will enable people to leave a shopping list attached to the grocery store for a spouse or interact with a virtual tour guide at a

Clockwise from top left: ©Information in Place, Inc., First image, artist: Daniel McDeavitt; second image, artist: Daniel McDeavitt, photographer: Keith Kramer

historical site. A person will choose what kind of information they want by tuning into channels of information relevant to their current activities.

Information in Place, Inc. (IIPI) is developing a prototype AR training system for the U.S. Army Simulation, Training, and Instrumentation Command. While this system will be used to train many kinds of skills, the focus is on enabling soldiers to learn battle skills in a realistic battle context by using computer-generated characters and events like those found in video games but which appear to be part of the "real world." For instance, when learning how to approach a high-rise building where hostages are being held, the soldiers must defend against virtual snipers, simulated mine fields, and the sounds of virtual bullets flying by their heads. This can make training more realistic and cost-effective.

This work is complimentary to the Naval Research Lab's work on the Battlefield Augmented Reality System, which is designed to provide soldiers with real-time information while in battle. For instance, the system might outline the window on a nearby buiding in which a sniper has been spotted.

In another example, IIPI is working with the U.S. Coast Guard to determine how ship navigation can be made safer and security can be increased. In this AR system, a virtual highway is displayed on the water that shows a ship's crew precisely where they should navigate, as well as labeling hazards and indicating where other ships are headed. Other uses include being able to instantly transmit security information by marking zones on the water, helping the Coast Guard keep vessels out of secure zones and defend against a terrorist threat.

Artist: Daniel McDeavitt

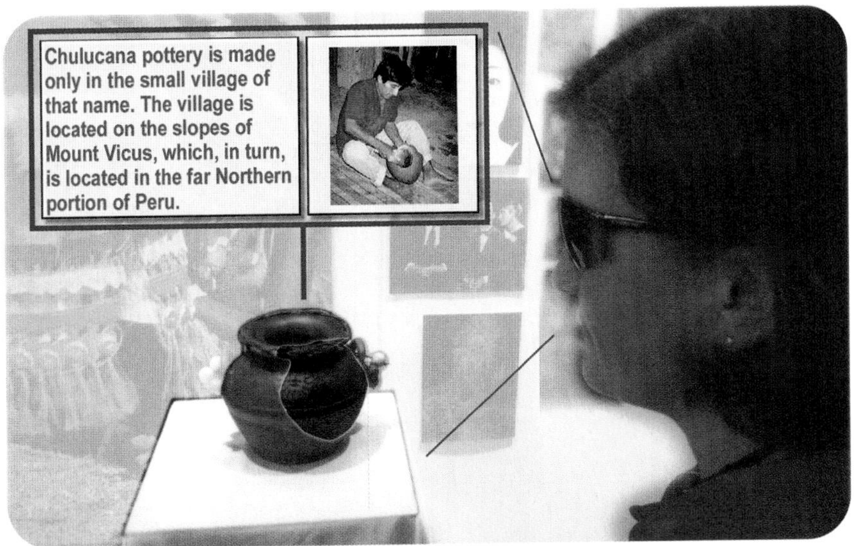

Chulucana pottery is made only in the small village of that name. The village is located on the slopes of Mount Vicus, which, in turn, is located in the far Northern portion of Peru.

X-RAY VISION. *In a museum people will be able to see what is behind the paint of a painting or the parts of an artifact that are missing. Additionally, personalized information can be presented to them.*

THE KILLER APPLICATION

Some have called mobile AR the killer application for mobile computing. We believe this is true. While today many discrete AR applications are being developed, we believe that within the decade a WorldBoard system will be in place to serve as a central infrastructure. In this world of 2012, AR technology will be as common as cell phones are today, and it will likely be the preferred mode of interaction with digital information via the communication device of the future.

This entirely new interface to computing enables the physical and digital worlds to be perceived as one, and this will radically alter our relationship with information. We will come to think of digital information as an integral part of our world. Today, we put physical tools and information where they are most needed. Tomorrow, as a mechanism to help us manage the ovewhelming amount of digital information, we will put digital information in its place and in doing so increase its usefulness.

PROVOCATIONS...

Will augmented reality enable us to change our mates' appearance, and then our own?

Will there have to be a 12-step program to help people "take off the glasses?"

—Sonny Kirkley and Chris Borland

WANT MORE?

WORLDBOARD FORUM
www.worldboard.org

INFORMATION IN PLACE, INC.
www.informationinplace.com

THE AUGMENTED REALITY HOMEPAGE
www.augmented-reality.org

A SURVEY OF AUGMENTED REALITY
www.cs.unc.edu/~azuma/ARpresence.pdf

RECENT ADVANCES IN AUGMENTED REALITY
www.cs.unc.edu/~azuma/cga2001.pdf

The Future of Transportation and Travel

About every two generations, we invent a new way to get around that changes our cities, our neighborhoods, our homes, and our lives.

It's hard to predict what's next. In a decade or so, we could all be riding magnetically levitated trains at 500mph between newly transformed cities or riding our personal, gyroscopically controlled scooter to a friend's house built around new scooter-accessible roadways.

But by looking at the past we can see how quickly we change, particularly in the United States. A century ago, or even 50 years ago, no one could have imagined that the huge passenger rail system, constructed with such an enormous amount of effort, would lie abandoned, almost unused.

Perhaps 50 years in the future, weeds may sprout from cracks in our interstate highways. Perhaps like "rails to trails," our sons and daughters will devise recreational uses for these mammoth concrete viaducts, when cars no longer course along their lanes.

If history is any indication, we will make a change soon. Since about 1800, we have developed and adopted a new way to move people, goods, and services about every two to three generations. Each change has revolutionized our society, inventing new cities, neighborhoods, and ways of life, while leaving the old ways to decay.

One thing is probable: The next new way to get around will not come through the lone inventor, laboring away in splendid isolation. It might start that way, but no new method of getting around has become a "system" without a government, that often disliked entity, pushing and subsidizing it. Technology alone does not drive change. You have to persuade someone, usually a government, to build supporting infrastructure on a wide basis. As one transportation engineer said, "Transportation is a system. You can't have a little bit of transportation."

THE PAST

We can see this by looking at the last 200 years, a wild, roller-coaster ride of a journey as far as changes in transportation and travel. It began about 1825, with canals, those seemingly simple wide ditches filled with water, used by horse-drawn barges. But in the 1800s, these canals were the equivalent of high-speed rail or a jet plane. Various states, particularly New York with the Erie Canal, subsidized their construction, and canals revolutionized the transport of goods and services. The price of inland shipping dropped by 90%.

Then came the railroads, which gradually replaced canals. Historians estimate state and federal governments in the 19th century gave away about a fifth of the total land area of the country to private railroad companies, as well as the power of eminent domain and the hundreds of millions of dollars in direct grants. The new rail system created new cities, like Atlanta, and enlarged existing ones, like Chicago. It also created hundreds of new towns. Soon afterward, the streetcar created thousands of new neighborhoods within cities and towns.

After World War I, the car and the plane, and their necessary companions the highway and the airport, gradually replaced the passenger railroad, the grand train station, and the humble streetcar.

Although the automobile dates to the 1890s, people did not use them regularly until towns and states began paving roads in earnest, which took awhile. In 1922, 80% of the roads in this country were dirt and gravel. The country's newly-established Bureau of Public Roads, a federal office, led the way in researching methods of producing cost-effective, durable, reliable roads.

After World War II came the elevated, limited-access freeway, which was to the simple paved road as a Formula One racecar is to a Model-T Ford. In 1956 President Eisenhower signed the National Highway and Defense Act, perhaps the largest public works project in world history.

Around these new roads and new highways came new ways to live. Early suburbs popped up around newly paved roads in the 1920s, while huge covered regional shopping centers in the 1960s popped up around the first cloverleafs around the elevated, limited-access highways.

Air travel had a similar history. The airplane began in the Wright Brothers' bicycle shop in the early 1900s but became a method of transportation only after cities built hundreds of municipal airports and the federal government subsidized the creation of passenger airline companies.

Now we are in the 21st century, and the car and the plane have dominated transportation for about 75 years. Which means we're due for a change.

THE FUTURE

An unstable combination of government subsidies, technological promise, and private profit will determine what comes next, and this will vary from place to place. Indicators like wealth will not always be reliable indicators of what transportation systems particular societies will adopt.

Consider the humble bicycle, invented in the 19th century and still in use. Right now, the Chinese and the Scandinavians use the bicycle extensively for daily travel, even though one nation has very low per capita income and the other region has very high per capita income. Meanwhile, people in the United States, a rich country, bicycle less and less, except for sport. The bicycle is a marvelous tool, a nearly perfect blend of technology and utility. But using it more in this country would mean taming some of the suburban sprawl that makes bicycle riding so difficult here. That's not likely.

New transportation trends, such as smart cars and intelligent highways, which build on existing infrastructure, have an advantage. In the United States, nearly driverless trucks may soon speed down special reserved lanes of the interstates equipped with magnets that guide the vehicles at 100mph-plus speeds.

More difficult to achieve in this country, although still possible, is a new network of high-speed trains, even though they are already in use in Europe and Japan. Trains powered by magnetic levitation, also proven technology, could reach 300–500mph. A hurdle in the United States would be the airline industry, which probably would oppose putting public money into a track system for its competitor.

The requirements of new infrastructure are one reason why personal space travel is probably a long way off to all but the most profligate millionaire or billionaire. To carry even a few thousand people annually into space would mean somebody would have to construct launch pads and space ships that we now don't have. Private enterprise is unlikely to do this, and government is unlikely to see the wider social or economic benefit.

But change is coming. If history is any guide, we will move on again to the next new thing soon, with scarcely a backward glance. Whether it's for personal jetpacks or high-speed trains, we will abandon our beloved Porsches and Fords and the highways we built for them. We will close up our municipal airports when the next new thing comes around the corner that promises to get us there faster, quicker, and easier.

—Alex Marshall

Personal Transporters...

It's the 21st Century, Do You Know Where Your Hoverboard Is?

THERE IS PROBABLY NO MORE FANCIFUL VISION OF THE *near future — as featured in science-fiction novels, movies, and other media — than the personal transport, zippy futuristic getabouts unbound by asphalt and oh-so-20th-century internal combustion engines. No vision of the near future is more perpetually trapped on "imagineers'" drawing boards than these air cars, hoverboards, jetpacks, and similar Jetsonian pipe dreams. Although the technology to realize such cool conveyances is tantalizingly close at hand, impediments such as high costs, public safety concerns, and a firmly entrenched gas-guzzling infrastructure have so far thwarted the best of developers' intentions.*

The Segway Human Transporter is probably the closest we've gotten to the type of high-tech transportation that science-fiction authors have been writing into our future for decades. Created by high-profile inventor Dean Kamen, the Segway, originally code-named "Ginger," caught the world's attention in early 2001 when it was leaked to the media that Kamen (who'd already stunned with iBot, his stair-climbing wheelchair) was working on some sort of revolutionary transportation device. After Steve Jobs, Jeff Bezos, and Bob Metcalfe fell for Ginger in a big way during a private demo, speculation about Ginger ran rampant until Kamen went public with his invention in early December 2001.

The battery-powered scooter looks like a push mower that you climb onto. Sports gyros, servos, and microprocessors allow you to steer the device simply by moving your body in the desired direction of travel. Kamen's brainchild is not likely to put Detroit out of business anytime soon, but it does point to a future in which environmentally friendly, single-person vehicles may finally become an option for around-town travel. Some U.S. postal services and city police departments are already testing the viability of the Segway for making their rounds. But will a criminal take a cop seriously when he tools up atop of what looks like a push mower?

A STIRLING FUTURE

One of the tantalizing speculations during the development of Ginger was that it might be powered by a Stirling engine.

THE SEGWAY HUMAN TRANSPORTER.
Currently available only to commercial customers for selected business applications.

Images courtesy of Segway LLC

COMMANDO CODY. *Sky Marshall of the Universe, blasting off in his jetpack in the 1949 B-movie* King of the Rocketmen.

Although the Stirling engine is often thought of as a futuristic power source, it is actually far from new. Invented in 1816 by Scottish clergyman Robert Stirling, various versions of the engine are already in use in specialty markets such as submarines and power generators for yachts. What makes a Stirling engine so desirable is that it makes far more efficient use of fuel, there's no combustion (which greatly reduces pollution and engine noise), and it can use any fuel source, from gasoline to methane to rotting plant matter. Unfortunately, there are drawbacks. The engines are currently very expensive to produce, they take awhile to warm up, and they don't accelerate quickly — all of which makes them undesirable for vehicles.

If manufacturing costs could come down and ways could be found around the warm-up and acceleration problems, Stirling engines could have a profound and positive impact on our future. Think of a world in which, not only could your car and commuter scooter be nonpolluting and free from foreign oil, but a Stirling plant in your basement could allow you to generate your own power.

The Stirling engine speculations related to Kamen and the Segway

INSIDE THE SEGWAY

How does Dean Kamen's self-balancing "human transporter" achieve its magic? Using the latest advances in gyros, tilt sensors and high-performance motors. Here's how it works:

Intelligent key A digital security code thwarts would-be thieves. Also sets speed limits

Kill switch

User interface Tells you the machine is on, what mode it's in and how much battery life is left

Turning control A single axle gives Segway something no other vehicle has: a turning radius of zero

Control shaft Die-cast aluminum, height adjustable

Motors Two of them drive each wheel independently. Emission free and fully redundant; if one fails, the other takes over

Batteries Two types available; NiCd and NiMH; rechargeable by plugging into any outlet

UNDER THE HOOD

"Sisterboards" A pair of circuit boards sends commands to the motors based on input from sensors. If one fails, the other can function by itself

Balance sensors Gyroscopes and tilt sensors work together to pick up tiny shifts of body weight and changes in terrain. The five gyros operate by committee, voting among themselves to eliminate errant readings

Chassis Houses Segway's electronic innards. Tested to withstand 7 tons of force—the weight of three SUVs

Rubber diaphragms Hidden beneath the rider's platform, they engage the machine's self-balancing systems. Step off; and the Segway stops

Tires Tubeless and resistant to flats. Treated for enhanced traction on wet surfaces and to leave no marks indoors

Source: Segway
TIME Graphic by Lon Tweeten

SOLOTREK HELICOPTER BACKPACK. *Expected to be used primarily for military, search and rescue, and other specialty applications.*

resurfaced in mid-2002 when his New Power Concepts company was issued several patents for Stirling engine technologies, including techniques for more inexpensive manufacturing. Segway could prove to be earth shattering after all. Such a Stirling-powered scooter may have been what Ethernet inventor Bob Metcalfe was talking about when he was quoted as saying that Kamen's invention would be "bigger than the Internet" and "almost as big as cold fusion would have been."

SOLOTREK HELICOPTER BACKPACK

Despite the media's obsession with Segway, it's not the only fledgling futuristic transportation device. Others, such as the SoloTrek, have enjoyed increased exposure in the wake of Kamen's device. Developed by Millennium Jet, Inc., the SoloTrek is what you might get if you stripped a small helicopter down to its blades and engine and strapped the remains onto your back. The occupant steps into the harness on the 325-pound craft, jacks the throttle, and off to work he goes. That's the vision anyway. This helicopter backpack is still in the prototype stage and has enjoyed only a few test flights (of a few feet for less than half a minute in duration). Even if the SoloTrek can overcome design and manufacturing obstacles, it's doubtful that it will ever be used for anything other than military, search and rescue, and other specialty applications.

AIRBOARD HOVERCRAFT

The hovercraft is another futuristic travel technology that never seems to catch on, but could soon, at least as a recreational vehicle. The electric scooter company ZAP has signed a distribution agreement with Australia's Arbortech Industries for rights to distribute the latter's personal hovercraft technology in North America. The AirBoard is also available from Hammacher Schlemmer. The AirBoard, a saucer-shaped contraption that you stand on to zip around, hovers some 4 inches

NILES GARDEN MONORAIL

Sometimes, you just can't sit around and wait for the future to arrive. Such was the impatience of Kim Pedersen, a monorail enthusiast from Niles, a historic district in Fremont, California. He built what he's dubbed a "garden monorail" in his backyard. The two-car monorail, constructed from wood, sheet metal, and a wheelchair motor, snakes through Pedersen's backyard on 300 feet of track, 8 feet above the ground at the highest point. The cars even have lights on them for cruising around and showing off the future to the neighbors at night.

MOLLER SKYCAR

If life were fair, we'd all be swooping into work in a Moller Skycar by now. Paul Moller has spent nearly three decades and untold millions of dollars developing his wheeled car/airplane combo vehicle and has just recently gotten to the point of tethered test flights. The vertical take-off and landing (VTOL) vehicle has been the darling of pop mechanics and futurist magazines since its inception, but real-world progress has been slow. Moller hopes that manufacturing can begin within the next few years. Given the complexity of the vehicle and its expense (initially it will cost nearly a million dollars), it could be decades before the vehicles are available to consumers. Developing an all-computerized, infallible flight control system will be required before the Skycar can ever be sold as a general consumer device. One thing that could help drive the success of such flying cars is NASA's "highway in the sky" initiative (officially known as The Small Aircraft Transportation System). This plan calls for a computerized "free flight" system to be created that will allow the average person to safely take to the sky in small personal aircraft such as the Moller Skycar. Skeptics of the plan abound, some of who have churlishly dubbed it "The George Jetson Plan." Money is perhaps the biggest impediment. NASA says it needs $69 million to realize its vision within 5 years.

MAGIC CARPET RIDE. *Be the first on your block to own an AirBoard, available as the "Levitating Hover Scooter" from Hammacher Schlemmer for $14,999.95.*

above the ground and travels up to 15mph. Unfortunately, the AirBoard currently costs a whopping $15,000, and you need a special permit to operate it in public.

As fun and bleeding edge as these technologies are, it is still unlikely that our means of personal transportation will radically change anytime soon. The Segway has the greatest chance of widespread success, and coupled with Stirling engine technology, that success could be far wider. If this happens, and laws and habits change to accommodate it, it could pave the way for some of the other technologies outlined here.

PROVOCATIONS...

What will PT traffic jams be like? What will the tricked-out "art car" versions look like? Will schools need a new form of drivers-ed classes?

—Gareth Branwyn

WANT MORE?

SEGWAY PERSONAL TRANSPORTER
www.segway.com

SOLOTREK
www.solotrek.com

ZAP ELECTRIC VEHICLES
www.zapworld.com

HAMMACHER SCHLEMMER
www.hammacher.com

ARBORTECH INDUSTRIES, LTD.
www.airboard.com.au

THE NILES GARDEN MONORAIL
www.monrails.org

MOLLER SKYCAR
www.moller.com/skycar

BICYCLES OF TOMORROW...
Miles of Possibilities, Two Feet at a Time

ELECTRIC BICYCLE KIT. *The ZETA III, from ZAP, enables you to convert your existing bike into an electric power-assisted cycle (above).*
BAMBOO BICYCLE. *Enthusiasts believe bamboo, as a bicycle-frame material, is as strong as aluminum (left).*

FOLD IT AND STOW IT. *Just remove the lug, fold it, put it in its case, and you're ready to fly.*

QUICK, WHAT'S YOUR TOP-OF-MIND ASSOCIATION WHEN *you hear the word "bike?" Is it some obscure shortstop clickety-clacking in the spokes? Is it the Wicked Witch of the West riding off with Toto? Or does the word conjure up images like hand-grips with tassels, banana seats, your first "wheelie," or the classic Schwinn Varsity 10-speed? Well, the odds are that your most innate two-wheeled perceptions are directly related to a kid-centric form of transportation. But there's a high-tech side to the bicycle that in many unexpected ways transforms the simplistic concept of a "bike" into a vast array of NASA-like conveyance systems.*

For sure, "extreme biking" is nothing new. Students of Leonardo da Vinci are said to have made sketches of bike-like contraptions as early as the 15th century. In the late 1800s the Wright brothers had a bike shop before they decided to take to the air, and they used many of the things they learned about bicycles to create their early airplanes. In 1914, aeronautical types started to experiment with a "bullet" bike, vividly illustrating that the bicycle has always been all about aerodynamics, innovation, and the wacky manifestations of the human mind.

Clockwise from top left: Photo courtesy of Bamboo Bike Company, LCC (503 650-5162) · Photo courtesy of ZAP. All rights reserved · Photo courtesy of Ev Global Motors Company (www.ebike.com) · Photo courtesy of Ev Global Motors Company (www.ebike.com)

Accordingly, having two wheels is about all the bikes of the future will have in common with those of the past. Some are at work creating the principles of personal rapid transit (PRT). PRT uses streamlined recumbent bicycles (riders travel lying down) that will travel along aerial (sky bikes) or land-based (bike trains) grid systems. These mass transit systems will deliver non-stop, station-to-station service at speeds from 30mph to 60mph. The bikes themselves will be small electric vehicles, and the leaning-back travel style and tightly spaced configuration of the bikes will provide maximized transport efficiency. Electricity is bound to be a common future theme. Combining the ease and mobility of a pedal bike with the power of a golf cart, electrics and electric hybrids can reach speeds of 20mph – but plan on limited range (20 miles) and a price tag of $1,000.

COMPUTER ON BOARD

Traditional or off-the-beaten path, smart bicycle ideas abound. Shimano has created what they call digital integrated intelligence. It essentially combines the high-performance, multispeed bicycle with an onboard computer. Riders will be able to view and control the automated action through a handlebar-mounted nerve center termed the "flight deck." Yet while one sphere of these bike revolutionaries focuses on brains, another contingent continues to focus on the sheer brawn (or lack thereof) – and for these people it's all about materials. Steel, aluminum, titanium, carbon fibers? All old hat. Tomorrow's bikes are made of stuff called Scandium or E5 or ZR 9000. They're the latest high-tech alloys in the pursuit of the bike-frame Holy Grail – frames that are super-light, but not dentable, and super-strong, yet still moldable. It should be noted, however, that some believe that bike frame nirvana occurs naturally in the form of bamboo. And once you find the perfect futuristic frame, you'll of course need the perfect futuristic tire. Specialized Bicycles and DuPont think they have the answer. Their Kevlar-based invention seals all gaps in the fabric weave to create what amounts to a flat-proof tire.

BIKE WITH BRAINS. *Shimano's Flight Deck computer has controls that are integrated into the bike's shift levers, enabling you to view gears and gear ratios without lifting your hands from the handlebars.*

SPORT UTILITY CYCLE (SUC)

Tomorrow's high-tech bikes promise to deliver unexpected forms, but what about more purposeful function? Are you ready for the sport utility cycle – the SUC? Xtracycle is fully prepared to convert your old mountain bike or cruiser into a real workhorse. By adding an extension to your existing frame, you can create an SUC capable of carrying a 200-pound payload, so you can pedal with, say, an ice chest and barbecue.

So you'll be able to go big, but what about going small? S and S Machine now builds a bike that comes with a precision lug built into the bike frame. The lug allows a full-size road or mountain bike to be folded and packed into a case that easily slides into a plane's overhead compartment. And for those with a fear of riding alone, Alternative Powered Vehicles has designed the Zero Emission Machine, a rig that accommodates four independent pedalers.

From its popular association with leisure living and paper routes, the staid little bicycle has traveled quite a distance, and it's nothing short of amazing how far two feet will ultimately take us.

PROVOCATIONS...

Will we have to impose speed limits on the bikes of tomorrow?

Could we see entirely new forms of "biker gangs" in the future?

If biking becomes a major form of travel, will it inspire new pop music tunes, the way cars, motorcycles, and skateboards did?

– Patrick Macke

WANT MORE?

SHIMANO
http://bike.shimano.com

FOLDING BIKE
www.sandsmachine.com

SPORT UTILITY CYCLE
www.xtracycle.com

FLATPROOF TIRES
www.specialized.com
www.contitires.com

EBIKES
www.primaricerca.it/laprima/england/powerbike.htm
www.zapworld.com
www.evglobal.com
www.apriliaenjoy.com

BIKE MATERIALS
www.trekbikes.com

BAMBOO BICYCLE
www.bamboobike.com

2000 2005 2010 2015 2020

risks rewards

The Drive of Tomorrow...

Trends in the Evolution of Cars and Roads

THANKFULLY, OUR AIR-TRAFFIC CONCERNS DO NOT CURRENTLY INCLUDE MILLIONS OF *small helicopters filled with commuters headed for work. However, several trends are working to make the cars of the mid-21st century as fantastic as personal helicopters would have been.*

FILL 'ER UP WITH H2, JOE

One thing about 21st-century cars is certain: They can't always run on gasoline. The world's supply of fossil fuels is finite, and at some point it will simply cost too much to extract the oil to refine into gasoline — maybe 20 years from now, maybe 50, maybe even 100. Fortunately, auto manufacturers are beginning to address this issue now.

At first, we thought electric cars would replace gasoline-fueled cars, but heavy batteries, limited range, and a lack of charging stations kept the electric car off the streets. The current trend is to pair gasoline and electric engines in hybrid cars. Both Honda and Toyota currently produce hybrid models, which use the gasoline and electric engines both independently and together during different types of driving. Excess energy created by the gasoline engine and during braking is used to charge the batteries — you don't need to plug these cars in. The primary benefits of the hybrid approach are reduced emissions and gasoline consumption.

But hybrid cars are really only a temporary solution. The real replacement for the internal combustion engine will likely be the fuel cell, which will generate power for electric motors that propel the car. Fuel cell technology has been around for a long time, but recent attention from government and industry has resulted in dramatic reductions in fuel cell size and cost. Every automaker in the world has at least some R&D activity focused on powering cars with fuel cells. However, the Bush administration recently scrapped an existing program that would have sought immediate increases in gasoline engine efficiency and replaced it with a program intended to jump-start the movement to hydrogen-powered cars. Oil companies also are trying to figure out how to get into the hydrogen business.

The problem with hydrogen-powered cars is the hydrogen, which is currently more expensive to produce and distribute than gasoline. Nor is it clear how to store the hydrogen once it's in the car — hydrogen stored in tanks would be bulky and likely trigger fears of explosion. An interim solution is to obtain the hydrogen from gasoline, through a process known as steam reforming. This would allow fuel cell cars to use the existing fuel infrastructure, and it does produce fewer emissions than burning gasoline in an internal combustion engine. For a long-term solution, engineers are exploring ways to store the

SAFETY CONCEPT CAR (SCC). *Volvo's SCC employs a variety of new technologies that enhance personal safety; many of these features help the driver make the right decision in difficult traffic situations (e.g., a collision warning system, among other features).*

Image by PRNewsFoto

hydrogen in metal hydrides, which can be made to chemically hold and then release hydrogen molecules to power the fuel cell.

INCREASED SAFETY

Even in this age of airplanes being used as weapons, you're still more likely to be killed or injured while driving your car than while flying in an airplane. This is not news to the carmakers, who started making seatbelts standard in the 1950s and 1960s, and have become increasingly aware of the marketing power of safety features. The recent trend of airbags everywhere will certainly continue – side and curtain airbags are becoming increasingly standard, and BMW has introduced a knee-area airbag on its top-of-the-line cars.

The crumple zones in today's cars absorb much of the shock of an accident before it can be transferred to the car's occupants. A new, super-strong and lightweight material, stabilized aluminum foam, increases the amount of force absorbed by as much as 600%. Made by blowing gas bubbles into a molten mixture of aluminum and ceramic particles, the foam would also increase fuel efficiency, as it is so much lighter than a solid metal. NASCAR officials see the foam as a good way to address their linked concerns of speed and safety and hope to be using it in the crumple zones of their cars sometime this year.

Information systems can play as large a part in auto safety as materials. Electronic sensors will monitor all aspects of a car's condition, from fluids to engine to tire pressure, and notify the driver if something needs attention. Critical information will likely be relayed by a heads-up display, which projects information onto the inside of the

MERCEDES BENZ MULTIMEDIA CAR.
Mercedes S-series include capabilities for wireless communications in their cars, including reading and sending email, surfing the Web, and more.

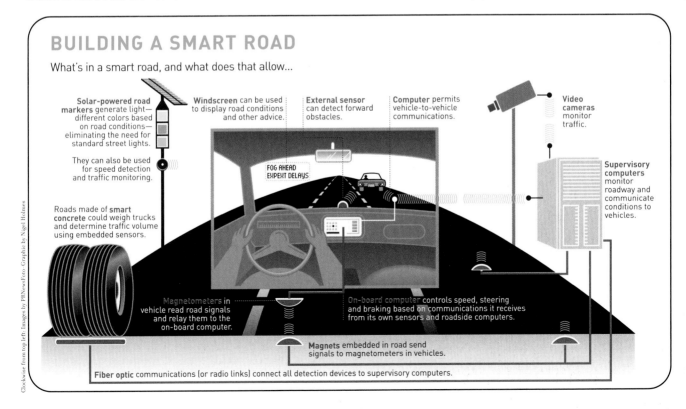

BUILDING A SMART ROAD

What's in a smart road, and what does that allow...

Solar-powered road markers generate light—different colors based on road conditions—eliminating the need for standard street lights.

They can also be used for speed detection and traffic monitoring.

Roads made of **smart concrete** could weigh trucks and determine traffic volume using embedded sensors.

Windscreen can be used to display road conditions and other advice.

External sensor can detect forward obstacles.

Computer permits vehicle-to-vehicle communications.

Video cameras monitor traffic.

Supervisory computers monitor roadway and communicate conditions to vehicles.

FOG AHEAD
EXPECT DELAYS

Magnetometers in vehicle read road signals and relay them to the on-board computer.

On-board computer controls speed, steering and braking based on communications it receives from its own sensors and roadside computers.

Magnets embedded in road send signals to magnetometers in vehicles.

Fiber optic communications (or radio links) connect all detection devices to supervisory computers.

Clockwise from top left: Images by PRNewsFoto · Graphic by Nigel Holmes

GM'S AUTONOMY

GM's AUTOnomy concept car is perhaps the most dramatic vision of the automobile of the future. GM engineers want to get rid of the steel chassis, the drive train, the internal-combustion engine, the steering column – all the hallmarks of today's cars – and replace them with a skateboard. Okay, not quite a skateboard, but a 6-inch thick automotive platform, containing a fuel cell power system, fuel storage facilities, front and rear crumple zones, electronic suspension arms, a computing infrastructure, and four wheels driven by four electronic motors, each contained in what used to be the hubcap. Onto this "skateboard," GM and its customers could snap whatever body style they want – or happened to need that day.

Fuel cells and software are what will make this happen. Since fuel cells create only power, water vapor, and heat, no exhaust system or catalytic converter would be needed. And since a steady stream of power would be delivered directly to the wheel-mounted engines, the transmission, drive shaft, and differential are no longer needed. The car would be controlled electronically. The brake pedal would no longer need to be hydraulically connected to the braking system – a sensor would detect the amount of braking requested and the car would transmit this information to the braking systems, which would then use motors and actuators to apply the braking force.

The software makes it possible to standardize the interface between the skateboard and the rest of the car. Commands for acceleration, braking, cornering, powering the interior heating and cooling – everything the car needs to do – would be adjusted specifically for the body currently riding the skateboard, but based upon the common capabilities designed into the chassis. Since the interior design no longer needs to accommodate an engine, drive train, or steering column, it essentially becomes a room that can be designed, and changed, like any other.

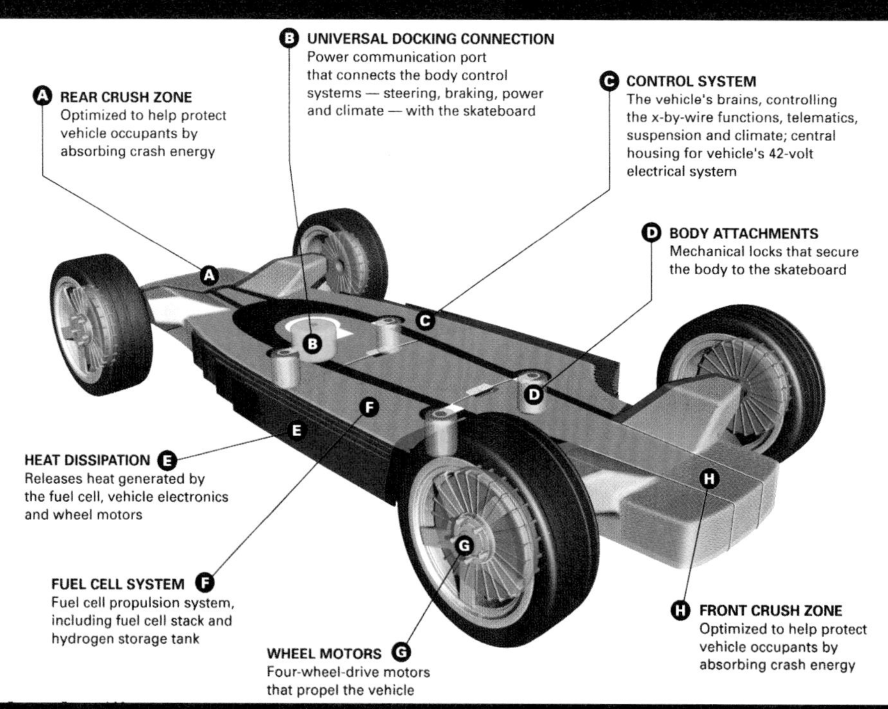

A REAR CRUSH ZONE
Optimized to help protect vehicle occupants by absorbing crash energy
B UNIVERSAL DOCKING CONNECTION
Power communication port that connects the body control systems — steering, braking, power and climate — with the skateboard
C CONTROL SYSTEM
The vehicle's brains, controlling the x-by-wire functions, telematics, suspension and climate; central housing for vehicle's 42-volt electrical system
D BODY ATTACHMENTS
Mechanical locks that secure the body to the skateboard
HEAT DISSIPATION E
Releases heat generated by the fuel cell, vehicle electronics and wheel motors
FUEL CELL SYSTEM F
Fuel cell propulsion system, including fuel cell stack and hydrogen storage tank
WHEEL MOTORS G
Four-wheel-drive motors that propel the vehicle
H FRONT CRUSH ZONE
Optimized to help protect vehicle occupants by absorbing crash energy

Image courtesy of General Motors Corporation

windshield, allowing drivers to more easily divide their attention between the car and the road. Cars will also make sure that their drivers are paying attention, using dash-mounted cameras and sophisticated software to detect the nodding head and droopy eyes of a driver about to fall asleep behind the wheel. Communication and navigation systems in cars are already retrieving information about road construction and conditions — a trend that's sure to increase. When fully linked into a wireless information network, a car could even make sure that the person trying to drive it is one of its owners or friends, that they're currently licensed, and that they're in an appropriate condition to drive.

ASSISTED DRIVING

The best way to make our cars safer is to stop humans from driving them. The Japanese Institute for Traffic Accident Research and Data Analysis determined that human error was the cause of 90% of the accidents on that country's densely-trafficked roads, and automakers are now extending their focus on safety to the driver. Standard cruise control makes long trips easier on the driver and can improve fuel economy, but you still need to react if the guy in front of you has his cruise control set 5mph lower than yours. Adaptive cruise control systems, now available on some luxury cars, use radar and microprocessors to adjust the car's cruising speed and remain a safe distance from other vehicles in the same lane.

...you're still more likely to be killed or injured while driving your car than... on an airplane.

Japanese car companies have taken this concept even further. Subaru's Active Driving Assist system will sound an alarm if the car starts to drift out of its lane and will downshift and sound an alarm if the car enters a curve too fast. Honda's Intelligent Driver Support system uses a network of laser sensors, digital video cameras, and electronic control units to track other vehicles and the car's lane position. It will adjust driving speeds and apply small steering corrections to keep the car in its correct lane and a safe distance away from other cars. Of course, the driver has ultimate control and can override these systems at any time, but carmakers hope that these systems will make driving safer and less stressful.

Drivers who are willing to give up complete control of their vehicles will gain both safety and speed when automated highway systems (AHSs) become available. AHS would likely consist of dedicated lanes in highways, equipped with data gathering and transmitting hardware that would help cars drive themselves. The driver would specify the desired destination, and the car's computer would check for AHS availability along the route it plans. When the car approaches an AHS-equipped lane, the car would signal the driver, who would steer the car into a transition lane and then relinquish control to the car, which would guide the car into the AHS lane and take over, following the road at its designated speed, accommodating other cars wanting to join the lane, and using brakes and steering to avoid any obstacles that do appear. The driver would be free to sit back, relax, even watch TV or browse the Internet – though some adjustment and experience would likely be needed before drivers reached living-room levels of comfort.

When enough AHS-capable roads and vehicles become available, cars could travel in "platoons." These would be groups of 10-20 vehicles whose travel is coordinated not just with the road, but with each other. This would allow them to travel very closely together – perhaps as little as 3 meters apart. Platoons would dynamically reform themselves at highway exits, as cars left and joined the platoon. Collisions could occur between vehicles in the event of mechanical failure, but they would be at very low relative velocities and the malfunctioning vehicle would be quickly guided out of the automated lane.

So imagine 50 years from now, traveling quietly but very quickly down the highway toward work while watching the morning news. You neighbor is in the car behind you (3 meters behind you!), and the heads-up system is telling you that the platoon will be taking a detour to avoid accident-related delays (from non-automated cars, of course) coming up ahead. The main computer display shows that your hydrogen storage is at about two-thirds of capacity and that all safety features are online and functioning. Oh, and the coffee's done brewing and the microwave says your breakfast's ready. Sure beats having to pilot a helicopter to work, huh?

PROVOCATIONS...

Could cars become so safe that we will lower the minimum age for a driver's license?

Will fewer accidents on the roads hurt the autobody business and drive up the cost of repairs?

Will deer populations rise?

– Bill Kaszubski

WANT MORE?

GM R&D
www.gm.com/automotive/innovations/rnd

SMART ROAD
www.virginiadot.org/projects/constsal-smartrd.asp

HYDROGEN/FUEL CELLS
www.hfcletter.com

INSTITUTE FOR ACCIDENT RESEARCH AND DATA ANALYSIS
www.itarda.or/jp/english/eg_home.htm

AUTONOMY
http://gm.com/company/gmability/environment/products/adv_tech/autonomy1_010702.html

MERCEDES
www.mercedesbenz.com

VOLVO
www.volvocars.com

HIGH-SPEED RAIL... The Iron Horse Goes Electric

"It's Century time! A minute ago, outside the station, you were in the heart of a great city, with crowds, blaring taxis, newsboys shouting the evening headlines. Now you're in a different world as you follow that crimson carpet down the platform of Grand Central Terminal toward the softly lighted, streamlined cars that will be your club on wheels for tonight."

—1948 advertisement for luxury rail service for the 20th Century Limited.

A different world indeed. A world of pillbox hats and fedoras, of Eva Marie Saint and Cary Grant, of cigarettes and cocktails. A world that's long over in America, killed by the interstate highway system and the freedom of the car. But now, from our 21st-century perspective of urban sprawl and energy crises, it seems that we may have lost more than just romance and elegance. Transportation planners are looking at rail with a fresh perspective, hoping to create systems that preserve the best aspects of the automotive experience while gaining the efficiency and economy of rail.

The age of rail never ended in Europe and Japan. With less space to cover and a more centralized approach to transportation planning, train systems there have not atrophied the way they have in the U.S. The Japanese Shinkansen – Bullet Train – went into service in 1964, with a top speed of 131mph. The high-speed TGV trains operating in France today routinely travel in excess of 180mph. These trains are powered by electric engines, are designed to be extremely aerodynamic and light, and run on dedicated tracks with long straightaways and gentle curves.

TRANSPORTATION HISTORY. *Maglev train arrives at Old Dominion University, April, 2002.*

The next generation of high-speed trains is evolving along three paths: incremental improvements to the existing high-speed designs, tilting trains that can travel at increased speeds on existing tracks, and maglev trains that

NEW DIRECTIONS IN MAGLEV TECHNOLOGY

The train hovers inches above the track, riding a cushion of air silently across the countryside at hundreds of miles per hour – the sci-fi vision of maglev trains is undeniably compelling. Unfortunately, commercial prospects for maglev are not. The problem is the huge expense of the track, which requires large amounts of electricity and expensive cooling systems to operate and costs more than twice as much to build as conventional rail.

Recent advances in technology could bring maglev closer. The Inductrack system uses permanent magnets arranged in a design known as a Halbach array, which takes the magnetic force emitted by permanent magnets and focuses it in one direction. Scientists have created as much as 50 pounds of repulsive force from just 1 pound of magnet. The competing LevX system also uses permanent magnets, but its developers have achieved physical changes in the magnetic material – neodymium – that produces a stronger magnetic force that doesn't degrade over time, like current maglev systems do. These technologies are beginning to receive government funding, including some from NASA, which wants to use Inductrack as a space-launching platform. Perhaps in the next decade the loudest thing on our trains will be the whistle.

float on a cushion of electromagnetic force and glide silently along their supercooled tracks. While tilting trains have been deployed in Sweden and on Amtrak's Eastern Seaboard route, maglev trains have yet to be proven commercially viable, chiefly because they require an entirely new, and expensive, kind of rail infrastructure.

Of course, Americans like their cars and don't tend to take too well to public transportation. Dual-mode transit systems hope to address this conflict. Travelers would drive their cars as usual in their neighborhoods and to run short errands. If they wanted to go farther – commute to work or travel to another city, say – their automobiles would become train cars, either by being driven onto a specially-designed train car or by activating maglev hardware in the car itself. Cars would then be controlled by the train system, moving at speeds very close to each other. Drivers could relax in the comfort of their own car, even take a nap behind the wheel. Arriving at their destination, drivers would regain control of their vehicles and drive back onto the street.

And that's the central question for an American rail renaissance: Will we be willing to give up control and let a train do the driving, even for part of the time? Developments in rail technology should make this less of a sacrifice, and resource depletion may leave us with no alternatives, but the American love affair with the car is a deep and passionate one. What remains to be seen is if we can once again find that passion in a sleeper car.

PROVOCATIONS...

If high-speed rail allows people to commute from greater distances, will this lead to bigger or smaller cities?

– Bill Kaszubski

THE NEXT GENERATION OF CABS

Personal Rapid Transit (PRT) systems hope to bring the efficiency of rail to travel within a city. Aimed at the transportation niche currently occupied by taxicabs and subways, PRTs would use train cars that accommodate two to four people, travel on an elevated guideway like those used for monorails, and be propelled by an electric motor. A traveler would go to a PRT station, select his destination station, and purchase a ticket. A car would pull forward from a queue, the passenger would enter and take a seat, the car would leave the station, enter the main track area, and be automatically routed to its destination station. The guideways could be much smaller than typical a monorail and could be constructed in the centers of existing roads.

A test system was constructed and operated in Marlboro, Massachusetts, from 1995–2000, and further prototypes are being developed in Minneapolis, Minnesota, and Irvine, California.

WANT MORE?

TGV SPOTTERS GUIDE
http://mercurio.iet.unipi.it/tgv/spotter.html

HIGH-SPEED RAIL WEBRING
http://p.webring.com/webring?index&ring=speedtrain

INNOVATIVE TRANSPORTATION TECHNOLOGIES OVERVIEW
http://faculty.washington.edu/jbs/itrans

INDUCTRACK
www.llnl.gov/str/Post.html

PRT SYSTEMS
www.taxi2000.com

2000 2005 2010 2015 2020

risks  rewards 

Air Travel... Fly the Smarter Skies

TAKE A LOOK AT ANY COPY OF *POPULAR MECHANICS* FROM *past decades and you're likely to come across at least one article about futuristic aircraft. ¶ Air travel has always been one of the most frequently used images to depict life in the future. For one thing, flying is a metaphor for escaping the world on the ground with all its problems and complexities. But it's also a practical goal. Being able to quickly, safely, and efficiently move people over great distances will always be a crucial aspect of life inthe global village.*

SONIC CRUISER. *Envisioned as being built largely from high-tech plastic, this dramatic concept aircraft from Boeing will fly at speeds up to Mach .98.*

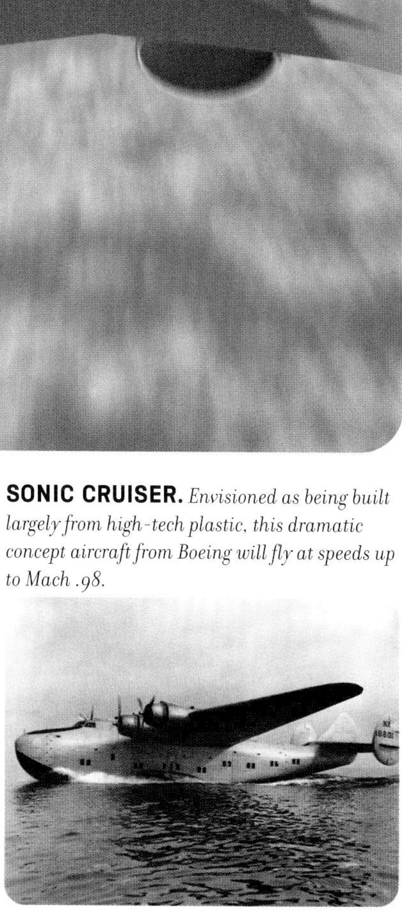

Not long after the Wright Brothers made their historic Kitty Hawk flight, futurists have been predicting the arrival of airships capable of carrying a thousand passengers, giant cargo blimps to replace ocean freighters, and skyway systems for personal aircraft and jetpacks. The problem is, nothing in the field of air travel innovation has made much of a splash since the invention of the Concorde in the early 1960s. We've been basically flying in the same passenger jets our grandparents flew in. That's about to change, thanks to a combination of technological achievements and societal imperatives.

TAKING A MEETING AT 30,000 FEET

The Boeing Business Jet (BBJ) is a member of the 737 family of airliners. The first BBJ was delivered in 1998, and more than 46 airliners are now in worldwide service. The highly configurable 807 ft. cabin can be customized to meet business needs for up to 149 passengers, replete with executive offices, conference rooms with a full contingent of AV capabilities, private offices, bedrooms, living rooms, dining rooms, and bathrooms. With the ability to fly 6,000 miles nonstop, the BBJ points the way to a new generation of corporate jets and business travel.

CHEAPER

The airlines are responding to increased passenger and cargo demand by introducing a wide variety of innovative systems and technologies. Newcomer airliner JetBlue, for instance, is using small, fuel-efficient jets, which are also wider than standard planes and therefore more comfortable. The airline uses touch-screen monitors for check-in. And rather than trying to offer flights between every conceivable city, JetBlue also restricts its route map to the most profitable trips. Best of all, JetBlue passengers can watch live television on video monitors mounted in the seat backs.

CEO David Neeleman's vision is paying off: JetBlue and Southwest airlines are the only airlines to turn a profit in the past two years. JetBlue's strategy is to offer affordable flights to the frequent traveler — a strategy that makes good sense in a much more pragmatic, cost-conscious, post-dotcom business climate.

FASTER

Of course, transcontinental passengers can only watch so many *Laverne & Shirley* reruns before getting antsy. That's where new high-speed jets come in. Today's commercial jets fly at about 80% the speed of sound (or Mach .80). A number of hyperjet technologies are currently under development promising to cut coast-to-coast flight times. Boeing is currently working on a radical passenger jet design that uses delta-shaped wings near the tail fin and a pair of small wings near the nose that will shave an hour from flights between coasts, and two hours from flights between the U.S. and Europe. Called the Sonic Cruiser, commercial service for this mostly plastic-built plane that will fly at speeds of up to Mach .98 could begin as early as 2008.

Looking further out, Scramjet engines, which are able to scoop up vast quantities of oxygen from the atmosphere without overheating the combustion chamber (which happens to ramjet engines above Mach 6 or so), will deliver speeds of up to Mach 10. Beyond that are space-orbiting rocketplanes, which could orbit the earth in a little over an hour.

SAFER

Even though air travel is relatively safe compared to other forms of transportation, there is definitely room for improvement. The biggest single cause of airplane accidents is pilot error. That's why airline companies are looking into computerized systems that can assist and, when necessary, take over the controls from human pilots. Researchers are looking into the idea of "swarming"

MODEL 314 "CLIPPER." *Once seen as the future of air travel, the "Clipper" got its name from the great sailing ships that plied the oceans in the 19th century. The Boeing Clipper was the 747 airplane of its era and made its first trans-Atlantic flight in the summer of 1939. Passengers rode and dined in comfort, with dressing rooms, seats that could be converted into overnight beds, and many other amenities. With today's renewed emphasis on comfort, airplane interior designers are studying the Clipper's luxurious conveniences as a source of inspiration for modern aircraft (left).*

FORCED TO FLY

Census reports reveal that freeways will become increasingly clogged with commuters, and more people are taking flight. The FAA projects that the number of air passengers will continue to soar, from 733 million in 2000 to 1.2 billion by 2012. Airbus projects that airborne cargo shipments will grow even faster in coming years.

AIRSTRIP-FREE ZONES

One of the biggest impediments to widespread use of personal aircraft has been the shortage of runways. With a few exceptions, neighborhoods are designed for cars, not planes that require a long strip of flat asphalt for take-off and landing. In recent years, the idea of airplanes that use vertical takeoff and landing (VTOL for short) technology is being taken seriously. In late 2002, Bell/Agusta began flight tests on the first commercially available "tiltrotor" aircraft, the BA609. The nine-passenger vehicle utilizes tiltable propellers that enable it to take off and land like a helicopter. Once airborne, the BA609's propellers can tilt back down like a conventional airplane.

FIRST COMMERCIAL TILTROTOR. *Bell/Agusta 609 tiltrotor demonstrates the application of Vertical Takeoff and Landing (VTOL) design to commercial aircraft for the first time.*

URBAN RESCUE. *The K004 ERV, designed by the Kulair, Inc., is a proposed VTOL emergency rescue vehicle uniquely suited for urban environments (artist's rendition).*

networks of planes that continually broadcast their velocity and position to neighboring planes, allowing the aircraft to automatically adjust their courses to avoid in-air collisions. Such a system will become essential when more small planes start filling the skies. NASA is proposing a system called SATS (Small Aircraft Transportation System) that will combine intelligent networks with a new crop of small planes, such as the Lancair Columbia 300 and the Cirrus SR-22, which are almost as easy to operate as automobiles and will open the skies up to almost everyone.

After the tragic events of 9-11, airplane safety is on everyone's mind. Many airlines have already installed reinforced doors between the cabin and the cockpit. To deter highjackers from taking over planes, and to prevent successful hijackers from using planes as missiles, airlines are looking at a number of other possibilities. These include on-the-ground deterrents such as increasing the number of National Guard troops in airports and improving security measures at check stations, as well as a number of in-the-air measures, such as putting armed federal air marshals on flights or allowing pilots to carry weapons. High-tech solutions being considered include retrofitting planes so that they could be

EASY TO FLY. *The Lancair Columbia 300 represents a new type of small plane that is much easier to pilot than its predecessors.*

Clockwise from top left: Image courtesy of Bell/Agusta Aerospace Company/ K004 Emergency Rescue Vehicle, Kulair, Inc., 2000–Image courtesy of the Lancair Company

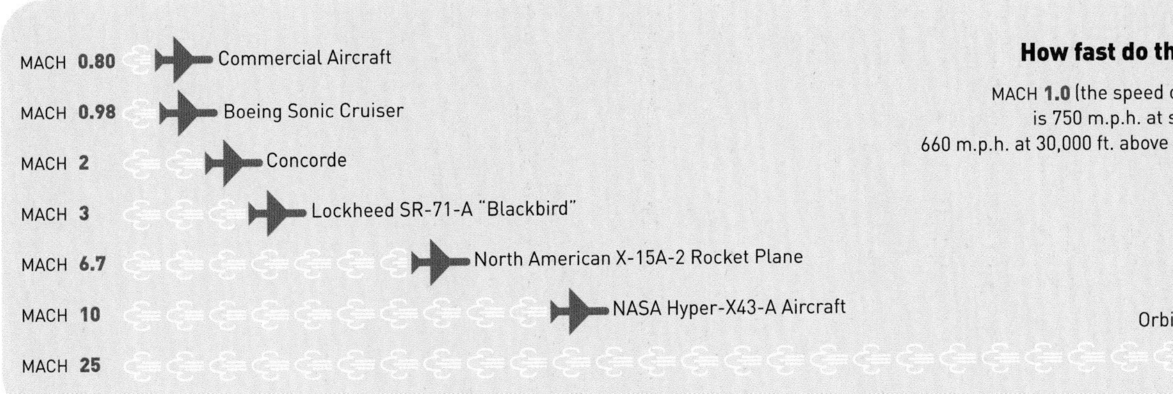

operated by pilots on the ground, stationing crews into compartments that can only be entered from the outside, installing video cameras that allow pilot monitoring of the cabin, and installing a "knock-out" gas system that would render the hijackers (and passengers) unconscious in case of a takeover attempt.

MORE COMFORTABLE

In recent years, airline designers have concentrated on coming up with new ways to increase passenger capacity on planes. Many of the solutions involved making seats narrower and reducing legroom. While cramming as many warm bodies into the fuselage as possible certainly increased revenues, the sardine-can approach has caused passengers to complain and has even been cited as the reason for increased incidences of "air rage" on planes. Now airlines are pulling back. Not only are they making the seats big enough for adults again, they're using soothing colors and gently curving contours to calm passengers' nerves. Boeing, for instance, is steering away from sharp corners and hard edges on its new planes, opting for curvy ceilings that convey a mood of gentle comfort to the passengers. And they've hired designers who employ principles of "color psychology" to give the cabin a feeling of spaciousness, security, and luxury. It may be an illusion, but if it keeps the drunk guy in aisle 23 from going berserk, we're all for it.

Somewhere, a former editor of *Popular Mechanics* is proclaiming, "I told you so!"

QUIET FLIGHTS. *So-called "fluidic wallpaper" under development could be used to make in-flight meetings, individual workspaces, and other areas of this Boeing Business Jet much quieter and more comfortable.*

Clockwise from top left: Graphic by Nigel Holmes; © The Boeing Company

PROVOCATIONS...

Will people literally "live on airplanes"?

In an age of superfast air travel, will the greatest luxury be to go slow?

Who cares about faster planes — when will airline meals stop tasting so bad?

—Mark Frauenfelder

WANT MORE?

FREEFLIGHT
www.jamesfallows.com/freeflight

BOEING, INC.
www.boeing.com

BELL HELICOPTER TEXTRON
www.bellhelicopter.com/index.html

JETBLUE AIRWAYS
www.jetblue.com

THE RAMJET/SCRAMJET ENGINE
www.aviation-history.com/engines/ramjet.htm

SATS OVERVIEW
www.sats.larc.nasa.gov/main.html

SONIC CRUISER
www.boeing.com/news/feature/concept

LANCAIR COLUMBIA
www.lancair.com

KULAIR, INC.
www.kulikovair.com/index.html

2000 2005 2010 2015 2020

Floating Cities... FROM ARK TO ARCOLOGY

THE BIBLICAL ARK IS PERHAPS MAN'S FIRST USE OF AN OCEAN-BORNE COMMUNITY TO *escape the problems of the land. Since then, our cities have reached into the sea to address a wide range of issues, other than a wrathful deity: overcrowding, lack of developable land, political discontent, environmental dangers, and a desire for leisure.*

THIS LAND IS MY LAND

The creation of some floating cities is motivated not by a lack of space, but of freedom. In 1967, Paddy Roy Bates and his wife Joan established the Principality of Sealand on an abandoned WWII anti-aircraft platform 7 miles off the English coast. At that time, British territorial waters extended only 3 miles from the shore, enabling Roy and Joan to declare themselves the sovereign Prince and Princess of Sealand – a claim that has never been formally contested, or accepted, by the British government. That may soon change, though, as Sealand has become a data haven – a Swiss bank of the Internet.

HavenCo, a corporation registered in Antigua, has set up Internet servers and claims to provide "better quality infrastructure [in] an environment free of unnecessary bureaucracy." This means that e-commerce companies (online casinos, say) can operate tax-free, that government censorship can be overcome (HavenCo hosts the Web site of the Tibetan government in exile), and that any type of group can exchange strongly encrypted email and files on any type of subject (except for spam and child pornography, which HavenCo does not allow). HavenCo's ultimate effect on Sealand's sovereignty has yet to be seen.

A more ambitious, and aesthetically pleasing, principality is coming into being in the Caribbean. Called New Utopia, it is being developed by its prince, Lazarus Long (formerly Howard Turney), in 1,000 square miles of ocean about 160 miles west of the Caymans. Long filed a claim to this area with the U.N. in 1996, and it has not been challenged. New Utopia's libertarian government is founded upon the philosophies of Robert Heinlein and Ayn Rand and will be constructed with simple landfill techniques and concrete pilings like those used in New Orleans and Miami Beach. Construction has begun, headquartered on a used oil-drilling platform. Optimistic estimates have a small airport, hotel, and (of course) casino opening as soon as December 2002.

BIGGER THAN THE QUEEN MARY. *At over 4,500 feet, a width of 750 feet, and a height of 350 feet, the Freedom Ship would be more than four times longer than the Queen Mary (above).*

Image courtesy of The Freedom Ship

FLOATING CITIES OF THE WAY-FUTURE

The most ambitious floating city concept is also the most beautiful. Architect and city planner Eugene Tsui envisions a truly mobile floating city, built from seawater mineral salts electrolytically deposited on steel rebar, powered by the temperature differences in ocean water, and inhabited by up to 50,000 people. Called Nexus, the island would be a sovereign state, existing in international waters outside of the 12-mile boundary of any nation. It would harvest ocean thermal energy, solar energy, and wind energy to drive 27 turboprops capable of propelling the island at speeds up to 5 kilometers per hour. A small mountain range at one end of the island would dissipate tsunami waves to minimize their impact. The island would travel the oceans of the world, to reduce its impact on any one ecosystem.

It would also be a laboratory for advances in manufacturing, government, and environmentally sensitive resource extraction. Tsui envisions small, self-governing communities on the island and a larger, consensus-based government to address the larger issues of concern for the island (i.e., where should we go?). The island would be self-supporting, deriving income from sources as diverse as tourism, mineral and metal dredging, fish farming, water desalinization, and marine research and exploration. Nexus is still a concept; in 1986, Tsui estimated that it could be built for $10 billion – $200,000 per resident. Construction would take about 9 years, but so far no plans have been initiated.

Drawing and Photo by Eugene Tsui

A VACATION THAT NEVER ENDS

Cruise ships are the closest we currently come to floating cities. The problem is, you do eventually have to go home. The developers of the Freedom Ship want to change that and are planning what would be the world's first arcology — a self-contained city aboard a massive ship.

Freedom Ship will be almost a mile long, as wide as two and a half football field stadiums, and as high as a 25-story building — the largest seafaring vessel ever built. The floating city would circle the earth roughly every 2 years and cater to the needs of global jetsetters with a 10,000-room hotel, a world-class hospital, an airport for private jets, a marina, a shopping mall, a golf course, and a school offering kindergarten through college education. And offering perhaps the greatest amenity of all, the Freedom Ship will also be the largest floating tax haven ever created, with no local taxes of any kind — although residents will have to abide by the federal tax laws of their own countries.

A fifth of the living units on Freedom Ship have already been sold — at a cost ranging from $170,000 to well over $11 million — and the developers are so sure of their success that they're planning at least three more mega-vessels to round out the fleet.

Such floating cities are something new in our geography — "places" that move — and, as such, they are beyond the bounds of our traditional ideas of "nations" or "countries." These floating cities naturally attract those who feel constrained by traditional notions of national identity and who also have extensive disposable income. Whether or not such folks will be able to form a true community, with its own forms of participatory government, remains to be seen. (The developers' plans on this point remain vague.) But regardless, such floating cities will doubtlessly be useful if another flood comes along.

PROVOCATIONS...

Will the libertarian governments of floating cities be sustainable?

Could they have a rebellion or a revolution?

Should they be allowed to?

Will traditional nations allow residents of floating cities to use them as tax shelters — or exile them?

If terrorists attack a floating city, who should be responsible for defending it?

—Bill Kaszubski

WANT MORE?

SEALAND AND HAVENCO

www.sealandgov.com

www.havenco.com

NEW UTOPIA

www.new-utopia.com

FREEDOM SHIP

www.freedomship.com

NEXUS

www.tdrinc.com/nexus

SPACE TOURISM...

A Whole New Meaning for Frequent Flyer Miles

VOMIT COMET. *"Look Ma, no hands!" Passengers on board the infamous Vomit Comet experiencing zero gravity.*

IMAGINE VACATION CRUISES THAT OFFER STUNNING VIEWS *of the Earth and the stars, dancing and floating in zero gravity, and a whole range of microgravity sports and acrobatics — in short, a truly "out-of-this-world" experience. The stuff of science fiction, you say? When wealthy California investor Dennis Tito blasted into space on a voyage to the International Space Station in 2001, a new era of space tourism was born.*

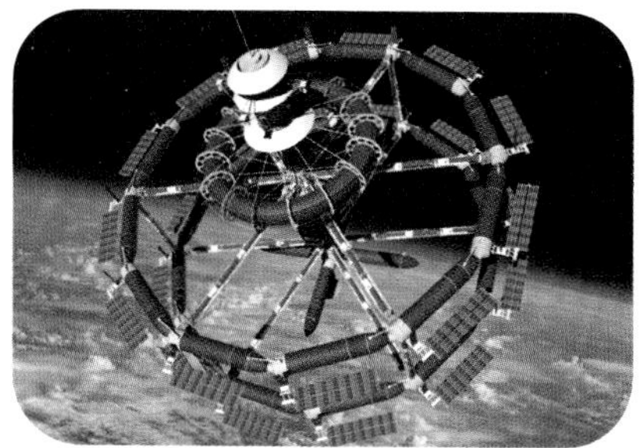

SPACE ISLAND GROUP. *This company has planned this orbiting space hotel and space station that will accommodate 400 people. The floating hotel will be constructed as a giant ring over 1/2 mile round, divided into 2 or 3 decks. It will include a casino, 4 restaurants, and a movie theater. Suites in the nonrotating central column would enable hotel guests to experience zero gravity.*

Clockwise from top left: Image courtesy of Incredible Adventures - Image courtesy of Space Island Group - Image courtesy of Space Island Group - Image courtesy of Space Island Group Image courtesy of Space Island Group

GROWING FOOD IN SPACE. *As part of a comprehensive research plan to prepare for vacations in space, the Space Island Group's Media and Design Center will house a fully operational facility or "living classroom" that will be used to grow fruit and vegetables hydroponically. The staff will consist of student interns from five or six major universities on loan to the Center who receive college credit for their work.*

WHEEL STATION INTERIOR. *The turning of the outer ring produces the "feel" of 1/3 normal gravity in the wheel station's interiors, which were inspired by* 2001: A Space Odyssey *and dedicated to Sir Arthur C. Clarke.*

If companies such as Space Adventures, the Space Island Group, XCOR Aerospace, and Bigelow Aerospace succeed, a chance to see the Earth from space may be within the safe reach of many people in the not-too-distant future. In fact, you can even apply your frequent flyer miles today to a trip into space in the future, thanks to a partnership between US Airways and Space Adventures of Arlington, Virgina. But the price of entry is not cheap, ranging from $98,000 for a suborbital flight all the way up to a whopping $20 million for a trip to the International Space Station.

SPACE TOURISM INDUSTRY

As space tourism becomes more commonplace, however, many expect prices to come down — just not anytime soon. International Space University President Karl Doetsch believes that a booming

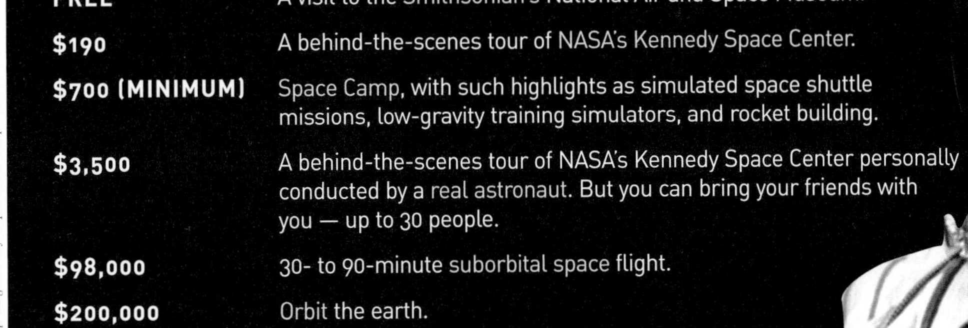

WHAT IT IS GOING TO COST YOU...

FREE	A visit to the Smithsonian's National Air and Space Museum.
$190	A behind-the-scenes tour of NASA's Kennedy Space Center.
$700 (MINIMUM)	Space Camp, with such highlights as simulated space shuttle missions, low-gravity training simulators, and rocket building.
$3,500	A behind-the-scenes tour of NASA's Kennedy Space Center personally conducted by a real astronaut. But you can bring your friends with you — up to 30 people.
$98,000	30- to 90-minute suborbital space flight.
$200,000	Orbit the earth.
$20,000,000	Trip to the International Space Station.

"I don't think anyone realizes just how beautiful space is."

—Dennis Tito, the world's first "space tourist."

Clockwise from left: Image courtesy of Space Island Group-Image courtesy of Space Island Group-Photo ITAR-TASS space tourism industry probably is 10 - 15 years off. To make this happen will require cooperation between the government and the private sector, with significant investment in research and development for reusable, safe, and inexpensive vehicles. In addition, there are legal issues because no specific space law has yet been defined for space tourism. Space tourists will also face issues of physical fitness and space motion sickness.

Companies such as Space Island Group, Hilton, and Budget are already designing hotel rooms, casinos, and guest rooms — right down to the color of the carpets and the international cuisine on the menus. Bigelow Aerospace envisions orbiting cruise ships built and financed entirely by the private sector by the year 2015. With something like 10,000 would-be space tourists willing today to spend $1 million each to visit the final frontier, the stakes are high.

ROCKET GUY

But some are not willing to wait until commercial space travel is available. Like some latter-day Edison, engineering-school dropout and toy inventor "Rocket Guy" Brian Walker of Bend, Oregon, is building his very own one-person rocket, which will be fueled by 90% pure hydrogen peroxide. His Project R.U.S.H. (Rapid Up Super High) is expected to be completed sometime in late 2002, when he plans to fulfill a childhood dream by going 30 miles straight up into space.

SPACE DEGREE

Before much longer you may even be able to get a degree in space tourism. The Rochester Institute of Technology's Hotel and Restaurant Management Program now offers a course in space tourism development. In this course, students "explore the unusual and often unique factors of hospitality and tourism management in an earth orbit habitat (like the international space station) or other celestial bodies (like the moon or an asteroid)."

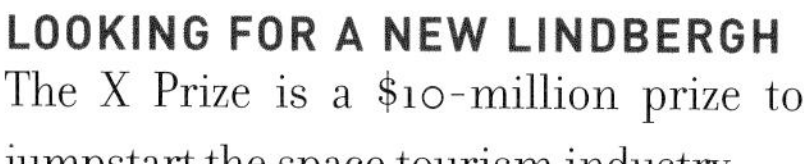

LOOKING FOR A NEW LINDBERGH

The X Prize is a $10-million prize to jumpstart the space tourism industry through competition between the most talented entrepreneurs and rocket experts in the world. The prize will go to the first team that privately finances, builds, and launches a spaceship able to carry three people up to 100 kilometers (62.5 miles). This spaceship has to return safely to Earth, and the launch must be repeated with the same ship

HOME BREW. *Inventor Brian Walker, "Rocket Guy," who plans his own homemade trip into space, 30 miles straight up.*

Space Travel Time Line

1961 Soviet cosmonaut Yuri Gargarin first person to travel in space

1969 Neil Armstrong and "Buzz" Aldrin walk on the moon

1986 Mir space station launched

1998 John Glenn the oldest person to fly in space

1998 International Space Station (ISS) established

within two weeks. The X Prize was inspired by the early aviation prizes of the 20th century, primarily the ground-breaking trans-Atlantic flight of Charles Lindbergh in The Spirit of St. Louis, which captured the $25,000 Orteig Prize.

PROVOCATIONS...

When will we see the first sneaker or fast food logo on the outside of a spaceship?

When will we send up the first artist? The first poet?

Will we need new transnational treaties governing ordinary citizens' activities in space?

—Charles O. Stewart III

THE VOMIT COMET

The "Vomit Comet" is a Space Adventures Zero Gravity experience in a Russian Illyushin-76 aircraft. Weightlessness is achieved when the Vomit Comet flies up to 34,000 feet at 45° and then powers back and glides over the top of the arch. At this point, everyone inside the padded interior of the aircraft experiences "free fall" for about 25-30 seconds.

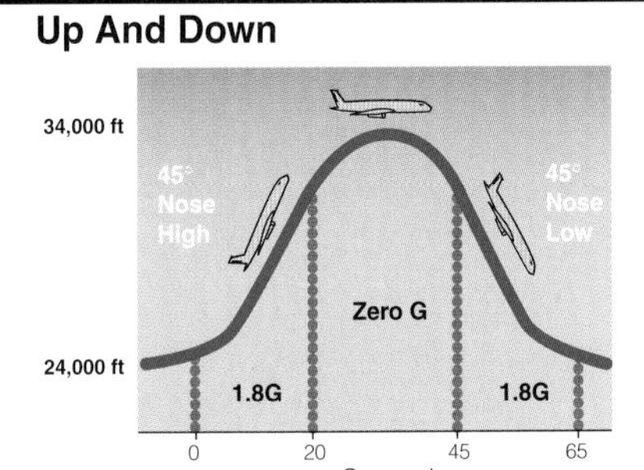

When the Vomit Comet pulls out of its dive, the people inside experience 1.8Gs, which is nearly twice normal body weight. This maneuver is usually repeated 8-12 times to give everyone their money's worth of free-fall experiences. But they don't call this the Vomit Comet for nothing! Roughly 30% of people experience significant motion sickness during the repeated up-and-down flight of the aircraft.

2001 — Dennis Tito the first space tourist

2002 — South African Mark Shuttleworth the second space tourist

2005 — Suborbital space tourism flights aboard Reusable Launch Vehicles

2015 — Space vacation cruise ship in orbit around the earth

Clockwise from top left: Image courtesy of Space Island Group - Photo ITAR-TASS

WANT MORE?

SPACE.COM
www.space.com

SPACE ADVENTURES, INC.
www.spaceadventures.com

INCREDIBLE ADVENTURES
www.incredible-adventures.com

FIRST AFRICAN IN SPACE PROJECT
www.africaninspace.com

SPACE FUTURE
www.spacefuture.com

SPACE DAILY
www.spacedaily.com

XCOR AEROSPACE
www.xcor.com

BIGELOW AEROSPACE
www.bigelowaerospace.com

ROCHESTER INSTITUTE OF TECHNOLOGY
www.rit.edu

SPACE ISLAND GROUP
www.spaceislandgroup.com

SPACE FRONTIER FOUNDATION
www.space-frontier.org

BRIAN WALKER, ROCKET GUY
www.rocketguy.com

U. S. SPACE TRANSPORTATION ASSOCIATION
www.spacetransportation.org

STARCHASER INDUSTRIES, LTD.
www.starchaser.co.uk

EUROPEAN SPACE AGENCY
www.esa.int

SPACE TOURISM SOCIETY
www.spacetourismsociety.org

The Future of Education

"Rip Van Winkle," a familiar tale by the American author Washington Irving, tells about an idle man who lived in the Catskill Mountains with his wife, young children, and loyal dog. One afternoon he fell asleep on a remote, grassy knoll and awoke 20 years later, complete with long, grizzled beard. When he returned to his town, he was confused by its many changes.

Now imagine a more recent Rip, a college lad who dozes off in 1932 and wakes up 70 years later. We escort him on a tour of his modern surrounds, wanting to impress our aged traveler with his new world. Our first stop is to observe a NASA shuttle launch. Not surprisingly, Rip is frightened and stunned by the size and power of the spacecraft. His last memory of air travel was Charles Lindbergh's 1927 trans-Atlantic flight. Next we take Rip to a cardiac surgical unit at City Hospital. He's curious and puzzled by the electronic gadgetry, the instruments used, and the procedures performed. His prior medical recollection was of a physician making house calls.

And finally we accompany our sleepy friend to a modern-day university. It's only here that Rip proudly proclaims, "Ah, a school!" At last Rip is relaxed as he strolls through this familiar setting of lecture halls and classrooms.

Technology impacts nearly every aspect of our lives, yet its effect on learning continues to be modest. That isn't to say there is neither investment in technology nor innovative uses. Indeed, we know that schools and corporations have spent billions of dollars building a complex digital network to provide "anytime, anyplace" access to the Internet. Nonetheless, if you walk the halls of schools or corporate America, you'll quickly see that the way we taught and learned before the "information revolution" is not significantly different from the way we teach and learn today. It seems that we've optimized our computer- and Web-based systems to reflect a model of schooling consistent with a bygone era, complete with central control, standardization, and top-down administration of courses, tests, and degrees. However, this is about to change.

In our post 9-11, post-Enron/WorldCom culture, a collective threshold has been crossed, awakening us to an unpredictable and impermanent world. While globalization has brought us the opportunities of genomic discovery, a worldwide technological infrastructure, and the democratic transformation of nations, it has also brought us the challenges of a global AIDS epidemic, computer viruses, and terrorism. Even though English has become the de facto language of trade and communication, increasingly we feel vulnerable because of our unfamiliarity with non-Western languages, cultures, and traditions. As pundits declare that a return to basics is what's needed in our schools, many teenagers have migrated from the linear tradition of the book to a nonlinear, synchronous mix of instant messaging, hypersurfing through Google hits, and tracking their last bid on eBay. Each of these factors contributes to a climate of change, a sense that the industrial view of schooling must give way to a view consistent with the challenges and opportunities of our time. At its core, the change will redefine the role of teacher, learner, and content.

No longer will the teacher disseminate information in the form of lectures and textbooks. Rather, the teacher will adopt the role of facilitator, tutor, and learner. Similarly, the student's role will change from a memorizer of facts and principles to that of a researcher, problem-solver, and strategist. The "keep your eyes on your own paper" value of independent scholarship will be augmented with learning communities and cooperative workgroups. Skilled collaboration, interpersonal communications, and project management will define successful learner teams.

Content will change as well. Traditionally, we organize content into disciplines—the "arts and sciences." We further divide these disciplines into smaller content silos, each to be mastered by the learner in a prescribed curriculum of courses and topics. Increasingly, however, this strategy will fail, given the exponential growth of information. Instead, students will be encouraged to examine the connectedness of information. Digital learning tools will promote multidisciplinary thinking and an appreciation for multiple perspectives while solving authentic, real-world problems. Overcoming the "tyranny of the disciplines," scholars will regroup themselves into new academic units with names such as "Informatics," and students will develop new specialties with titles such as "genetics software engineer" and "interaction designer."

To overcome a growing sense of "information anxiety" — the uneasy feeling of understanding less about what we want to know more — cognitive tools will help us visualize concepts as variations of larger themes. Big-concept thinking, systemic analysis, and model building will replace the less useful memorization of disconnected facts. Sophisticated online search engines will lead learners to specific details, discarded after their use and resurrected when necessary. Unlike the end-of-chapter problems students solve in today's textbooks, future learners will engage in problems that are context-dependent, complicated, messy, and that reappear in diverse guises.

Lest you think this new Digital Learning Environment lacks the rigor of today's best curriculum designs, consider this: Intelligent software tutors will ensure that students acquire basic skills — not through the textbook-imitative exercises of today's e-learning, but through sophisticated algorithms of concept presentation, simulation, correction, and review. These skills will be mastered when they're needed. For example, most of us learned how to add two fractions with unlike denominators because it was the next topic in the teacher's curriculum plan. Our major motivation for paying attention and learning the procedure was to achieve a high score on the Friday afternoon quiz. Now imagine the same concepts introduced in the context of a problem-centered environment. A student team may be constructing a 3D model, including measuring and adding components of varying lengths. In this case, the students are motivated to access instruction on fractions because it will help them produce their model. And it's not only motivation that will change. Rates of comprehension and retention will increase as well.

Ensuring that "no child is left behind," management systems will track learner proficiencies. Teachers will provide support and guidance to individuals, probing here, questioning there, and emphasizing learning how rather than learning what. In time, software-generated, personal learning assistants will "accompany" each student through a lifetime of learning. Like an alter ego or "über-me," these intelligent agents, accessing a personalized, life-cumulative profile, will provide options for the learner: "On Friday, you'll be in Chicago. You have three hours between appointments. Given your interest in Mies Van Der Rohe, shall I reserve tickets for the East Pier Architectural Boat Tour? (East Pier docents score 22% higher approval ratings than docents from competing tour companies.) The weather agent predicts a sunny day and low humidity. By the way, I've prepared a videography of Chicago architects. I know you like to impress others with little-known facts."

As we look forward, might there be other trends signaling the Digital Learning Environment? Look for new tools, databases, and settings. There will be less use of productivity tools and more use of cognitive tools for conversation, analysis, prototype construction, scenarios, simulation, reflection, and insight. These new tools will lead to ethical debates, the development of personal standards and evaluation criteria, and the contribution to team norms.

The Web-as-learning-tool will be used less as a global database and more as a global "learningbase," indexed with generations of recursive commentary, a kind of "Global Talmud." Learners will explore interpretations, rules, and cases. Scenario building and computer imaginative forms of interactive narrative will lead to the integration of academic skills and "practical intelligence" or tacit knowledge. Learning spaces, whether formal or informal, virtual or real, will become safe environments for experimentation and failure. Throughout a lifetime of learning, each person will function as both a learner and a coach.

When Rip went to school, his reading comprehension task was simple: a paragraph or two with a multiple-choice question. He knew that the answer could always be found in the paragraphs above. Tomorrow's students will consider the appropriateness of the question, whether it is part of a larger problem, the likelihood that an answer exists, and the trustworthiness of the sources found. Students will examine their findings from multiple perspectives, and they will develop criteria by which to judge their conclusions. One might argue that the best teachers have always guided their students with these considerations. Yet the new digital tools will allow learners and teachers to access information in ways, quantities, and speeds never imagined by Rip's most prominent professors.

If you want Rip Van Winkle to recognize your school, you had better wake him up now because in another 30 years he'll have no idea what he's looking at — let's hope!

– Martin Siegel

The Future of the Classroom...
New Modes of Teaching and Learning

IT IS 2015 AND YOU ARE A VISITOR TO THE Under the Sea Learning Center in San Diego, California. The Center resembles a combination workshop, museum, library, and science lab, replete with colorful images of aquatic life, from kelp forests and whales to wetlands and marshes. Touch screens flash images of students' local work to preserve the Batiquitos and San Elijo Lagoons with their underwater "seabots" that collect marine data in real-time.

The students work in different configurations — some are talking with one of the center teachers about their projects, while others are either writing or working in small groups on experiments. They use digital paper to record their ideas or plans, with wireless connections to their computer workspace. Learners of different ages in the center make it harder to spot the expert learners, the teachers, who seem as engaged as the students.

This "classroom of the future" suggests new roles for both teachers and students, as well as new conceptions of the physical settings in which learning occurs. Imagine schools where students enter learning communities with peers of various ages and stay with this group for three years. Students advance through primary, elementary, middle, and high-school learning communities based on their own rate of progress. Students that need more learning may stay in a center longer than three years as "experts" helping the new students. These multi-age settings make peer learning and mentoring a natural function of the community.

Students need the continuity of instruction that results from having a teacher who knows them well across time and in various contexts, but they benefit also from interaction with different teachers. Schools can be structured to address both these needs. In the school of the future, each learning community might contain three types of instructors: a "community teacher," an expert in learning and assessment, and a paraprofessional "learning guide." In addition, a resource expert in each center could provide specialized assistance to both teachers and students.

These migratory communities of learners and teachers move through a series of theme-organized learning centers. After completing an immersion in a particular learning center, the community — students, community teacher, and their learning guide — moves on to a new center, while the center teachers remain to welcome the next group.

HIGH TECH HIGH. *Many parts of the learning center model described here are in place in an innovative charter school, High Tech High, in San Diego, California. In this learning center, students tackle math, science, humanities, and the arts through project-based learning. The top photo shows students doing project-based learning around glider construction and aerodynamics. Internships and personalized learning plans help to address the learning needs of every student, with the goal of helping all students find their path to college.*

Photos courtesy of High Tech High, San Diego, CA

In these new spaces for learning,

community teachers need to have a background in learning sciences and learning assessment. They design educational experiences that have as their primary goal student evaluation. Working with the center teachers, the community teachers develop a rich set of strategies to monitor student progress. They help the center teachers align their teaching with the needs of the student community. They also help the center teachers find and assign resource teachers to help groups or individuals with their specialized learning needs. Their major role is to organize the teaching team to monitor the learning profile for each student in their community.

Stationed in each learning center are curriculum expert "center teachers," who team with the community teacher and learning guide to create a 12-week team. Center teachers are curriculum specialists with expertise in two to three disciplines. They are responsible for knowing the best strategies for teaching their content areas.

Learning guides are paraprofessionals who help students learn, but they do not have all the added responsibility of teachers. The guides do not develop curricula, plan lessons, or create student reports. Instead, they supervise and facilitate independent and group work. Because they stay with the same community of students, learning guides know the students well and create a consistent set of expectations for appropriate center behavior. Learning guides also help create cohesiveness and trust among the student community.

Each center also includes "resource" teachers who can be called in to facilitate the specific learning needs of the particular team. Resource experts provide special work in a particular subject area (chemistry), for a particular group (bilingual students), or with special equipment (multimedia). Planning the learning center environment means coordination of expertise in academic disciplines, knowledge of the student community, and integration of resources both local and distant.

The redesign of teaching described in this vision of the classroom of the future includes a career path from entry-level teacher to master teacher. In this model, teachers are engaged in professional work inside and outside of the classroom. These changes in the teacher's roles and their responsibilities make it possible for a teacher to develop expertise through continual change in teaching partners and learning communities.

In a period of about 20 years at the turn of the last century, schooling changed from one-room, multi-age classrooms to the graded, K-12 system of the present. Although the new battle cry of the Department of Education is "No Child Left Behind," current educational programs tend to reinforce the existing structure, a structure that was designed to sort students into tracks leading either to entry into the workforce or opportunities for continued education. We could, if we had the vision and will, change schools again so that, truly, no child is left behind.

WHAT'S HOLDING US BACK?

Schools are not built for personalizing learning. Schools are designed to support a single speed of learning. Much of the current model of education is built on a model appropriate to the industrial age — not the information age.

Teaching is not attracting and retaining qualified teachers. In the current model, there is little room for advancement.

One teacher cannot reach all students in a group. Team-teaching increases the skill base of teachers who work with a set of students.

High- stakes "norm" testing labels students, teachers, and schools in non-productive ways. Norm-referenced testing doesn't help schools create successful learning contexts for all students.

PROVOCATIONS...

How will wireless Internet computing impact standardized testing?

Will it mean the end of the SAT?

Will one e-book be ALL your textbooks?

If computers do all our memorizing for us, will we no longer learn things by rote?

—Margaret Riel

WANT MORE?

SCHOOL RENEWAL
www.schoolrenewal.org

NO CHILD LEFT BEHIND ACT OF 2001
www.ed.gov/legislation/ESEA02/107-110.pdf

CARROLL, T. G. (2000).
IF WE DIDN'T HAVE THE SCHOOLS WE HAVE TODAY, WOULD WE CREATE THE SCHOOLS WE HAVE TODAY?
www.citejournal.org/vol11/iss1/currentissues/general/article1.htm

RIEL, M. (1995).
THE FUTURE OF TEACHING.
http://gsep.pepperdine.edu/~mriel/office/papers/Future_of_teaching.pdf

DISTANCE EDUCATION... LEARNING ANYWHERE, ANYTIME

RECENT TRENDS IN DIStance education indicate that we are on the threshold of an exciting new era for education, educational technology, and society at large. The tools and opportunities for distance education are changing the way we work, learn, and socialize. As Samuel Dunn predicted at the start of this decade, 95% of the academic courses in the U.S. will be digitally enhanced in some manner by 2010. To meet these needs, many new companies and institutions are emerging to provide distance learning content, services, and technologies. Enrollment trends and projections are staggering as forecasts for distance education and training extend into billions of dollars.

Although there is general agreement that learning at a distance will not completely replace face-to-face instruction—indeed, there are some who see online learning as a boon to traditional instruction — learners of all ages will increasingly rely on electronic technologies for learning. In fact, in corporate and military training settings, blended or hybrid learning (a mix of online and face-to-face) already dominates discussion. In higher education, Linda Harasim and her colleagues in Canada have found that such mixed forms of delivery are the most common. In Australia, "flexible learning" is used to describe the trend toward greater educational opportunity and choice represented by distance education combined with other modes of learning.

Distance education in the 21st century will offer many new learning opportunities. To cope with rapid change and the emergence of many new occupations ("information taxonomist," "usage anthropologist," and others), you will have increasing opportunities to create or declare your own unique major or program of study. And as the human lifespan continues to lengthen, you will see most people seeking multiple degrees in multiple delivery formats. Advances in wireless and wearable technologies will make mobile, remote learning an exciting possibility for many. With an Internet connection, you will be able to mix and match academic courses to obtain a degree or certificate across a consortium of universities. Universitas 21 represents a consortium of 18 member universities in 10 countries, with a total enrollment of 500,000 students. The online offerings of Universitas 21 will enable qualified students around the globe to receive a quality education, even

ARMING SOLDIERS WITH LAPTOPS

The eArmyU was conceived to develop educated, technology-savvy soldiers who will succeed on the battlefields of the 21st century. Launched January 16, 2001, eArmyU is a partnership of 23 colleges and universities offering more than 4,000 online courses and 90 post-secondary degrees and certificates. Within the first year of its inception, eArmyU enrolled more than 12,000 students.

The eArmyU provides access to online courses and degrees for each soldier. Each enrollee is entitled to a laptop, free tuition, an Internet connection, a printer, and books and fees to complete these courses. Assigned Program Mentors provide valuable academic guidance to each soldier. Students are provided with program links specific to their fields of study, a link to their home institution, and important Program Mentor contact information. Using this information, soldiers can begin to establish a distance-learning community with their Program Mentor and other students pursuing degrees in the same or similar areas of study.

in areas where the actual supply of world-class education is rare. With a market for higher education that could top 160 million by 2025, distance learning represents one of the few ways to meet this explosive global demand.

Some of my own research indicates that freelance online instruction will increase five-fold during the next decade in both higher education and corporate training. Imagine dialing into the Web and picking among a range of experts to teach you something that you want at that moment. Of course, as technology becomes more intelligent, other instructors will be trained to assume roles wherein they counsel online students about their course choices and options. And, naturally, some will be trained as course facilitators. Important skills here include flexibility, risk taking, innovation, providing timely feedback, building relationships, motivating and engaging learners, and individualizing instruction.

How will established schools respond to the increasing trend toward online learning? Some will find unique niche markets or program specialties, while others, such as Universitas 21, will form consortia that capitalize on the strengths of each. In addition, much publicized and somewhat controversial online "cyber" universities such as Jones International University and Capella University have sprung up to meet the demands of adult learners seeking new credentials and life-long learning opportunities.

Distance learning will not just affect colleges and universities, but will drastically change primary and secondary schools as well as corporate and military training. The Florida Virtual High School is leading the way in the secondary school arena with over 5,000 online students. Companies in the corporate training world, such as SmartForce and NETg, offer extensive training-related content on the Web. Even though computer technology skills and applications are the focus today, soft skills such as leadership and ethics training are on the rise.

Distance learning at the end of the 20th century put learners in touch with each other and with experts in some of the most remote parts of the globe. Interplanetary chats with explorers and remote views from distant satellites or space ships will enhance and intrigue learners in the 21st century. Entire cultures may change due to online technologies that immerse learners in more authentic learning experiences. It's a sure bet that the explosive need for continuous, lifelong learning will continue to drive the development of online learning offerings in university settings as well as in business, government, and industry.

PROVOCATIONS...

Will distance learning mean the end of class clowns, and the start of class cartoonists?

Will there still be class reunions? If so, in classrooms or chatrooms?

Will students get intelligent agents to cheat for them?

—Curt Bonk

WANT MORE?

CAPPELLA UNIVERSITY
www.capella.edu

EARMYU
www.earmyu.com

JONES INTERNATIONAL UNIV.
http://jiu-web-a.jonesinternational.edu

DISTANCE EDUCATION CLEARINGHOUSE
www.uwex.edu/disted

DISTANCE LEARNING RESOURCE NETWORK
www.dlrn.org

ONLINE LEARNING MAGAZINE
www.onlinelearningmag.com

DISTANCE LEARNING
www.hoyle.com/distance.htm

COURSESHARE.COM
www.courseshare.com

PUBLICATIONSHARE.COM
www.publicationshare.com

2000 2005 2010 2015 2020

risks rewards

NEW COLLABORATIVE TOOLS... Constructing Shared Meanings

COLLABORATION HAS *become increasingly important — indeed, absolutely essential — in the modern world, and the digital revolution continues to give us a wide array of tools for constructing shared meanings.*

Consider Carrie Keller, a new accounting professor at Delta College, who is struggling with her new responsibilities and deadlines. The recent turmoil in the accounting industry requires her to teach a course on the "Ethics of Auditing." On merlot.org and the World Lecture Hall, she finds several relevant course syllabi, case activities, and links to videoclips and audio files. In a manner similar to how one selects movies from a hotel room, these reusable learning objects (RLOs) can be used by anyone with access to the Internet. Simply put, RLOs are small, reusable chunks of flexible instructional media that can be mixed and matched by instructors.

Collaboration tools and reusable learning objects for instructors are just a start. During the semester, Carrie's auditing students use tools such as Groove, TeamThink, ThoughtShare, SurveyShare, Smart Ideas, and OurProject to collaborate with others around the world on course papers and research projects. These students organize their research schedules using OurProject, generate survey questions within TeamThink, collect survey research data in SurveyShare, and map out their findings with collaborative concept mapping tools like Smart Ideas.

INTERNET PROTOCOL-BASED VIDEOCONFERENCING. *This photo from the Indiana University School of Education shows IP-based videoconferencing at work. It's cheaper, doesn't require any special network connections, allows for easier ad-hoc point-to-point and multipoint connections, and can include connections to home and off-campus offices, among other benefits.*

Carrie's students will not rely exclusively on outdated textbooks and an instructor to interpret current events. Instead, they will have live feeds into the corporate world. In fact, as Carrie assigns the tasks for the semester, a few of her students have volunteered to use wearable computing devices that will enable them to transmit images of their field setting (with permission, of course) to a designated course Web site.

Carrie also wants her students to read current news and journal articles that relate to the class. Her students will use the "intelligent agents," or "bots," that came with their laptops to help with research on the Web and to individualize the articles that are collected. Among these online software agents, there are more than 30 personality types to choose from, from ones that simply report the facts they find online, to those that act like high-level coaches or guides. These intelligent agents take requests and ask questions when they don't understand something, using "natural language" processing. Collaborative intelligent agents are all about autonomy. They glide across networks and out into the Web to work on your behalf with other agents. As artificial intelligence continues to advance, we'll see an increasing use of these intelligent agents.

Image courtesy of Curt Bonk

Carrie's class also illustrates the shift in our society from competition to collaboration. Although you probably have used various collaboration tools such as email, computer networks, live chat, whiteboards, and bulletin board systems, within the next 5 years the options in education will expand to extensive mentoring networks and exchanges for nearly every discipline imaginable. Within 10–20 years, collaboration will extend to interplanetary chat networks from astronauts commissioned on the moon, space stations, and Mars or one of the other planets. NASA is already making plans for a system of Internet networks and interplanetary gateways.

Back here on Earth, tools for creating a shared space to collaborate will continue to proliferate. In public schools, students from different hemispheres might jointly track and report on asteroids, comets, and planets revolving around stars millions of light years away. In the performing arts areas, young students might create and perform plays with sister schools. More typically, however, small, rural schools in North America might provide international feedback on student papers from Japan, Iran, or Nigeria and vice versa. Students might also participate in a global peace project wherein they share cultural ideas and perspectives using the Key Pals program or the Intercultural Pen Pals exchange. Within a few years, such global collaboration on student papers will be the norm, not the exception.

Digital tools for collaboration also allow distant explorers to discuss research findings and ask for student insights and opinions. Explorers and experts can already send field notes and images from remote regions such as the Arctic tundra or Mayan ruins in different online adventures or quests. Collaborative initiatives such as the Global Learning and Observations to Benefit the Environment (GLOBE) Program allow students to collect and share information such as weather patterns and bird migration instantaneously across the planet.

The corporate training world is in the midst of similar trends intended to speed up product design and development through online communities of practice and knowledge management. For instance, electronic meeting software is emerging from Smart Technologies that will help global teams set goals, record ideas, and make key decisions. In addition, tools such as Groove allow employees to open windows on their computer screens and discuss edits, collect additional information, and view shared data with others. Translation tools such as Déjà Vu will spark even greater opportunities for global document collaboration and product design. By the end of the decade, collaboration waiting and collaboration forwarding features may be as common as call waiting is today.

We are entering a time where everyone will be affected by advances in collaborative educational tools. But even as we continue to develop increasingly flexible and sophisticated digital tools for collaboration, what will remain most important will be the types of interactions made possible by these technologies.

PROVOCATIONS...

How will credit be awarded for global collaborative projects?

Who will own the materials shared online?

How will teacher training be affected by collaborative tools and activities?

—Curt Bonk

WANT MORE?

CENTRA
www.centra.com

CLASSROOM CONNECT (QUESTS)
www.classroomconnect.com

COLLABORATIVE TOOLS
www.voght.com/cgi-bin/pywiki?CollabTools

GROOVE
www.groove.net

HORIZON LIVE
www.horizonlive.com

THE GLOBE PROGRAM
www.globe.gov

MERLOT
www.merlot.org/Home.po

MENTERGY
www.mentergy.com

ONLINE COLLABORATIVE LEARNING IN HIGHER EDUCATION
http://musgrave.cqu.edu.au/clp/clpsite/index.htm

OURPROJECT.COM
www.ourproject.com

SMART TECHNOLOGIES
www.smartboard.co.uk

SURVEYSHARE
www.surveyshare.com

THOUGHTSHARE COMMUNICATIONS
www.thoughtshare.com

WORLD LECTURE HALL
www.utexas.edu/world/lecture

AGENTLAND.COM
www.agentland.com

BOTSPOT
www.botspot.com

What's Next for War?

IF YOU WANT TO UNDERSTAND THE American way of war, just read the newspaper. No, not the first section, with its chronicle of global conflicts. Go instead to the sports section, and note the numbing statistical detail with which every game of whatever sport is analyzed. Baseball, football, basketball – and beyond – all are subjected to a kind of scientific, operational study that diminishes the memory of great sportswriters like Ring Lardner. But at the same time this approach speaks volumes about our belief that in such study lies mastery – of sports or strategy. In victory and defeat, American strategic planners have adhered to the notion that war, like sports or manufacturing, can be understood and mastered in statistical terms.

From World War II to the Gulf War half a century later, this meant figuring out how to move convoys of troops and weapons to far-flung fronts as quickly as possible – or at least faster than the enemy could mass his forces. Success at Normandy depended upon reinforcing our beachhead faster than the Germans could build up their counterattacking forces. My early experience as a defense analyst began with calculating whether, in case of Soviet attack, we would be able to reinforce our NATO allies fast enough to offset the waves of Red Army forces that would be coming. Later, I helped calculate first how long it would take to put enough troops into Saudi Arabia to defend against a further Iraqi advance and then figured out how long it would take to mass enough forces and weapons to go on the offensive. War seemed so very calculable to me.

But there were always holes in the scientific orthodoxy about war. Vietnam is the prime example – though many other insurgencies have made the point, too – that God isn't always on the side of the big battalions. The outcomes of many guerrilla wars have shown that, no matter how much pain can be inflicted by a mass-oriented modern military, endurance and morale can win through in the end. Though Bush père announced, in the wake of Desert Storm in 1991, that the Gulf War had finally "exorcised" the ghost of Vietnam, nobody has fought us straight up since. And in 1993, swarms of irregular Somali "technicals" shot down some of our best helicopters and killed or wounded many of our special forces, causing us to withdraw from their sad land. Now we are chasing terrorist shadows all over Afghanistan, with no end in sight. And we're not alone in our troubles. Over the past 10 years, small groups of Hezbollah fighters have driven the Israelis out of southern Lebanon, and al Aqsa suicide squads have also given the Israeli Defense Forces fits during the intifadah. The Russians too have had a very hard time in Chechnya, where they lost the 1994-96 war to ragtag bands of Chechen fighters, and later reasserted control only with great difficulty.

Clearly, the destructive and disruptive power of small, armed groups is on the rise. Beyond the successes of various guerrilla movements over the past half-century, we have also seen, in the recent attacks on America, that a handful of dedicated zealots can shake the world. Even individuals can get into the act– anonymously and virtually, if they like – as the economic damage done by computer worms and viruses often runs into the hundreds of millions of dollars. Imagine a campaign in which a Nimda or a Code Red is released each week – for a year. Then add occasional real-world attacks, perhaps also being perpetrated anonymously, and you'll see that we have moved ineluctably from the Cold War world to a dark new "Cool War" world.

All this grows from the empowerment of the few, and sometimes the one, a process that has been accelerated by the information revolution. But the nuclear shadow remains as well, the worst residue of the arms racing of the Cold War. And while deterrence was stable during the Soviet-American rivalry – because there was somebody to retaliate against – it lies in tatters when the nuclear "power" may be a small group of fanatics with apocalyptic dreams and no country of their own to worry about. Beyond nuclear weapons, there is bioterror to worry about as well, because just a few zealots willing to serve as human vectors of disease – if needed – could have effects as great as 9-11.

The challenge now is for those of us steeped in mutual deterrence and other mass-oriented notions of war to reinvent our security and military organizations along the lines shown to us by these new adversaries. If they work in small, distributed networks, then so must we. Given that the U.S. security and defense establishment is the world's largest bureaucracy, the likelihood of this shift occurring seems remote. Beyond the sheer inertia that guides and governs defense procurement, there is the apparently legitimate concern that we need to keep our industrial-age tanks, ships, guns, and planes — just in case another big war comes along.

If we could only encourage our national security elite to cast aside their habits of mind and institutional interests — even briefly — they would see that current technological trends all point the way to smaller, nimbler, networked forces. The great technological change in the nature of war going on right now has to do with the sharp rise in the information content of weaponry. Previously, weapons were almost all about hurling mass and energy at the foe, with accuracy severely delimited by range. Today, we can embed a great deal of information in weapons — note that computer viruses are almost all information and no mass — so much so that, for the first time in history, we have in effect decoupled range from accuracy. This is what empowers the small unit in a conflict. And note that, while we Americans focus on software and other technical guidance mechanisms, our terrorist enemy has stolen a march on us, increasing the information content of their weapons by using human beings as "guidance systems," whether on hijacked planes or as walking bombs on crowded streets.

What does all this mean? It means that most of our military is structured to fight wars that are highly unlikely to recur. The Navy still rallies around the aircraft carrier and daydreams about costly, huge "arsenal ships" that can carry 500 missiles. Both types of vessels should have their numbers painted over and replaced with big bull's eyes, as they'll soon be sitting ducks for supersonic cruise missiles and high-speed, supercavitation torpedoes. The Air Force, rather than concentrating on providing close support to our special forces, continues to pursue the elusive, costly notion that "strategic bombardment" can work — though it is hard to point to any decisive strategic bombing campaigns waged over the past 90 years. The Army wants to embrace "digitization" — so that commanders can know where every soldier and weapons system is at all times — but without making any real changes in its organizational structure, guaranteeing that a flood of data will hinder rather than enhance field operations.

All this old thinking persists at a time when war is coming to be waged by the small and the many, not the few and the large. These notions persist at a time when unmanned weapons systems — autonomous or tele-operated — can ably support small sea, air, and land combat units. All this resistance to the new prevents change at a time when the increasing information content of weapons means we can do well — better, actually — with far, far less mass, saving billions each year. For the tools and technologies that will enable us to master the looming threats ahead are already out there — often in the private sector, where most research and development now occurs. Very strong encryption must be used routinely, making us all less vulnerable to cyberterror; and a range of "back hacking" devices to help track terror networks are also coming on line. Scanners capable of looking straight through ship containers, detecting radiological or other materials, are already available — and will do much more than ballistic missile defense ever will to protect the homeland. Finally, in the field, our forces have increasing access to information systems — e.g., sharing live video feeds in real-time between troops on the ground and Predators and attack aircraft above — that will empower "hunter networks" in the terror war and other future conflicts. We can improve, only if we're willing to embrace transformational change.

Sadly, most of the nearly $400 billion U.S. defense budget — nearly half of global military expenditures — is wasted, as we pay over and over again each year to sustain capabilities that are less and less relevant to the future of war. It means that we will keep trying to force future conflicts to fit into our existing, costly mold, rather than reshaping our forces to deal with the irregular threats that already confront us — even though the nimble new force would also hedge against the return of old-style warfare. And trust me, after Saddam's misadventure in the last Gulf War, nobody is lining up to challenge American power in a conventional way. Waiting for a reprise of that war is like keeping the landing lights on for Amelia Earhart.

What comes next? Unless we engage in meaningful debate about the changing nature of war, we shall find ourselves ever less prepared for the kinds of conflicts that will confront us. So don't just ask what the future will bring. Instead, join me in demanding of our government that we build a new military for a new era in warfare. And don't be intimidated by the somber, knowing tones of the military-industrial mouthpieces who warn against change. We know, even they know, deep down, that change must come to war. Our adversaries know that it already has.

—John Arquilla

2000 2005 2010 2015 2020

risks  rewards 

Army of the Future... G.I. Dot Joe

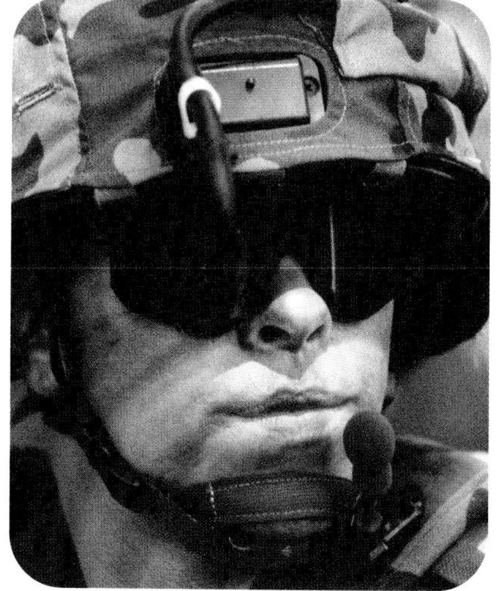

THE LAND WARRIOR SYSTEM. *The fighting fatigues of tomorrow.*

THE CONTEXT AND PURPOSE OF *our military forces is changing – from fighting grand wars like World War II, to engaging in smaller, focused conflicts and more peacekeeping missions like Kosovo or Afghanistan. The joint forces of tomorrow must not only be prepared to meet armies on the battlefield, but to meet rogue combatants in complex, populated urban landscapes. They must be able to withstand not only major artillery, but a broader spectrum of nontraditional threats such as chemical, biological, and cyber attacks. And they must do all this while keeping both civilian and our own casualties to an absolute minimum.*

That's the tallest order ever given to any fighting force in the history of humanity. And the key to fulfilling it will be the use of new technologies that make our forces smarter, faster, more lethal, and more precise.

A major step forward toward fulfilling this vision is the development of the Land Warrior system, the next-generation "individual fighting system" now being prototyped for use by the infantry, marines, and other soldiers in close combat.

The Land Warrior system is to traditional Army fighting gear what a Porsche is to the Model T. Land Warrior's helmet, for example, includes a global positioning system antenna, video and infrared cameras, a visor with the heads-up display, transmitters to identify the soldier as an American to other fighters, as well as chemical and biological weapons detectors and a gas mask. An integrated mic, radio, and wireless LAN devices allow each soldier to know the precise locations of fellow soldiers, enemies, and targets; let soldiers see real-time maps of the battlefield terrain; and allow commanders to send text messages to each soldier's helmet-mounted displays.

Clockwise from top left: Photo courtesy of U.S. Department of Defense-Photo courtesy of U.S. Department of Defense-Photo by Jim Caldwell, courtesy of U.S. Army Training and Doctrine Command

The protective clothing and individual equipment subsystem incorporate modular body armor and upgrade plates that can stop small-arms rounds fired at point-blank range. It includes chemical/biological protective garments and is 35% lighter than traditional "flak jackets."

The weapons system is built around the traditional M-16 but includes a host of advances, including a laser range finder, a digital compass, a thermal sight, and a daylight video sight – an attached camera that not only allows soldiers to literally "shoot around corners," but to take pictures that are relayed to other soldiers in the field.

Future enhancements to the Land Warrior system will include thermal controls that allow soldiers to maintain their body temperature in extreme environments and built-in medical sensors that allow commanders and remote medics to check on a soldier's vital signs with the push of a button.

These technologies don't just make soldiers more effective and immune killing machines — they actually change the nature of military actions. They allow for more distributed, real-time decision making by forces on the ground, and allow individual soldiers to better understand the behavior of their entire platoon. A new kind of "swarm" behavior emerges, as the soldiers, both peers and commanders, can take advantage of massive amounts of information in real-time.

Clockwise from top left: Photo courtesy of U.S. Department of Defense- Video images courtesy of America's Army

"AMERICA'S ARMY: OPERATIONS"

Tomorrow's digital-savvy infantry men and women are today's teenagers – that's why the Army has recently launched a free top-of-the-line video game as a recruitment tool. "America's Army: Operations" seeks to recruit young people by presenting an authentic sense of structure, processes, and technology of today's army missions.

The cost of the Land Warrior system is kept low by using off-the-shelf technologies whenever possible. Each Land Warrior is powered by ruggedized off-the-shelf technologies including a Pentium processor and Windows operating system. The program will cost $2 billion when 45,000 sets of the equipment are fielded over the next 15 years.

Land Warrior is just the beginning, however. The military is also just beginning to test a variety of new technologies that will revolutionize every aspect of force deployment. At the Army's Soldier Systems Center, for example, engineers are developing a Transdermal Nutrient Delivery System (TNDS)– a patch that will keep soldiers fed when they are in extreme situations where they can't get a meal for an extended period of time. Like a nicotine patch, the TNDS delivers nutrients directly to the soldier's bloodstream until help arrives.

And at the newly created Institute for Soldier Nanotechnologies at MIT, scientists are exploring the revolutionary applications of nanotechnology to every aspect of soldiering, including the creation of uniforms that change colors to camouflage the wearer, that provide super-human performance enhancements, and that can become a rigid cast when a soldier breaks his or her leg. While these kinds of technologies are not expected to be fully developed for another 15 years, they point the way to an era when "military intelligence" is no longer dismissed by some as an oxymoron.

PROVOCATIONS...

Will drill sergeants scream at privates to move their joysticks?

Will a dying soldier one day send his spouse instant messages from the battlefield?

—Andrew Zolli

WANT MORE?

SOLDIER SYSTEMS CENTER
www.natick.army.mil

PM SOLDIER SYSTEMS
www.pmsoldiersystems.army.mil/public/default.asp

AMERICA'S ARMY
www.americasarmy.com

Non-Lethal Weapons...Stop or I'll Goo You

THE WORLD NOW HAS AT ITS DISPOSAL MORE KILLING POWER THAN HAS BEEN USED OR *possessed throughout the entire course of human history. We can send a bomb across the world and destroy one specific building. We can bring destruction from air, land, sea, and space. And, of course, we can use nuclear weapons to destroy our planet many times over. Fortunately, the mission of the world's most powerful armies is evolving beyond straightforward destruction.*

From military involvement in international peacekeeping missions to police ensuring relative peace at demonstrations and economic conferences, there are more and more situations where killing is simply too extreme an answer. As such, defense researchers have turned their attentions to the development of non-lethal weapons. The U.S. Department of Defense defines non-lethal weapons (NLW) as "weapons that are explicitly designed to and primarily employed so as to incapacitate personnel and material, while minimizing fatalities, permanent injury to personnel, and undesired damage to property and the environment." The most basic and elegant NLW are as old as warfare. Espionage, deception, and propaganda were the cornerstones of Sun Tzu's *Art of War*, written in the 4th century B.C. The new generation of NLW attempts to add a physical equivalent to Sun's information-based strategies.

KNOCK IT OFF

Crowd and riot control is a common police mission, but the traditional tear gas and water cannons can be crude and sometimes harmful tools in that mission. Pepperball guns allow targeted dispersal of pepper spray, in paintball-like pellets that explode on impact, causing tearing and loss of breath. Laser dazzlers, also used in Somalia, create bright and pulsing flashes of light to disorient and temporarily blind their targets. Problem is, sometimes the blindness is not temporary, and these weapons have been condemned by human rights organizations as a violation of international law.

HOLD IT RIGHT THERE

A primary use of a handgun, especially in law-enforcement contexts, is to stop someone who is advancing toward the gunholder. It usually works quite well, but with the unfortunate side effects of injury, pain, or death. The standard remedy is to replace a lead bullet with a plastic or rubber bullet, but these munitions have been known to blind targets – pushing the envelope of non-lethality. Foam and beanbag bullets hope to minimize damage but don't always succeed. Replacing mechanical force with electrical current yields the taser gun, which incapacitates its target by drowning out the electrical signals between the brain and the body. The problem with the taser weapon is range: The current required is so significant that the projectile portion of the weapon, two metal barbs, must be connected to the gun by two wires, forcing the shooter to be within 21 feet of the target and making reloading awkward. The Mission Research Company is working on a pulsed-energy gun that will wirelessly transmit enough energy to superheat the air around a target so that it explodes, creating a bright flash of light and a loud bang. HSV Technologies' Tetanizing Beam Weapon replaces the taser's wires with a beam of ultraviolet light, sending a powerful jolt of electricity as far as 2 kilometers.

Newer immobilizing weapons rely on materials technology to achieve their objectives. A web gun will shoot a Kevlar net capable of entangling a human or larger adversary. The Army's Portable Vehicle Arresting Barrier will stop a 7,500-pound vehicle traveling at 45mph in about 200 feet, wrapping around the vehicle to keep the occupants inside. First used in Somalia to inauspicious results, the foam gun sprays its targets with a foam that expands and hardens. The problem? When sprayed on heads and faces, the foam had a tendency to suffocate its target; new protocols call for the foam to be sprayed on targets' legs, but the foam is still very difficult to remove once the target has been apprehended. The ultimate evolution of this type of weaponry is likely to be a "goo gun," which will fire an expanding polymer blob to both knock down and immobilize its target.

DON'T GO THERE

A security force might also want to keep people out of a certain area altogether. Traditional military doctrine would call for the use of machine guns, mines, mortars, and (in the old days) mustard gas. Today's non-lethal equivalents include an update on the stink bomb that could smell like vomit, burnt hair, or rotting flesh. The U.S. Army has used a "suds gun" that creates a dense, stable stream of soap bubbles that can be used to create barriers or fill rooms. And the Marines have been investigating super lube – a sprayable antitraction gel described as liquid ball bearings that can cordon areas off from vehicle and foot traffic or render a doorknob unturnable.

Instead of light, the newest ranged NLW use microwaves and sound waves. The microwave versions of these weapons create an intense burning sensation in the target and can induce nausea or even vomiting, all without causing permanent damage, in most cases. Sonic pulse weapons hope to use focused waves of sound and air pressure to both disorient and physically displace their targets. A prototype device developed by the American Technology Corporation is described by its inventor as able to "virtually knock a cow on its back," though no human-bovine conflicts seem to be in the works.

PROVOCATIONS...

Will there be a non-lethal arms race?

How will the toy industry change if non-lethals become the preferred mode of force?

Will we see trailers for *Non-lethal Weapon 4*?

—Bill Kaszubski

WANT MORE?

PENTAGON NON-LETHAL WEAPONS PROGRAM
www.jnlwd.usmc.mil

AMERICAN TECHNOLOGY CORPORATION
www.atcsd.com/index.html

MISSION RESEARCH COMPANY
www.mrcsb.com/atech.html

Military Robots...

SAY THE WORD "BATTLEBOTS" TODAY AND *you'll likely conjure up images of the popular TV show of the same name where teams of players pit their remote-controlled fighting machines against each other. If development proceeds apace, it won't be long before a "battlebot" is something far more ominous, an autonomous robot that can roll onto a battlefield and engage an enemy. Defense developers have a long ways to go before they get to this point, but there have been some recent advances in battlefield robotics that, at least for the moment, are more about helping soldiers than taking lives.*

Imagine a robot that a soldier can carry in a backpack and toss through a window like a grenade. Once deployed, the 'bot becomes an extension of the soldier's senses, scoping out enemy units, using special sensors to sniff for biological and chemical weapons, and assessing other 21st-century battlefield hazards. This is what "throwbots" are all about. One such throwbot, called Spike, was developed at Draper Laboratory in Cambridge, Massachusetts, as part of the Defense Departments's Tactical Mobile Robots (TMR) program. Spike looks something like the copper float inside your toilet tank. Once tossed, its center expands to form an axle that remains stationary while the half-sphere wheels move the 'bot around. Inside the thick axle is a video camera. An operator, out of harm's way, can see what the robot sees. If Spike encounters rough terrain, such as rubble, a set of spiky wheels can be deployed to give the robot greater traction.

Another type of man portable robot, called a PackBot, is being developed at iRobot, a company founded by well-known M.I.T. robotics pioneer Rodney Brooks. Looking not

NON-LETHAL WEAPONIZED ROBOT. *Although this robot may look menacing, the right arm of this experiment by the Space and Naval Warfare Systems Command is equipped with a six-barreled tranquilizing dart gun.*

Image courtesy of Space and Naval Warfare Systems Center, San Diego unlike a remote-controlled kid's toy tank, PackBot is really a platform to accommodate different types of tactical robot configurations. It can be outfitted with numerous environmental sensors, for reconnaissance and threat assessment, and it can be used to haul ordinance or supplies. It's even been tested as a robotic ambulance where, towing a stretcher, it can pull up alongside a wounded soldier who then rolls onto it before being hauled out of harm's way. iRobot is also working on a number of other DoD-funded projects, such as MUMS (Micro Unattended Mobility System), a semi-autonomous 'bot similar to Draper's Spike that can even be fired from a grenade launcher, and Swarm, a project to develop the software needed to coordinate data between distributed groups of autonomous robots.

The Tactical Mobile Robot program was hastily put to the test after 9-11. Lt. Col. John Blitch, who had retired as the head of the TMR program the day before the terrorist attacks, quickly assembled a team of operators and 'bots from various TMR developers. Seventeen robots in all (including iRobot's PackBots) worked Ground Zero, searching for survivors.

The success of the robot recovery workers at the World Trade Center and the achievements of the unmanned Predator planes over the skies of Afghanistan have opened many people's eyes to the real-world potential of robotic and tele-operated machines to do what Michael Toscano of the Pentagon's Joint Robotics Program calls the "dirty, dangerous, and dull." While this attention is leading to stepped-up activity in the field, there is still a long way to go before robotic battlefield assistants become commonplace. Wartime periods have a way of accelerating technological innovations, and the war on terrorism is likely no exception, so we may be seeing 'bots on the battlefield sooner than we thought.

PACKBOT. *Designed to accommodate different types of tactical robot configurations.*

THROWBOT. *"Spike" extends a soldier's eyes and ears by means of special sensors.*

Clockwise from top left: Image courtesy of iRobot-Source-The Charles Stark Draper Laboratory, Inc.

PROVOCATIONS...

Will we one-day turn over lethal combat decisions to robotic warriors?

—Gareth Branwyn

WANT MORE?

DOD JOINT ROBOTICS PROGRAM
www.jointrobotics.com

DARPA TACTICAL MOBILE ROBOTS
www.darpa.mil/ato/programs/tmr.htm

DARPA DISTRIBUTED ROBOTICS
www.darpa.mil/mto/drobotics

SPACE AND NAVAL WARFARE SYSTEMS COMMAND
www.spawar.navy.mil/robots

MOBILE ROBOT DATABASE
http://robot.spawar.navy.mil/MobileRobotKB

IROBOT
www.irobot.com

FUTURE COMBAT SYSTEM
www.darpa.mil/fcs/index.html

SAIC
www.saic.com

CYBERWAR AND CYBERTERRORISM... DANGER ON THE DESKTOP

HIDDEN INFORMATION. *Before-and-after versions of a drawing of Shakespeare, one normal and one with a steganographic message inserted using a program called White Noise Storm. The images are identical to the unaided eye and serve as a good illustration of how Al Qaeda is alleged to have hidden messages in harmless-looking imagery.* **VISUAL ENCRYPTION.** *This Al Hirschfeld drawing (top right) of The Bard is a simple example of visual encryption. You should be able to find five instances of "Nina" hidden in this drawing. The Pentagon used Hirschfeld drawings to test acuity in finding targets. Subjects had to indentify the NINAs.*

Image courtesy of Neil F. Johnson

ON SEPTEMBER 11, 2001, A SMALL, LOOSELY-ORGANIZED *group of terrorists pulled off a sudden, complex attack on the World Trade Center in New York City that killed thousands and caused immediate, radical shifts in many nations' policies. What would be next? Many worry that the encore could be an "electronic Pearl Harbor" as devastating in the digital world as the September 11 attacks were in the physical world. Could terrorists hack into the banking system? The Pentagon? A nuclear power plant?* ¶ *For years, military theorists have looked at how to fight wars in which computer programmers are the generals, laptops the infantry, and software the weaponry. They've coined terms like* information warfare *for the ancient art of using data to gain advantage. Capturing messengers in ancient Greece and breaking Nazi codes were both information warfare; those*

who learned their enemies' secrets could make better, faster decisions and multiply their soldiers' impact.

Cyberwar is a modern subset of information warfare: using computer networks and other electronic tools to both assess a battlefield and destroy an enemy — or that enemy's will to fight in the first place. NATO's 1998 operation against Serbia is a prime example. The Alliance monitored and disrupted Serb phone calls, email exchanges, radio and TV transmissions, and computer networks to cripple the Serbian military's confidence in its communications, just as the threat of bombing destroyed its ability to move heavy weapons. Pro-Serb hackers tried doing the same to U.S. and European networks, blurring the "front line" of the conflict.

While cyberwar can be thought of as nations fighting nations, cyberterrorism is what non-state groups do to everyone else. Cyberterrorists use technology to generate fear that causes citizens or governments to change their actions and goes far beyond merely jamming an e-commerce site or defacing a government Web page. For example, in 2001, an Australian rejected for a local government job avenged this slight by hacking into the computer that controlled the local sewage system. Using a two-way radio and a laptop, Vitek Boden caused the facility to dump about 1 million liters of sewage onto a nearby resort. "It had very serious

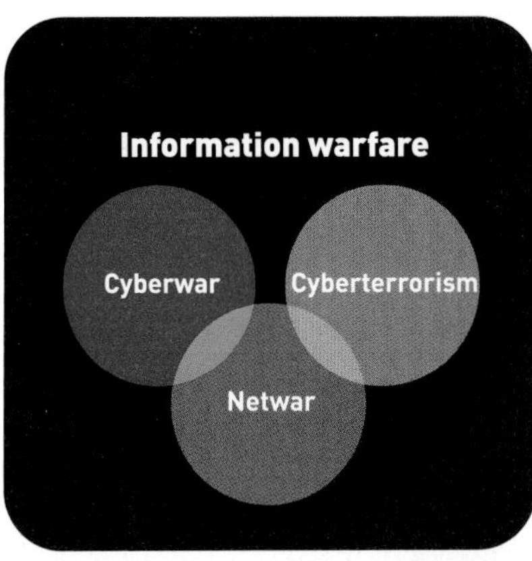

AN INFOWAR PRIMER

INFORMATION WARFARE: An umbrella term for any offensive or defensive use of information to shorten your decision-making cycle while disrupting an opponent's. Breaking an enemy's codes is one example.

INFORMATION DOMINANCE: The achievement of a clearer picture of a battlefield than an opponent has. The combination of satellite photography, drone reconnaissance, and ground observers helped U.S. forces achieve this in Afghanistan.

CYBERWAR: The use of computers and other electronic tools to increase your ability to destroy an opponent or his ability or will to fight. The 1998 NATO campaign against Serbia was partly a cyberwar.

CYBERTERROR: The use of computer networks to damage physical or information infrastructure and cause fear among a citizenry or government. Cyberterror could range from destruction of bank records to sabotaging computers at a nuclear power plant.

Axes of information warfare

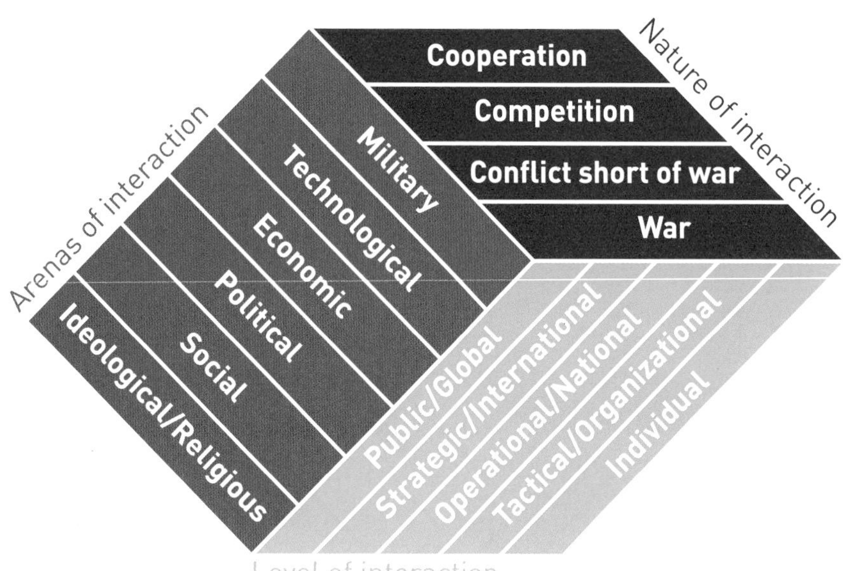

SCOPE OF INFOWAR. *As David Alberts explains in* Defensive Information Warfare *(1996): "The scope, or battlespace, of information warfare and strategy (IWS) can be defined by the players and three dimensions — the nature of their interactions, the level of their interactions, and the arena of their interactions. Nation states or combinations of nation states are not the only players. Non-state actors (including political, ethnic, and religious groups; organized crime; international and transnational organizations; and even individuals empowered by information technology) are able to engage in information attacks and to develop information strategies to achieve their desired ends."*

consequences," says Dr. Dorothy Denning, a Georgetown University professor who is a leading computer-security expert. "If Hamas had done that, we would call it terrorism." Could cyberterrorists hack into, say, the air-traffic control system or a nuclear plant? It's possible, just as it's possible they could shoot their way in; computer networks are so complex that they'll always have some vulnerability. But terrorists might rather hack into a company's payroll system or a bank's records.

NETWAR AND "SWARMING"

Some cyberterrorism and cyberwar may also be netwar, a concept explored and popularized by John Arquilla and David Ronfeldt, in which antagonists use networked organizations and technologies to achieve their goals. Unlike traditional military or business enterprises with their top-down chains of command, these networked organizations may be loosely structured or even leaderless, with members independently pursuing various causes.

Benign examples include Jody Williams' email-based International Campaign to Ban Landmines, which succeeded despite powerful opposition, and the Open Source movement, in which computer programmers worldwide collaborate on better software (such as Linux). A contrasting, obviously non-benign, example would be Al Qaeda, which uses email and cryptography extensively and whose members can act without central direction.

Computer networks enable these small groups to quickly "swarm" at targets via letter-writing campaigns, innovative computer code, or destructive terrorist attacks. The result? Big political and economic impacts from relatively few people. Security experts face the problem of a large-scale netwar: a decentralized but wired enemy making a coordinated series of electronic feints and punches against business and government, from railway signaling

122° 24' 36" W, 37° 46' 26" N

Most security systems are based on something you know (a password) and perhaps something you have (a passkey or other device). But so-called geo-encryption would demand that you also be in a particular place at a given moment, as checked by global positioning system (GPS) signals. This would help verify that you're in a CIA building rather than a Central Asian cave. Beyond worries about Osama dot Laden, geo-encryption could also ensure that a DVD is played only at your home — rather than on the black market — or that your record collection didn't migrate to an online music-sharing operation. The idea has problems, however. The federal government, which operates the GPS network, sometimes degrades the accuracy of commercially available GPS signals from roughly 1-5 meters to as many as 100 — the difference between you logging in or the guy at the phone booth down the block. Also, critics worry about criminals mimicking GPS signals from afar. Even with these problems, some experts believe that "being in the right place at the right time" will soon have a whole new meaning.

Image by Nigel Holmes

systems to the computers at the New York Stock Exchange. Such a careful combined attack could generate chaos, forcing the victims to shut down their systems until damage can be assessed. Everyday life could become extremely difficult for awhile. "If they were able to obliterate your bank account, that would seriously scare people," Dorothy Denning says.

But don't start hoarding food or stuffing money into your mattress just yet. While it's healthy to be aware of what cyberterrorists could do to our electronic or physical infrastructure, both the government and corporate America have a vested interest in keeping records safe and critical systems working. Numerous public and private efforts are underway to share information about threats — and to create new obstacles to thwart would-be cyberterrorists before they even log in.

PROVOCATIONS...

Will developed countries develop a "cyberwarfare" nonproliferation treaty similar to current agreements on nuclear weapons?

If a government stopped a cyberattack, would it be justified in responding militarily in the real world?

How severely?

Will cyberwarriors become a fifth branch of the military?

Will a computer programmer win the Medal of Honor?

—Paul D. Kretkowski

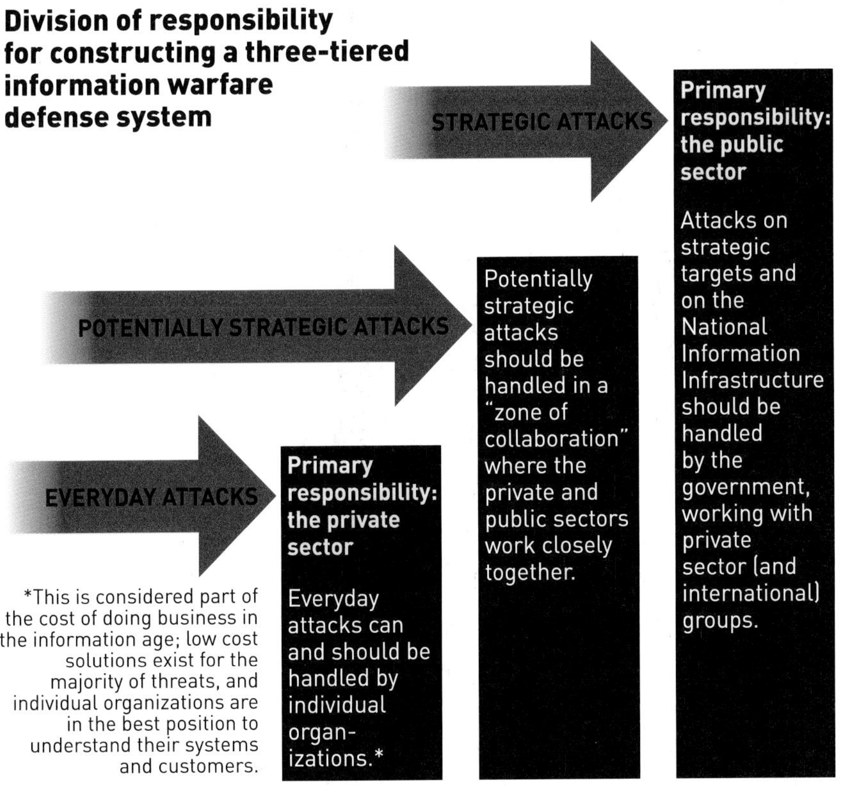

Division of responsibility for constructing a three-tiered information warfare defense system
STRATEGIC ATTACKS
Primary responsibility: the public sector
Attacks on strategic targets and on the National Information Infrastructure should be handled by the government, working with private sector (and international) groups.
POTENTIALLY STRATEGIC ATTACKS
Potentially strategic attacks should be handled in a "zone of collaboration" where the private and public sectors work closely together.
EVERYDAY ATTACKS
Primary responsibility: the private sector
Everyday attacks can and should be handled by individual organ-izations.*
*This is considered part of the cost of doing business in the information age; low cost solutions exist for the majority of threats, and individual organizations are in the best position to understand their systems and customers.

Image by Nigel Holmes

DEFENSE IN DEPTH. *A comprehensive defense strategy covers three lines of defense — everyday attacks, potentially strategic attacks, and strategic attacks — with responsibility shared between public and private organizations (Alberts,* Defensive Information Warfare, *1996).*

WANT MORE?

DEFENSIVE INFORMATION WARFARE, BY DAVID ALBERTS
www.ndu.edu/ndu/inss/books/diw/index.html

DOROTHY DENNING AND GEO-ENCRYPTION
www.smartbusinessmag.com/article/0,3658,apn=2&s=101&a=24832&ap=1,00.asp

DENNING'S LINKS
www.cs.georgetown.edu/~denning/links.html

INFORMATION WARFARE
www.infowar.com

FED. OF AMERICAN SCIENTISTS
ww.fas.org/irp/wwwinfo.html

RAND ARTICLES
www.rand.org/publications/MR/MR661

www.rand.org/publications/MR/MR789

"AN ELECTRONIC PEARL HARBOR?"
http://205.130.85.236/issues/15.1/smith.htm

INST. FOR THE ADVANCED STUDY OF INFORMATION WARFARE
www.psycom.net/iwar.1.html

INFO WAR SITE
www.iwar.org.uk

BAN LANDMINES CAMPAIGN
www.icbl.org

OPEN SOURCE INITIATIVE
www.opensource.org

OPEN SOURCE DEVELOPMENT NETWORK
www.osdn.com

Biowarfare...

WHAT YOU CAN'T SEE, CAN KILL YOU

AT FIRST WE JUST THOUGHT IT WAS THE SMELL. WE *thought it was the smell of decaying bodies that killed people. And so we used the dead – horses, cows, humans – to catapult death in a basket over high city walls. Effective enough. A dead cat down a well, a bubonic rat rocket: This was germ warfare in the 1300s. But in 1763 America, we have a milestone of morbidity: what is likely the first use of a deadly disease (in this case, smallpox) for genocide.*

It is 1763. The French have surrendered what will become Canada to England, the Ottawa Indians have mounted a punishing uprising against a string of British forts, and a European import – smallpox – is making the rounds at Fort Pitt.

"Could it not be contrived to send the Small Pox among those disaffected tribes of Indians?" writes General Amherst to Colonel Bouquet. "We must on this occasion use every stratagem in our power to reduce them." While we cannot be certain Bouquet carried this out, there is evidence that a Captain Ecuyer did, as the commander of the besieged Fort Pitt wrote: "...Out of our regard for them [two Indian chiefs] we gave them two Blankets and an Handkerchief out of the Small Pox Hospital. I hope it will have the desired effect."

It did. In fact, of the pestilence known to generations of man, smallpox holds all records – killing over 300 million people in the 20th century alone – which is why it makes such an effective weapon – and why biological warfare in general continues to thrive. It's cheap, it's fast, and it spreads like, well, like a virus.

Two World Wars and a Cold one provided us with a dark agenda: improve military technology and apply it to delivering biological agents of death. The Geneva Protocol of 1925 outlawed the use – though not the development – of chemical and biological weapons. Japan was notably absent from the adopters of the Protocol, and during World War II its Imperial Army began to weaponize various disease agents, including anthrax, typhoid, and cholera, and to test these developments on the inhabitants of occupied Manchuria. Historical

Clockwise from top left: Photo© Prentice Hall, Inc.; Photo© Imperial War Museum, used with permission

estimates of the death toll from Japan's experiments reach 10,000 people.

The Cold War provided an ideal opportunity for the world's governments to apply the advances in military technology achieved during the two World Wars to the delivery of biological agents of death. In a trial that concluded in April 2002, the head of South Africa's biowarfare research program, Dr. Wouter Basson (known in his country as "Dr. Death"), confirmed the extent of his country's explorations. These included research into a race-specific bacterial weapon, the development of a bizarre array of delivery devices for bioweapons (from anthrax cigarettes to salmonella sugar to poisoned t-shirts), and research into a vaccine that would block human fertility, with which the government hoped to "inoculate" the country's black population. A white judge acquitted Dr. Death of all 67 charges against him, largely on the grounds that he was just following orders. The activities came to light due to the efforts of South Africa's Truth and Reconciliation Commission; unfortunately, no such commissions have illuminated the Cold War biowarfare research of the United States and the USSR, which presumably took place on a much larger scale.

In 1972, the U.S. and more than 100 nations signed the Biological and Toxin Weapons Convention – the world's first treaty banning an entire class of weapons – which bars possession of deadly biological agents, except for defensive research. Unfortunately, no clear mechanisms to enforce the treaty exist. And the provisions for defensive research allow the creation and possession of offensive agents, to test the efficacy of the defenses. Moreover, many countries have chosen not to join the Convention, including "rogue states" like Iran and Syria and U.S. allies like Israel and Egypt. No international terrorist states have signed the accord.

THE STATE OF BIOWARFARE

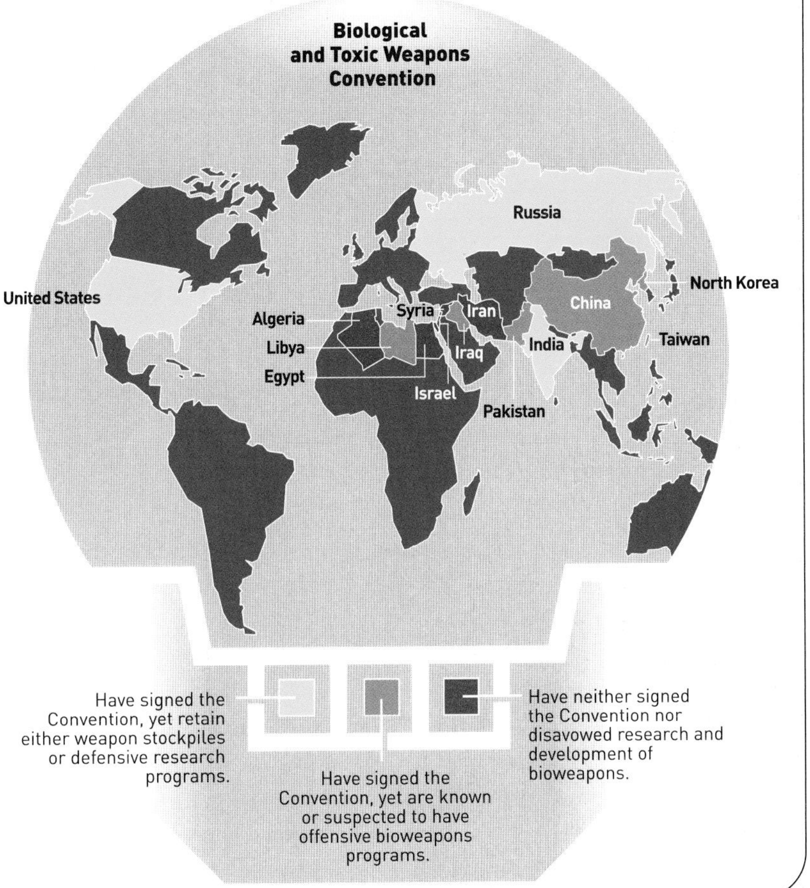

Biological and Toxic Weapons Convention

United States
Russia
North Korea
China
Taiwan
India
Pakistan
Algeria
Libya
Egypt
Syria
Iran
Iraq
Israel

Have signed the Convention, yet retain either weapon stockpiles or defensive research programs.

Have signed the Convention, yet are known or suspected to have offensive bioweapons programs.

Have neither signed the Convention nor disavowed research and development of bioweapons.

Graphic by Nigel Holmes

MAKE ROOM FOR ANTHRAX DETECTORS

A researcher working under an Office of Naval Research grant is just a couple of months away from completing a prototype detector designed to sound the alarm when airborne microbes such as anthrax are in the air. Dr. Jeanne Small, a biophysicist and professor of chemistry and biochemistry at Eastern Washington University in Cheney, Washington, has come up with a detector that continuously samples the air, offering analysis in under a half-hour. Dr. Small has successfully tested biological particles ranging in size from 1 to 10 microbes by using lasers and acoustic sensors to detect and identify microbes. Working with Dr. Small is InnovaTek, a Richland, Washington, company, that makes the air sampler, and Quantum Northwest in Spokane, Washington, which builds the sensor component.

THE BIO-H-BOMB

Two recent experiments offer a chilling look at the intersection of biotechnology and biowarfare. An Australian team has discovered a way to dramatically increase the lethality of the mousepox virus, a close cousin to smallpox, and an American team has synthesized the polio virus from scratch.

The Australians were hoping to control rodent populations on the island nation by triggering an immune response that would render female mice infertile. They located a protein that would trigger the immune response and a hormone — Interleukin-4 — that would throw the mice's immune systems out of balance, suppressing the creation of the killer cells that destroy invading pathogens. To introduce their new genetic material, they used a strain of the mousepox virus they believed the mice were resistant to. A few days later, half of their mice were dead — their imbalanced immune systems unable to defend against a virus they had been vaccinated for. Interleukin-4 is known to have similar effects on the human immune system, leading scientists to predict a similar increase in lethality for a modified smallpox virus.

The American researchers, working under a Pentagon grant, chemically combined genetic fragments (ordered from a bioresearch supply company) according to the polio genome map (available on the Internet) to create the first artificial virus. The purpose of the experiment, according to both the researchers and the Pentagon, was to show that such a thing could be done, and with relative ease. The experiment took two years to complete, but they estimate it could be re-created in as little as 6 months.

Fortunately, we're not quite past the point of no return – the polio virus is dramatically less complex than a more deadly virus like smallpox (7,500 base pairs in polio versus 200,000 base pairs for smallpox), which could not be synthesized using the same method. And to test the efficacy of the Interleukin-4 enhancement, researchers would risk exposure to a hyper-deadly virus, an activity most biochemists would not sign up for. Of course, history has shown that once humans get a little knowledge, they hunger for more. Hopefully, the hunger for a deadlier form of biowarfare will remain unsated.

And so the future of biowarfare lies along two paths: smaller states and terrorist organizations seeking to develop (or steal) the kinds of offensive capabilities already possessed by the Superpowers, and a race to counter these efforts, undertaken largely by the U. S.

Recent advances in genomics provide a powerful defense against bacterial and viral pathogens. The research of Stephen A. Johnston of the University of Texas's Southwestern Medical Center is typical. Johnston breaks pathogens into hundreds of genetic fragments and tests them as vaccines, determining which parts of the pathogen's genetic structure actually perform the work of the vaccination. This is leading to more rapid development of vaccines and the likelihood of creating a single, broadly effective immunization.

Biowarfare Time Line

1300s — Bubonic plague spread throughout Europe

1770s — Smallpox used by British in first act of biowarfare

1925 — Geneva Convention adopted: outlawed use of chemical and biological weapons

1925 — Japanese bioweapons researchers kill 10,000 in Manchuria during WWII

THE BLACK DEATH

In October of 2001, scientists at Britain's Sanger Center (one of the participants in the Human Genome Project), announced that they had sequenced all 4,012 genes of the bacterium that causes bubonic plague. The plague, known as the Black Death when it killed a third of Europe's population in the 14th century, is feared to be in the arsenals of most countries with advanced biowarfare programs.

About 3,000 cases of bubonic plague are still reported each year, with symptoms that include painful swelling under the arms and around the groin, chills, exhaustion, and fever. Antibiotics are an effective treatment, and vaccines are available, but the vaccine supply is limited and the disease can still be fatal if not treated promptly. Fortunately, the sequencing of the genome will not make it easier to weaponize the plague, and it will greatly assist efforts to defend against it. Scientists will be much more able to determine which portion of the bacterium functions as an effective vaccine, increasing the quality of the vaccines and the speed at which they can be produced.

Mankind's advances mean we no longer have to throw dead cats over walls to slaughter enemy populations. Instead, we can lob a ballistic missile or send a virus carrier on an intercontinental airplane flight. As we continue to fight on this unseen battlefield, the visible casualties remind us that while the world's governments may guide the defense against biowarfare, the ultimate responsibility for the protection of the human body lies with its owner.

PROVOCATIONS...

Will the race to defend against biological agents produce unintended breakthroughs, such as a cure for cancer? Will there be a boom in air purifiers? Will the government ever have to enforce quarantine? How should it do so?

—Bill Kaszubski

WANT MORE?

U.S. CENTERS FOR DISEASE CONTROL AND PREVENTION
www.cdc.gov

U.S. NATIONAL INST. FOR HEALTH
www.nih.gov

CDC SPECIAL PATHOGENS
www.cdc.gov/ncidod/dvrd/spb/index.htm

BIOWEAPON NEWS FROM NATIONAL LIBRARY OF MEDICINE
www.nlm.nih.gov/medlineplus/biologicalandchemicalweapons.html

FED. OF AMER. SCIENTISTS, CHEMICAL AND BIOLOGICAL ARMS CONTROL
www.fas.org/bwc

TEXT OF THE BIOLOGICAL AND TOXIN WEAPONS CONVENTION
www.state.gov/t/ac/bw/10431.htm

INNOVATEK
www.tekkie.com

QUANTUM NORTHWEST
www.qnw.com

1945-1989 Cold War

1972 Biological and Toxin Weapons Convention adopted: outlawed research into and possession of offensive bioweapons materials

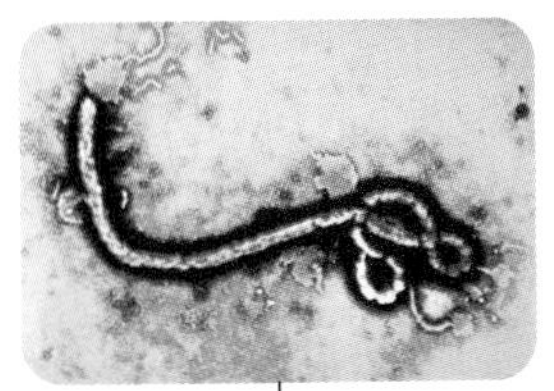

1976 First outbreak of Ebola; research into hemorrhagic fever viruses begins, possibly in violation of Biological and Toxin Weapons Convention

2001 Anthrax outbreaks in continental United States

Clockwise from top: Photo© Dorling Kindersley · Photo© Dorling Kindersley · Photo© Corbis · Photo© Dorling Kindersley

2000 2005 2010 2015 2020

risks  rewards 

Automatic Face Recognition... THE ID YOU CAN'T FORGET

The walls have eyes

Security cameras in stores, banks and even parks may soon start scanning for fugitives. The new Mugspot system uses pattern-recognition software to watch crowds at airports, bus stations and other busy places.

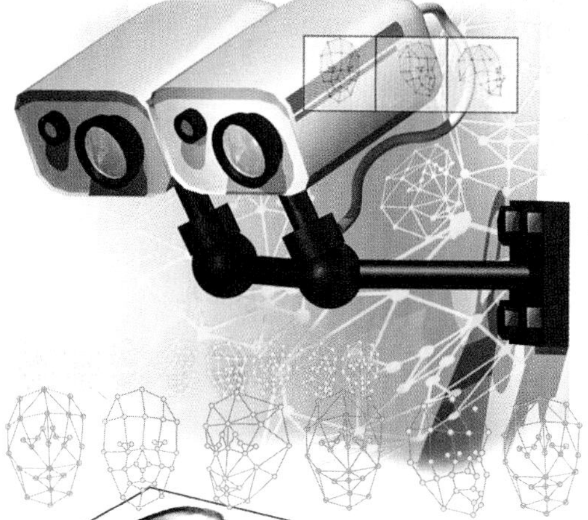

How it works

In about 13 seconds, Mugspot scans a crowd and compares the faces to a database of pictures. Future refinement may cut that time in half. Airports and bus terminals are prime locations, but Mugspot can watch cars at traffic intersections.

Computer picks out the heads of people and tracks them, watching for the best view of the subject's face.

A geometric grid of 45 points is plotted. Because Mugspot examines facial proportions, hair or disguises won't throw it off. If the computer has only a partial view of the face, it can't plot all 45 points, and the identification is harder.

Three-dimensional facial grids of eight different people

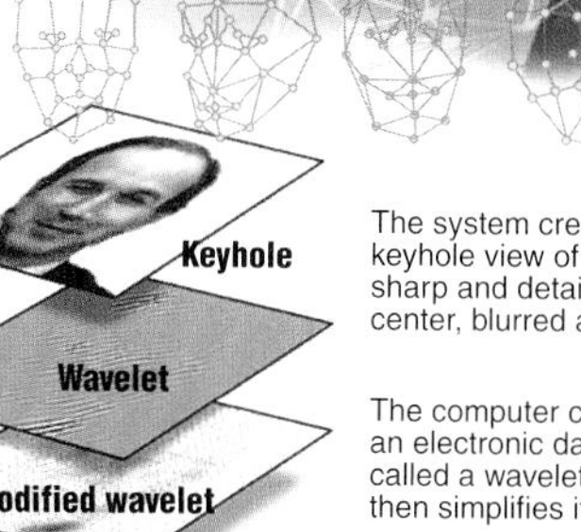

The system creates a keyhole view of each person – sharp and detailed at the center, blurred at the sides

The computer creates an electronic data file called a wavelet transform, then simplifies it into a grid

Software compares each facial grid its database of grids of several hundred wanted criminals

People with matching grids are displayed on a monitor, and security is alerted

Cunanan test

Researchers had Mugspot scan and analyze a photo of serial killer Andrew Cunanan

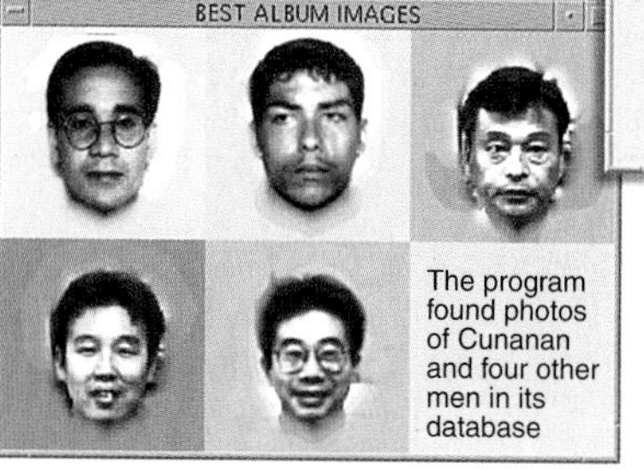

The program found photos of Cunanan and four other men in its database

It ranked the matches, showing the best one at top left

Other ID checking methods

Finger identification: Being tested by MasterCard. When a person opens an account, his or her fingerprint is scanned and a numeric value is loaded onto a microchip on the credit card. To use the card, the holder presses a finger against a small screen, which compares it to the record in the chip.

Hand recognition: The system scans fingers and tops and sides of a hand. It's now in use at San Francisco International Airport, the Colombian legislature and sperm banks, which use it to verify donors.

Face recognition: Software keeps unauthorized people from using a personal computer. A small video camera takes a picture of person, and the computer compares it to images of approved users.

SOURCES: University of Southern California, Los Angeles; MasterCard; FaceIt; Wired; Salk Institute for Biological Studies

Graphic by R. Scott Horner/Newscom

WHEN SOME PEOPLE *encounter facial recognition technology, they don't like it. "My face is my password? That's too Big Brother for me!" Actually, human beings have used facial recognition as a form of ID for millions of years. But it's only been in the last few years that the technology to determine who you are by your facial features has begun to catch up with our innate ability to differentiate each other at a glance.*

Like fingerprints, no two people have the exact facial characteristics. Facial recognition software takes advantage of this by identifying dozens of measurable features, such as the contour of a jaw and chin, the distance between eyes, and the width of a nose. Each of these features is called a *nodal point*.

When a digital camera takes a picture of your face, the facial recognition software turns all the nodal points into one long string of numbers, called a *faceprint*. Your faceprint is then compared against all the faceprints in a database to determine who you are. The database might be a "whitelist" containing faceprints and names of employees who work in a high security building. Or it might be a "blacklist" containing the identities of wanted terrorists and criminals. A blacklist of at-large suspects was famously used by Tampa Bay, Florida, police to search for criminals at Super Bowl XXXV, which was dubbed "Snooperbowl" by privacy rights advocates who decry the use of face recognition. The attendees weren't aware that their faces were being monitored and matched up against a database. At the end of the day, the system succeeded in identifying just 19 petty criminals, such as ticket scalpers and pickpockets.

Facial recognition is already being put to use in airports and other public places. Boston's Logan Airport has been testing facial recognition systems to catch terrorists. The Mexican government is using it to prevent voters from voting more than once. The Foxwoods, Trump, and Stratosphere casinos use them to nail suspected cheaters. The Wisconsin Department of Corrections uses it to keep a log of prison visitors and to verify inmates' identities. The Massachusetts Department of Transitional Assistance is using it to crack down on welfare fraud.

While facial recognition is an excellent way to prevent unauthorized people from entering a workplace, some security experts have their doubts about its effectiveness as a way to nab criminals at sporting events and terrorists at airports. Bruce Schneier, chief technology officer and Founder of Counterpane Internet Security, Inc., says even a system with a 99.99% accuracy rate will set off 10,000 false alarms for each terrorist it identifies, assuming one in every billion people passing by the video camera is a terrorist. Such a system would create a "boy who cried wolf scenario," he says, because security personnel would stop taking the alarms seriously. But facial recognition companies argue that the deterrent factor of facial recognition companies is an important feature that isn't taken into account in Schneier's analysis.

A noncontroversial use for facial recognition technologies is in air bag deployment. A Los Angeles-based company called Eyematic is working with air bag manufacturers to include tiny video cameras and facial recognition technologies into their equipment. The software wouldn't try to tell who the rider is; it would simply determine the location of a rider's face and aim the air bag to deploy in the proper place on the rider's body. This system would prevent children and small adults from getting injuries from airbags that might otherwise hit them in the face and neck.

PROVOCATIONS...

With automatic facial recognition do you have the right not to be recognized?

Will Halloween be the most confusing day of the year?

If you come home with a black eye, will your house let you in?

—Mark Frauenfelder

BLURRY RESULTS

In May 2002, The American Civil Liberties Union obtained results of a facial recognition technology test used to screen employees at the Palm Beach International Airport. The system, called FaceIt, failed to identify the employees 53% of the time. The facial recognition system's manufacturer, Identix, defended itself by saying the system was used with the incorrect lighting and that similar tests in other airports reported only 10% false negatives. FaceIt takes video photographs of people and converts them into digital faceprint codes, which are then compared to a database containing faceprint codes.

NICE TO SEE YOU, TOO!

Researchers at NCR and the USC Integrated Media Systems Center are developing computers that can recognize how you're feeling. A digital camera and specialized software pinpoint facial features and create a map of your emotional state. NCR is interested in applying the technology to ATMs to make them more responsive. Forgot your glasses and can't see the numbers? The computer can detect this and make the type larger. Hate annoying advertisements? Emotion-sensing ATMs could help ease your irritation. But all this begs the question: Do you want a cash machine that can read your mind?

WANT MORE?

VIISAGE
www.viisage.com/facialrecog.htm

IDENTIX
www.identix.com

EYEMATIC
www.eyematic.com

ACLU ON FACIAL RECOGNITION
www.aclu.org/issues/privacy/facial_recognition_faq.html

EPIC ON FACIAL RECOGNITION
www.epic.org/privacy/facerecognition

OMRON TECHNOLOGY VENTURES
www.society.omron.com/faceid

CRIME INVESTIGATION...

"Just Lots More Facts, Ma'am"

"IT IS GLUE, WATSON," SAID HE. "*Unquestionably it is glue. Have a look at these scattered objects in the field!" I stooped to the eyepiece and focused for my vision. "Those hairs are threads from a tweed coat. The irregular gray masses are dust. There are epithelial scales on the left. Those brown blobs in the centre are undoubtedly glue.*"

— Sir Arthur Conan Doyle, *The Casebook of Sherlock Holmes.*

The year is 1927, and Sherlock Holmes has determined that the cap found next to the dead policeman in St. Pancras Station is undoubtedly the hat of the accused: "a picture-frame maker who habitually handles glue." Seventy-five years later, the technologies available for finding connections between crimes, criminals, and evidence would cause Holmes's famous pipe to slip from his lips and crash to the floor – taking with it, of course, a treasure trove of DNA, hair, and fiber evidence.

The tools that scientists have used to learn nature's secrets of natural and

ARE FINGERPRINTS RELIABLE?

If you've ever been arrested, applied for a security clearance, or gotten a job in a casino or a day-care center, odds are that your fingerprints are in Clarksburg, West Virginia — with about 43 million others — in the F.B.I.'s Integrated Automated Fingerprint Identification System. On its Web site, the F.B.I. states, "Fingerprints offer an infallible means of personal identification." Since no two people have ever been shown to have identical fingerprints, there's almost no contesting this statement on a theoretical basis. However, the everyday practice of fingerprint identification diverges from its theoretical promise in two main areas: getting a good fingerprint sample from a crime scene and making a definitive match to an already-known fingerprint.

In 2001 U.S. District Court Judge Louis H. Pollak ruled that while fingerprint experts could testify to their opinion about a fingerprint, they could not definitively identify it as belonging to a defendant. As you might expect, the law enforcement community was not happy with this standard and appealed the decision. Judge Pollak held a series of hearings to gather further background on the science and practice of fingerprint analysis as practiced by the F.B.I., and in 2002, he vacated his earlier judgment, ruling that the F.B.I.'s standards were sufficiently scientific and allowing the evidence in the case under consideration. He did not, however, make any statements about the general reliability of fingerprint evidence, and new challenges by defense attorneys have since increased. It seems that the ultimate fate, and utility, of the 43 million fingerprints in Clarksburg will be determined by the courts.

Photo from the collection of Gregory Goldsmith www.geocities.com/hollywood/academy/9648

biological science – infrared cameras, mass spectrometers, and polymerase chain reactions, for example – also have enabled law enforcement agencies to detect and discover the true nature of crimes, and they have also helped innocent citizens prove that they had been unjustly convicted.

Advances in infrared sensing have given police the ability to detect minute differences in temperature – a technology known as thermal imaging. This technology's usefulness extends far beyond the well-known night-vision goggles. Police use thermal imaging to detect evidence that a fleeing suspect may have removed from their pockets and discarded, like an incriminating breadcrumb trail. Motor vehicle accident investigators use thermal imaging to see the full extent and direction of tire skids, including those of cars with anti-lock braking systems, which don't leave the usual trail of burnt rubber. And, of course, drug enforcement agents use thermal imagers and helicopters to locate the heat emitted by hidden drug cultivation and processing facilities. These advances hasten the arrival of police at the true scene of a crime, but they may not help prove the guilt or innocence of a suspect – that is the realm of forensics.

The primary objective of forensic analysis is individualization. It is used to answer questions like: Did this specimen come from that person? Was this specimen part of that object? Is the physical evidence consistent with a particular sequence of events? Answering these questions requires that forensic detectives examine their evidence at truly fundamental levels: the atom and the genome.

Fingerprints© Corbis

Mass spectrometry allows investigators to determine the atomic constituents of a substance found at a crime scene, even if just a trace amount is recovered. The specimen is vaporized by an ion beam, and the various atoms emitted can be separated and identified by measuring the relationship between their masses and electrical charges. Once a specimen is identified, the same substance may be found on other pieces of evidence, perhaps on a suspect or their belongings. In one experiment, x-ray analysis was used to locate evidence: bullet fragments lodged deep in clothing. Mass spectrometry may also be able to help with ballistic analysis. Since the lead used in bullets decays into specific isotopes at known rates, samples from fired bullets can be matched to batches of ammunition or residue found in guns, substantiating the results of traditional ballistic analysis.

When the evidence comes not from objects but people, forensic investigators turn to the technology of the biochemist. The polymerase chain reaction (PCR) process allows a minute sample of a DNA-bearing substance (saliva from a cigarette butt, skin from a hair follicle) to be amplified to an amount that can be easily analyzed. The genetic patterns of small regions of DNA can then be matched with other samples found at the crime scene or found in a database of previous offenders. The sequencing of the entire human genome has allowed forensic geneticists to identify more portions of our genome that lend themselves most readily to this type of comparison. The National Institute of Justice is even applying this technique to the domestic cat genome, enabling the innumerable hairs found in the homes of cat owners to be used as evidence. Current research in genomic analysis will allow identifications to be made from still smaller samples, increase the number of markers contained in genetic databases, and allow the creation of smaller and faster DNA analysis machines, one day permitting this analysis to be performed right at the scene of the crime.

Of course, none of this technology is a replacement for the staple of Holmes's method: deduction. But it does allow investigators to bring much more information to bear on the solving of a crime, and it provides them with the evidence to support their conclusions in court.

PROVOCATIONS...

Will everyone be required to register their DNA with the FBI?

Will the cost of crime labs create a "justic disparity" between rich and poor communities?

—Bill Kaszubski

WANT MORE?

FORENSIC EVIDENCE IN THE NEW MILLENNIUM
www.forensic-evidence.com

NATIONAL LAW ENFORCEMENT AND CORRECTIONS TECHNOLOGY LIBRARY
www.justnet.org/virlib

EVIDENCE: THE TRUE WITNESS
http://library.thinkquest.org/17049/gather

LATENT PRINT INVESTIGATION
http://onin.com/fp

Lie Detection...Truth or Consequences

IN THE OPENING SCENE OF Blade Runner (1982), Ridley Scott's masterful science-fiction movie set in L.A. circa 2019, we see a man — actually a replicant, or genetically-engineered human cyborg — being given something called a Voigt-Kampff exam, a futuristic polygraph test. The test monitors the subject for certain involuntary physical responses to key questions, which makes it very similar to current polygraphs.

POLYGRAPHS: Do they detect lies?

State law kept polygraph, or "lie detector," evidence out of the murder trial of O.J. Simpson, but it's been used in the civil lawsuit against him.

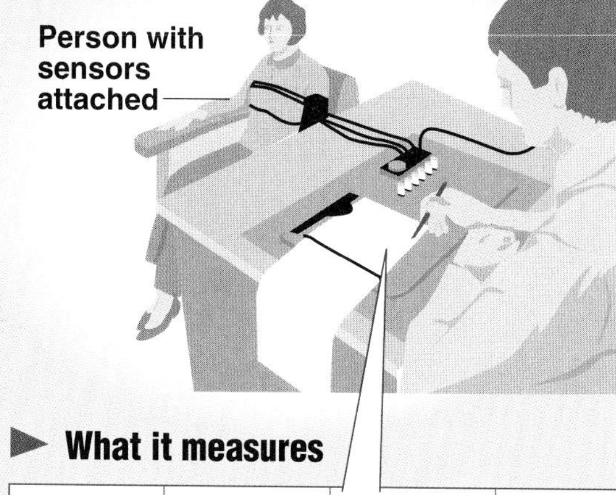

► How it works

Sensors measure body changes as person answers yes-no questions; data is recorded on moving strip of paper

► How reliable?

- Person can't be forced to take polygraph; usually barred as evidence in criminal trials; used in civil trials if parties agree
- Skill of testers varies; some claim 95% accuracy; test can't tell guilt from fear
- Guilty are usually detected; major problem is number of innocent people who fail test

SOURCE: World Book, Science and Invention Encyclopedia

► What it measures

Body movements

Breathing (diaphragm)

Breathing (chest)

Perspiration

Pulse and blood pressure

Pattern indicates probable lie

Graphic credit: KRT. Illustrator: Quin Tian

The polygraph, often simply called a "lie detector," was invented in 1917 by William M. Marston. It's based on an old assumption: That a guilty person will have emotional reactions to incriminating questions. Polygraphs measure a person's breathing rate, perspiration, and blood pressure. The theory goes that when asked questions relating to a crime, a guilty person will have an involuntary physical reaction that can be measured by some combination of the machine's detectors. That's the theory. The reality is that the readings can be fooled by, for example, a subject who bites her tongue (pain reactions make it hard to establish a baseline to compare truth to lies), or by anyone who knows simple relaxation techniques, such as yoga or meditation.

RECENT DEVELOPMENTS

More recent developments in machine-aided interrogation have tried to measure other involuntary responses. For example, Truster software, developed by the Israeli military and sold in the U.S. by Truster USA, uses Computerized Voice Stress Analysis (CVSA) to measure micro-changes in a subject's voice that might indicate a lie. Truster messages include: "Truth," "False Statement," "Subject is Not Sure," "Outsmart," "Inaccuracy," "Avoidance – Voice Manipulation," "High Stress," "Excitement," and "Extreme Excitement." Truster was actually used by *Time* magazine reporter Martin Lewis during the 2000 U.S. presidential campaign, somewhat tongue-in-check, as a kind of "cyber truth serum" for the candidates.

Marian Stewart Bartlett of the

Institute for Neural Computation in San Diego has developed a video system that maps a face onto a grid and measures changes in unconscious "micro-expressions." These split-second facial changes are alleged to be a giveaway that someone is lying.

BRAIN FINGERPRINTING

The most intriguing development in this area is "brain fingerprinting," a new scientific technology that detects whether specific information is stored in a person's brain. First developed in the early 1990s by Lawrence Farwell, Ph.D., brain fingerprinting has been used to detect with 100% accuracy which people in a group were FBI agents by measuring brain responses to words or pictures that only FBI agents would recognize. Someone already familiar with those words or pictures will show different brainwave activity than someone who is new to the information.

Brain fingerprinting is based on the principle that the brain is central to all human acts. In a criminal act, there may or may not be many kinds of peripheral evidence, but the brain is always there, planning, executing, and recording the crime. The fundamental difference between a perpetrator and a falsely accused, innocent person is that the perpetrator, having committed the crime, has the details of the crime stored in his brain, and the innocent suspect does not. This is what brain fingerprinting scientifically detects. Brain fingerprinting was found to be 100% accurate in tests for the CIA and the U.S. Navy.

To test a subject, words or pictures relevant to a crime, terrorist act, or terrorist training are flashed on a computer screen, along with other, irrelevant words or pictures. Electrical brain responses are measured non-invasively through a patented headband equipped with sensors. A specific brain wave response called a MERMER (memory and encoding related multifaceted electroencephalographic response) is elicited when the brain processes noteworthy information it recognizes. (The MERMER contains another, well-known and scientifically established brain response known as a P300.) When details of the crime that only the perpetrator would know are presented, a MERMER/P300 is emitted by the brain of a perpetrator, but not by the brain of an innocent suspect. A computer analyzes the brain response to detect the MERMER/P300, and thus determines scientifically whether or not the specific crime-relevant information is stored in the brain of the suspect. Brain fingerprinting does not measure whether someone is lying, but rather whether or not the record of a crime is stored in his or her brain.

Brain fingerprinting has been ruled admissible in court in Iowa, in the case of Terry Harrington, who was convicted of murder in 1978 and has been serving a life sentence since then. Brain fingerprinting proved that the record stored in Harrington's brain did not match the crime scene, but did match his alibi. Faced with the brain fingerprinting evidence, the only alleged witness to the crime recanted and in a sworn statement admitted he had lied in the original trial to avoid being prosecuted for the crime himself.

CONVICTING A SERIAL KILLER/RAPIST

Brain fingerprinting was used to help convict a serial killer/rapist by proving that the record stored in the brain of JB Grinder matched the scene of the murder of Julie Helton. Faced with a certain conviction and probable death sentence, Grinder pled guilty in exchange for life without parole. He also confessed to the murders of three other young women.

For the test, Grinder wore a special

THE HOME INTERROGATOR

It's not just law enforcement and the FBI who get to play with lie detectors. There are a number of companies who will happily sell you lie-detection equipment. Most of these devices do voice stress analysis, measuring micro-tremors in a person's voice that can indicate stress. Companies such as Truster USA and the Spy Shop sell VSA equipment, and a few Web sites even give you schematics so that you can build your own homemade (albeit primitive) lie detector.

Photo courtesy of Brain Fingerprinting Laboratories, Inc.

THE BRAINS BEHIND BRAIN FINGERPRINTING. *Dr. Lawrence Farwell, one of the developers of "brain fingerprinting," which directly reads brain activity and might just be the next big thing in the fight against terrorism.*

THE EYES HAVE IT

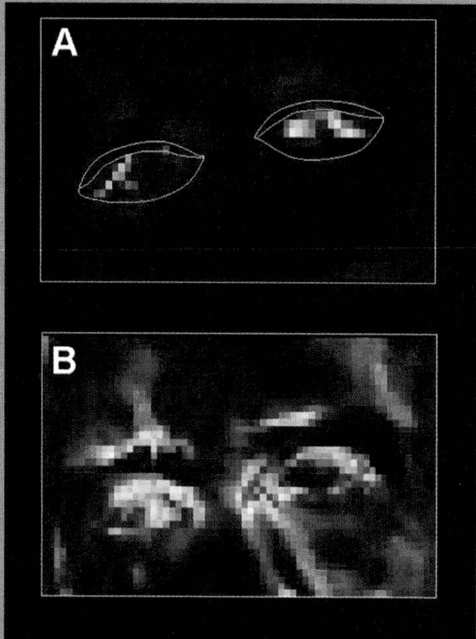

THERMAL IMAGING. *The changes around the eyes after telling the truth (upper image) and telling a lie (lower image) are detected (Photo: Pavlidis, et al.).*

How do you screen a lot of people quickly at, say, an airport, to see if they're carrying weapons or telling the truth? Giving each of them a polygraph test and then trying to analyze the results would take days. What if you could just look into their eyes? Or, more specifically, around their eyes? Using a high-resolution thermal imaging camera developed by Norman Eberhardt and James Levine of the Mayo Clinic and Ioannis Pavlidis of Honeywell Laboratories, you can do just that.

It's well known by security professionals that the temperature around a person's eyes can rise several degrees when they're lying. With this new camera, it's easy to monitor for that change. After a series of tests at the Department of Defense's Polygraph Institute, the camera identified 75% of test subjects who were lying and 90% of those telling the truth, about the same accuracy as a polygraph test, but done faster. "The technology represents a new and potentially accurate method of lie detection," says Dr. Levine. "The development holds promise for practical application in high-level security operations, such as airport security and border checkpoints."

Not everyone is sold on the technology, however. Aldert Vrij of the Department of Psychology at Portsmouth University in England, who has done a number of important studies of lying and lie detection, believes that the system has all the same flaws as regular polygraphs. Both tests rely on an emotional response by the liar, which means people who can lie calmly might not be detected at all.

headband equipped with sensors that measured activity from three areas of his brain. The headband was connected to an electroencephalograph, which fed the data into a computer for analysis. A combination of words and pictures flashed on the monitor in front of Grinder.

As the headband collected Grinder's brainwaves, investigators were looking for a brainwave called a MERMER. In this case, a MERMER would prove that Grinder knew something significant about Julie Helton's murder.

As the graph on the next page illustrates, each of the three lines on Grinder's brain fingerprint represents a different kind of information. The green line corresponds to random words and images and shows no significant response. The red line, for information that the investigators had given Grinder, shows a MERMER wave, so he remembered those details. What's most significant is the blue MERMER. This corresponds to "probe" questions about information that only the killer would know. The investigators concluded from this that Grinder knew critical details about the murder and was probably guilty.

While a lie detector that can see directly into a brain seems foolproof, brain fingerprinting has its critics. Dr. Emanuel Donchin, one of Dr. Farwell's former collaborators, believes that the MERMER wave doesn't always indicate guilt. Donchin says that a seemingly damning piece of evidence can produce a MERMER in an innocent brain if the evidence reminds that person of something about which they have particularly strong feelings.

COUNTERTERRORISM

In counterterrorism applications, brain fingerprinting can identify the perpetrators and planners of terrorist acts and can also detect a trained terrorist even before he or she strikes.

According to a study by psychology professor Gerald Jellison of the University of Southern California, Americans tell an average of 200 large and small lies every day. While most of these are the harmless little social evasions that we hardly think twice about, other lies hold the keys to robberies, thefts, even murder and treason. In a post-9-11 world, lie detection is sure to remain a major security research area.

Images courtesy of Dr. Ioannis Pavlidis from Honeywell Laboratories

SERIAL KILLER. *Dr. Larry Farwell conducts a brain fingerprint examination of serial killer JB Grinder. Brain fingerprinting uses a modified electroencephalograph to read brainwave activity and detect whether or not information is stored in a person's brain. In tests, it has been proven much more accurate than traditional polygraph tests.*

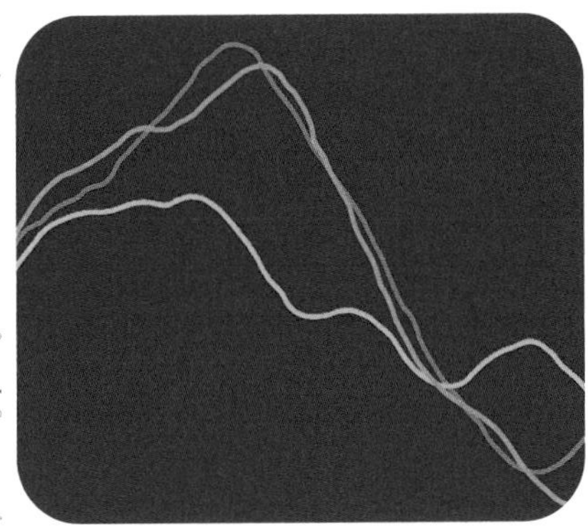

EVIDENCE OF GUILT. *This graph shows the brain response of serial killer JB Grinder to information relevant to the murder of Julie Helton. The graph indicates that the record stored in JB Grinder's brain matches details from the actual crime scene.*

PROVOCATIONS...

Will politicians need to get their voices scrambled?

Will men or women want to use this software more?

What happens to the "little white lie"?

Will people simply talk less?

—Richard Kadrey

WANT MORE?

LIE DETECTION RESOURCES
www.nettrace.com.au/resource/associated/liedetection.htm

AMERICAN POLYGRAPH ASSOCIATION (APA)
www.polygraph.org

HISTORY OF POLYGRAPH
www.crimelibrary.com/forensics/polygraph/2.htm

NATIONAL INSTITUTE FOR TRUTH VERIFICATION (NITV™)
www.cvsa1.com/product.php

BRAIN FINGERPRINTING
www.brainwavescience.com

HONEYWELL LABORATORIES
www.honeywell.com

TRUSTER LIE DETECTION SYSTEM
www.trusterusa.com

LEARNING TO SEE MICRO-EXPRESSIONS (WITH VIDEO)
www.bbc.co.uk/science/humanbody/humanface/exp_deceit3.shtml

LAFAYETTE INSTRUMENT
www.lafayetteinstrument.com

AARON CAKE'S SIMPLE LIE DETECTOR
www.aaroncake.net/circuits/lie.htm

DIOGENES COMPANY
www.diogenesgroup.com

THE SPY SHOP
www.spyshopinc.com

TODAY'S PRISONS...

Lock 'em Up and Throw Away the Swipe Card

IN 1791, THE PHILOSOPHER JEREMY BENTHAM PROPOSED A *design for a new type of prison he called a Panopticon (approximately Greek for "all-seeing place"). It was a semi-circular building with guards at the center and cells around the perimeter, allowing prisoners to be observed by guards, but not vice versa. Not knowing whether they were being watched or not, obedience was the prisoner's only rational option. Bentham's Panopticon was never built; however, technology has now enabled us to create prisons that demand the same level of obedience from their occupants, without relying on their rationality.* ¶ *Following this precedent, modern prison designers have combined the architecture of prisons with sophisticated control and containment systems to create prisons that provide more livable environments for inmates and ensure maximum secuity for guards and the surrounding community. Los Angeles County's Twin Towers jail is the*

SMILE, YOU'RE ON JAILCAM: PRIVACY AND "AMERICA'S TOUGHEST SHERIFF"

Joe Arpaio wants to make you suffer. In a 1995 interview, the Maricopa County Sheriff explained his corrections philosophy with chilling bluntness: "I aim to make this place so unpleasant that [prisoners] won't even think about doing something that could bring them back."

His tactics have included tent-campt jails in the middle of the desert, 20-cent meals for prisoners, and, starting in July 2000, a live Webcast of four interior views of the county jail, hosted by crime.com. Lacking the drama of a structure of, say, Oz, Arpaio's production was nevertheless heavy on the humanity: prisoners bound in restraint chairs; strip searches; female prisoners using the toilet.

Arpaio saw the Webcam as a way to both discourage crime and combat charges of cruelty and mistreatment that had been leveled against his department. Problem was, the views from all cameras were of processing and holding areas — none of the "stars" had been convicted of a crime.

Middle Ground Prison Reform files suit against the county and the sheriff in May 2001, and although the case is still pending, it seems to have had the desired effect: The bathroom camera was disconnected soon after the suit was filed, and crime.com has gone out of business. Sheriff Joe says he is looking for another host for the cameras, but as of now the only people watching the feeds from the Maricopa County Jail are the jailors.

AP/Wide World Photos

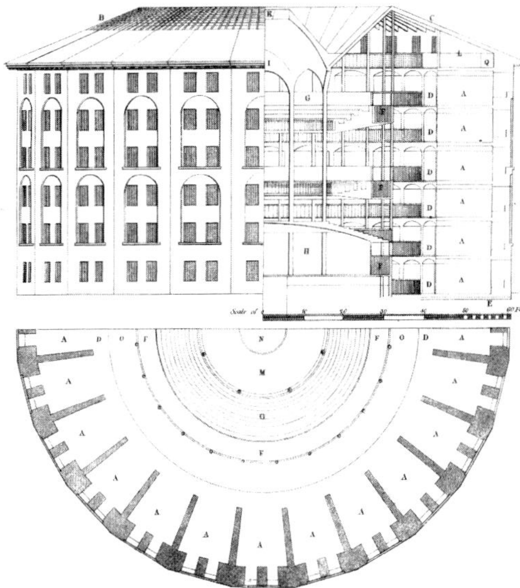

PANOPTICON, ANYONE? *An architect's rendering of Bentham's idea for a prison (left).* **LA COUNTY JAIL.** *A lone guard walks the perimeter of the jail (far left).*

largest in the world, and a 21st-century Panopticon, featuring a circular design; shatterproof glass instead of bars; electronically-controlled locks instead of large, clanky keyrings; and completely pervasive camera and intercom systems, all controlled from isolated, ergonomically-designed guard stations.

California has long been a frontier of prison development. The California Department of Corrections (CDoC), which deployed the first lethal electric perimeter fence in the 1980s, has now developed electronic wrist monitors that tell prison officials the location of every person in their facility. If an inmate tries to remove or damage their wrist unit, gets too close to a perimeter fence, or engages in any behavior that is not allowed, an alarm will sound at both the central control and in the inmate's unit, resulting in almost immediate response.

"This kind of technology... converts the information of a thousand eyes," says Larry Cothran of the CDoC. "It takes away all the guesswork of investigations. If inmate A is stabbed, we now can see exactly who was standing next to him at the time. Will it change almost every facet of prison life? I think so."

For offenders out on parole, there are high-tech monitoring tools that can track individuals around the clock. For example, Pro Tech Monitoring's SMART® System uses an ankle bracelet that transmits signals to a Portable Tracking Device (PTD), which has a GPS receiver, cellular modem and land-line communications capability, motion detectors, and tamper-detection circuitry. The PTD incorporates a computer that contains the "Rules of Supervision" for the offender and any off-limit areas. This system notifies the supervising agency and the offender of violations in real time.

Although the Panopticon model may discourage inmate misbehavior, it will still occur. Prisons are now deploying less-than-lethal weapons technology, such as Taser guns, bean-bag guns, and "Pepperball" guns, to stop incidents and control the inmate population. A less-than-lethal water restraint system operates like a fire hose, shooting a spray of water laced with pepper spray over the heads of fighting inmates, breaking up fights a lot more effectively than a group of guards with nightsticks. Pepper spray is also used to "extract" prisoners who have barricaded themselves in their cells. Prison administrators are also relying on more training to help guards control unruly prisoners, even staging an annual Mock Prison Riot at a converted prison in West Virginia, which drew over 1,350 people in 2001.

The trouble with Bentham's Panopticon is that it required a fundamentally moral and rational prisoner, one who behaved all the time even while knowing that there was no way the guard could be watching everyone all the time. Perhaps that's why it was never built. Bentham's heirs have overcome this limitation through technology, creating modern Panopticons with countless unsleeping eyes and ears. The ultimate effect on prisoner morality has yet to be seen.

PROVOCATIONS...

Should prisoners have rights to a video record of their incarceration for their own protection?

Could banishment from certain Internet services become a new form of virtual prison?

—Bill Kaszubski

WANT MORE?

JUSTICE TECH INFO CENTER
www.nlectc.org/justnet.html

OFFICE OF LAW ENFORCEMENT TECH COMMERCIALIZATION
www.oletc.org

CA DEPT. OF CORRECTIONS
www.cdc.state.ca.us

PRO TECH MONITORING
www.ptm.com/home.htm

THE SENTENCING PROJECT
www.sentencingproject.org

PRISON PRIVATIZATION SITE
www.ucc.uconn.edu/~logan

BUREAU OF JUSTICE STATISTICS
www.ojp.usdoj.gov/bjs

LOS ANGELES COUNTY JAILS
www.lasd.org/custody/index.html

Our Planet

Meeting Global Challenges in the 21st Century

I AM PERSUADED THAT WHAT WE DO OR FAIL to do in the first quarter of this new century will set the direction, perhaps decisively, for the future of life on Earth as we know it. I am at a stage in my life in which I will likely be spared the worst consequences of our failure to respond to the many serious challenges that confront our world today — such as conserving our dwindling natural resources; healing our environment; and addressing the ever-increasing need for food, water, shelter, sanitation, energy, education, health, and economic security among the world's peoples. Yet when I look at my grandchildren and think of the world that is in store for them and those who follow them if we fail to act, I am reinforced in my determination to do everything possible in the remainder of my life to ensure that they may have a secure, sustainable, and promising future.

Our awareness of these challenges is not new. The United Nations Conference on the Human Environment, held in Stockholm almost 30 years ago, put the environment issue on the global agenda and established the inextricable link between environment and the development aspirations and priorities of developing countries. Stockholm, in its historic Declaration, stated that "to defend and improve the human environment for present and future generations has become an imperative goal for mankind — a goal to be pursued together with, and in harmony with, the established and fundamental goals of peace and of world-wide economic and social development." It thus pointed up the systemic linkages between the environment and the issues of peace, security, economic and social development through which human activities are shaping our common future.

The 1992 Earth Summit, held in Brazil, was a landmark experience which produced the Rio Declaration and framework Conventions on Climate Change and Biodiversity, mandated a negotiating process which has since resulted in a Convention on Desertification, and agreed on Agenda 21 as a comprehensive program — the transition to a sustainable development pathway. Now as we approach the next milestone, the United Nations World Summit on Sustainable Development in Johannesburg, it is important that we reflect on the lessons and experiences of the past 30 years and discern how this can guide us in setting our directions and global priorities for the new millennium.

A wide range of success stories demonstrates that when the will exists, impressive progress can be made. Across the globe, progress is more evident today in the actions of civil society than of governments. More than 3,000 cities and towns in every part of the world have adopted their own local sustainable development agenda, based on the Global Agenda 21 developed at the 1992 Earth Summit; National Councils for Sustainable Development have been established in some 100 countries; women and youth have taken more and more leadership; there have been impressive advances in the fields of science and education; the special role and experience of indigenous people has become increasingly appreciated; and more and more business leaders have found that a commitment to sustainable development is good for their own bottom line.

Dramatic improvements have been effected in the environmental performance of industry, and technologies have been developed which promise solutions to many environmental problems, as the prospect of emission-free motor vehicles and the transition to a hydrogen-based energy economy attest. At the same time, developing countries have become more aware of and concerned with the environmental problems which inhibit their own development and undermine their struggle to eradicate poverty — exacting such immense human and economic costs as deteriorating conditions in their cities, destructive exploitation of the natural resources on which future development depends, the immense challenge of meeting their growing needs for water and ensuring its quality, prevention and care of destructive and debilitating disease, and most of all their primary need to lift their people out of the quagmire of poverty. As former Indian Prime Minister Indira Gandhi said at the Stockholm Conference, "Poverty is the greatest polluter."

Yet developing countries, which are custodians of most of the world's precious biodiversity resources, are expected to care for them with only sporadic and limited support from industrialized countries. As their economies grow, they will contribute increasingly to the more remote and less visible global problems for which the industrialized countries are largely responsible, notably the risk of climate change, which affects the interests and the future of all nations.

The tragic events of 9-11 demonstrated dramatically the vulnerabilities of even the most advanced and powerful of societies to destructive attacks, however misguided, by relatively small groups of alienated people. This underscores the need for international cooperation, not only to conduct the war against terrorism, but also to deal with the whole complex of issues integral to the globalization process. These include eradication of poverty, environmental protection, notably the risk of climate change, meeting the development and security needs of developing countries, redressing the gross, and growing, imbalances that divide rich and poor and nourish the enmities and frustrations that are the seedbeds of conflict.

International cooperation is as indispensable to the effective management of the other elements of the globalization process as it is to the prevention of terrorism. But cooperation based on coercion will not long be effective. Sustainable cooperation requires truly shared decision-making and responsibility on the part of the majority of nations, and this can only be achieved if the dominant nations of the world take the lead. Many of the world's governments regret but cannot be immobilized by the retreat from multilateral leadership on these issues on the part of the United States, which has performed an immensely valuable service to the world community by leading it effectively through much of the period since World War II. No individual nation is in the position to replace the United States in this role. And while world leaders continue to hope for and work for the return of the United States' leadership, they cannot afford at this critical time to allow a vacuum to prevail which would put at risk the very multilateral cooperation this is now badly needed to ensure the sustainability of life on Earth as we know it.

The need for new and revitalized leadership is reinforced by the sobering realization that much of what has been agreed in the past has not been implemented, and there is a disturbing tendency even to backtrack on past agreements. This dichotomy between aspiration and action is a reflection of the conflict between the world's ecosystems and its ego systems. Putting ego aside, learning to cooperate; to take proportional responsibility; and to create social, economic, and technological values that foster a sustainable world is at the very heart of the challenge that will face the next generation of global leaders.

We have, for the first time in history, the capacity to meet these monumental challenges. Indeed, on a global basis we are the wealthiest civilization ever and are producing material wealth at an unprecedented rate. Yet we do this while running down our natural capital and undermining the life-support systems on which all life on Earth depends. And this situation cannot be sustained much longer. As Britain's Prime Minister Tony Blair said recently, "You don't have to be an expert to realize that sustainable development is going to become the greatest challenge we face this century."

Much of what we must do has already been identified, articulated, and agreed upon at Stockholm, Rio, and various other international forums. But implementation depends on motivation — and this is at the heart of our current dilemma. Most of the changes we must make are in our economic life. The system of taxes, subsidies, regulations, and policies through which governments motivate the behavior of individuals and corporations continues to incent unsustainable behavior. At the deepest level, all people and societies are motivated by their moral, ethical, and spiritual values. To build on these a set of basic moral and ethical principles that are broadly acceptable is certainly not easy. A process that has taken several years and involved millions of people around the world has succeeded in producing a "people's" Earth Charter as a major contribution to articulating the moral and ethical foundations for sustainable development. At the Johannesburg World Summit on Sustainable Development, world leaders will be challenged to recognized the Earth Charter as an important expression of the commitment of millions of people throughout the world to these basic ethical and moral principles.

Amidst all of the uncertainty, one thing is certain — this is the most critical time for the planet Earth and its people in our shared history. Many of the challenges we confront will become crippling crises without focused and sustained action, and this puts a special burden on all of us, especially our leaders. We must look to them, gathered in Johannesburg, and thereafter in every nation, for the will and the wisdom to rise to the awesome responsibilities that our times have conferred upon us all.

—Maurice Strong

Biodiversity...Variety Is Life's Main Course

A recent U.N. report, prepared ahead of a summit next month in Johannesburg on the environment and poverty, warned that 12 percent of birds and nearly a quarter of all mammal species are regarded as globally threatened

Species under threat

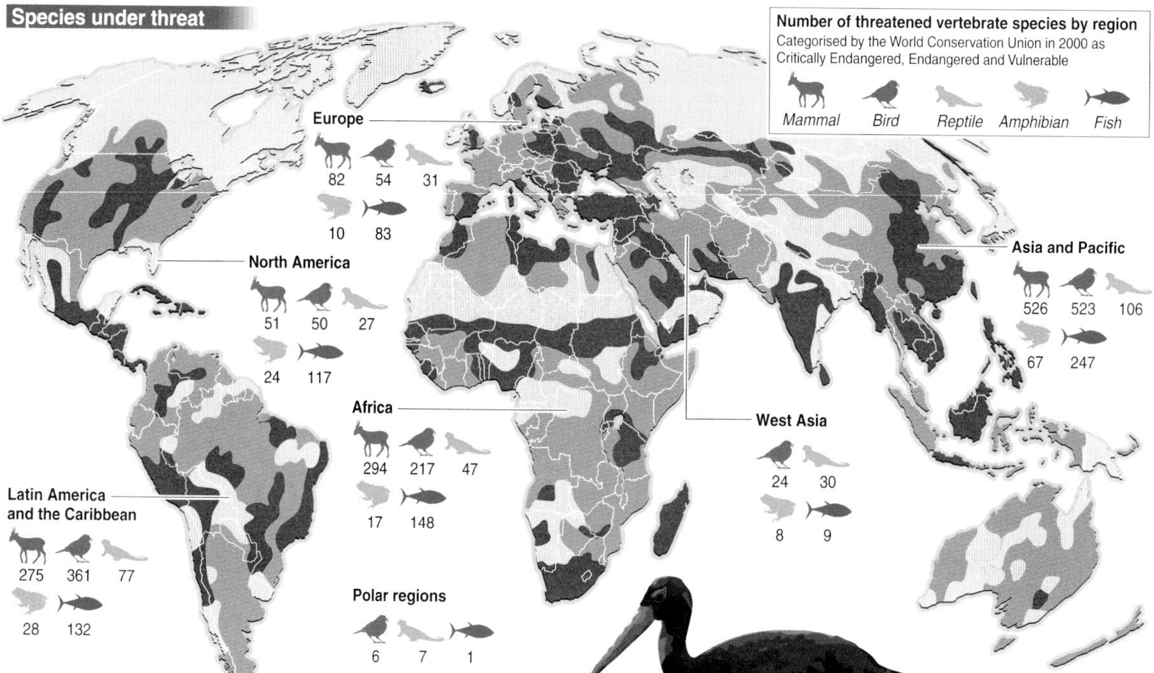

Number of threatened vertebrate species by region
Categorised by the World Conservation Union in 2000 as Critically Endangered, Endangered and Vulnerable

Region	*Mammal*	*Bird*	*Reptile*	*Amphibian*	*Fish*
Europe	82	54	31	10	83
North America	51	50	27	24	117
Africa	294	217	47	17	148
Latin America and the Caribbean	275	361	77	28	132
Polar regions		6	7		1
West Asia		24	30	8	9
Asia and Pacific	526	523	106	67	247

Very degraded soil *Degraded soil* *Stable soil* *Without vegetation*

Land degradation is probably the main reason behind the decline of species. Human activities such as deforestation, overgrazing, fuelwood consumption, agricultural mismanagement and urbanisation are all causes of land degradation

Black stork a rare elusive bird, one of many species which could soon become extinct because of human activities such as logging, farming and damning

Percentage of land degradation by region

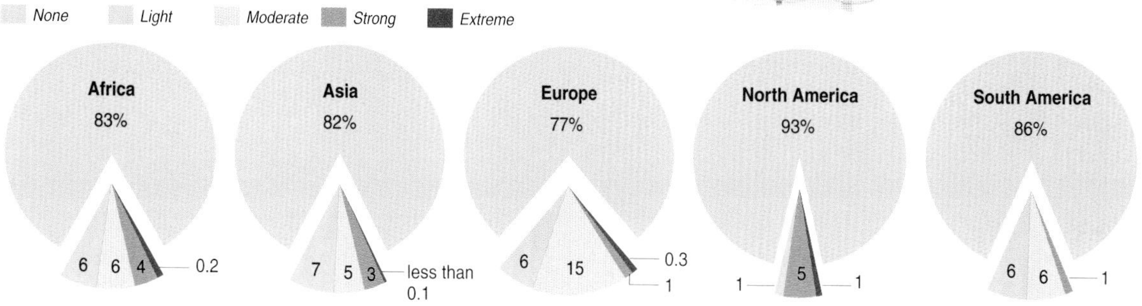

None *Light* *Moderate* *Strong* *Extreme*

Africa 83% — 6, 6, 4, 0.2

Asia 82% — 7, 5, 3, less than 0.1

Europe 77% — 6, 15, 0.3, 1

North America 93% — 1, 5, 1

South America 86% — 6, 6, 1

"Biodiversity" was coined in 1988 by the noted sociobiologist E.O. Wilson to *describe the variety of life on Earth. No one knows for certain how many species of life there are, but about 2 million have been described, and the United Nations Environment Program (UNEP) Global Biodiversity Assessment estimates that there could be around 13 million. (Other estimates range from 10 million to 100 million.)*

The world thrives on its wide variety of biological variation because all plants and animals depend on one other to some degree. But in the last century or so, human beings have been exploiting plant and animal species at an accelerated rate. Species are dying out faster than any time in history — except during the extinction of the dinosaurs and other life forms 65 million years ago. In the past few years, biologists and zoologists have noted an alarming increase in the rate of animal extinctions. The World Conservation Union reports that human activities are making plant and animal species disappear 50 times faster than the natural rate. According to a researcher at The University of Texas at Austin, half the living bird and mammal species will be extinct in 200–300 years.

When a species disappears, several things are irrevocably lost. First, the unique genetic information describing that plant or animal, the result of billions of years of evolution, is gone forever. Who knows if a recently eradicated species of tropical fern contained the cure for cancer or AIDS? Second, there's the loss to the ecosystem. Each plant and animal is part of an interdependent network. Kill a plant, and you kill the animals that feed on it, and in turn those animals' predators. There are certain plants and animals called *keystone* species, whose existence has tremendous impact on the biosphere. The sea otter, for instance, is a keystone species. It eats sea urchins, which in turn eat large quantities of kelp. If the sea otter population drops, then sea urchins will proliferate and eat more kelp. Then, the many species of marine animals that live in the kelp forest will die. Coastlines will also begin to crumble when they are hit by waves that were buffered by the offshore kelp.

BIODIVERSITY DISAPPEARING

The UNEP recently cited four main causes for the decrease in biodiversity. The major factor is land use. Human beings currently use about 25% of the Earth's land for agriculture. Land that once held hundreds or thousands of varieties of animal plant life now support just a few. The wild plants and animals that formerly lived in these areas must move to new land or perish. The second factor is overexploitation of biological resources. Over fishing has decimated many marine animal populations, and farming has pulled nutrients from the ground. The other two factors — the introduction of alien species into new areas (intentionally or unintentionally) and pollution — were also cited in the report as major factors for the decline in biological diversity.

PRESERVING BIODIVERSITY

Because species are dependent on one another for their survival, a single extinction creates a hardship on directly dependent species. If too many species become extinct in a short period of time, it could result in a runaway situation of mass extinctions. That's why it's important to educate people and companies whose businesses have the greatest impact on the environment.

The threat of catastrophic species extinction may not be enough to convince people to start working on ways to preserve biodiversity. What's needed, say some experts, is an economic incentive. If it can be demonstrated that promoting biodiversity can yield short- and long-term profits to companies, they'll work toward curbing extinctions. For example, farmers are learning that by planting several different species of a crop at the same time can dramatically reduce the need for pesticides, because specific insects often favor just one species of plant. The concept of sustainable agriculture is becoming increasingly common in rainforest areas as a way to preserve native species while giving farmers tools and information to increase crop yields.

PROVOCATIONS...

How many species' extinctions are you willing to tolerate each year: 1,000? 10,000? 100,000?

Some farmers say that the only way they can survive is by "slashing and burning" large swaths of rainforest. What can be done about it?

Would you be willing to pay twice as much for food, shelter, clothing, and fuel if it meant putting a stop to mass species extinctions?

—Mark Frauenfelder

WANT MORE?

RAINFOREST ALLIANCE
www.rainforest-alliance.org

BIODIVERSITY (FREE ONLINE BOOK, BY EDWARD O. WILSON)
http://books.nap.edu/books/0309037395/html/index.html

ALL SPECIES FOUNDATION
www.all-species.org

BIODIVERSITY SUPPORT PROGRAM
www.bsponline.org

BIODIVERSITY ACTION NETWORK
www.bionet-us.org

BIOLOGICAL DIVERSITY
www.biodiv.org

GLOBAL BIODIVERSITY FORUM
www.gbf.ch

ANIMALINFO.ORG
www.animalinfo.org

CLIMATE CHANGES...

Changing Weather, Weathering Change

IN THE 17TH CENTURY THE *French mathematician and theologian Blaise Pascal put forward a simple argument for why it was wise to believe in God. According to Pascal, behaving as if God existed had huge (potentially eternal) benefits with no real downside, while behaving as if God did not exist could literally cost you your soul. Acting like a believer was simply the less risky course.* ¶ *As in Pascal's time, the debate about global warming is also about the outcome of a gamble. Today, we are betting that the benefits of our industrial and agricultural*

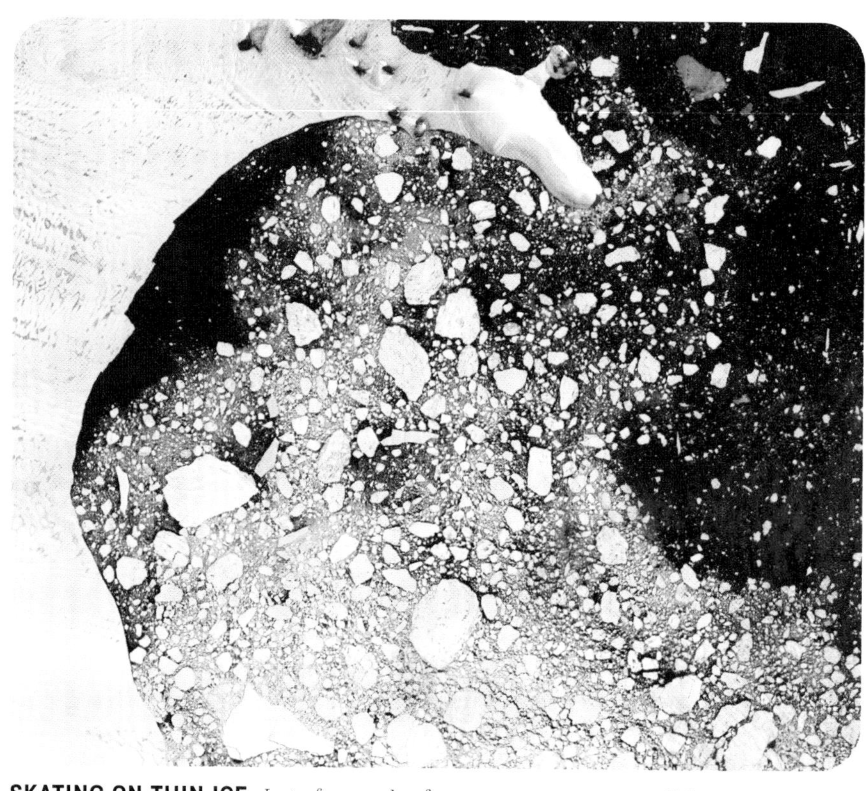

SKATING ON THIN ICE. *Just a few months of warmer temperatures were all that was required to disintegrate the Larsen ice shelf, one of Antarctica's largest, and send it into the sea. The shelf is enormous — big enough to fill 29 trillion bags of party ice.* **GETTING WARMER, GETTING WARMER.** *This is the Hadley Centre's "business as usual" scenario for climate change from 1900 to 2075. Assuming no change in our behavior, average temperatures across the globe could rise more than 3°C, or 5.4°F.*

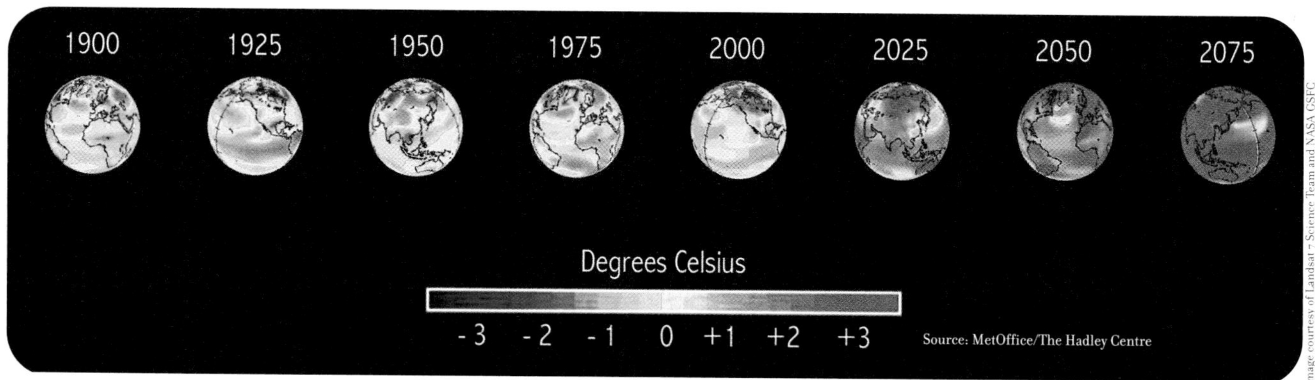

Image courtesy of Landsat 7 Science Team and NASA GSFC

activities – increasing standards of living for the rich and poor alike – will outweigh the negative consequences of those activities – a buildup of so-called "greenhouse gases" in the atmosphere that could lead to disastrous global climate changes.

The only problem is that the evidence is not in our favor.

While not absolutely unequivocal, there is overwhelming scientific consensus that the earth is warming, that this warming trend will worsen, and that human activity plays a significant, if not primary, role. The Earth's average temperature has always fluctuated, but recent evidence suggests that this trend is accelerating: The 1990s was the hottest decade of the millennia, and the past five years were among the seven hottest ever recorded. The globally averaged temperature of the air at the Earth's surface has warmed between 0.3 and 0.6°C (about 0.5 and 1°F) since the late 19th century. The current best estimate is that temperatures will rise between 1 and 3.5°C (about 2 to 6°F) by the year 2100, with continued increases thereafter.

The primary suspects in this warming are the "greenhouse gases," such as carbon dioxide (CO_2), that act as an atmospheric insulator for the planet and are released in massive quantities when fossil fuels are burned.

Carbon dioxide is released to the atmosphere by a variety of sources, and over 95% percent of these emissions would occur even if human beings were not present on Earth. But these natural sources are nearly balanced by physical and biological processes, called natural sinks, which remove CO_2 from the atmosphere. For example, some CO_2 dissolves in sea water, and some is removed by plants as they grow.

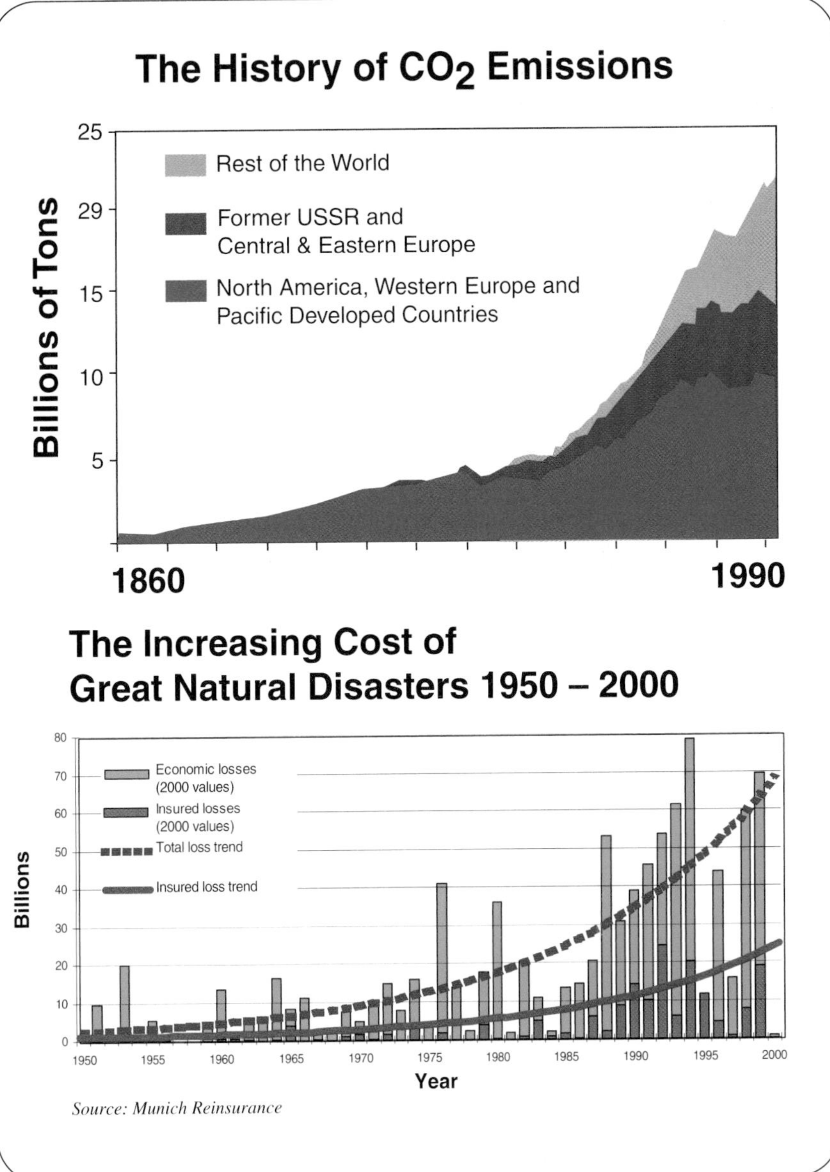

Source: Munich Reinsurance

THE COST OF FOOLING WITH MOTHER NATURE. *Natural disasters are becoming more significant and costlier.*

As a result of this natural balance, CO_2 levels in the atmosphere would have changed little if human beings had not undertaken to do two things: create more CO_2 by burning ever more fossil fuels and systematically cut down some of the largest natural sink – the old growth forests. As a result of this "one-two" punch, we've slowly added to the amount of CO_2 in the atmosphere. This addition, presently about 3% over annual natural emissions, is sufficient to exceed the balancing effect of the sinks, and CO_2 has gradually accumulated in the atmosphere. Today, atmospheric CO_2 is more than 30% above preindustrial levels.

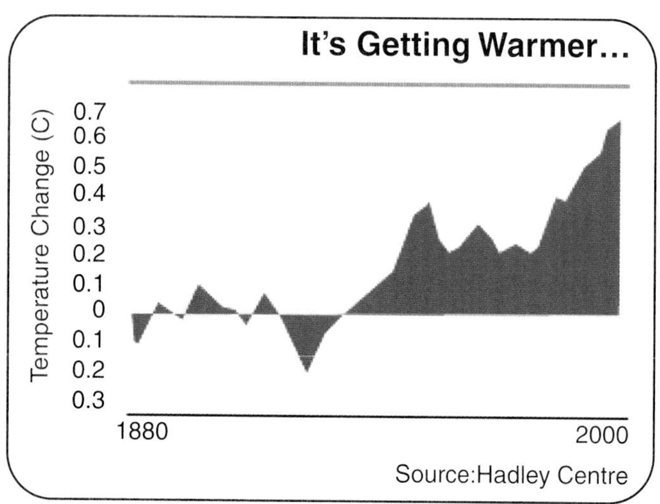

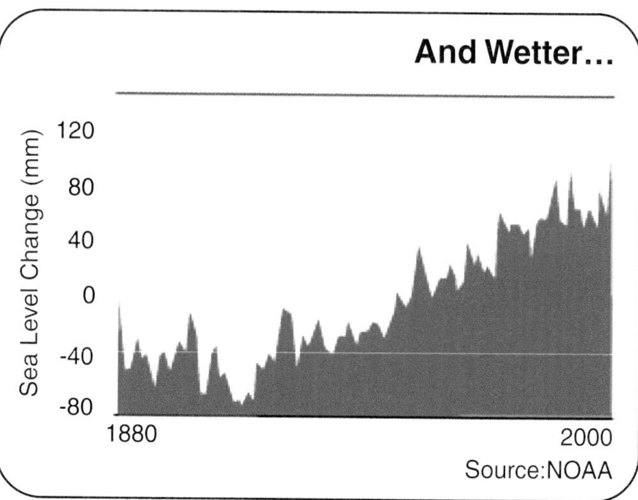

The consequence of this buildup is the same as adding more stuffing to a blanket – things get toastier – which means an environment that's warmer in some places, wetter in others, and wilder all over.

Temperatures around Antarctica have risen five times faster than the global average over the past 50 years, going up by around 2.5°C since the 1940s. Around the world, ice sheets and glaciers are melting at a rate unprecedented since recordkeeping began: In the Tien Shan Mountains, in central Asia, 22% of glacial ice volume has disappeared in the last 40 years. And three Antarctic ice shelves, each formed millennia ago, have disintegrated within the last decade.

As temperatures rise, so do sea levels and the number of storms and coastal flooding. The National Oceanographic and Atmospheric Adminstration reported that increasing incidence of El Niño in recent decades correlated with rising temperatures. With 50%-70% of the global human population currently living in coastal areas, future sea level rises, alterations in storm patterns, and higher storm surges could have significant effects. Already, two South Pacific islands have disappeared beneath the waves, as climate change raises sea levels to new heights. They are Tebua Tarawa and Abanuea – which ironically mean "the beach which is long-lasting" – in the island state of Kiribati. In the Indian Ocean, the beaches of a third of the 200 inhabited islands of the Maldives are being swept away. And experts say if the sea level goes up by 1 meter, Bangladesh, one of the poorest and overcrowded nations, could lose 17% of its land. Closer to home, much of lower Manhattan, built on landfill, could be submerged.

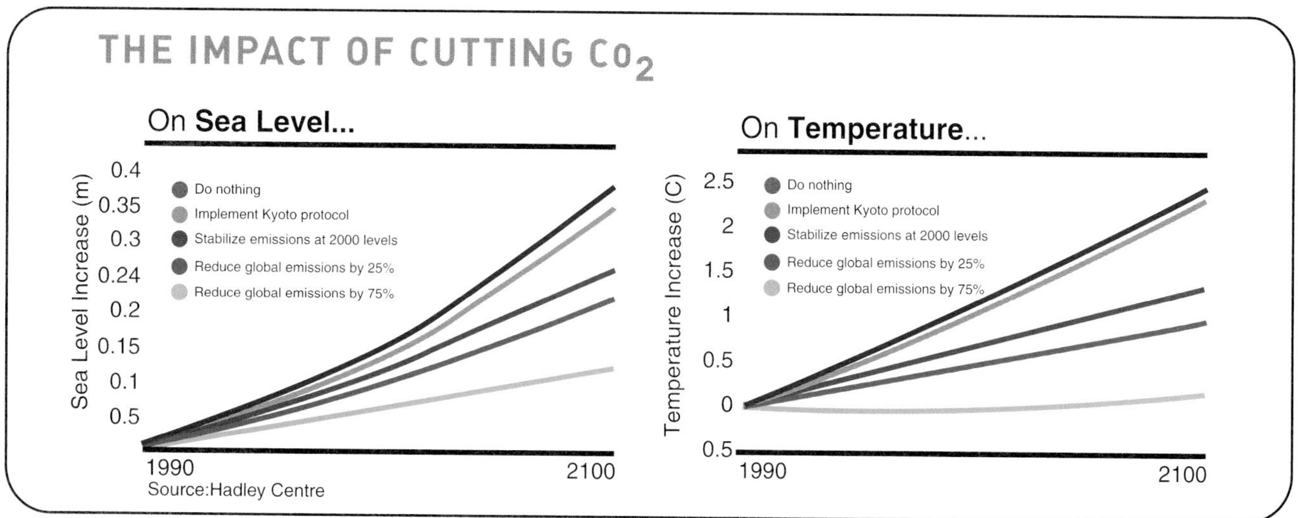

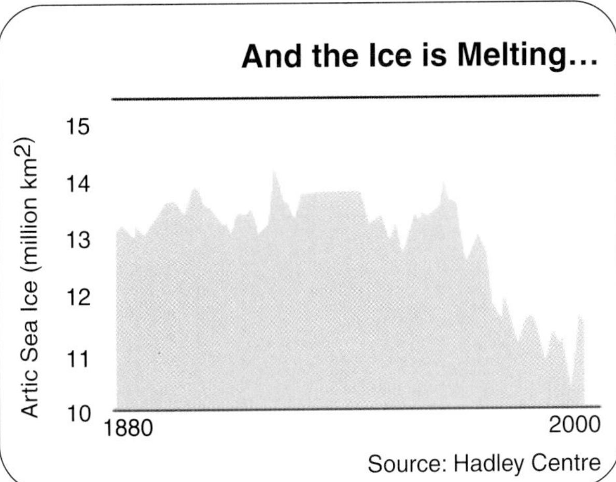

Increased CO_2 directly affects the oceans as well. Researchers in the U.S. suspect rising CO_2 levels in the atmosphere could reduce worldwide coral growth by almost half. A Greenpeace report predicts that the Great Barrier Reef in Australia will be dead within 30 years if urgent action is not taken to prevent the effects of climate change.

The cost of all of climate change – estimated by the United Nations at more than $300 billion per year – has caught the attention of the world's industrial and economic leaders. When the Conference Board polled its members in 2000, they identified global warming as the number-one strategic environmental threat facing the planet. According to Eileen Claussen, president of the Pew Center for Climate Change, "there is a sea-change going on around this issue that cuts across political parties, industries, and generations."

The U.S. pollutes more, absolutely, and per head, than any other country (it also produces more wealth). Its greenhouse emissions have risen by more than 11% since 1990.

"This problem didn't arise quickly, and it won't go away quickly – but there are things we must begin to do now," says Claussen. In the next 10 years, she foresees a greater focus on so-called efficiency technologies – making better use of the fossil fuels we use in our cars, factories, and power plants and making more efficient use of the electricity that we produce with those fuels.

Other approaches may be more unusual. Consider the problem of "urban heat islands." An abundance of dark pavement and black roofs, which soak up sunlight rather than reflect it, can make some cities 2 to 8°F hotter than surrounding areas and aggravate smog problems. A "cool communities" approach would lower air-conditioning use and make the air healthier. Planting more greenery, painting roofs white, and using lighter-colored pavement can alleviate air pollution, heat, and the need for air conditioning.

A long-term, comprehensive approach will require not only reductions in fossil fuel use, but beneficial technologies to replace those fuels. On the 20-year horizon, Claussen sees a slow migration from fossil-fuel-based transportation to fuel cells and reliance on new forms of energy production. "Ultimately, climate change won't be comprehensively addressed until technology, the marketplace, global governments, and world opinion are all aligned. But we're beginning to see that happen."

Photo courtesy of NASA

THE OLD AIR FILTERS. *Old-growth forests act like giant air filters, pumping excess carbon dioxide out of the atmosphere. Every minute, humans cut down about 150 acres of such forest, creating spaces like these in Bolivia.*

PROVOCATIONS...

Will we abandon carols that dream of white Christmases?

Will summer start in April and last until October?

Will Americans have to go to Canada to ski?

—Andrew Zolli

WANT MORE?

PEW CENTER ON GLOBAL CLIMATE CHANGE
www.pewclimate.org

HADLEY CENTRE
www.hadleycentre.com

INTERGOVERNMENTAL PANEL ON CLIMATE CHANGE
www.ipcc.ch

WORLD RESOURCES INSTITUTE
www.wri.org

GHG PROTOCOL INITIATIVE
www.ghgprotocol.org

PERSONAL GREENHOUSE GAS CALCULATOR
www.epa.gov/globalwarming/tools/ghg_calc.html

2000 2005 2010 2015 2020

risks  rewards 

Population Growth...
Here Comes the Neighborhood

"Population growth is the primary source of environmental damage."
— Jacques Cousteau

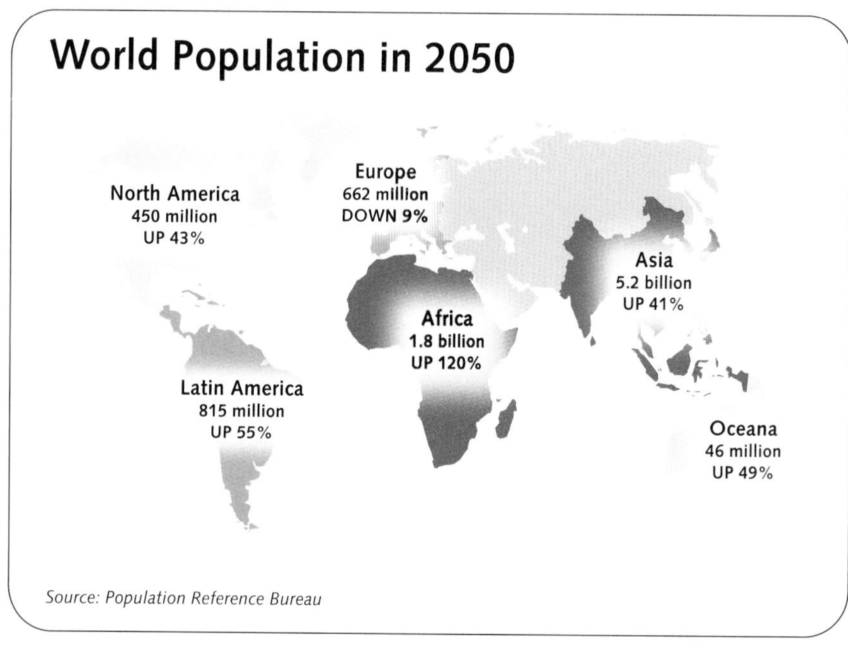

IN THE TIME IT TOOK YOU to read the above quote (for most people, about a second), four people were added to the world's population and two people died. This simple ratio attests to one of the most crucial challenges we will collectively face in the coming century.

According to population researcher Joel Cohen of Rockefeller University, 2,000 years ago there were about 250 million people on Earth. It took almost 1,700 years to double that number to about one-half billion. The next doubling took less than two centuries, from the middle of the 17th century to around 1800. The next doubling took a little over 100 years, and the next took only about 39 years. The second half of the 20th century is the first time in all of human history in which the Earth's population doubled within a single lifetime — a fortyfold acceleration in the population growth rate. Today, every year, the world adds a little over 76 million people — roughly the population of Germany — to its number. While the population growth rate has slowed, from about 2% annually in 1960 to 1.4% in 2000, the absolute number of people continues to increase by about 1 billion every 13 years.

Those new entrants into the human experience don't all come from the same place. "Only 1 million are in the industrialized countries," say demographers Carl Haub and Diana Cornelius of the Population Reference Bureau. The rest come from the developing world — in fact, in the post-industrial West, many countries are experiencing negative population growth — their numbers are shrinking, due to lowered fertility rates, longer lifespans, access to birth control, and a higher standard of living, which has reduced the need for offspring as a source of agricultural labor.

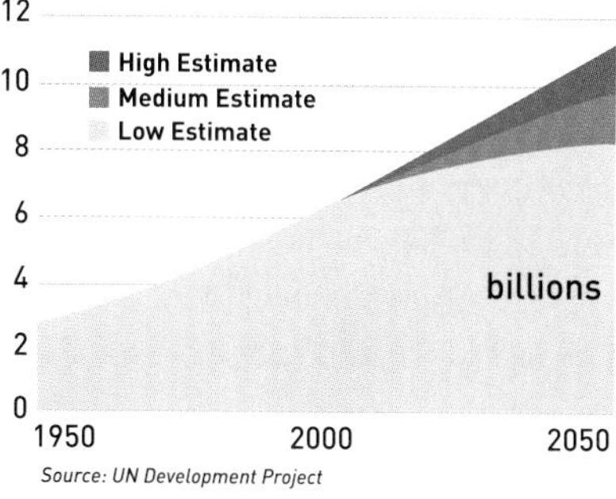

Extend these trends over 25 or 50 years, and the world's population picture looks dramatically different. "In 1950, there were twice as many people in the less developed countries," say Haub and Cornelius. "By 2050, that difference could be almost six to one. The developing world's population is projected to increase by 2.9 billion by 2050, compared with only 49 million in the more developed countries." By that time, there will likely be 10 billion people on the planet, and 7 billion of us will be African or Asian. Moreover, there will increasingly be an age gap between the wealthy and graying West, whose citizens are living longer thanks to advanced healthcare and life extension, and the (on average) much younger and more impoverished developing world.

The extra feet will make it difficult to tread lightly on the Earth and will drive up demand for food and clean water. In 64 of 105 developing countries studied by the U.N. Food and Agriculture Organization, the population has been growing faster than food supplies. Population pressures have degraded some 5 billion acres of arable land — an area the size of Canada and the United States put together.

The supply of freshwater is finite — only a tiny fraction of the world's water is currently drinkable, and the vast majority of that goes to agricultural uses. Global demand for water has increased more than sixfold over the last century, compared with a threefold increase in world population, as we fail to replenish supplies. The United Nations estimates that two out of three people will be living with water shortages by 2025. Over the next two decades, it is expected that the world will need 17% more water to grow food for increasing populations in developing countries and that total water use will increase by 40%. International disputes are already brewing over water rights, and at least a few are likely to develop into full-blown conflicts. Several corporations, looking ahead to a day when fresh water is more valuable than oil, are looking to privatize, and capitalize on, dwindling supplies.

One of the few counters to global population growth is also one of the most brutal. The two centers of greatest population growth — Africa and Asia — are the hardest hit by the HIV virus — close to 90% of all AIDS-related deaths occur in Sub-Saharan Africa and Asia. Today, more than 70% of all infections are in Sub-Saharan Africa — in some countries, such as Botswana, more than 30% of adults are infected with the virus, and their populations are expected to decline as a direct result. According to the United Nations, Asia may overtake Africa as the AIDS leader as early as 2005. The terrible irony is that a wholesale cure for the disease may unlock even more accelerated population growth.

Toward the end of the 21st century, many demographers expect the population to stabilize and return to more modest numbers, as standards of living and technologies improve. In the meantime, we will confront a host of challenges that will define much of the politics and technological agenda of the coming decades — not only easing suffering, but creating the conditions for our neighbors to lead meaningful, productive, and more equitable lives.

PROVOCATIONS...

Will population growth inevitably transform the debate over bioengineered food?

Will we ever see a population treaty as we have environmental treaties?

—Andrew Zolli

Income Disparity Will Remain Large

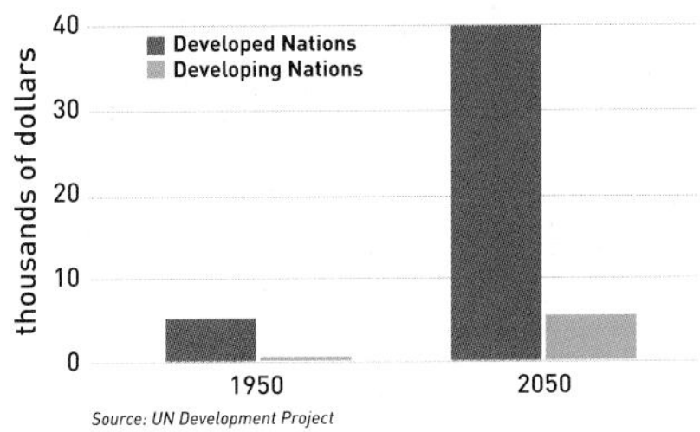

Source: UN Development Project

The Life Expecancy Gap Is Closing

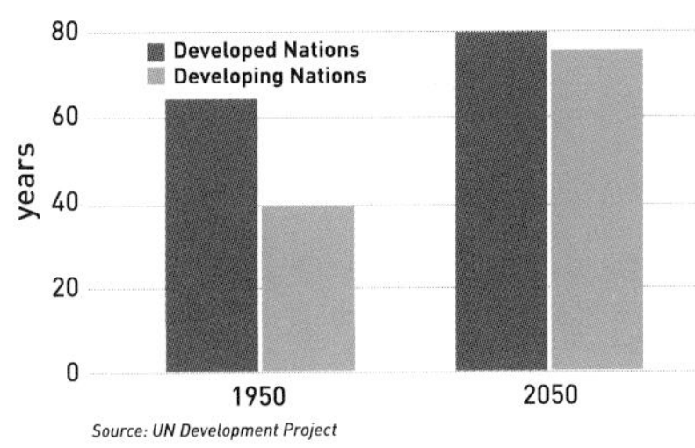

Source: UN Development Project

More Urban Dwellers In The Future

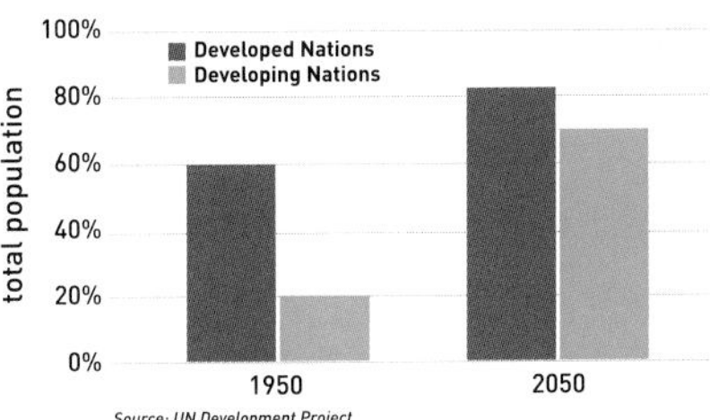

Source: UN Development Project

WANT MORE?

POPULATION REFERENCE BUREAU
www.prb.org

UN POPULATION INFORMATION NETWORK
www.un.org/popin

POPULATION PYRAMIDS
www.census.gov/ipc/www/idbpyr.html

POPULATION RESEARCH CENTER
www.prcdc.org

The Future of Literacy...
CHANGING MEANINGS, CHANGING LIVES

IT USED TO BE ENOUGH TO just know how to read and write. Spend a few years in grammar school, work through McGuffy's Reader, learn a perfect Palmer script and the multiplication tables, and you could consider yourself literate. Think again. The "Three Rs" alone just won't cut it anymore – literacy must now be thought of as the ability to access, analyze, evaluate, and communicate messages in a variety of forms.

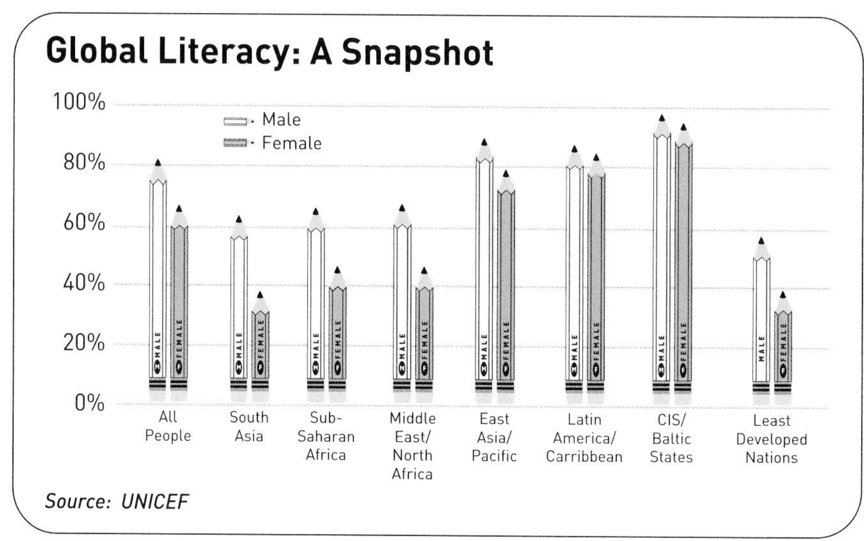

Technology has given us many more ways to communicate, and our increasingly complex and urban society has given us many more reasons to want or need to. These forces, combined with the increased economic impact of communication, have created an explosion in the volume and forms of information in the life of a person in the developed world. Now our definition of literacy

HAND-CRANKED POWER

You work 12 hours each day, trying to feed everyone and maybe send someone to school. You've witnessed multiple acts of violence as civil unrest tears your country apart. You're 13. And the most precious thing you can think of is the radio you crank up every day to listen to news and maybe your soap opera. This is reality for hundreds of thousands of African children. The Freeplay Foundation is working to bring the power of radio to this shattered generation. Distributing the hand-powered radios pioneered by the for-profit Freeplay Radio, the foundation has thrown a lifeline to children drowning in responsibility. In partnership with the other British charities War Child UK and Refugee Trust, the Freeplay Foundation has distributed tens of thousands of radios throughout Africa. It also teaches the radios' new owners how to operate them and broadcasts information about healthcare, clean water, animal husbandry, improved farming methods, children's rights, as well as news, music, sports, and the occasional soap opera.

Photo courtesy of FreePlay Foundation

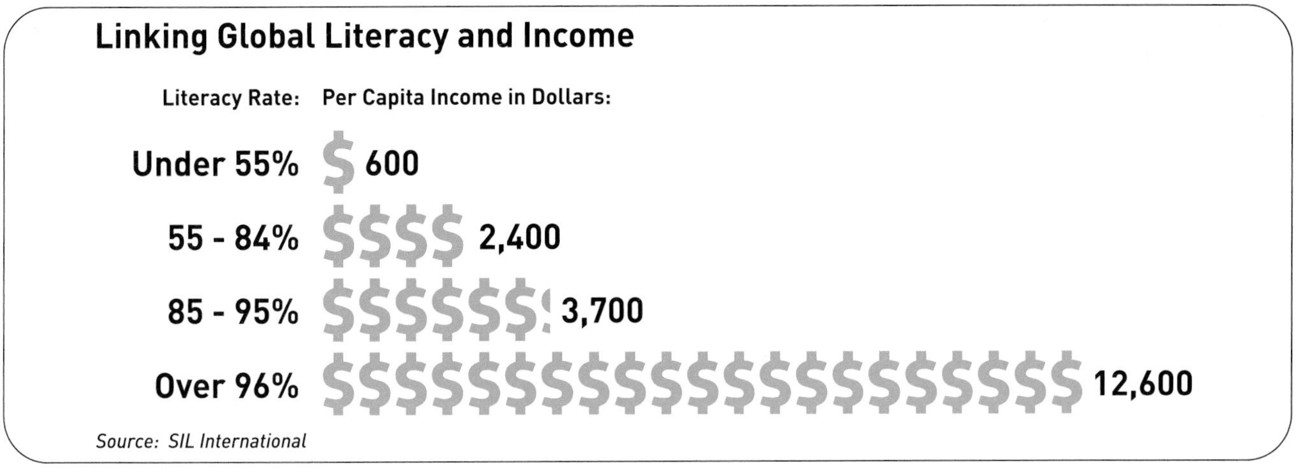

Linking Global Literacy and Income

Literacy Rate:	Per Capita Income in Dollars:
Under 55%	600
55 - 84%	2,400
85 - 95%	3,700
Over 96%	12,600

Source: SIL International

must include the ability to distinguish fact from propaganda, to educate ourselves about healthcare options, to participate in a democratic society.

But while technology has widened the definition of literacy, it has also increased the options for becoming literate. Computer-based instruction makes it possible for adults to access literacy education at their own pace and in contexts that are less threatening than a traditional classroom. The Internet has made distance learning feasible, bringing literacy education and teacher training to rural areas and other isolated communities, such as prisons. And wireless technology has made it possible to deliver literacy education to regions of the developing world without traditional communication infrastructures.

Because illiteracy keeps people from so much more than just the latest Danielle Steele novel, especially in the developing world, literacy has a direct effect on a person's life and income expectancy. According to UNESCO, there are about 1 billion illiterate people in the world — 26% of the world's adult population that cannot, with understanding, both read and write a short, simple statement on their everyday life. The vast majority (98%) of these illiterates live in the developing world, with 52% in India and China alone. Two-thirds of illiterates are women—one out of every three women in the world. These same women are responsible for 70% of the food production in Africa, and the largely patriarchial societies in which they live keep them from information that could greatly improve the yield and sustainability of their agriculture.

While the developed world does not face the same crushing burden of basic illiteracy that the developing world does, it does have to deal with a vision of literacy that changes with each new generation that enters the school system. From the new math to computers in the classroom to the Internet, the tactics in our defense of the literacy of Western society must constantly shift.

Media literacy programs will be an increasingly important component of a secondary education in a society of people who spend 1,000 hours each year consuming television programming alone. As film and television become both mature (film will be 125 years old in 2025) and easier to produce (you can become a digital filmmaker for about $3,000), the grammar of images will be as much a component of literacy as the grammar of words. As our knowledge of our bodies and our ability to maintain and improve them continue to explode, health literacy will help us not just feel better but live longer. And as democratic, deregulated capitalism becomes the way of life for more and more countries, people will be increasingly responsible for the decisions that determine the content and quality of their lives — decisions that simply cannot be made without good information.

PROVOCATIONS...

When will the SAT measure visual literacy?

Will the downfall of autocratic governments be a cause or a consequence of a literate developing world?

When will the first Nobel Prize be awarded to a hypertext novel?

—Bill Kaszubski

WANT MORE?

LITERACY AT THE UN
www.unesco.org/education

LITERACY RESEARCH
www.literacy.org

SCIENTIFIC EVIDENCE IN LEARNING
www.nifl.gov/partnershipforreading

RADIO EMPOWERMENT
www.freeplayfoundation.org

Garbage and Pollution...

The Effluence of Our Affluence: Garbage In, Energy Out?

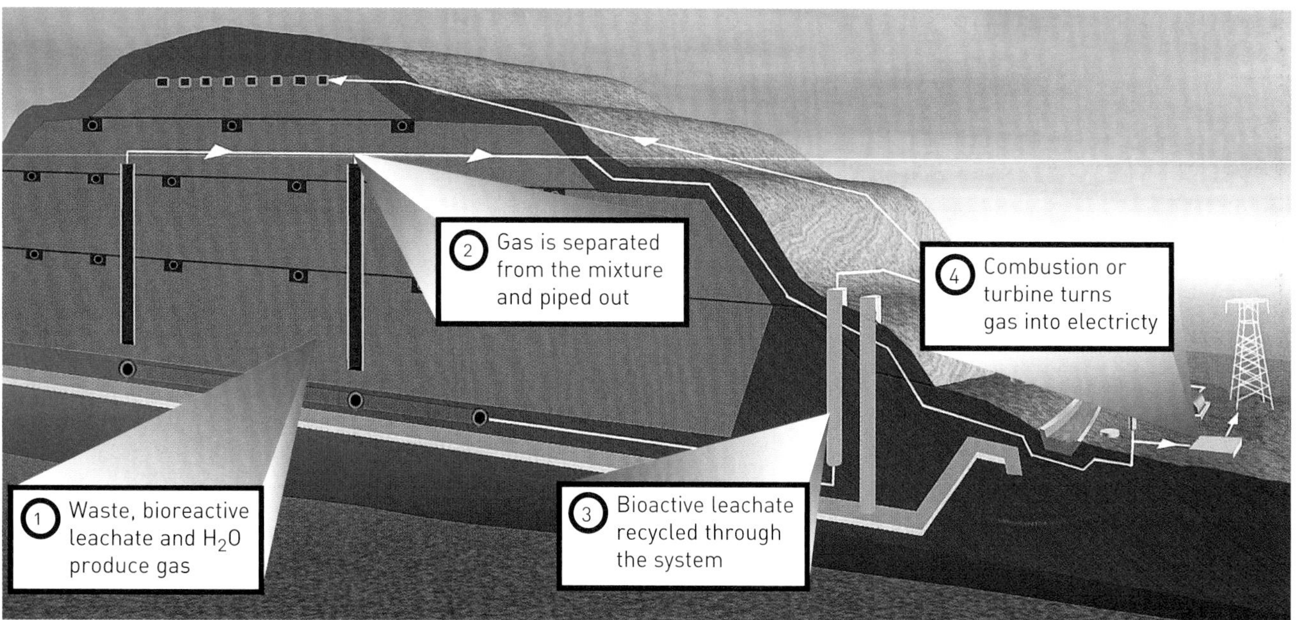

1 Waste, bioreactive leachate and H_2O produce gas
2 Gas is separated from the mixture and piped out
3 Bioactive leachate recycled through the system
4 Combustion or turbine turns gas into electricty

GARBAGE, EAT THYSELF. *In a bioreactor landfill, water along with leachate from the decomposing waste is recirculated back through the waste, accelerating further decomposition. Accomplished under anaerobic (no oxygen) conditions, the process enhances the production of methane — roughly 50% of the gas generated by the landfill — which can then be used for energy production. Since landfills must be monitored for as long as biodegradation is present, accelerated decomposition can reduce environmental risks, at the same time reducing long-term monitoring costs.*

Graphic courtesy of John Trotti, Municipal Solid Waste Magazine

PRODUCING WASTE IS THE WORLD'S MOST INCLUSIVE ACTIVITY. EVERY DAY, SLIGHTLY OR *significantly, we all use more of* something *than we need to meet our needs. The rest is tossed, flushed, dumped, or simply... lost. Progress, for all of its benefits, is hardly efficient.*

According to the U.S. Environmental Protection Agency, our society produces over 10 billion tons of waste per year. Of that, nearly 232 million tons are municipal solid waste, or MSW — what most of us think of as common "garbage." That translates into more than 1,640 pounds per person, roughly 4 1/2 pounds of garbage every day — a rate that is twice that of any other nation on Earth. And that's just the benign waste: Ever year American industries release more than 3 million tons of toxic waste into the water, air, and ground — enough to fill almost a thousand Olympic swimming pools.

And as the volume and the toxicity of our waste increases, the number of politically and environmentally sound places to dispose of our waste is dwindling. We are using more and more of our natural resources, and along with our trash, we are also throwing away valuable energy.

For a generation, the mantra of waste disposal has been "Reduce, Reuse, Recycle." This approach has been an unparalleled success. More than 23% of our municipal waste is now recycled, and another 22% — more than 50 million tons — never becomes waste at all. The amount of waste we recycle and compost grew by more than 75% during the 1990s alone.

There's still tremendous room to improve. Already, Europe is far ahead of the U.S. in its political commitment to recycling, having recently proposed "take-back" laws that require product manufacturers to fully recycle the products they manufacture, in the hopes that such requirements will lead to more efficiency and more environmentally friendly designs.

But even so, the "Reduce, Reuse, Recycle" mantra is beginning to show its age. Recycled products, for example, have to compete with heavily-subsidized "virgin" product industries, often making the market for such recycled goods unstable, and thus less attractive to local governments. And for all of its many benefits, large-scale composting of organic material has a nasty side effect — methane gas — which is 21 times more powerful than carbon dioxide in its greenhouse effects.

"Now we need to broaden our spectrum of responses to waste," says John Trotti, editor-in-chief of the industry journal *MSW Management*. "Zero waste is impossible, but close to zero isn't. But it's going to take radical new approaches to get there — thinking beyond traditional modes of recycling and embracing new technologies."

In the last scene of *Back to the Future*, Dr. Emmett Brown, just back from the year 2015, slips a banana peel into his time-traveling DeLorean to give it the energy it will need to literally fly through time. The scene got a chuckle in 1988, but it turns out Steven Spielberg wasn't quite so off-base.

As waste decomposes over many years, it gives off "landfill gas," or LFG, which is a major contributor to greenhouse emissions. Each year, more than 4 trillion square feet of energy-rich LFG are flared worldwide, mostly because no economic use has been developed for it.

That may be changing, thanks to a new waste management technology called bioreactors. These self-contained systems accelerate the natural decomposition of organic waste by promoting the growth of microorganisms that "eat" the waste placed inside. Bioreactors turn waste inert, reducing air pollution, and reduce the waste's overall volume, cutting the use and extending the life of landfills. But most importantly, by capturing, cleaning, and processing LFG, the next generation of bioreactors will allow waste managers to capture a valuable — and renewable — source of energy that can be used for electricity production. And this electricity would be far cheaper than most produced today because it would not have to be transmitted long distances to customers. A major city like New York, which produces 11,000 tons of municipal waste every day, could be outfitted with dozens of bioreactive power plants, dramatically cutting the amount of waste it has to export, becoming almost electrically self-sufficient in the process. "We spend billions digging natural gas out of the ground, and here's a major source just sitting there unused, and worse still, contributing to global warming," says Trotti.

That gas could play another powerful role in the next economy — providing the hydrogen to power the fuel cells of tomorrow's automobiles or cleanly run turbines that produce power for electrical grids. Such an approach would solve a major obstacle to fuel cell adoption — where to make and how to transport all that hydrogen. The answer could be your local dump. "Such an approach would be transformational," says Trotti. "It would move us from an almost exclusively hydrocarbon-based economy based on petroleum back to a carbohydrate-based economy based on organics."

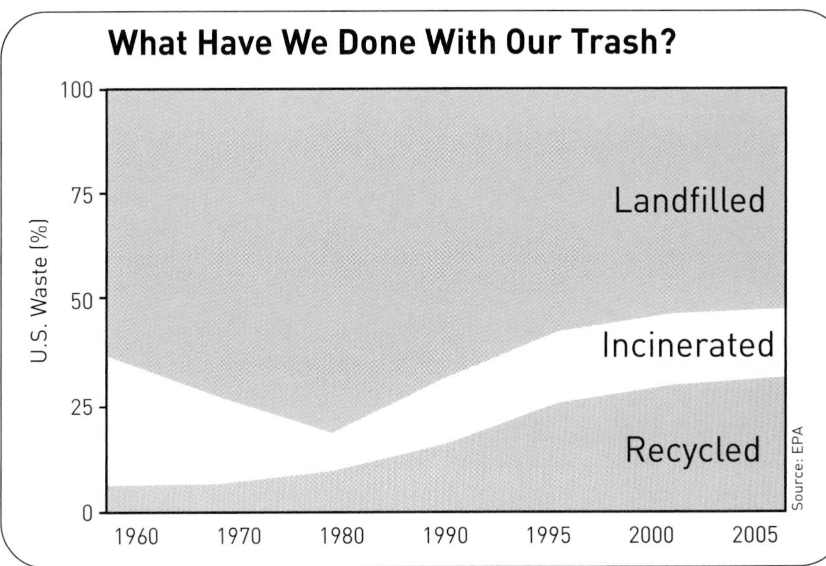

PROVOCATIONS...

Will there be a 21st-century "Henry Ford of Garbage?"

Will the trash man have to pay us to take the garbage away?

— Andrew Zolli

WANT MORE?

GRASS ROOTS RECYCLING NETWORK
www.grrn.org

MSW MANAGEMENT MAGAZINE
www.forester.net/msw.html

WASTE MANAGEMENT IN 2020
www.epa.gov/epaoswer/osw/vision.htm

HUMAN ENERGY: A Dependable, Renewable Resource

MANY PEOPLE AROUND THE WORLD agree that a new global energy strategy needs to be devised and adopted. Conventional thinking focuses mostly on the diminishing reserves of fossil fuels and the negative implications that the consumption of these fuels have on the Earth's atmosphere. Many people also acknowledge that the reliance placed today on non-renewable fuels is dangerous and that if the current burn rate continues, energy crises will most certainly continue.

It is natural, therefore, that most technological efforts are directed toward the harnessing of renewable sources of energy and toward eventually restraining the use of energy to the degree to which it may be satisfactorily renewed. Commercial activities have focused on a macro scenario, the creation of alternative forms of energy on a large scale, e.g. power stations supplying electrical power to cities and large communities and for transportation.

This thinking is important, but it does not take into account the need for remote communities to have access to usable forms of energy, especially to take advantage of the massive technological achievements that have taken place in recent decades. Very little attention has been given to providing alternative energy sources on a micro scale to the millions of households and small communities on the planet that have no access to electricity.

Electricity offers the rural poor more than just the obvious things like refrigeration and lighting — it brings education, information, and the opportunity for new kinds of healthcare and new levels of economic prosperity. The challenge is that the rural poor typically lack the very economic and political clout, and often the education, needed to get rural areas wired to the power grid. And in developing nations with extremely tight resources, the cities take priority because that's where the people are. It's a catch-22.

In the last decade, efforts have been made to address this problem, focusing primarily on the use of solar energy, with some peripheral work being done on wind and the conversion of biomass into a useful form of energy. All three of these methodologies require fairly sophisticated and expensive technology, and other than solar are immature technologies.

More recently, another form of renewable energy has received attention: human energy. Human energy is readily available to benefit human beings: It's a battery we always carry with us. For centuries, human energy has been used to draw water, provide transportation, and extract nutritious components from various staple foods. Until recently there was no way to turn the mechanical energy of our bodies into useful electricity.

Technology has now been developed that converts human mechanical energy directly into electricity in sufficient quantities for it to be used to power a wide range of modern electrical equipment. The Freeplay Energy Group in South Africa developed the world's first practical mechanized radio, which was aimed at using communication to combat the spread of AIDS through Africa. This seed has germinated into a full-fledged program to provide technology for converting human mechanical energy to electricity, thereby making electrical power available to billions of people who otherwise would not have access to electricity except from prohibitively expensive commercial sources like batteries.

Electronics have permeated almost every facet of human existence and provide an enormous benefit to man. Examples include radios, TV, recorded media, computers, light (both incandescent and fluorescent) sources, and medical curative and diagnostic machines. As electronics have evolved, they have become more sophisticated and less power hungry. The amount of electricity required to power an electronic device is compatible with the energy available from harnessed human activity.

If you worked hard enough and long enough, you could provide sufficient energy (for conversion into electricity) to power a wide range of appliances. But the reward available from the use of this electricity needs to be worth the effort expended in the first place. This, in a practical sense, restricts the useful realm of electricity generated from human power. A rough rule of thumb would eliminate heating devices such as hairdryers, refreshment coolers, and cathode-ray television screens. Nevertheless, a wide range of electrical appliances do offer an effort/reward relationship that is attractive. Broadly speaking, these fall into the categories of radios, illumination devices (such as flashlights and small desktop lamps), mobile phones, two-way radios, personal computers, and home stereos.

Using human energy requires that it be harnessed from the human being in the first place, so attention needs to be given to the ergonomics that interface a human with a "self-powered" machine. The perceived effort delivered to the machine needs to be minimized while providing an activity that both attends to the stress on the human being and encourages the range of practical situations where the harvesting of the energy is not an obstacle. The intention is to extract work from the human being most efficiently and to redeliver this work as electrical energy on demand.

Work implies expending a force over a particular distance. The most common methodology of extracting work from a human being in this case is a simple crank mechanism, and a balance between the effort and speed (i.e. distance over time) applied to the crank is fairly easy to determine. Another methodology that uses the larger muscles of the body is a pedal or treadle action of the legs. The larger muscles of the body in the legs have the ability to exert a higher force over a longer distance, thereby applying a greater amount of work to the receiving machine.

Once expended, human mechanical energy needs to be stored mechanically and immediately converted into electricity, or stored electrochemically (e.g. battery) to be converted later into electricity.This stored energy can then be redelivered on demand as electricity to a wide range of appliances.

The earlier human electromechanical systems used a steel spring to store human energy in mechanical format. Springs offer an excellent ergonomic relationship with the human being and return the energy back into the system very efficiently. However, springs are bulky and expensive and only allow a particular amount of energy to be stored (with the spring fully wound, it is not able to store anymore energy). Fully charged springs were then discharged through a transmission into an electromagnetic generator, which converted this energy into electricity. The release of the spring was controlled to deliver electricity at the correct rate applicable to the particular use for which it was designed. Other human electrical systems convert human mechanical energy directly into electricity and store this electricity in batteries for later use on demand.

The future looks bright for the self-powered appliance industry. It won't be long before the World Wide Web will be accessible across the entire planet via wireless technology. Computers and the next generation of Internet terminals will be electronic devices using a lower power level than is currently the norm. The incentive for remote communities to join in this new phenomenon of social and economic interaction will be enormous, and the only restriction will be a source of electrical energy to power their connections. With human-powered electrical systems, this will no longer be a problem. Power systems will most likely be integrated with other alternative sources of power such as solar, wind, and biomass energy.

Audio and illumination appliances also require less power, which means that people all over the world are now able to listen to local, regional, and intercontinental radio broadcasts for long periods of time using alternative sources of power. By using human power and possibly integrating this source with other alternative energies, communities are now able to light their homes and workplaces during the hours of darkness, thereby increasing their productivity and social interaction.

Particularly in remote regions, new forms of renewable energy that can be converted into electricity are really the only solutions to the global demand for power for those small electronic devices that enhance the quality of life. These energy sources are multiple – biomass, wind, solar, and human energy — but the only one that is reliable and always available is the human itself.

—Rory Stear

Energy Generation and Storage... MAKE IT, STORE IT, FIND IT IN THE AIR

In 1882, Thomas Edison opened the first commercial power plant in the U.S., on Pearl Street in New York City. Edison wanted to sell light bulbs, so he created a coal-fired plant to provide steady, reliable power for a single neighborhood. Unfortunately, the station also produced a lot of noise, dirt, and clouds of black smoke.

LIGHT MY BULB. *Power flows from the dynamo room at Edison's Pearl Street Station.*

CLEANING UP COAL

Not much has changed in the last 120 years. Power plants have gotten larger and a lot more efficient, but they still pump out pollutants – over two billion tons each year – and contribute to acid rain, smog, and global warming. Nuclear power plants, while less polluting in the short term, produce waste that will remain toxic for 10,000 years.

The U.S. Department of Energy's Vision 21 program aims to change all that, and do it within 15 years. Forty percent of our electricity comes from one of our oldest and most abundant energy resources: coal. While greenhouse emissions from coal plants have been cut by a factor of three over the last 20 years, Vision 21 could bring about virtually pollution-free plants.

The idea is to create a series of technology "modules" in power plants that can use multiple fuels, including coal, natural gas, biomass, coke waste from oil refineries, and municipal waste. Combined with gasification systems, high-efficiency furnaces, new gas turbines, and air scrubbing technology, the plants could be virtually pollution-free. Vision 21 plants would also produce multiple products – perhaps electricity in combination with liquid fuels and chemicals or hydrogen or industrial process heat.

By most estimates, the world has about 80 years of oil and 70 years of natural gas left. Coal, however, could last us another 300 years. And the U.S. has the largest known coal reserves in the world. If we're going to use this potent energy source without turning the Earth into a sooty, acid-washed mess, we're going to have to learn to do it a lot more efficiently. Vision 21 might not be the answer to all our energy worries, but it's better than anything we have now.

YOU CAN NEVER BE TOO THIN

Imagine an animated demo on an appliance box. Imagine mini-speakers on a CD cover playing samples from the disk. Imagine drug patches that deliver doses through your skin automatically. Imagine smart fabrics that evaporate sweat away from you.

All of these possibilities are closer to reality because of batteries that can be printed directly onto paper, plastic, or fabric. Invented by Power Paper Ltd., a company based in Tel Aviv, Israel, the batteries aren't a breakthrough in design or materials. They use zinc and manganese dioxide, common battery chemicals, structured in a way that's similar to ordinary batteries.

CLEAN MACHINE. *The energy plant of the future will be twice as efficient, able to use multiple fuels, and produce many different energy products — but will create no air or water pollution (above).*
POWERING FLATLAND. *The structure of a PowerPaper battery (below).*

Clockwise from top left: Image courtesy of U.S. Department of Energy's Office of Fossil Energy - Image courtesy of PowerPaper, Inc.

The trick is that the company has figured out a way to make the components from an ink-like material, producing a dry battery that doesn't need a traditional hermetically-sealed case. The batteries are non-toxic and can be thrown away with harming the environment. Currently they're begin used in smart credit cards, but PowerPaper has signed a partnership deal with the International Paper Company. Soon, you could see dancing logos and singing french fry wrappers at your favorite fast food joint.

PowerPaper isn't the only outfit exploring skinny power. The Korea Institute of Science and Technology and Johns Hopkins University are both experimenting with tiny lithium-polymer batteries. These are more powerful than zinc and manganese dioxide batteries, but more expensive, too. The John Hopkins plastic battery is rechargeable. PowerPaper is currently developing a rechargeable version of their design.

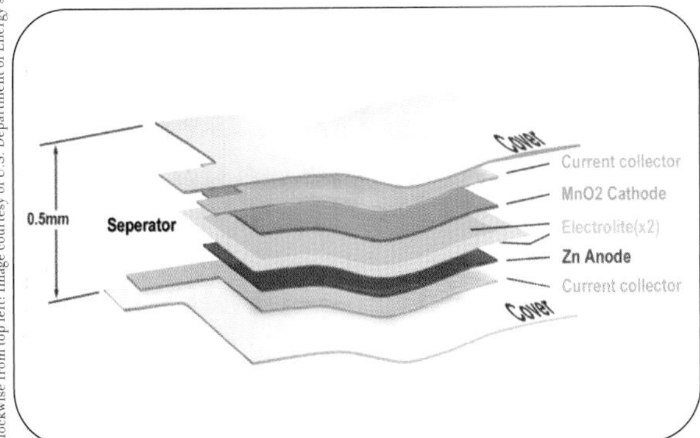

SOME LIKE IT HOT

Back in 1883, Thomas Edison noticed that, under certain conditions, heat can "boil" free electrons off of an electrode placed in a vacuum. He theorized that those electrons could be captured and used as a power source – a process known as thermionics. Today, physicists at MIT have a working microchip that can convert heat into electricity. By replacing the vacuum with a semiconducting material, they lowered the temperature required for the reaction from about 1000°C to about 200°C. This means that in a few years, a car engine could provide the power to run its own electronics, and maybe recharge your laptop. You might even recharge your PDA by leaving it in the sun on the dashboard – provided that someone else is working on non-melting plastic.

PROVOCATIONS...

Will we stop using fossil fuels because they run out, or because of the damage they do to the environment?

What other uses could self-powered paper be put to?

When every surface can display an advertisement, will we have to pay to escape them?

—Richard Kadrey

WANT MORE?

VISION 21
www.fe.doe.gov/coal_power/vision21/index.shtml

THE HISTORY OF ELECTRIC POWER PRODUCTION IN THE US
www.eia.doe.gov/cneaf/electricity/page/electric_kid/append_a.html

POWERPAPER CO.
www.powerpaper.com

DISTRIBUTED POWER NEWS
www.buscom.com/letters/dpnpromo/dpn/dpn.html

THERMIONICS
www.eneco-usa.com/technology

Wind Power... The Answer May Be Blowin' in the Wind

RENEWABLE RESOURCE. *Wind turbine farm in Nevada.*

BIG ENERGY AND THE U.S. GOVERNMENT HAVE FINALLY BEGUN TO TAKE WIND POWER *seriously. This renewable source of energy currently accounts for less than 1% of electricity production in the U.S., but in 2002, when the Department of Energy made a record purchase of renewable power for its offices, 25% of that power was slated to come from the wind. The U.S. added 1,700 megawatts of wind-generating capacity in 2001, or nearly $1.7 billion worth of new generating capacity, making it the second largest wind power producer in the world, just behind Germany.*

Wind power comes from "wind farms," which are clusters of wind-driven turbines that generate electricity. Wind farms range in size from the 6,000 wind turbines in California's Altamont Pass to a single turbine on a farm or ranch. At 230 feet tall and with blades bigger than the wings of a jumbo jet, the biggest offshore wind turbines in the world do an efficient job of converting wind energy into electricity. Most of the interest in wind power over the last decade has come from northern Europe, where you have strong winds from the North Sea and thousands of miles of coastline.

In 2001, the Department of Energy announced a new program, Wind Powering America, aimed at using wind to provide at least 5% of U.S. electricity by 2020, increasing the federal use of wind power to 5% by 2010, and to have 24 states producing more than 20 megawatts via wind power in the same year. The Department of Energy estimates that there is enough potential wind energy in the Great Plains to generate enough electricity for the entire country. Toward that, wind power pioneer Jim Dehlsen is developing a massive 3,000-megawatt wind farm across 222,000 acres in rural South Dakota. When it's complete, the wind farm will transmit power across Iowa, and on to Illinois and other Midwestern states.

ALTAMONT PASS

The 6,000 wind turbines at California's

Zuma Press/Mike Valdez

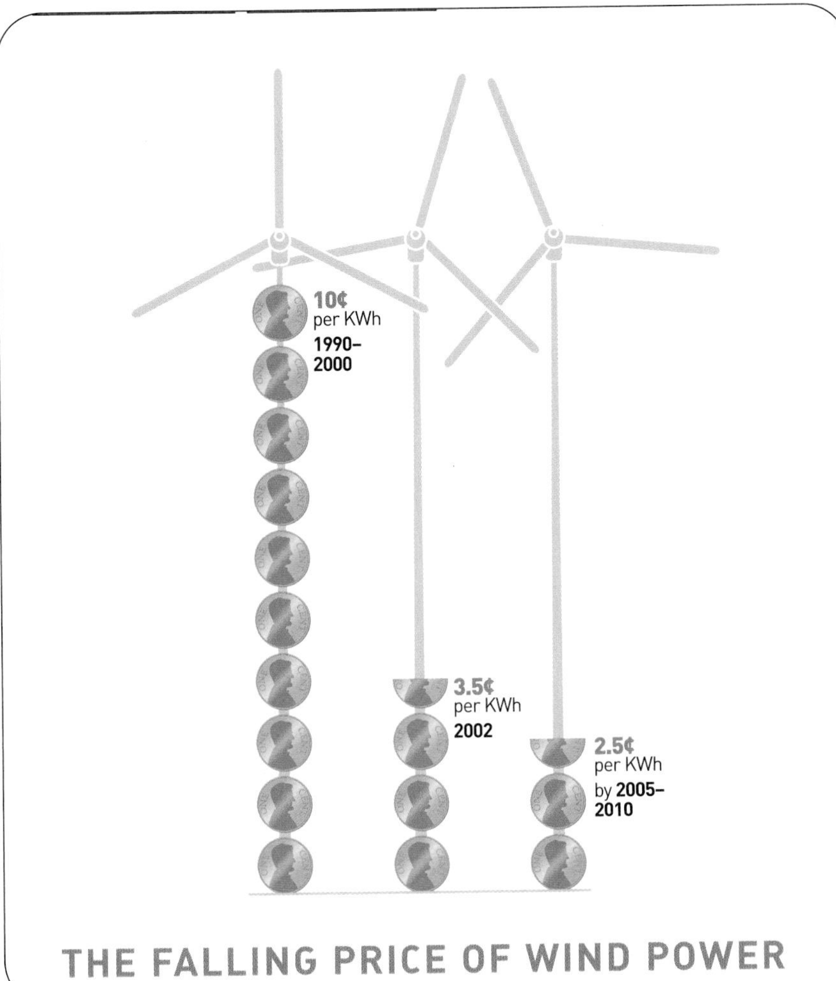

Graphic by Nigel Holmes

Altamount Pass mark the most famous wind farm in the country. Two other wind power plants in the Tehachapi Mountains in Kern County and at San Gorgonio Pass, north of Palm Springs, combine to give California the largest collection of wind turbines in the world, generating over 1,600 megawatts of electricity.

Many of these turbines are being replaced with larger and more efficient models. At the beginning of 2002, between California's large farms and smaller ones scattered around the country, the total U.S. power capacity from wind was 4,250 megawatts.

NEXT-GENERATION TURBINES

The size and power output of wind turbines have increased tremendously since the technology was first introduced. Twenty years ago, a large wind turbine produced around 150 kilowatts. Newer models can produce five times that power.

One of the ways wind turbines increase their efficiency is by using new, lighter materials to increase their size. Older models are around 100 feet tall. The new models being installed at Denmark's Horns Rev Wind Farm will average 230 feet. Not only does this taller design allow for larger rotors to generate power, but being farther from the ground means that the structure can catch a larger amount of the wind's energy.

The Union of Concerned Scientists described wind power as "the fastest growing energy source on the planet," with global wind capacity more than tripling by 2004. Governmental policies, technology improvements, cost reductions, high natural gas prices, and environmental concerns are all converging to support the development of wind power in the U.S. and elsewhere. Wind power is here to stay.

PROVOCATIONS...

Will eco-conscious consumers pay more (in the medium term) for electricity that comes exclusively from renewable sources like wind?

When will we see the first major renewable-only energy brand?

Could small windmills crop up in urban areas like satellite dishes?

—Richard Kadrey

WANT MORE?

NATIONAL WIND TECH CENTER
www.nrel.gov/wind

D.O.E. WIND POWERING AMERICA
www.eren.doe.gov/windpoweringamerica

AMERICAN WIND ENERGY ASSOC.
www.awea.org

WIND FARMS WORLD TOUR
www.chelseagreen.com/Wind/images/windfarm.htm

WIND FARM MAPS
http://rotor.fb12.tu-berlin.de/windfarm/location.html

WINDMILLS IN THE SKY
www.techtv.com/tomorrowsworld/story/0,24330,3364982,00.html

Geothermal... Ancient Sources, Hot Prospects

Heat from the Earth

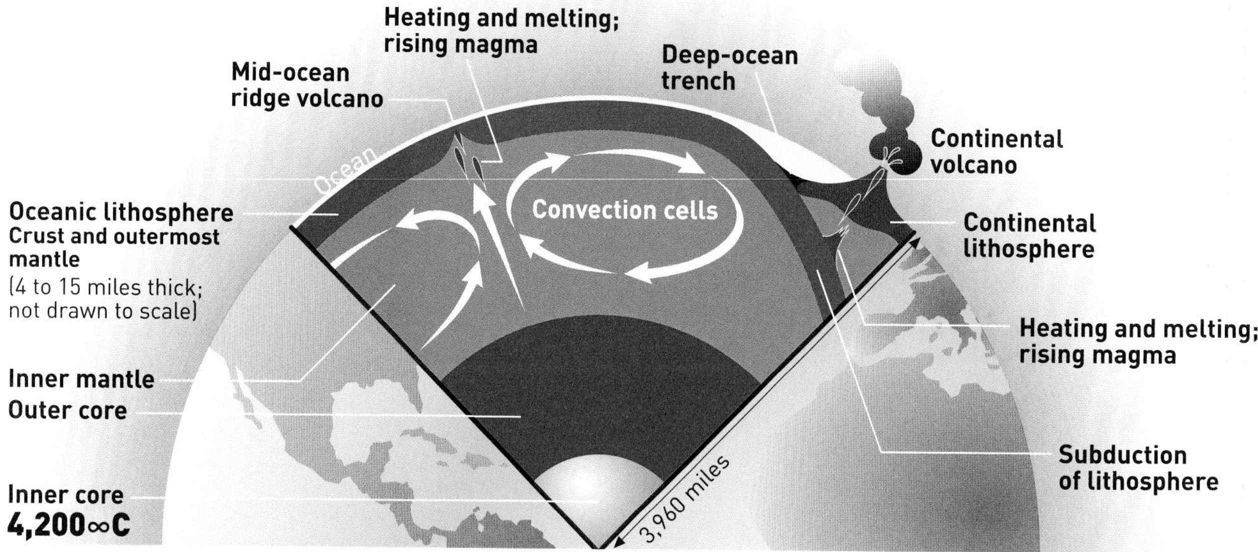

As a power source, *geothermal energy is hardly news. Tribal people were using natural hot springs to cook food 10,000 years ago. Two thousand years ago, at Pompeii, the Romans used geothermal springs to soak in and to heat their buildings.*

Geothermal power is well suited to address many current concerns about clean and sustainable energy. Geothermal stations use little land, provide continuous and reliable power, and conserve the use of fossil fuels. Geothermal energy can be used in modular and incremental development to offer power locally to remote sites and communities that are not easily connected to regional power grids and is available in one form or another over 95% of the Earth's surface. And geothermal energy is highly renewable – once underground steam is extracted from below ground to power a turbine, it can be pumped back into the ground, cycling endlessly. As long as this recharge rate matches the rate of extraction, a geothermal resource can be used almost indefinitely.

Geothermal energy is used in several ways – directly as a source of heat and indirectly as a raw material for producing electricity in turbines. Using geothermal energy directly for heat is highly efficient, using 50%–70% of the energy stored in deep hot rocks and superheated water. When turned into electricity, up to 20% of the energy is transferred.

Geothermal is not without some risk, however. Extracting geothermal energy can create some air pollution from radon gas, hydrogen sulfide, methane, ammonia, and carbon dioxide, although CO_2 emissions are only 5% of those from fossil fuel plants. These emissions can be controlled with technology that injects the waste gases and fluids back into the ground.

According to the U.N., about 9,000 megawatts of electricity is currently generated from geothermal resources, and the equivalent of another 9,000 megawatts is recovered for direct heating applications. Total investment in geothermal energy from 1973 to 1995 was about $22 billion, and the industry continues to grow at about 16% a year in electricity generation and about 6% a year for heat generation. Currently Costa Rica, El Salvador, Kenya, and Nicaragua generate 10%–20% of their electricity from geothermal resources, while the Phillipines generates 22% and plants to increase this amount by 30% by 2008. If present trends continue, geothermal electricity generating capacity could increase to about 58,000 megawatts worldwide by 2020.

Geothermal has more domestic uses, and can be used to lower the costs of heating

Graphic by Nigel Holmes

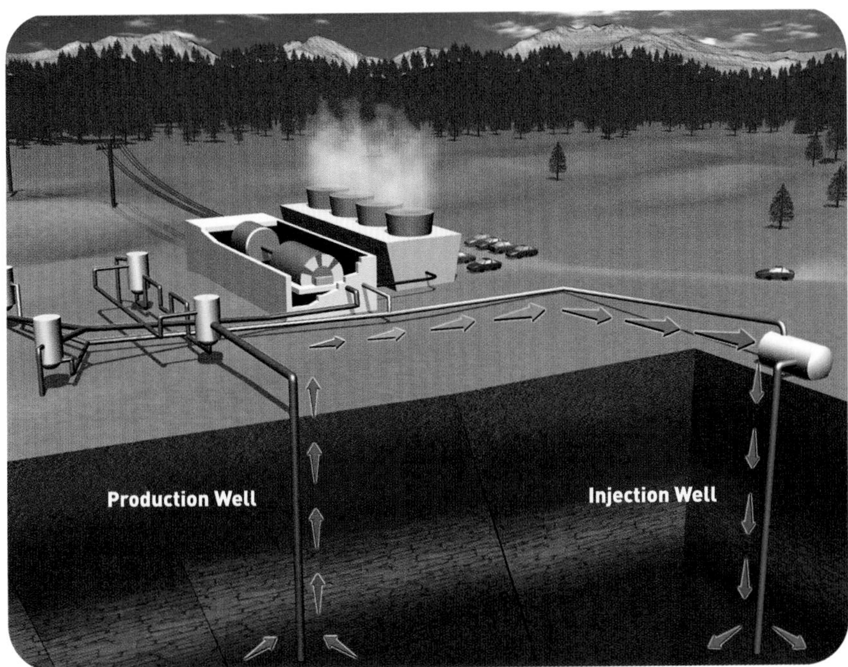

ENERGY FROM THE GROUND. *Geothermal plants produce energy by pulling steam from deep within the earth, using it to power electrical turbines and pumping it back into the ground.*

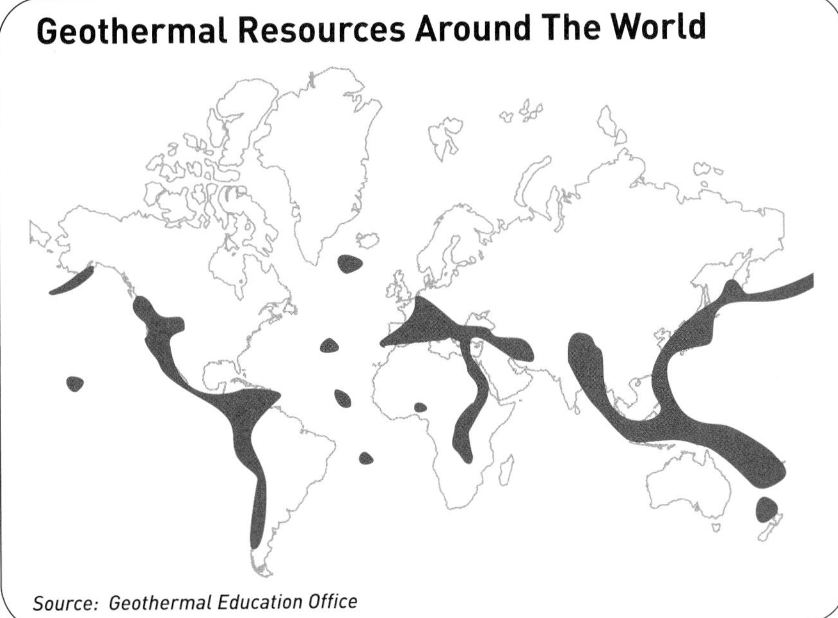

Image courtesy of Geothermal Education Office, Tiburon, CA

and cooling a building. Almost everywhere, the upper 10 feet of the earth's surface maintains a nearly constant temperature between 50° and 60°F (10° and 16°C). A geothermal heat pump system consists of pipes buried in the shallow ground near the building, a heat exchanger, and ductwork into the building. In winter, heat from the relatively warmer ground goes through the heat exchanger into the house. In summer, hot air from the house is pulled through the heat exchanger into the relatively cooler ground. Heat removed during the summer can be used as no-cost energy to heat water.

These technologies use only a tiny fraction of the total geothermal resource. Several miles everywhere beneath the earth's surface is hot, dry rock being heated by the molten magma directly below it. Funded by the U.S. Department of Energy, several projects are underway to develop technologies to drill into this rock; inject cold water down one well; circulate it through the hot, fractured rock; and draw off the heated water from another well. One day, we might also be able to recover heat directly from the molten magma far below the surface of the earth. We're all standing on an energy resource that could supply the entire world for centuries.

PROVOCATIONS...

If, ultimately, we can fuel the earth without polluting the environment, when will it happen?

As other countries become leaders in the fields of renewable energy, will the U.S. realize it's missing the boat and encourage utilities to invest in clean energy via tax credits?

—Andrew Zolli and Richard Kadrey

WANT MORE?

GEOTHERMAL EDUCATION OFFICE
http://geothermal.marin.org

GEOTHERMAL ENERGY ASSOCIATION
www.geo-energy.org

ALTERNATIVE ENERGY INSTITUTE, INC.
www.altenergy.org

Ocean Power... Lightning from the Sea

Image courtesy of Ocean Power Delivery Ltd.

THE BIGGEST SOLAR COLLECTOR IN THE WORLD HAS BEEN AROUND ABOUT AS LONG AS THE *Earth itself—the ocean. Every year, the world's oceans absorb heat energy equivalent to about 37 trillion kilowatts. If less than 0.1% of this renewable energy within the oceans could be converted into electricity, it would satisfy the present world demand for energy more than five times over.*

The question is how? Technologies for deriving electrical power from the ocean include tidal power, wave power, ocean thermal energy conversion, ocean currents, ocean winds, and salinity gradients. Of these, the three most well-developed technologies are tidal power, wave power, and ocean thermal energy conversion.

A large amount of energy is stored in the tides. The tides go in and out, and we can capture energy from this with tidal power stations. Tidal power stations can stretch over a delta, estuaries, beaches, or other places that are affected by the tides. When high tide comes in, water flows through a turbine to create electricity. Now some of the water is up behind the barrage. A gate is lowered from the barrage, capturing the water above it. When low tide comes, the gate is raised and the water flows out, first transferring its energy through turbines. This way, electricity is created with a two-way turbine. Some tidal power stations can produce 320 megawatts of electricity, and future improvements in design and efficiency could raise this amount dramatically.

In tropical seas, ocean thermal energy converter (OTEC) plants exploit the temperature difference between warm surface waters and the frigid deep waters to generate steam and drive

POWERFUL PELAMIS. *Ocean Power Delivery Ltd. is developing a novel offshore wave energy converter called Pelamis. Floating across the waves, the Pelamis is a long, thin, semi-submerged structure composed of four cylindrical sections linked by hinged joints. The wave-induced motion of the joints is resisted by hydrolic rams which power a generator. An array of 40 Pelamis machines could produce enough energy to power 20,000 homes (left).*

Available Wave Energy

low high

Source: Wavegen

turbines. OTEC uses the warm waters to evaporate a liquid that boils at a very low temperature, such as ammonia or freon. The steam produced is forced through turbines to create electricity. The gas is then put in a storage tank where cold water from the ocean floor is brought up to turn it back into a liquid. Then the process starts all over again. Although environmentally friendly, OTEC plants face substantial hurdles: Located far from shore, they must transport their electricity back to land, dramatically increasing its cost, and the plants themselves consume much of the power they produce.

The most exciting ocean energy method may come from harnessing the waves. When the wind hits the water, it transfers massive amounts of potential energy to the water. One of the best ways to recapture some of this energy is the oscillating water column (OWC). When waves hit an OWC, the air inside is compressed and forced through air turbines, powering a generator. OWCs are still mostly experimental, but one is already in use in Tofteshallen, Norway. It is one of the most advanced wave-to-energy devices in the world, creating 500 kilowatts of electricity.

In the U.S., communities' ocean power options are largely driven by where they are located. Tidal power requires large differences between low and high tide which, in the U.S., occur only in Maine and Alaska. Ocean thermal energy conversion is limited to tropical regions, such as Hawaii, and to a portion of the Atlantic coast. Wave energy has a more general application, with potential along the California coast. The western coastline has the highest wave potential in the U.S.; in California, the greatest potential is along the northern coast.

THE MIGHTY LIMPET

A Scottish company, Wavegen, has built the world's first commercial wave-powered electric plant on the Scottish island of Islay. Called the LIMPET (land installed marine powered energy transformer), Wavegen's system generates 500 kilowatts of power using seawater to compress air, which then drives a turbine. Not surprisingly, most research on wave systems comes from places such as Japan, Australia, England, and New Zealand — countries with a lot of coastline. In the U.S., the California Energy Commission is studying the viability of bringing wave power to the state.

Photo courtesy of Wavegen

PROVOCATIONS...

Will northern California energy needs one day be pitted against northern California coastal real estate needs? Will wave energy slow or accelerate coastal environmental protections?

— Andrew Zolli and Richard Kadrey

WANT MORE?

OCEAN POWER DELIVERY
www.oceanpd.com

DOE HYDROPOWER DATA
http://hydropower.inel.gov

WHAT IS OTEC?
www.nrel.gov/otec/what.html

WAVEGEN
www.wavegen.co.uk

Solar Power... Lighten Your Electric Bill

SOLAR IS THE SINGLE *most abundant source of renewable energy, yet it accounts for less than 1% of current U.S. energy production. Even more surprising, we've understood the basic concept of stealing electricity from light — the Photovoltaic Effect — since it was discovered in 1839 by French physicist Edmund Becquerel.*

However, it wasn't until the mid-1950s that researchers at Bell Labs produced useful silicon solar cells. This early cell only captured about 4.5% of the solar energy that hit, but within a few months, another team had raised the percentage to 6%. Current solar cells range in efficiency from 7% to 32%, though the most efficient cells are very expensive and are only used in satellites.

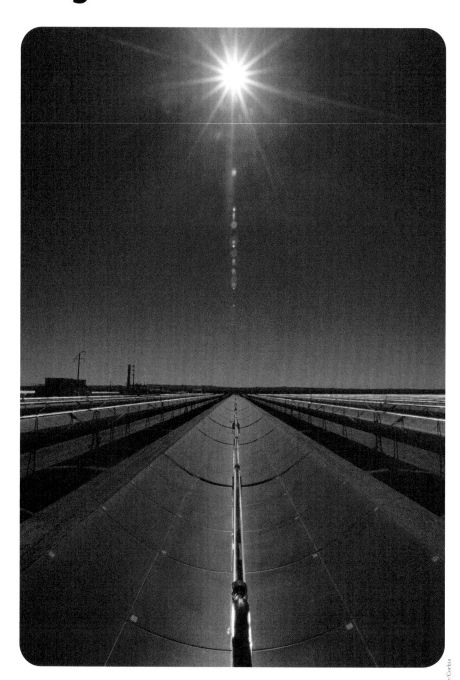

While their efficiency increases at a glacial pace, the price of cells has fallen dramatically. In the 1970s, when solar cells first went into mass production, they were so expensive that solar power wasn't an option for individuals, and the few photo cells you saw were on low-power novelty items, such as toys and portable radios. Back then, solar electric power cost about $200 per watt. Today, the price is down to around $4. Not only does this open up a whole range of products to consumers in developed countries, but it means that in the developing world solar power could bring electricity to places where it was out of the question to build and maintain power lines costing thousands of dollars per mile.

Photo © Roger Ressmeyer/Corbis

What can solar power do for you right now? Chances are, photo cells won't get you completely off the electric grid any time soon. But they can help. Several manufacturers have developed

THE MILLION SOLAR ROOFS INITIATIVE

Announced by President Clinton in 1997, this is a plan to install solar energy systems on 1 million roofs in the U.S. by 2010. The initiative covers two types of solar technology: photovoltaics, which convert solar energy directly into electricity, and solar thermal panels, which collect heat for homes, hot water, and swimming pools. The Department of Energy is working with industry and local governments to raise awareness and bring solar power to schools, business, and individual homes by lowering costs and creating federal lending and financing programs. By 2010, a million solar roofs could reduce carbon emissions by the same amount as the annual emissions of 850,000 cars. The program also hopes to create 70,000 new jobs by raising the demand for the manufacture and installation of solar energy systems.

SMART ENERGY. *Solar panels blanket the roof of Sussex Central Middle School in Delaware, a participant in the Million Solar Roofs program.*

photovoltaic panels that look like ordinary roof tiles and can even provide power on cloudy days. The panels aren't cheap — between $7,000 and $11,500 to fill approximately 20% of your electric power needs. The good news is that with photo cell prices still falling, the same roof setup should be half the price by 2004. A few experimental homes have actually generated more power than they need on a daily basis and fed the excess power back to the utility company for credit.

Every minute of sunlight that hits the earth contains more energy than all the humans and industries in the world use in a year, and it's the only form of renewable power that requires no fuel and has no moving parts. We're eventually going to learn to use solar power — we have to.

PROVOCATIONS...

If solar cars make driving free, will we have traffic jams all day?

Will power companies disappear when all houses generate their own energy?

Will the "sun belt" become more politically powerful?

—Richard Kadrey

THREE FLAVORS OF SUN

When most people talk about solar power, they're really talking about photovoltaics, which are specially treated wedges of silicon, cadmium, or other elements. When light hits a photovoltaic cell, it knocks an electron loose, which the cell captures to convert light directly into electricity.

Passive Solar uses simple "passive" technology such as skylights and windows set high into walls to increase the amount of sun that enters a building, saving power by using the sun's light and warmth to heat a space, without the aid of any mechanical devices.

Solar Thermal systems use the warmth from sunlight to heat water enclosed in tubing for kitchens, bathrooms, and swimming pools or provide radiant heat for rooms. Larger, industrial solar thermal systems use an array of mirrors to collect sunlight at a central point. The heat from this concentrated sun produces electricity by boiling water to create steam, which powers a generator turbine.

There's one more theoretical kind of solar power: electricity beamed from the moon. Dr. David Criswell wants to build the Lunar Solar Power (LSP) System, a collection of 20–40 lunar power bases, built across the eastern and western edges on the moon's sunny side. The bases would capture vast amounts of solar energy and beam it back to earth as microwaves. Earth antennae would then capture and feed the power into the local grid.

WANT MORE?

NATIONAL CENTER FOR PHOTOVOLTAICS
www.nrel.gov/ncpv

SOLAR POWER FROM THE EREN
www.eren.doe.gov/RE/solar.html

HOMEBREW POWER INFO
www.homepower.com

THE SOLAR ELECTRIC POWER ASSOCIATION (SEPA)
www.SolarElectricPower.org

FLORIDA SOLAR ENERGY CENTER
www.fsec.ucf.edu/PVT

NATIONAL SOLAR ARCHITECTURE RESEARCH UNIT
www.fbe.unsw.edu.au/units/solarch

Fuel Cells... The Next Big Thing?

UNDER THE HOOD. *A microchannel fuel processor can extract hydrogen from gasoline, to power a fuel cell (above).* **SUM OF THE PARTS.** *A fuel cell is combined with cooling and air supply systems to make a car engine (left).*

WHAT'S A HYDROGEN FUEL CELL? IT COULD BE THE NEXT REVOLUTION IN ENERGY PRO-*duction. And the idea behind it couldn't be simpler. ¶ Imagine a battery that never runs out of power. That's essentially what a fuel cell is: Like a battery, it generates electricity through an internal chemical reaction. The difference is that as long as the fuel cell gets a supply of fresh hydrogen, it will put out electricity indefinitely.*

The cell does this by stealing electrons from hydrogen atoms. Hydrogen and oxygen enter a fuel cell from opposite ends. The hydrogen atoms are chemically split and the electrons siphoned off, producing electricity. At the end of the process, the oxygen and hydrogen come together to form the primary fuel cell waste product: pure water.

Today, fuel cells are pricey items used by utility and industrial companies. NASA even uses fuel cells to provide power on the Space Shuttle. However, prices are dropping and durability is going up. In the next decade, we're going to see fuel cells replace conventional batteries in small appliances and mobile electronics, such as cell phones. The U.S. government is sponsoring studies of fuel cells as a power source for ultra-efficient, nonpolluting cars. We might also see them in homes, letting us live off of the electrical grid or providing backup power in case of a blackout.

RACING IN THE STREETS

With fuel cells reaching new levels of power and efficiency, the race is on to see who can successfully create a commercially viable fuel cell car.

Daimler-Chrysler unveiled an experimental fuel cell SUV back in the winter of 2000. Since then, GM unveiled a mock-up of its AUTOnomy concept car at the 2002 Detroit Car Show. Both Toyota and Honda plan to have small fleets of fuel cell vehicles on the streets by 2003. By 2004, Ford plans to market a fuel cell-gas hybrid version of its Focus Fuel Cell Vehicle (FCV).

There are still a lot of challenges in the way of these designs, including bringing down the price of the fuel cells and increasing their power. Honda's new model has an impressive top speed of 87mph, but its range is still under 200 miles. Plus, no one knows how to deliver the hydrogen fuel to the cars. But with both industry and the DOE backing new research, these are problems that are bound to be solved in the next few years.

MEGA FUEL CELLS AND MICRO POWER PLANTS

"This new technology has the potential to alter the landscape of tomorrow's power

Clockwise from top left: Photo courtesy of Ballard Power Systems; Photo courtesy of Pacific Northwest National Lab

INSIDE A FUEL CELL

A fuel cell creates electricity through a chemical reaction, just like a convention battery, but the chemicals and the results are very different.

In a fuel cell, hydrogen is forced through a catalyst — porous carbon paper coated with platinum — which strips away electrons from the hydrogen atoms. The electrons are siphoned off by the negative anode so they can be used as electricity. On the positive cathode side, oxygen enters the cell and mixes with the returning hydrogen to produce pure water.

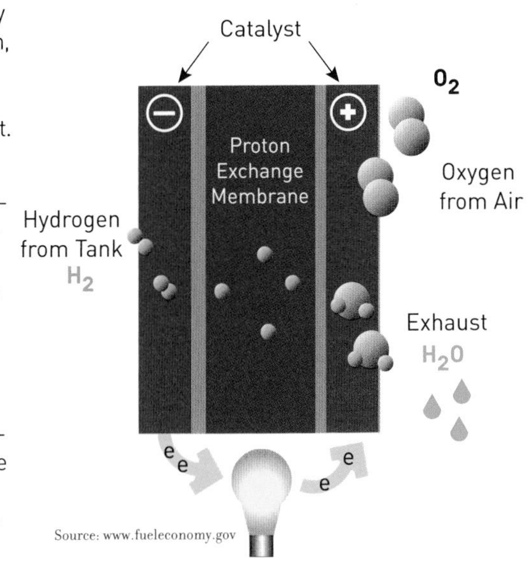

Source: www.fueleconomy.gov

A single fuel cell only produces about 0.7 volts. To get a useful amount of voltage, a large number of fuel cells are combined to create a fuel cell stack. When people refer to "a fuel cell," they're usually referring to one of these stacks.

industry," said Secretary of Energy Spencer Abraham, talking about the world's first fuel cell-gas turbine hybrid power plant as it came online at the National Fuel Cell Research Center on the campus of the University of California-Irvine.

Built as a joint project between Siemens Westinghouse and Southern California Edison, the generator combines fuel cells with small, high-speed microturbines to produce enough power for around 200 homes. This gas-fuel cell hybrid has set a new record in electrical efficiency, around 53%. Conventional internal combustion engines are only about 25% efficient. With improvements, researchers think they can raise the efficiency to 60% for smaller systems and 70% for larger ones.

TWICE AS EFFICIENT. *The world's first fuel cell-gas turbine system generates 220KW and has operated for 900+ hours at more than 50% efficiency.*

Photo © Siemens AG, Munich/Berlin

PROVOCATIONS...

Are fuel cells the beginning of the end for big oil companies, or will they find a way to shift into the hydrogen market? Will your next house power itself? Will the demand for fuel cell catalysts create a "platinum crisis"?

—Richard Kadrey

WANT MORE?

FUEL CELL INFO CENTER
www.fuelcells.org

HYDROGEN ENERGY CENTER
www.h2eco.org

FUEL CELL TODAY
www.fuelcelltoday.com

THE HYDROGEN & FUEL CELL LETTER
www.hfcletter.com

NATIONAL FUEL CELL RESEARCH CENTER (NFCRC)
www.nfcrc.uci.edu/fuelcellinfo_index.htm

FUEL CELLS IN SPACE AND DEFENSE
www.internationalfuelcells.com/spacedefense/overview.shtml

FUEL CELLS: GREEN POWER
http://education.lanl.gov/resources/fuelcells/

Nuclear Power... Smaller Is Better

THE FIRST COMMERCIAL nuclear power plant was built in Shippingport, Pennsylvania, in 1957. Back then, what sold the idea was that nuclear power was "too cheap to meter." Things didn't work out quite that way. And now, coupled with accidents at Three Mile Island and Chernobyl, the nuclear industry has been in a fallow period for over a decade with few new reactors coming online. However, with the hunger for power growing and with innovative new designs on the drawing boards, nuclear energy may be ready for a comeback.

Generation IV, the U.S. Department of Energy's program aimed at finding and developing new ideas in nuclear power, is charged with finding new designs that are both safer and cheaper than the big money, big science nuclear plants of the past. The pebble-bed reactor is one of the popular designs being studied. Pebble-beds are smaller and simpler to build than current reactors and cheaper to run. They're part of a new generation of reactors called "inherently safe," meaning a Chernobyl-style meltdown is almost impossible. The Westinghouse AP-600 is another "inherently safe" design under study. Instead of using mechanical pumps that move cooling water to the plant's hot core, the AP-600 stores

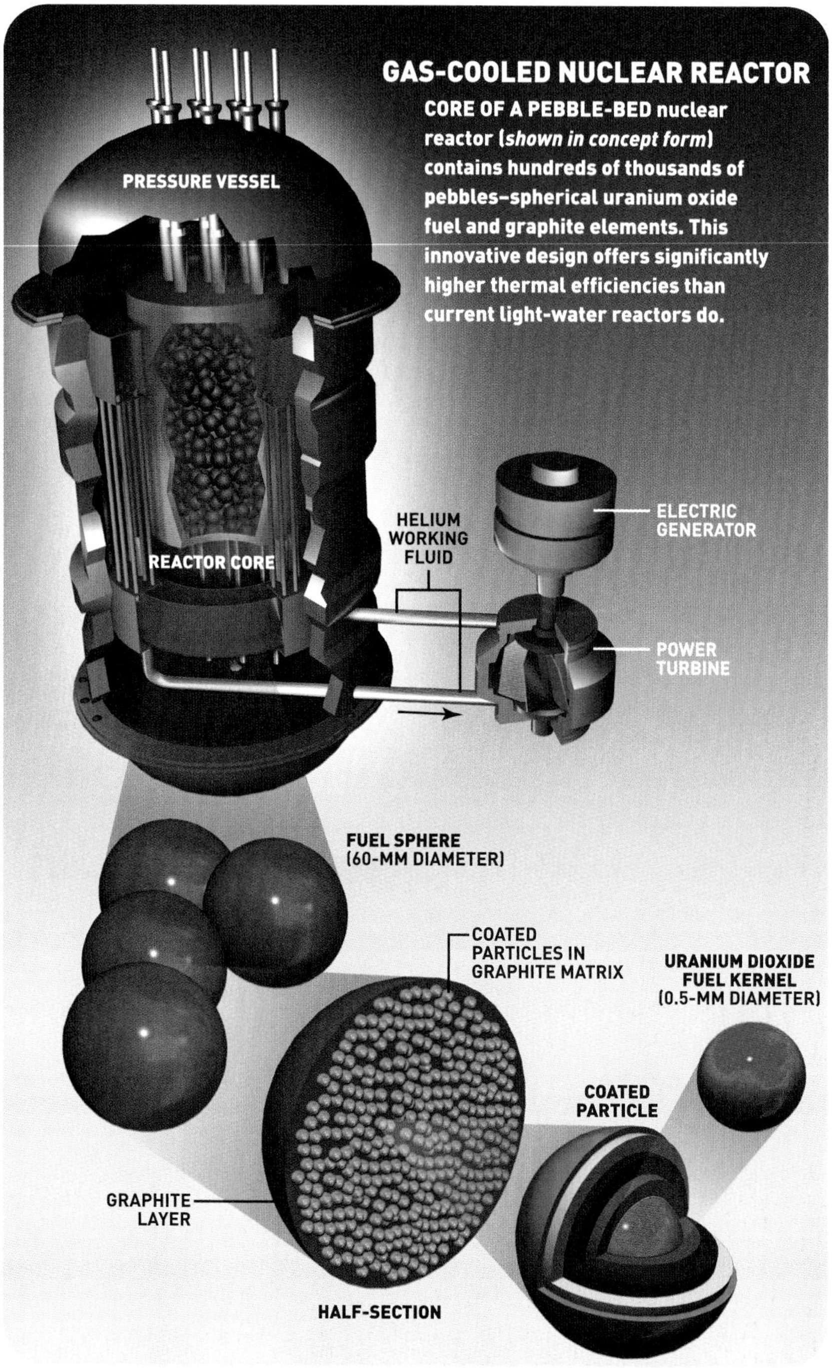

GAS-COOLED NUCLEAR REACTOR

CORE OF A PEBBLE-BED nuclear reactor (*shown in concept form*) contains hundreds of thousands of pebbles–spherical uranium oxide fuel and graphite elements. This innovative design offers significantly higher thermal efficiencies than current light-water reactors do.

THE UNUSUAL FUEL THAT FEEDS A PEBBLE-BED REACTOR. *The nuclear fuel for this reactor is contained in tennis-ball-size graphite "pebbles." Because the individual pebble can't get hot enough to cause a meltdown, a Chernobyl-style accident is nearly impossible.*

Graphic by Don Foley

NUCLEAR WASTE

Radioactive waste has always been the elephant in the corner for the nuclear power industry. Currently, the U.S. Department of Energy is trying to decide what to do with a 12-million-ton pile of radioactive uranium waste lying unprotected in Moab, Utah. And that's not the only pile of unprocessed radioactive waste. Add that to the 70,000 tons of nuclear power plant waste the government would like to store in the proposed Yucca Mountain repository in Nevada. It's obvious that waste disposal remains the biggest problem facing the nuclear power industry. In whatever form, the high-level waste that comes from nuclear plants will remain radioactive for 10,000 years. That's one of the reasons the government chose Yucca Mountain as its new waste storage facility. The site is isolated and the soil is purportedly stable and not prone to leakage or earthquakes — though even the DOE's own scientific advisors have questioned whether the studies have proven conclusively that Yucca Mountain's geology can successfully contain the waste. If the current plans continue, waste will begin moving there in 10 years.

water above the reactor so that in case of an accident, gravity will dump thousands of gallons of specially treated water directly into the core. This passive water system also means that the reactor is easier to build and cheaper to maintain than conventional plants.

For government and business, though, the brass ring of nuclear power remains fusion power. Fusion is more efficient than the fission reactors we now use because most of its fuel could come from ordinary seawater, thereby producing less waste than current reactors.

But fusion power has been much harder to develop than anyone expected. After nearly 50 years of work, even the best fusion reactors can only return about 65% of the power used to run them. The development of fusion has been expensive, too. The U.S. was an original partner in the International Thermonuclear Experimental Reactor (ITER), a joint EU, Russian Federation, and Japanese project, but we pulled out when the budget topped $8 billion. We're in talks to rejoin the partnership in a scaled-down version of the ITER, but nothing is certain.

One contender in the pricey fusion research arena is the British MAST (Mega Amp Spherical Tokamak) reactor. It's smaller than most fusion reactors, and it is its compactness, British scientists argue, that makes it much more energy efficient than the giant reactors that are the industry norm. The small MAST reactor keeps the plasma that's the power source of a fusion reactor in a tighter bundle than a large reactor. This tight configuration produces more bang for the megawatt buck. The United Kingdom Atomic Energy Authority is betting that its MAST reactors will be easier to develop, cheaper to build, and quicker to come online than fusion's old-school behemoths.

KRT Photos

YUCCA MOUNTAIN. *The location of the proposed Yucca Mountain nuclear waste storage facility in Nevada, 100 miles northwest of Las Vegas. Within 10 years, the facility could be ready to begin receiving the 70,000 tons of waste the government would like to store there.*

PROVOCATIONS...

Will Big Energy still control nuclear power?

Will future generations use our nuclear waste as a resource?

—Richard Kadrey

WANT MORE?

NUCLEAR ENERGY RESEARCH INITIATIVE (NERI)
http://neri.ne.doe.gov

NUCLEAR OPTIMIZATION (NEPO)
http://nepo.ne.doe.gov

GENERATION IV
http://gen-iv.ne.doe.gov

NUCLEAR REGULATORY COMMISSION
www.nrc.gov

RADWASTE.ORG
www.radwaste.org

NUCLEAR POWER PLANT DEMO
www.ida.liu.se/~her/npp/demo.html

MAST
www.fusion.org.uk/culham/mast.htm

YUCCA MOUNTAIN PROJECT
www.ymp.gov

YUCCA WATCHDOG SITE
www.yuccamountain.org

Exploration... A Remedy for Cosmic Loneliness

We live in a rich and wonderful universe, full of incredible phenomena. Ask the question: What is the strangest, most complex, most capable phenomenon in the universe? It seems a very hard question, which should be the province of the wisest of scientists and philosophers. But it is not.

All of us encounter that most wonderful known phenomenon in the universe. It is we! Were it not for the fact that we are almost constantly in the presence of other human beings, we would immediately guess this. Were we some other form of intelligence, biological or machine, and encountered a human for the first time, we would be stunned by such a phenomenon. Such talents! We have a memory that can hold countless detailed records of events that occurred many, many years before. We possess the ability to manipulate complicated concepts in the mind, leading to mind-boggling technologies and social systems. And there is consciousness — that most mysterious and powerful ability of humans. The list goes on and on.

No wonder we yearn to discover other creatures like ourselves in the universe. If we are so remarkable, and yet the product of a brief and unfinished expression of evolution, what even more remarkable creatures and civilizations exist in space? They could be literally billions of years ahead of us in their biological, intellectual, and social evolution. What could we learn about possible futures for us, of Earth-enriching technologies, of aesthetics, of the breadth of physiologies that can provide conscious, intelligent creatures? And, of course, just as has always been the case on Earth, it would be a great adventure to encounter a culture that had developed independently from our own. How different it would be!

These are old thoughts. They have been around since the time of the earliest philosophers, and especially since the time, some 400 years ago, when we first realized that the sun was a star, and perhaps a myriad of stars, like our sun, had planetary systems. We have longed to know of intelligent life, or even any form of life, on other planets. But in science, as in everyday life, wishing does not make it so! To detect any form of life on planets at the great distances to the stars has been far beyond the ability of any of even the greatest telescopes on Earth. Until now.

Indeed, the means to detect life elsewhere in the solar system or on the planets of other stars has grown out of the steady march of improvement in telescope capabilities. More than that, we have learned much about the possible origins of life and how life adapts to ranges of environments, and all of this has encouraged us to believe that life can easily arise and evolve in an enormous range of circumstances. We have found microbial life living miles down in the Earth; indeed, perhaps more life than exists on the surface of the planet. It boggles the mind to think that perhaps all the life we have known until now was just a minor constituent of a much bigger system of living things that was here all the time, but we didn't know it. It boggles the mind to find life everywhere: from the frozen arctic, to the summit of Mt. Everest, to the steaming, boiling water of hot springs. There is a strong message here — life is adaptable and opportunistic, and we can expect to find it in every habitable site and in many sites which we would think must be sterile.

The best news encouraging a search for extraterrestrial life has been the discovery of more than 100 other planetary systems, some much like our own, with more of those to come as the search methods become more suited to finding solar systems. Yes, there are habitable worlds out there.

What will the future bring in the search for life? In the long run, it is intelligent life that we most want to find. For 40 years we have been slowly testing the waters, building ever better, more powerful instruments capable of detecting civilizations now more advanced than ourselves. The key instrument through all of these years has been the radio telescope. Sensitive to the weakest of signals, seeing clearly through the dust clouds of the Milky Way, exploiting the quietness of space in the radio spectrum, the radio telescope has been the instrument of choice. Still, the stars are far away, and even the most optimistic scientist does not expect detectable signals to be coming from more that a handful of civilizations among the perhaps a million or more stars we must search. The signals will be weak. Realism forces us to call for much more powerful instruments than we now have.

The good news is that we know how to build what is necessary, and the means to do this is not preposterous. Right now the SETI Institute is building a new form of radio telescope, probably the wave of the future for all radio telescopes, which will enable a better search by far than any previous one. This telescope, the Allen Telescope Array, will use 350 20-foot diameter antennas, all connected together under computer control, to duplicate the performance of a traditional telescope more than 300 feet in size. And the cost will be perhaps one-quarter of the cost of a telescope built in the traditional way. That is reason enough to pursue this approach. But there are other major advantages, such as the ability for the instrument to look at several different places in the sky at once. In addition, this form of telescope can "grow" indefinitely by simply adding more antennas. We can build whatever it takes to find that elusive signal we all hope for. It is not out of the question to build a telescope that is effectively miles in size. We even have done preliminary planning of a telescope on the far side of the moon, the ideal place to search for extraterrestrial radio signals.

If you really want to hear of the dreams of the distant future, one great dream is to place a small telescope so far from the sun, about 600 billion miles, that it can use the gravitational field of the sun as a lens to create a telescope many thousands of times more powerful than what we could build on Earth. The gravitational field of the sun would provide this simple system with the image quality that would be given by a lens somewhat larger than the sun itself. This telescope could not only photograph the planets of stars hundreds of light years away, but it could resolve continents and oceans on them. But it will be a long time before our space technology is adequate to meet this challenge.

Certainly such systems are expensive. But in contrast, the resources put into other efforts, even in simply expanding a small section of highway, for example, are far greater.

SETI can carry out a magnificent project with the efforts of only, say, a few hundred people. Funds equal to the cost of a single launch of the space shuttle would build a SETI system beyond our most wild dreams. Surely these costs are trivial compared not only to what else we do, but to the value of the benefits that will accrue from the discovery of even one extraterrestrial civilization. And keep in mind: If there is one to be found, there are many. A wise civilization would easily see the wisdom in devoting the necessary but relatively miniscule resources needed to conduct serious, high-powered searches. Many people, particularly those in the high-tech industries, know this and support SETI. The public at large understands and supports the project. It is somewhat sad to have to say that governmental bodies have not yet grasped the importance of this enterprise.

Why does even the highly educated U.S. Congress fail to see that a small investment in SETI will, in the long run, provide benefits beyond our imagining, not just to the U.S., but to the world as a whole? The answer is that science education, despite great efforts by dedicated teachers, has failed to create a rapport between the public at large and the vast, so different, so vexing, yet so fantastic and tantalizing grandeur of the greater universe. We still live naively in that universe, with all its potential to create a myriad of phenomena, some of them just amazing, others extremely relevant to our own welfare. We grope for understanding and, indeed, make tremendous progress. But there is so far to go. We must glimpse, in fine detail, distant worlds. We must study, also in fine detail, the nature and lives of beings in places very far away. In many, perhaps most, cases, these creatures will be far older and wiser than we.

Science educators know this and are driven by the importance of success to provide an ever improving public understanding of the glories of the universe. In time, this will produce not only many more talented scientists and engineers, but political bodies willing to make "it," the great discoveries, happen. The wave of the future is moving clearly in this direction. It seems certain that the greatest and most important era of exploration lies just before us.

—Frank Drake

2000 2005 2010 2015 2020

risks  rewards 

EXTREME ENVIRONMENTS... The Lake at the End of the World

SOMETIMES IT SEEMS AS IF THERE ARE NO SECRET PLACES LEFT ON EARTH – NO "TERRA *incognita" to spark the imaginations of intrepid explorers. But don't tell that to the teams of scientists studying Lake Vostok – the frozen Antarctic lake near the magnetic South Pole.*

Explorations into this supremely remote environment, in one of the most inhospitable places imaginable, may soon transform our understanding of the history of life on our planet and lead to new techniques for seeking out life elsewhere in the solar system.

Imagine a body of water the size of Lake Ontario, and twice as deep. Now cover it with a layer of ice nine times the height of Chicago's Sears Tower, and put it in the coldest spot on Earth – where the temperature recently dipped to a balmy -128°F/-89°C.

That's Lake Vostok, a "subglacial" lake at the South Pole that vanished under the first advancing frosts of an Ice Age some 15 million years ago – at a time when our ape-like ancestors were still roaming the border forests of Asia and Africa. Ever since, this last pristine corner of the Earth's ecosystem has been an island unto itself, a lost world.

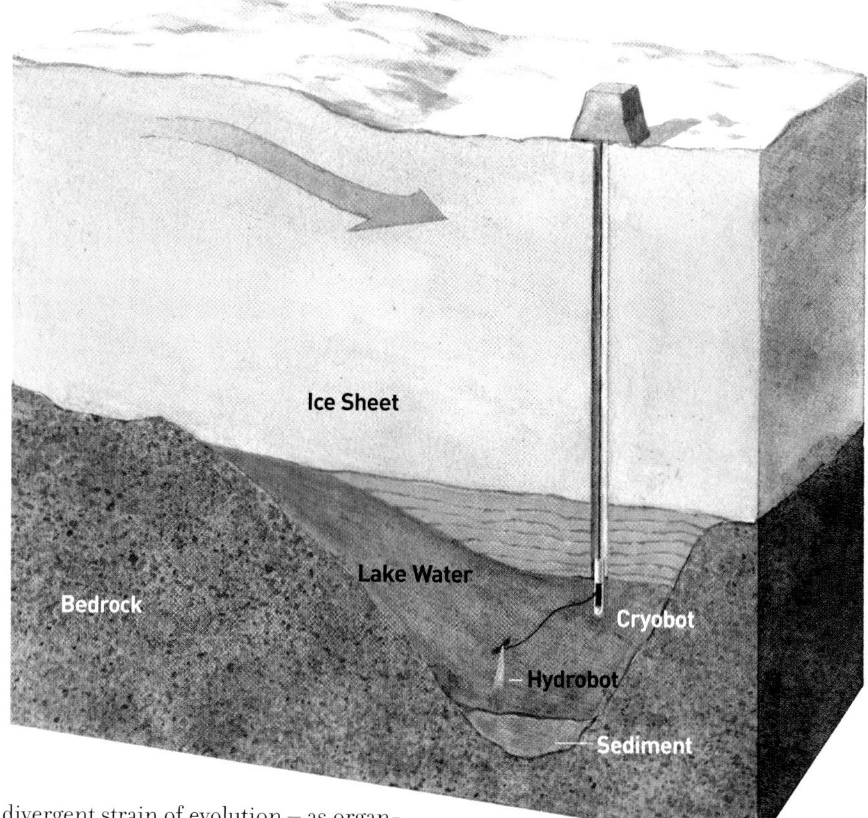

Rob Wood © Wood Ronsaville Harlin, Inc., Annapolis, MD

Cloaked in perpetual darkness, with near-freezing temperatures, a massive ice sheet preventing nutrients from reaching its waters, and pressure 360 times those at the surface, the lake would seem devoid of the sunlight, food, and warmth we consider to be requirements for all living things. But recent research suggests that this lake could contain exotic forms of life unlike any seen before – a divergent strain of evolution – as organisms from the distant past adapted to this harshest of environments.

There is more than a passing chance. The lake's waters, today kept liquid by heat rising from the earth's interior, were not always so cold. "30 million years ago, Antarctica was green," says John Priscu, an environmental biologist from the University of Montana who is examining life in the lake. "At that point, the lake would have been teeming with life – fish, vegetation, and the like." This organic material could have been sufficient to support microbial forms of life as it decomposed. Recent evidence suggests that Vostok may also be geothermically active – and life has been found thriving in the black abyss of the deep oceans around geothermal vents elsewhere on the planet. Either way, the discovery of life in this 15-million-year-old Petri dish would be, in the words of one researcher, "the biological discovery of the millennium."

The lake is so remote that it remained unknown when the Soviets built a base directly above it in 1957; its existence was only confirmed in 1996, with the advent of new forms of satellite and seismic imaging technology. Simply living at Vostok Station is a challenge – the nearest supply station is a 1,000km tractor ride away – not the sort of place where you can easily run out for spare parts.

The layers of ice, built up over millennia, contain chemical clues to Earth's climate stretching back millennia, much as the layers of rock and sediment provide clues to our geological history. By analyzing "ice cores," Russian scientists already have reconstructed the Earth's climate going back some 420,000 years. The ice cores from deepest in the ice – only some 100 meters above the liquid lake – have already turned up new, unclassified microbes frozen in the ice. Priscu's team is currently sequencing the DNA to see if the organisms are unique.

The real challenge will be to drill all the way through the ice to the lake below – without introducing chemical or microbial contamination. "The question is not whether the question of life under the ice is compelling," says Frank Carsey, of Jet Propulsion Laboratory. "It's whether we can discover the answer without harming the very thing we're investigating."

E.T., YOU'RE HOME. *Strange, new kinds of microbes, with nicknames like Mickey Mouse and Klingon, have been found trapped in Vostok's ancient ice.*

THE ANTI-ICE CUBE. *Cryobots like this one may melt their way to the discovery of new life.*

Clockwise from top left: Image courtesy of NASA Marshall Space Flight Center–Image courtesy of NASA/JPL/Caltech

To solve that problem, Carsey and his team are exploring radical new approaches to gaining access to the lake – cryobots. These lozenge-shaped robots melt their way through the ice as they descend, refreezing it above them, ensuring no contamination. When a cryobot breaks through the ceiling of ice, it may release a variety of sensors, video cameras, and other apparatus. Cryobot technology is still being perfected, but it's precisely the kind of technology that could determine if life exists, or existed, under the ice.

PROVOCATIONS...

Will Antarctica become a new eco-tourism magnet?

Will Vostok's ice cores alter the debate about climate change?

—Andrew Zolli

WANT MORE?

EXTREME ENVIRONMENTS
www.nsf.gov/home/crssprgm/lexen/
www.resa.net/nasa/antarctica.htm

NATIONAL SCIENCE FOUNDATION OFFICE OF POLAR PROGRAMS
www.nsf.gov/od/opp/start.htm

LAKE VOSTOK
www.bbc.co.uk/science/horizon/2000/vostok.shtml

SCIENTIFIC COMMITTEE ON ANTARCTIC RESEARCH
www.scar.org

SUBGLACIAL LAKE EXPLORATION
http://salegos-scar.montana.edu

CRYOBOTS HOME PAGE
http://fuego.jpl.nasa.gov

2000 2005 2010 2015 2020

risks  rewards 

Deep Sea Exploration...
The Next Frontier Is As Close As the Coast

IN THE 20TH CENTURY, *we extended our reach up and out to the birth of time 15 billion years past—and in and down to the frozen motion of molecules. But the Hubble space telescope and scanning electron microscopes are merely tools to let us see. What we really want to do is visit. Just as we are pushing up and out of the gravity well with spaceflight, we are also pushing in and down to the bottoms of our oceans.*

We already live on Waterworld: Oceans cover over 70% of the Earth's surface. With scuba gear, divers routinely swim to depths of 300 feet. But everything below that is considered "deep sea," and deep sea comprises 60% of our oceans. Here, then, is both the opportunity and the risk: The ocean depths offer more daunting technical challenges than deep space.

But, you think, the vacuum! Temperature fluctuations of several hundred degrees! Radiation! Space vehicles must tolerate sunside temperatures of 250°F in tandem with lows of –250°F

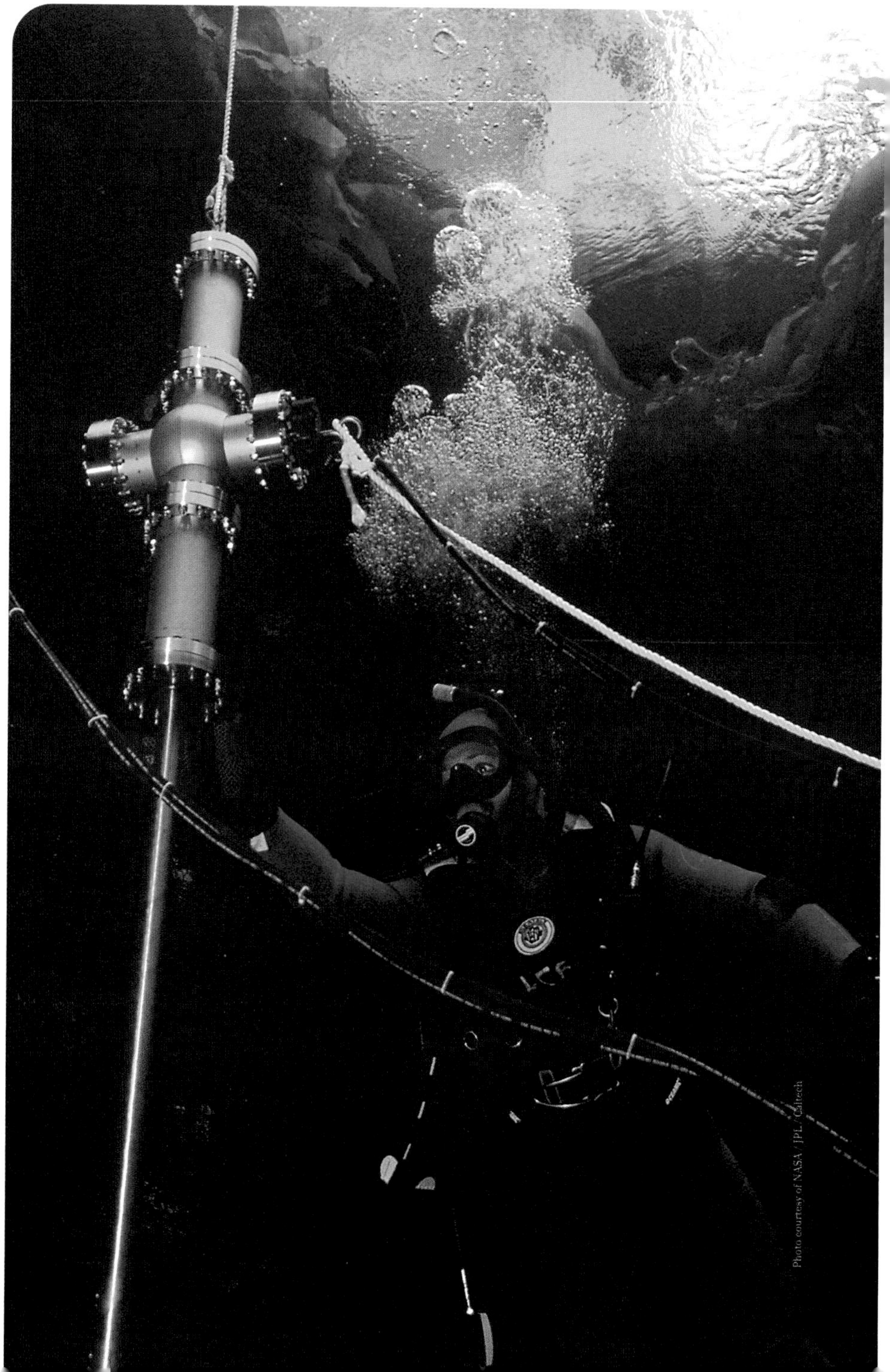

PROBING THE DEEP. *Researchers in Monterey, California, prepare a deep ocean probe.*

Photo courtesy of NASA/JPL/Caltech

and shield their contents against both radiation and space debris. Yet deep ocean vehicles must tolerate a similar temperature variance—35°F in the coldest depths to 750°F near hydrothermal vents — as well as protect against one of the most corrosive substances on Earth: saltwater. Where astronauts need only suit up for a one-atmosphere difference in pressure, divers endure a one-atmosphere increase in pressure for every 33 feet (10 meters) they descend.

Furthermore, as Marcia McNutt, CEO of MBARI (Monterey Bay Aquarium Research Institute), reminds us, "Solar panels are capable of powering most interplanetary voyages, but sunlight does not penetrate beyond the uppermost regions of the ocean. Space is virtually transparent to the transmission of electromagnetic energy, while the oceans are opaque to [it]." Consequently, many deep sea exploration devices are tethered to their launch platforms. Imagine this limitation in space.

Given these constraints, why bother? Scientists would answer, for data: What is the largest animal on the planet, and what is its life cycle? (The blue whale – also, at 188dB, the loudest animal on Earth.) How might plankton and algae offset rising carbon dioxide levels in our atmosphere? (By absorbing excess.) What role do coral reefs play in maintaining viable fish stocks? (Approximately 10% of fish caught annually for food live in reefs.) Investors would answer, for profit: minerals on the ocean floor and dissolved in sea water itself; biochemicals indigenous to marine plants and animals; new food sources. And archaeologists, anthropologists, and historians would answer, for the ancient artifacts and the stories: of sunken cities, of lost ships, of old wars.

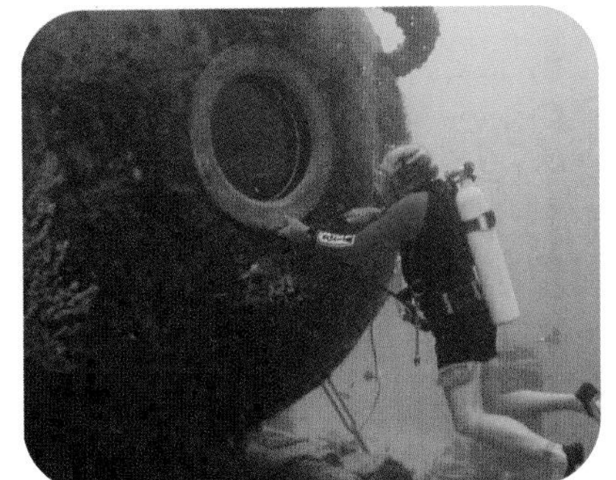

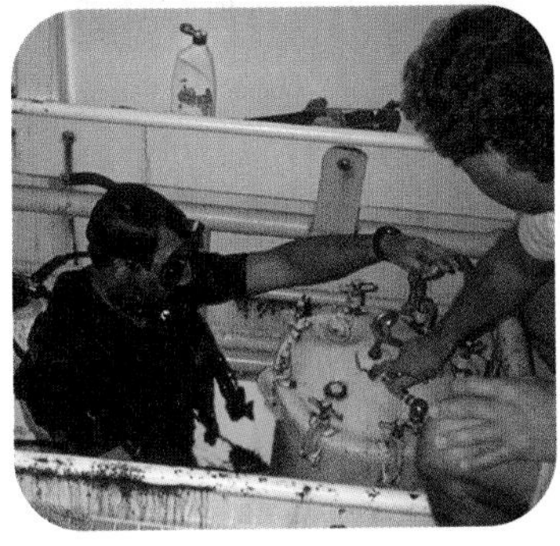

Photos courtesy of NOAA / University of North Carolina at Wilmington

INNERSPACE STATION. *Since 1993, the National Oceanic and Atmospheric Administration and the University of North Carolina at Wilmington have been conducting research in Aquarius, located in the Florida Keys National Marine Sanctuary. Scientists use Aquarius to study coral reefs and the coastal ocean. Starting in 2001, NASA astronauts also began using Aquarius as a space station analogue for training. Aquarius is unique: it's the only underwater research laboratory operating in our oceans - on planet earth.*

How do we get there? Basically, we have three choices. We can visit the ocean depths virtually, piggy-backing on the senses of aquatic robots and remotely operated exploration tools. Or we can build vessels that withstand the temperatures, the saltwater, and the pressures, and visit the sea depths in the nautilus shell of our own inventiveness. On the horizon, emerging technologies might one day enable us to build "sea suits" and explore in conditions more nearly skin to sea.

We extend our virtual reach beneath the waves with three kinds of tools. Using cables, we lower sensor arrays from ships, as the oceanographer Robert Ballard did to explore the Titanic with the sensor sled Argo. We build undersea robots, like Japan's Aqua Explorer 2000 or Woods Hole's ABE (Autonomous Benthic Explorer). Or we deploy sensor stations on the ocean floor, like the GEOSTAR station of the Mediterranean "Biodeep" project. Economics and durability both support continued use of towed equipment arrays, but microminiaturization, chip design, new materials research, and biomimetic robotics point to autonomous undersea vehicles (AUVs) and robots as key marine tools of tomorrow.

In essence, we are designing the next benthic life-form: It will hunt anomalies, taste its surroundings, excrete data, and return to us periodically to ingest energy for continued existence. It may not even need batteries, using heat engines to generate energy from ocean temperature differentials,

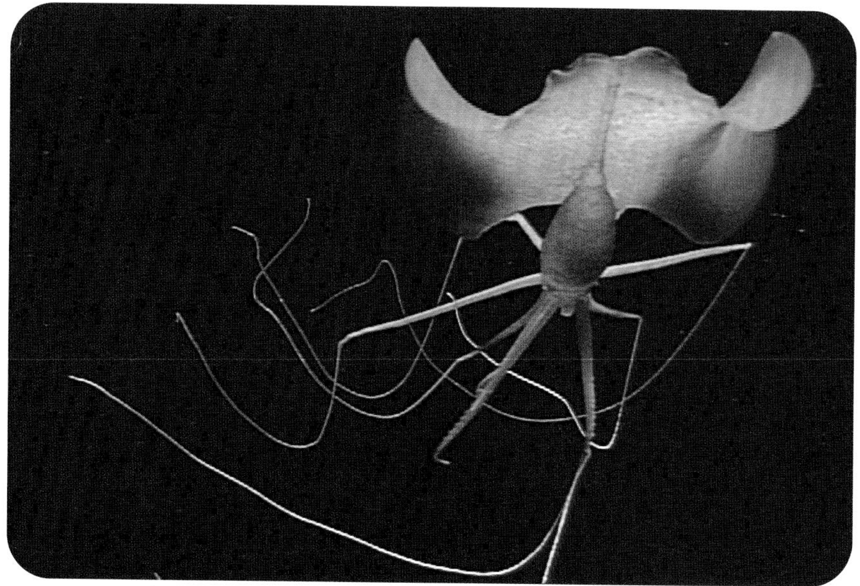

ALIEN INVADERS. *We're the alien invaders of its world. And what is it, exactly? A new kind of squid, 13-16 feet long and as delicate as a flower, discovered recently in the deep ocean by the Monterey Bay Aquarium Research Institute. It is estimated that there are up to 10 million such undescribed species of organisms in the abyssal ocean.* **UNDERSEA SENSOR.** *GEOSTAR is an unmanned automatic observation and monitoring station that has been successfully tested in the Tyrrhenian Sea off the island of Ustica, Italy. The station was submerged to a depth of 2,000 meters between September 2000 and May 2001, providing scientists with a mobile underwater research base.*

UNDERWATER FLYER. *Graham Hawkes's Deepflight submersibles may open the way for popular deep sea ocean exploration. In a "reverse Everest" expedition, one such sub, now in development, will explore the deepest part of the ocean – the Mariana trench.*

like the new Slocum Glider. For the sake of efficient propulsion, this silicon seabeast will mimic its organic neighbors in design. Draper Laboratory's newest autonomous ocean robot is modeled after a yellowfin tuna. Simpler additions to our technological aquarium will drift along passively collecting data: Tiny, free-floating robots will include chemical sensors on their microchips and buckytubes to filter particulates for analysis. These zooplankton mimics will trade and pool data among themselves and store observations until sucked up by a larger robofish for collection.

All this robotic sea life will function within an ecosystem of instrumentation rather than kelp, an ecosystem emerging from initiatives like the Neptune project. An underwater observatory stretching from Vancouver Island to northern California, the Neptune project will feature 2,000 miles of fiber-optic cable, a host of free-roaming AUVs, and high-definition television cameras. As of 2006, your video wallpaper could display a live feed from the deep ocean (of course, by 2015 the opposite wall may feature a live feed from Mars).

In 1953 Auguste Piccard and his son Jacques dove nearly 2 miles into the ocean depths in the bathyscaph Trieste. The newest three-passenger exploration submersibles, Japan's Shinkai 6500, are sleeker, more maneuverable, safer, and can reach depths of 6,500 meters. But these submersibles use 20th-century technology. Graham Hawkes, a private entrepreneur and inventor, believes that "closer and endlessly richer in life, resources and mysteries... it is earth's oceans – not space – that will fuel man's future into the next century." His response to this imperative is the world's first underwater "aircraft," Deep Flight. A single-person submersible, the pilot plunges into the deep in a prone position. Inverted wings on the craft create "negative" lift, pulling the sub into the ocean depths without need for ballast. This enables a fast descent, optimizing "bottom time" for exploration purposes. Deep Flight II will be proven to over 12,000 meters with an "Ocean Everest" expedition to the Marianas Trench.

Deep Flight's smaller cousins will basically be atmospheric dive suits with attitude. Atmospheric dive suits (ADS) are by definition jointed, human-shaped, single-person submersibles which can descend to almost 760 meters while maintaining internal pressure close to one atmosphere. This eliminates the need for compression or decompression schedules but requires a suit so heavy the wearer moves it using built-in propulsion. The next generation of ADS will easily reach depths of 1,000 meters; include directional thrusters for increased maneuverability; and carry enhanced sensor, data, and communication arrays onboard. But the Exosuit, designed by Dr. Phil Nuytten, represents the most promising future for ADS – a lightweight, non-tethered dive suit so flexible that divers will be able to swim wearing it.

Scuba gear and wetsuits come as close to swimming like fish as humans can get. New materials developments may allow us literally to swim like fish – or like sharks and dolphins. But access to the ocean depths requires more than streamlining the hydrodynamically clumsy human form. It means addressing the dangers inherent in being an air-breathing mammal in a high-pressure environment. One potential answer would be a fluid breathing apparatus, like that spotlighted in the movie *Abyss*. Replacing the air in our lungs with a highly oxygenated fluid would sidestep the decompression difficulties arising from breathing gases under pressure. Such a liquid – perflubron (perfluorooctyl bromide) – is currently undergoing clinical trials for therapeutic use with patients suffering respiratory failure from infection, burns, toxic substances, or premature birth. Significant technical problems – circulating the liquid easily through the lungs, eliminating the carbon dioxide that is exhaled, draining the lungs in the transition back to breathing air – mean this technology will take a decade or more to develop. But its development will allow humans much greater freedom of the depths.

NO SWEAT. *The Pompeii worm is the most heat-tolerant animal on Earth, able to survive an environment nearly hot enough to boil water. Covering this deep-sea worm's back is a fleece of bacteria. These microbes may possess heat-stable enzymes useful in a variety of applications, such as pharmaceutical production, food processing, paper and textile manufacture, and others.*

In the very long term, beyond the scope of this book, we may know enough not only about ourselves, but also about our marine neighbors – dolphins, orcas, blue whales – to understand how they survive plummeting to great depths and rising again to the sun and the sky in one breath. We may then apply that understanding to redesigning our own physiognomy. And so, in some far future, we may need to paraphrase Shakespeare to visualize our childrens' lives:

Full fathom five our daughters dive,
and all their bones of coral made;
deep ocean pearls delight their eyes,
and nothing of them doth fade
but celebrates a sea-change
into something rich and strange.

PROVOCATIONS...

Will sea floor mining and seawater filtering replace land-based mining?
Will tomorrow's kids want to be aquanauts?
Will the "Mile High Club" have a matching "Mile Below Club?"

—Wendy Schultz

WANT MORE?

DOE HYDROPOWER DATA
http://hydropower.inel.gov/index.html

WHAT IS OTEC?
www.nrel.gov/otec/what.html

OCEAN POWER OVERVIEW
www.eren.doe.gov/consumerinfo/refbriefs/nb1.html

WAVEGEN
www.wavegen.co.uk

JAPANESE MIGHTY WHALE PROJECT
www.jamstec.go.jp/jamstec/MTD/Whale

WAVE POWER GROUP, UNIVERSITY OF EDINBURGH
www.mech.ed.ac.uk/research/wavepower/index.htm

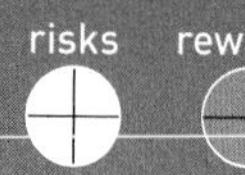

SPACE EXPLORATION... Homo Sapiens to Homo Stellae

"The Earth is the cradle of the mind, but we cannot live forever in a cradle."
—Konstantin Tsiolkovsky, father of astronautics, 1911

REDUCE, REUSE, RECYcle. Oddly enough, this mantra of environmental sustainability also sums up the requirements for economically viable spaceflight: reduce weight; reuse the rockets, vehicles, and tools; and recycle the components. Innovations in materials science coupled with the march of Moore's Law – faster, smaller, cheaper, more interconnected microprocessors – will unlock the doors of space for scientists, businesspeople, tourists, even students and their teachers. Especially if the technological innovations can be combined with design enabling

DON'T ROLL OVER, MARTIAN ROVER. *At the end of 2003, half a dozen years after the last Martian exploration, not one but two rovers are being sent to the Red Planet - the twin Mars Exploration Rovers. The rovers will lay the groundwork for the permanent robotic presence on the planet.*

"continuous intact abort capability" – that is, the ability to abort a flight safely at any point during the flight, and return home. Then a safe path to space will finally be accessible to all.

Our first tours of Mars will be online. A sash of satellites in orbit above Mars will relay commands to sensor stations and robots on the Red Planet and transmit data and visuals back to Earth. The first node of a system-wide "Interplanetary Internet," this communications network will allow scientists to explore via telepresence and

Image courtesy of NASA

teleoperation—and allow the rest of us to kibbitz.

By 2015, an entire silicon ecology of robots could act as online tour guides on Olympus Mons or through Valles Marineris. The prototypes are already there: Pathfinder and its mobile unit, Sojourner, as well as the Mars Global Surveyor. But the world's space agencies have even more robots in the works, ready for launch over the next decade. In 2003, ESA will launch the Mars Express, and NASA will launch twins: the identical Athena geological rovers, building on the success of Sojourner. Space scientists are also borrowing from nature to design autonomous, insect-like robots that could be deployed in large numbers and nanoscale information sensors that could be dusted across the landscape.

Rovers, however, can only rove so far. The subsequent generation of Mars explorers could be airborne and inflatable. NASA—and students at MIT—are designing robotic airplanes and gliders to skim through the valleys and canyons of Mars and ride thermals over its mountains. Hot air balloons, which would rise in the relative warmth of day to land again at night, are also on the drawing boards. All these designs rely on inflatable structures. The Jet Propulsion Laboratory's Gossamer

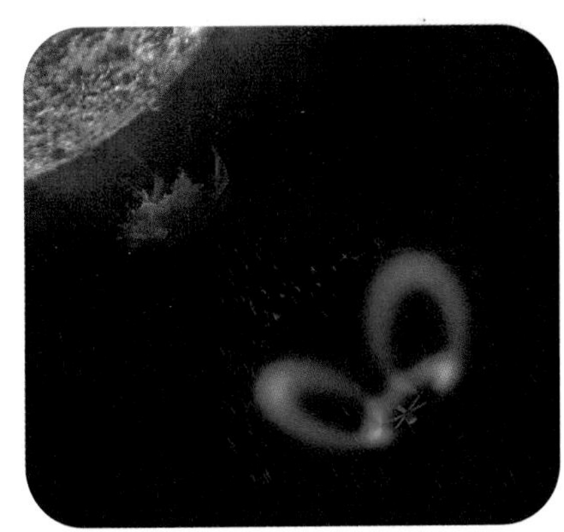

SOLAR SAILER. *Tomorrow's space probes will use entirely new forms of propulsion. On such a system, Mini-Magnetospheric Plasma Propulsion creates a dense field of charged particles around the spacecraft that catch the "solar wind." This system, being prototyped at the University of Washington, would be 10 times faster than the space shuttle and could zip by Voyager I, launched in 1977 and currently 6.8 billion miles away.*

Post 2003 Mission Plans
are being developed for
Launch Opportunities in 2005, 2007, 2009, 2011, etc. at 26 month intervals
are being re-evaluated in light of
Mission Failures in 1999
involving
Mars Climate Orbiter
Mars Polar Lander
may include
will be
Low Cost "Scout" Missions
Science Driven
Technology Enabled
defined by
Science Principal Investigator
means following
Science Priorities from Mars Exploration Program Analysis Group
Subsurface Exploration
is essential for
Landers
launching in
2007
requiring improved
Navigation Surface Targets
Hazard Avoidance
Hazard Tolerance
will establish need for improved
Mars Ascent Vehicle
will seek to characterize
Biological Potential
Climate & Geological History
Current Environment
require
Sample Return
needs
Earth Return Vehicle
to launch in
2011
Orbiters
enable
Very High Resolution Imaging
High Rate Communications
Near IR Spectral Mapping
Subsurface Mapping
allows choice of
Landing Sites
involves
Ground-Penetrating Radar
to be carried in
ESA's Mars Express
to launch in
2005
Source: NASA

FROM SPAGHETTI TO SPACEFLIGHT. *A manned mission to Mars will be the most complex effort undertaken by human beings ever. The number of considerations is enormous - this flowchart is just a tiny fraction of the total picture.*

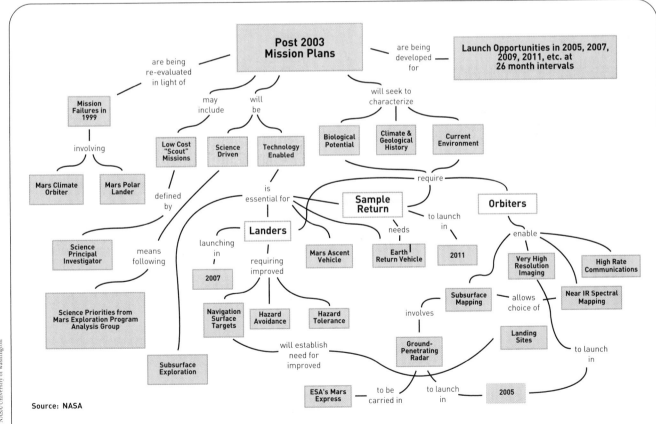

Image courtesy of NASA/University of Washington

NEW HORIZONS IN SPACE TRAVEL. *Although we've explored much of the solar system since the 1970s, one target remains shrouded in mystery — Pluto and its ghostly moon Charon. The New Horizons spacecraft, being developed by NASA, Johns Hopkins, and others, will remedy this. Launching in 2006, it will fly by Pluto and Charon as early as 2015 and pass the Kuiper Belt by 2026.*

Image courtesy of Johns Hopkins University Applied Physics Laboratory/Southwest Research Institute (JHUAPL/SWRI)

Spacecraft Initiative explores these uses as well as designs for lightweight, inflatable telescopes, "ballutes" (balloon parachutes), and heat shields.

NASA cancelled the X-33 spaceplane prototyping but continues its search for transportation systems to carry people and equipment safely and reliably to orbit — as are over 20 private engineering teams. While spaceplanes like the Pan Am spaceplane seen in *2001: A Space Odyssey* represent one design path, we may one day simply take an elevator to orbit. Tsiolkovsky and colleagues in Russia suggested "space towers" to lift passengers and cargos out of Earth's gravity well, and Arthur C. Clarke portrayed the idea in his novel *The Fountains of Paradise*. New high-tensile strength, self-healing composites will not only make our spaceplanes safer, but could make the idea of a floating tether — a cable dangling down, and stretching out, from a "buoy" in orbit — feasible. The lower docking station would be suborbital, allowing simpler, lower-cost spaceplanes to ferry people to the "elevator's" lowest point. Passengers would then ride for several hours in large, comfortable gondolas up the cable to a space station at mid-point. Interplanetary cargo would continue up the cable to the high end, where it would be flung off the cable at speeds exceeding escape velocity.

With weight one of the biggest constraints in launch costs, designers are also using advanced materials such as highly heat-resistant, featherweight carbon mesh to make inflatable interplanetary and interstellar spacecraft, such as solar sailers. Solar will rely on the faint push of the solar wind on carbon mesh sails miles wide to accelerate lightweight, unmanned craft to speeds as high as 10% lightspeed. Scientists are also working on solar sailers whose "sails" will simply be bubbles of magnetic force. On the far edge of interstellar spacecraft design are even more breakthrough propulsion projects — theoretically intriguing but requiring revolutionary insights into physics and the fabric of space-time. These include ideas to utilize "zero point energy" — essentially, the background buzz of the universe; to explore possible applications of black hole physics; to understand the relationship between the electromagnetic spectrum and gravity; and to theorize about warping the spacetime continuum.

Armstrong's boot hit moon dust on July 20, 1969. Thirty-three years later, we have not yet visited any other planets. This is not a lack of technology, but a lack of public and political will. Space exploration is expensive, and, given real and serious problems here on Earth, less politically aerodynamic than it was during the Cold War. Early NASA culture had internalized the von Braun strategy for interplanetary exploration: This assumed a monumental staged effort, stairstepping from large infrastructure to large infrastructure — build rockets, then build a space station, next a moon base, and finally launch to Mars. Obviously, the magnitude of this

UNVEILING A COSMIC DARK AGE

The Next Generation Space Telescope (NGST) is an orbiting infrared observatory that will take the place of the Hubble Space Telescope at the end of this decade. It will study the universe at the important but previously unobserved epoch of galaxy formation, peering through ancient dust to witness the birth of stars and planetary systems similar to our own.

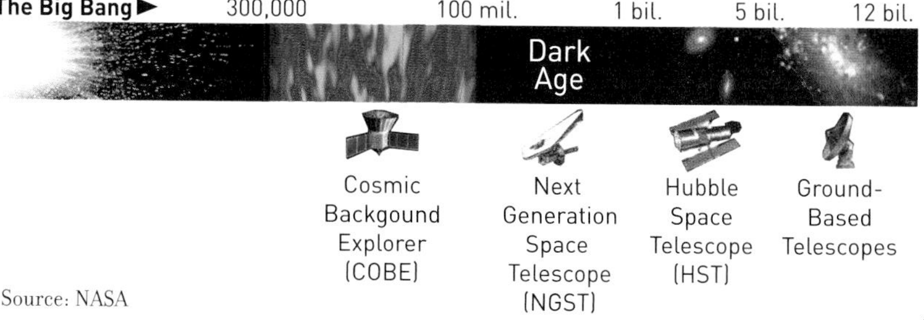

Source: NASA

MARS BY 2020!

2003 Japan's Nozumi orbiter reaches Mars in December.

Mars makes its closest approach to Earth in 17 years.

European Space Agency's (ESA) Mars Express mission launched in June with arrival on Mars planned for December — the lander Beagle 2 designed to look for water and life.

Mars Exploration Rover mission, featuring two flights sending identical Athena geological sciences payloads to Mars, launches.

2004 MER two-rover mission arrives on Mars.

2005 Mars Reconnaissance Orbiter launched.

Self-healing, evolvable onboard flight computers increase system reliability and safety.

Telecom satellites "piggyback" on biannual Mars missions.

First Mars lander/rover missions with built-in terrestrial Internet capabilities.

2007 CNES (French Space Agency) launches orbiter and "Netlanders".

ASI (Italian Space Agency) launches a communications orbiter.

NASA "Scout" missions.

Permanent robotic presence on Mars.

2009 NASA plans a Mars launch of a "smart" lander, a long-range rover, and a radar satellite.

2015 Proposed joint international manned mission to Mars.

2016 Launch window for "fast transit" (130 days) to Mars.

2020 NASA's proposed horizon for a manned Mars mission.

approach renders it astronomically expensive. The manned Mars proposal Bush rejected so resoundingly in 1989 featured $450 billion worth of expenses. The "smaller, faster, cheaper" use of robotic exploration devices during the 1990s reflected the resulting innovation of economic necessity.

An alternate strategy for manned missions to Mars, called the Mars Direct approach, was championed by Robert Zubrin in his 1996 book *The Case for Mars*. Taking lessons from history — successful explorers lived off the land — it proposes unmanned flights to Mars in advance of manned flights: First send robots to Mars to process fuel from the immediate environment, to build habitats, and to land return vehicles. Then send people. Could we mount a manned expedition by 2015? NASA estimates it will cost $50 billion and does not wish even to consider it until 2020. Yet on July 5, 2002, the Russians suggested a $20 billion collaborative effort between NASA, ESA, and themselves aimed at launching a manned mission by 2015.

The engineering talent and technology to go to Mars already exists — now what is required is the political will. Putting people on Mars is expensive, and there are many more competing needs on Earth. But politics attend every one of humanity's adventures, and they are always overcome. The first person to set foot on Mars has already been born: The rest of us must simply commit to sending her.

PROVOCATIONS...

With more international cooperation, when will we again see a major "first" by a non-American in space?

When will the first baby be born in zero gravity?

—Wendy Schultz

WANT MORE?

INTERPLANETARY INTERNET SPECIAL INTEREST GROUP
www.ipnsig.org

NASA INSTITUTE FOR ADVANCED STUDIES
www.niac.usra.edu

NASA BREAKTHROUGH PROPULSION PROJECTS
www.grc.nasa.gov/WWW/bpp

MARS
cmex-www.arc.nasa.gov/CMEX

www.marstoday.com

www.marsacademy.com

www.marssociety.org

INTERNATIONAL SPACE UNIVERSITY
www.isunet.edu

2000 2005 2010 2015 2020

risks  rewards 

The Search for Extraterrestrial Intelligence...
ACCELERATING THE COSMIC CONVERSATION

ALL SETI, ALL THE TIME. *It's one of the most persistently enticing sirens to beckon the SETI community: a major telescope that can be dedicated to the search. Despite the seductiveness of this idea, construction of an instrument designed to meet the requirements of full-time SETI has always foundered on the large costs. In the next few years, that situation is going to change. Thanks to the far-sighted benevolence of technologists Paul Allen (co-founder of Microsoft) and Nathan Myhrvold (former chief technology officer for Microsoft), a new telescope will be constructed that will allow a targeted SETI search to proceed 24 hours a day, 7 days a week. The new instrument, appropriately called the Allen Telescope Array, known formerly as the One Hectare Telescope, or 1hT, is a joint effort by the SETI Institute and the University of California, Berkeley. Because of its novel construction – an array of inexpensive antennas – it can be simultaneously used for both SETI and cutting-edge radio astronomy research.*

Image courtesy of SETI Institute

Tired of the alien-of-the-week as depicted by *Star Trek*? Jar-Jar Binks bugging you? Are you wondering where the real space sentients are, and if they are weirder than we can even imagine? You are not alone – and in all probability, we are not alone either. At least, that's what the folks at SETI – the Search for Extra-Terrestrial Intelligence – are betting.

If you were Jimmy the Greek, would you take the bet? If you knew as

HOW MANY ETs?

How many civilizations might exist among the stars for us to communicate with? Dr. Frank Drake developed an approach to estimate the answer, by calculating the odds of specific factors thought to play a role in the development of such civilizations.

The equation is usually written:

N = R* • fp • ne • fl • fi • fc • L

Where

N = The number of civilizations in the Milky Way Galaxy whose electromagnetic emissions are detectable

R* =The rate of formation of stars suitable for the development of intelligent life

fp = The fraction of those stars with planetary systems

ne = The number of planets, per solar system, with an environment suitable for life

fl = The fraction of suitable planets on which life actually appears

fi = The fraction of life-bearing planets on which intelligent life emerges

fc = The fraction of civilizations that develop a technology that releases detectable signs of their existence into space

L = The length of time such civilizations release detectable signals into space

Slightly different values for each of these values can lead to wildly differing results — from a few dozen civilizations to hundreds of thousands. But calculated this way, the wildest and least conservative estimate is that we're alone.

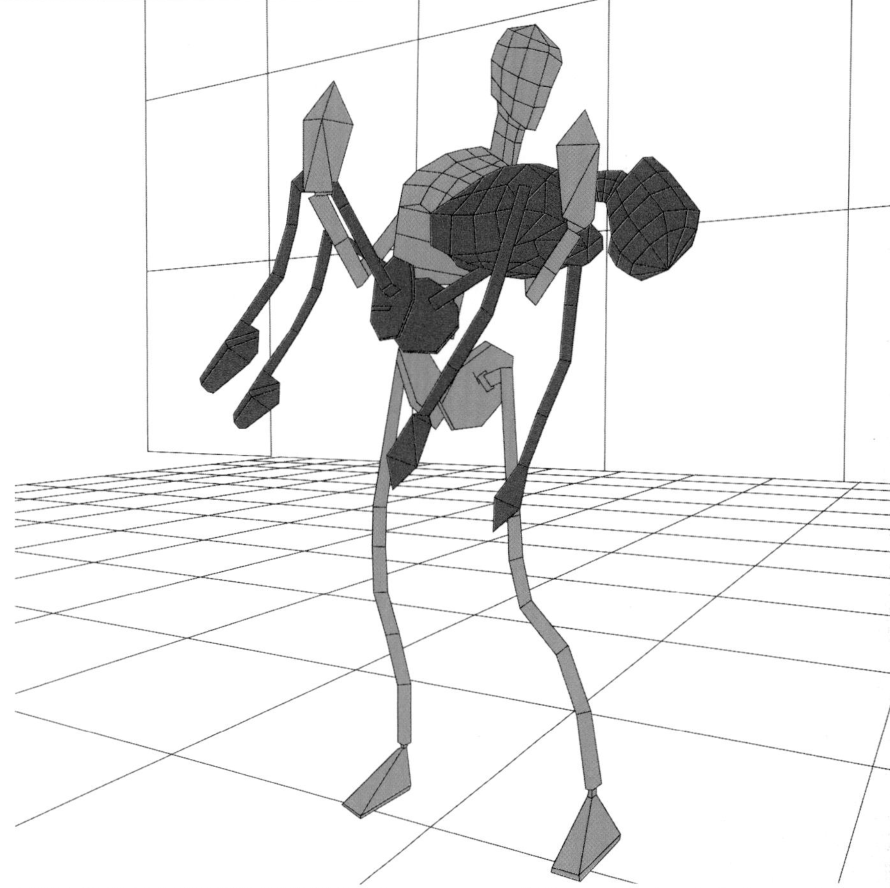

Image courtesy of Doug Vakoch

THE VALUES ARE THE MESSAGE. *For a generation, SETI researchers have looked to encode and decode messages written in the language of science. But how do we encode more abstract values, like altruism or beauty? Doug Vakoch, of the SETI Institute, is leading a community of researchers looking to answer this complex question.*

much about the universe as bookies know about horse racing, you could figure the odds. First, how many stars does our galaxy have? Of those, how many have planets? Of the stars with planets, how many include planets with thermal activity and water (characteristics enabling the evolution of organic life)? Where life emerged, how often did signal-generating intelligence evolve? Frank Drake, an eminent astronomer, neatly bundled the applicable assumptions into an equation which calculates how many stars might have detectable intelligent life. Unfortunately, the answer depends entirely upon your assumptions and the values you enter into Drake's equation: The answer could be a million – or none.

So we are propelled from Drake's Equation to Fermi's Paradox: Surely our situation is not unique; assuming other intelligent lifeforms evolved, why haven't we heard from them? Maybe they evolved – and self-destructed once they reached the nuclear age. Or perhaps they moved quickly through their radio and TV eras and are now using laser-based communication systems, or quantum broadcasting, or technologies as yet unimagined by us. Given that a billion-year age gap could potentially exist between their evolution and ours, their use of "magic" communication technologies is not at

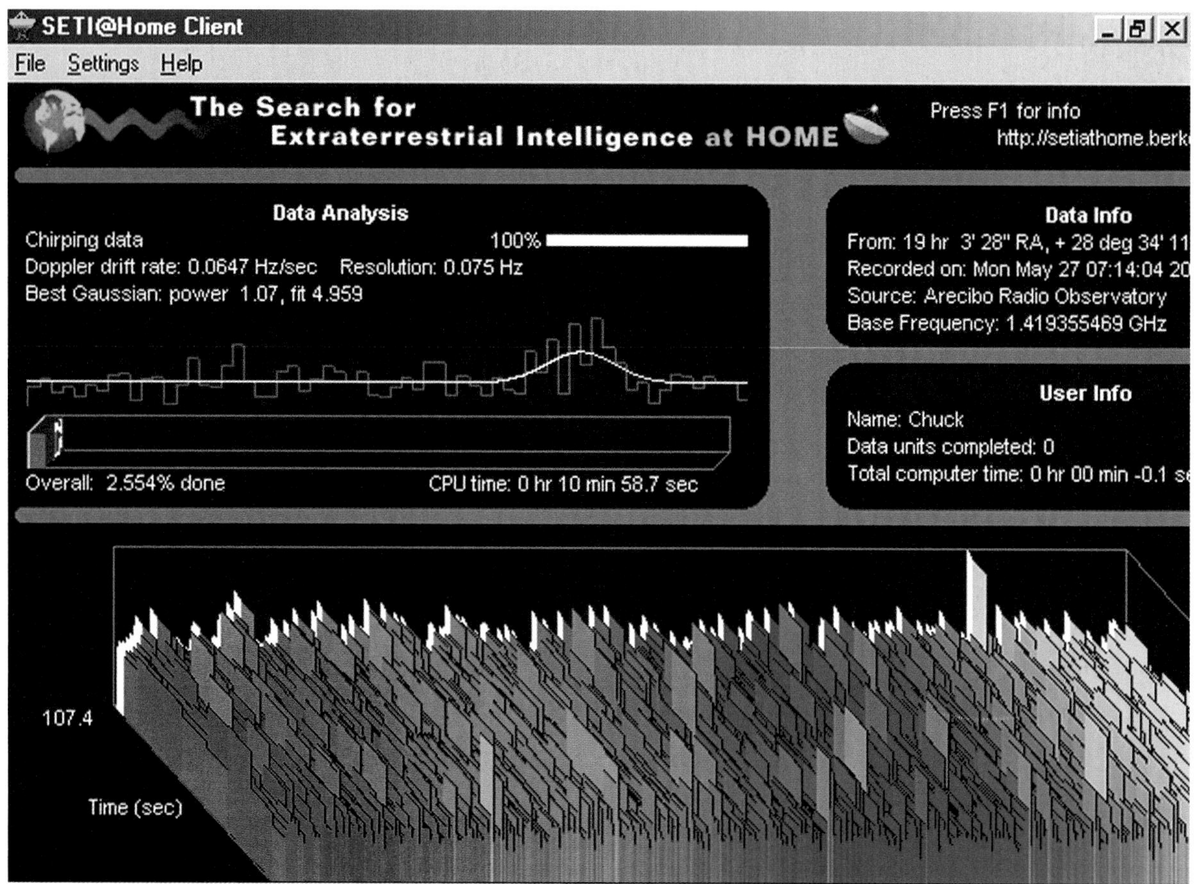

SETI ON YOUR COFFEE BREAK. *The SETI@home project, which began operation in April 1999, uses Internet distributed computing to help identify signals from the stars. Small segments of data from the Arecibo radio telescope are downloaded by the SETI@home program, which typically runs as a screen-saver, then they are processed and returned to researchers at UC Berkeley. In its first 2 years of operation, SETI@home has attracted 3.5 million users from around the world, and together they have contributed over 890,000 years of computer time to analyzing radio data.*

all unlikely (any sufficiently advanced technology is indistinguishable from magic, according to Arthur C. Clarke).

Thus we need to be clever in scanning stars. Our strategies include focusing on wavelengths which the universe leaves "quiet," making it easier to hear artificial signals; wide-field surveys which scan big sections of sky; targeted searches which focus only on 1,000 nearby "sun-like" stars; and "piggyback" searches of data collected from ordinary radio astronomy – which borrow processing power from thousands of volunteers' desktop PCs via the SETI@home screensaver. In the next decade, our search will expand in two dimensions. First, the new Allen Telescope Array in northern California will provide 24/7/365 SETI radio scans via 350 linked 6-meter dishes. Second, projects like COSETI (Columbus Optical SETI) will reinvigorate the search for optical messages beamed at Earth via high-energy, pulse lasers.

On August 15, 1977, Dr. Jerry Ehrman looked through a stack of printouts from Ohio State University's Big Ear Radio Observatory and printed "WOW!" next to a strong signal spike. Unfortunately, that signal never recurred. If it had, what would have happened? Think the movie *Contact* rather than *The X-Files*: Any potential "hits" are double-checked against a database of potential Earth-based signal sources and then referred to other radio telescope observatories for independent confirmation. If confirmation occurs, international protocols for next steps – and possible responses – are being jointly devised by astronomers, diplomats, and space lawyers.

Once we receive an interstellar message, we must interpret it and respond. In both deciphering alien messages and designing our own for

CULTURES OF THE IMAGINATION

How do we develop protocols for contact with alien cultures when we don't know any yet? We could combine cultural observation strategies developed by anthropologists with the exploration of "cultures of the imagination" (COTI). Sound like fun to you? You can play, too, by attending CONTACT, an annual conference that combines cutting-edge updates on space science and space exploration with role-playing alien contact.

Featuring an eclectic mix of anthropologists, space scientists, physicists, NASA engineers, science-fiction authors, and artists as participants, COTI teams at the conference extrapolate a future human space-faring society and "evolve" an alien society based on a plausible planetary environment. The human "first contact team" then tests out possible communications protocols with the newly met alien society.

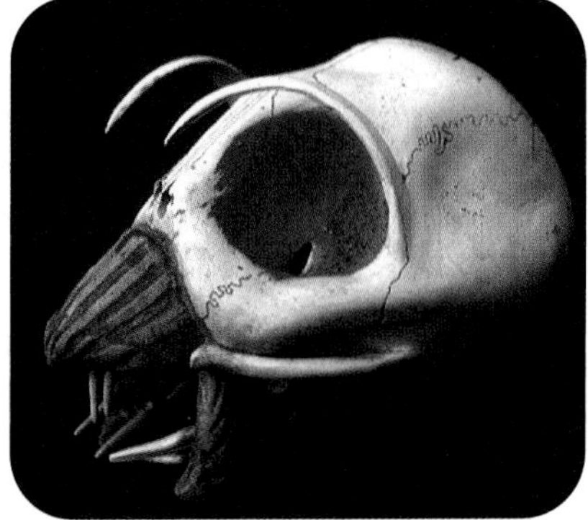

OTHERWORLDLY PALEONTOLOGY. *Rooted in cutting-edge science and his own imagination, artist Joel Hagen envisions the skeletons of alien civilizations. Hagen's work is informed by the science, and in turn influences that science.*

Clockwise from top left: Graphic by Pamela Lee; logo © 1983 by CONTACT: Cultures of the Imagination–Alien skull sculpted by Joel Hagen © 1983 by CONTACT: Cultures of the Imagination

transmission, we need a clearly understandable reference point. For example, the Rosetta Stone gave us Greek and Egyptian script alongside Egyptian hieroglyphs; Mayan glyphs were understood first in reference to numerals and their calendar. In sending greetings via Voyager and the 1974 transmission from Arecibo, we included numerals, chemical formulae, and stick figures depicting the human body. But starting with math and the elements of the universe does not ensure cross-cultural understanding. Doug Vakoch, the SETI Institute's Interstellar Message Group Leader, has been working with scientists, artists, and schoolchildren to create messages conveying human intention as well. And every year participants at the CONTACT conference explore different protocols for human communication with alien cultures.

But let's be honest with ourselves. While we find us endlessly fascinating, that could just be Terran narcissism. What's to say a billion-year-old, highly evolved, intelligent species would find us any more interesting than we find the average earthworm? Or, culturally, any more understandable or admirable? Our home definitions of progress might not be shared by the Galaxy. Yet whatever the communication difficulties and cultural barriers involved, the effort alone transforms us.

PROVOCATIONS...

Would contact with ETs lead to less violence on Earth?

Could ETs one day contact us through the Internet?

—Wendy Schultz

WANT MORE?

THE SETI INSTITUTE
www.seti.org

SETI AT HOME:
http://setiathome.ssl.berkeley.edu

DRAKE'S EQUATION, EXPLAINED AND COMPUTED
www.seti.org/science/drake-bg.html

www.msnbc.com/modules/drake/default.asp

SERENDIP (SEARCH FOR EXTRATERRESTRIAL RADIO EMISSIONS FROM NEARBY DEVELOPED INTELLIGENT POPULATIONS)
http://seti.ssl.berkeley.edu/serendip

SPACE.COM'S SETI CHANNEL
www.space.com/searchforlife/index.html

ASTROBIOLOGY AT NASA
http://astrobiology.arc.nasa.gov

THE CONTACT CONFERENCE
www.cabrillo.cc.ca.us/contact

Tomorrow and Tomorrow and Tomorrow

If time is a river, this book is but a dip in the shallows. Important shallows to be sure, as what happens in the next few years will have a huge impact on all our lives, but shallows nonetheless. A decade is the proper interval to consider a stage in one's life, the future of a company, the challenges facing a nation, or the evolution of new industries, but all these things occur against the backdrop of larger, deeper time.

Society today suffers from an almost pathological obsession with the short-term. It is why a decade's glance seems so bold. This is an age when executives can't see past the next quarter, politicians the next election, and harried parents the next soccer practice or house payment. But having read to this point, you, gentle reader, understand that looking ahead is not a novelty but a necessity, and the farther the look the better.

Treat this book as a chapter in a longer forecast of your own making. Pick an explicit time period and tie it to a central player. Half a century might be suitable for considering one's personal future, or a century for contemplating what the future holds for one's children. But don't hesitate to tackle larger intervals: Contemplate the next two centuries and the prospects for one's grandchildren, one's community, or one's country. And don't be afraid to go farther, to one thousand, or even ten thousand years, and consider the future of all the life we share this planet with.

The speculations in this book afford a solid jumping-off point for explorations into larger time horizons. Begin by considering which trends identified here will last beyond the decade, which will take a different course, and what entirely new developments will appear that were never mentioned here at all. What follows are a few simple suggestions to consider as you explore.

Always look back twice as far as you look forward. If you are trying to make sense of 2010, look back to 1980 and imagine the changes from then to 1990 and from 1990 to the present. Is an entirely new automotive fuel-cell revolution likely within the next 10 years? Comparatively smaller changes have taken longer: PCs were obscure hobbyist tools in 1980, popular gizmos for a minority of consumers in 1990, and ubiquitous appliances in 2000. Can the auto industry evolve as quickly as the computer industry, or will its progress be slower despite the forces afoot for change?

The farther out you look, the more valuable this double look-back becomes. 2102 seems unimaginable, but 2002 once was the distant future for people in 1902. There was talk then of electrical brains (computers), monster bombs (nukes), and space travel (Apollo). In some areas such as communications, reality shot far past their imaginings, while in others, visions like Mars travel seem as far off as ever. Or consider what 1900 looked like from 1802, the year before Lewis and Clark set out on their westward expedition.

Do not confuse the desired for the likely. Every forecaster is tempted to depict the future they hope for — or the future they most fear. But the eventual reality is usually entirely different. Futurists in the 1960s told us that computers and robots were going to deliver us into a future "leisure society," in which the greatest social challenge would be figuring out what to do with all our spare time. It is a vision that makes today's calendar-toting, time-starved, overstressed mouse potatoes weak with envy.

Our fears can also mislead us. The future from the 1950s held nuclear war as a near-certainty. Imagine telling someone then that half a century would pass without a nuke delivered in anger, the USSR would no longer exist, and both sides would exchange diplomats rather than missiles. How is the new obsession with terrorism skewing our views of the future today?

Consider what won't change. Even in periods of rapid change, novelties emerge atop a deeper set of unchanging constants. Our homes may be filled with computer gizmos, but we still build houses with nostalgic fireplaces and long for "quality time" with our children. The contents of our houses have changed rapidly and repeatedly, but the way we build our houses has evolved very slowly. We gobble down dietary supplements, but we still eat three times a day, and our food looks largely like food looked a century ago. Religion is the mother of all constants. A decade ago, forecasters spoke of the death of religion, yet today there is a resurgence of religious participation worldwide.

Tracking these constants is useful for more than identifying when a possible innovation will be rejected, for often as not, they serve as the platform for breathtaking innovation. The Internet took off among parents eager to stay in touch with their college-age offspring, and now students can email Dad to transfer more cash to them at electronic speeds. The desire for leisure and recreation has fueled an enormous outdoor industry in a commercial arms race to deliver ever more intense vacations and lighter, faster, higher-performance recreational gear.

Even the most expected futures tend to arrive late and in utterly unexpected ways. Change is rarely linear — more often than not, events unfold suddenly after long periods of seeming stability. Consumers anticipated television for decades before it finally rocketed into American homes in 1951. Will a long-awaited wireless future arrive as suddenly?

And when the change finally arrives, expect to be utterly surprised by the details. As futurist Peter Schwartz notes, the difference between a forecast and reality is that a good forecast is plausible and internally consistent. Reality labors under no such constraints. The mid-1990s arrival of the World Wide Web was the wildest of improbabilities that triggered even greater surprises. In the late 1980s, the consensus was that interactive TV would dazzle us all. Imagine telling them that 1980s interactive TV would fail and, instead, a vast electronic hypermedia would arrive, triggering an online purchasing revolution — and the hottest thing being sold would be books.

Last, but not least, do not forget that the purpose of forecasting is not merely to anticipate what lies ahead. Rather, an understanding of the future leads to better decisions in the present. Listening for the hint of rapids around the next bend in time's river may help one avoid white water, and imagining where the river leads could open up vast new horizons.

—Paul Saffo

A TOUR OF TECHTV

TechTV is the only 24-hour cable television network dedicated to showcasing the impact technology has on our everyday lives and on the world at large. By creating and delivering entertaining and insightful programming regarding today's and tomorrow's technology news, events, products, and people, TechTV enables viewers to stay current and connected with all things related to technology.

Offering more than a cable television channel, TechTV delivers a fully integrated Web site. TechTV.com enhances the TV viewing experience with compelling companion content and interactivity.

TechTV is owned by Vulcan, Inc.

NETWORK PROGRAM GUIDE

BIG THINKERS

Big Thinkers

www.techtv.com/bigthinkers

Explore the future of technology through insightful and down-to-earth interviews with the industry's most influential thinkers and innovators of our time.

CALL FOR HELP

www.techtv.com/callforhelp

Host Chris Pirillo translates technical jargon into plain English, provides computing tips, answers live viewer questions, and interviews guests who help demystify technology. It's interactive, informative, and above all, fun.

CYBERCRIME

www.techtv.com/cybercrime

Hosts Alex Wellen and Jennifer London take an inside look at fraud, hacking, viruses, identity theft, and invasions of privacy to keep users secure and aware of the potential dangers on the Internet.

EXTENDED PLAY

www.techtv.com/extendedplay

Host Adam Sessler provides comprehensive reviews of the hottest new games on the market and previews games in development and tips on how to score the biggest thrills and avoid the worst spills in gaming.

EYE DROPS

www.techtv.com/eyedrops

Breathtaking, beautiful, compelling, insightful, and sometimes even a little scary, but always entertaining, Eye Drops has something for everyone. Eye Drops showcases today's best computer-generated animated short subjects.

FRESH GEAR

www.techtv.com/freshgear

Host Sumi Das takes an in-depth look at the coolest new products out there from color PDAs to ultra-light notebooks, digital cameras to PVRs, virtual operating rooms to wearable computers. Catch reviews of the latest products, get advice on what to buy and what to bypass, and explore the technologies of tomorrow.

FUTURE FIGHTING MACHINES

www.techtv.com/futurefightingmachines

Future Fighting Machines takes a look at the latest in military hardware and gadgets, from electromagnetic energy weapons, to high-tech soldiers' uniforms with built-in mine detection, to flying spying micro-robots.

MAX HEADROOM

www.techtv.com/maxheadroom

In a cyberpunk future where television is the fabric that binds society, Max Headroom is a computer-generated TV host at Network 23.

THE SCREEN SAVERS

www.techtv.com/screensaver

TechTV's daily live variety show hosted by Leo Laporte and Patrick Norton features guest interviews and celebrities, remote field pieces, product advice and demos, and software reviews.

THE TECH OF...

www.techtv.com/thetechof

From the food we eat, to the sports we play, to buildings where we work, technology has a profound impact on the way we live. *The Tech Of...* is an engaging series that goes behind the scenes of modern life and shows you the technology that makes things tick.

TECH LIVE

www.techtv.com/news

Tech Live focuses on the technology world's most important people, companies, products, and issues and how they affect consumers, investors, and the industry through interviews, product reviews, advice, and technology analysis.

TECHNOGAMES

www.techtvcom/technogames

Homemade machines, robots, and electronic devices face off in a high-tech international competition from London's Millennium Dome. Innovation and technical excellence are tested as robots compete at cycling, swimming, high jump, rope climb, solar-powered marathon, and shot put.

TECHTV'S TITANS OF TECH

www.techtv.com/titansoftech

Through insightful interviews and in-depth profiles, *Titans of Tech* offers viewers an informed look at where the new economy is headed. These specials profile technology's most important movers and shakers — the CEOs, entrepreneurs, and visionaries driving today's tech economy.

TOMORROW'S WORLD

TOMORROW'S WORLD

www.techtv.com/tomorrowsworld

The BBC's *Tomorrow's World* takes a look at the latest innovations and discoveries in medicine, space, entertainment, sports, transportation, and law enforcement. Featuring reports from every corner of the globe, *Tomorrow's World* is a fascinating, informed, and fact-based view of the future of technology.

Index

NUMBERS

A

F

G

J

K

L

M

Q

R

S

T

U

V

W

X-Y

Z